B.M. Harwani

Android™ Programming

UNLEASHED

SAMS | **800 East 96th Street, Indianapolis, Indiana 46240 USA**

Android™ Programming Unleashed

ISBN-13: 978-0-672-33628-7
ISBN-10: 0-672-33628-6

The Library of Congress cataloging-in-publication data is on file.

Printed in the United States of America

First Printing: December 2012

Trademarks

All terms mentioned in this book that are known to be trademarks or service marks have been appropriately capitalized. Sams Publishing cannot attest to the accuracy of this information. Use of a term in this book should not be regarded as affecting the validity of any trademark or service mark.

Warning and Disclaimer

Every effort has been made to make this book as complete and as accurate as possible, but no warranty or fitness is implied. The information provided is on an "as is" basis. The author and the publisher shall have neither liability nor responsibility to any person or entity with respect to any loss or damages arising from the information contained in this book or programs accompanying it.

Bulk Sales

Sams Publishing offers excellent discounts on this book when ordered in quantity for bulk purchases or special sales. For more information, please contact

U.S.Corporate and Government Sales
1-800-382-3419
corpsales@pearsontechgroup.com

For sales outside of the U.S., please contact

International Sales
international@pearsoned.com

Editor-in-Chief
Mark Taub

Acquisitions Editor
Laura Lewin

Development Editor
Songlin Qiu

Managing Editor
Kristy Hart

Project Editor
Jovana San Nicolas-Shirley

Copy Editor
Geneil Breeze

Indexer
Joy Dean Lee

Proofreader
WriteOrWrong Proofreading Services

Technical Editors
Douglas Jones
Joseph Annuzzi
Roman Irani

Editorial Assistant
Olivia Basegio

Cover Designer
Mark Shirar

Compositor
Gloria Schurick

Contents at a Glance

Table of Contents

I: Fundamentals of Android Development

III: Building Menus and Storing Data

7   Creating Interactive Menus and ActionBars   323

8   Using Databases   385

About the Author

B.M. Harwani is founder and owner of Microchip Computer Education (MCE), based in Ajmer, India, that provides computer education in all programming and web developing platforms. He graduated with a BE in computer engineering from the University of Pune, and also has a C Level (master's diploma in computer technology) from DOEACC, Government of India. Being involved in the teaching field for more than 18 years, he has developed the art of explaining even the most complicated topics in a straightforward and easily understandable fashion. To know more, visit his blog http://bmharwani.com/blog.

Dedication

Dedicated to my mother, Mrs. Nita Harwani, Ray Tomlinson, and Dr. V. A. Shiva Ayyadurai.

My mother is next to God for me. Whatever I am today is just because of the moral values taught by her.

I admire and appreciate Ray Tomlinson and Dr. V. A. Shiva Ayyadurai's invention—Internet-based email.
They have revolutionized the mode of communication. In fact, their achievement has changed the life of millions of people around the world, including me.

Acknowledgments

I owe a debt of gratitude to Laura Lewin, Acquisitions Editor, for her initial acceptance and giving me an opportunity to create this work. I am highly grateful to the whole team at Pearson Technology Group for their constant cooperation and contribution to create this book.

My gratitude to Songlin Qiu, who as a Development Editor, offered a significant amount of feedback that helped to improve the chapters. She played a vital role in improving the structure and quality of information.

I must thank Douglas Jones, Joseph Annuzzi, and Romin Irani, the Technical Reviewers, for their excellent, detailed reviewing of the work and the many helpful comments and suggestions they made.

Special thanks to Geneil Breeze, Copy Editor, for first-class structural and language editing. I appreciate her efforts in enhancing the contents of the book and giving it a polished look.

I also thank Gloria Schurick, Compositor, for doing excellent formatting and making the book dramatically better.

Big and ongoing thanks to Jovana Shirley, Project Editor, for doing a great job and for the sincere efforts of the whole team to get the book published on time.

A great big thank you to the editorial and production staff and the entire team at Pearson Technology Group who worked tirelessly to produce this book. Really, I enjoyed working with each of you.

I am also thankful to my family, my small world: Anushka (my wife) and my two little darlings, Chirag and Naman, for inspiring me to work harder.

I should not forget to thank my dear students who have been good teachers for me as they make me understand the basic problems they face in a subject and enable me to directly hit at those topics. The endless interesting queries of my students help me to write books with a practical approach.

We Want to Hear from You!

As the reader of this book, *you* are our most important critic and commentator. We value your opinion and want to know what we're doing right, what we could do better, what areas you'd like to see us publish in, and any other words of wisdom you're willing to pass our way.

We welcome your comments. You can email or write to let us know what you did or didn't like about this book—as well as what we can do to make our books better.

Please note that we cannot help you with technical problems related to the topic of this book.

When you write, please be sure to include this book's title and author as well as your name and email address. We will carefully review your comments and share them with the author and editors who worked on the book.

Email: errata@informit.com

Mail: Addison-Wesley/Prentice Hall Publishing
          ATTN: Reader Feedback
          1330 Avenue of the Americas
          35th Floor
          New York, New York, 10019

Reader Services

Visit our website and register this book at informit.com/register for convenient access to any updates, downloads, or errata that might be available for this book.

Introduction

Android is Google's open source and free Java-based platform for mobile development. It enables developers to build real-world mobile applications using the Android SDK and publish them on Google Play.

The huge demand for developing Android applications inspired me to write this book. Like any good book, it begins by explaining the usage of basic UI controls one at a time, configuring them by applying different attributes, and writing applications to understand how they respond to user actions. Gradually, once the reader is acquainted with the basic UI controls, the book explains how to use the advanced controls, resources, dialogs, and different types of menus.

The book addresses intermediate to advanced users and teaches different components provided by the Android SDK through examples. The book will be beneficial for developers and instructors too who want to learn or teach Android programming. For practical implementation the book also explains using the back-end databases for storing and fetching information. In short it is a useful reference book for anyone who wants to understand all key aspects of Android programming and to apply them practically into developing Android applications.

Key Topics That This Book Covers

This book is comprehensive and covers each topic in detail. Key topics covered are

- ▶ Understanding basic controls and event handling.
- ▶ Using resources, media, audio, and video.
- ▶ Creating of different types of menus with XML as well as through Java code.
- ▶ Accessing databases in Android applications.
- ▶ Using Internet, Google Maps, and Location-Based Services.
- ▶ Different types of layouts and selection widgets.
- ▶ Sending and receiving SMS messages and emails.
- ▶ Everything required for developing applications—for example, UI controls, containers, databases, menus—and accessing the Internet is available in one place.
- ▶ The book is completely up to date with the latest Jelly Bean.

Key Benefits That This Book Provides

By the time you finish the book, you will be able to

▶ Use and configure UI controls to develop Android applications

▶ Understand the technique of organizing controls in different layouts

▶ Use different resources in developing feature-rich Android applications

▶ Use different dialogs for getting data from the user

▶ Store, fetch, and update database records, and to access databases through menus

▶ Display web pages and Google Maps

▶ Send and receive SMS messages and emails

▶ Use the Telephony Manager for making phone calls

▶ Create your own custom service and also learn to consume SOAP Services

▶ Draw graphics, apply animation, and use interpolators

▶ Create, use, and register Content Providers

▶ Execute events automatically through Alarm Manager

▶ Use device sensors

▶ Publish Android applications

How This Book Is Organized

This book is structured in four parts:

▶ Part I: "Fundamentals of Android Development"

In Chapter 1, "Introduction to Android," you learn to install the Android SDK Starter Package, add platforms and other components, and install Eclipse and the Android Developer Tools (ADT) plug-in. You learn to make the ADT plug-in functional and create Android Virtual Devices to run and deploy Android applications. You also learn to create and run your first Android project, and you learn to set the layout of the application and the usage of the TextView control in an Android application.

Chapter 2, "Basic Widgets," focuses on the basic widgets used in an Android application. You learn about folders and files that are automatically created by the ADT plug-in, activities, the Android Activity life cycle, usage of the Android Manifest file, commonly used layouts and controls, and how event handling is performed. You learn how to create an anonymous inner class, implement the OnClickListener interface, and declare the event handler in the XML definition of the control. The chapter shows how to create a new Activity, register the new Activity, and start the Activity, and how to use three controls—EditText, CheckBox, and RadioButton—to develop Android applications.

▶ Part II: "Building Blocks for Android Application Design"

In Chapter 3, "Laying Out Controls in Containers," you learn about containers—the different types of layouts used to organize and arrange the controls of an application. You learn to use LinearLayout, RelativeLayout, AbsoluteLayout, FrameLayout, and TableLayout, and you learn to adapt to the screen orientation. In addition, you learn the usage of different attributes that help in laying out controls in different layouts. The chapter shows you how to apply different attributes in the layouts such as the Orientation attribute, Height and Width attribute, Padding attribute, Weight attribute, and Gravity attribute.

Chapter 4, "Utilizing Resources and Media," discusses the different types of resources and the procedures to apply them in Android applications. You learn to apply Dimension resources, Color resources, styles, and themes. You also learn to use String and Integer arrays. To display images in an Android application, you learn to use Drawable resources and create an Image Switcher application using the ToggleButton control. Also, you learn to implement scrolling through ScrollView and to play audio and video. Finally, the chapter explains using ProgressBar and assets.

Chapter 5, "Using Selection Widgets and Debugging," focuses on selection widgets. You learn to use the ListView, Spinner, AutoComplete, and GridView controls in Android applications. You learn how to use display options in selection widgets through string arrays and the ArrayAdapter, and you also see how to extend ListActivity and use styling for the standard ListAdapters. You learn to create an Image Gallery using Gallery Control and the procedure to use the debugging tool, Dalvik Debug Monitor Service (DDMS). The chapter also explains the procedure involved in debugging applications, placing breakpoints in an application, and using Debug perspective. And you learn to adding logging support to Android applications.

In Chapter 6, "Displaying and Fetching Information Using Dialogs and Fragments," you learn to use different dialogs in Android applications. You learn to use the AlertDialog to display important messages to the user, as well as to receive input from the user. You also learn to display and select dates and times with the DatePicker and TimePicker dialog boxes. The chapter explains fragments, their life cycles, and the procedure for creating them through XML and with Java code. You also learn about specialized fragments: ListFragment, DialogFragment, and PreferenceFragment.

▶ Part III: "Building Menus and Storing Data"

In Chapter 7, "Creating Interactive Menus and ActionBars," you learn about different types of menus. You learn to create options menus, expanded menus, submenus, and context menus with XML as well as Java code. You also learn to use check boxes/radio buttons in menus, handle menu selections, add shortcut keys, and assign icons to menu items. You learn to use the ActionBar, display action items, and create a tabbed ActionBar and a drop-down list ActionBar.

In Chapter 8, "Using Databases," you learn to use databases in Android applications. In the chapter you use the SQLite `SQLiteOpenHelper` to fetch desired rows from a table, and you learn to use cursors. You also learn to access databases through ADB and menus, and you learn to create data entry forms and display table rows through `ListView`.

▶ Part IV: "Advanced Android Programming: Internet, Entertainment, and Services"

Chapter 9, "Implementing Drawing and Animation," focuses on understanding animation. You learn to use `Canvas` and `Paint`, measure screen coordinates, and apply frame-by-frame animation. You also learn about tweening animation and the use of interpolators.

In Chapter 10, "Displaying Web Pages and Maps," you learn to display web pages through `WebView` controls, handle page navigation, and add permissions for Internet access. You see how to use the `WebViewClient`, use Google Maps, get Google Keys, and install the Google API. You learn to create AVDs for map-based applications, use location-based services, supply latitude and longitude values through DDMS, add zooming, and display map markers.

In Chapter 11, "Communicating with SMS and Emails," you learn about broadcast receivers. You see how to broadcast and receive the broadcasted `intent`. You also see how the Notification system is used, created, configured, and displayed in the status bar. You learn the procedure for sending and receiving SMS messages programmatically. Finally, you learn how to send email and use the Telephony Manager to make phone calls.

In Chapter 12, "Creating and Using Content Providers," you learn how to define, create, use, and register Content Providers. You also learn to define a database, Content URI, and MIME types. Also you learn to implement the `getType`, `query`, `insert`, `update`, and `delete` methods. Finally, the chapter explains how to use loaders.

In Chapter 13, "Creating and Consuming Services," you learn to move processes to the background threads using the `Handler` and `AsyncTask` classes. You learn to download and display images from the Internet. The chapter also explains how to create your own Bind Service and the procedure to consume SOAP Services. You also learn to use Alarm and Sensor Managers.

In Chapter 14, "Publishing Android Applications," you learn how to publish Android applications. You learn about versioning and digitally signing your applications, deploying APK files, and publishing your applications to the Google Play Store.

Code Examples for This Book

All the Android projects discussed in this book are available to download from the www. informit.com/title/ 9780672336287. Download the code bundle provided in the site and unzip it. Follow these steps to use the provided code:

1. Launch Eclipse.

2. Select the `File`, `Import` option. From the `Import` dialog that opens, select the `Existing Projects into Workspace` option and click the `Next` button.

3. In the next dialog, click the `Browse` button to locate and select the folder where you unzipped the code bundle.

4. After you select the code bundle, all the Android projects enclosed in it appear in the `Projects` box. By default all the projects are checked. Uncheck projects that you don't want to import and click `Finish`. That's it. The projects are imported into Eclipse and are ready to run.

PART I

Fundamentals of Android Development

CHAPTER 1

Introduction to Android

Android is Google's open source and free Java-based platform for mobile development. It enables developers to build real-world mobile applications using the Android software development kit (SDK) and publish them to the Android market. Android comes with several application programming interfaces (APIs) that make the task of developing full-featured applications easy. You can even use a camera, accelerometer, or GPS in an Android application. Moreover, Android is cross-compatible—it can run on Android phone/tablet/devices of different screen sizes and resolutions. Using Android, you can develop applications for a wide variety of devices, including phones, e-book readers, netbooks, and GPS units. Android was initially developed by Android, Inc., a small Palo Alto, California, company. Google bought this company in July 2005 and released the Android SDK in November 2007. Periodically, Google releases Android SDK updates. At the time of this writing, the latest version is 4.1.

> **NOTE**
>
> Android offers support for Bluetooth, EDGE, 3G, WiFi, Camera, GPS, compass, and accelerometer.

The Android 4.1 Jelly Bean SDK

The Android 4.1 Jelly Bean SDK was released with new features for developers in July 2012. It improves the beauty and simplicity of Android 4.0 and is a major platform release that adds a variety of new features for users and app developers. A few of the big features of this release include the following:

▶ **Project Butter**—Makes the Jelly Bean UI faster and more responsive. Also CPU Touch Responsiveness is added, which increases CPU performance whenever the screen is touched. It uses the finger's speed and direction to predict where it will be located after some milliseconds, hence making the navigation faster.

▶ **Faster speech recognition**—Speech recognition is now faster and doesn't require any network to convert voice into text. That is, users can dictate to the device without an Internet connection.

▶ **Improved notification system**—Besides text, the notifications include pictures and lists too. Notifications can be expanded or collapsed through a variety of gestures, and users can block notifications if desired. The notifications also include action buttons that enable users to call directly from the notification menu rather replying to email.

▶ **Supports new languages**—Jelly Bean includes support for several languages including Arabic, Hebrew, Hindi, and Thai. It also supports bidirectional text.

▶ **Predictive keyboard**—On the basis of the current context, the next word of the message is automatically predicted.

▶ **Auto-arranging Home screen**—Icons and widgets automatically resize and realign as per the existing space.

▶ **Helpful for visually impaired users**—The Gesture Mode combined with voice helps visually impaired users to easily navigate the user interface.

▶ **Improved Camera app**—The Jelly Bean Camera app includes a new review mode of the captured photos. Users can swipe in from the right of the screen to quickly view the captured photos. Also, users can pinch to switch to a new film strip view, where they can swipe to delete photos.

▶ **Better communication in Jelly Bean**—Two devices can communicate with Near Field Communication (NFC); that is, two NFC-enabled Android devices can be tapped to share data. Also, Android devices can be paired to Bluetooth devices that support the Simple Secure Pairing standard by just tapping them together.

▶ **Improved Google Voice search**—Jelly Bean is equipped with a question and answer search method that helps in solving users' queries similar to Apple's popular Siri.

▶ **Face Unlock**—Unlocks the device when the user looks at it. It also prevents the screen from blacking out. Optionally "blink" can be used to confirm that a live person is unlocking the device instead of a photo.

▶ **Google Now**—Provides users "just the right information at just the right time." It displays cards to show desired information automatically. For example, the Places card displays nearby restaurants and shops while moving; the Transit card displays information on the next train or bus when the user is near a bus stop or railway station; the Sports card displays live scores or upcoming game events; the Weather card displays the weather conditions at a user's current location, and so on.

> ▶ **Google Play Widgets**—Provides quick and easy access to movies, games, magazines, and other media on the device. It also suggests new purchases on Google Play.

> ▶ **Faster Google Search**—Google Search can be opened quickly, from the lock screen and from the system bar by swiping up and also by tapping a hardware search key if it is available on the device.

> ▶ **Supports antipiracy**—This feature supports developers in the sense that the applications are encrypted with a device-specific key making it difficult to copy and upload them to the Internet.

Understanding the Android Software Stack

The Android software stack consists of a Linux kernel and a collection of C/C++ libraries that are exposed through an application framework for application development.

The Android software stack consists of four main layers, as shown in Figure 1.1.

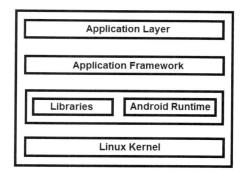

FIGURE 1.1   Android software stack

The following list gives a brief description of each of the layers in the software stack:

> ▶ **Linux kernel**—The kernel on which Android is based contains device drivers for various hardware components of an Android device, including Display, Camera, Keypad, Wi-Fi, Flash Memory, and Audio.

> ▶ **Libraries**—The next layer on top of the Linux kernel is the libraries that implement different Android features. A few of these libraries are listed here:

>> ▶ **WebKit library**—Responsible for browser support.
>> ▶ **FreeType library**—Responsible for font support.
>> ▶ **SQLite library**—Provides database support.
>> ▶ **Media libraries**—Responsible for recording and playback of audio and video formats.
>> ▶ **Surface Manager library**—Provides graphics libraries that include SGL and OpenGL for 2D and 3D graphics support.

▶ **Android runtime**—The engine at the same layer as the libraries. It provides a set of core Android libraries and a Dalvik virtual machine that enable developers to write Android applications using Java. The core Android libraries provide most of the functionality available in the core Java libraries, as well as the Android-specific libraries. Dalvik VM is explained in detail later in this chapter.

▶ **Application framework**—Provides the classes that enable application developers to develop Android applications. It manages the user interface, application resources, and abstraction for hardware access.

▶ **Application layer**—Displays the application developed and downloaded by users, along with the built-in applications provided with the Android device itself.

Installing the Android SDK

For developing native Android applications that you can publish on the Google Play marketplace, you need to install the following four applications:

▶ **The Java Development Kit (JDK)** can be downloaded from http://oracle.com/ technetwork/java/javase/downloads/index.html.

▶ **The Eclipse IDE** can be downloaded from http://www.eclipse.org/downloads/.

▶ **The Android Platform SDK Starter Package** can be download from http:// developer.android.com/sdk/index.html.

▶ **The Android Development Tools (ADT) Plug-in** can be downloaded from http:// developer.android.com/sdk/eclipse-adt.html. The plug-in contains project templates and Eclipse tools that help in creating and managing Android projects.

The Android SDK is not a full development environment and includes only the core SDK Tools, which are used to download the rest of the SDK components. This means that after installing the Android SDK Tools, you need to install Android platform tools and the other components required for developing Android applications. Go to http:// developer.android.com/sdk/index.html and download the package by selecting the link for your operating system. For Windows users, the provided .exe file is named `installer_ r18-windows.exe`. After downloading the file, double-click it to initiate the installation process. The Android SDK Manager window opens. The dialog boxes that you see from now on are from the Windows installer, and the screens may vary from other operating systems' installers.

The first screen is a Welcome screen. Select the `Next` button to move to the next screen. Because the Android SDK requires the Java SE Development Kit for its operation, it checks for the presence of JDK on your computer. If JDK is already installed, you see the screen shown later in Figure 1.4. If the JDK is not found, it displays a button with the caption *Visit* `java.oracle.com`, which you can use to download and install JDK. On selecting the button, you are taken to http://www.oracle.com/technetwork/java/javase/downloads/ index.html. This site shows links to download *Java Platform, Standard Edition, Java SE*

Development Kit (JDK) bundles, and additional resources. The latest version of Java available at the time of this writing is JDK version 1.7. Select the *JDK* link that suits your platform (Windows, Linux, or Mac) and double-click the downloaded file to begin JDK installation. You will probably see a Security Warning dialog box, asking whether you want to run or cancel the execution of the file. Select the `Run` button to initiate JDK installation. The first screen that you see is a `Java Setup Wizard Welcome` screen. Select the `Next` button to see the `Custom Setup` dialog box for selecting optional JDK features that you want to install, as shown in Figure 1.2.

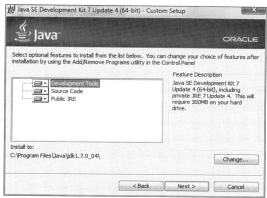

FIGURE 1.2   The Custom Setup dialog box

Three categories of features (Development Tools, Source Code, and Public JRE) are displayed, and you can select from the respective drop-down lists to choose the list of features in the category you want to install. The dialog box also asks for a drive location where you want to install the JDK. The default location displayed is `C:\Program Files\Java\jdk1.7.0_04\`, but you can use the `Change` button to select another location. Keep the default settings and click the `Next` button to continue. The selected program features are installed, followed by a dialog box that prompts for the destination folder to install the Java runtime environment (JRE), as shown in Figure 1.3.

FIGURE 1.3   Dialog box prompting for the JRE installation location

The dialog box displays the default location for installing the JRE (C:\Program Files\Java\jre7). Use the Change button to place the program elsewhere. Keep the default location and select the Next button to continue. The Java files are copied and installed on your machine. If the installation is successful, a confirming dialog box is displayed. Select Finish to exit the wizard. After Java installation, the Android SDK Tools Setup Wizard automatically resumes.

If Java is already installed on your computer before beginning with Android SDK installation, the wizard detects its presence and displays the version number of the JDK found on the machine, as shown in Figure 1.4.

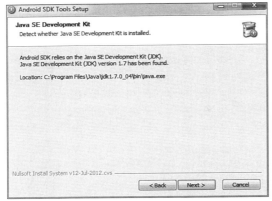

FIGURE 1.4   Dialog box informing you that the JDK is already installed on the computer

Select the Next button. You get a dialog box asking you to choose the users for which Android SDK is being installed. The following two options are displayed in the dialog box:

► Install for anyone using this computer

► Install just for me

Select the Install for anyone using this computer option and click Next. The next dialog prompts you for the location to install the Android SDK Tools, as shown in Figure 1.5. The dialog also displays the default directory location for installing Android SDK Tools as C:\Program Files (x86)\Android\android-sdk, which you can change by selecting the Browse button. Keep the default directory for installing Android SDK Tools unchanged; then select the Next button to continue.

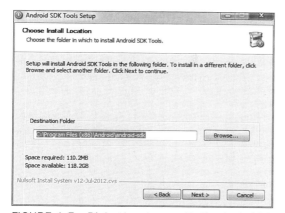

FIGURE 1.5   Dialog box to specify the Android SDK Tools installation location

The next dialog box asks you to specify the `Start Menu folder` where you want the program's shortcuts to appear, as shown in Figure 1.6.

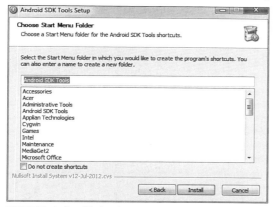

FIGURE 1.6   Dialog box to select the Start menu shortcut folder

A default folder name appears called `Android SDK Tools`. If you do not want to make a `Start Menu folder`, select the `Do not create shortcuts` check box. Let's create the `Start Menu folder` by keeping the default folder name and selecting the `Install` button to begin the installation of the Android SDK Tools. After all the files have been downloaded and installed on the computer, select the `Next` button. The next dialog box tells you that the `Android SDK Tools Setup Wizard` is complete and the Android SDK Tools have successfully installed on the computer. Select `Finish` to exit the wizard, as shown in Figure 1.7.

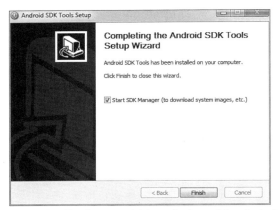

FIGURE 1.7   Successful installation of the Android SDK Tools dialog box

Note that the check box Start SDK Manager (to download system images) is checked by default. It means that after the Finish button is clicked, the Android SDK Manager, one of the tools in the Android SDK Tools package, will be launched. Android SDK is installed in two phases. The first phase is the installation of the SDK, which installs the Android SDK Tools, and the second phase is installation of the Android platforms and other components.

Adding Platforms and Other Components

In this step you see how to use the Android SDK Manager to download and install the important SDK packages required for the development environment. The Android SDK Manager (see Figure 1.8) that opens up shows the list of all the packages and their installation status. The dialog box shows that the Android SDK Tools package is already installed on the machine. To install any other package, you just need to check its check box. The Android SDK Manager recommends a platform by checking the Android 4.1 (API 16) and Google USB Driver package by default, which means the six components beneath the node will also be checked.

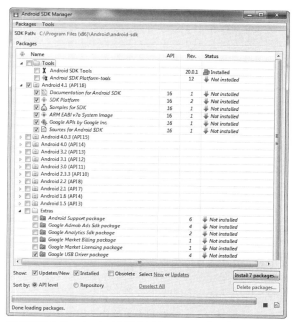

FIGURE 1.8   Android SDK Manager showing the list of packages and their current status

You can check more packages and uncheck existing packages to determine which API
you want to install. Because you want to work with the latest Android API, leave the
default selected. Select all the packages listed under the Extras node as well, and choose
the Install 7 packages button at the bottom to initiate installation. The next dialog
box you see shows the list of the packages that you have selected to install, the package
description, and license terms. You need to select the Accept All option, followed by the
Install button to begin installation, as shown in Figure 1.9.

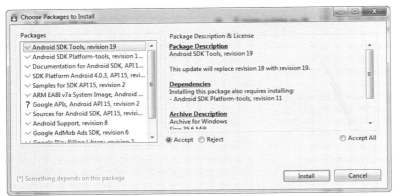

FIGURE 1.9   Dialog box to accept the license terms for the selected packages and to begin installation

An `Android SDK Manager Log` window appears showing the downloading and installation progress. It also shows the list of packages that have been loaded, Android SDK Platform tools that have been downloaded and installed on the machine, and the ones that are still being downloaded (see Figure 1.10—left). After you select the `Close` button, the next dialog window is the `ADB Restart` window that provides information about updates and asks whether you want to restart ADB, as shown in Figure 1.10 (right). Select the `Yes` button in the dialog to restart ADB.

You learn about ADB in detail later in this chapter. For now, it's enough to know that ADB (Android Debug Bridge) is a command-line tool popularly used to communicate with emulator and Android devices.

FIGURE 1.10   Android SDK Manager Log showing the status of different packages (left), and the ADB Restart dialog box, prompting you to restart ADB (right)

The next dialog box is the `Android SDK Manager`, as shown in Figure 1.11. The dialog box confirms that the Android SDK Platform tools, Android 4.1 (API16), and its components have been successfully installed on your machine.

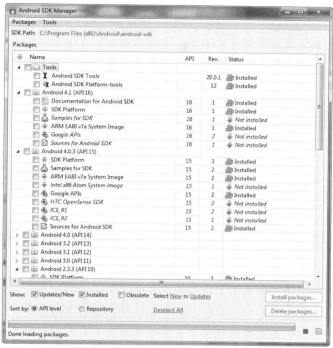

FIGURE 1.11   Android SDK Manager showing that all the desired packages have been successfully installed on the machine

You don't need the Android SDK Manager window for now, so you can go ahead and close it.

An Android application is a combination of several small components that include Java files, XML resource and layout files, manifest files, and much more. It would be very time-consuming to create all these components manually. So, you can use the following applications to help you:

▶ **Eclipse IDE**—An IDE that makes the task of creating Java applications easy. It provides a complete platform for developing Java applications with compiling, debugging, and testing support.

▶ **Android Development Tools (ADT) plug-in**—A plug-in that's added to the Eclipse IDE and automatically creates the necessary Android files so you can concentrate on the process of application development.

Before you begin the installation of Eclipse IDE, first set the path of the JDK that you installed, as it will be required for compiling the applications. To set the JDK path on Windows, right-click on My Computer and select the Properties option. From the System Properties dialog box that appears, select the Advanced tab, followed by the Environment

`Variables` button. A dialog box, `Environment Variables`, pops up. In the `System vari-ables` section, double-click on the `Path` variable. Add the full path of the JDK (`C:\Program Files\Java\jdk1.7.0_04\bin\java.exe`) to the `path` variable and select `OK` to close the windows.

Installing Eclipse

Eclipse IDE is a multilanguage software development platform commonly used for developing Java applications. You can add plug-ins to extend its features for developing applications in other languages. Eclipse can be downloaded from the following URL: http://www.eclipse.org/downloads/. The *Eclipse Classic* and the *Eclipse IDE for Java Developers* are recommended. Just remember that both the JDK and Eclipse must be for the same version, either 32 bit or 64 bit. The latest version, Eclipse Classic 3.7, is available at the time of this writing.

> **NOTE**
>
> To develop Android applications with Eclipse IDE, you need to extend its features by adding the Android Development Tools (ADT) plug-in to it.

Eclipse is a self-contained executable file—that is, all you need to do to install Eclipse is to unzip the downloaded file to any desired folder. To launch Eclipse, run the `Eclipse.exe` file. Eclipse IDE starts by displaying its logo, followed by a `Workspace Launcher` dialog box, as shown in Figure 1.12. The `Workspace Launcher` dialog prompts for the location of the workspace folder where the Eclipse project files will be stored. A default location is displayed that you can change by selecting the `Browse` button.

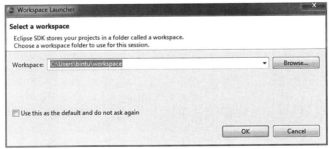

FIGURE 1.12   The first screen you see after launching Eclipse IDE, asking for the Workspace location to save applications

The `Use this as the default and do not ask again` box can be checked if you don't want Eclipse to prompt for the workspace every time it is launched. I recommend not checking this box, as it is better to have a separate workspace for each project to keep them organized. Select the `OK` button to continue. When `Eclipse` finishes loading, an Eclipse Welcome screen is displayed, as shown in Figure 1.13.

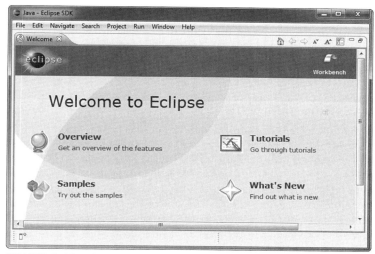

FIGURE 1.13   Eclipse Welcome screen

Select the curved-arrow icon at the top right of the screen to go to the `Workbench`, as shown in Figure 1.14.

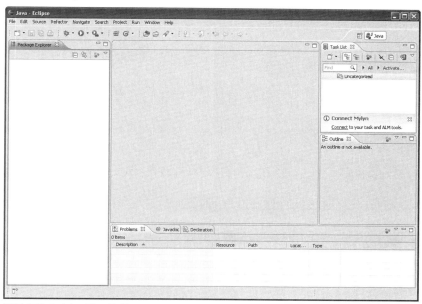

FIGURE 1.14   The Eclipse `Workbench`, showing windows and panels

You can see that all the windows in the `Workbench` (`Package Explorer`, `Editor window`, `Debug window`, and `Task List`), are blank at the moment. These windows update their content as you develop Android applications. One more step is needed before you begin Android application development: installing the Android Development Tools (ADT) plug-in.

Installing the Android Development Tools (ADT) Plug-in

Android Development Tools (ADT) is a plug-in for the Eclipse IDE that provides a powerful, integrated environment to build Android applications. It makes the task of developing Android applications easy. It integrates with Eclipse to add functionality for creating, testing, debugging, and deploying Android applications.

> **NOTE**
>
> The ADT plug-in creates all the necessary base files required by the application.

To install the ADT plug-in, select the `Help, Install New Software...` option from the Eclipse IDE. You see a dialog box asking for the location of the website from which you want to install new software, as shown in Figure 1.15 (left). Select the `Add` button to add a website or repository location. An `Add Repository` dialog box appears, as shown in Figure 1.15 (right). Enter the name of the repository in the `Name` text box. Specify the name of the repository as `ADT Plug-in`, although it can be any other address. In the `Location` box, specify the location of the repository as https://dl-ssl.google.com/android/eclipse/ and click `OK`.

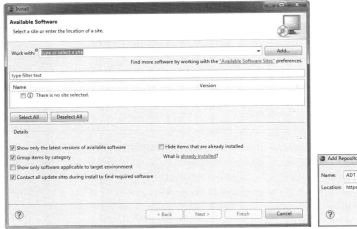

FIGURE 1.15   The dialog box prompting for the location of the software installation website (left), and the dialog box to add the new repository information (right)

Eclipse accesses the list of developer tools available at the specified site and displays it, as shown in Figure 1.16. In the figure, you can see that an entry named `Developer Tools` is displayed, along with four child nodes: `Android DDMS`, `Android Development Tools`, `Android Hierarchy Viewer`, and `Android Traceview`. You need to install all four tools, so select the parent node, `Developer Tools` (its child nodes will be auto-selected), and select the `Next` button.

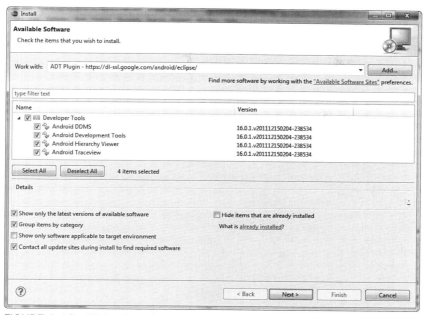

FIGURE 1.16   Dialog box displaying the list of developer tools available in the added repository

You see a dialog box to `Review Licenses` for the ADT. Read the License Agreement, select the `I accept the terms of the license agreements` radio button if you agree with the terms and conditions, and select the `Finish` button, as shown in Figure 1.17.

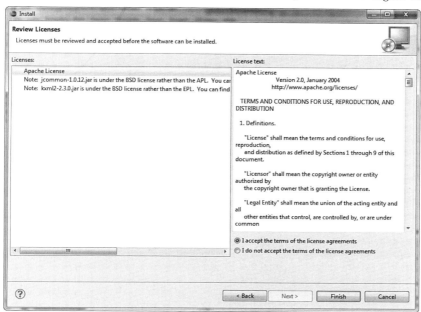

FIGURE 1.17   Dialog box to review and accept/reject the license agreement

The ADT plug-in is then downloaded and installed in Eclipse. After installation of the ADT plug-in, you get a `Software Updates` dialog box asking to restart Eclipse. To make the ADT plug-in show up in the IDE, you need to restart Eclipse. Select the `Restart Now` button from the `Software Updates` dialog box to make the installation changes take effect.

> **NOTE**
>
> If an older version of ADT is already installed in Eclipse, then instead of reinstalling, you just need to update it. Select `Help, Check for Updates` option. A new version of ADT is displayed, and you can update the ADT plug-in by copying and installing the new version.

Making the ADT Plug-in Functional

To make the ADT plug-in functional inside Eclipse, the plug-in needs to point to the Android SDK. Launch the Eclipse IDE and select the `Window, Preferences` option. In the `Preferences` dialog box, select the `Android` node (see Figure 1.18—left) and set the `SDK Location` field to specify the path where the Android SDK is installed on your disk (see Figure 1.18—right).

FIGURE 1.18   (left) The `Preferences` window to specify the location of Android SDK installation, and (right) the list of supportable platforms displayed after specifying the location of the Android SDK installation

On specifying the path of the Android SDK, a list of `SDK Targets` is displayed. You can now develop and test Android applications against any of the displayed targets. You need to select the `Apply` button and click `OK` to reload the `SDK Targets` and close the `Preferences` window. Eclipse now has the ADT plug-ins attached.

The Android applications that you develop need to be tested and debugged before they are loaded on the actual Android device. The Android SDK provides several virtual devices that you can use to test and debug your applications.

Creating Android Virtual Devices

An Android Virtual Device (AVD) represents a device configuration. There are many Android devices, each with different configuration. To test whether the Android application is compatible with a set of Android devices, you can create AVDs that represent their configuration. For example, you can create an AVD that represents an Android device running version 4.1 of the SDK with a 64MB SD card. After creating AVDs, you point the emulator to each one when developing and testing the application. AVDs are the easiest way of testing the application with various configurations.

To create AVDs in Eclipse, select the `Window, AVD Manager` option. An `Android Virtual Device Manager` dialog opens, as shown in Figure 1.19. The dialog box displays a list of existing AVDs, letting you create new AVDs and manage existing AVDs. Because you haven't yet defined an AVD, an empty list is displayed.

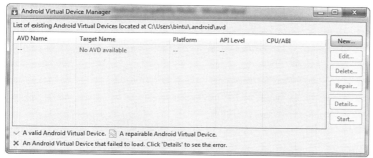

FIGURE 1.19   The AVD Manager dialog

Select the `New` button to define a new AVD. A `Create new Android Virtual Device (AVD)` dialog box, appears (see Figure 1.20—left). The fields are as follows:

▶ `Name`—Used to specify the name of the AVD.

▶ `Target`—Used to specify the target API level. Our application will be tested against the specified API level.

▶ `CPU/ABI`—Determines the processor that we want to emulate on our device.

▶ `SD Card`—Used for extending the storage capacity of the device. Large data files such as audio and video for which the built-in flash memory is insufficient are stored on the SD card.

▶ `Snapshot`—Enable this option to avoid booting of the emulator and start it from the last saved snapshot. Hence, this option is used to start the Android emulator quickly.

▶ `Skin`—Used for setting the screen size. Each built-in skin represents a specific screen size. You can try multiple skins to see if your application works across different devices.

▶ `Hardware`—Used to set properties representing various optional hardware that may be present in the target device.

In the AVD, set the `Name` of the AVD to `demoAVD`, choose `Android 4.1—API Level 16` for the `Target`, set `SD Card` to `64 MiB`, and leave the `Default (WVGA800)` for `Skin`. In the `Hardware` section, three properties are already set for you depending on the selected target. The `Abstracted LCD density` is set to `240`; the `Max VM application heap size` is set to

48, and the `Device RAM size` is set to `512`. You can select these properties and edit their values, delete them, and add new properties by selecting the `New` button. New properties can include `Abstracted LCD density`, `DPad support`, `Accelerometer`, `Maximum horizontal camera pixels`, `Cache partition size`, `Audio playback support`, and `Track-ball support`, among others. Finally, select the `Create AVD` button (see Figure 1.20—right) to see how to create the virtual device called `demoAVD`.

NOTE

You learn about the API and its different levels in Chapter 2, "Basic Widgets."

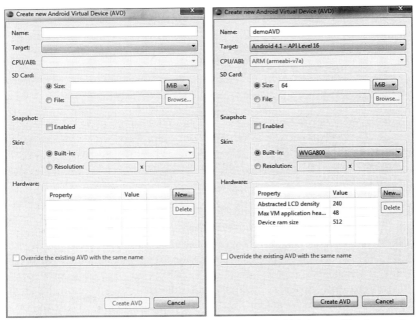

FIGURE 1.20   (left) Dialog to create new AVD, and (right) specifications of new AVD, `demoAVD`

The new AVD, `demoAVD`, is created and displayed in the list of existing AVDs, as shown in Figure 1.21.

NOTE

The larger the allocated SD Card space, the longer it takes to create the AVD. Unless it is really required, keep the SD Card space as low as possible. I would recommend keeping this small, like 64MiB.

FIGURE 1.21   The newly created AVD listed in the AVD Manager

You now have everything ready for developing Android applications—the Android SDK, the Android platform, the Eclipse IDE, the ADT plug-in, and an AVD for testing Android applications. You can now create your first Android application.

Creating the First Android Project

To create an application, open Eclipse and choose `File, New, Android Application Project` or click the `Android Project Creator` icon on the Eclipse toolbar, or select the `File, New, Other` option. A dialog box appears asking you to select the wizard you want to use for the new application. Select `Android Application Project` and click `Next`. You see a dialog box asking for information about the new Android application, as shown in Figure 1.22 (left). In the `Application Name` box, enter the name of the application. Let's name the application `HelloWorldApp`. The `Project Name` box shows the name of the project automatically by default. The project name assigned is the same as the application name, that is, `HelloWorldApp`. You can change the project name if desired. The `Package Name` box shows the default package name, `com.example.helloworldapp`. Let us enter the package name as `com.androidunleashed.helloworldapp`. The package name serves as a unique identifier for the application. A package name may contain uppercase or lowercase letters, numbers, and underscores. The parts of the package name may only begin with letters. The package name must be unique across all packages installed on the Android system. We use the syntax `com.androidunleashed.project_name` for the package names assigned to all the applications in this book. Remember, once an application is published, you cannot change the package name. If you change the application name, then it is considered to be a different application.

From the `Build SDK` drop-down, select the version of Android that represents the device most commonly used by your target audience. Let's select the `Android 4.1 (API 16)` as the target platform. From the `Minimum Required SDK` select the minimum version of the Android platform that is required by the application to run. That is, the application will not run if the device's API level is lower than the API level specified through this drop-down list. Select `API 8: Android 2.2 (Froyo)` from the `Minimum Required SDK` drop-down. It also means the application requires at least API 8 to run. Because this is a new project, select the `Create Project in Workspace` check box. By default, the `Location` where the application is stored on our disk drive is set to the workspace specified when opening Eclipse for the first time. Click `Next` to move further.

The next dialog, `Configure Launcher Icon` (see Figure 1.22—right), is used for configuring the icon for the application. The dialog shows three options—`Image`, `Clipart`, and `Text`—to define the icon for our application. The `Clipart` option is selected by default showing one of the built-in clipart. Select the `Choose` button to open the list of available clipart and then select one of them as our application's icon. We can also select the `Image` option to specify the custom image to be used as our application's icon. The `Text` option, when selected, displays a text box where we can enter text to represent our application. Select the `Font` button to change the font of the text and also to specify the font size and style. The dialog box also shows a `Trim Surrounding Blank Space` check box that we can select to remove the extra blank space around the chosen image, clipart, or text. A scrollbar is also provided to specify the padding around the icon. The icon can be set to appear at the center of the assigned space or can be cropped to accommodate the assigned space. The dialog also shows buttons to make the icon appear in a square or circle shape. Also, two buttons, `Background Color` and `Foreground Color`, are provided that display different colors that can be used as the foreground and background color of the icon. After defining the icon, click `Next` to move further.

> **NOTE**
>
> The Android Project Wizard automatically creates all the required files for the Android application.

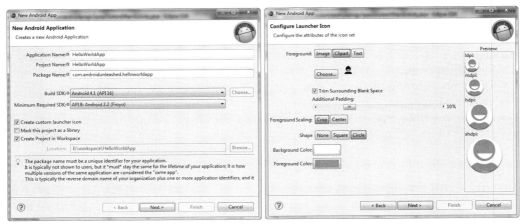

FIGURE 1.22   Dialog box to specify the new project information (left), and configuring the launcher icon (right)

The next dialog prompts us to select whether we want to create an activity. If we want to create an activity, the dialog box asks whether we want to create a `BlankActivity` or `MasterDetailFlow` activity (see Figure 1.23—left). The `BlankActivity` option creates a new blank activity, whereas the `MasterDetailFlow` option creates two master and detail fragments and two activities. We discuss activities and fragments later. To keep things simple, we go for blank activity for this application. Because, we want to create a blank activity, select the `Create Activity` check box and the `BlankActivity` option from the list and then click `Next`. The next dialog confirms the creation of the activity. The Android SDK assigns the default name `MainActivity` to the newly created activity. Also, the layout file is assigned the default name as `activity_main`. The `Title` assigned to the activity by default is `MainActivity` (see Figure 1.23—right). Let's name the activity `HelloWorldAppActivity`. The layout filename and title name automatically change to reflect the newly assigned activity name. The layout name becomes `activity_hello_world_app`, and the `Title` of the application also changes to `HelloWorldAppActivity`. We can always change the auto-assigned layout filename and title of the application. Keeping the auto-assigned layout filename and the title unchanged, create the application by clicking `Finish`.

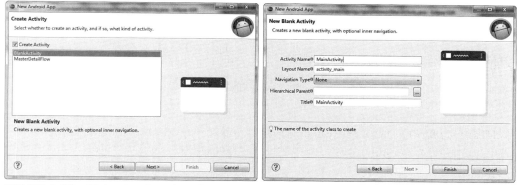

FIGURE 1.23   Dialog box to select the type of activity to create (left), and specifying information of the newly created activity (right)

NOTE

The AVDs with newer SDKs can run applications that require older SDKs. The opposite is not true; that is, an application that requires a newer SDK will not run on an AVD with an older SDK.

The application is created, and the `Package Explorer` shows the files automatically created by the ADT plug-in, as shown in Figure 1.24.

FIGURE 1.24   The `Package Explorer` displaying all the directories, subdirectories, and files automatically created for the application `HelloWorldApp` by ADT

You learn about the role of the different folders and their respective content in the next chapter. For now, we concentrate on the two files that play important roles in almost all Android applications:

▶ **The XML file, activity_hello_world_app.xml, found in the `res/layout` folder**—The file that defines the user interface of the application. It contains controls such as `TextView`, `Button`, `EditText`, and `CheckBox` that are arranged on the display. The definitions in this file control how the user interacts with the application.

▶ **The Java file, HelloWorldAppActivity.java, found in the `src` folder**—The file where action code of the controls defined in the layout file `activity_hello_world_app.xml` is written. Different events that occur via the controls in the layout file are handled with Java code. The data entered by the user is fetched and processed with this Java file.

The idea of separating the user interface from the action code is to isolate the presentation layer from the business logic, allowing developers to change the user interface without rewriting the code itself. As I talk about the XML and Java files, I will frequently use several terms described in Table 1.1.

TABLE 1.1   Common Terms

Term	Description
View	Views are user interface (UI) controls that collectively make up the screen of an application. `TextView`, `Buttons`, and `EditText` controls are all individually known as `Views`, and each is meant to perform a specific task. Views are placed inside containers also known as `layouts` and are configured by setting properties.
ViewGroup	ViewGroups are extensions of the `View` class that can contain multiple child `Views`. They can combine several views into an atomic component and can also arrange or organize child views in a desired manner. Examples of ViewGroup include `LinearLayout`, `AbsoluteLayout`, `TableLayout`, `RelativeLayout`, `FrameLayout`, and `ScrollView`. The ViewGroup that does the job of arranging and organizing child views is known as `layouts`.
Activity	Android applications are made up of one or more activities. An Android application must have at least one activity. An activity usually represents a single screen in an application and consists of one or more views. An activity enables user interaction with the application. If there is more than one activity in the application, they work independently. An activity is created automatically by the Android Project Wizard when you create a new project through the Android Project Wizard. Activities in Android are usually started with an `Intent`.
Intent	An `Intent` is a message-passing mechanism telling the Android application what the user is asking it to do. That is, it notifies the application of the occurrence of a certain event and also represents the action to execute in response to the event, along with the data on which to perform the action.

Laying Out the Application

The screen of the application is defined by an XML file. The controls through which the desired information is displayed to the user and through which the user interacts with the application are defined in XML code. To define a screen of an application, you open the `activity_hello_world_app.xml` file, which is automatically created by the ADT plug-in in the `res/layout` folder. You can create more layout files to represent different screens of an application. All layout files are stored in the `res/layout` directory of the Android project. When you double-click on the `activity_hello_world_app.xml` file, you see the graphical layout of the application in the center window, as shown in Figure 1.25. The layout that you see is the default created by the ADT plug-in. There are two tabs at the bottom of the panel: `Graphical Layout` and `activity_hello_world_app.xml`. The `Graphical Layout` tab shows the layout in the `Eclipse's Visual Designer`, and the `activity_hello_world_app.xml` tab shows the XML code of the layout file.

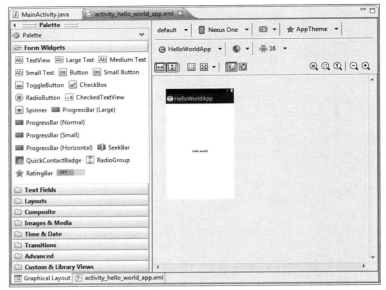

FIGURE 1.25   The layout file `activity_hello_world_app.xml` in the Visual Designer

Using the Visual Designer

The Visual Designer provided by Eclipse displays the layout file graphically. On the left side of the display, the designer shows a list of controls categorized in different categories. Through these controls, you can quickly design a screen. All you need to do is drag the desired control from the left side and drop it on the layout file. You can also configure the controls by settings their properties. The `Properties` panel is hidden by default. To make the `Properties` panel visible, select the `Window`, `Show View`, `Other`, `General`, `Properties` option. After you select a control, all its properties are displayed in the `Properties` panel.

Understanding the XML Version of the Layout File

The XML code of the layout file `activity_hello_world_app.xml` can be seen by selecting the `activity_hello_world_app.xml` tab at the bottom of the panel. The default code is shown in Listing 1.1.

LISTING 1.1   Default Code in the Layout File `activity_hello_world_app.xml`

```
<RelativeLayout                                              #1
    xmlns:android="http://schemas.android.com/apk/res/android"    #2
    xmlns:tools="http://schemas.android.com/tools"
    android:layout_width="match_parent"                      #3
    android:layout_height="match_parent">
    <TextView                                                #4
        android:layout_width="wrap_content"
        android:layout_height="wrap_content"
```

```
        android:layout_centerHorizontal="true"
        android:layout_centerVertical="true"
        android:text="@string/hello"                          #5
        tools:context=".HelloWorldAppActivity" />
</RelativeLayout>
```

Statement #1 declares that all the controls are laid out in `RelativeLayout`. The `RelativeLayout` is the default layout and arranges the controls in relation to the existing controls. Layouts are also known as `containers`, as they hold and arrange the controls within them. You learn about the layouts in detail in Chapter 3, "Laying Out Controls in Containers." Statement #2 defines the Android namespace. This attribute should always be set to http://schemas.android.com/apk/res/android. Namespaces are for assigning unique identifications to application elements, thus avoiding any collisions between element names. Even if you define another element in an XML schema with a name already in use in the Android API (to define its elements), collision will not occur, as they are defined in their respective namespaces.

Statement #4 defines the most basic UI control, `TextView`, which is commonly used for displaying information. In Android, the control that shows up on the screen and is used for displaying information and handling events is known as a `View`. The `TextView` that you see in the layout file (see Listing 1.1) is one of the most common views. You learn about more `Views` later in this book. All the `Views` are placed inside a container. The most common attributes required for laying out a screen view are `layout_width` and `layout_height`. These attributes are also known as `LayoutParams` in the Android SDK. The `layout_width` and `layout_height` attributes specify the width and height that a `View` can have. The two most common values for `layout_width` and `layout_height` are `match_parent` and `wrap_content` constants. The `match_parent` value in statement #3 tells the Android system to fill as much space as possible on the screen based on the available space of the parent layout. The `wrap_content` value tells the Android system to take up only as much space as needed to show the `View`. As the view's content grows, the `View`'s viewable space also grows. Remember, the `layout_width` and `layout_height` attributes are essential attributes, and if you don't provide values for these attributes, the Android application will crash when rendering the view. The value of the attributes `android:layout_centerHorizontal` and `android:layout_centerVertical` are set to `"true"` to make the `TextView` control's text appear at the horizontal and vertical center of the view.

Statement #5 requires that the text to be displayed via the `TextView` control must be fetched from the strings resource file, `strings.xml`, defined in `res/values` folder. The text defined in the `hello` resource in the `strings.xml` file is assigned to the `TextView` for display. For now, let's leave the resource files alone and talk about action code.

NOTE

For Android 2.2 and lower versions, `match_parent` was used as `fill_parent`. The option `fill_parent` is deprecated but is still supported for backward compatibility.

Defining Action Code Through Java

Recall that the Android application Java file is the `Activity` automatically created in the `src` folder by the ADT plug-in. An `Activity` represents a screen of the application and enables user interaction. While creating the application, you defined the `Activity` name as `HelloWorldAppActivity`; hence the Java file is named `HelloWorldAppActivity.java`. The default code in the Java activity file `HelloWorldAppActivity.java` is shown in Listing 1.2.

LISTING 1.2   Default Code in the Java Activity File `HelloWorldAppActivity.java`

```
package com.androidunleashed.helloworldapp;

import android.os.Bundle;
import android.app.Activity;
import android.view.Menu;

public class HelloWorldAppActivity extends Activity {
    @Override
    public void onCreate(Bundle savedInstanceState) {          #1
        super.onCreate(savedInstanceState);                    #2
        setContentView(R.layout.activity_hello_world_app);     #3
    }

    @Override
    public boolean onCreateOptionsMenu(Menu menu) {            #4
        getMenuInflater().inflate(R.menu.activity_hello_world_app, menu);
        return true;
    }
}
```

The Java file is created and maintained in the package `com.androidunleashed.helloworldapp` that you defined at the time of application creation. The first statement of the code in Listing 1.2 confirms it. The file imports the desired class files and also inherits the `Activity` class. The `onCreate()` method is invoked when the `Activity` is started. It calls the `onCreate()` method of the super class (the `Activity` class) for initializing an activity.

In statement #1, the parameter `Bundle savedInstanceState` refers to a bundle used to pass information between different activities. Statement #2 is essential for activity initialization. If you don't write this statement into the Java file, you get a runtime exception.

Statement #3 defines the screen (user interface) of the activity `HelloWorldAppActivity`. Basically, the user interface defined in the layout file `activity_hello_world_app.xml` is set as the content of an activity file. The parameter `R.layout.activity_hello_world_app` in the `setContent()` method refers to the `activity_hello_world_app.xml` file of the project's `res/layout` folder. The character `R` in the parameter refers to the auto-generated `R.java` class file, which we discuss in the next chapter.

Statement #4 defines the `onCreateOptionsMenu()` method that is meant for dealing with menus. We learn about the menus in detail in Chapter 7, "Creating Interactive Menus and ActionBars."

Let's keep the existing default code of `activity_hello_world_app.xml` and `HelloWordlAppActivity.java` and run the application to see the output.

To run the application, you need to create an `Eclipse launch configuration` and choose a virtual device on which to run the application. The Android ADT provides two options for creating `launch configurations`:

▶ **Run configuration**—Used to run an application on a given device

▶ **Debug configuration**—Used to debug an application while it's running on a given device

To create an `Eclipse launch configuration`, select the `Run, Debug Configurations` option. A `Debug Configurations` dialog box opens. Double-click the `Android Application` in the left pane (see Figure 1.26—left). The wizard inserts a new configuration named `New_configuration`, as shown in Figure 1.26 (right).

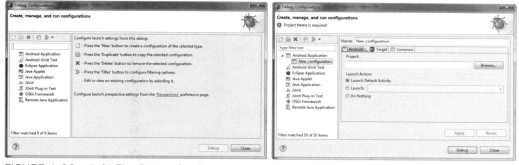

FIGURE 1.26   (left) The Debug Configurations window, and (right) defining a new configuration through the Debug Configurations window

Let's rename the configuration to `HelloWorldApp_configuration`. You need to specify the Android project name that you want to launch in the `Project` box. So, click the `Browse` button and choose the Android project `HelloWorldApp`. From the `Launch` drop-down list in the `Launch Action` section, select the Activity file `com.androidunleashed.helloworldapp.HelloWorldAppActivity` option, followed by the `Apply` button (see Figure 1.27—left). Next, you need to define a device on which to run the application. Select the `Target` tab in the same dialog box. You get the screen shown in Figure 1.27 (right).

The Deployment Target Selection Mode displays the following three options:

▶ `Always prompt to pick device`—Allows you to choose the device or AVD to connect to when using this launch configuration.

▶ `Launch on all compatible devices/AVDs`—Deploys the application automatically on all the compatible AVDs or devices available.

▶ **Automatically pick compatible device**—Deploys the application on the AVDs that are selected. If none of the AVDs are selected, the application is launched on the compatible AVDs or devices available.

Select the third option, `Automatically pick compatible device`, followed by selecting the `demoAVD` that we created earlier to deploy the application automatically on this virtual device (see Figure 1.27—right). We select the `demoAVD` check box because we want to test the application against the Android 4.1 target. You can create more AVDs targeting other platforms from the `AVD Manager` window, and all the defined AVDs automatically appear in this dialog box, allowing you to select the desired target to test the application. After selecting the AVD, select the `Apply` button, followed by `Close` button, to save the launch configuration file.

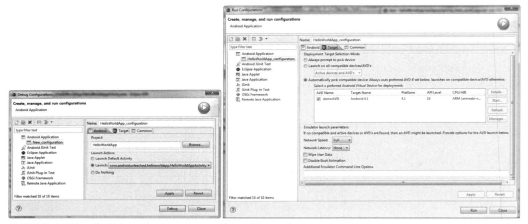

FIGURE 1.27   (left) Creating a new configuration called `HelloWorldApp_configuration`, and (right) defining the target AVD for the new configuration

Running the Application

Once the `launch configuration` file has been made, you can run the Android application by either selecting the `Run` icon from the Eclipse IDE toolbar, selecting the `Run` option from the `Run` menu, or pressing the `Ctrl+F11` keys. Before displaying the application output, the emulator displays several boot screens. The first is shown in Figure 1.28 (left). The window's title bar contains the port number of your computer on which the emulator is running (5554) and the AVD name (`demoAVD`). The second screen shows the Android logo, which is the same logo Android OS users see when they boot their phones. The second screen shows that the loading phase is complete and then displays the default locked Home screen, as shown in Figure 1.28 (right).

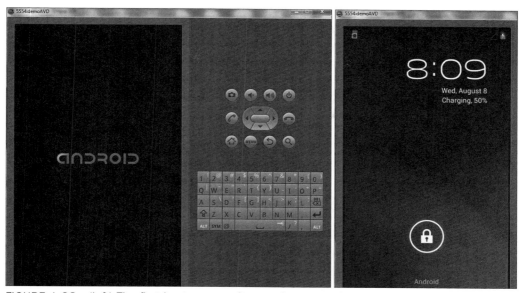

FIGURE 1.28   (left) The first boot screen after running an application showing the Android logo, and (right) the second boot screen showing the default locked Home screen

To unlock the Home screen, either select the Menu button on the emulator, press the F2 key on your computer, or drag the lock to the right side and drop it over the other lock that appears there, as shown in Figure 1.29 (left). After the emulator is unlocked, the Home screen appears (see Figure 1.29—middle), followed by the output of the application, as shown in Figure 1.29 (right).

FIGURE 1.29   (left) Dragging the lock to the right to unlock the Home screen, (middle) the emulator showing the Home screen, and (right) the output of the HelloWorldApp application

You can see that the application's title, HelloWorldAppActivity, appears in the title bar of the emulator, and a text message, Hello world!, is displayed via the TextView control. The text to the TextView is assigned via the strings resource file, strings.xml. The output of the application confirms that the Activity is running correctly in the emulator.

If you feel that the screen shown by the emulator is too big, you can reduce it to the actual device size by selecting the Window, AVD Manager option. From the Android Virtual Device Manager dialog box that opens up (see Figure 1.30—left), select demoAVD and click the Start button. Select the Scale display to real size check box (see Figure 1.30—right) and then click the Launch button to start the emulator.

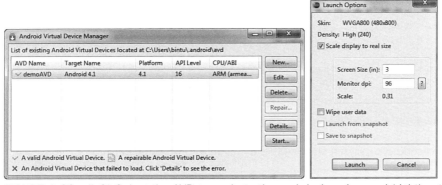

FIGURE 1.30   (left) Select the AVD to scale to the real device size, and (right) setting options in the Launch Options dialog.

Don't close the emulator screen; let it stay active to save the emulator's loading time for running other applications. Whenever you run an application, the ADT checks for a running emulator and deploys it if found.

The Dalvik Virtual Machine (Dalvik VM)

While running Android applications, the Android runtime provides the Dalvik virtual machine that provides an environment to deploy and run Android applications. Dalvik VM is the Android platform's virtual machine written by Dan Bornstein, who named it after a town in Iceland. Android applications run under this virtual machine. It is a specialized virtual machine designed specifically for Android and optimized for mobile devices with limited battery, memory, and computation capability. When you run an application, the Android SDK accesses all the layout and variable information in the XML files, converts it into Java source code, and places it in the R.java file. The Java code in the R.java class file is compiled into the Java byte code files (.class files), which, with the help of a tool named dx (included in the Android SDK), is converted into Dalvik byte code and stored in .dex format. The Dalvik Executable (.dex) format is optimized for efficient storage and low memory consumption.

Android applications are not deployed in dex format. Instead, the dex code is bundled into an APK file.

The Application Package (APK) File

The dex code that you get after converting the Java files is bundled with other required data and resources, including the manifest file AndroidManifest.xml into an Application Package (APK) file, which has an .apk extension. An APK file usually represents a single application and is used to distribute an Android application and install it on a mobile device or emulator. Each APK installed on an Android device is given its own unique ID that remains unchanged for as long as the APK resides on that device. An APK must be signed with a certificate whose private key is held by its developer.

> **NOTE**
>
> The Android Manifest file is an essential Android application configuration file. It contains the application startup information and its different components. You learn about the Android Manifest file and its content in detail in Chapter 2.

Using the TextView Control

So far, our HelloWorldApp contains default code. We simply ran the application whose default structure and code was created for us by the ADT plug-in. Now we learn to use the TextView control, removing the default text and entering our own. You can assign text to the TextView in two ways:

▶ Direct assignment to the TextView control as defined in the layout file activity_ hello_world_app.xml

▶ Indirectly through the Java Activity file HelloWorldAppActivity.java

Assigning the Text Directly in the Layout File

The text that you want to be displayed through the TextView control can be assigned to it in its XML definition in the layout file activity_hello_world_app.xml. From the Package Explorer window, open activity_hello_world_app.xml by double-clicking it in the res/ layout folder. Modify activity_hello_world_app.xml to appear as shown in Listing 1.3.

LISTING 1.3   Code Written in the Layout File activity_hello_world_app.xml

```
<RelativeLayout
    xmlns:android="http://schemas.android.com/apk/res/android"
    xmlns:tools="http://schemas.android.com/tools"
    android:layout_width="match_parent"
    android:layout_height="match_parent">
    <TextView
        android:layout_width="wrap_content"
        android:layout_height="wrap_content"
        android:layout_centerHorizontal="true"
        android:layout_centerVertical="true"
```

```
        android:text="Hello World!"
          tools:context=".HelloWorldAppActivity" />
</RelativeLayout>
```

Notice that only the statement in bold has been modified. In the statement, `android:text="Hello World!"`, the `android:text` is an attribute that is used for assigning a text to the given control. The text `Hello World!` is assigned to the `TextView` control through the `android:text` attribute. You learn about more attributes later in this chapter. Let's run the application to see the impact of changing the `TextView` control's text. You get the output shown in Figure 1.31 (left). The output displays the text, `Hello World!`, that you assigned to the `TextView` control. To make the message "Hello World!" appear at the top-left corner of the screen (see Figure 1.31—right), remove the two attributes `android:layout_centerHorizontal` and `android:layout_centerVertical` from the `<TextView>` tag in the preceding layout file followed by running the application.

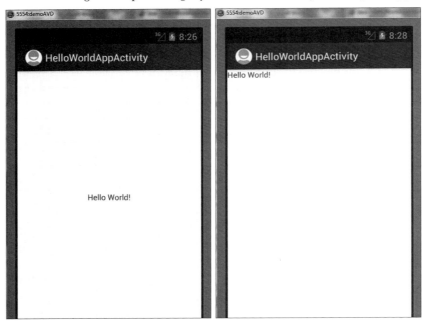

FIGURE 1.31   (left) Text message Hello World! displayed at the center of the screen by setting an attribute in the XML definition, and (right) text message Hello World! appears at the top-left corner of the screen.

Let's now try out the alternate method of assigning text to the `TextView` control by using the Java `Activity` file.

Assigning Text Through the Activity File

To assign text to the `TextView` control through the Java `Activity` file `HelloWorldAppActivity.java` you need to do the following two things:

▶ **Remove the text from XML definition**—The first thing that you need to do is to remove the text that was assigned to the `TextView` control in the layout file `activity_hello_world_app.xml`. Open the `activity_hello_world_app.xml` file and remove the statement `android:text="Hello World!"`. The `TextView` control will appear blank and will not display anything on execution.

▶ **Assign an ID to the `TextView` control**—To access the `TextView` control in the `Activity` file, you have to uniquely identify it by assigning it an ID. To assign an ID to a control, use the `android:id` attribute. Add the following statement to the `TextView` tag in the `activity_hello_world_app.xml` file:

```
android:id="@+id/message"
```

This statement declares that a constant called `message` is assigned as an ID to the `TextView` control and will be used to uniquely identify it from other `Views`. The plus sign (+) in `@+id/message` means that the ID, `message`, must be created if it doesn't already exist.

After you remove the `android:text` and add the `android:id` attribute to the `TextView` tag, the layout file `activity_hello_world_app.xml` appears as shown in Listing 1.4.

LISTING 1.4   Code Written in the Layout File `activity_hello_world_app.xml`

```
<RelativeLayout
    xmlns:android="http://schemas.android.com/apk/res/android"
    xmlns:tools="http://schemas.android.com/tools"
    android:layout_width="match_parent"
    android:layout_height="match_parent" >
    <TextView
        android:id="@+id/message"
        android:layout_width="wrap_content"
        android:layout_height="wrap_content"
        tools:context=".HelloWorldAppActivity" />
</RelativeLayout>
```

After you assign an ID to the `TextView` control, it will be accessible in the `Activity` file. To assign text to the `TextView` control through `HelloWorldAppActivity.java`, modify it to appear as shown in Listing 1.5.

LISTING 1.5   Code Written in the Java Activity File `HelloWorldAppActivity.java`

```
package com.androidunleashed.helloworldapp;

import android.app.Activity;
import android.os.Bundle;
import android.widget.TextView;
```

```
public class HelloWorldAppActivity extends Activity {
@Override
    public void onCreate(Bundle savedInstanceState) {
        super.onCreate(savedInstanceState);
        setContentView(R.layout.main);
        TextView mesg = (TextView)findViewById(R.id.message);    #1
        mesg.setText("Hello World!");                            #2
    }
}
```

Statement #1 locates the control with the message ID in the layout file by using the find-ViewById method of the Activity class and maps it to the TextView object, mesg. It means the mesg object now represents the TextView control with the message ID in the layout file. Statement #2 assigns the text Hello World! to mesg object and hence to the TextView control. Because we are not dealing with any menu, we erased the onCreateOptionsMenu() method from the preceding activity file, which was provided by default.

On running the application, you see the same output shown in Figure 1.31 (right). Let's assign a few more attributes to the TextView control and change its height, width, color, style, background, and alignment. Android provides several units of measurement for specifying the dimension when setting the size of controls. Before you begin applying different attributes to the TextView control, let's have a brief look at the allowable units of measurements used in dimensioning controls.

Applying Dimensions to Controls

Dimensions are commonly used to specify the size and other properties for the controls and layouts. As you design the user interface, you often specify a dimension for a control or layout. The following units of measurements are used:

- ▶ **px (pixels)**—Corresponds to the actual pixels on the screen.

- ▶ **in (inches)**—Based on the actual size of the screen.

- ▶ **mm (millimeters)**—Based on actual size of the screen.

- ▶ **pts (points)**—Points are a fixed dimension—1/72 of an inch.

- ▶ **dip or dp (device-independent pixels)**—Based on the physical density of the screen. This unit is relative to a 160 dpi screen, so one dp is one pixel on a 160 dpi screen. The ratio of dp to pixel changes with the screen density. For example, on a 240 dpi screen, 1 dp is equal to 1.5 pixels.

- ▶ **sp (scale independent pixels)**—Similar to the dp unit, but also depends on the user's font size settings. Hence this unit is preferred while specifying font sizes.

> **NOTE**
>
> Using the px unit is not recommended, as the UI may not render correctly on a device with a different screen resolution.

To align the content within the control, the gravity attribute is used. Let's go ahead and discuss it.

Aligning Content with the Gravity Attribute

The gravity attribute is used for aligning the content within a control or its container. For example, to align the text of the `TextView` control to the center, you set the value of its `android:gravity` attribute to `center`. Some of the valid values for the `android:gravity` attribute are shown in Table 1.2.

TABLE 1.2   Values Used in the Gravity Attribute

Value	Description
top	Aligns the content to the top of the container. In terms of `TextView`, this value makes the text align at the top of the `TextView` control.
bottom	Aligns the content to the bottom of the container.
left	Aligns the content to the left of the container.
right	Aligns the content to the right of the container.
center_horizontal	Places the content at the horizontal center of its container's width.
center_vertical	Places the content at the vertical center location of its container.
fill_horizontal	Grows the horizontal size of the content to fill its container.
fill_vertical	Grows the vertical size of the container to fill its container.
center	Places the content at the center of its container (at the horizontal and vertical center position).

You can combine two or more values of any attribute using the ' | ' (pipe character). For example, the following example centrally aligns the text horizontally as well as vertically within a control:

```
android:gravity="center_horizontal|center_vertical"
```

If you want to apply the gravity attribute to any control through the Java activity file, the Java method used for this purpose is `setGravity()`.

Commonly Used Attributes

Table 1.3 lists the attributes commonly applied to configure the controls.

TABLE 1.3   List of Commonly Used Attributes

Attribute	Java Method	Description
android:width	setWidth()	Sets the width of the control equal to the specified value. The value can be in any of the units of measurement discussed in Dimensions. For example, `android:width="150dp"`
android:height	setHeight()	Sets the height of the control equal to the given value. For example: `android:height="200dp"`
android:text	setText()	Sets the text to display in the given control. For example: `android:text="Hello World!"`
android:textColor	setTextColor()	Sets the color of the text. The color value is specified in the form of hexadecimal RGB values, preceded by an optional alpha channel. Formats for specifying color are `"#RGB"`, `"#ARGB"`, `"#RRGGBB"`, or `"#AARRGGBB"`. You learn more about colors in Chapter 4, "Utilizing Resources and Media." For example: `android:textColor="#0F0"`
android:textSize	setTextSize()	Sets the size of the text. For example: `android:textSize="25dp"`
android:ellipsize	setEllipsize()	If set, causes text that is longer than the width of the container to be ellipsized instead of breaking it in the middle. Ellipsized means an ellipsis (...) will appear that represents text that could not be accommodated in the available width. Valid options are `none`, `start`, `middle`, `end`, and `marquee`, where `none` will not ellipsize and break the text in the middle. The options `start`, `middle`, and `end` display dots at the beginning, middle, and end of the container's width. The marquee makes the text to scroll horizontally in the available width of the container. For example: `android:ellipsize="end"`

Attribute	Java Method	Description
android:singleLine	setTransformationMethod()	Decides whether the control is supposed to be a single-line input or multiple-line input. Assigning the Boolean value *true* to this attribute creates a single horizontal scrollable line instead of wrapping it into multiple lines. For example: android:singleLine="true"
android:background	setBackgroundResource()	Sets the background color of a control or makes an image appear in the background of the control. An image from the drawable resource can be specified to appear in the control's background. More on drawable resources and images can be found in Chapter 4. For example: android:background="#0000ff"
android:textStyle	setTypeface()	Applies a style to the text. The valid values are bold, italic, bold-italic. For example: android:textStyle="italic"
android:typeface	setTypeface()	Sets the text to appear in a given font style. The valid options are normal, sans, serif, and monospace. For example: android:typeface="serif"

Let's apply some of the attributes shown in the Table 1.3 to the TextView control (in activity_hello_world_app.xml) of the HelloWorldApp application, as shown in the following example:

```
<TextView
    android:id="@+id/message"
    android:layout_width="match_parent"
    android:layout_height="wrap_content"
    tools:context=".HelloWorldAppActivity"
    android:typeface="serif"
    android:textColor="#0F0"
    android:textSize="25dp"
    android:textStyle="italic"
    android:gravity="center_horizontal" />
```

This code makes the text of the `TextView` control appear in `serif` font, green color, 25dp size, italic, and at the horizontal center of the container, as shown in Figure 1.32 (left).

> **NOTE**
>
> The "dp" unit represents density-independent pixels based on a 160-dpi (pixel density per inch) screen. We learn more about units in Chapter 4.

Let's apply a few more attributes to the `TextView` control here:

```
<TextView
        android:id="@+id/message"
        android:layout_width="wrap_content"
        android:layout_height="wrap_content"
        tools:context=".HelloWorldAppActivity"
        android:gravity="center"
        android:height="200dp"
        android:width="150dp"
        android:typeface="serif"
        android:textColor="#0F0"
        android:textSize="25dp"
        android:textStyle="bold"   />
```

This code makes the content of the `TextView` wrap move to the next line if the width assigned to it is insufficient. The `TextView` control is assigned the `height` and `width` of 200dp and 150dp, respectively, and its text is set to appear at the center of its assigned size. The text appears in `serif` font, green color, 25dp font size, and bold. The text in the `TextView` appears as shown in Figure 1.32 (right).

FIGURE 1.32   (left) Text message formatted with different attributes and displayed via `TextView` control, and (right) the text of `TextView` wrapped to the next line

Using the Android Emulator

The Android emulator is used for testing and debugging applications before they are loaded onto a real handset. The Android emulator is integrated into Eclipse through the ADT plug-in.

Limitations of the Android Emulator

The Android emulator is useful to test Android applications for compatibility with devices of different configurations. But still, it is a piece of software and not an actual device and has several limitations:

▶ Emulators no doubt help in knowing how an application may operate within a given environment, but they still don't provide the actual environment to an application. For example, an actual device has memory, CPU, or other physical limitations that an emulator doesn't reveal.

▶ Emulators just simulate certain handset behavior. Features such as GPS, sensors, battery, power settings, and network connectivity can be easily simulated on a computer.

▶ SMS messages are also simulated and do not use a real network.

▶ Phone calls cannot be placed or received but are simulated.

▶ No support for device-attached headphones is available.

▶ Peripherals such as camera/video capture are not fully functional.

▶ No USB or Bluetooth support is available.

The emulator provides some facilities too. You can use the mouse and keyboard to interact with the emulator when it is running. For example, you can use your computer mouse to click, scroll, and drag items on the emulator. You can also use it to simulate finger touch on the soft keyboard or a physical emulator keyboard. You can use your computer keyboard to input text into UI controls and to execute specific emulator commands. Some of the most commonly used commands are

▶ Back [ESC button]

▶ Call [F3]

▶ End [F4]

▶ Volume Up [KEYPAD_PLUS, Ctrl-5]

▶ Volume down [KEYPAD_MINUS, Ctrl-F6]

▶ Switching orientations [KEYPAD_7, Ctrl-F11/KEYPAD_9, Ctrl-F12]

You can also interact with an emulator from within the DDMS tool. Eclipse IDE provides three perspectives to work with: *Java perspective, Debug perspective,* and *DDMS perspective.* The Java perspective is the default and the one with which you have been working up to now. You can switch between perspectives by choosing the appropriate icon in the top-right corner of the Eclipse environment. The three perspectives are as follows:

▶ **The Java perspective**—It's the default perspective in Eclipse where you spend most of the time. It shows the panes where you can write code and navigate around the project.

▶ **The Debug perspective**—Enables application debugging. You can set breakpoints; step through the code; view LogCat logging information, threads, and so on.

▶ **The Dalvik Debug Monitor Service (DDMS) perspective**—Enables you to monitor and manipulate emulator and device status. It also provides screen capture and simulates incoming phone calls, SMS sending, and GPS coordinates.

The Debug perspective and DDMS are discussed in detail in Chapter 5, "Using Selection Widgets and Debugging." To manage content in the device or emulator, you can use the ADB (Android Debug Bridge).

The Android Debug Bridge (ADB)

The Android Debug Bridge (ADB) is a client-server program that is part of the Android SDK. It is used to communicate with, control, and manage the Android device and emulator.

It consists of three components:

▶ **Client**—Runs on a computer machine. It can be invoked from the command prompt using the `adb` command.

▶ **Daemon**—Runs as a background process in either an emulator instance or in the device itself.

▶ **Server**—Runs in a computer machine in the background. It manages the communication between the client and the daemon.

When you install the Android SDK, the Android Debug Bridge is also automatically installed along with it. When the Android Debug Bridge is active, you can issue `adb` commands to interact with one or more emulator instances. You can install applications, push and pull files, and run shell commands on the target device. Using the shell commands, you can perform several tasks such as listing existing applications, deleting applications, and querying or modifying SQLite databases available on the device.

To access ADB through Windows, open the command prompt and navigate to the folder where `adb.exe` is located by using the `cd` command. By default, `adb.exe` is installed in `C:\ Program Files (x86)\Android\android-sdk\platform-tools`. When you are in the folder where `adb` is found, you can issue the following commands to interact with the device or emulator:

▶ **adb** `devices`—Displays the list of devices attached to the computer. Figure 1.33 shows the currently running emulator on your computer, *emulator-5554*.

▶ **adb** `push`—Copies files from your computer to the device/emulator.

Syntax:

```
adb push source destination
```

where *source* refers to the file along with its path that you want to copy, and *destination* refers to the place in the device or emulator where you want to copy the file. Figure 1.33 copies the mp3 file, `song1.mp3`, from local disk drive D: to the `sdcard` folder of the running emulator.

▶ **adb** `pull`—Copies files from the device/emulator to your computer.

Syntax:

```
adb pull source [destination]
```

Figure 1.33 shows how the `song1.mp3` file can be copied from the sdcard of the emulator to the android folder on local disk drive E:.

▶ **adb** `shell`—Displays the shell prompt where you can issue Unix commands. You can see the names of different files and folders of the emulator after issuing an `ls` command (see Figure 1.33).

You can issue the commands to list, rename, and delete applications from the emulator. For example, to delete the file `song1.mp3` that you pushed into the emulator, you issue the `rm` command, as shown in Figure 1.33.

Leave the shell; press `Ctrl+D`.

▶ **adb** `install`—Installs an application from your computer to the device/emulator.

Syntax:

```
adb install appname.apk
```

This code

```
C:\Program Files (x86)\Android\android-sdk\platform-tools>adb install D:\
androidunleashed\loginApp.apk
```

installs the application package file `loginApp.apk` into the emulator.

```
C:\Program Files (x86)\Android\android-sdk\platform-tools>adb devices
List of devices attached
emulator-5554   device

C:\Program Files (x86)\Android\android-sdk\platform-tools>adb push D:\song1.mp3 /sdcard
61 KB/s (8414449 bytes in 133.836s)

C:\Program Files (x86)\Android\android-sdk\platform-tools>adb pull /sdcard/song1.mp3 E:\android
72 KB/s (8414449 bytes in 112.807s)

C:\Program Files (x86)\Android\android-sdk\platform-tools>adb shell
# ls
ls
sqlite_stmt_journals
cache
sdcard
etc
system
sys
sbin
proc
init.rc
init.goldfish.rc
init
default.prop
data
root
dev
# cd sdcard
cd sdcard
# pwd
pwd
/sdcard
# ls
ls
song1.mp3
# rm song1.mp3
rm song1.mp3
# ls
ls
# ^D
C:\Program Files (x86)\Android\android-sdk\platform-tools>
```

FIGURE 1.33   Output of different commands issued through ADB

Let's conclude the chapter by understanding how an Android application is launched on a physical device.

Launching Android Applications on a Handset

To load an application onto a real handset, you need to plug a handset into your computer, using the USB data cable. You first confirm whether the configurations for debugging your application are correct and then launch the application as described here:

1. In Eclipse, choose the Run, Debug Configurations option.

2. Select the configuration HelloWorldApp_configuration, which you created for the HelloWorldApp application.

3. Select the Target tab, set the Deployment Target Selection Mode to Manual. The Manual option allows us to choose the device or AVD to connect to when using this launch configuration.

4. Apply the changes to the configuration file by clicking the Apply button.

5. Plug an Android device into your computer, using a USB cable.

6. Select Run, Debug in Eclipse or press the F11 key. A dialog box appears, showing all available configurations for running and debugging your application. The physical device(s) connected to the computer are also listed. Double-click the running Android device. Eclipse now installs the Android application on the handset, attaches a debugger, and runs the application.

Summary

In this chapter, you saw how to install the Android SDK Starter Package, add platforms and other components, and install Eclipse and the Android Development Tools (ADT) plug-in. You made the ADT plug-in functional and created Android Virtual Devices to run and deploy Android applications. You learned how to create a First Android Project and set the layout of the application. The XML version of the layout file was described, and you learned how to define action code through Java. You were introduced to the concept and usage of different tools such as Dalvik VM, APK, ADB, and the Android Emulator. You learned to use the `TextView` control in the application and assign text to it via the layout and activity files. You also learned about the usage of commonly used attributes of controls, including the gravity attribute. Finally, you learned the steps to launch an application on a handset.

The next chapter focuses on the basic widgets used in an Android application. You learn about

▶ Folders and files that are automatically created by the ADT plug-in

▶ `Activities`, the Android Activity life cycle, usage of `Android Manifest` file, commonly used layouts and controls, and how event handling is performed

▶ How to create an anonymous inner class, implement the `OnClickListener` interface, and declare the event handler in the XML definition of the control

▶ How to create and start your own `Activity`, `Intent`, create your own layout file, create a new `Activity`, register the new `Activity`, and start the `Activity`

▶ How to use three controls—`EditText`, `CheckBox`, and `RadioButton`—and develop Android applications using these controls

CHAPTER 2

Basic Widgets

Almost all popular applications are interactive. These applications interact with the user, and, depending on the data supplied by the user, desired actions and/or processing are performed. The user interface controls thus play a major role in getting feedback from the user. In this chapter, we learn about the basic widgets supplied by the Android SDK for creating simple user interfaces. In later chapters, we learn about complex widgets for creating sophisticated user interfaces. Also, for better understanding of the Android application, we discuss different Android Project files and Activities that are automatically created for us by the Android Eclipse plug-in to reduce the work needed to develop an Android application.

Understanding the Role of Android Application Components

To gain an understanding of the role and functionality of different components that make up an Android application, you create a new Android application and study each of its components.

Let's start by creating an application that prompts the user to enter a name and displays a Welcome message in return. The Android Project Wizard creates all the required files for an Android application. To create an application, open Eclipse and choose, File, New, Android Application Project or click the Android Project Creator icon on the Eclipse toolbar. You see a dialog box, as shown in Figure 2.1 (left).

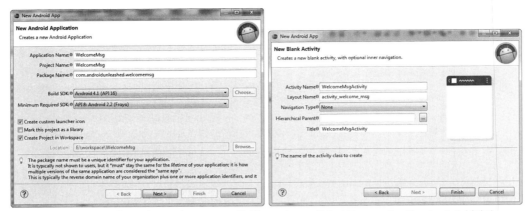

FIGURE 2.1   Specifying the project name (left), and specifying the application target (right)

▶ In the `Application Name` box, enter the name of the Android project. Let's name the application `WelcomeMsg`. The `Project Name` is automatically assigned, which is the same as the application name by default. Being a unique identifier, the `Package Name` is `com.androidunleashed.welcomemsg`.

▶ From the `Build SDK` drop-down, select `Android 4.1 (API 16)` as the target platform as we expect it to be the version commonly used by your target audience.

▶ Select `API 8: Android 2.2 (Froyo)` from the `Minimum Required SDK` drop-down to indicate that the application requires at least API level 8 to run.

▶ Because this is a new project, select the `Create Project in Workspace` check box to create the project files at the Workspace location specified when opening Eclipse for the first time. The `Create custom launcher icon` check box is selected by default and enables us to define the icon of our application. Click the `Next` button to move to the next dialog box.

▶ The next dialog is `Configure Launcher Icon`, which is meant for configuring the icon for the application. Because we want to have a default icon for our application, keeping the default options selected in the dialog box, click the `Next` button to move further.

▶ The next dialog prompts us to select whether we want to create an activity. Also, it prompts for the type of activity. Because we want to create a blank activity, select the `Create Activity` check box and the `BlankActivity` option from the list and then click `Next`.

▶ The next dialog (see Figure 2.1—right) asks us to enter information about the newly created activity. Name the activity `WelcomeMsgActivity`. The layout filename and title name automatically change to reflect the newly assigned activity name. The layout name becomes `activity_welcome_msg`, and the `Title` of the application also changes to `WelcomeMsgActivity`. We can always change the auto-assigned layout file-name and title of the application.

▶ Keeping the auto-assigned layout filename and the title unchanged, click the `Finish` button after supplying the required information. The application is created by ADT, along with all the necessary files.

Understanding the Utility of Android API

The Android platform provides a framework API that applications can use to interact with the underlying Android system. The framework API consists of a core set of packages and classes; XML elements for declaring layouts, resources, and so on; a manifest file to configure applications; permissions that applications might require; intents; and much more. The framework API is specified through an integer called API level, and each Android platform version supports exactly one API level, although backward compatibility is there; that is, earlier API levels are supported. The initial release of the Android platform provided API Level 1, and subsequent releases have incremented the API level.

Table 2.1 shows the API level supported by each version of the Android platform.

TABLE 2.1   The Android Platform and Corresponding API Levels

Platform Version	API Level	Code Name
Android 4.1	16	Jelly Bean
Android 4.0.3	15	Ice Cream Sandwich
Android 4.0	14	Ice Cream Sandwich
Android 3.2	13	Honeycomb
Android 3.1	12	Honeycomb
Android 3.0	11	Honeycomb
Android 2.3.3	10	Gingerbread
Android 2.3.1	9	Gingerbread
Android 2.2	8	Froyo
Android 2.1	7	Eclair
Android 2.0.1	6	Eclair
Android 2.0	5	Eclair
Android 1.6	4	Donut
Android 1.5	3	Cupcake
Android 1.1	2	
Android 1.0	1	

Each Android API level shows the maximum framework API revision that the Android platform supports. You need to select the *Target Name*, and hence the API level for the application, as doing so helps the application specify the framework API revision it requires to operate.

Remember that to enable applications to run on a maximum number of platforms, you can set the applications to target the lowest platform, Android 1.0. Because of backward compatibility, the application that supports the Android 1.0 platform can easily run on all the devices, even on the devices with the Android 4.0 platform. However, the opposite is not true. There is a cost to selecting the lowest platform too: you cannot use features supported in higher platforms. Thus, all the applications that you create in this book target platform 4.1 to exploit the latest features added to the API.

After creating the new Android application by name, `WelcomeMsg`, the ADT creates a `WelcomeMsg` directory in the default Eclipse workspace for the project. It also creates subdirectories for keeping source files, compiled or generated files, resource files, and so on. Certain default content is also created in these subdirectories that are required in an Android application. Several files, such as `AndroidManifest.xml` and `project.properties`, are also automatically created to make the job of configuring the Android application easier. You can have a look at the files and directories created by ADT if you expand the project tree in the `Package Explorer` window (see Figure 2.2).

FIGURE 2.2   Package Explorer window showing different directories, subdirectories, and files automatically created by ADT

Let's take a quick look at the different folders and files created by ADT.

Overview of the Android Project Files

The following files and directories are created for the Android application. The list below is just an overview of the files and directories. We will talk about these files and directories in detail as we move further in the book:

▶ **/src folder**—The folder that contains the entire Java source file of the application. The folder contains a directory structure corresponding to the package name supplied in the application. The folder contains the project's default package: `com.androidunleashed.welcomemsg`. On expanding the package, you find the Activity of the application, the `WelcomeMsgActivity.java` file, within it.

▶ **/src/com.androidunleashed.welcomemsg**—Refers to the package name of the application. To avoid any collision among the class names, variable names, and so on used in the application with those of other Android applications, each application has to be packaged in a unique container.

▶ **/src/com.androidunleashed.welcomemsg/WelcomeMsgActivity.java**—The default Activity file of the application. Recall that each application has at least one Activity that acts as the main entry point to the application. The Activity file is automatically defined as the default launch Activity in the Android Manifest file.

▶ **/gen folder**—Contains Java files generated by ADT on compiling the application. That is, the `gen` folder will come into existence after compiling the application for the first time. The folder contains an `R.java` file that contains references for all the resources defined in the `res` directory. It also contains a `BuildConfig.java` file that is used to run code only in debug mode. It contains a `DEBUG` constant that helps in running debug-only functions.

▶ **/gen/com.androidunleashed.welcomemsg/R.java**—All the layout and other resource information that is coded in the XML files is converted into Java source code and placed in the `R.java` file. It also means that the file contains the ID of all the resources of the application. The `R.java` file is compiled into the Java byte code files and then converted into `.dex` format. You should never edit this file by hand, as it is automatically overwritten when you add or edit resources.

▶ **Android SDK `jar` file**—The `jar` file for the target platform.

▶ **/assets folder**—The `assets` folder is empty by default. It stores raw asset files that may be required in the application. It may contain fonts, external JAR files, and so on to be used in the application. The `assets` folder is like a resource folder where uncompiled resources of the project are kept and no IDs are generated for the resources kept here.

▶ **/bin folder**—The folder that stores the compiled version of the application.

▶ **/res folder**—The folder where all application resources (images, layout files, and string files) are kept. Instead of hard coding an image or string in an application, a better approach is to create a respective resource in the `res` folder and include its reference in the application. This way, you can change the image or string or any other resource anytime without disturbing the code. Each resource is assigned a unique resource ID, which automatically appears in the `R.java` file and thus in the `R` class after compilation, enabling us to refer to the resource in the code. To categorize and arrange the resources, three subdirectories are created by default: `drawable`, `layout`, and `values`.

▶ **/res/drawable-xhdpi, /res/drawable-hdpi, /res/drawable-mdpi, /res/drawable-ldpi**—the application's icon and graphic resources are kept in these folders. Because devices have screens of different densities, the graphics of different resolutions are kept in these folders. Usually, graphics of 320dpi, 240dpi, 160dpi, and 120dpi are used in Android applications. The graphics with 320dpi, 240dpi, 160dpi, and 120dpi are stored in the `res/drawable-xhdpi`, `res/drawable-hdpi/`, `res/drawable-mdpi`, and `res/drawable-ldpi` folders, respectively. The application picks up the graphic from the correct folder after determining the density of the current device.

▶ **/res/layout**—Stores the layout file(s) in XML format.

▶ **/res/values**—Stores all the values resources. The values resources include many types such as string resource, dimension resource, and color resource.

▶ **/res/layout/activity_welcome_msg.xml**—The layout file used by `WelcomeMsgActivity` to draw views on the screen. The views or controls are laid in the specified layout.

▶ **/res/values/strings.xml**—Contains the string resources. String resources contain the text matter to be assigned to different controls of the applications. This file also defines string arrays.

▶ **AndroidManifest.xml**—The central configuration file for the application.

▶ **proguard.cfg**—Defines how ProGuard optimizes the application's code. ProGuard is a tool that removes unused code from the Android application and optimizes it, which increases performance. It is also used to obfuscate the code to help protect it from decompilation.

▶ **project.properties**—A build file used by Eclipse and the Android ADT plug-in. It contains project settings such as the build target. You can use this file to change various properties of the project. If required, the file should not be edited directly but through editors available in Eclipse.

Other folders that may become the part of an Android application include `bin`, `libs`, and `referenced libraries`. The `bin` folder is hidden. The `libs` and `referenced libraries` folders don't appear until a third-party library and reference are added to the project.

It's clear that the Java Activity file is the main file that drives the entire Android application. The default content of the Activity file `WelcomeMsgActivity.java` is shown in Listing 2.1.

LISTING 2.1   Default Code in the `WelcomeMsgActivity.java` File

```java
package com.androidunleashed.welcomemsg;

import android.os.Bundle;
import android.app.Activity;
import android.view.Menu;

public class WelcomeMsgActivity extends Activity {

    @Override
    public void onCreate(Bundle savedInstanceState) {
        super.onCreate(savedInstanceState);
        setContentView(R.layout.activity_welcome_msg);
    }

    @Override
    public boolean onCreateOptionsMenu(Menu menu) {
        getMenuInflater().inflate(R.menu.activity_welcome_msg, menu);
        return true;
    }
}
```

Understanding Activities

Every unique screen the user interacts with in an application is displayed through an Activity—one Activity for each screen. Users can interact with an application by performing different actions with the visual controls found in the Activity. A simple application may consist of just one Activity, whereas large applications contain several Activities. Each Activity of an application operates independently of the others. A stack of Activities is maintained while running an application, and the Activity at the top of the stack is the one currently being displayed. When the `Back` button is pressed, the Activity is popped from the stack, making the previous Activity the current Activity, which therefore displays the previous screen. The transition from one Activity to another is accomplished through the use of asynchronous messages called `intents`. Intents can be used to pass data from one Activity to another. All of the Activities in the application must be defined in the Application's manifest file, an XML file that keeps track of all the components and permissions of the application. Each Activity in an Android application is either a direct subclass of the `Activity` base class or a subclass of an `Activity` subclass.

Activities have life cycles and inherit a set of life cycle methods from the `Activity` base class that are executed when the corresponding life cycle state of the Activity is reached.

Understanding the Android Activity Life Cycle

The Android Activity life cycle defines the states or events that an Activity goes through from the time it is created until it finishes running. The Activity monitors and reacts to these events by executing methods that override the `Activity` class methods for each event. Table 2.2 lists the methods executed during the different events that occur during an Android Activity life cycle.

TABLE 2.2   List of Methods Instantiated During Different Events of an Android Activity Life Cycle

Method	Description
onCreate()	The method called when the Activity is first created. It initializes the Activity and is used to create views of the application, open persistent data files required by the Activity, and so on.
onStart()	The method called just before the Activity becomes visible on the screen. An Activity can be either in a foreground or background state. When an Activity switches to the background state, the onStop() method is executed, and when it switches to foreground, the onResume() method is invoked.
onResume()	The method called whenever the Activity becomes the foreground Activity, whether it is right after the execution of the onStart() method or when some other foreground Activity exits and the Activity appears at the top of the Activity stack, making it a foreground Activity. A foreground Activity interacts with the user, that is, receives keyboard and touch inputs and accordingly generates the response.
onPause()	The method called when the Activity is stopped and no longer visible in the foreground and some other Activity is switched to the foreground. Because the Activity is not visible. This method contains commands to minimize consumption of resources and to store the Activity state, which will be used when the Activity resumes to the foreground. You can use this method to suspend any action that consumes CPU cycles or battery.
onStop()	The method called when the Activity is no longer visible, either because another Activity is switched to the foreground or because the Activity is being destroyed.
onDestroy()	The method used when the Activity is completed and is about to get destroyed. The method may or may not be called; that is, the system may simply terminate the process. You can use this method to release the resources consumed by the Activity.

All the activities of an application, permissions, and intents are defined through the XML-structured manifest file `AndroidManifest.xml`. For each Activity, there needs to be an entry in the `AndroidManifest.xml` file, where you can define labels, permissions, and so on. In fact, the manifest file is the configuration file where all the different components of the application are defined.

Role of the Android Manifest File

The configuration file `AndroidManifest.xml` is created by ADT when creating a new Android project and is kept in the project's root directory. It's an XML file that defines the overall structure and information about the application, for example, the activities, services, and intents used in the application. It also contains the permissions that the application might need to run. The manifest also defines metadata of the application such as its icon and label. Besides this, the file also contains the information required in building and packaging the application for installing and deploying it on an Android device or the emulator. To sum up, the application manifest file contains all the essential information required by the Android system to run the application.

> **NOTE**
>
> *Services* refers to the processes that run in the background with no visual user interface. Services are used for the tasks that you want to run quietly in the background without user action and that supply some data or information to other applications. Services start when an Activity starts or when a device boots up, keeps running in the background, and stops automatically on finishing its task. Music playing in the background, a program displaying stock market figures, and a GPS tracking program that monitors the location of the device are few examples of services.

Listing 2.2 shows the manifest file for the application that you just created.

LISTING 2.2   Default Code in the Android Manifest File

```
<manifest xmlns:android="http://schemas.android.com/apk/res/android"
package="com.androidunleashed.welcomemsg"
    android:versionCode="1"
    android:versionName="1.0" >
    <uses-sdk
        android:minSdkVersion="8"
        android:targetSdkVersion="15" />
    <application
        android:icon="@drawable/ic_launcher"
        android:label="@string/app_name"
        android:theme="@style/AppTheme" >
        <activity
            android:name=".WelcomeMsgActivity"
            android:label="@string/title_activity_welcome_msg" >
            <intent-filter>
                <action android:name="android.intent.action.MAIN" />
                <category android:name="android.intent.category.LAUNCHER" />
            </intent-filter>
        </activity>
    </application>
</manifest>
```

The `<manifest>` tag, is the root element of this XML document and contains several attributes:

- ▶ `android`—Identifies the Android namespace used to provide several system attributes used within the application.

- ▶ `package`—Its value is set to the application's Java package. The name of the application package acts as the unique identifier for the application in the Android device.

- ▶ `versionCode/versionName`—The `versionCode` attribute is used to define the current application version. The version is used internally to compare application versions. The `versionName` attribute is used to specify a version number that is displayed to users.

- ▶ `<uses-sdk>`—This tag is optional and is used to specify the maximum, minimum, and preferred API level required for the application to operate. Three attributes are used with this tag as follows:

  - ▶ `android:minSdkVersion`—Used to specify the minimum API level required for this application to run. The default value is "1." For example, the following attribute says that the minimum API level required by the application is 15:
    ```
    android:minSdkVersion="15"
    ```
    Hence, the application will run on API Level 15 and above, but will not run on API Level 14 or below.

  - ▶ `android:targetSdkVersion`—Used to specify the preferred API level on which the application is designed to run.
  - ▶ `android:maxSdkVersion`—Used to specify the maximum API level supportable by the application; that is, the application cannot run on an API level higher than the one specified in this attribute. While installing the application, the Android system checks the `<uses-sdk>` attributes defined in the application's manifest files and compares it with its own internal API level. The application can be installed only if

    The value of the `android:minSdkVersion` attribute of the application must be less than or equal to the system's API level. If the `android:minSdkVersion` attribute is not declared, it is assumed that the application requires API Level 1.

    The value of the `android:maxSdkVersion` attribute of the application (if it is declared) must be equal to, or greater than, the system's API level.

- ▶ `<application>` tag—Nested within `<manifest>` is `<application>`, which is the parent of application control tags. The `icon` and `label` attributes of the `application` tag refer to icon and label resources that will be displayed in Android devices to represent the application. In Chapter 4, "Utilizing Resources and Media," you learn about the resources in detail. For the time being, it is enough to understand that `@string` and `@drawable` refer to the strings and drawable resources, respectively. The term `"@drawable/icon"` refers to the image file `icon.png` in the `res/drawable` folder, and `"@string/app_name"` refers to the control resource with ID `app_name` in the `strings.xml` file that is stored in the `res/values` folder of the application.

▶ **`<activity>` tag**—Nested within `<application>` is the `<activity>` tag, which describes an Activity component. This tag's name attribute identifies a class that is an Activity, `WelcomeMsgActivity`. This name begins with a period character to show that it's relative to the `com.androidunleashed.welcomemsg` package. That is, the `WelcomeMsgActivity` is relative to `<manifest>`'s package value, `com.androidunleashed.welcomemsg`. Remember that on creating the new Android project `WelcomeMsg`, an Activity named `WelcomeMsgActivity` was automatically created for us in the specified package `com.androidunleashed.welcomemsg` by the ADT.

▶ **`<intent- filter>`**—Nested within `<activity>` is the `<intent-filter>`. The intents are used to interact with the applications and services. By default, the intent specifies the action as MAIN and the category as LAUNCHER; that is, it makes this Activity available from the application launcher, allowing it to launch when the application starts. Basically, the `<intent-filter>` tag declares the capabilities of different components through the nested `<action>` and `<category>` tags.

Besides the preceding default tags used in the manifest file, the following are some of the most commonly used tags:

▶ **`<service>` tags**—Used for declaring services. Services refer to the processes that run in the background without a user interface. They perform required processing and handle events silently without user interaction.

▶ **`<receiver>` tags**—Used for declaring broadcast receivers. Broadcast receivers are used to listen and respond to broadcast announcements. Applications initiate broadcasts for the interested applications when some event occurs that requires attention; for example, essential information or confirmation is required from the user before taking some destructive action. An application can have any number of broadcast receivers. A broadcast receiver responds by taking a specific action.

▶ **`<provider>` tags**—Used for declaring content providers. Content providers provide content, that is, data to applications. They help in handling, storing, and sharing data such as audio, images, video, and contact lists with other applications. Android ships with a number of content providers that the applications can use to access and share data with other applications.

▶ **`<uses-permission>` tags**—Used for declaring the permissions that the application needs.

Example:

`<uses-permission android:name="android.permission.CAMERA" />`—Used for the application that needs to use the camera.

`<uses-permission android:name="android.permission.INTERNET"/>`—Used for the application that needs to access the Internet

NOTE

The `<uses-permission>` tags are nested within `<manifest>` tags. They appear at the same level as the `<application>` tag.

Using the Manifest Editor

To configure the application, you don't have to manipulate the XML code of the `AndroidManifest.xml` file manually; instead you can take the help of the Manifest Editor provided by the Android Development Tools (ADT) plug-in. To use the Manifest Editor in Eclipse, right-click the `AndroidManifest.xml` file in the Package Explorer window, and select `Open With, Android Manifest Editor`. This presents the Android Manifest Overview screen, as shown in Figure 2.3.

FIGURE 2.3   Manifest Editor

The screen provides a user-friendly interface to configure the application, enabling you to set the application version information and root-level manifest nodes, including `uses-sdk` and `uses-permission`, for example. It also provides shortcut links to the Application, Permissions, Instrumentation, and raw XML screens. In short, the task of managing the application—setting icons, setting the theme, applying security, testing settings, and so on—becomes easy through Manifest Editor.

Creating the User Interface

There are three approaches to creating user interfaces in Android. You can create user interfaces entirely in Java code or entirely in XML or in both (defining the user interface in XML and then referring and modifying it through Java code). The third approach, the combined approach, is highly preferred and is the one used in this book. The XML file in which you create the user interface is `activity_welcome_msg.xml` found in the `res/layout` folder. In the `activity_welcome_msg.xml` file, different controls or views that you want to interact with the user are defined. The controls or views in `activity_welcome_msg.xml` have to be laid out in some way. The default layout in which the controls or views are usually arranged is `RelativeLayout`. The `activity_welcome_msg.xml` file is also referred to as the Activity layout file.

Listing 2.3 shows the original content of the layout file `activity_welcome_msg.xml`.

LISTING 2.3   Default Code in the `activity_welcome_msg.xml` File

```
<RelativeLayout xmlns:android="http://schemas.android.com/apk/res/android"
    xmlns:tools="http://schemas.android.com/tools"
    android:layout_width="match_parent"
    android:layout_height="match_parent" >
    <TextView
        android:layout_width="wrap_content"
        android:layout_height="wrap_content"
        android:layout_centerHorizontal="true"
        android:layout_centerVertical="true"
        android:text="@string/hello_world"
        tools:context=".WelcomeMsgActivity" />
</RelativeLayout>
```

Recall that in this application you want to prompt the user to enter a name, and in return the application displays a welcome message along with the entered name. So, if the name entered is "Kelly," the application displays "Welcome Kelly!" For the current application, you only need to work with two files: `activity_welcome_msg.xml` and the Activity file `WelcomeMsgActivity.java`. Let's begin with the `activity_welcome_msg.xml` file. Double-click the `activity_welcome_msg.xml` file and overwrite its default content with the code shown in Listing 2.4.

LISTING 2.4   Code Written in the `activity_welcome_msg.xml` File

```
<LinearLayout xmlns:android="http://schemas.android.com/apk/res/android"
    android:orientation="vertical"
    android:layout_width="match_parent"
    android:layout_height="match_parent">
    <TextView
        android:layout_width="match_parent"
        android:layout_height="wrap_content"
        android:text="Enter your name:"/>
    <EditText
        android:layout_width="match_parent"
        android:layout_height="wrap_content"
        android:id="@+id/user_name"/>
```

```
<Button
        android:layout_width="match_parent"
        android:layout_height="wrap_content"
        android:id="@+id/click_btn"
        android:text="Click Me"/>
<TextView
        android:layout_width="match_parent"
        android:layout_height="wrap_content"
        android:id="@+id/response"/>
</LinearLayout>
```

In the preceding XML file, four controls are used: two `TextViews`, one `EditText`, and one `Button` control. The first `TextView` prompts the user to enter a name by displaying the message *Enter your name:* and the second `TextView` is used to display the *Welcome* message to the user. The `EditText` control provides a blank text box, allowing the user to enter a name. The `Button` control is for generating an event; that is, only when the user selects the `Button` control will a welcome message be displayed through the second `TextView` control. The `EditText`, `Button`, and one of the `TextView` controls are assigned the IDs user_name, click_btn, and response, respectively. These IDs are used to access these controls in the Java Activity file. The `Button` control is assigned the caption `Click Me`. The four controls are laid out in `LinearLayout`—a placement that arranges the controls contained in it either horizontally or vertically.

Commonly Used Layouts and Controls

The views or the controls that we want to display in an application are arranged in an order or sequence by placing them in the desired layout. The layouts also known as Containers or ViewGroups are used for organizing the views or controls in the required format. Examples of layouts are `LinearLayout`, `FrameLayout`, and so on. A brief description of layouts follows:

▶ `LinearLayout`—In this layout, all elements are arranged in a descending column from top to bottom or left to right. Each element contains properties to specify how much of the screen space it will consume. Depending on the orientation parameter, elements are either arranged in row or column format.

▶ `RelativeLayout`—In this layout, each child element is laid out in relation to other child elements. That is, a child element appears in relation to the previous child. Also, the elements are laid out in relation to the parent.

▶ `AbsoluteLayout`—In this layout, each child is given a specific location within the bounds of the parent layout object. This layout is not suitable for devices with different screen sizes and hence is deprecated.

▶ **FrameLayout**—This is a layout used to display a single view. Views added to this are always placed at the top left of the layout. Any other view that is added to the FrameLayout overlaps the previous view; that is, each view stacks on top of the previous one.

▶ **TableLayout**—In this layout, the screen is assumed to be divided in table rows, and each of the child elements is arranged in a specific row and column.

▶ **GridLayout**—In this layout, child views are arranged in a grid format, that is, in the rows and columns pattern. The views can be placed at the specified row and column location. Also, more than one view can be placed at the given row and column position.

2

NOTE

The three terms used to represent user interface elements are *view*, *widget*, and *control*. They are used interchangeably in this book.

The following list highlights some of the controls commonly used in Android applications:

▶ **TextView**—A read-only text label. It supports multiline display, string formatting, and automatic word wrapping.

▶ **EditText**—An editable text box that also accepts multiline entry and word-wrapping.

▶ **ListView**—A ViewGroup that creates and manages a vertical list of views, displaying them as rows within the list.

▶ **Spinner**—A TextView and an associated list of items that allows us to select an item from the list to display in the text box.

▶ **Button**—A standard command button.

▶ **CheckBox**—A button allowing a user to select (check) or unselect (uncheck).

▶ **RadioButton**—A mutually exclusive button, which, when selected, unselects all other buttons in the group.

Event Handling

In our sample application, you want the user to enter a name in the EditText control. After the user has entered the name and clicks the Button control, a welcome message displays on the screen. The action of clicking a Button, pressing the Enter key, or performing any action on any control is considered an event. The reaction to the event, that is, the action to be taken when the event occurs, is called event handling. To handle an event, you use the listeners that wait for an event occurrence. When an event occurs, the listeners detect it and direct the program to the appropriate routine.

An event listener is an interface in the `View` class that contains a single callback method, called an event occurrence. For example the callback method `onClick()` is called when the user clicks on a button. For event handling, the event listener is either implemented in the `Activity` class or is defined as an `anonymous` class. Thereafter, an instance of the implementation is passed to the respective control through the `setOnClickListener()` method.

> **NOTE**
>
> *Click* is just one type of an event.

In this chapter we discuss three ways of event handling:

▶ Creating an anonymous inner class

▶ Implementing the `OnClickListener` interface

▶ Declaring the event handler in the XML definition of the control

Creating an Anonymous Inner Class

In this method of event handling, you implement a listener inline; that is, an `anonymous` class is defined with an `OnClickListener` interface, and an `onClick(View v)` method is implemented in it. The anonymous inner class is passed to the listener through the `setOnClickListener()` method. To implement the concept of `anonymous inner` class for event handling, the Java activity file `WelcomeMsgActivity.java` is modified to appear as shown in Listing 2.5.

LISTING 2.5   Code Written in the `WelcomeMsgActivity.java` File

```
package com.androidunleashed.welcomemsg;

import android.app.Activity;
import android.os.Bundle;
import android.widget.TextView;
import android.widget.EditText;
import android.widget.Button;
import android.view.View;

public class WelcomeMsgActivity extends Activity {
    @Override
    public void onCreate(Bundle savedInstanceState) {
        super.onCreate(savedInstanceState);
        setContentView(R.layout.activity_welcome_msg);
        Button b = (Button)this.findViewById(R.id.click_btn);
```

```
      b.setOnClickListener(new Button.OnClickListener(){
          public void onClick(View v)   {
                  TextView resp = (TextView) findViewById(R.id.response);
                  EditText name = (EditText) findViewById(R.id.user_name);
                  String str = "Welcome " + name.getText().toString() + " !";
                  resp.setText(str);
          }
      });
   }
}
```

You can see that a listener is implemented inline through an anonymous class with an onClickListener interface. A callback method onClick(View v) is implemented in the class, and, finally, the anonymous class is associated with the Button object b. Now, whenever the Button control is clicked in the application, the onClick() method is invoked. In the onClick() method, you fetch the TextView and the EditText controls defined in the layout file with the IDs response and user_name, and then map them to the TextView and EditText objects resp and name, respectively. That is, the objects resp and name represent the TextView and EditText controls defined in the layout file. The name entered by the user in the EditText control is accessed, and, after it is prefixed with a Welcome message, is assigned to a String object, str. Finally, the str object is assigned to the TextView object, resp, to display the Welcome message, along with the user's name on the screen.

NOTE

The class method onCreate() is called when the Activity is first created. It is used to initialize the Activity and to create views of the application.

The application is complete. Let's run it to see its output.

Running the Application

To run the application, you can create an Eclipse launch configuration as described in Chapter 1, "Introduction to Android." If you run the application without creating a launch configuration, you see the Run As dialog box shown in Figure 2.4. Choose Android Application, and a launch configuration is automatically created.

FIGURE 2.4   Run As dialog box asking the way to run the current application

The ADT compiles the application and then deploys it to the emulator with the default launch configuration.

The Android emulator is loaded showing the output of the application. You can see in the emulator that a prompt message `Enter your name:` appears via the `TextView` control. In addition, a blank text box appears via the `EditText` control where you will enter a name, and a button appears via `Button` control (see Figure 2.5—top). After you enter the user name `Kelly` and select the `Click Me` button, a welcome message, `Welcome Kelly!`, appears via the `TextView` control (see Figure 2.5—bottom). Recall that you defined all these controls in the file `activity_welcome_msg.xml`.

FIGURE 2.5   (top) Application asking for the username, and (bottom) Welcome message displayed along with the username

You have seen the use of the anonymous inner class in event handling. Next, you try another method of event handling, the Activity Implementing OnClickListener interface.

Activity Implementing the OnClickListener Interface

In this method of event handling, the Activity class implements the OnClickListener interface, which requires us to implement the onClick() method in this class. The onClick() method is declared inside the class, and the listener is set by passing a reference to the class by the following statement: b.setOnClickListener(this);

To implement the OnClickListener interface, the activity file WelcomeMsgActivity.java is modified to appear as shown in Listing 2.6.

LISTING 2.6   Implementing the OnClickListener Interface in the WelcomeMsgActivity.java File

```
package com.androidunleashed.welcomemsg;

import android.app.Activity;
import android.os.Bundle;
import android.widget.TextView;
import android.widget.EditText;
import android.widget.Button;
```

```java
import android.view.View;
import android.view.View.OnClickListener;

public class WelcomeMsgActivity extends Activity implements OnClickListener {
    @Override
    public void onCreate(Bundle savedInstanceState) {
        super.onCreate(savedInstanceState);
        setContentView(R.layout.activity_welcome_msg);
        Button b = (Button)this.findViewById(R.id.click_btn);
        b.setOnClickListener(this);
    }

    public void onClick(View v) {
        TextView resp = (TextView)this.findViewById(R.id.response);
        EditText name = (EditText)this.findViewById(R.id.user_name);
        String str = "Welcome " + name.getText().toString() + " !";
        resp.setText(str);
    }
}
```

This code locates the `Button` control that you created in the `activity_welcome_msg.xml` file (with the ID `click_btn`), assigns it to the instance `b`, and attaches an event listener to it. When the event occurs via a button click, the `onClick()` method is executed. The `TextView` and `EditText` controls of `activity_welcome_msg.xml` are located and accessed via the `resp` and `name` objects, respectively. The username entered in the `EditText` control is fetched and displayed along with a welcome message via the `TextView` control; that is, we get the same output as shown previously in Figure 2.5.

In the `WelcomeMsg` application, an event such as `Click` occurs via the `Button` control, which, in turn invokes the respective event handler that does the desired action.

Besides the Java code, you can define the event handler in the XML file too. That is, you can declare the event handler in the XML definition of the control and define the event handler in the Activity class. Let's discuss this process in detail.

Declaring the Event Handler in the XML Control Definition

Since Android SDK 1.6, there has been another way to set up a click handler for the `Button` controls. In the XML definition of a `Button` in the layout file `activity_welcome_msg.xml`, you can add an `android:onClick` attribute. This attribute is used to represent the method you want to execute when a click event occurs via the `Button` control. For example, the following statement declares the `dispMessage()` method as the event handler for the button when a click event occurs:

```
android:onClick="dispMessage"
```

All you need to do is define the `dispMessage()` in the Activity class to perform the desired action.

Remember, to try out this method of event handling, you need to modify the layout file `activity_welcome_msg.xml` of the application. The code that we write in the `activity_welcome_msg.xml` file is as shown in Listing 2.7. The statement in bold is the newly added code; the rest is the same as Listing 2.4.

LISTING 2.7   Declaring an Event Handler in the `activity_welcome_msg.xml` File

```
<LinearLayout xmlns:android="http://schemas.android.com/apk/res/android"
    android:orientation="vertical"
    android:layout_width="match_parent"
    android:layout_height="match_parent">
    <TextView
        android:layout_width="match_parent"
        android:layout_height="wrap_content"
        android:text="Enter your name:"/>
    <EditText
        android:layout_width="match_parent"
        android:layout_height="wrap_content"
        android:id="@+id/user_name"/>
    <Button
        android:id="@+id/click_btn"
        android:layout_width="match_parent"
        android:layout_height="wrap_content"
        android:text="Click Me"
        android:onClick="dispMessage" />
    <TextView
        android:layout_width="match_parent"
        android:layout_height="wrap_content"
        android:id="@+id/response"/>
</LinearLayout>
```

In this code block, the attribute `android:onClick` means that the `dispMessage()` method must be invoked when the button is clicked. Note that you can declare the same event handler for several controls; that is, you can declare the `dispMessage()` method as the event handler for multiple buttons.

In the Java Activity file `WelcomeMsgActivity.java`, the method `dispMessage()` is defined. This method performs the task of accessing the name entered in the `EditText` control and displaying a welcome message along with the entered name. After you add the method `dispMessage()`, the Activity file `WelcomeMsgActivity.java` appears as shown in Listing 2.8.

LISTING 2.8   Adding the `dispMessage()` Method to the `WelcomeMsgActivity.java` File

```
package com.androidunleashed.welcomemsg;

import android.app.Activity;
import android.os.Bundle;
import android.view.View;
import android.widget.TextView;
import android.widget.EditText;

public class WelcomeMsgActivity extends Activity {
    @Override
    public void onCreate(Bundle savedInstanceState) {
        super.onCreate(savedInstanceState);
        setContentView(R.layout.activity_welcome_msg);
    }
    public void dispMessage(View v) {
        TextView resp = (TextView) findViewById(R.id.response);
        EditText name = (EditText) findViewById(R.id.user_name);
        String str = "Welcome " + name.getText().toString() + " !";
        resp.setText(str);
    }
}
```

You can see in the `dispMessage()` method that the `TextView` and `EditText` controls with the IDs response and user_name are accessed from the layout file, `activity_welcome_msg.xml` and mapped to the `TextView` and `EditText` objects resp and name, respectively. The username entered in the `EditText` control is accessed through the name object (`EditText` control) and is assigned to the resp object (`TextView` control) along with the welcome message for display. On running the application, you get the same output shown previously in Figure 2.5 (top and bottom).

Can you define the same event handler method in more than one `Button` control? The answer is yes. But you might think that if the same event handler, `dispMessage`, is declared in more than one `Button` control, then how does the application know which control has invoked it? The solution is the `View` object; that is, the control on which the event has occurred is also passed to the event handler. In the event handler, the `getId()` method of the `View` object can be used to discover the button from which the event has occurred and an appropriate action can be taken, as shown in the following code snippet:

```
public void dispMessage(View v) {
    if (v.getId()==R.id.id1) {

    }
    if (v.getId()==R.id.id2) {

    }
```

```
    . . . . . .
    . . . . .
}
```

`id1` and `id2` are the IDs of the button controls that declare the same event handler.

Previously in Listing 2.7, notice that we used two `TextView` controls. The first `TextView` control is used for displaying the text *Enter your name*. The second `TextView` does the task of displaying a welcome message to the user.

Is there any other way of displaying a response in an Android application besides using the `TextView` control? Yes, you can use `Toast` class for displaying output.

Displaying Messages Through `Toast`

A `Toast` is a transient message that automatically disappears after a while without user interaction. It is usually used to inform the user about happenings that are not very important and does not create a problem if they go unnoticed. A `Toast` is created by calling the static method, `makeText()`, of the `Toast` class. The syntax of the `makeText()` method is shown here:

```
Toast.makeText(activity_context, string_to_display, duration)
```

The method needs the `Activity` (`Context`) `String` to display, as well as the `duration` for which the message is displayed on the screen. You can also supply the ID of the String resource that you want to display. The duration is expressed in the form of constants, such as `Toast.LENGTH_SHORT` or `Toast.LENGTH_LONG`, to determine the duration for which the string's message remains on the screen. The method returns a `Toast` instance. You call the `show()` method on the returned `Toast` instance to display the containing string or message. You learn about string resources in Chapter 4.

To display the welcome message through `Toast`, modify the Java activity file `WelcomeMsgActivity.java` as shown in Listing 2.9. Only the code in bold is new.

LISTING 2.9   `WelcomeMsgActivity.java` File for Displaying a Message Through `Toast`

```
package com.androidunleashed.welcomemsg;

import android.app.Activity;
import android.os.Bundle;
import android.widget.EditText;
import android.view.View;
import android.widget.Toast;

public class WelcomeMsgActivity extends Activity {
    @Override
    public void onCreate(Bundle savedInstanceState) {
        super.onCreate(savedInstanceState);
```

```
        setContentView(R.layout.activity_welcome_msg);
    }
    public void dispMessage(View v) {
        EditText name = (EditText) findViewById(R.id.user_name);
        String str = "Welcome " + name.getText().toString() + " !";
        Toast.makeText(WelcomeMsgActivity.this, str, Toast.LENGTH_SHORT).show();
    }
}
```

You can see that a `String` object, `str`, is defined, which contains a `Welcome` message and the name entered by the user in the `EditText` control with the ID `user_name`. The text in the `String` object, `str`, is displayed via `Toast`, as shown in Figure 2.6. The message `Welcome Kelly !` automatically disappears after a while.

FIGURE 2.6   Displaying a Welcome message through `Toast`

Since a `Toast` is transient, it is not visible for an extensive period, and you don't receive any confirmation that the user actually saw it. Therefore, we continue to use the `TextView` control in Android applications to display information to the user.

In Listing 2.9, you saw that the Activity of the application is automatically created by the ADT that drives the application. Can we create our own activity? Let's see how in the next section.

Creating and Starting an Activity

The structure that is used to start, stop, and transition between Activities within an application is called an `Intent`.

Describing Operations Through Intent

An intent is a data structure that describes operations to perform in an Android application. It consists of an action that the application needs to perform, data to operate on, and other information helpful in executing the operation. Intent can be explicit or implicit as follows:

▶ **Explicit Intent**—In an explicit intent, you specify the Activity required to respond to the intent; that is, you explicitly designate the target component. Because the developers of other applications have no idea of the component names in your application, an explicit intent is limited to be used within an application—for example, transferring internal messages.

▶ **Implicit Intent**— In an implicit intent, you just declare intent and leave it to the platform to find an Activity that can respond to the intent. That is, you don't specify the target component that should respond to the intent. This type of intent is used for activating components of other applications. It is the job of the Android platform to search for the most suitable component to handle the implicit intent.

Method Used to Start an Activity

The method used to start an activity is `startActivity()`. First create an implicit or explicit intent object and pass it to the `startActivity()` method in the format shown here:

```
startActivity(my_intent);
```

where `my_intent` refers to the intent that is passed to the method as a parameter. The `startActivity()` method finds and starts the single Activity that best matches the given intent.

To explicitly specify the Activity that you want to start through an intent, create a new intent specifying the current application context and the class name of the activity you want to launch and pass this `Intent` to the `startActivity()` method, as shown here:

```
startActivity(new Intent(this, Welcome.class));
```

In the preceding statement, you created an explicit intent and initialized it by passing the Activity context, this and the `Welcome`'s class instance, which is the activity that you want to launch. The `Intent` object is passed to the `startActivity()` method, which launches the activity described by `Welcome.class`. If `startActivity()` is unable to find the specified activity, an `android.content.ActivityNotFoundException` is thrown.

Let's explore the concept of creating and starting your own activity using an example. You create an application similar to the `WelcomeMsg` application but with the following two differences:

▶ Instead of using the default Activity automatically created by the ADT, you create your own Activity in this application.

▶ You create and use your own layout file instead of the default layout file.

Launch Eclipse and create a new Android Project called `WelcomeApp` with the following settings:

▶ Select `Android 4.1` as the `Target` platform.

▶ Let the application name be the default, which is `WelcomeApp`.

▶ Let the package name be `com.androidunleashed.welcomeapp`.

▶ Let the Activity name be the default, which is `WelcomeAppActivity`.

From now on, we call the settings shown here the default settings. Almost all applications in this book will be created with these default settings unless otherwise specified.

In any new Android project that you create, ADT creates a layout file `activity_welcome_app.xml` by default. But as mentioned earlier, in this application you learn to create and use your own layout file.

Creating Your Own Layout File

To create a new layout file, from the `Package Explorer` window, right click the `res/layout` folder and select the `New, Android XML File` option. A dialog box appears asking for information about the new Android XML File. In the `File` text box, enter the filename as `welcome` (no need to add the `.xml` extension). Select the option `LinearLayout` from the `Root Element`, which denotes that you want to create a linear layout file, and finally, select the `Finish` button. The layout file, `welcome.xml`, is created in the `res/layout` folder. The initial content of the file is shown in Listing 2.10.

LISTING 2.10   Default Code in the `welcome.xml` File

```xml
<?xml version="1.0" encoding="utf-8"?>
<LinearLayout xmlns:android="http://schemas.android.com/apk/res/android"
    android:layout_width="match_parent"
    android:layout_height="match_parent"
    android:orientation="vertical" >
</LinearLayout>
```

Let's add two `TextView` controls, an `EditText` and a `Button` control, to the layout file (the same controls as in the `WelcomeMsg` application). After you add these controls, the contents of the `welcome.xml` file will be as shown in Listing 2.11.

LISTING 2.11   Code Written in the `welcome.xml` File

```xml
<?xml version="1.0" encoding="utf-8"?>
<LinearLayout xmlns:android="http://schemas.android.com/apk/res/android"
    android:orientation="vertical"
    android:layout_width="match_parent"
    android:layout_height="match_parent">
    <TextView
```

```
        android:layout_width="match_parent"
        android:layout_height="wrap_content"
        android:text="Enter your name:"/>
    <EditText
        android:layout_width="match_parent"
        android:layout_height="wrap_content"
        android:id="@+id/user_name"/>
    <Button
        android:layout_width="match_parent"
        android:layout_height="wrap_content"
        android:id="@+id/click_btn"
        android:text="Click Me"/>
    <TextView
        android:layout_width="match_parent"
        android:layout_height="wrap_content"
        android:id="@+id/response"/>
</LinearLayout>
```

After the layout file is completed, it's time to create a new Activity.

Creating a New Activity

You know that an Activity file is in the form of a Java file. So, you need to add a Java file to the package `com.androidunleashed.welcomeapp` that's inside the `src` folder of the application. Click the `src` node in the `Package Explorer` window to expand it. The package `com.androidprogrs.welcomeapp` is displayed, showing the default Activity file `WelcomeAppActivity.java` inside it. To create an Activity, right-click the package `com.androidunleashed.welcomeapp` and select the `New`, `Class` option. A `New Java Class` dialog box appears, requesting you to enter the name of the Java file. In the `Name` text box, enter the name of the Activity file, `Welcome` (no need to add the `.java` extension). Keeping all the default options selected, select the `Finish` button to create the Java file.

The Activity `Welcome.java` is added to the package with the default content, as shown here:

```
package com.androidunleashed.welcomeapp;
public class Welcome {
}
```

Let's add some action to the Activity file. Recall that this application is similar to the `WelcomeMsg` application that you created before; that is, it prompts the user to enter a name and prints a welcome message when the `Button` control is selected. So, let's add the code shown in Listing 2.12 to the newly created Activity file.

LISTING 2.12   Code Written in the `Welcome.java` File

```java
package com.androidunleashed.welcomeapp;

import android.app.Activity;
import android.os.Bundle;
import android.widget.TextView;
import android.widget.EditText;
import android.widget.Button;
import android.view.View;

public class Welcome extends Activity {
    @Override
    protected void onCreate(Bundle savedInstanceState) {
        super.onCreate(savedInstanceState);
        setContentView(R.layout.welcome);
        Button b = (Button)this.findViewById(R.id.click_btn);
        b.setOnClickListener(new Button.OnClickListener() {
            public void onClick(View v) {
                TextView resp = (TextView) findViewById(R.id.response);
                EditText name = (EditText) findViewById(R.id.user_name);
                String str = "Welcome " + name.getText().toString() + " !";
                resp.setText(str);
            }
        });
    }
}
```

Registering the New Activity

Only the components declared in the application's manifest file `AndroidManifest.xml` are visible to Android and hence can be used to run the application. This means that the new Activity `Welcome.java` must be declared in the `AndroidManifest.xml` file to make it visible to Android and start it. The `AndroidManifest.xml` file is shown in Listing 2.13. The statement in bold is added to register the newly created activity, `Welcome.java`.

LISTING 2.13   The `AndroidManifest.xml` File

```xml
<manifest xmlns:android="http://schemas.android.com/apk/res/android"
    package="com.androidunleashed.welcomeapp"
    android:versionCode="1"
    android:versionName="1.0" >
    <uses-sdk
        android:minSdkVersion="8"
        android:targetSdkVersion="15" />
    <application
```

```
        android:icon="@drawable/ic_launcher"
        android:label="@string/app_name"
        android:theme="@style/AppTheme" >
        <activity
            android:name=".WelcomeAppActivity"
            android:label="@string/title_activity_welcome_app" >
            <intent-filter>
                <action android:name="android.intent.action.MAIN" />
                <category android:name="android.intent.category.LAUNCHER" />
            </intent-filter>
        </activity>
        <activity android:name=".Welcome" android:label="@string/app_name" />
    </application>
</manifest>
```

Starting the Activity

After registering the Activity `Welcome.java` in the `AndroidManifest.xml` file, you can now start it by using the `startActivity()` method discussed at the beginning of the section. Because the new Activity is started from the default activity file of the application `WelcomeAppActivity.java`, the `startActivity()` method needs to be added to the same file. The code in the default Activity file `WelcomeAppActivity.java`, after adding the `startActivity()` method, appears as shown in Listing 2.14.

LISTING 2.14   The `WelcomeAppActivity.java` File

```
package com.androidunleashed.welcomeapp;

import android.app.Activity;
import android.os.Bundle;
import android.content.Intent;

public class WelcomeAppActivity extends Activity {
    @Override
    public void onCreate(Bundle savedInstanceState) {
        super.onCreate(savedInstanceState);
        setContentView(R.layout.activity_welcome_app);
        startActivity(new Intent(this, Welcome.class));
    }
}
```

The statements in bold are the statements just added to the file; the remainder is the default code provided by ADT. The `startActivity()` method creates an explicit intent, which explicitly specifies that the Activity file `Welcome.java` is to be run at the start. When the application is run, you see the same output as that of the `WelcomeMsg` application (see Figure 2.5, left and right).

Before we move on to the next application, let's have a quick look at the attributes that can be used in XML definitions of the `EditText` and `Button` controls to configure them.

Using the `EditText` Control

The `EditText` control is a subclass of `TextView` and is used for getting input from the user. You can use several attributes to configure the `EditText` control to suit your requirements. For example, you can implement the scrolling feature to scroll the text when the user types beyond the width of the control or the auto text feature to correct common spelling mistakes while the user types. The default behavior of the `EditText` control is to display text as a single line and run over to the next line when the user types beyond the width of the control. By applying attributes, you can constrain the `EditText` control to remain on a single line only and let the text scroll to the left. You can also hide the characters typed by the user for security purposes, that is, convert the characters into dots, which you usually see while typing passwords.

Example:

```
<EditText
    android:layout_width="match_parent"
    android:layout_height="wrap_content"
    android:hint="Enter your name"
    android:singleLine="false"
    android:id="@+id/user_name" />
```

The preceding example sets the `EditText` control to expand to multiple lines when the user types beyond the width of the control. Also, the control displays the hint text `Enter your name`, which is automatically erased as the user types data.

The list of attributes that can be used to configure `EditText` control are discussed in the following section.

Attributes Used to Configure the `EditText` Control

The following is a list of attributes that can be used to configure the `EditText` control:

▶ **`android:layout_width`**—Used to set the width of the `EditText` control. The two valid values are `wrap_content` and `match_parent`. The value `wrap_content` sets the width of the `EditText` control to accept only a single character. When the user types text, the width of the `EditText` control automatically increases to accommodate the new content. Also, the cursor moves to the next line when the boundary of the container is reached. No text scrolling takes place unless the `android:scrollHorizontally` attribute is set to `"true"`. In this case, instead of moving to the next line, the text scrolls left to accommodate the newly typed content. If the value of the `android:layout_width` attribute is set to `match_parent`, the width of the `EditText` control is set equal to the width of its container. When the user types the text beyond the available width, the cursor moves to the next line.

▶ **android:layout_height**—Used to set the height of the `EditText` control. Valid values are `wrap_content` and `match_parent`. When the value `wrap_content` is assigned to the control, the height of the `EditText` control increases when typing text beyond the width of the control. If the value `match_parent` is assigned to the control, text expands the height of the control to fill up the height of the container.

▶ **android:singleLine**—When set to `true`, forces the `EditText` control to remain on a single line. That is, on reaching the end of the available width, the text that is typed in scrolls to the left. If the value is set to `false`, the cursor moves to the next line when the end of the available width of the control is reached.

▶ **android:hint**—Displays helpful text in the `EditText` control to guide user entry. The text automatically disappears when the user enters data. For example, `android:hint="Enter your name"` displays the text `Enter your name` in the `EditText` control to indicate that a name has to be entered in this `EditText` control.

▶ **android:lines**—Sets the height of the `EditText` control to accommodate the specified number of lines. For example, `android:lines="5"` sets the height of `EditText` control to accommodate five lines. Typing text beyond the fifth line causes the text to scroll up to accommodate input.

▶ **android:textSize**—Sets the size of the text typed in the `EditText` control. You can specify the size in any of the following units of measurement: `px`, `in`, `mm`, `pts`, `dip`, and `sp`. For example, `android:textSize="15px"` sets the size of text typed in the `EditText` control to 15 pixels. The recommended unit for text size is `sp` as it works correctly across different screen sizes and densities.

▶ **android:autoText**—When set to `true` enables the `EditText` control to correct common spelling mistakes.

▶ **android:capitalize**—Automatically converts typed text into capital letters. The valid values are `none`, `characters`, `words`, and `sentences`. The value `none` does not capitalize anything. The value `characters` capitalizes every character. The value `words` capitalizes the first character of every word. The value `sentences` capitalizes the first character of the first word of each sentence.

▶ **android:password**—When set to `true`, the attribute converts the typed characters into dots to hide entered text.

▶ **android:minWidth**—Used to specify the minimum width of the control.

▶ **android:maxWidth**—Used to specify the maximum width of the control. Text typed beyond the maximum width scrolls if the `android:scrollHorizontally` attribute is set to `true`; otherwise, it moves onto the next line.

▶ **android:minHeight**—Used to specify the minimum height of the control.

▶ **android:maxHeight**—Used to specify the maximum height of the control.

▶ **android:scrollHorizontally**—When set to `true`, makes the text scroll horizontally if typed beyond the specified width of the control.

▶ `android:inputType`—Specifies the type of data that will be typed in the `EditText` control. This attribute configures the onscreen keyboard too. There are many possible values that include `number`, `phone`, `text`, `textCapCharacters`, `textCapWords`, `textEmailAddress`, `datetime`, `date`, `time`, `textAutoCorrect`, `textMultiLine`, and `textPassword`. Figure 2.7 (first through fifth image) shows how the onscreen keyboard changes when the values `number`, `phone`, `text`, `textCap Characters`, and `textEmailAddress` are assigned to this attribute, respectively. This single attribute actually replaces many attributes such as `android:password`, `android:singleLine`, `android:numeric`, `android:phoneNumber`, `android:capitalize`, and `android:autoText`.

FIGURE 2.7   (first) Keyboard when `inputType` is `number`, (second) keyboard when `inputType` is `phone`, (third) keyboard when `inputType` is `text`, (fourth) keyboard when `inputType` is `text-CapCharacters`, and (fifth) keyboard when `inputType` is `textEmailAddress`

In the `WelcomeMsg` application that you created earlier, you saw that an event listener was associated with the `Button` control; that is, the application performs an action when the user performs an event (clicks) on the `Button` control. Is it essential to have a `Button` control to initiate action? Can't you initiate an action by pressing the Enter key on the `EditText` control? In other words, can you add an event listener to the `EditText` control? The answer is yes! Let's see how.

Adding an Event Listener to the `EditText` Control

In this section, you learn how to add an event listener to the `EditText` control that checks for the occurrence of an event in the `EditText` control and executes the callback method accordingly. You use a practical approach by creating a new Android application to perform this action. In this application, an `EditText` control is displayed on the screen asking the user to enter a name. After the user enters a name and presses the Enter key, a welcome message displays via the `TextView` control.

First launch Eclipse and create a new Android project called `EditTextApp`, and modify `activity_edit_text_app.xml` as shown in Listing 2.15.

LISTING 2.15 The `activity_edit_text_app.xml` File

```xml
<LinearLayout xmlns:android="http://schemas.android.com/apk/res/android"
    android:orientation="vertical"
    android:layout_width="match_parent"
    android:layout_height="match_parent">
    <EditText
        android:layout_width="match_parent"
        android:layout_height="wrap_content"
        android:hint="Enter your name"
        android:id="@+id/user_name"/>
    <TextView
        android:layout_width="match_parent"
        android:layout_height="wrap_content"
        android:id="@+id/response"/>
</LinearLayout>
```

You can see that the layout contains two controls: `EditText` for getting the name from the user and `TextView` for displaying a welcome message. The `EditText` and `TextView` controls are assigned the `user_name` and `response` IDs, respectively. The `EditText` control displays hint text, `Enter your name`, to indicate that a name must be entered in the `EditText` control.

To add an action, that is, to display the welcome message when the user presses the Enter key after entering a name, we need to write code in the Activity file. Let's put the code shown in Listing 2.16 into the Activity file `EditTextAppActivity.java`.

LISTING 2.16 The `EditTextAppActivity.java` File

```java
package com.androidunleashed.edittextapp;

import android.app.Activity;
import android.os.Bundle;
import android.widget.EditText;
import android.widget.TextView;
import android.view.View;
import android.view.View.OnKeyListener;
import android.view.KeyEvent;

public class EditTextAppActivity extends Activity {

    @Override
    public void onCreate(Bundle savedInstanceState) {
        super.onCreate(savedInstanceState);
        setContentView(R.layout.activity_edit_text_app);
        final TextView resp = (TextView)this.findViewById(R.id.response);
        final EditText username = (EditText) findViewById(R.id.user_name);
```

```
username.setOnKeyListener(new OnKeyListener() {
    public boolean onKey(View v, int keyCode, KeyEvent event) {
        if ((event.getAction() == KeyEvent.ACTION_UP) && (keyCode ==
            KeyEvent.KEYCODE_ENTER)) {
            resp.setText("Welcome "+username.getText()+" !");
            return true;
        }
        return false;
    }
});
}
}
```

In Listing 2.16, the `EditText` control from the layout is captured and mapped to the user-name `EditText` object. To display the welcome message to the user, the `TextView` control with the `response` ID is captured from the layout and assigned to the `TextView` object `resp`. An event listener, `OnKeyListener`, is added to the `EditText` object username so that the callback method `onKey()` is invoked whenever a key is pressed. The `onKey()` method is implemented, and it checks whether the Enter key is pressed. When the Enter key is pressed, a welcome message is displayed to the user through the `TextView` object, `resp`. The `onKey()` method is set to return `false` until the Enter key is pressed. The `onKey()` method is set to return `true` when the Enter key is pressed by the user.

NOTE

The `onKey()` method is set to return `true` if the event is handled and you want no other handler to listen to the events. You set this method to return `false` if the event is not handled and you want the method to listen for more key presses and to continue handling events.

You see the output shown in Figure 2.8 (top). You can see the hint text `Enter your name` in the `EditText` control. After the user has entered a name and pressed the Enter key, the username and the welcome message appear, as shown in Figure 2.8 (bottom).

FIGURE 2.8   `EditTextApp` displaying the hint text `Enter your name` (top), and welcome message displayed when the Enter key is pressed (bottom)

While developing applications, you may encounter a situation where you want to display certain options for the user to select. The two controls that enable you to do this are `CheckBox` and `RadioButton`.

Choosing Options with CheckBox

A `checkbox` control has two states: `checked` and `unchecked`. When the check box is selected, it toggles its state from checked to unchecked and vice versa. A check box is created via an instance of `android.widget.CheckBox`.

In Java, the following methods can be used with `Checkbox` controls:

▶ `isChecked()`—Determines whether the check box is checked

▶ `setChecked()`—Sets or changes the state of the check box

▶ `toggle()`—Toggles the state of the check box from checked to unchecked or vice versa

To add an event listener, you can implement the `OnCheckedChangeListener` interface that invokes the callback method `onCheckedChanged()` when the state of the check box changes. In addition, you can also use the traditional implementation, the `OnClickListener` interface, that invokes the `onClick()` method when any of the `CheckBox` controls are clicked.

Example:

```
<CheckBox
    android:id="@+id/purchase"
```

```
        android:layout_height="wrap_content"
        android:layout_width="match_parent"
        android:text="Purchase" />
```

The preceding example shows a Purchase check box that the user can select to indicate that he or she wants to purchase an item.

To learn the concept of `CheckBox`, let's create an Android application based on these controls. In this application, you create three `CheckBox` controls, each representing a food item along with its price (see Figure 2.9—left). When the food items are selected, the total price is displayed. The application shows us how `CheckBox` controls are displayed, how event listeners are attached to them, and whether the `CheckBox` is in a checked or unchecked state. Let's start with the application.

Launch Eclipse, create a new Android project called `CheckBoxApp`, and add three `CheckBox` controls to the Activity layout file `activity_check_box_app.xml`, as shown in Listing 2.17.

LISTING 2.17   The `activity_check_box_app.xml` File

```xml
<LinearLayout xmlns:android="http://schemas.android.com/apk/res/android"
    android:orientation="vertical"
    android:layout_width="match_parent"
    android:layout_height="match_parent">
    <TextView
        android:layout_width="match_parent"
        android:layout_height="wrap_content"
        android:text="Select Items you want"/>
    <CheckBox
        android:id="@+id/checkbox_pizza"
        android:layout_height="wrap_content"
        android:text="Pizza    $15"
        android:layout_width="match_parent" />
    <CheckBox
        android:id="@+id/checkbox_hotdog"
        android:layout_height="wrap_content"
        android:text="Hot Dog   $5"
        android:layout_width="match_parent" />
    <CheckBox
        android:id="@+id/checkbox_burger"
        android:layout_height="wrap_content"
        android:text="Burger   $10"
        android:layout_width="match_parent" />
    <Button
        android:layout_width="match_parent"
        android:layout_height="wrap_content"
        android:id="@+id/bill_btn"
```

```
        android:text="Calculate Bill"/>
    <TextView
        android:layout_width="match_parent"
        android:layout_height="wrap_content"
        android:id="@+id/amount"/>
</LinearLayout>
```

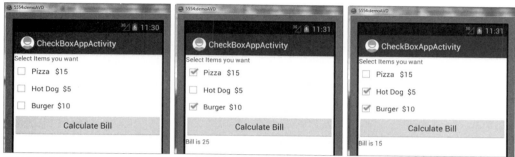

FIGURE 2.9   `CheckBox` controls displayed on application startup (left), price displayed when the first and last `CheckBox` controls are selected (middle), and price displayed when the last two `CheckBox` controls are selected (right)

You can see that two `TextViews`, three `CheckBoxes`, and a `Button` control are defined in Listing 2.17. The first `TextView` is for displaying a message, `Select Items you want`, asking the user to select the food items using the `CheckBox` controls. The three `CheckBoxes` are assigned unique IDs—`checkbox_pizza`, `checkbox_hotdog`, and `checkbox_burger`—and they represent the food items, `Pizza`, `HotDog`, and `Burger`, respectively. The caption and ID assigned to the `Button` control are `bill_btn` and `Calculate Bill`, respectively. The second `TextView` is assigned the ID `amount` and is meant for displaying the total price of the food items selected by the user.

To add an action to the application, that is, to check the status of each of the `CheckBox` controls and to print the sum of the food items selected, you need to write some Java code in the Activity file. Let's write the code shown in Listing 2.18 in the Activity file `CheckBoxAppActivity.java`.

LISTING 2.18   The `CheckBoxAppActivity.java` File

```
package com.androidunleashed.checkboxapp;

import android.app.Activity;
import android.os.Bundle;
import android.widget.Button;
import android.widget.TextView;
import android.widget.CheckBox;
import android.view.View;
import android.view.View.OnClickListener;
```

```java
public class CheckBoxAppActivity extends Activity implements OnClickListener {
    CheckBox c1,c2,c3;
        TextView resp;

    @Override
    public void onCreate(Bundle savedInstanceState) {
        super.onCreate(savedInstanceState);
        setContentView(R.layout.activity_check_box_app);
        Button b = (Button)this.findViewById(R.id.bill_btn);
        resp = (TextView)this.findViewById(R.id.amount);
        c1 = (CheckBox)findViewById(R.id.checkbox_pizza);
        c2 = (CheckBox)findViewById(R.id.checkbox_hotdog);
        c3 = (CheckBox)findViewById(R.id.checkbox_burger);
        b.setOnClickListener(this);
    }

    public void onClick(View v) {
        int amt=0;
        if (c1.isChecked()) {
            amt=amt+15;
        }
        if (c2.isChecked()) {
            amt=amt+5;
        }
        if (c3.isChecked()) {
            amt=amt+10;
        }
        resp.setText("Bill is " +Integer.toString(amt));

    }
}
```

The Button control with the ID bill_btn is accessed from the layout file and is mapped to the Button object b. The TextView control with the ID amount is accessed from the layout file and is mapped to the TextView object resp. Similarly, the three CheckBoxes with the IDs checkbox_pizza, checkbox_hotdog, and checkbox_burger are accessed from the layout file and mapped to the CheckBox objects c1, c2, and c3, respectively. An event handler, setOnClickListener, is attached to the button. Hence, whenever the button is clicked, the onClick() method is called. In the onClick() method, an integer variable amt is initialized to 0. The state of each check box is checked through the isChecked() method. The isChecked() method returns the Boolean value true if the check box is checked; otherwise, it returns false. The three check boxes represent the food items Pizza, HotDog, and Burger, respectively. The state of each check box is checked, and if any of them is selected, the amount associated with that food item is added to the amt variable. That is, the total amount of the selected food item is computed and stored in the amt variable. The total in the amt variable is displayed on the screen by assigning it to the

TextView object resp. When the application is run, you get the screen shown in Figure 2.9 (left). No total is displayed, as no food item has been selected. When a check box is selected, the total price of the selected food items is displayed, as shown in Figure 2.9 (middle and right).

What if you want users to select only a single option from a group? The solution is using the RadioButton control.

Choosing Mutually Exclusive Items Using RadioButtons

RadioButton controls are two-state widgets that can be in either a checked or unchecked state. The difference between check boxes and radio buttons is that you can select more than one check box in a set, whereas radio buttons are mutually exclusive—only one radio button can be selected in a group. Selecting a radio button automatically deselects other radio buttons in the group.

To make them mutually exclusive, RadioButton controls are grouped together into the RadioGroup element so that no more than one can be selected at a time. To create a group of radio buttons, first create a RadioGroup and then populate the group with few RadioButton controls, as shown in the following example:

```
<RadioGroup
    android:id="@+id/group_hotel"
    android:layout_width="match_parent"
    android:layout_height="wrap_content"
    android:orientation="vertical" >
        <RadioButton android:id="@+id/radio_fivestar"
            android:layout_width="wrap_content"
            android:layout_height="wrap_content"
            android:text="Five Star " />
        <RadioButton android:id="@+id/radio_threestar"
            android:layout_width="wrap_content"
            android:layout_height="wrap_content"
            android:text="Three Star" />
</RadioGroup>
```

In the preceding code block, a RadioGroup with the group_hotel ID is defined, which contains two RadioButton controls with the IDs radio_fivestar and radio_threestar, respectively. Because only a single radio button in a group can be in a checked state, checking a radio button automatically unchecks the other radio button in the group.

In Java, the following methods can be applied to RadioButtons:

▶ isChecked()—Detects whether the RadioButton control is selected.

▶ toggle()—Toggles the state of the RadioButton from selected to unselected and vice versa.

▶ **check()**—Checks a specific `RadioButton` whose ID is supplied in the method.

▶ **getCheckedRadioButtonId()**—Gets the ID of the currently selected `RadioButton` control. It returns –1 if no `RadioButton` control is checked.

Let's create an application using the concept of radio buttons. In this application, you define two `RadioButton` controls in a `RadioGroup`. Each `RadioButton` represents a hotel type, and whenever a `RadioButton` is selected, the hotel type represented by it will be displayed through a `TextView` control (see Figure 2.9—middle). It is obvious that when a `RadioButton` representing a hotel type is selected, any other previously selected `RadioButton` is automatically unselected. The application shows how `RadioButton` controls are defined, how they are nested in `RadioGroup` controls, and how an event listener is attached to them. Let's start with the application.

Launch Eclipse, create a new Android project called `RadioButtonApp`, and add two `RadioButton` controls to the Activity layout file `activity_radio_button_app.xml`, as shown in Listing 2.19.

LISTING 2.19   The `activity_radio_button_app.xml` File

```
<LinearLayout xmlns:android="http://schemas.android.com/apk/res/android"
    android:orientation="vertical"
    android:layout_width="match_parent"
    android:layout_height="match_parent">
    <TextView
        android:layout_width="match_parent"
        android:layout_height="wrap_content"
        android:text="Select the type of hotel"/>
    <RadioGroup
        android:layout_width="match_parent"
        android:layout_height="wrap_content"
        android:orientation="vertical">
    <RadioButton android:id="@+id/radio_fivestar"
        android:layout_width="wrap_content"
        android:layout_height="wrap_content"
        android:text="Five Star " />
    <RadioButton android:id="@+id/radio_threestar"
        android:layout_width="wrap_content"
        android:layout_height="wrap_content"
        android:text="Three Star" />
    </RadioGroup>
    <TextView
        android:layout_width="match_parent"
        android:layout_height="wrap_content"
        android:id="@+id/hoteltype"/>
</LinearLayout>
```

In Listing 2.19, you can see that two `RadioButton` controls with the `radio_fivestar` and `radio_threestar` IDs are grouped inside a `RadioGroup`. This means that the two radio buttons have become mutually exclusive—selecting one radio button automatically deselects the other radio button.

To add an event listener action to the two `RadioButton` controls, you need to write some Java code in the Activity file. Let's write the code shown in Listing 2.20 in the Activity file `RadioButtonAppActivity.java`.

LISTING 2.20   The `RadioButtonAppActivity.java` File

```
package com.androidunleashed.radiobuttonapp;

import android.app.Activity;
import android.os.Bundle;
import android.widget.TextView;
import android.widget.RadioButton;
import android.view.View;
import android.view.View.OnClickListener;

public class RadioButtonAppActivity extends Activity {
    @Override
    public void onCreate(Bundle savedInstanceState) {
        super.onCreate(savedInstanceState);
        setContentView(R.layout.activity_radio_button_app);
        RadioButton radioFivestar = (RadioButton) findViewById(R.id.radio_fivestar);
        RadioButton radioThreestar = (RadioButton) findViewById(R.id.radio_threestar);
        radioFivestar.setOnClickListener(radioListener);
        radioThreestar.setOnClickListener(radioListener);
    }

    private OnClickListener radioListener = new OnClickListener() {
        public void onClick(View v) {
            TextView selectedHotel = (TextView) findViewById(R.id.hoteltype);
            RadioButton rb = (RadioButton) v;
            selectedHotel.setText("The hotel type selected is: " +rb.getText());
        }
    };
}
```

The two `RadioButton` controls are captured from the layout and mapped to the `RadioButton` objects `radioFivestar` and `radioThreestar`. The `View.OnClickListener` interface is implemented to listen to the click events on the `RadioButton` controls. The `onClick()` callback method is implemented. This is the method that is executed when any of the `RadioButton` controls are selected. In the `onClick()` callback method, the `TextView` control from the layout is captured and mapped to the `TextView` object `selectedHotel`.

Also, the text content of the `RadioButton` control that is selected by the user is fetched through the `getText()` method and is displayed through the `TextView` object `selected-Hotel`. On execution of the application, you see two `RadioButton` controls on the startup screen, as shown in Figure 2.10 (left). When the user selects the five star `RadioButton`, the `TextView` displays the message `The hotel type selected is: Five Star` (see Figure 2.10—middle). Similarly, when the user selects the three star `RadioButton`, the `TextView` displays the message `The hotel type selected is: Three Star` (see Figure 2.10—right).

FIGURE 2.10   `RadioButton` controls displayed on application startup (left), `TextView` display-ing the message when the Five Star `RadioButton` is selected (middle), and `TextView` displaying the message when the Three Star `RadioButton` is selected (right)

In the preceding application you have a single set of `RadioButton` controls nested inside a `RadioGroup`. What if you want to display two sets of `RadioButton` controls, asking the user to select a `RadioButton` from both sets? For example, the user needs to select the type of the hotel, as well as the type of room. In that case, you need to create two `RadioGroup` controls: one to represent hotel types and the other to represent room types. The `RadioGroup` that represents hotel types will have two `RadioButton` controls showing the text Five Star and Three Star. Similarly, the other `RadioGroup` that represents room types will have three `RadioButton` controls to show three options: Ordinary Room, Luxury Room, and Grand Suite. The layout file with two `RadioGroup` controls appears as shown in Listing 2.21.

LISTING 2.21   The `activity_radio_button_app.xml` File with Two `RadioGroup` Controls

```
<LinearLayout xmlns:android="http://schemas.android.com/apk/res/android"
    android:orientation="vertical"
    android:layout_width="match_parent"
    android:layout_height="match_parent">
    <TextView
        android:layout_width="match_parent"
        android:layout_height="wrap_content"
        android:text="Select the type of hotel"/>
    <RadioGroup android:id="@+id/group_hotel"
        android:layout_width="match_parent"
        android:layout_height="wrap_content"
        android:orientation="vertical">
        <RadioButton android:id="@+id/radio_fivestar"
            android:layout_width="wrap_content"
            android:layout_height="wrap_content"
```

```
                android:text="Five Star " />
        <RadioButton android:id="@+id/radio_threestar"
                android:layout_width="wrap_content"
                android:layout_height="wrap_content"
                android:text="Three Star" />
    </RadioGroup>
    <TextView
        android:layout_width="match_parent"
        android:layout_height="wrap_content"
        android:text="Select the type of room"/>
    <RadioGroup android:id="@+id/group_room"
        android:layout_width="match_parent"
        android:layout_height="wrap_content"
        android:orientation="vertical">
        <RadioButton android:id="@+id/radio_suite"
                android:layout_width="wrap_content"
                android:layout_height="wrap_content"
                android:text="Grand Suite " />
        <RadioButton android:id="@+id/radio_luxury"
                android:layout_width="wrap_content"
                android:layout_height="wrap_content"
                android:text="Luxury Room" />
        <RadioButton android:id="@+id/radio_ordinary"
                android:layout_width="wrap_content"
                android:layout_height="wrap_content"
                android:text="Ordinary Room" />
    </RadioGroup>
    <TextView
        android:layout_width="match_parent"
        android:layout_height="wrap_content"
        android:id="@+id/hoteltype" />
</LinearLayout>
```

To make two independent sets of radio buttons, one to represent hotel types and another to represent room types, you create two RadioGroup controls with the group_hotel and group_room IDs. The first RadioGroup, group_hotel, contains two RadioButton controls with the radio_fivestar and radio_threestar IDs to represent five star and three star hotels. Similarly, the next RadioGroup, group_room, contains three RadioButton controls with the radio_suite, radio_luxury, and radio_ordinary IDs to represent the suite, luxury, and ordinary room types. The two TextView controls are used to display the messages Select the type of hotel and Select the type of room, asking the user to select the type of hotel and room. The third TextView with the hoteltype ID is used to display the options selected by the user. To make the two RadioGroups functional and to display the hotel and room type selected by the user, write the code shown in Listing 2.22 in the Java activity file RadioButtonAppActivity.java.

LISTING 2.22   The `RadioButtonAppActivity.java` File

```
package com.androidunleashed.radiobuttonapp;

import android.app.Activity;
import android.os.Bundle;
import android.widget.TextView;
import android.widget.RadioButton;
import android.view.View;
import android.view.View.OnClickListener;

public class RadioButtonAppActivity extends Activity {
    String str1="";
    String str2="";

    @Override
    public void onCreate(Bundle savedInstanceState) {
        super.onCreate(savedInstanceState);
        setContentView(R.layout.activity_radio_button_app);
        RadioButton radioFivestar = (RadioButton) findViewById(R.id.radio_fivestar);
        RadioButton radioThreestar = (RadioButton) findViewById(R.id.radio_threestar);
        RadioButton radioSuite = (RadioButton) findViewById(R.id.radio_suite);
        RadioButton radioLuxury = (RadioButton) findViewById(R.id.radio_luxury);
        RadioButton radioOrdinary = (RadioButton) findViewById(R.id.radio_ordinary);
        radioFivestar.setOnClickListener(radioListener1);
        radioThreestar.setOnClickListener(radioListener1);
        radioSuite.setOnClickListener(radioListener2);
        radioLuxury.setOnClickListener(radioListener2);
        radioOrdinary.setOnClickListener(radioListener2);
    }

    private OnClickListener radioListener1 = new OnClickListener() {
        public void onClick(View v) {
            TextView selectedOptions = (TextView) findViewById(R.id.hoteltype);
            RadioButton rb = (RadioButton) v;
            str1="The hotel type selected is: " +rb.getText();
            selectedOptions.setText(str1+"\n"+str2);
        }
    };

    private OnClickListener radioListener2 = new OnClickListener() {
        public void onClick(View v) {
            TextView selectedOptions = (TextView) findViewById(R.id.hoteltype);
            RadioButton rb = (RadioButton) v;
            str2="Room type selected is: " +rb.getText();
            selectedOptions.setText(str1+"\n"+str2);
```

```
        }
    };
}
```

The `RadioButton` controls with IDs `radio_fivestar`, `radio_threestar`, `radio_suite`, `radio_luxury`, and `radio_ordinary` are captured from the layout file and mapped to the `RadioButton` objects `radioFivestar`, `radioThreestar`, `radioSuite`, `radioLuxury`, and `radioOrdinary`, respectively. Two event listener interfaces are created, `radioListener1` and `radioListener2`. One checks for event occurrences in the `RadioButton` controls in `group_hotel`, and the other checks for the occurrence of events in the `RadioButton` controls in `group_room`. Both the interfaces have the callback method `onClick()` implemented in them.

When any of the `RadioButton` controls in the first `RadioGroup`, `group_hotel`, is selected, the callback method `onClick()` of `radioListener1` is executed and text is assigned to the string `str1` to represent the `RadioButton` selected in that radio group. Similarly, when any `RadioButton` control from the second `RadioGroup`, `group_room`, is selected, the callback method `onClick()` of `radioListener2` is executed. This assigns text to the string `str2` to represent the `RadioButton` selected in that radio group. The `TextView` with the `hotel-type` ID is captured from the layout file and is mapped to the `TextView` object `selected Options`. The text messages in both the `str1` and `str2` strings are assigned to the `TextView` control `selectedOptions` for display. On running the application, you see two sets of `RadioButton` controls in their respective `RadioGroups` (see Figure 2.11—left). When the five star `RadioButton` from the `RadioGroup` `group_hotel` and the `RadioButton` luxury room from the `RadioGroup` `group_room` are selected, the `TextView` displays the message The hotel type selected is: Five Star Room; Type selected is: Luxury Room (see Figure 2.11— middle). Similarly, when the three star `RadioButton` control from the `RadioGroup` `group_hotel` and the grand suite `RadioButton` from the `RadioGroup` `group_room` are selected, the `TextView` displays the message The hotel type selected is: Three Star and Room type selected is: Grand Suite (see Figure 2.11—right).

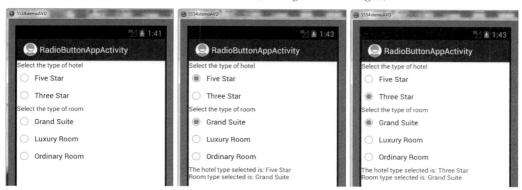

FIGURE 2.11   `RadioButton` controls in two `RadioGroups` (left), `TextView` informing that the Five Star `RadioButton` and the Grand Suite Room `RadioButton` are selected (middle), and `TextView` informing that the Three Star `RadioButton` and the Grand Suite `RadioButton` are selected (right)

Summary

The main focus of this chapter was to understand the working of basic widgets such as EditText, CheckBox, and RadioButton, and to develop Android applications using these controls. You also learned the role of the folders and files automatically created by the ADT plug-in. You learned about Activities, the Android Activity life cycle, the usage of the Android Manifest file, commonly used layouts and controls, and how events are handled in Android applications. To respond to different events, you learned to create anonymous inner classes, implement the OnClickListener interface, and declare the event handler in the XML definition of the control. You also saw how to describe operations through Intent, create your own layout file, create a new Activity, register the new Activity, and finally, the steps needed to start the Activity.

In the next chapter, you learn about containers—the different types of layouts used to organize and arrange the controls of an application. You learn to use LinearLayout, RelativeLayout, AbsoluteLayout, FrameLayout, and TableLayout. Also you learn to adapt to the screen orientation. In addition, you learn the usage of different attributes that help in laying out controls in different layouts. You learn to apply different attributes in the layouts such as the Orientation attribute, Height and Width attributes, Padding attribute, Weight attribute, and Gravity attribute.

PART II

Building Blocks for Android Application Design

Laying Out Controls in Containers

A container is a view used to contain other views. Android offers a collection of view classes that act as containers for views. These container classes are called layouts, and as the name suggests, they decide the organization, size, and position of their children views.

Let's start the chapter with an introduction to different layouts used in Android applications.

Introduction to Layouts

Layouts are basically containers for other items known as Views, which are displayed on the screen. Layouts help manage and arrange views as well. Layouts are defined in the form of XML files that cannot be changed by our code during runtime.

Table 3.1 shows the layout managers provided by the Android SDK.

TABLE 3.1   Android Layout Managers

Layout Manager	Description
LinearLayout	Organizes its children either horizontally or vertically
RelativeLayout	Organizes its children relative to one another or to the parent
AbsoluteLayout	Each child control is given a specific location within the bounds of the container

Layout Manager	Description
FrameLayout	Displays a single view; that is, the next view replaces the previous view and hence is used to dynamically change the children in the layout
TableLayout	Organizes its children in tabular form
GridLayout	Organizes its children in grid format

The containers or layouts listed in Table 3.1 are also known as `ViewGroups` as one or more `Views` are grouped and arranged in a desired manner through them. Besides the `ViewGroups` shown here Android supports one more `ViewGroup` known as ScrollView, which is discussed in Chapter 4, "Utilizing Resources and Media."

LinearLayout

The LinearLayout is the most basic layout, and it arranges its elements sequentially, either horizontally or vertically. To arrange controls within a linear layout, the following attributes are used:

▶ `android:orientation`—Used for arranging the controls in the container in horizontal or vertical order

▶ `android:layout_width`—Used for defining the width of a control

▶ `android:layout_height`—Used for defining the height of a control

▶ `android:padding`—Used for increasing the whitespace between the boundaries of the control and its actual content

▶ `android:layout_weight`—Used for shrinking or expanding the size of the control to consume the extra space relative to the other controls in the container

▶ `android:gravity`—Used for aligning content within a control

▶ `android:layout_gravity`—Used for aligning the control within the container

Applying the `orientation` Attribute

The `orientation` attribute is used to arrange its children either in horizontal or vertical order. The valid values for this attribute are `horizontal` and `vertical`. If the value of the `android:orientation` attribute is set to `vertical`, the children in the linear layout are arranged in a column layout, one below the other. Similarly, if the value of the `android:orientation` attribute is set to `horizontal`, the controls in the linear layout are arranged in a row format, side by side. The orientation can be modified at runtime through the `setOrientation()` method. That is, by supplying the values `HORIZONTAL` or `VERTICAL` to the `setOrientation()` method, we can arrange the children of the LinearLayout in row or column format, respectively.

Applying the `height` and `width` Attributes

The default height and width of a control are decided on the basis of the text or content that is displayed through it. To specify a certain height and width to the control, we use the `android:layout_width` and `android:layout_height` attributes. We can specify the values for the `height` and `width` attributes in the following three ways:

▶ By supplying specific dimension values for the control in terms of `px` (pixels), `dip`/`dp` (device independent pixels), `sp` (scaled pixels), `pts` (points), `in` (inches), and `mm` (millimeters). For example, the `android:layout_width="20px"` attribute sets the width of the control to 20 pixels.

▶ By providing the value as `wrap_content`. When assigned to the control's height or width, this attribute resizes the control to expand to fit its contents. For example, when this value is applied to the width of the `TextView`, it expands so that its complete text is visible.

▶ By providing the value as `match_parent`. When assigned to the control's height or width, this attribute forces the size of the control to expand to fill up all the available space of the enclosing container.

> **NOTE**
>
> For layout elements, the value `wrap_content` resizes the layout to fit the controls added as its children. The value `match_parent` makes the layout expand to take up all the space in the parent layout.

Applying the `padding` Attribute

The `padding` attribute is used to increase the whitespace between the boundaries of the control and its actual content. Through the `android:padding` attribute, we can set the same amount of padding or spacing on all four sides of the control. Similarly, by using the `android:paddingLeft`, `android:paddingRight`, `android:paddingTop`, and `android:paddingBottom` attributes, we can specify the individual spacing on the left, right, top, and bottom of the control, respectively.

The following example sets the spacing on all four sides of the control to 5 pixels:

```
android:padding="5dip"
```

Similarly, the following example sets the spacing on the left side of the control to 5 pixels:

```
android:paddingLeft="5dip"
```

> **NOTE**
>
> To set the padding at runtime, we can call the `setPadding()` method.

Let's see how the controls are laid out in the LinearLayout layout using an example. Create a new Android Project called `LinearLayoutApp`. The original default content of the layout file `activity_linear_layout_app.xml` appears as shown in Listing 3.1.

LISTING 3.1   Default Code in the Layout File `activity_linear_layout_app.xml`

```
<RelativeLayout xmlns:android="http://schemas.android.com/apk/res/android"
    xmlns:tools="http://schemas.android.com/tools"
    android:layout_width="match_parent"
    android:layout_height="match_parent" >
    <TextView
        android:layout_width="wrap_content"
        android:layout_height="wrap_content"
        android:layout_centerHorizontal="true"
        android:layout_centerVertical="true"
        android:text="@string/hello_world"
        tools:context=".LinearLayoutAppActivity" />
</RelativeLayout>
```

Let's apply the LinearLayout and add three `Button` controls to the layout. Modify the `activity_linear_layout_app.xml` to appear as shown in Listing 3.2.

LISTING 3.2   The `activity_linear_layout_app.xml` File on Adding Three `Button` Controls

```
<LinearLayout xmlns:android="http://schemas.android.com/apk/res/android"
    android:layout_width="match_parent"
    android:layout_height="match_parent"
    android:orientation="vertical" >
    <Button
        android:id="@+id/Apple"
        android:text="Apple"
        android:layout_width="match_parent"
        android:layout_height="wrap_content" />
    <Button
        android:id="@+id/Mango"
        android:text="Mango"
        android:layout_width="match_parent"
        android:layout_height="wrap_content" />
    <Button
        android:id="@+id/Banana"
        android:text="Banana"
        android:layout_width="match_parent"
        android:layout_height="wrap_content" />
</LinearLayout>
```

The `orientation` of LinearLayout is set to `vertical`, declaring that we want to arrange its child elements vertically, one below the other. The height and width of the layout are set to expand to fill up all the available space of the enclosing container, that is, the device screen. Three `Button` controls are added to the layout, which appear one below the other. The IDs and text assigned to the three `Button` controls are `Apple`, `Mango`, and `Banana`, respectively. The `height` of the three controls is set to `wrap_content`, which is enough to accommodate the text. Finally, the `width` of the three controls is set to `match_parent`, so that the width of the three controls expands to fill up the available space of the LinearLayout container. We see the output shown in Figure 3.1.

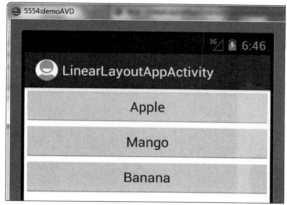

FIGURE 3.1   Three `Button` controls arranged vertically in LinearLayout

To see the controls appear horizontally, set the `orientation` attribute of the LinearLayout to `horizontal`. We also need to set the `layout_width` attribute of the three controls to `wrap_content`; otherwise, we will be able to see only the first `Button` control, the one with the `Apple` ID. If the `layout_width` attribute of any control is set to `match_parent`, it takes up all the available space of the container, hiding the rest of the controls behind it. By setting the values of the `layout_width` attributes to `wrap_content`, we make sure that the width of the control expands just to fit its content and does not take up all the available space. Let's modify the `activity_linear_layout_app.xml` to appear as shown in Listing 3.3.

LISTING 3.3   The `activity_linear_layout_app.xml` File on Setting Horizontal Orientation to the `Button` Controls

```
<LinearLayout xmlns:android="http://schemas.android.com/apk/res/android"
    android:layout_width="match_parent"
    android:layout_height="match_parent"
    android:orientation="horizontal" >
    <Button
        android:id="@+id/Apple"
        android:text="Apple"
        android:layout_width="wrap_content"
        android:layout_height="wrap_content" />
```

```
    <Button
        android:id="@+id/Mango"
        android:text="Mango"
        android:layout_width="wrap_content"
        android:layout_height="wrap_content" />
    <Button
        android:id="@+id/Banana"
        android:text="Banana"
        android:layout_width="wrap_content"
        android:layout_height="wrap_content" />
</LinearLayout>
```

The controls are arranged horizontally, as shown in Figure 3.2.

FIGURE 3.2   Three `Button` controls arranged horizontally in LinearLayout

Applying the `weight` Attribute

The `weight` attribute affects the size of the control. That is, we use `weight` to assign the capability to expand or shrink and consume extra space relative to the other controls in the container. The values of the `weight` attribute range from `0.0` to `1.0`, where `1.0` is the highest value. Let's suppose a container has two controls and one of them is assigned the `weight` of `1`. In that case, the control assigned the `weight` of `1` consumes all the empty space in the container, whereas the other control remains at its current size. If we assign a `weight` of `0.0` to both the controls, nothing happens and the controls maintain their original size. If both the attributes are assigned the same value above `0.0`, both the controls consume the extra space equally. Hence, `weight` lets us apply a size expansion ratio to the controls. To make the middle `Button` control, `Mango`, take up all the available space of the container, let's assign a `weight` attribute to the three controls. Modify the `activity_linear_layout_app.xml` file to appear as shown in Listing 3.4.

LISTING 3.4   The `activity_linear_layout_app.xml` File on Applying the `weight` Attribute to the `Button` Controls

```
<LinearLayout xmlns:android="http://schemas.android.com/apk/res/android"
    android:orientation="horizontal"
    android:layout_width="match_parent"
    android:layout_height="match_parent">
    <Button
        android:id="@+id/Apple"
        android:text="Apple"
        android:layout_width="wrap_content"
        android:layout_height="wrap_content"
        android:layout_weight="0.0" />
    <Button
        android:id="@+id/Mango"
        android:text="Mango"
        android:layout_width="wrap_content"
        android:layout_height="wrap_content"
        android:layout_weight="1.0" />
    <Button
        android:id="@+id/Banana"
        android:text="Banana"
        android:layout_width="wrap_content"
        android:layout_height="wrap_content"
        android:layout_weight="0.0" />
</LinearLayout>
```

By setting the `layout_weight` attributes of `Apple`, `Mango`, and `Banana` to `0.0`, `1.0`, and `0.0`, respectively, we allow the `Mango` button control to take up all the available space of the container, as shown in Figure 3.3 (left). If we set the value of `layout_weight` of the `Banana` button control to `1.0` and that of `Mango` back to `0.0`, then all the available space of the container is consumed by the `Banana` button control, as shown in Figure 3.3 (middle). Similarly if we set the `layout_weight` of all controls to `1.0`, the entire container space will be equally consumed by the three controls, as shown in Figure 3.3 (right).

FIGURE 3.3   (left) The `weight` attribute of the Mango `Button` control set to 1.0, (middle) the `weight` attribute of the Banana `Button` control set to 1.0, and (right) all three `Button` controls set to the same `weight` attribute

Similarly if we set the weight of `Apple`, `Mango`, and `Banana` to `0.0`, `1.0`, and `0.5`, respectively, we get the output shown in Figure 3.4.

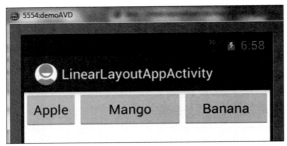

FIGURE 3.4   The `weight` attribute of the Apple, Mango, and Banana `Button` controls set to 0.0, 1.0, and 0.5

We can see that the text of the three controls is center-aligned. To align the content of a control, we use the `Gravity` attribute.

Applying the `Gravity` Attribute

The `Gravity` attribute is for aligning the content within a control. For example, to align the text of a control to the center, we set the value of its `android:gravity` attribute to `center`. The valid options for `android:gravity` include `left`, `center`, `right`, `top`, `bottom`, `center_horizontal`, `center_vertical`, `fill_horizontal`, and `fill_vertical`. The task performed by few of the said options is as follows:

▶ `center_vertical`—Places the object in the vertical center of its container, without changing its size

▶ `fill_vertical`—Grows the vertical size of the object, if needed, so it completely fills its container

▶ `center_horizontal`—Places the object in the horizontal center of its container, without changing its size

▶ `fill_horizontal`—Grows the horizontal size of the object, if needed, so it completely fills its container

▶ `center`—Places the object in the center of its container in both the vertical and horizontal axis, without changing its size

We can make the text of a control appear at the center by using the `android:gravity` attribute, as shown in this example:

```
android:gravity="center"
```

We can also combine two or more values of any attribute using the | operator. The following example centrally aligns the text horizontally and vertically within a control:

```
android:gravity="center_horizontal|center_vertical"
```

Figure 3.5 shows the `android:gravity` attribute set to left and right for the `Button` controls `Mango` and `Banana`.

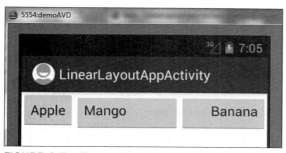

FIGURE 3.5   The text in the Mango and Banana `Button` controls aligned to the left and right, respectively, through the `android:gravity` attribute

Besides the `android:gravity` attribute, Android provides one more similar attribute, `android:layout_gravity`. Let's explore the difference between the two.

Using the `android:layout_gravity` Attribute

Where `android:gravity` is a setting used by the `View`, the `android:layout_gravity` is used by the container. That is, this attribute is used to align the control within the container. For example, to align the text within a `Button` control, we use the `android:gravity` attribute; to align the `Button` control itself in the LinearLayout (the container), we use the `android:layout_gravity` attribute. Let's add the `android:layout_gravity` attribute to align the `Button` controls themselves. To see the impact of using the `android:layout_gravity` attribute to align the `Button` controls in the LinearLayout, let's first arrange them vertically. So, let's modify `activity_linear_layout_app.xml` to make the `Button` controls appear vertically, one below the other as shown in Listing 3.5.

LISTING 3.5   The `activity_linear_layout_app.xml` File on Arranging the `Button` Controls Vertically

```
<LinearLayout xmlns:android="http://schemas.android.com/apk/res/android"
    android:orientation="vertical"
    android:layout_width="match_parent"
    android:layout_height="match_parent">
    <Button
        android:id="@+id/Apple"
        android:text="Apple"
        android:layout_width="wrap_content"
        android:layout_height="wrap_content" />
    <Button
        android:id="@+id/Mango"
        android:text="Mango"
        android:layout_width="wrap_content"
        android:layout_height="wrap_content" />
    <Button
        android:id="@+id/Banana"
        android:text="Banana"
```

```
                android:layout_width="wrap_content"
                android:layout_height="wrap_content" />
</LinearLayout>
```

The preceding code arranges the `Button` controls vertically, as shown in Figure 3.6 (left). To align the `Button` controls `Mango` and `Banana` to the center and to the right of the LinearLayout container, add the following statements to the respective tags in the `activity_linear_layout_app.xml` layout file:

```
android:layout_gravity="center"
```

and

```
android:layout_gravity="right"
```

The two `Button` controls, `Mango` and `Banana`, are aligned at the center and to the right in the container, as shown in Figure 3.6 (middle).

FIGURE 3.6   (left) The three `Button` controls vertically aligned with the `width` attribute set to `wrap_content`, (middle) the Mango and Banana `Button` controls aligned to the center and right of container, and (right) the width of the three `Button` controls expanded to take up all the available space

At the moment, the `layout_width` attribute of the three controls is set to `wrap_content`. The width of the three controls is just enough to accommodate their content. If we now set the value of the `android:layout_width` attribute for all three controls to `match_parent`, we find that all three `Button` controls expand in width to take up all the available space of the container, as shown in Figure 3.6 (right). Now we can apply the `android:gravity` attribute to align the text within the controls. Let's add the following three attributes to the `Button` controls `Apple`, `Mango`, and `Banana`:

```
android:gravity="left"
android:gravity="center"
```

and

```
android:gravity="right"
```

These lines of code align the content of the three `Button` controls to the `left`, to the `center`, and to the `right` within the control, as shown in Figure 3.7 (left). Because the three `Button` controls are arranged vertically in the layout (the orientation of the LinearLayout is set to vertical), the application of the `weight` attribute makes the controls expand vertically instead of horizontally as we saw earlier. To see the effect, let's add the following statement to the tags of all three `Button` controls:

```
android:layout_weight="0.0"
```

As expected, there will be no change in the height of any control, as the `weight` value assigned is `0.0`. Setting an equal value above `0.0` for all three controls results in equal division of empty space among them. For example, assigning the `android:layout_weight="1.0"` to all three controls results in expanding their height, as shown in Figure 3.7 (middle).

FIGURE 3.7   (left) The three `Button` controls with their text aligned to the left, center, and right, (middle) the vertical available space of the container apportioned equally among the three `Button` controls, and (right) the text of the three `Button` controls vertically aligned to the center

In the middle image of Figure 3.7, we see that the text in the `Apple` and `Banana` controls is not at the vertical center, so let's modify their `android:gravity` value, as shown here:

`android:gravity="center_vertical"` for the `Apple` control

`android:gravity="center_vertical|right"` for the `Banana` control

The `center_vertical` value aligns the content vertically to the center of the control, and the `right` value aligns the content to the right of the control. We can combine the values of the attribute using the | operator. After applying the values as shown in the preceding two code lines, we get the output shown in Figure 3.7 (right).

RelativeLayout

In RelativeLayout, each child element is laid out in relation to other child elements; that is, the location of a child element is specified in terms of the desired distance from the existing children. To understand the concept of relative layout practically, let's create a new Android project called `RelativeLayoutApp`. Modify its layout file `activity_relative_layout_app.xml` to appear as shown in Listing 3.6.

LISTING 3.6   The `activity_relative_layout_app.xml` File on Arranging the `Button` Controls in the RelativeLayout Container

```xml
<RelativeLayout xmlns:android="http://schemas.android.com/apk/res/android"
    android:orientation="vertical"
    android:layout_width="match_parent"
    android:layout_height="match_parent">
    <Button
        android:id="@+id/Apple"
        android:text="Apple"
        android:layout_width="wrap_content"
        android:layout_height="wrap_content"
        android:layout_marginTop="15dip"
        android:layout_marginLeft="20dip" />
    <Button
        android:id="@+id/Mango"
        android:text="Mango"
        android:layout_width="match_parent"
        android:layout_height="wrap_content"
        android:padding="28dip"
        android:layout_toRightOf="@id/Apple"
        android:layout_marginLeft="15dip"
        android:layout_marginRight="10dip"
        android:layout_alignParentTop="true" />
    <Button
        android:id="@+id/Banana"
        android:text="Banana"
        android:layout_width="200dip"
        android:layout_height="50dip"
        android:layout_marginTop="15dip"
        android:layout_below="@id/Apple"
        android:layout_alignParentLeft="true" />
    <Button
        android:id="@+id/Grapes"
        android:text="Grapes"
        android:layout_width="wrap_content"
        android:layout_height="match_parent"
        android:minWidth="100dp"
        android:layout_alignParentRight="true"
        android:layout_below="@id/Banana" />
    <Button
        android:id="@+id/Kiwi"
        android:text="Kiwi"
```

```
        android:layout_width="100dip"
        android:layout_height="wrap_content"
        android:layout_below="@id/Banana"
        android:paddingTop="15dip"
        android:paddingLeft="25dip"
        android:paddingRight="25dip" />
</RelativeLayout>
```

Before we understand how the controls in the previous code block are placed, let's have a quick look at different attributes used to set the positions of the layout controls.

Layout Control Attributes

The attributes used to set the location of the control relative to a container are

- ▶ **android:layout_alignParentTop**—The top of the control is set to align with the top of the container.

- ▶ **android:layout_alignParentBottom**—The bottom of the control is set to align with the bottom of the container.

- ▶ **android:layout_alignParentLeft**—The left side of the control is set to align with the left side of the container.

- ▶ **android:layout_alignParentRight**—The right side of the control is set to align with the right side of the container.

- ▶ **android:layout_centerHorizontal**—The control is placed horizontally at the center of the container.

- ▶ **android:layout_centerVertical**—The control is placed vertically at the center of the container.

- ▶ **android:layout_centerInParent**—The control is placed horizontally and vertically at the center of the container.

The attributes to control the position of a control in relation to other controls are

- ▶ **android:layout_above**—The control is placed above the referenced control.

- ▶ **android:layout_below**—The control is placed below the referenced control.

- ▶ **android:layout_toLeftOf**—The control is placed to the left of the referenced control.

- ▶ **android:layout_toRightOf**—The control is placed to the right of the referenced control.

The attributes that control the alignment of a control in relation to other controls are

- ▶ android:layout_alignTop— The top of the control is set to align with the top of the referenced control.

▶ `android:layout_alignBottom`—The bottom of the control is set to align with the bottom of the referenced control.

▶ `android:layout_alignLeft`—The left side of the control is set to align with the left side of the referenced control.

▶ `android:layout_alignRight`—The right side of the control is set to align with the right side of the referenced control.

▶ `android:layout_alignBaseline`—The baseline of the two controls will be aligned.

For spacing, Android defines two attributes: `android:layout_margin` and `android:padding`. The `android:layout_margin` attribute defines spacing for the container, while `android:padding` defines the spacing for the view. Let's begin with padding.

▶ `android:padding`—Defines the spacing of the content on all four sides of the control. To define padding for each side individually, use `android:paddingLeft`, `android:paddingRight`, `android:paddingTop`, and `android:paddingBottom`.

▶ `android:paddingTop`—Defines the spacing between the content and the top of the control.

▶ `android:paddingBottom`—Defines the spacing between the content and the bottom of the control.

▶ `android:paddingLeft`—Defines the spacing between the content and the left side of the control.

▶ `android:paddingRight`—Defines the spacing between the content and the right side of the control.

Here are the attributes that define the spacing between the control and the container:

▶ `android:layout_margin`—Defines the spacing of the control in relation to the controls or the container on all four sides. To define spacing for each side individually, we use the `android:layout_marginLeft`, `android:layout_marginRight`, `android:layout_marginTop`, and `android:layout_marginBottom` options.

▶ `android:layout_marginTop`—Defines the spacing between the top of the control and the related control or container.

▶ `android:layout_marginBottom`—Defines the spacing between the bottom of the control and the related control or container.

▶ `android:layout_marginRight`—Defines the spacing between the right side of the control and the related control or container.

▶ `android:layout_marginLeft`—Defines the spacing between the left side of the control and the related control or container.

The layout file `activity_relative_layout_app.xml` arranges the controls as follows:

The `Apple` button control is set to appear at a distance of `15dip` from the top and `20dip` from the left side of the `RelativeLayout` container. The width of the `Mango` button control is set to consume the available horizontal space. The text `Mango` appears at a distance of `28dip` from all sides of the control. The `Mango` control is set to appear to the right of the `Apple` control. The control is set to appear at a distance of `15dip` from the control on the left and `10dip` from the right side of the relative layout container. Also, the top of the `Button` control is set to align with the top of the container.

The `Banana` button control is assigned the `width` and `height` of `200dip` and `50dip`, respectively. The control is set to appear `15dip` below the `Apple` control. The left side of the control is set to align with the left side of the container.

The `Grapes` button control is set to appear below the `Banana` button control, and its width is set to expand just enough to accommodate its content. The height of the control is set to take up all available vertical space. The text `Grapes` is automatically aligned vertically; that is, it appears at the center of the vertical height when the `height` attribute is set to `match_parent`. The minimum width of the control is set to `100dip`. The right side of the control is set to align with the right side of the container.

The `Kiwi` Button control is set to appear below the `Banana` control. Its width is set to `100dip`, and the height is set to just accommodate its content. The text `Kiwi` is set to appear at the distance of `15dip`, `25dip`, and `25dip` from the top, left, and right boundary of the control.

We don't need to make any changes to the `RelativeLayoutAppActivity.java` file. Its original content is as shown in Listing 3.7.

LISTING 3.7   The Default Code in the Activity File `RelativeLayoutAppActivity.java`

```
package com.androidunleashed.relativelayoutapp;

import android.app.Activity;
import android.os.Bundle;

public class RelativeLayoutDemoActivity extends Activity {
    @Override
    public void onCreate(Bundle savedInstanceState) {
        super.onCreate(savedInstanceState);
        setContentView(R.layout.activity_relative_layout_app);
    }
}
```

When the application is run, we see the output shown in Figure 3.8.

FIGURE 3.8   The five `Button` controls' layout relative to each other

We can make the text `Grapes` appear centrally at the top row by adding the following line:

```
android:gravity="center_horizontal"
```

So, its tag appears as follows:

```
<Button
    android:id="@+id/Grapes"
    android:text="Grapes"
    android:layout_width="wrap_content"
    android:layout_height="match_parent"
    android:minWidth="100dp"
    android:layout_alignParentRight="true"
    android:layout_below="@id/Banana"
    android:gravity="center_horizontal" />
```

The output is modified to appear as shown in Figure 3.9.

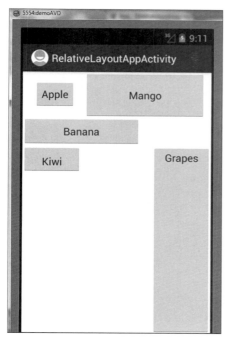

FIGURE 3.9   The Grapes Button control aligned horizontally at the center

Let's explore the concept of laying out controls in the RelativeLayout container by writing an application. The application that we are going to create is a simple Login Form application that asks the user to enter a User ID and Password. The TextView, EditText, and Button controls in the application are laid out in a RelativeLayout container (see Figure 3.10—left). If either the User ID or Password is left blank, the message The User ID or password is left blank. Please Try Again is displayed. If the correct User ID and Password, in this case, guest, are entered, then a welcome message is displayed. Otherwise, the message The User ID or password is incorrect. Please Try Again is displayed.

So, let's create the application. Launch the Eclipse IDE and create a new Android application called LoginForm. Arrange four TextView controls, two EditText controls, and a Button control in RelativeLayout, as shown in the layout file activity_login_form.xml displayed in Listing 3.8.

LISTING 3.8   The activity_login_form.xml on Laying Out the TextView, EditText, and Button Controls in the RelativeLayout Container

```
<RelativeLayout
    xmlns:android="http://schemas.android.com/apk/res/android"
    android:orientation="horizontal"
    android:layout_width="match_parent"
    android:layout_height="match_parent" >
    <TextView
        android:id="@+id/sign_msg"
```

```xml
    android:text = "Sign In"
    android:layout_width="wrap_content"
    android:layout_height="wrap_content"
    android:typeface="serif"
    android:textSize="25dip"
    android:textStyle="bold"
    android:padding="10dip"
    android:layout_centerHorizontal="true"/>
<TextView
    android:id="@+id/user_msg"
    android:text = "User ID:"
    android:layout_width="wrap_content"
    android:layout_height="wrap_content"
    android:layout_margin="10dip"
    android:layout_below="@+id/sign_msg" />
<EditText
    android:id="@+id/user_ID"
    android:layout_height="wrap_content"
    android:layout_width="250dip"
    android:layout_below="@+id/sign_msg"
    android:layout_toRightOf="@+id/user_msg"
    android:singleLine="true" />
<TextView
    android:id="@+id/password_msg"
    android:text = "Password:"
    android:layout_width="wrap_content"
    android:layout_height="wrap_content"
    android:layout_below="@+id/user_msg"
    android:layout_margin="10dip"
    android:paddingTop="10dip"/>
<EditText
    android:id="@+id/password"
    android:layout_height="wrap_content"
    android:layout_width="250dp"
    android:singleLine="true"
    android:layout_below="@+id/user_ID"
    android:layout_toRightOf="@+id/password_msg"
    android:password="true" />
<Button
    android:id="@+id/login_button"
    android:text="Sign In"
    android:layout_width="wrap_content"
    android:layout_height="wrap_content"
    android:layout_centerHorizontal="true"
    android:layout_marginTop="10dip"
    android:layout_below="@+id/password_msg"/>
```

```
    <TextView
        android:layout_width="match_parent"
        android:layout_height="wrap_content"
        android:id="@+id/response"
        android:layout_below="@+id/login_button"/>
</RelativeLayout>
```

The controls in the application are arranged in the RelativeLayout, as explained here:

▶ Through the `TextView` control `sign_msg`, the text `Sign In` is displayed horizontally centered at the top. It is displayed in bold serif font, `25 dip` in size. The text is padded with a space of `10dip` on all four sides of its container.

▶ Another `TextView` control, `user_msg`, displays the text `User ID` below the `TextView` `sign_msg`. The `TextView` is placed `10dip` from all four sides.

▶ An `EditText` control `user_ID` is displayed below `sign_msg` and to the right of `user_msg`. The width assigned to the `TextView` control is `250 dip` and is set to `single-line` mode, so if the user types beyond the given width, the text scrolls to accommodate extra text but does not run over to the second line.

▶ A `TextView` `password_msg` control displaying the text `Password:` is displayed below the `TextView` `user_msg`. The `TextView` control is placed at a spacing of `10dip` from all four sides, and the text `Password:` is displayed at `10dip` from the control's top boundary.

▶ An `EditText` control `password` is displayed below the `EditText` `user_ID` and to the right of the `TextView` `password_msg`. The `width` assigned to the `TextView` control is `250 dip` and is set to `single-line` mode. In addition, the typed characters are converted into dots for security.

▶ A `Button` control `login_button` with the caption `Sign In` is displayed below the `TextView` `password_msg`. The button is horizontally centered and is set to appear at `10dip` distance from the `EditText` control `password`.

▶ A `TextView` control `response` is placed below the `Button` `login_button`. It is used to display messages to the user when the `Sign In` button is pressed after entering `User ID` and `Password`.

To authenticate the user, we need to access the `User ID` and `Password` that is entered and match these values against the valid `User ID` and `Password`. In addition, we want to validate the `EditText` controls to confirm that none of them is blank. We also want to welcome the user if he or she is authorized. To do all this, we write the code in the activity file `LoginFormActivity.java` as shown in Listing 3.9.

LISTING 3.9   Code Written in the Java Activity File `LoginFormActivity.java`

```java
package com.androidunleashed.loginform;

import android.app.Activity;
import android.os.Bundle;
import android.view.View.OnClickListener;
import android.widget.Button;
import android.widget.EditText;
import android.view.View;
import android.widget.TextView;

public class LoginFormActivity extends Activity implements OnClickListener  {
    @Override
    public void onCreate(Bundle savedInstanceState) {
        super.onCreate(savedInstanceState);
        setContentView(R.layout.activity_login_form);
        Button b = (Button)this.findViewById(R.id.login_button);
        b.setOnClickListener(this);
    }

    public void onClick(View v) {
        EditText userid = (EditText) findViewById(R.id.user_ID);
        EditText password = (EditText) findViewById(R.id.password);
        TextView resp = (TextView)this.findViewById(R.id.response);
        String usr = userid.getText().toString();
        String pswd = password.getText().toString();
        if(usr.trim().length() == 0 || pswd.trim().length() == 0){
            String str = "The User ID or password is left blank \nPlease Try Again";
            resp.setText(str);
        }
        else{
            if(usr.equals("guest") && pswd.equals("guest")) resp.setText("Welcome " +
            usr+ " ! ");
            else resp.setText("The User ID or password is incorrect \nPlease Try Again");
        }
    }
}
```

The `Button` control is accessed from the layout file and is mapped to the `Button` object b. This activity implements the `OnClickListener` interface. Hence, the class implements the callback method `onClick()`, which is invoked when a click event occurs on the `Button` control.

In the `onClick()` method, the `user_ID` and `password` `EditText` controls are accessed from the layout file and mapped to the `EditText` objects `userid` and `password`. Also, the `TextView` control `response` is accessed from the layout file and is mapped to the `TextView` object resp. The User ID and password entered by the user in the two EditText controls are accessed through the objects userid and password and assigned to the two Strings usr and pswd, respectively. The data in the usr and pswd strings is checked for authentication. If the user has left any of the EditText controls blank, the message The User ID or password is left blank. Please Try Again is displayed, as shown in Figure 3.10 (left). If the User ID and password are correct, then a welcome message is displayed (see Figure 3.10—right). Otherwise, the message The User ID or password is incorrect. Please Try Again is displayed, as shown in Figure 3.10 (middle).

FIGURE 3.10   (left) The Login Form displays an error if fields are left blank, (middle) the Password Incorrect message displays if the user ID or password is incorrect, and (right) the Welcome message displays when the correct user ID and password are entered.

AbsoluteLayout

Each child in an AbsoluteLayout is given a specific location within the bounds of the container. Such fixed locations make AbsoluteLayout incompatible with devices of different screen size and resolution. The controls in AbsoluteLayout are laid out by specifying their exact X and Y positions. The coordinate 0,0 is the origin and is located at the top-left corner of the screen.

Let's write an application to see how controls are positioned in AbsoluteLayout. Create a new Android Project called AbsoluteLayoutApp. Modify its layout file, activity_absolute_layout_app.xml, as shown in Listing 3.10.

LISTING 3.10   The Layout File activity_absolute_layout_app.xml on Arranging Controls in the AbsoluteLayout Container

```
<AbsoluteLayout xmlns:android="http://schemas.android.com/apk/res/android"
    android:orientation="vertical"
    android:layout_width="match_parent"
    android:layout_height="match_parent">
    <TextView
        android:layout_width="wrap_content"
        android:layout_height="wrap_content"
        android:text="New Product Form"
        android:textSize="20sp"
```

```
        android.textStyle="bold"
        android:layout_x="90dip"
        android:layout_y="2dip"/>
    <TextView
        android:layout_width="wrap_content"
        android:layout_height="wrap_content"
        android:text="Product Code:"
        android:layout_x="5dip"
        android:layout_y="40dip" />
    <EditText
        android:id="@+id/product_code"
        android:layout_width="wrap_content"
        android:layout_height="wrap_content"
        android:minWidth="100dip"
        android:layout_x="110dip"
        android:layout_y="30dip" />
    <TextView
        android:layout_width="wrap_content"
        android:layout_height="wrap_content"
        android:text="Product Name:"
        android:layout_x="5dip"
        android:layout_y="90dip"/>
    <EditText
        android:id="@+id/product_name"
        android:layout_width="200dip"
        android:layout_height="wrap_content"
        android:minWidth="200dip"
        android:layout_x="110dip"
        android:layout_y="80dip"
        android:scrollHorizontally="true" />
    <TextView
        android:layout_width="wrap_content"
        android:layout_height="wrap_content"
        android:text="Product Price:"
        android:layout_x="5dip"
        android:layout_y="140dip" />
    <EditText
        android:id="@+id/product_price"
        android:layout_width="wrap_content"
        android:layout_height="wrap_content"
        android:minWidth="100dip"
        android:layout_x="110dip"
        android:layout_y="130dip" />
    <Button
        android:layout_width="wrap_content"
        android:layout_height="wrap_content"
```

```
        android:id="@+id/click_btn"
        android:text="Add New Product"
        android:layout_x="80dip"
        android:layout_y="190dip" />
</AbsoluteLayout>
```

The controls in `activity_absolute_layout_app.xml` are as follows:

▶ The `New Product Form` TextView is set to appear 90dip from the left and 2dip from the top side of the container. The size of the text is set to 20sp, and its style is set to bold.

▶ The `Product Code` TextView is set to appear 5dip from the left and 40dip from the top side of the container.

▶ The `product_code` EditText control is set to appear 110dip from the left and 30dip from the top side of the container. The minimum width of the control is set to 100dp.

▶ The `ProductName` TextView control is set to appear 5dip from the left and 90dip from the top side of the container.

▶ The `product_name` EditText control is set to appear 110dip from the left and 80dip from the top side of the container. The minimum width of the control is set to 200dip, and its text is set to scroll horizontally when the user types beyond its width.

▶ The `Product Price` TextView is set to appear 5dip from the left and 140dip from the top side of the container.

▶ The `product_price` EditText control is set to appear 110dip from the left and 130dip from the top side of the container. The minimum width of the control is set to 100dip.

▶ The `click_btn` Button, `Add New Product`, is set to appear 80dip from the left and 190dip from the top side of the container.

If we don't specify the x, y coordinates of a control in AbsoluteLayout, it is placed in the origin point, that is, at location 0,0. If the value of the x and y coordinates is too large, the control does not appear on the screen. The values of the x and y coordinates are specified in any units, such as sp, in, mm, and pt.

After specifying the locations of controls in the layout file `activity_absolute_layout_app.xml`, we can run the application. There is no need to make any changes in the file `AbsoluteLayoutAppActivity.java`. When the application is run, we get the output shown in Figure 3.11.

FIGURE 3.11   Different controls laid out in AbsoluteLayout

The AbsoluteLayout class is not used often, as it is not compatible with Android phones of different screen sizes and resolutions.

The next layout we are going to discuss is FrameLayout. Because we will learn to display images in FrameLayout, let's first take a look at the ImageView control that is often used to display images in Android applications.

Using ImageView

An ImageView control is used to display images in Android applications. An image can be displayed by assigning it to the ImageView control and including the android:src attribute in the XML definition of the control. Images can also be dynamically assigned to the ImageView control through Java code.

A sample ImageView tag when used in the layout file is shown here:

```
<ImageView
    android:id="@+id/first_image"
    android:src = "@drawable/bintupic"
    android:layout_width="wrap_content"
    android:layout_height="wrap_content"
    android:scaleType="fitXY"
    android:adjustViewBounds="true"
    android:maxHeight="100dip"
    android:maxWidth="250dip"
    android:minHeight="100dip"
    android:minWidth="250dip"
    android:resizeMode="horizontal|vertical" />
```

Almost all attributes that we see in this XML definition should be familiar, with the exception of the following ones:

▶ **android:src**—Used to assign the image from drawable resources. We discuss drawable resources in detail in Chapter 4. For now, assume that the image in the `res/drawable` folder is set to display through the `ImageView` control via this attribute.

Example:

```
android:src = "@drawable/bintupic"
```

You do not need to specify the image file extension. JPG and GIF files are supported, but the preferred image format is PNG.

▶ **android:scaleType**—Used to scale an image to fit its container. The valid values for this attribute include `fitXY`, `center`, `centerInside`, and `fitCenter`. The value `fitXY` independently scales the image around the X and Y axes without maintaining the aspect ratio to match the size of container. The value `center` centers the image in the container without scaling it. The value `centerInside` scales the image uniformly, maintaining the aspect ratio so that the width and height of the image fit the size of its container. The value `fitCenter` scales the image while maintaining the aspect ratio, so that one of its X or Y axes fits the container.

▶ **android:adjustViewBounds**—If set to `true`, the attribute adjusts the bounds of the `ImageView` control to maintain the aspect ratio of the image displayed through it.

▶ **android:resizeMode**—The `resizeMode` attribute is used to make a control resizable so we can resize it horizontally, vertically, or around both axes. We need to click and hold the control to display its resize handles. The resize handles can be dragged in the desired direction to resize the control. The available values for the `resizeMode` attribute include `horizontal`, `vertical`, and `none`. The `horizontal` value resizes the control around the horizontal axis, the `vertical` value resizes around the vertical axis, the `both` value resizes around both the horizontal and vertical axes, and the value `none` prevents resizing.

FrameLayout

FrameLayout is used to display a single `View`. The `View` added to a FrameLayout is placed at the top-left edge of the layout. Any other `View` added to the FrameLayout overlaps the previous `View`; that is, each `View` stacks on top of the previous one. Let's create an application to see how controls can be laid out using FrameLayout.

In the application we are going to create, we will place two `ImageView` controls in the FrameLayout container. As expected, only one `ImageView` will be visible, as one `ImageView` will overlap the other `ImageView`, assuming both `ImageView` controls are of the same size. We will also display a button on the `ImageView`, which, when selected, displays the hidden `ImageView` underneath.

Let's start with the application. Create a new Android project called `FrameLayoutApp`. To display images in Android applications, the image is first copied into the `res/drawable` folder and from there, it is referred to in the layout and other XML files. We look at the procedure for displaying images, as well as the concept of drawable resources, in detail in Chapter 4. For the time being, it is enough to know that to enable the image(s) to be referred to in the layout files placed in the `res/drawable` folder, the image needs to exist in the `res/drawable` folder. There are four types of drawable folders: `drawable-xhdpi`, `drawable-hdpi`, `/res/drawable-mdpi`, and `/res/drawable-ldpi`. We have to place images of different resolutions and sizes in these folders. The graphics with the resolutions 320 dpi, 240dpi, 160 dpi, and 120dpi (96 x 96 px, 72 x 72 px, 48 x 48 px, and 36 x 36 px), are stored in the `res/drawable-xhdpi`, `res/drawable-hdpi`, `res/drawable-mdpi`, and `res/drawable-ldpi` folders, respectively. The application picks up the appropriate graphic from the correct folder. So, if we copy two images called `bintupic.png` and `bintupic2.png` of the preceding size and resolution and paste them into the four `res/drawable` folders, the `Package Explorer` resembles Figure 3.12.

FIGURE 3.12   The `Package Explorer` window showing the two images, `bintupic.png` and `bintupic2.png`, dropped into the `res/drawable` folders

To display two `ImageViews` and a `TextView` in the application, let's write the code in the layout file `activity_frame_layout_app.xml` as shown in Listing 3.11.

LISTING 3.11   The Layout File `activity_frame_layout_app.xml` on Arranging the `ImageView` and `TextView` Controls in the FrameLayout Container

```
<FrameLayout xmlns:android="http://schemas.android.com/apk/res/android"
    android:orientation="vertical"
    android:layout_width="match_parent"
    android:layout_height="match_parent">
    <ImageView
        android:id="@+id/first_image"
        android:src = "@drawable/bintupic"
        android:layout_width="match_parent"
        android:layout_height="match_parent"
        android:scaleType="fitXY" />
    <ImageView
        android:id="@+id/second_image"
        android:src = "@drawable/bintupic2"
        android:layout_width="match_parent"
        android:layout_height="match_parent"
        android:scaleType="fitXY" />
    <TextView
        android:layout_width="wrap_content"
        android:layout_height="wrap_content"
        android:text="Click the image to switch"
        android:layout_gravity="center_horizontal|bottom"
        android:padding="5dip"
        android:textColor="#ffffff"
        android:textStyle="bold"
        android:background="#333333"
        android:layout_marginBottom="10dip" />
</FrameLayout>
```

The `first_image` and `second_image` ImageView controls are set to display the images `bintupic.png` and `bintupic2.png`, respectively. To make the two images stretch to cover the entire screen, the `scaleType` attribute in the `ImageView` tag is set to `fitXY`. A `TextView`, `Click the image to switch`, is set to display at the horizontally centered position and at a distance of `10dip` from the bottom of the container. The spacing between the text and the boundary of the `TextView` control is set to `5dip`. The background of the text is set to a dark color, the foreground color is set to white, and its style is set to bold. When a user selects the current image on the screen, the image should switch to show the hidden image. For this to occur, we need to write code in the activity file as shown in Listing 3.12.

LISTING 3.12   Code Written in the Java Activity File `FrameLayoutAppActivity.java`

```java
package com.androidunleashed.framelayoutapp;

import android.app.Activity;
import android.os.Bundle;
import android.widget.ImageView;
import android.view.View.OnClickListener;
import android.view.View;

public class FrameLayoutAppActivity extends Activity {
    @Override
    public void onCreate(Bundle savedInstanceState) {
        super.onCreate(savedInstanceState);
        setContentView(R.layout.activity_frame_layout_app);
        final ImageView first_image = (ImageView)this.findViewById(R.id.first_image);
        final ImageView second_image = (ImageView)this.findViewById(R.id.second_image);
        first_image.setOnClickListener(new OnClickListener(){
            public void onClick(View view) {
                second_image.setVisibility(View.VISIBLE);
                view.setVisibility(View.GONE);
            }
        });
        second_image.setOnClickListener(new OnClickListener(){
            public void onClick(View view) {
                first_image.setVisibility(View.VISIBLE);
                view.setVisibility(View.GONE);
            }
        });
    }
}
```

The two `first_image` and `second_image` `ImageView` controls are located through the `findViewById` method of the Activity class and assigned to the two `ImageView` objects, `first_image` and `second_image`, respectively. We register the click event by calling the `setOnClickListener()` method with an `OnClickListener`. An anonymous listener is created on the fly to handle click events for the `ImageView`. When the `ImageView` is clicked, the `onClick()` method of the listener is called. In the `onClick()` method, we switch the images; that is, we make the current `ImageView` invisible and the hidden `ImageView` visible. When the application runs, we see the output shown in Figure 3.13 (left). The application shows an image, and the other image is hidden behind it because in FrameLayout one View overlaps the other. When the user clicks the image, the images are switched, as shown in Figure 3.13 (right).

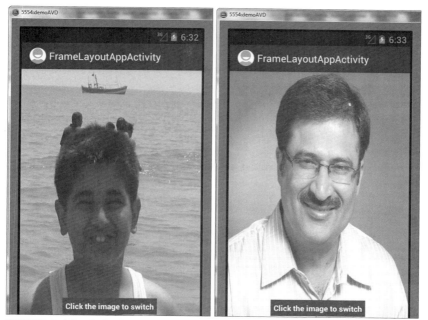

FIGURE 3.13   (left) An image and a `TextView` laid out in FrameLayout, and (right) the images switch when clicked

TableLayout

The TableLayout is used for arranging the enclosed controls into rows and columns. Each new row in the TableLayout is defined through a `TableRow` object. A row can have zero or more controls, where each control is called a `cell`. The number of columns in a TableLayout is determined by the maximum number of cells in any row. The width of a column is equal to the widest cell in that column. All elements are aligned in a column; that is, the width of all the controls increases if the width of any control in the column is increased.

> **NOTE**
>
> We can nest another TableLayout within a table cell, as well.

Operations Applicable to TableLayout

We can perform several operations on TableLayout columns, including stretching, shrinking, collapsing, and spanning columns.

Stretching Columns

The default width of a column is set equal to the width of the widest column, but we can stretch the column(s) to take up available free space using the `android:stretchColumns` attribute in the TableLayout. The value assigned to this attribute can be a single column number or a comma-delimited list of column numbers. The specified columns are stretched to take up any available space on the row.

Examples:

▶ `android:stretchColumns="1"`—The second column (because the column numbers are zero-based) is stretched to take up any available space in the row.

▶ `android:stretchColumns="0,1"`—Both the first and second columns are stretched to take up the available space in the row.

▶ `android:stretchColumns="*"`—All columns are stretched to take up the available space.

Shrinking Columns

We can shrink or reduce the width of the column(s) using the `android:shrinkColumns` attribute in the TableLayout. We can specify either a single column or a comma-delimited list of column numbers for this attribute. The content in the specified columns word-wraps to reduce their width.

NOTE

By default, the controls are not word-wrapped.

Examples:

▶ `android:shrinkColumns="0"`—The first column's width shrinks or reduces by word-wrapping its content.

▶ `android:shrinkColumns="*"`—The content of all columns is word-wrapped to shrink their widths.

Collapsing Columns

We can make the column(s) collapse or become invisible through the `android:collapseColumns` attribute in the TableLayout. We can specify one or more comma-delimited columns for this attribute. These columns are part of the table information but are invisible. We can also make column(s) visible and invisible through coding by passing the `Boolean` values `false` and `true`, respectively, to the `setColumnCollapsed()` method in the TableLayout. For example:

▶ `android:collapseColumns="0"`—The first column appears collapsed; that is, it is part of the table but is invisible. It can be made visible through coding by using the `setColumnCollapsed()` method.

Spanning Columns

We can make a column span or take up the space of one or more columns by using the `android:layout_span` attribute. The value assigned to this attribute must be `>=1`. For example, the following value makes the control take or span up to two columns:

```
android:layout_span="2"
```

Let's try arranging controls in a TableLayout with an example. Create a new Android project called `TableLayoutApp`. Make its layout file `activity_table_layout_app.xml` appear as shown in Listing 3.13.

LISTING 3.13   The Layout File `activity_table_layout_app.xml` on Arranging Controls in a TableLayout Container

```xml
<TableLayout xmlns:android="http://schemas.android.com/apk/res/android"
    android:orientation="vertical"
    android:layout_width="match_parent"
    android:layout_height="match_parent"
    android:stretchColumns="1">
    <TableRow android:padding="5dip">
        <TextView
            android:layout_height="wrap_content"
            android:text="New Product Form"
            android:typeface="serif"
            android:layout_span="2"
            android:gravity="center_horizontal"
            android:textSize="20dip" />
    </TableRow>
    <TableRow>
        <TextView
            android:layout_height="wrap_content"
            android:text="Product Code:"
            android:layout_column="0"/>
        <EditText
            android:id="@+id/prod_code"
            android:layout_height="wrap_content"
            android:layout_column="1"/>
    </TableRow>
    <TableRow>
        <TextView
            android:layout_height="wrap_content"
            android:text="Product Name:"
            android:layout_column="0"/>
        <EditText
            android:id="@+id/prod_name"
            android:layout_height="wrap_content"
            android:scrollHorizontally="true" />
```

```
    </TableRow>
    <TableRow>
        <TextView
            android:layout_height="wrap_content"
            android:text="Product Price:" />
        <EditText
            android:id="@+id/prod_price"
            android:layout_height="wrap_content" />
    </TableRow>
    <TableRow>
        <Button
            android:id="@+id/add_button"
            android:text="Add Product"
            android:layout_height="wrap_content" />
        <Button
            android:id="@+id/cancel_button"
            android:text="Cancel"
            android:layout_height="wrap_content" />
    </TableRow>
</TableLayout>
```

We cannot specify the `layout_width` attribute for the controls enclosed within the TableLayout, as their width will be always set to `match_parent` by default. We can specify the `layout_height` attribute for the enclosed controls (the default value is `wrap_content`). The `layout_height` attribute of the `TableRow` is always `wrap_content`.

Cells are added to a row in increasing column order. Column numbers are zero-based. If we don't specify a column number for any cell, it is considered to be the next available column. If we skip a column number, it is considered an empty cell in that row. We can make a cell span columns. Besides `TableRow`, we can use any `View` subclass as a direct child of `TableLayout`. The `View` is displayed as a single row that spans all the table columns.

NOTE

TableLayout does not display border lines for rows, columns, or cells.

In Listing 3.13, we specify that the second column of each row should be stretched to take up any available space in the row. The row contents are

▶ The first row of the table has a single control, New Product Form TextView. The TextView is set to span two columns and is set to appear at the center of the horizontal space. The `font` of the text displayed through TextView is set to `serif`, 20dip in size.

▶ In the second row, a `TextView` and an `EditText` control are displayed. The `TextView` control with text `Product Code` is set to appear at the column 0 location (the first column), and the `EditText` control is set to appear at column 1 (the second column).

▶ In the third row, again two controls, `TextView` and `EditText`, are displayed. The `TextView` control with the text `Product Name` is set to appear in column 0. If the user types text beyond the width of the `EditText` control, the content scrolls horizontally.

▶ In the fourth row, the `TextView` control with the text `Product Price` is displayed in the first column, and the `EditText` control is displayed in the second column.

▶ In the fifth row, a `Button` control with the caption `Add Product` is displayed in the first column, and a `Button` control with the caption `Cancel` is displayed in the second column.

When the application is run, the controls are laid out in rows and columns, as shown in Figure 3.14.

FIGURE 3.14   Different controls arranged in TableLayout

GridLayout Layout

GridLayout lays out views in a two-dimensional grid pattern, that is, in a series of rows and columns. The intersection of row and column is known as a grid cell, and it is the place where child views are placed. It is easier to use GridLayout when compared to TableLayout. Without specifying intermediate views, we can flexibly place the views randomly in the grid by specifying their row and column positions. More than one view can be placed in a grid cell. Besides this, views can span multiple grid cells too.

> **NOTE**
>
> No need to specify `layout_height` and `layout_width` for the GridLayout child views as they default to `WRAP_CONTENT`.

Specifying Row and Column Position

The two attributes that are used to specify the row and column position of the grid cell for inserting views are `android:layout_row` and `android:layout_column`. Together, they specify the exact location of the grid cell for placing the view. For example, the following statements place the view at the first row and column position of the grid:

```
android:layout_row="0"
android:layout_column="0"
```

When either or both of the preceding attributes are not specified, GridLayout uses the next grid cell by default for placing the view.

Spanning Rows and Columns

Views can span rows or columns if desired. The attributes used for doing so are `android:layout_rowSpan` and `android:layout_columnSpan`. For example, the following statement spans the view to two rows:

```
android:layout_rowSpan="2"
```

Similarly, the following statement spans the view to three columns:

```
android:layout_columnSpan="3"
```

Inserting Spaces in the GridLayout

For inserting spaces, a spacing view called Space is used. That is, to insert spaces, the Space view is inserted as a child view. For example, the following statements insert a space at the second row in the GridLayout. The width and height of the blank space are 50dp and 10dp:

```
<Space
    android:layout_row="1"
    android:layout_column="0"
    android:layout_width="50dp"
    android:layout_height="10dp" />
```

Similarly, the following statements insert a space at the third row in the GridLayout that spans three columns:

```
<Space
android:layout_row="3"
```

```
android:layout_column="0"
android:layout_columnSpan="3"
android:layout_gravity="fill" />
```

Let's apply the knowledge gained so far in arranging controls in a GridLayout. The application has controls arranged in the same way as we saw in TableLayout (see Figure 3.14) but in GridLayout instead. So, let's create a new Android project called GridLayoutLayoutApp. Make its layout file, `activity_grid_layout_app.xml`, appear as shown in Listing 3.14.

LISTING 3.14   The Layout File `activity_grid_layout_app.xml` on Arranging Controls in a GridLayout Container

```
<GridLayout xmlns:android="http://schemas.android.com/apk/res/android"
    xmlns:tools="http://schemas.android.com/tools"
    android:layout_width="match_parent"
    android:layout_height="match_parent"
    android:orientation="horizontal"
    android:rowCount="7"
    android:columnCount="2" >
    <TextView
        android:layout_row="0"
        android:layout_column="0"
        android:text="New Product Form"
        android:typeface="serif"
        android:layout_columnSpan="2"
        android:layout_gravity="center_horizontal"
        android:textSize="20dip"   />
    <Space
        android:layout_row="1"
        android:layout_column="0"
        android:layout_width="50dp"
        android:layout_height="10dp" />
    <TextView
        android:layout_row="2"
        android:layout_column="0"
        android:text="Product Code:"   />
    <EditText
        android:id="@+id/prod_code"
        android:layout_width="100dip"   />
    <TextView
        android:text="Product Name:"    />
    <EditText
        android:layout_row="3"
        android:layout_column="1"
        android:id="@+id/prod_name"
        android:layout_width="200dip"     />
```

```
<TextView
    android:layout_row="4"
    android:layout_column="0"
    android:text="Product Price:"    />
<EditText
    android:layout_row="4"
    android:layout_column="1"
    android:id="@+id/prod_price"
    android:layout_width="100dip" />
<Space
    android:layout_row="5"
    android:layout_column="0"
    android:layout_width="50dp"
    android:layout_height="20dp" />
<Button
    android:layout_row="6"
    android:layout_column="0"
    android:id="@+id/add_button"
    android:text="Add Product"    />
<Button
    android:id="@+id/cancel_button"
    android:text="Cancel"    />
</GridLayout>
```

In the preceding code, the GridLayout is defined as consisting of seven rows and two columns. The orientation of GridLayout is set to horizontal; that is, controls are placed in rows. It means that while specifying the grid location of a view, if we don't specify the column number, the next available column is assigned to it. As said earlier, the layout_width and layout_height attributes are not specified for any of the views laid in GridLayout because the default value wrap_content is considered for them. Remember, the row and column numbers are zero-based. In Listing 3.14, the controls are positioned in the grid as follows:

▶ A TextView with the text New Product Form is set to appear at the first row and column position of the grid. The text appears in serif font and in 20dip size. The text spans two columns and appears at the center of the row.

▶ A blank space is inserted at the second row and first column position. The width and height of the blank space are 50dp and 10dp, respectively.

▶ A TextView with the text Product Code: is set to appear at the third row and first column position of the grid.

▶ An EditText control with the ID prod_code of width 100dip is set to appear at the third row and second column position of the grid, that is, to the right of the text Product Code:. The question is even though we didn't specify row and column position for the EditText control, how it will appear at the third row and second column position? The answer is because the orientation of the GridLayout is horizontal, the current row (if it is not full) and the next column (if available) are considered the default location for the control to be inserted.

▶ A TextView with the text Product Name: is set to appear at the fourth row and first column position of the grid. Because both columns of the third row are full, the fourth row is considered the location for this view.

▶ An EditText control with the ID prod_name of width 200dip is set to appear at the fourth row and second column of the grid, that is, to the right of the text Product Name:.

▶ A TextView with the text Product Price: is set to appear at the fifth row and first column of the grid.

▶ An EditText control with the ID prod_price of width 100dip is set to appear at the fifth row and second column position of the grid, that is, to the right of the text Product Price:.

▶ A blank space is inserted at the sixth row and first column position. The width and height of the blank space are 50dp and 20dp, respectively.

▶ A Button control with the caption "Add Product" is set to appear at the seventh row and first column of the grid.

▶ A Button control with the caption "Cancel" is set to appear at the seventh row and second column of the grid.

There is no need to write any code in the Java activity file GridLayoutAppActivity.java. When the application is run, the controls are laid out in the grid pattern as shown in Figure 3.15.

FIGURE 3.15   Controls organized in the GridLayout

Adapting to Screen Orientation

As with almost all smartphones, Android supports two screen orientations: `portrait` and `landscape`. When the screen orientation of an Android device is changed, the current activity being displayed is destroyed and re-created automatically to redraw its content in the new orientation. In other words, the `onCreate()` method of the activity is fired whenever there is a change in screen orientation.

`Portrait` mode is longer in height and smaller in width, whereas `landscape` mode is wider but smaller in height. Being wider, `landscape` mode has more empty space on the right side of the screen. At the same time, some of the controls don't appear because of the smaller height. Thus, controls need to be laid out differently in the two screen orientations because of the difference in the height and width of the two orientations.

There are two ways to handle changes in screen orientation:

▶ **Anchoring controls**—Set the controls to appear at the places relative to the four edges of the screen. When the screen orientation changes, the controls do not disappear but are rearranged relative to the four edges.

▶ **Defining layout for each mode**—A new layout file is defined for each of the two screen orientations. One has the controls arranged to suit the `Portrait` mode, and the other has the controls arranged to suit the `Landscape` mode.

Anchoring Controls

For anchoring controls relative to the four edges of the screen, we use a RelativeLayout container. Let's examine this method by creating an Android project called `ScreenOrientationApp`. To lay out the controls at locations relative to the four edges of the screen, write the code in the layout file `activity_screen_orientation_app.xml` as shown in Listing 3.15.

LISTING 3.15   The Layout file `activity_screen_orientation_app.xml` on Laying Out Controls Relative to the Four Edges of the Screen

```
<RelativeLayout xmlns:android="http://schemas.android.com/apk/res/android"
    android:orientation="vertical"
    android:layout_width="match_parent"
    android:layout_height="match_parent">
    <Button
        android:id="@+id/Apple"
        android:text="Apple"
        android:layout_width="wrap_content"
        android:layout_height="wrap_content"
        android:layout_marginTop="15dip"
        android:layout_marginLeft="20dip" />
    <Button
        android:id="@+id/Mango"
```

```
        android:text="Mango"
        android:layout_width="match_parent"
        android:layout_height="wrap_content"
        android:padding="28dip"
        android:layout_toRightOf="@id/Apple"
        android:layout_marginLeft="15dip"
        android:layout_marginRight="10dip"
        android:layout_alignParentTop="true" />
    <Button
        android:id="@+id/Banana"
        android:text="Banana"
        android:layout_width="200dip"
        android:layout_height="50dip"
        android:layout_marginTop="15dip"
        android:layout_below="@id/Apple"
        android:layout_alignParentLeft="true" />
    <Button
        android:id="@+id/Grapes"
        android:text="Grapes"
        android:layout_width="wrap_content"
        android:layout_height="match_parent"
        android:minWidth="100dp"
        android:layout_alignParentRight="true"
        android:layout_below="@id/Banana" />
    <Button
        android:id="@+id/Kiwi"
        android:text="Kiwi"
        android:layout_width="100dip"
        android:layout_height="wrap_content"
        android:layout_below="@id/Banana"
        android:paddingTop="15dip"
        android:paddingLeft="25dip"
        android:paddingRight="25dip" />
</RelativeLayout>
```

Listing 3.15 shows five Button controls arranged in a RelativeLayout container. The controls are aligned relative to the edges of the container or in relation to each other. Let's keep the activity file ScreenOrientationAppActivity.java unchanged with the default code, as shown in Listing 3.16.

LISTING 3.16   Default Code in the Java Activity File ScreenOrientationAppActivity.java

```
package com.androidunleashed.screenorientationapp;

import android.app.Activity;
import android.os.Bundle;
```

```
public class ScreenOrientationAppActivity extends Activity {
    @Override
    public void onCreate(Bundle savedInstanceState) {
        super.onCreate(savedInstanceState);
        setContentView(R.layout.activity_screen_orientation_app);
    }
}
```

When the application is run while in the default `portrait` mode, the controls appear as shown in Figure 3.16 (left). Because the five `Button` controls are placed in relation to the four edges of the container and in relation to each other, none of the `Button` controls disappear if the screen is rotated to `landscape` mode, as shown in Figure 3.16 (right). To switch between `portrait` mode and `landscape` mode on the device emulator, press the `Ctrl+F11` keys.

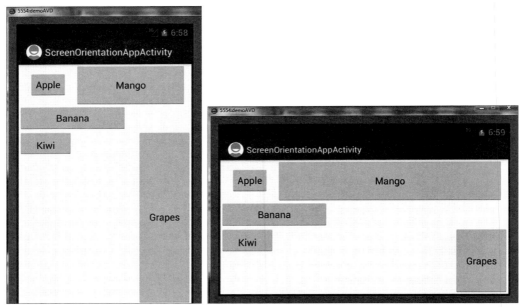

FIGURE 3.16   (left) Controls in `portrait` mode, and (right) the controls in `landscape` mode

Now that we understand the concept of adapting to screen orientation through anchoring controls, let's have a look at another approach.

Defining Layout for Each Mode

In this method, we define two layouts. One arranges the controls in the default `portrait` mode, and the other arranges the controls in `landscape` mode. To understand this, let's write code as shown in Listing 3.17 for laying out the controls for `portrait` mode in the default layout file `activity_screen_orientation_app.xml` (found in the `res/layout` folder).

LISTING 3.17   The Layout File `activity_screen_orientation_app.xml` on Laying Out
Controls in `portrait` Mode

```xml
<LinearLayout xmlns:android="http://schemas.android.com/apk/res/android"
    android:orientation="vertical"
    android:layout_width="match_parent"
    android:layout_height="match_parent">
    <Button
        android:id="@+id/Apple"
        android:text="Apple"
        android:layout_width="300dp"
        android:layout_height="wrap_content"
        android:padding="20dip"
        android:layout_marginTop="20dip" />
    <Button
        android:id="@+id/Mango"
        android:text="Mango"
        android:layout_width="300dp"
        android:layout_height="wrap_content"
        android:padding="20dip"
        android:layout_marginTop="20dip" />
    <Button
        android:id="@+id/Banana"
        android:text="Banana"
        android:layout_width="300dip"
        android:layout_height="wrap_content"
        android:padding="20dip"
        android:layout_marginTop="20dip"  />
    <Button
        android:id="@+id/Grapes"
        android:text="Grapes"
        android:layout_width="300dip"
        android:layout_height="wrap_content"
        android:padding="20dip"
        android:layout_marginTop="20dip"   />
    <Button
        android:id="@+id/Kiwi"
        android:text="Kiwi"
        android:layout_width="300dip"
        android:layout_height="wrap_content"
        android:padding="20dip"
        android:layout_marginTop="20dip"  />
</LinearLayout>
```

In Listing 3.17, we can see that five `Button` controls are vertically arranged in a LinearLayout container, one below the other. This vertical arrangement makes a few of the `Button` controls disappear when the screen is in `landscape` mode.

If we run the application without defining the layout for the `landscape` mode, we find the controls arranged in `portrait` mode, as shown in Figure 3.17 (left). But when we switch the screen orientation to `landscape`, we find the last two `Button` controls have disappeared, as shown in Figure 3.17 (right). This is because in `landscape` mode, the screen becomes wider but shorter in height.

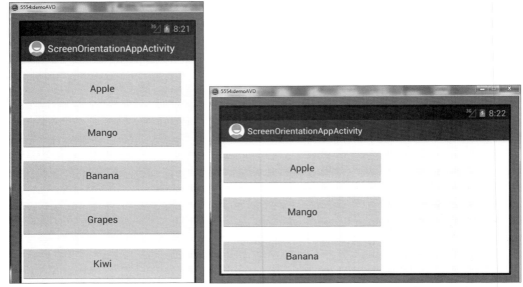

FIGURE 3.17   (left) Controls in `portrait` mode, and (right) some controls disappear in `landscape` mode.

To use the blank space on the right side of the screen in `landscape` mode, we need to define another layout file, `activity_screen_orientation_app.xml`, created in the `res/layout-land` folder. The `layout-land` folder has to be created manually inside the `res` folder. Right-click on the `res` folder in the `Package Explorer` window and select the `New`, `Folder` option. A dialog box opens, asking for the name for the new folder. Assign the name `layout-land` to the new folder, and click the `Finish` button. Copy the `activity_screen_orientation_app.xml` file from the `res/layout` folder and paste it into `res/layout-land` folder. Modify the `activity_screen_orientation_app.xml` file in the `res/layout-land` folder so as to arrange the controls in `landscape` mode. The code in the newly created `activity_screen_orientation_app.xml` is modified as shown in Listing 3.18.

LISTING 3.18   The Layout File `activity_screen_orientation_app.xml` in the `res/layout-land` Folder

```
<RelativeLayout xmlns:android="http://schemas.android.com/apk/res/android"
    android:orientation="vertical"
```

```
    android:layout_width="match_parent"
    android:layout_height="match_parent">
    <Button
        android:id="@+id/Apple"
        android:text="Apple"
        android:layout_width="250dp"
        android:layout_height="wrap_content"
        android:padding="20dip"
        android:layout_marginTop="20dip" />
    <Button
        android:id="@+id/Mango"
        android:text="Mango"
        android:layout_width="250dp"
        android:layout_height="wrap_content"
        android:padding="20dip"
        android:layout_marginTop="20dip"
        android:layout_toRightOf="@id/Apple" />
    <Button
        android:id="@+id/Banana"
        android:text="Banana"
        android:layout_width="250dip"
        android:layout_height="wrap_content"
        android:padding="20dip"
        android:layout_marginTop="20dip"
        android:layout_below="@id/Apple" />
    <Button
        android:id="@+id/Grapes"
        android:text="Grapes"
        android:layout_width="250dip"
        android:layout_height="wrap_content"
        android:padding="20dip"
        android:layout_marginTop="20dip"
        android:layout_below="@id/Apple"
        android:layout_toRightOf="@id/Banana"  />
    <Button
        android:id="@+id/Kiwi"
        android:text="Kiwi"
        android:layout_width="250dip"
        android:layout_height="wrap_content"
        android:padding="20dip"
        android:layout_marginTop="20dip"
        android:layout_below="@id/Banana" />
</RelativeLayout>
```

In this code block, we can see that, to fill up the blank space on the right side of the screen, the `Mango` and `Grapes` button controls are set to appear to the right of the `Apple` and `Banana` button controls.

We can also detect the screen orientation via Java code. Let's modify the activity file `ScreenOrientationAppActivity.java` to display a toast message when the screen switches between `landscape` mode and `portrait` mode. The code written in the Java activity file `ScreenOrientationappActivity.java` is shown in Listing 3.19.

LISTING 3.19   Code Written in the Java Activity File `ScreenOrientationappActivity.java`

```java
package com.androidunleashed.screenorientationapp;

import android.app.Activity;
import android.os.Bundle;
import android.widget.Toast;

public class ScreenOrientationAppActivity extends Activity {

    @Override
    public void onCreate(Bundle savedInstanceState) {
        super.onCreate(savedInstanceState);
        setContentView(R.layout.activity_screen_orientation_app);
    if(getResources().getDisplayMetrics().widthPixels>getResources().getDisplayMetrics().
            heightPixels)
        {
            Toast.makeText(this,"Screen switched to Landscape mode",Toast.LENGTH_SHORT).
            show();
        }
        else
        {
            Toast.makeText(this,"Screen switched to Portrait mode",Toast.LENGTH_SHORT).
show();
        }
    }
}
```

Now, when we run the application, the controls appear in `portrait` mode as shown in Figure 3.18 (left) and in `landscape` mode as shown in Figure 3.18 (right). We can see that none of the `Button` controls are now hidden in `landscape` mode.

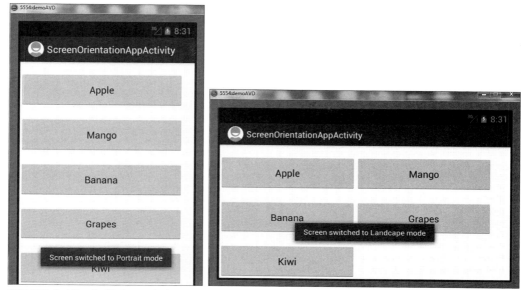

FIGURE 3.18   (left) Controls in `portrait` mode, and (right) all controls are visible in `landscape` mode.

Summary

In this chapter, you learned how to lay out controls for different orientations. You also learned to apply attributes such as `Orientation`, `Height`, `Width`, `Padding`, `Weight`, and `Gravity` to arrange the controls and their content. You saw how to create individual Android applications dedicated to each layout, `LinearLayout`, `RelativeLayout`, `AbsoluteLayout`, `FrameLayout`, and `TableLayout`.

In the next chapter, you learn about different types of resources and the procedures to apply them in Android applications. You learn to apply `Dimension` resources, `Color` resources, `Styles`, and `Themes` and also learn to use `String` and `Integer` arrays. To display images in the Android application, you learn to use `Drawable` resources and create an Image Switcher application using the `ToggleButton` control.

# CHAPTER 4

Utilizing Resources and Media

Resources include text data, bitmaps, audio, videos, and other items used by the Android application. Most commonly resources are kept separately in XML files and accessed in Java code through the IDs assigned to them. In this chapter you learn to access media too, that is, access and use images, audio, and video in Android applications.

Resources

Resources in Android refer to the external files that hold the information, such as strings, images, layouts, and audio, to be supplied to an Android application. Because resources are external, we can maintain and modify them whenever we want without disturbing the code. For example, the strings resource keeps the strings used in an Android application. Changing the string content in the resource file is easier when compared to applying changes to hard-coded strings that are scattered in the application code. Also, by creating several resource files, each supporting different hardware, we can make our applications applicable to diverse hardware systems. For example, we can have several layouts for screen size and orientation and use them dynamically when we want.

Resources are broadly divided into three categories—values, drawable, and layout—and are stored in the `res` folder of our project hierarchy. The values resources in turn represent resources such as strings, colors, dimensions, styles, and string or integer arrays. All resource types have a respective subfolder in the `res` folder. The ADT Wizard automatically creates a `res` folder that contains subfolders for the values, drawable, and layout resources, as shown in Figure 4.1.

FIGURE 4.1   The `res` folder showing the nested drawable (`drawable-hdpi`, `drawable-ldpi`, `drawable-mdpi`) layouts and values folders and their content

Types of Resources

A brief outline of the three folders is provided here:

▶ **`drawable` folder**—Depending on the target platform chosen, our application can have either a single directory, `drawable`, or four directories, `drawable-ldpi`, `drawable-mdpi`, `drawable-hdpi`, and `drawable-xhdpi`, where we can store the images used in our application. If our application has a single directory, `drawable`, then the images to be used in our application, regardless of resolution, are stored in it. If our application has four directories, then the images with different screen resolutions are stored in the respective directories. That is, the images of low, medium, high, and extra high resolutions are stored in the `drawable-ldpi`, `drawable-mdpi`, `drawable-hdpi`, and `drawable-xhdpi` directories, respectively. Android chooses the image(s) from the respective directory, depending on the density of the device used to run the application.

▶ **`layout` folder**—This folder contains a layout file automatically created for us. The default name assigned to this file is `activity_main.xml`, but we can assign any name to it. In Chapter 3, "Laying Out Controls in Containers," we saw how to use this file to lay out `Views` in the desired format.

▶ **`menu` folder**—This folder contains XML file(s) that represent application menus. Again, the default name assigned to the menu file that is automatically created for us is `activity_main.xml`, but we can change the name if we want.

▶ **`values` folder**—This folder by default contains a `strings.xml` file that we can use to define values resources that include strings, colors, dimensions, styles, and string or integer arrays. We can also create individual XML files for each of these resources instead. The folder also contains the `styles.xml` file that declares the standard platform's default light theme. The following is a list of some XML files that we can create in the values folder:

- ▶ `arrays.xml`—For defining `arrays` resources
- ▶ `colors.xml`—For defining `color` resources that define color values
- ▶ `dimens.xml`—For defining dimension resources to standardize certain application measurements
- ▶ `strings.xml`—For defining string resources
- ▶ `styles.xml`—For defining styles resources to format or change the appearance of our views and application

There are many Android devices with different Android versions, and managing themes across them is a critical task. To manage themes for different Android versions, different `values` folders in the `/res` folder containing individual themes are maintained. The idea is that on the basis of the platform version, the desired theme will be automatically selected from the respective folder.

- ▶ `values-v11`—The folder contains the `styles.xml` file that declares the holographic theme, which is used when the application runs on Android 3.0 (API Level 11) or higher. That is, if the API level of the device is 11 or higher, the `styles.xml` file present in this folder overrides the `styles.xml` file present in the `res/values` folder.

- ▶ `values-v14`—The folder contains the `styles.xml` file that declares the DeviceDefault theme, which is used when the application runs on Android 4.0 (API Level 14) or higher.

Besides these default subdirectories automatically created by ADT, there are several subdirectories that we can manually create in the `res` folder to categorize and keep our resources tidy. Table 4.1 shows the list of supported subdirectories in the `res` folder.

TABLE 4.1   Supported Subdirectories of the `res` Folder

Subdirectory Name	Stores
`anim`	Files that define animations.
`color`	XML files that define a list of colors.
`drawable-xhdpi`	Extra high resolution images. The `xhdpi` stands for extra high dots per inch.
`drawable-hdpi`	High-resolution images. The `hdpi` stands for high dots per inch.
`drawable-ldpi`	Low-resolution images. The `ldpi` stands for low dots per inch.
`drawable-mdpi`	Medium-resolution images. The `mdpi` qualifier stands for medium dots per inch.
`menu`	XML files that represent application menus.
`raw`	Non-XML data such as audio files.
`xml`	Additional XML files used in our application.
`libs`	Reference libraries.

When our application is built, all resources are compiled and included in our application package. On compilation, an `R class` file is created that contains references to all the resources created and hence enables us to reference them in the Java code. For each of the resource types, the `R class` contains static subclasses for `string`, `drawable`, and `layout` resource types. The subclasses created are `R.string`, `R.drawable`, and `R.layout`, respectively. Through these subclasses, we can access their associated resources in Java code.

> **NOTE**
>
> Don't edit the `R.java` file, as it is regenerated every time something gets changed, added, or deleted in the `/res/*` subdirectory.

Creating Values Resources

The resources in the `values` directory include different types, such as `strings`, `colors`, `dimensions`, and `string` or `integer` arrays. All the values are stored in XML files in the `res/values` folder. It is preferred to have a separate XML file for each type of resource in the `values` directory. The filename can be anything, but most commonly, the string resources file is named `strings.xml`. Remember, the resource filenames should contain only lowercase letters, numbers, period (.), and underscore (_) symbols.

> **NOTE**
>
> We can have any number of XML files to represent resources, provided they reside in the `/res/values` subdirectory. Never save resource files directly inside the `res/` folder—it will cause a compiler error.

To create Values resources, let's create an Android project called `ValuesResourcesApp`. The `strings.xml` file that is automatically created for us by the ADT Wizard contains the default content shown in Listing 4.1.

LISTING 4.1   Default Code in the `strings.xml` File

```
<resources>
    <string name="app_name">ValuesResourcesApp</string>
    <string name="hello_world">Hello world!</string>
    <string name="menu_settings">Settings</string>
    <string name="title_activity_values_resources_app">ValuesResourcesAppActivity</string>
</resources>
```

The two string resources with the name attributes `hello` and `app_name` are assigned to the `TextView` (in `main.xml`) and `label` attribute of the `Activity` tag (in `AndroidManifest.xml`) to display the name of the activity and the application name, respectively, while running the project. Let's modify the `strings.xml` file to appear as shown in Listing 4.2.

LISTING 4.2   Code Written in the `strings.xml` File

```xml
<resources>
    <string name="app_name">ValuesResourcesApp</string>
    <string name="menu_settings">Settings</string>
    <string name="title_activity_values_resources_app">ValuesResourcesAppActivity</string>
    <string name="str_name">XYZ Restaurant</string>
    <string name="str_address">11, Hill View Street, New York</string>
    <string name="str_message"><b>Welcome</b></string>
</resources>
```

We can see that the string resources file has a root element, `<resources>`, followed by one or more child elements, `<string>`. Each `<string>` element represents one string resource. Besides the text for the string resource, it contains a `name` property used to assign a unique resource ID to the string. That is, the names assigned to the four string resources, `app_name`, `str_name`, `str_address`, and `str_message`, are the resource IDs of the respective strings, and we can use these resource IDs in other resource files or the Java code for accessing the respective string resources.

We can use the string resources of the preceding XML file in other resource files by using the following syntax:

`@string/resource_ID`

For example, to access the string resource with the resource ID `str_address` in another resource file, we use the following code:

`@string/str_address`

All the string resources mentioned in the preceding string resource file will be compiled and placed in the `R.java` file. In the Java code, we can access the resources from the `R.java` file, using the following syntax:

`R.string.resource_ID`

In preceding syntax, the `string` refers to the resource type; that is, every resource ID needs to be prefixed by the resource type. Likewise, to access the `drawable` and `layout` resources, we prefix the resource ID by `R.drawable` and `R.layout`, respectively. There is no need to add any prefix while accessing any control from the layout. The resource ID is enough. The syntax is

`R.id.resource_ID`

Hence, to access the string resource with the resource ID `str_address` in the Java code, we use the following statement:

`R.string.str_name`

We use the `getString()` method and pass the resource ID of the concerned string resource to access it in Java code. Hence, the complete command to access the string resource with the resource ID `str_address` is

```
getString(R.string.str_address);
```

In the `strings.xml` file shown in Listing 4.2, we can also use HTML tags `<b>`, `<i>`, and `<u>` to make a string appear bold, italicized, or underlined. To access the string resources defined in the file `strings.xml` and to apply them to the `TextView` controls, the layout file `activity_values_resources_app.xml` may be modified to appear as shown in Listing 4.3.

LISTING 4.3   Code Written in the Layout File `activity_values_resources_app.xml`

```
<LinearLayout xmlns:android="http://schemas.android.com/apk/res/android"
    android:orientation="vertical"
    android:layout_width="match_parent"
    android:layout_height="match_parent" >
    <TextView
        android:id="@+id/name_view"
        android:layout_width="match_parent"
        android:layout_height="wrap_content"
        android:text="@string/str_name" />
    <TextView
        android:id="@+id/address_view"
        android:layout_width="match_parent"
        android:layout_height="wrap_content" />
    <TextView
        android:id="@+id/message_view"
        android:layout_width="match_parent"
        android:layout_height="wrap_content"
        android:text="@string/str_message" />
</LinearLayout>
```

In this code block, the statement `android:text="@string/str_name"` accesses a string resource from a resource file `res/values/strings.xml`, whose `name` property is `str_name`. The text in the string resource `str_name` is assigned to the `TextView` for display. Similarly, the string resource `str_message` is accessed and assigned to the `TextView` `message_view`. Hence, the text `XYZ Restaurant` and the `Welcome` message appear on the screen through the first and third `TextView` controls, `name_view` and `message_view`, respectively. But the middle `TextView`, `address_view`, does not display any text, as it is not assigned any string resource. Why?

The answer is that we will learn to assign a string resource to this `TextView` through Java code. The code written in the Java file `ValuesResourcesAppActivity.java` may appear as shown in Listing 4.4.

LISTING 4.4   Code Written in the Java Activity File `ValuesResourcesAppActivity.java`

```java
package com.androidunleashed.valuesresourcesapp;

import android.app.Activity;
import android.os.Bundle;
import android.widget.TextView;

public class ValuesResourcesAppActivity extends Activity {
    @Override
    public void onCreate(Bundle savedInstanceState) {
        super.onCreate(savedInstanceState);
        setContentView(R.layout.activity_values_resources_app);
        String strAddress=getString(R.string.str_address);
        TextView addressView=(TextView)findViewById(R.id.address_view);
        addressView.setText(strAddress);
    }
}
```

The string resource with the resource ID `str_address` is accessed and assigned to the String object `strAddress`. The `TextView` with the ID `addressView` is accessed from the layout and is mapped to the `TextView` object `addressView`. The content of the string resource that is saved in the `strAddress` object is assigned to the `TextView` to display. That is, the content of the string resource `str_address` is assigned to a `TextView` so it will be displayed on the screen. We get the output shown in Figure 4.2.

FIGURE 4.2   The three `TextView`s displaying the text assigned to them via String resource and Java code

Let's change the size of the text in these `TextView` controls via dimension resources.

Dimension Resources

Dimension resources are used for standardizing certain application measurements. These resources can be used to specify the sizes for fonts, layouts, and widgets. Also, we can modify the size of any control in the application without changing the code. Besides this, we can define dimensions for different screen resolutions and densities to support different hardware.

To try out dimension resources, let's open the application `ValuesResourcesApp` and add an XML file called `dimens.xml` to the `values` folder. To the `dimens.xml` file, add the code as shown in Listing 4.5.

LISTING 4.5   Code Written in the `dimens.xml` File

```xml
<?xml version="1.0" encoding="utf-8"?>
<resources>
    <dimen name="small_size">15dp</dimen>
    <dimen name="medium_size">15sp</dimen>
    <dimen name="large_size">20pt</dimen>
</resources>
```

We can see that the dimension resource is defined through the `dimen` element. The `dimen` element contains a numerical value followed by unit of measurement. Like other resources, it includes the `name` property to specify the ID of the resource.

We can use any of the following units of measurement:

▶ **px**—Pixels

▶ **in**—Inches

▶ **mm**—Millimeters

▶ **pt**—Points

▶ **dp**—Density-independent pixels based on a 160-dpi (pixel density per inch) screen

▶ **sp**—Scale-independent pixels

In the `strings.xml` file, we have defined three dimension resources: `15dp`, `15sp`, and `20pt`, represented by the three resource IDs `small_size`, `medium_size`, and `large_size`, respectively. Let's apply the dimension resources to our `TextView` controls `name_view`, `address_view`, and `message_view`. First, we learn to apply dimension resources through the layout file followed by Java code. To apply dimension resources to the `TextView` controls, modify `activity_values_resources_app.xml` to appear as shown in Listing 4.6.

LISTING 4.6   The Layout File `activity_values_resources_app.xml` on Applying Dimension Resources to `TextView` Controls

```xml
<LinearLayout xmlns:android="http://schemas.android.com/apk/res/android"
    android:orientation="vertical"
    android:layout_width="match_parent"
    android:layout_height="match_parent" >
    <TextView
        android:id="@+id/name_view"
        android:layout_width="match_parent"
        android:layout_height="wrap_content"
        android:text="@string/str_name"
```

```
            android:textSize="@dimen/small_size" />
    <TextView
            android:id="@+id/address_view"
            android:layout_width="match_parent"
            android:layout_height="wrap_content" />
     <TextView
            android:id="@+id/message_view"
            android:layout_width="match_parent"
            android:layout_height="wrap_content"
            android:text="@string/str_message"
            android:textSize="@dimen/large_size" />
</LinearLayout>
```

In the preceding code block, the two statements

```
android:textSize="@dimen/small_size"
```

and

```
android:textSize="@dimen/large_size"
```

access the two dimension resources `small_size` and `large_size` and apply to the two `TextViews` with the IDs `name_view` and `message_view`, respectively. Their text size is set to `15px` and `20sp`, respectively. Now let's see how to apply dimension resources to a `View` via Java code.

To apply the dimension resource `medium_size` to our `TextView` `address_view`, add these statements to the Java file `ValuesResourcesAppActivity.java`:

```
float addressSize= this.getResources().getDimension(R.dimen.medium_size);
addressView.setTextSize(addressSize);
```

The `TextView` to which we want to apply the dimension resource is accessed from the layout file and mapped to the `TextView` object `addressView`. Thereafter, we access our Resources object by calling the `getResources()` method on our activity object. Then, through the Resources object, we access the dimension by supplying its resource ID to the `getDimension()` method. The dimension accessed is then applied to the `TextView` using the `setTextSize()` method. After the application is run, we find that the three `TextView` controls appear in the sizes defined in the dimension resources, as shown in Figure 4.3.

FIGURE 4.3   Different dimensions applied to the three `TextView`s via dimension resources

Let's now see how to apply colors to our `View`s via `color` resources.

Color Resources

To define a `color` resource, we use the `color` element. The color value is specified in the form of hexadecimal RGB values preceded by an optional `Alpha` channel. The `Alpha` channel represents the transparency. We can specify the color either through single-character hex values or double-character hex values formats, as shown here:

▶ **#RGB**—For example, #F00 for a Red color.

▶ **#RRGGBB**—For example, #FF0000 for a Red color

▶ **#ARGB**—For example, #5F00 for a Red color with an Alpha of 5.

▶ **#AARRGGBB**—For example, #50FF0000 for a Red color with an Alpha of 50.

To apply `color` resources to our application `ValuesResourcesApp`, let's add an XML file called `colors.xml` to the `values` folder. In the `colors.xml` file, define a few color resources by writing the following lines of code in it:

```
<?xml version="1.0" encoding="utf-8"?>
<resources>
    <color name="red_color">#F00</color>
    <color name="green_color">#00FF00</color>
    <color name="blue_alpha_color">#500000FF</color>
</resources>
```

This code block defines three color resources that represent the three colors `red`, `green`, and `blue` (bit transparent) through the resource IDs `red_color`, `green_color`, and `blue_alpha_color`, respectively. Again, we learn to apply color resources to our `View`s with two methods: via the layout file and Java code. To apply `color` resources via the layout file `activity_values_resources_app.xml`, let's modify it to appear as shown in Listing 4.7.

LISTING 4.7   The Layout File `activity_values_resources_app.xml` on Applying Color
Resources

```xml
<LinearLayout xmlns:android="http://schemas.android.com/apk/res/android"
    android:orientation="vertical"
    android:layout_width="match_parent"
    android:layout_height="match_parent" >
    <TextView
        android:id="@+id/name_view"
        android:layout_width="match_parent"
        android:layout_height="wrap_content"
        android:text="@string/str_name"
        android:textSize="@dimen/small_size"
        android:textColor="@color/red_color"/>
    <TextView
        android:id="@+id/address_view"
        android:layout_width="match_parent"
        android:layout_height="wrap_content" />
     <TextView
        android:id="@+id/message_view"
        android:layout_width="match_parent"
        android:layout_height="wrap_content"
        android:text="@string/str_message"
        android:textSize="@dimen/large_size"
        android:textColor="@color/blue_alpha_color"/>
</LinearLayout>
```

In the preceding code block, the two statements

```
android:textColor="@color/red_color"
```

and

```
android:textColor="@color/blue_alpha_color"
```

access the `color` resources with the IDs `red_color` and `blueAlpha_color`, from the
resource file and assign them to the text of the two `TextViews`, `name_view` and `message_
view`. This changes their color to red and blue, respectively.

To apply the `color` resource to the `TextView` `address_view`, we use Java code. Add the
following lines of code to the Java file `ValuesResourcesAppActivity.java` to access the
color resource and apply it to the desired View:

```
int addressColor=this.getResources().getColor(R.color.green_color);
addressView.setTextColor(addressColor);
```

Here, the Resources object is accessed by calling the `getResources()` method. The Resources object, the `getColor()` method, is called to access the color resource by supplying its resource ID. The color accessed is then applied to the `addressView TextView` by using the `setTextColor()` method. The complete code in `ValuesResourcesAppActivity.java` is shown in Listing 4.8.

LISTING 4.8   The Code Written in the Java Activity File `ValuesResourcesAppActivity.java`

```java
package com.androidunleashed.valuesresourcesapp;

import android.app.Activity;
import android.os.Bundle;
import android.widget.TextView;

public class ValuesResourcesAppActivity extends Activity {
    @Override
    public void onCreate(Bundle savedInstanceState) {
        super.onCreate(savedInstanceState);
        setContentView(R.layout.activity_values_resources_app);
        String strAddress=getString(R.string.str_address);
        TextView addressView=(TextView)findViewById(R.id.address_view);
        addressView.setText(strAddress);
        float addressSize= this.getResources().getDimension(R.dimen.medium_size);
        addressView.setTextSize(addressSize);
        int addressColor=this.getResources().getColor(R.color.green_color);
        addressView.setTextColor(addressColor);
    }
}
```

When the application is run, we see the three `TextView` controls appearing in the colors defined in the `color` resources, as shown in Figure 4.4. Because the print book is in black and white, the `TextView` controls are distinguished through different sizes.

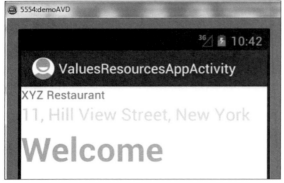

FIGURE 4.4   The three `TextView`s displayed in different colors applied via the Color Resource. The `TextView` controls are distinguished through different sizes.

Styles and Themes

A style is a collection of attributes such as color, font, margin, and padding that we can apply collectively to our Views, Activity, or an entire application. That is, instead of applying attributes individually to the components of our application, we can create a style incorporating all these attributes and quickly apply it instead. Through styles, we can apply a consistent dynamic look to our Views, Activity, and to the overall application. Also, we can easily change the appearance of our Views and application by simply specifying a different style or modifying the properties of the existing style, all without disturbing the Java code.

A style is created by using a style element with one or more item child elements. The style element includes a name property to specify the resource ID. Each item element includes a name property to define the attributes such as color, font, and so on. An item element defines an attribute and its value shown in this syntax:

```
<resources>
    <style name="resource_ID">
        <item name="attribute_name">value </item>
    </style>
</resources>
```

Styles support inheritance; that is, the attributes of any existing style can be accessed and included in the current style by using the parent property of the style element. For example, the attributes defined in a style named style1 can be included in the style named style2 by making use of the parent property in style2 as shown here:

```
<style name="style2" parent="style1" >
```

To apply styles to the individual Views in the layout file, open the styles.xml file that already exists in the values folder. In the styles.xml file, define the styles as shown in Listing 4.9.

LISTING 4.9   The Code Written in the styles.xml File

```
<resources>
    <style name="AppTheme" parent="android:Theme.Light" />
    <style name="style1">
        <item name="android:textColor">#00FF00 </item>
        <item name="android:typeface">serif</item>
        <item name="android:textSize">30sp </item>
    </style>
    <style name="style2" parent="style1" >
        <item name="android:textColor">#0000FF</item>
        <item name="android:typeface">sans</item>
        <item name="android:background">#FF0000</item>
        <item name="android:padding">10dip</item>
    </style>
```

```
    <style name="style3" parent="style2" >
        <item name="android:textColor">#00FF00</item>
        <item name="android:background">#00000000</item>
        <item name="android:typeface">monospace</item>
        <item name="android:gravity">center</item>
    </style>
</resources>
```

We can see that three styles are defined with IDs: `style1`, `style2`, and `style3`, respectively. The `style1` defines three attributes that

▶ Set the text color to `green`

▶ Set the font (typeface) to `serif`

▶ Set the font size to `30sp`

The `style2` inherits `style1`; hence it automatically gets the preceding three attributes. The `style2` overrides the `font` and `text color`, changing them to `sans` and `blue`, respectively. Also, `style2` includes the attributes to set the background color of the text to `red` and the text spacing to `10dip` from all four sides of the container. Thus, it also means that `style 2` now has the attributes that

▶ Set the font size to `30sp` (inherited from `style1`)

▶ Set the text color to `blue`

▶ Set the font (typeface) to `sans`

▶ Set the text background color to `red`

▶ Set the padding (text spacing from all four sides of the container) to `10dip`

The `style3` inherits `style2`, which means it receives all these attributes. It overrides certain attributes redefining the text color, background color, and the font to `green`, `black`, and `monospace`, respectively. Also, `style3` includes the `gravity` attribute set to `center` that makes the content of a `View` appear at the center. Hence, the `style3` has the following attributes that

▶ Set the font size to `30sp`

▶ Set the text color to `green`

▶ Set the background color of the text to `black`

▶ Set the font (typeface) to `monospace`

▶ Set the padding (text spacing from all four sides of the container) to `10dip`

▶ Make the content appear at the center of the `View`

Let's apply the three styles to the three `TextView` controls. Modify `activity_values_resources_app.xml` to appear as shown in Listing 4.10.

LISTING 4.10   The Layout File `activity_values_resources_app.xml` on Applying Styles to `TextView` Controls

```
<LinearLayout xmlns:android="http://schemas.android.com/apk/res/android"
    android:orientation="vertical"
    android:layout_width="match_parent"
    android:layout_height="match_parent">
    <TextView
        android:id="@+id/name_view"
        style="@style/style1"
        android:layout_width="match_parent"
        android:layout_height="wrap_content"
        android:text="@string/str_name"/>
    <TextView
        android:id="@+id/address_view"
        style="@style/style2"
        android:layout_width="match_parent"
        android:layout_height="wrap_content"
        android:text="@string/str_address" />
    <TextView
        android:id="@+id/message_view"
        style="@style/style3"
        android:layout_width="match_parent"
        android:layout_height="wrap_content"
        android:text="@string/str_message" />
</LinearLayout>
```

We can see that `style1`, `style2`, and `style3` are applied to the three `TextView` controls `name_view`, `address_view`, and `message_view`, respectively. Hence, the content of the first `TextView` appears in `green`, `serif` font and `30sp` in size. Similarly, the content of the second `TextView` appears in a blue foreground color, red background color, `sans` font, `30sp` in size, and the spacing (padding) between the text and the `TextView` on all four sides is `10dip`. The content in the third `TextView` appears in monospace font, green foreground color, black background color, size `30sp` in and the text appears at the center of the `TextView`.

> **NOTE**
>
> The `padding` attribute value will be overridden by the `gravity` attribute, making the text appear at the center of the `TextView`.

We don't need any code in the Java activity file. So remove all the code that we have been adding to it. That is, modify the Java file `ValuesResourcesAppActivity.java` to appear as shown in Listing 4.11.

LISTING 4.11   Code in the Java Activity File `ValuesResourcesAppActivity.java`

```java
package com.androidunleashed.valuesresourcesapp;

import android.app.Activity;
import android.os.Bundle;

public class ValuesResourcesAppActivity extends Activity {
    @Override
    public void onCreate(Bundle savedInstanceState) {
        super.onCreate(savedInstanceState);
        setContentView(R.layout.activity_values_resources_app);
    }
}
```

When the application is run, we get the output as shown in Figure 4.5.

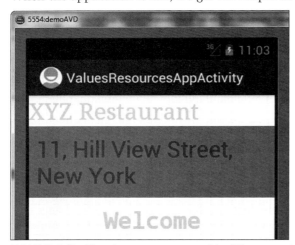

FIGURE 4.5   The three `TextView`s with different styles applied to them

Applying Themes

We can apply the `style` element to an entire Activity or application by adding the `android:theme` attribute to the Android manifest. For example, after we add the `android:theme` attribute to the `<activity>` element in the Android manifest, all the attributes of the `style` are applied to every `View` within the Activity. Similarly, after we add the `android:theme` attribute to the `<application>` element in the Android manifest, all the attributes of the `style` are applied to all the activities in the application.

The `AndroidManifest.xml` file of our application `ValuesResourcesApp` originally appears as shown in Listing 4.12.

LISTING 4.12   Default Code in the `AndroidManifest.xml` File

```xml
<manifest xmlns:android="http://schemas.android.com/apk/res/android"
    package="com.androidunleashed.valuesresourcesapp"
    android:versionCode="1"
    android:versionName="1.0" >
    <uses-sdk
        android:minSdkVersion="8"
        android:targetSdkVersion="15" />
    <application
        android:icon="@drawable/ic_launcher"
        android:label="@string/app_name"
        android:theme="@style/AppTheme" >
        <activity
            android:name=".ValuesResourcesAppActivity"
            android:label="@string/title_activity_values_resources_app" >
            <intent-filter>
                <action android:name="android.intent.action.MAIN" />

                <category android:name="android.intent.category.LAUNCHER" />
            </intent-filter>
        </activity>
    </application>
</manifest>
```

Let's apply `style3`, which we defined in the `styles.xml` file, to the entire application by modifying the `android:theme` attribute in `AndroidManifest.xml` file, as shown in bold in Listing 4.13.

LISTING 4.13   Code in the `AndroidManifest.xml` File on Modifying the `android:theme` Attribute

```xml
<manifest xmlns:android="http://schemas.android.com/apk/res/android"
    package="com.androidunleashed.valuesresourcesapp"
    android:versionCode="1"
    android:versionName="1.0" >
    <uses-sdk
        android:minSdkVersion="8"
        android:targetSdkVersion="15" />
    <application
        android:icon="@drawable/ic_launcher"
        android:label="@string/app_name"
        android:theme="@style/style3" >
```

```
        <activity
            android:name=".ValuesResourcesAppActivity"
            android:label="@string/title_activity_values_resources_app" >
            <intent-filter>
                <action android:name="android.intent.action.MAIN" />
                <category android:name="android.intent.category.LAUNCHER" />
            </intent-filter>
        </activity>
    </application>
</manifest>
```

To see the impact of applying the style to the entire application, we need to remove the styles in the layout file that were applied to the individual `TextView` controls. So, modify `activity_values_resources_app.xml` to appear as shown in Listing 4.14.

LISTING 4.14 The Layout file `activity_values_resources_app.xml` on Removing Styles

```
<LinearLayout xmlns:android="http://schemas.android.com/apk/res/android"
    android:orientation="vertical"
    android:layout_width="match_parent"
    android:layout_height="match_parent">
    <TextView
        android:id="@+id/name_view"
        android:layout_width="match_parent"
        android:layout_height="wrap_content"
        android:text="@string/str_name" />
    <TextView
        android:id="@+id/address_view"
        android:layout_width="match_parent"
        android:layout_height="wrap_content"
        android:text="@string/str_address" />
    <TextView
        android:id="@+id/message_view"
        android:layout_width="match_parent"
        android:layout_height="wrap_content"
        android:text="@string/str_message" />
</LinearLayout>
```

After the application is run, we find that the content of all three `Views` appears in `monospace` font, `green` foreground color, `black` background color, `30sp` in size, and the text appears at the center of the container, as shown in Figure 4.6.

FIGURE 4.6   The three `TextViews` styled by the application of a theme

We now know how to deal with values resources. Before we move onto drawable resources, let's have a quick look at one more form of string resources, known as the string array.

Arrays

Arrays refer to a collection of values or elements. Arrays are known for their capability of direct reference; that is, any element in an array can be referenced directly by specifying its `index/subscription` value. Arrays are considered to be one of the most flexible data sources for an application. Arrays can be in the form of strings or integers and are used for storing the data of their respective data type.

Using String Arrays

As the name suggests, the string array provides an array of strings. Such a resource is popularly used with selection widgets such as `ListView` and `Spinner` that need to display a collection of selectable items to the user. To define a string array, we use the following syntax:

```
<string-array name="array_name">
    <item>text1</item>
    <item>text2</item>
    . . .
    . . .
</string-array>
```

The `name` property acts as the resource ID and `text1`, `text2`, and so on represent the elements of the string. The syntax for defining an integer array is shown here:

```
<integer-array name="array_name">
    <item>number1</item>
    <item>number2</item>
    . . .
    . . .
</integer-array>
```

First we learn to use `string-array` in an Android application, and then we learn to use `integer-array`. To understand how `string-array` is defined and how it can be used to display a list of items, let's create a new Android project called `StringArrayApp`. In the strings resource file `strings.xml`, define a `string-array` called `fruits` and assign a few strings to it. After we add a `string-array`, the `strings.xml` file appears as shown in Listing 4.15.

LISTING 4.15   Code in the `strings.xml` File on Adding a String Array

```
<resources>
    <string name="app_name">StringArrayApp</string>
    <string name="menu_settings">Settings</string>
    <string name="title_activity_string_array_app">StringArrayAppActivity</string>
    <string-array name="fruits">
        <item>Apple</item>
        <item>Mango</item>
        <item>Orange</item>
        <item>Grapes</item>
        <item>Banana</item>
    </string-array>
</resources>
```

We can see that the string array `fruits` consists of five string elements, namely `Apple`, `Mango`, `Orange`, `Grapes`, and `Banana`. Let's make these string elements appear in a `TextView`. Add a `TextView` to the layout file. The code appears as shown in Listing 4.16.

LISTING 4.16   Code in the Layout File `activity_string_array_app.xml` on Adding the `TextView` Control

```
<LinearLayout xmlns:android="http://schemas.android.com/apk/res/android"
    xmlns:tools="http://schemas.android.com/tools"
    android:orientation="vertical"
    android:layout_width="match_parent"
    android:layout_height="match_parent">
    <TextView
        android:id="@+id/fruits_view"
        android:layout_width="match_parent"
        android:layout_height="wrap_content" />
</LinearLayout>
```

A `TextView` with an ID `fruits_view` is added to the layout file `activity_string_array_app.xml`. To access the elements of the string array and to display them via the `TextView`, we write the code in the Java file `StringArrayAppActivity.java` as shown in Listing 4.17.

LISTING 4.17   Code Written in the Java Activity File `StringArrayAppActivity.java`

```
package com.androidunleashed.stringarrayapp;

import android.app.Activity;
import android.os.Bundle;
import android.widget.TextView;

public class StringArrayAppActivity extends Activity {
    @Override
    public void onCreate(Bundle savedInstanceState) {
        super.onCreate(savedInstanceState);
        setContentView(R.layout.activity_string_array_app);
        TextView fruitsView = (TextView)findViewById(R.id.fruits_view);
        String[] fruitsArray = getResources().getStringArray(R.array.fruits);
        String str = "";
        for(int i = 0; i < fruitsArray.length; i++){
            str += fruitsArray[i] + "\n";
        }
        fruitsView.setText(str);
    }
}
```

The `fruitsView` `TextView` is accessed from the layout file `main.xml` and is assigned to the `TextView` object `fruitsView`. Also, the string array `fruits` from the layout file is accessed and assigned to the string array `fruitsArray`. That is, we can now access the string elements of the string array from the layout file in the Java code via the string array `fruitsArray`. An empty string, `str`, is created. When we use a `for` loop, each element of `fruitsArray` is accessed and appended to the string `str`. A new-line character, `\n`, is added between every string element to display them on separate lines. The string elements collected in the `str` element are assigned to the `TextView` `fruitsView` for display. After the application is run, all the string elements are displayed in the `TextView`, as shown in Figure 4.7.

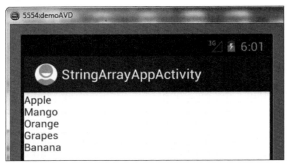

FIGURE 4.7   The content of the string array displayed through a `TextView`

Let's now take a look at creating and displaying integer array elements.

Using Integer Arrays

Creating an integer array is similar to creating a string array; the only difference is that the tag `string-array`, which we used for creating the string array, is replaced by `integer-array`. The elements of the integer array are defined with the help of the child tag `items`, the same as those used for string arrays. Let's define an integer array consisting of a few elements in the resource file `strings.xml` file. After we define an integer array, the `strings.xml` file appears as shown in Listing 4.18.

LISTING 4.18   The `strings.xml` File on Defining an Integer Array

```
<resources>
    <string name="app_name">StringArrayApp</string>
    <string name="menu_settings">Settings</string>
    <string name="title_activity_string_array_app">StringArrayAppActivity</string>
    <integer-array name="OddNumbers">
        <item>1</item>
        <item>3</item>
        <item>5</item>
        <item>7</item>
        <item>9</item>
    </integer-array>
</resources>
```

We display the integer array elements through a `TextView`. Since the integer array is representing odd numbers, let's change the resource ID of the `TextView` in `main.xml` to `oddnums_view`. The `activity_string_array_app.xml` file now appears as shown in Listing 4.19.

LISTING 4.19   The Layout File `activity_string_array_app.xml` on Changing the Resource ID of the `TextView` Control

```
<LinearLayout xmlns:android="http://schemas.android.com/apk/res/android"
    xmlns:tools="http://schemas.android.com/tools"
    android:orientation="vertical"
    android:layout_width="match_parent"
    android:layout_height="match_parent">
    <TextView
        android:id="@+id/oddnums_view"
        android:layout_width="match_parent"
        android:layout_height="wrap_content" />
</LinearLayout>
```

The code that we write in the activity file `StringArrayAppActivity.java` to access the elements of the integer array and to display them via `TextView` is shown in Listing 4.20.

LISTING 4.20   Code Written in the Java Activity File `StringArrayAppActivity.java` to Access Array Elements

```
package com.androidunleashed.stringarrayapp;

import android.app.Activity;
import android.os.Bundle;
import android.widget.TextView;

public class StringArrayAppActivity extends Activity {

    @Override
    public void onCreate(Bundle savedInstanceState) {
        super.onCreate(savedInstanceState);
        setContentView(R.layout.activity_string_array_app);
        TextView oddNumsView = (TextView)findViewById(R.id.oddnums_view);
        int[] oddNumsArray = getResources().getIntArray(R.array.OddNumbers);
        String str = "";
        for(int i = 0; i < oddNumsArray.length; i++){
            str += oddNumsArray[i] + "\n";
        }
        oddNumsView.setText(str);
    }
}
```

The `oddNumsView` `TextView` from the layout file is accessed and mapped to the `TextView` object `oddNumsView`. Also, the `OddNumbers` integer array that we defined in the resource file `strings.xml` is accessed and mapped to the integer array `oddnumsArray`. Through a `for` loop, all the array elements are accessed and appended to an empty string, `str`. Between each array element, a line feed character, \n, is inserted to make them appear on separate lines. The content of the string str is then assigned to the TextView, oddNumsView for display. After the application is run, we get the output shown in Figure 4.8.

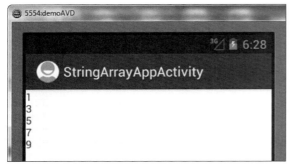

FIGURE 4.8   The content of a numeric array displayed through a TextView

We have learned to use values resources. The next resource, drawable, is helpful in displaying images in an Android application.

Using Drawable Resources

When it comes to displaying images, Android supports three common image formats: PNG, JPG, and GIF. The images for the Android application are stored in the directory res/drawable. Depending on the target platform chosen while creating a new application, ADT either creates a single directory, res/drawable, or several: drawable-ldpi, drawable-mdpi, drawable-hdpi, and drawable-xhdpi. Each directory is meant for storing images of different screen resolutions. To support devices of different densities, we can store the images of low, medium, high, and extra high resolutions in the drawable-ldpi, drawable-mdpi, drawable-hdpi, and drawable-xhdpi directories, respectively. The images with resolutions of 320dpi, 240dpi, 160dpi, and 120dpi and sizes 96x96px, 72x72px, 48x48px, and 36x36px are usually stored in the res/drawable-xhdpi, res/drawable-hdpi, res/drawable-mdpi, and res/drawable-ldpi folders, respectively. At runtime, depending on the density of the device on which the application is run, Android automatically chooses the correct resolution image. For example, if the application is running on a high-density device and the requested drawable resource is available in the drawable-hdpi folder, Android uses it in the application. If Android doesn't find the image in the drawable-hdpi folder, it searches for the image in other directories to find the closest match.

Displaying images is easy. We just put our image in the res/drawable folders and then refer to it in the code. In this section, we learn to display images in an Android application.

Let's create a new Android project called DispImageApp. As we said earlier, to display an image in an application, the file needs to be added to the res/drawable folder. Android supports images of almost all formats, but it prefers to use the PNG format. Copy a few images, for example, bintupic.png of 96x96px, 72x72px, 48x48px, and 36x36px in size and resolutions of 320dpi, 240dpi, 160dpi, and 120dpi, respectively, into the res/drawable-xhdpi, res/drawable-hdpi, res/drawable-mdpi, and res/drawable-ldpi folders, respectively. Remember, all image filenames should be lowercase and contain only letters, numbers, and underscores. After we add images to the res/drawable folders, the gen folder is regenerated where the R.java file resides. The R.java file includes a reference to the newly added image and hence can be used in the layout file or other Java code. The syntax for referencing the image in the layout file is

```
@drawable/image_filename
```

In Java code, the image can be referenced using the following syntax:

```
R.drawable.image_filename
```

Remember, the image_filename in the syntax shown refers to the base name of the file, that is, the filename without the extension. For example, the image file, bintupic.png, that we just added to the res/drawable folder is accessed as @drawable/bintupic in the layout file and other resources and as R.drawable.bintupic in the Java code. The extension of the image file, .png is never used when referencing it.

NOTE

Any subdirectories inside /res/drawable are ignored.

To display the image, let's add an ImageView control to the layout file. Write the code in the layout file activity_disp_image_app.xml as shown in Listing 4.21.

LISTING 4.21   The Layout File activity_disp_image_app.xml on Adding the ImageView Control

```
<LinearLayout xmlns:android="http://schemas.android.com/apk/res/android"
    xmlns:tools="http://schemas.android.com/tools"
    android:orientation="vertical"
    android:layout_width="match_parent"
    android:layout_height="match_parent">
    <ImageView
        android:id="@+id/image_toview"
        android:src="@drawable/bintupic"
        android:layout_width="match_parent"
        android:layout_height="match_parent"/>
</LinearLayout>
```

We can see that an ImageView control is defined with the ID image_toview. To make our image display through an ImageView control, we reference it via its src attribute. That is, we use the following statement to assign or refer the image in the res/drawable folder:

```
android:src="@drawable/bintupic"
```

This statement loads the image `bintupic.png`, which we pasted into the `res/drawable` folder. We don't need to write any Java code for displaying the image. After the application is run, the image is displayed, as shown in the Figure 4.9.

FIGURE 4.9   The image displayed through an `ImageView` control using a drawable resource

We can also specify the image for the `ImageView` control through Java code. To try this, let's remove the reference to the `bintupic` image in the `ImageView` control that we made through the `src` attribute:

```
android:src="@drawable/bintupic"
```

After we remove the image reference from the `ImageView` control, the layout file, `activity_disp_image_app.xml`, appears as shown in Listing 4.22.

LISTING 4.22   The Layout file `activity_disp_image_app.xml` on Removing the Image Reference from the `ImageView` Control

```
<LinearLayout xmlns:android="http://schemas.android.com/apk/res/android"
  xmlns:tools="http://schemas.android.com/tools"
    android:orientation="vertical"
    android:layout_width="match_parent"
    android:layout_height="match_parent">
    <ImageView
        android:id="@+id/image_toview"
        android:layout_width="match_parent"
```

```
                android:layout_height="match_parent"/>
</LinearLayout>
```

If we run the application now, nothing appears on the screen, as no image has been referenced by the `ImageView` control. Let's write the code in the Java activity file `DispImageAppActivity.java` to assign an image to the `ImageView` control as shown in Listing 4.23.

LISTING 4.23   The Java Activity File `DispImageAppActivity.java`

```
package com.androidunleashed.dispimageapp;

import android.app.Activity;
import android.os.Bundle;
import android.widget.ImageView;

public class DispImageAppActivity extends Activity {
    @Override
    public void onCreate(Bundle savedInstanceState) {
        super.onCreate(savedInstanceState);
        setContentView(R.layout.activity_disp_image_app);
        ImageView image = (ImageView) findViewById(R.id.image_toview);
        image.setImageResource(R.drawable.bintupic);
    }
}
```

In the preceding Java file, the statement

```
ImageView image = (ImageView) findViewById(R.id.image_toview);
```

gets the `ImageView` control from the layout file and stores it in an `ImageView` object called `image`. That is, the `image` is an `ImageView` object that now refers to the `ImageView` control placed in the layout file.

Via the `setImageResource()` method used in this statement

```
image.setImageResource(R.drawable.bintupic);
```

the image `bintupic.png` stored in the `res/drawable` folder is assigned to the `ImageView` control for display. After the application is run, we get the same output as shown previously in Figure 4.9.

We have now learned that the `setImageResource()` method can be used to change the image of the `ImageView` control dynamically at runtime. Let's use this method to modify our application so that it switches images when a button is clicked. When the button is clicked again, the previous image is redisplayed in the `ImageView` control. The button that is most suitable for this type of application is a `ToggleButton`, which flips between two states.

Switching States with Toggle Buttons

As the name suggests, the `ToggleButton` toggles between the two states, something like a radio button. A `ToggleButton` can only be in one state out of two mutually exclusive states, for example, `On` and `Off`. To display a `ToggleButton`, we use the `<ToggleButton>` tag in the layout file. To set the text for the button, the two attributes `android:textOn` and `android:textOff` are used. The default values for the two attributes are `ON` and `OFF`, respectively. The following code shows how to create a toggle button using the `ToggleButton` tag:

```
<ToggleButton
    android:layout_width="wrap_content"
    android:layout_height="wrap_content"
    android:textOn="Play"
    android:textOff="Stop" />
```

This code block defines a toggle button that shows the text `Play` in the `On` state and shows `Stop` in the `Off` state.

Let's create a new Android project called `ToggleButtonApp`. This project consists of a `TextView` and a `ToggleButton`. The `TextView` initially displays some text on startup. After we select the `ToggleButton`, the text displayed through `TextView` changes, and after we select the `ToggleButton` again, the previous text is redisplayed in the `TextView` control. So in all, we need to define two controls in the layout file, `TextView` and a `ToggleButton`. After we define the two controls, the code in the layout file `activity_toggle_button_app.xml` appears as shown in Listing 4.24.

LISTING 4.24   Code in Layout File `activity_toggle_button_app.xml` on Adding the `TextView` and `ToggleButton` Controls

```
<LinearLayout xmlns:android="http://schemas.android.com/apk/res/android"
    xmlns:tools="http://schemas.android.com/tools"
    android:orientation="vertical"
    android:layout_width="match_parent"
    android:layout_height="match_parent">
    <TextView
        android:layout_width="match_parent"
        android:layout_height="wrap_content"
        android:text="Select the Play button"
        android:id="@+id/response"/>
     <ToggleButton android:id="@+id/playstop_btn"
        android:layout_width="wrap_content"
        android:layout_height="wrap_content"
        android:textOn="Play"
        android:textOff="Stop"/>
</LinearLayout>
```

We can see that the `TextView` control is assigned the ID `response` and is set to display the default text: `Select the Play button`. The `ToggleButton` is assigned the ID `playstop_btn` and is set to display `Play` and `Stop` in the `On` and `Off` states, respectively. We want the text of the `TextView` control to change on the click of the `ToggleButton`. To enable the `ToggleButton` to switch text via the `TextView` control when it is clicked, we need to write some Java code in the `ToggleButtonAppActivity.java` file as shown in Listing 4.25.

LISTING 4.25   Code Written in the Java Activity File `ToggleButtonAppActivity.java`

```
package com.androidunleashed.togglebuttonapp;

import android.app.Activity;
import android.os.Bundle;
import android.widget.TextView;
import android.widget.ToggleButton;
import android.view.View.OnClickListener;
import android.view.View;

public class ToggleButtonAppActivity extends Activity {

    @Override
    public void onCreate(Bundle savedInstanceState) {
        super.onCreate(savedInstanceState);
        setContentView(R.layout.activity_toggle_button_app);
        final TextView resp = (TextView)this.findViewById(R.id.response);
        final ToggleButton playStopButton = (ToggleButton)
            findViewById(R.id.playstop_btn);
        playStopButton.setChecked(true);
        playStopButton.setOnClickListener(new OnClickListener() {
            public void onClick(View v) {
                if (playStopButton.isChecked()) {
                    resp.setText("Stop button is toggled to Play button");
                }
                else {
                    resp.setText("Play button is toggled to Stop button");
                }
            }
        });
    }
}
```

In the preceding code, we can see that the `response` TextView and `playstop_btn` ToggleButton are accessed from the layout file and are mapped to the `TextView` object `resp` and to the `ToggleButton` object `playStopButton`, respectively. The `ToggleButton` is initially set to the `checked` (On) state on startup. An event handler `OnClickListener` is added to the `ToggleButton` `playStopButton`. Its callback method, `onClick()`, is implemented, which executes when the `ToggleButton` is clicked. In the `onClick()` method, we check the state of the `ToggleButton` and change the text displayed through the `TextView` control accordingly. That is, when the `ToggleButton` is in the `On` state, the text displayed through the `TextView` control is set to `Stop button is toggled to Play button`. Similarly, when the `ToggleButton` is in the `Off` state, the text displayed through the `TextView` is set to `Play button is toggled to Stop button`. The state of the `ToggleButton` changes between the `checked` (On) and `unchecked` (Off) state on every click.

After the application is run, we get the output shown in Figure 4.10 (left). We can see that the `TextView` control displays the default text `Select the Play button`, and the caption displayed in the `ToggleButton` is `Play`. When the `ToggleButton` is selected, its caption changes to `Stop`, and the text in the `TextView` changes to `Play button is toggled to Stop button`, as shown in Figure 4.10 (middle). When the `ToggleButton` is selecte again, the caption in the `ToggleButton` changes back to `Play`, and the text in the `TextView` control changes to `Stop button is toggled to Play button`, as shown in Figure 4.10 (right). That is, the caption in the `ToggleButton`, as well as the text in the `TextView` controls, changes on every click of the `ToggleButton`.

FIGURE 4.10   (left) The `ToggleButton` and `TextView` on application startup, (middle) the text on `ToggleButton` and `TextView` changes on selecting the `ToggleButton`, and (right) the original text on `ToggleButton` reappears on clicking the `ToggleButton` again.

We can add the `android:gravity` and `android:layout_gravity` attributes to the `<TextView>` and `<ToggleButton>` tags in the layout file to center the text in the `TextView` control and to align the `ToggleButton` at the center position in respect to its container. The following statement centrally aligns the text in the `TextView` control:

```
android:gravity="center"
```

The following statement makes the `ToggleButton` appear at the center of the `LinearLayout` container:

```
android:layout_gravity="center"
```

We can also add a background image to the `ToggleButton` by adding the `android:background` attribute to the `<ToggleButton>` tag in the layout file. The following statement sets the `ic_launcher.png` image as the background image of the `ToggleButton`:

```
android:background="@drawable/ic_launcher"
```

The `ic_launcher.png` image is the built-in image resource provided by ADT that can be seen in the `res/drawable` folder. After we add the `android:layout_gravity` and `android:background` attributes, the `ToggleButton` appears with a background image and at the center of the `LinearLayout` container, as shown in Figure 4.11 (left). Figure 4.11 (middle and right) shows how the `ToggleButton`'s text and `TextView`'s text change with a click of the `ToggleButton`.

FIGURE 4.11   (left) The `ToggleButton` with background image applied and a `TextView` on application startup, (middle) the text on the `ToggleButton` and `TextView` changes on selecting the `ToggleButton`—the background image remains the same, and (right) the original text on the `ToggleButton` reappears on clicking the `ToggleButton` again.

In Figure 4.11, we notice that, although the `ToggleButton`'s text changes on every click, its background image remains the same. This is so because we defined the common background of the `ToggleButton` (for both of its states) through the `android:background` attribute. To display different background images for the `On` and `Off` states of the `ToggleButton`, we need to add two images to the application. Let's paste two images called, `play.png` and `stop.png`, into the `res/drawable` folders (`res/drawable-xhdpi`, `res/drawable-hdpi`, `res/drawable-mdpi`, and `res/drawable-ldpi`). To make these pasted images display as background images in the `ToggleButton` control's `On` and `Off` states, let's add some Java code to our `ToggleButtonAppActivity.java` file as shown in Listing 4.26. Only the statements in bold are newly added code; the rest of the code is the same as we saw in Listing 4.25.

LISTING 4.26   Code in the Java Activity File `ToggleButtonAppActivity.java`

```
package com.androidunleashed.togglebuttonapp;

import android.app.Activity;
import android.os.Bundle;
import android.widget.TextView;
import android.widget.ToggleButton;
import android.view.View.OnClickListener;
import android.view.View;

public class ToggleButtonAppActivity extends Activity {

    @Override
    public void onCreate(Bundle savedInstanceState) {
        super.onCreate(savedInstanceState);
        setContentView(R.layout.activity_toggle_button_app);
        final TextView resp = (TextView)this.findViewById(R.id.response);
        final ToggleButton playstopbutton = (ToggleButton)
            findViewById(R.id.playstop_btn);
```

```
        playstopbutton.setChecked(true);
        playstopbutton.setOnClickListener(new OnClickListener() {
            public void onClick(View v) {
                if (playstopbutton.isChecked()) {
                    playstopbutton.setBackgroundDrawable(getResources().getDrawable(R.
                    drawable.play));
                    resp.setText("Stop button is toggled to Play button");
                }
                else {
                    playstopbutton.setBackgroundDrawable(getResources().getDrawable(R.
                    drawable.stop));
                    resp.setText("Play button is toggled to Stop button");
                }
            }
        });
    }
}
```

We can see that the newly added code accesses the `Resources` object through the `getRe-sources()` method, and the `Drawable resources` are accessed by supplying the resource ID of the `play.png` and `stop.png` images to the `getDrawable()` method. The images accessed are then applied as the background of the `ToggleButton`'s `On` and `Off` states, respectively. Because we don't want any text to appear on top of the images of the `ToggleButton`, let's remove the text of the `On` and `Off` states. Modify the `android:textOn` and `android:textOff` attributes in the `<ToggleButton>` tag of the layout file `main.xml`. We make the two attributes appear as shown here:

```
android:textOn=""
android:textOff=""
```

These statements prevent the default text from appearing on the `ToggleButton` in its `On` and `Off` states. Now we replace the `ic_launcher.png` image with the `play.png` image by setting the following attribute:

```
android:background="@drawable/play"
```

This attribute displays the `play.png` image on application startup. The layout file `main.xml` on applying these changes appears as shown in Listing 4.27.

LISTING 4.27   Code Written in the Layout File `main.xml`

```
<?xml version="1.0" encoding="utf-8"?>
<LinearLayout xmlns:android="http://schemas.android.com/apk/res/android"
    android:orientation="vertical"
    android:layout_width="match_parent"
    android:layout_height="match_parent">
    <TextView
```

```
        android:layout_width="match_parent"
        android:layout_height="wrap_content"
        android:text="Select the Play button"
        android:id="@+id/response"
        android:gravity="center" />
    <ToggleButton android:id="@+id/playstop_btn"
        android:layout_width="wrap_content"
        android:layout_height="wrap_content"
        android:layout_gravity="center"
        android:textOn=""
        android:textOff=""
        android:background="@drawable/play"/>
</LinearLayout>
```

After the application is run, we find the `play.png` image appears in the `ToggleButton` (see Figure 4.12—left). After we select the Play button, the `stop.png` image appears to represent the `ToggleButton`'s `Off` state. Figure 4.12 (middle and right) shows how the text displays when the `TextView` changes after clicking the `ToggleButton`.

FIGURE 4.12   (left) The `ToggleButton` with a background image (no text) and the `TextView` on application startup, (middle) the background image of the `ToggleButton` and `TextView` changes on selecting the `ToggleButton`, and (right) the original background image reappears on the `ToggleButton` on clicking the `ToggleButton` again.

Creating an Image Switcher Application

We just learned how the `ToggleButton` works, so let's use it to modify our earlier application, `DispImageApp`, into an Image Switcher application. On startup, this application initially displays an image through an `ImageView` control with a `ToggleButton` at the bottom of the screen. When the `ToggleButton` is clicked, the image displayed in the `ImageView` control changes. After we click the `ToggleButton` again, the previous image is redisplayed in the `ImageView` control.

Because we want the application to switch images, we need to add one more image to the application. Recall that we have already added an image, `bintupic.png`, in the `res/drawable` folders of our application. Let's add one more image called `bintupic2.png` by dragging it to the `res/drawable` folders (`res/drawable-xhdpi`, `res/drawable-hdpi`, `res/drawable-mdpi`, and `res/drawable-ldpi`). Again, as expected, after we add image(s) to the `res/drawable` folder(s), the Java class `R.java` is regenerated, allowing us to refer to the newly added image in the layout file, as well as in Java code. After we add the two images, the application `Package Explorer` appears as shown in Figure 4.13.

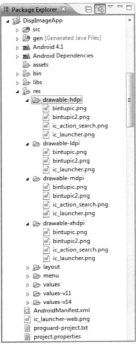

FIGURE 4.13   The `Package Explorer` window, showing the images dropped in the `res/drawable` folders

We want the application to show an image on startup (`bintupic.png`) through the `ImageView` control, along with a `ToggleButton` at the bottom of the display. We need to modify our layout file, `main.xml`, to do the following two things:

▶ Assign the `bintupic.png` image to an `ImageView` control to be displayed on startup.

▶ Add a `ToggleButton` to initiate image switching.

After we implement these tasks, our `activity_disp_image_app.xml` file appears as shown in Listing 4.28.

LISTING 4.28   Code in the Layout File `activity_disp_image_app.xml` on Adding a `ToggleButton` and Assigning an Image to the `ImageView` Control

```
<LinearLayout xmlns:android="http://schemas.android.com/apk/res/android"
    xmlns:tools="http://schemas.android.com/tools"
    android:orientation="vertical"
    android:layout_width="match_parent"
    android:layout_height="wrap_content">
    <ImageView
```

```
            android:id="@+id/image_toview"
            android:src="@drawable/bintupic"
            android:layout_width="wrap_content"
            android:layout_height="wrap_content"
            android:adjustViewBounds="true" />
    <ToggleButton android:id="@+id/change_image"
            android:layout_width="wrap_content"
            android:layout_height="wrap_content"
            android:textOn="Previous Image"
            android:textOff="Next Image"
            android:layout_gravity="center"
            android:layout_marginTop="10dip" />
</LinearLayout>
```

We can see that the image_toview ImageView control is set to display bintupic.png.
Below the ImageView control, a change_image ToggleButton is displayed at the center. The
ToggleButton is set to appear at a distance of 10dip from the ImageView control. The text
of the ToggleButton for its On and Off states is set to Previous Image and Next Image,
respectively. Now that we have all the Views set, it's time to add some actions to them.
To enable the ToggleButton to switch images, we need to write some Java code in the
DispImageAppActivity.java file as shown in Listing 4.29.

LISTING 4.29   Code Written in the Java Activity File DispImageAppActivity.java

```
package com.androidunleashed.dispimageapp;

import android.app.Activity;
import android.os.Bundle;
import android.widget.ImageView;
import android.widget.ToggleButton;
import android.view.View;
import android.view.View.OnClickListener;

public class DispImageAppActivity extends Activity {
    @Override
    public void onCreate(Bundle savedInstanceState) {
        super.onCreate(savedInstanceState);
        setContentView(R.layout.activity_disp_image_app);
        final ImageView image = (ImageView) findViewById(R.id.image_toview);
        final ToggleButton changeButton=(ToggleButton)findViewById(R.id.change_image);
        changeButton.setOnClickListener(new OnClickListener(){
            public void onClick(View v){
                if (changeButton.isChecked()) {
                    image.setImageResource(R.drawable.bintupic2);
                }
                else {
```

```
                    image.setImageResource(R.drawable.bintupic);
                }
            }
        });
    }
}
```

The `image_toview` `ImageView` control is accessed from the layout file and is mapped to the `ImageView` object `image`. Similarly, the `ToggleButton` control is accessed from the layout file and is mapped to the `ToggleButton` object `changeButton`. An event handler, `OnClickListener`, is added to the `ToggleButton`. Its callback method, `onClick()`, is implemented, which is executed when the `ToggleButton` is clicked. In the `onClick()` method, we check the state of the `ToggleButton` and accordingly change the image being displayed through the `ImageView` object. The state of the `ToggleButton` changes between `checked` and `unchecked` on every click. After the application is run, we find that the first image, `bintupic.png`, is displayed through the `ImageView` control along with the `ToggleButton`, and the text `Next Image` is displayed at the bottom (see Figure 4.14—left). When the `ToggleButton` is clicked, the image displayed through the `ImageView` control switches to `bintupic2.png`, and the button text of the `ToggleButton` changes to `Previous Image`, as shown in Figure 4.14 (right).

FIGURE 4.14   (left) An image displayed through the `ImageView` control with a `ToggleButton` below it, and (right) the image in the `ImageView` switches when the `ToggleButton` is selected.

When the `Previous Image` button is clicked, the earlier image is redisplayed in the `ImageView` control. What if the images being viewed are too long to accommodate in a single screen? The solution is to apply the `ScrollView` control to scroll the images. Let's learn more.

Scrolling Through `ScrollView`

A `ScrollView` is a special type of control that sets up a vertical scrollbar in a `View` container. This control is used when we try to display `Views` that are too long to be accommodated in a single screen. The `ScrollView` can have only one child view, so usually a `View` container layout is used as a child, which in turn contains other child controls that we want to scroll through. All the child controls in the layout have one continuous scrollbar.

Let's create a new Android project called `ScrollViewApp`. In this application, we place three images, one below the other. It is obvious that all the three images cannot fit into a single screen, so we use the `ScrollView` control to scroll them vertically. First copy the three images, `bm1.png`, `bm2.png`, and `bm3.png`, that we want to display in the `res/drawable` folders. To display the three images on low, medium, high, and extra high resolution devices, copy their low, medium, high, and extra high resolution versions into the `res/drawable-ldpi`, `res/drawable-mdpi`, `res/drawable-hdpi`, and `res/drawable-xhdpi` folders, respectively.

> **NOTE**
>
> To display images on devices of different sizes and resolutions and to ensure that your app looks great on any device, the `96x96px`, `72x72px`, `48x48px`, and `36x36px` images with resolutions of `320dpi`, `240dpi`, `160dpi`, and `120dpi`, respectively, are copied into the `res/drawable-xhdpi`, `res/drawable-hdpi/`, `res/drawable-mdpi`, and `res/drawable-ldpi` folders, respectively.

To display images in the application, we use the `ImageView` control and set the `android:src` attribute of each of them to refer to the files `bm1.png`, `bm2.png`, and `bm3.png` that we copied into the `res/drawable` folder. The layout file `activity_scroll_view_app.xml` with the three `ImageView` controls appears as shown in Listing 4.30.

LISTING 4.30   Code in the Layout File `activity_scroll_view_app.xml` on Defining Three `ImageView` Controls

```
<LinearLayout xmlns:android="http://schemas.android.com/apk/res/android"
    xmlns:tools="http://schemas.android.com/tools"
    android:layout_width="match_parent"
    android:layout_height="match_parent"
    android:orientation="vertical" >
    <ImageView
        android:id="@+id/image_toview"
        android:src="@drawable/bm1"
        android:layout_width="200dip"
        android:layout_height="250dip"
```

```
        android:layout_gravity="center" />
    <ImageView
        android:id="@+id/image_toview2"
        android:src="@drawable/bm2"
        android:layout_width="200dip"
        android:layout_height="250dip"
        android:layout_gravity="center"
        android:layout_marginTop="10dip" />
    <ImageView
        android:id="@+id/image_toview3"
        android:src="@drawable/bm3"
        android:layout_width="200dip"
        android:layout_height="250dip"
        android:layout_gravity="center"
        android:layout_marginTop="10dip" />
</LinearLayout>
```

We didn't use the `ScrollView` control in this code block, so you could see how images appear without it. We will, however, add it later. We don't have to write any code into the activity file `ScrollViewAppActivity.java`. The default code is shown in Listing 4.31.

LISTING 4.31   Default Code in the Java Activity File `ScrollViewAppActivity.java`

```
package com.androidunleashed.scrollviewapp;

import android.app.Activity;
import android.os.Bundle;

public class ScrollViewAppActivity extends Activity {
    @Override
    public void onCreate(Bundle savedInstanceState) {
        super.onCreate(savedInstanceState);
        setContentView(R.layout.activity_scroll_view_app);
    }
}
```

After the application is run, we see the output shown in Figure 4.15 (left). The first two images are visible, and the third one is hidden. The application does not scroll, so there is no way to see the hidden image. To add scrolling to the application, we add the `ScrollView` control to the layout file and make it the parent of the existing `LinearLayout` container. The `ScrollView` is set to wrap the `LinearLayout`, which contains the three `ImageView` controls on which we want to apply the scrolling effect. After we add the `ScrollView` control, the layout file `activity_scroll_view_app.xml` appears as shown in Listing 4.32.

LISTING 4.32   The Layout File `activity_scroll_view_app.xml` on Adding the `ScrollView` Control

```
<ScrollView xmlns:android="http://schemas.android.com/apk/res/android"
    android:id="@+id/scrollwid"
    android:layout_width="match_parent"
    android:layout_height="match_parent"
    android:fillViewport="true"
    android:orientation="vertical" >
    <LinearLayout xmlns:android="http://schemas.android.com/apk/res/android"
        xmlns:tools="http://schemas.android.com/tools"
        android:layout_width="match_parent"
        android:layout_height="match_parent"
        android:orientation="vertical" >
        <ImageView
            android:id="@+id/image_toview"
            android:src="@drawable/bm1"
            android:layout_width="200dip"
            android:layout_height="250dip"
            android:layout_gravity="center" />
        <ImageView
            android:id="@+id/image_toview2"
            android:src="@drawable/bm2"
            android:layout_width="200dip"
            android:layout_height="250dip"
            android:layout_gravity="center"
            android:layout_marginTop="10dip"    />
        <ImageView
            android:id="@+id/image_toview3"
            android:src="@drawable/bm3"
            android:layout_width="200dip"
            android:layout_height="250dip"
            android:layout_gravity="center"
            android:layout_marginTop="10dip"    />
    </LinearLayout>
</ScrollView>
```

In the preceding code block, the attribute `android:fillViewport` used in the `ScrollView` control needs an explanation.

Use of the `android:fillViewport` Attribute

When the size of the child control(s) is larger than the display, the `ScrollView` behaves naturally by applying a scrolling effect to the child controls. However, if the size of the child control(s) is smaller than the display, the `ScrollView` automatically shrinks to match the size of its content and take as much space as the size of its content. When set to `true`, the `android:fillViewPort` attribute makes the child control(s) of the `ScrollView` expand to the size of the display. If the size of child control(s) is already larger than the display, the attribute has no effect. We can see that in the `main.xml` file, the `LinearLayout` container holding the three `ImageView` controls is made child of a `ScrollView` control. The vertical scroller therefore appears on the right side of the images, as shown in Figure 4.15 (right).

FIGURE 4.15   (left) Two fixed images are displayed, and (right) scrolling images are displayed.

The `ScrollView` control is used for vertical scrolling. For horizontal scrolling, `HorizontalScrollView` is used. The `HorizontalScrollView` acts the same as the `ScrollView` except that it scrolls child controls horizontally.

> **NOTE**
>
> You shouldn't put a `ListView` inside a `ScrollView` because the `ListView` class implements its own scrolling and is optimized for dealing with large lists. The gestures on `ListView` will not be received by `ListView`, but by the parent `ScrollView`.

We just learned how to display images in Android applications. Next we see how to play audio files.

Playing Audio

In this section, we learn to play audio in Android applications. We also learn the methods used to pause and resume the audio. Let's make a new Android project called `PlayAudioApp`. The audio that we want to play needs to be added to this application.

Adding Audio to the Application

The audio file that we want to play must be located in the `res/raw` folder of our application. The `raw` folder isn't created automatically, so we need to create it manually. The `raw` folder is a special folder that is not processed at all; hence the content of the files copied in this folder is retained. Right-click the `res` folder in the `Package Explorer` window and select `New`, `Folder`. In the dialog box that opens, enter the name of the new folder as `raw` and click the `Finish` button.

In the `raw` folder, let's copy an audio file called `song1.mp3`. The Java class `R.java` file is automatically regenerated after the audio file is added to the application allowing us to access it. The `res` folder looks like Figure 4.16.

FIGURE 4.16   The newly added `raw` folder showing the audio, `song1.mp3`, which was added to it

In this application, we want to display a `TextView` and a `Button` control. `TextView` displays instruction(s), and the `Button` control initiates an action. To add the two controls, write the code in the layout file `activity_play_audio_app.xml` as shown in Listing 4.33.

LISTING 4.33   The Layout File `activity_play_audio_app.xml` on Adding the `TextView` and `Button` Controls

```
<LinearLayout xmlns:android="http://schemas.android.com/apk/res/android"
    xmlns:tools="http://schemas.android.com/tools"
    android:orientation="vertical"
    android:layout_width="match_parent"
    android:layout_height="match_parent">
```

```
<TextView
    android:layout_width="match_parent"
    android:layout_height="wrap_content"
    android:text="Playing Audio" />
<Button android:id="@+id/playbtn"
    android:layout_width="match_parent"
    android:layout_height="wrap_content"
    android:text="Play" />
</LinearLayout>
```

The `TextView` is set to display the text `Playing Audio`. The ID and the caption assigned to the `Button` control are `playbtn` and `Play`, respectively. To play the audio when the button is clicked, write the code as shown in Listing 4.34 into the activity file `PlayAudioAppActivity.java`.

LISTING 4.34   Code Written in the Java Activity File `PlayAudioAppActivity.java`

```java
package com.androidunleashed.playaudioapp;

import android.app.Activity;
import android.os.Bundle;
import android.widget.Button;
import android.view.View;
import android.media.MediaPlayer;

public class PlayAudioAppActivity extends Activity {
    @Override
    public void onCreate(Bundle savedInstanceState) {
        super.onCreate(savedInstanceState);
        setContentView(R.layout.activity_play_audio_app);
        Button playButton = (Button) findViewById(R.id.playbtn);
        playButton.setOnClickListener(new Button.OnClickListener() {
            public void onClick(View v) {
                MediaPlayer mp =
                    MediaPlayer.create(PlayAudioAppActivity.this,R.raw.song1);
                mp.start();
            }
        });
    }
}
```

The `playbtn` `Button` control is captured from the layout and mapped to the `Button` object `playButton`. An event handler, `OnClickListener`, is added to the `playButton` object. Its callback method, `onClick()`, is implemented, which is executed when the `playButton` is clicked. In the `onClick()` method, we create an instance, `mp`, of the `MediaPlayer` by calling the `MediaPlayer.create()` method. To the `MediaPlayer` instance `mp`, we pass the reference of our MP3 song, `song1.mp3`, that we placed in the `raw` folder. Finally, we call the MediaPlayer's `start()` method to play the song. After the application is run, we get a `TextView` showing the text `Playing Audio` and a `Button` control with the text `Play`, as shown in Figure 4.17. When the `Play` button is clicked, the audio, `song1.mp3`, is played.

FIGURE 4.17   The `TextView` and a `Play Button` control on application startup

We can control the volume of the audio with the volume switches on the side of the Android emulator. And we can also display an image on the `Button` control by adding the following attributes to the `<Button>` element:

▶ `android:drawableTop`—The image is displayed above the button text.

Example:

```
android:drawableTop="@drawable/ic_launcher"
```

This statement displays the `ic_launcher.png` image above the button text, as shown in Figure 4.18 (upper-left).

▶ `android:drawableBottom`—The image is displayed below the button text as seen in Figure 4.18 (upper-right).

▶ `android:drawableLeft`—The image is displayed to the left of the button text as shown in Figure 4.18 (bottom-left).

▶ `android:drawableRight`—The image is displayed to the right of the button text as shown in Figure 4.18 (bottom-right).

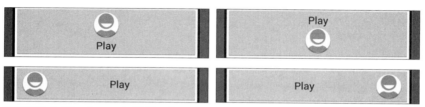

FIGURE 4.18   (upper-left) The image drawn above the button text, (upper-right) the image drawn below the button text, (bottom-left) the image drawn to the left of the button text, and (bottom-right) the image drawn to the right of the button text

PlayAudioApp works fine, but it doesn't have a `Stop` or `Pause` button to stop and resume playing the audio. To switch the status of the audio from play to stop and vice versa, we replace the `Button` control with the `ToggleButton` control. The layout file `activity_play_audio_app.xml` now appears as shown in Listing 4.35.

LISTING 4.35   The Layout File `activity_play_audio_app.xml` on Replacing `Button` with the `ToggleButton` Control

```
<LinearLayout xmlns:android="http://schemas.android.com/apk/res/android"
    xmlns:tools="http://schemas.android.com/tools"
    android:orientation="vertical"
    android:layout_width="match_parent"
    android:layout_height="match_parent">
    <TextView
        android:layout_width="match_parent"
        android:layout_height="wrap_content"
        android:gravity="center"
        android:id="@+id/response"/>
    <ToggleButton android:id="@+id/playstop_btn"
        android:layout_width="wrap_content"
        android:layout_height="wrap_content"
        android:textOn="Stop"
        android:textOff="Play"
        android:layout_gravity="center" />
</LinearLayout>
```

We can see that a `playstop_btn` `ToggleButton` is defined and assigned the text `Stop` and `Play` for its `On` and `Off` states. The `ToggleButton` is set to appear at the center of the LinearLayout container through the `android:layout_gravity="center"` attribute. Similarly, the text in the `TextView` control is aligned at the center through the `android:gravity="center"` attribute. Also, an ID `response` is assigned to the `TextView` so that we can access it and can change its text dynamically at runtime. To stop and resume the audio with a click of the `ToggleButton`, we write the Java code as shown in Listing 4.36 in the `PlayAudioAppActivity.java` file.

LISTING 4.36   Code Written in the Java Activity File `PlayAudioAppActivity.java`

```
package com.androidunleashed.playaudioapp;

import android.app.Activity;
import android.os.Bundle;
import android.widget.ToggleButton;
import android.view.View;
import android.widget.TextView;
import android.media.MediaPlayer;
import android.view.View.OnClickListener;
```

```
public class PlayAudioAppActivity extends Activity {
    @Override
    public void onCreate(Bundle savedInstanceState) {
        super.onCreate(savedInstanceState);
        setContentView(R.layout.activity_play_audio_app);
        final TextView response = (TextView)this.findViewById(R.id.response);
        response.setText("Select Play button to play audio");
        final MediaPlayer mp = MediaPlayer.create(PlayAudioAppActivity.this,R.raw.song1);
        final ToggleButton playStopButton = (ToggleButton)
            findViewById(R.id.playstop_btn);
        playStopButton.setOnClickListener(new OnClickListener() {
            public void onClick(View v) {
                if (playStopButton.isChecked()) {
                    response.setText("Select Stop button to stop audio");
                    mp.start();
                }
                else {
                    response.setText("Select Play button to play audio");
                    mp.pause();
                }
            }
        });
    }
}
```

The TextView and ToggleButton controls with the IDs response and playstop_button are accessed from the layout file and mapped to the TextView and ToggleButton objects response and playStopButton, respectively. The TextView is set to display the text Select Play button to play audio. An instance, mp, of the MediaPlayer is created by calling MediaPlayer's create() method. To the create() method, the reference of the MP3 song, song1.mp3, which we stored in the raw folder, is passed. An event handler, OnClickListener, is added to the ToggleButton object. Whenever, the ToggleButton is clicked, its callback method, onClick(), is executed. In the onClick() method, we check the status of the ToggleButton. If the ToggleButton is in the On state, we call the MediaPlayer's start() method to play the audio and set the text of the TextView to Select Stop button to stop audio to inform the user that if the ToggleButton is clicked, the audio is stopped. If the ToggleButton is in the Off state, the MediaPlayer's pause() method is called to stop the audio. The text of the TextView is set to Select Play button to play audio to inform the user that if the ToggleButton is clicked again, the audio resumes. After the application is run, we get a TextView and a ToggleButton shown in Figure 4.19 (left). The text on the ToggleButton, Play, and the text shown through the TextView, Select Play button to play audio, directs the user to click the ToggleButton if she wants to play the audio. After we select the ToggleButton, the audio begins playing, the text on the `ToggleButton` changes to `Stop`, and the text displayed through the `TextView` is changed to `Select Stop button to stop audio`, as shown in Figure 4.19 (right). If we select the `ToggleButton` again, the audio stops and the text on the `ToggleButton` and that of `TextView` changes to that shown in Figure 4.19 (left).

FIGURE 4.19   (left) The `TextView` and a `Play` Toggle Button control—audio plays on selecting the `ToggleButton`, and (right) the text on the `ToggleButton` and `TextView` changes on selecting the `ToggleButton`.

The preceding application is almost perfect, but let's change it so that it displays `Play` and `Stop` images in the `ToggleButton` instead of plain text. It's easy to do.

We need to add two images, `play.png` and `stop.png`, to the four `res/drawable` folders of this project. After we add the two images, the Java class, `R.java`, is regenerated containing the reference to the two images, so we can access them through code.

Because we want only the play and stop images to appear in the `ToggleButton` without text, we need to reset the `android:textOn` and `android:textOff` attributes of the `<ToggleButton>` tag in the layout file `main.xml`, as shown here:

```
android:textOn=""
android:textOff=""
```

These statements remove any text in the `ToggleButton` that is displayed in its `On` and `Off` states. Also, we need to use the `android:background` attribute to display the `play.png` image in the `ToggleButton` on startup. To do this, we need to add the following statement in the `<ToggleButton>` tag:

```
android:background="@drawable/play"
```

After we apply these modifications, the layout file `activity_play_audio_app.xml` appears as shown in Listing 4.37. Only the code in bold is modified; the rest is the same as we saw in Listing 4.35.

LISTING 4.37   Code in the Layout File `activity_play_audio_app.xml` on Adding the Background Image to the `ToggleButton`

```
<LinearLayout xmlns:android="http://schemas.android.com/apk/res/android"
    xmlns:tools="http://schemas.android.com/tools"
    android:orientation="vertical"
```

```
        android:layout_width="match_parent"
        android:layout_height="match_parent">
    <TextView
        android:layout_width="match_parent"
        android:layout_height="wrap_content"
        android:gravity="center"
        android:id="@+id/response"/>
    <ToggleButton android:id="@+id/playstop_btn"
        android:layout_width="wrap_content"
        android:layout_height="wrap_content"
        android:textOn=""
        android:textOff=""
        android:layout_gravity="center"
        android:background="@drawable/play" />
</LinearLayout>
```

To change the background image of the `ToggleButton` from `play.png` to `stop.png` when clicked, we need to add two statements to the Java activity file `PlayAudioAppActivity.java`, as shown in Listing 4.38. Only the statements shown in bold are the newly added code; the rest of the code is the same as we saw in Listing 4.36.

LISTING 4.38   Code in the Java Activity File `PlayAudioAppActivity.java`

```java
package com.androidunleashed.PlayAudioApp;

import android.app.Activity;
import android.os.Bundle;
import android.widget.ToggleButton;
import android.view.View;
import android.widget.TextView;
import android.media.MediaPlayer;
import android.view.View.OnClickListener;

public class PlayAudioAppActivity extends Activity {
    @Override
    public void onCreate(Bundle savedInstanceState) {
        super.onCreate(savedInstanceState);
        setContentView(R.layout.activity_play_audio_app);
        final TextView response = (TextView)this.findViewById(R.id.response);
        response.setText("Select Play button to play audio");
        final MediaPlayer mp = MediaPlayer.create(PlayAudioAppActivity.this,R.raw.song1);
        final ToggleButton playStopButton = (ToggleButton)
            findViewById(R.id.playstop_btn);
        playStopButton.setOnClickListener(new OnClickListener() {
            public void onClick(View v) {
```

```
        if (playStopButton.isChecked()) {
            response.setText("Select Stop button to stop audio");
            playStopButton.setBackgroundDrawable(getResources().getDrawable(R.
            drawable.stop));
            mp.start();
        }
        else {
            response.setText("Select Play button to play audio");
            playStopButton.setBackgroundDrawable(getResources().getDrawable(R.
            drawable.play));
            mp.pause();
        }
    }
});
    }
}
```

We can see that the newly added code allows access to the `stop.png` and `play.png` images from the drawable resources by supplying the image filenames to the `getDrawable()` method of the `Resources` object. Depending on the current state of the `ToggleButton` (`On` or `Off`), the accessed images are assigned to appear as its background. After the application is run, we see the `TextView` and a `ToggleButton` showing the `play.png` image (Figure 4.20—left). The text in the `TextView` control tells the user that when the `Play` button is clicked, an audio file is played. The audio begins playing, and the `ToggleButton`'s background changes from `play.png` to `stop.png`. The text in `TextView` also changes to tell the user that the `Stop` button can be pressed to stop the audio, as shown in Figure 4.20 (right).

FIGURE 4.20   (left) The `TextView` and a Toggle Button control representing an audio play button—audio plays when selecting the `ToggleButton`, and (right) the `ToggleButton`'s image changes to a Stop button when selected, informing the user that audio stops if selected again.

NOTE

If we want to play a song available on the Internet, we can use its URI.

Let's now see how video can be run in an Android application.

Playing Video

To play video in an application, Android provides a `VideoView` control, which, along with the MediaController, provides several buttons for controlling video play. These buttons allow us to play, pause, rewind, and fast-forward the video content displayed via the `VideoView` control. To understand the steps for playing a video, let's create a new Android project called `PlayVideoApp`. We can play a video that is available on the Internet or one that is loaded onto an SD card of our device or emulator.

> **NOTE**
>
> Unlike audio, the video doesn't play when placed in the `raw` folder. Instead it needs to be placed in the `SDCARD` folder.

Loading Video onto an SD Card

An emulator must be running while loading video onto an SD Card. Switch on the emulator by selecting the `Window, AVD Manager` option. Select the `demoAVD` virtual device—the one we created in Chapter 1, "Introduction to Android"—and select the `Start` button. We get a dialog box showing the Launch Options of the emulator. Select the `Launch` button to run the emulator. Remember, only the emulator with an `sdcard` option should be run. After you select the `Launch` button, the emulator starts. Close the `AVD Manager` dialog. To load a video onto an SD card, follow these steps:

1. Open the `DDMS perspective` by selecting the `Window, Open Perspective, DDMS` option.

2. In the `DDMS perspective`, open the `File Explorer` by selecting `Window, Show View, File Explorer`.

3. If you can't see the running emulator anywhere, open the `Devices` view by selecting `Window, Show View, Devices` option. We are able to see all the running emulators, and we can select the one that we want to use for playing the video.

4. In the `File Explorer` view, we see different folders and files in the emulator (see Figure 4.21).

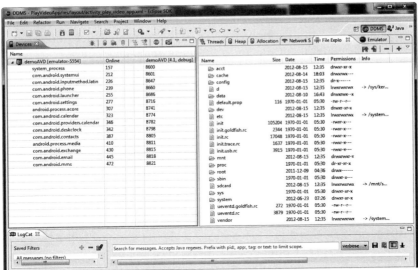

FIGURE 4.21   The DDMS showing different folders in the emulator through the File Explorer

Navigate the tree and expand the `mnt` node. In the `mnt` node, select the `sdcard` node. If you hover your mouse over the two buttons on the top right side of `File Explorer`, you see the messages `Pull a file from the device` and `Push a file onto the device`. Figure 4.22 (left) shows these marked with ellipses.

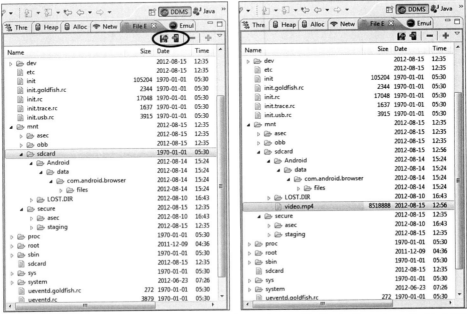

FIGURE 4.22   (left) The folders in the emulator along with the buttons to pull video from and push it to the `sdcard`, and (right) the File Explorer displaying the video, `video.mp4`, inserted onto the `sdcard` of the emulator

Click the button `Push a file onto the device`. We see a dialog box for choosing a video from the disk drive. After selecting a video, select the `OK` button to load the selected video onto the SD Card. Figure 4.22 (right) shows the `File Explorer` after `video.pm4` has been loaded onto the SD card.

Now we can go ahead and add a `VideoView` control to our layout file to view the loaded video. After we define the `VideoView` and `Button` controls in `activity_play_video_app.xml`, it appear as shown in Listing 4.39.

LISTING 4.39   Code in the Layout File `activity_play_video_app.xml` on Adding `VideoView` and `Button` Controls

```
<LinearLayout xmlns:android="http://schemas.android.com/apk/res/android"
    xmlns:tools="http://schemas.android.com/tools"
    android:orientation="vertical"
    android:layout_width="match_parent"
    android:layout_height="match_parent" >
    <VideoView android:id="@+id/video"
        android:layout_width="320dip"
        android:layout_height="240dip"/>
    <Button android:id="@+id/playvideo"
        android:text="Play Video"
        android:layout_height="wrap_content"
        android:layout_width="match_parent" />
</LinearLayout>
```

We can see that a `VideoView` and a `Button` control have been added to the application, where the `VideoView` widget is used for displaying video, and the `Button` control plays the video when selected.

To assign the video to the `VideoView` control, which is used to perform a variety of functions, write the code as shown in Listing 4.40 in the Java activity file `PlayVideoAppActivity.java`.

LISTING 4.40   Code in the Java Activity File `PlayAudioAppActivity.java`

```
package com.androidunleashed.playvideoapp;

import android.app.Activity;
import android.os.Bundle;
import android.widget.Button;
import android.view.View.OnClickListener;
import android.view.View;
import android.widget.MediaController;
import android.widget.VideoView;

public class PlayVideoAppActivity extends Activity {
```

```
@Override
public void onCreate(Bundle savedInstanceState) {
    super.onCreate(savedInstanceState);
    setContentView(R.layout.activity_play_video_app);
    Button playVideoButton=(Button)findViewById(R.id.playvideo);
    playVideoButton.setOnClickListener(new OnClickListener() {
        public void onClick(View view){
            VideoView videoView=(VideoView)findViewById(R.id.video);
            videoView.setMediaController(new
                MediaController(PlayVideoAppActivity.this));
            videoView.setVideoPath("sdcard/video.mp4");
            videoView.requestFocus();
            videoView.start();
        }
    });
}
}
```

We capture the `VideoView` control from the layout and map it to the `videoView` object. Then we use a `MediaController` and set it the media controller of the `videoView` object.

The `videoView` object is used for displaying video content and the button controls that enable us to perform play, pause, rewind, or fast-forward actions on the video. A MediaController provides these buttons. Hence the `VideoView`'s media controller is set by calling `setMediaController()` to display the different button controls. Then, we use the `setVideoPath()` method of the `VideoView` object to refer to an SD card (`sdcard`) for the `video.mp4` file. We can also use `setVideoURI()` method to access the video from the Internet. After setting the focus to the `VideoView` control through `requestFocus()` method, we use its `start()` method to start the video.

Run the application. We get the output showing a button, `Play Video`, as shown in Figure 4.23 (left). After we select the `Play Video` button, the video is displayed in the `VideoView` control, along with the button controls displayed via the MediaController, as shown in Figure 4.23 (right). The buttons enable stop, resume, rewind, and fast-forward. The progress bar at the bottom shows our location in the video.

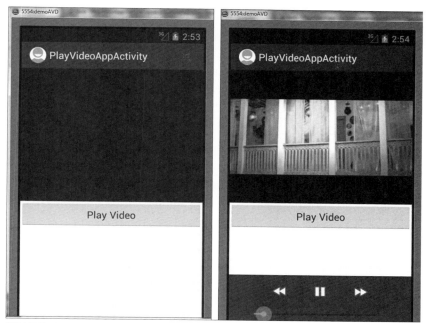

FIGURE 4.23   (left) The `button` control with the caption, `Play Video`, displayed on application startup, and (right) the video displayed in the `VideoView` control on selecting the `Play Video` button. Video control buttons appear at the bottom via the MediaController.

Displaying Progress with `ProgressBar`

Certain tasks, such as downloading a file, installing software, executing complex queries, and playing audio and video, take time to execute. While executing such tasks, we need to continually inform the user about the task progress by displaying a progress indicator. The `ProgressBar` is a control commonly used for displaying the progress of execution of tasks. The default mode of the `ProgressBar` view is a circular indicator that animates to show that a task is active but doesn't show actual progress. This icon is used when there is no specific duration for completion of the task. A more informative solution is a horizontal progress bar that displays an indicator showing the amount of a task that is completed (or is left to complete). To make the `ProgressBar` display in the form of a horizontal bar, set its style attribute to `@android:style/Widget.ProgressBar.Horizontal`, as shown in this example:

```
<ProgressBar android:id="@+id/progressbar"
android:layout_width="match_parent"
android:layout_height="wrap_content"
style="@android:style/Widget.ProgressBar.Horizontal" />
```

The following styles can be applied to the `ProgressBar`:

▶ `Widget.ProgressBar.Horizontal`

▶ `Widget.ProgressBar.Small`

▶ `Widget.ProgressBar.Large`

▶ `Widget.ProgressBar.Inverse`

▶ `Widget.ProgressBar.Small.Inverse`

▶ `Widget.ProgressBar.Large.Inverse`

The `ProgressBar` for `Widget.ProgressBar.Horizontal`, `Widget.ProgressBar.Small`, and `Widget.ProgressBar` appears as shown in Figure 4.24 (left, middle, and right, respectively).

FIGURE 4.24   (left) Horizontal style `ProgressBar`, (middle) small style `ProgressBar`, and (right) large style `ProgressBar`

The `inverse` style is used when our application uses a light-colored theme, such as a white background. The minimum value of the `ProgressBar` is by default 0. The maximum value of the `ProgressBar` is set by the `android:max attribute`. For example, the following statement, when applied to the `ProgressBar` control in the layout file, sets the maximum value of the `ProgressBar` to 100:

```
android:max="100"
```

We can also set the maximum value of the `ProgressBar` through a `setMax()` Java method. The following code sets the maximum value of the `ProgressBar` to 100:

```
progressBar.setMax(100);
```

To display progress through an indicator in the `ProgressBar` control, we call the `setProgress()` method of the `ProgressBar` class, passing in an integer value to indicate the progress. For example, the following statement sets the progress to 60, making the indicator appear at the 60 percent complete mark:

```
progressBar.setProgress(60);
```

where `progressBar` is an object that represents the `ProgressBar` control.

Let's create an Android project to understand the `ProgressBar`. Name the new Android project `ProgressBarApp`. In this application, we play an audio, and the `ProgressBar` displays the progress of the audio, showing how much has been played and how much is left. For this application, we use a `TextView`, a `ToggleButton`, and a `ProgressBar` control. The `TextView` control is used to have the user select the `ToggleButton` to play or stop the audio. The `ToggleButton` plays and stops the audio, and a horizontal bar `ProgressBar` displays the audio's progress. After we add the `ToggleButton` and `ProgressBar` controls, the layout file `activity_progress_bar_app.xml` appears as shown in Listing 4.41.

LISTING 4.41   Code Written in Layout File `activity_progress_bar_app.xml` on Adding the `ToggleButton` and `ProgressBar` Controls

```
<LinearLayout xmlns:android="http://schemas.android.com/apk/res/android"
    xmlns:tools="http://schemas.android.com/tools"
    android:layout_width="match_parent"
    android:layout_height="match_parent"
    android:orientation="vertical" >
    <TextView
        android:layout_width="match_parent"
        android:layout_height="wrap_content"
        android:gravity="center"
        android:id="@+id/response"/>
    <ToggleButton android:id="@+id/playstop_btn"
        android:layout_width="wrap_content"
        android:layout_height="wrap_content"
        android:textOn=""
        android:textOff=""
        android:layout_gravity="center"
        android:background="@drawable/play"   />
    <ProgressBar android:id="@+id/progressbar"
        android:layout_width="match_parent"
        android:layout_height="wrap_content"
        style="@android:style/Widget.ProgressBar.Horizontal"
        android:layout_marginTop="20dip" />
</LinearLayout>
```

To display Play and Stop images in the `ToggleButton` (see Figure 4.25), we copy the images `play.png` and `stop.png` to the `res/drawable` folders. For playing audio, create a folder called `raw` in the `res` folder and then copy the audio file `song1.mp3` into it.

To play and stop the audio with the `ToggleButton` control and to display the progress of the audio in the `ProgressBar` control, write the code as shown in Listing 4.42 in the activity file `ProgressBarAppActivity.java`.

LISTING 4.42   Code Written in the Activity File `ProgressBarAppActivity.java`

```
package com.androidunleashed.progressbarapp;

import android.app.Activity;
import android.os.Bundle;
import android.widget.ToggleButton;
import android.view.View;
```

```java
import android.widget.TextView;
import android.media.MediaPlayer;
import android.view.View.OnClickListener;
import android.widget.ProgressBar;
import android.os.Handler;

public class ProgressBarAppActivity extends Activity {
    MediaPlayer mp;
    ProgressBar progressBar;
    private final Handler handler = new Handler();

    @Override
    public void onCreate(Bundle savedInstanceState) {
        super.onCreate(savedInstanceState);
        setContentView(R.layout.activity_progress_bar_app);
        final TextView response = (TextView)this.findViewById(R.id.response);
        response.setText("Select Play button to play audio");
        progressBar=(ProgressBar)findViewById(R.id.progressbar);
        mp = MediaPlayer.create(ProgressBarAppActivity.this,R.raw.song1);
        final ToggleButton playStopButton = (ToggleButton)
        findViewById(R.id.playstop_btn);
        progressBar.setProgress(0);
        progressBar.setMax(mp.getDuration());

        playStopButton.setOnClickListener(new OnClickListener() {
            public void onClick(View v) {
                if (playStopButton.isChecked()) {
                    response.setText("Select Stop button to stop audio");
                    playStopButton.setBackgroundDrawable(
                        getResources().getDrawable(R.drawable.stop));
                    mp.start();
                    updateProgressBar();
                }
                else {
                    response.setText("Select Play button to play audio");
                    playStopButton.setBackgroundDrawable(
                        getResources().getDrawable(R.drawable.play));
                    mp.pause();
                }
            }
        });
    }

    private void updateProgressBar() {
        progressBar.setProgress(mp.getCurrentPosition());
        if (mp.isPlaying()) {
```

```
        Runnable notification = new Runnable() {
            public void run() {
                updateProgressBar();
            }
        };
        handler.postDelayed(notification,1000);
    }
}
}
```

In this code block, we can see that the `TextView`, `ProgressBar`, and `ToggleButton` controls with the IDs `response`, `progressbar`, and `playstop_btn` are accessed from the layout file `main.xml` and assigned to their respective button objects (`response`, `progressBar`, and `playStopButton`). The `TextView` is initially set to display `Select Play button to play audio` to tell the user what is supposed to be done. An instance (`mp` of the `MediaPlayer`) is created by calling the `MediaPlayer`'s `create()` method. The MP3 song reference, `song1.mp3`, which we stored in the `raw` folder, is passed to the `create()` method. The minimum value of the `ProgressBar` control is set to 0, and its maximum value is set equal to the duration of the audio.

An object handler of the `Handler` class is made, as we use it to send and process a `Runnable` object. `Handler` is the preferred threading technique used to perform tasks in the background. We talk about the threading technique in detail in Chapter 13, "Creating and Consuming Services." A `Handler` object processes `Message` and `Runnable` objects associated with the current thread's `MessageQueue`. A `MessageQueue` is a queue of messages (in `FIFO` order) where each message is a task that we want to be performed. When a message or runnable object is passed to the `Handler`, it is saved into the message queue. The UI thread pulls the message or runnable object from the queue and executes it. The `UI thread` is the main thread that is automatically created when an application is launched and is the one that handles events related to the widgets or controls used in the application.

An event handler, `OnClickListener`, is added to the `ToggleButton` object `playStopButton`. Whenever the `ToggleButton` is clicked, its callback method, `onClick()`, is executed.

In the `onClick()` method, we check the status of the `ToggleButton`. If the `ToggleButton` is set to the `On` state, we call the `MediaPlayer`'s `start()` method to play the audio and set the `TextView` to display the text `Select Stop button to stop audio` to tell the user that if the `ToggleButton` is pressed again, the audio will be stopped. The image `stop.png` from drawable resources is accessed and displayed as the background image of the `ToggleButton` `playStopButton`. The `updateprogressbar()` method is called to update the `ProgressBar` indicator.

In the `updateprogressbar()` method, we update the progress bar indicator to set it at the location decided by the `MediaPlayer` instance, `mp`. That is, the duration of audio played is displayed by updating the progress bar indicator periodically. For periodic execution of the `updateprogressbar()` method, we use threading.

A `Runnable` object `notification` is created and added to the message queue through the `postDelayed()` method of the `handler` object. The `runnable` object is scheduled to run after 1000 milliseconds. The `runnable` object is run on the thread to which this handler is attached—the main UI thread. The `run()` method, which is executed after every 1000 milliseconds, calls the `updateprogressbar()` method to update the progress bar indicator periodically.

If the `ToggleButton` is in the `Off` state, the `MediaPlayer`'s `pause()` method is called to `stop` the audio. The text of the `TextView` is set to display the message `Select Play button to play audio` to tell the user that, on clicking the `ToggleButton` again, the audio resumes playing. The image, `play.png`, from drawable resources is accessed and displayed as the background image of the `ToggleButton playStopButton`.

After the application is run, we get a `TextView`, a `ToggleButton`, and a `ProgressBar`, as shown in Figure 4.25 (left). The text message shown through `TextView`, `Select Play button to play audio`, directs the user to click the `ToggleButton` to play the audio. After the user selects the `ToggleButton`, the audio begins playing, and the image on the `ToggleButton` changes to display the `stop.png` file, and the text displayed through the `TextView` changes to `Select Stop button to stop audio`. The indicator in the `ProgressBar` shows the duration of the audio played, as shown in Figure 4.25 (right).

FIGURE 4.25   (left) `ProgressBar` on application startup, and (right) `ProgressBar` showing the duration of audio played

Using Assets

We have already seen how resources are used in Android applications. The external files containing information such as strings, images, and audio that reside in the `res/` folder are considered resources. Besides the `res/` directory, Android provides another directory, `assets/`, where we can keep asset files to be included in our application. The difference between resources and assets is that the resources are accessible in an Android application through the resource IDs generated in the `R.java` file. Android automatically generates an `R.java` file that contains the IDs of the resources found in `res/` folder, making it possible to access them through Java code. Content placed in the `assets/` directory is maintained in raw file format, and no IDs are generated for these files. To read the content from the `assets/` folder in an Android application, we use the `AssetManager`, which reads the content from the external files in the form of a stream of bytes.

In the application that we are going to create as an example, we add a text file asset. The content in the text file added to the `assets` folder is accessed using the `AssetManager` and is displayed in a `TextView`. Launch the Eclipse IDE and create a new Android project called `AssetsApp`. Add a file called `info.txt` (it should obviously contain some text) to the project by copying and pasting it into the `assets` folder in the `Package Explorer` window. Because we want the content of `info.txt` be displayed through a `TextView`, let's modify the layout file `activity_assets_app.xml` to appear as shown in Listing 4.43.

LISTING 4.43   Code in Layout File `activity_assets_app.xml` on Adding the `TextView` Control

```
<LinearLayout xmlns:android="http://schemas.android.com/apk/res/android"
   xmlns:tools="http://schemas.android.com/tools"
    android:layout_width="match_parent"
    android:layout_height="match_parent"
    android:orientation="vertical" >
    <TextView
        android:id="@+id/file_view"
        android:layout_width="match_parent"
        android:layout_height="wrap_content"
        android:textSize="15dip"
        android:textStyle="bold" />
</LinearLayout>
```

We can see that the layout file `activity_assets_app.xml` contains a `file_view` `TextView` control. The content to be displayed via `TextView` is set to appear in bold, 15dip text. To read the content from the file, `info.txt` is placed in the `assets` folder and is displayed via the `TextView` control. Code shown in Listing 4.44 is written in the Java activity file `AssetsAppActivity.java` for reading the content from the file placed in the `assets` folder and displaying it through the `TextView` control.

LISTING 4.44   Code in the Java Activity File `AssetsAppActivity.java`

```
package com.androidunleashed.assetsapp;

import android.app.Activity;
import android.os.Bundle;
import android.widget.TextView;
import java.io.InputStream;
import android.content.res.AssetManager;
import java.io.IOException;

public class AssetsAppActivity extends Activity {
    @Override
    public void onCreate(Bundle savedInstanceState) {
        super.onCreate(savedInstanceState);
        setContentView(R.layout.activity_assets_app);
```

```
TextView fileView=(TextView)findViewById(R.id.file_view);
InputStream input;
AssetManager assetManager = getAssets();
try {
    input = assetManager.open("info.txt");
    int fileSize = input.available();
    byte[] buffer = new byte[fileSize];
    input.read(buffer);
    input.close();
    String textForm = new String(buffer);
    fileView.setText(textForm);
} catch (IOException e) {
    fileView.setText("Some exception has occurred");

}
}
}
```

We can see in this code block that the TextView is accessed from the layout file and is mapped to the TextView object fileView. Because the assets are read using an AssetManager, we get a reference to the AssetManager instance by calling the getAssets() method. Basically, the getAssets() method opens the Assets folder and returns a handle to this folder. To read content from a file, we need an InputStream object, so the open() method of the AssetManager class is called, passing the filename info.txt to it as the parameter. The open() method opens the file info.txt in the assets folder and returns it in the form of the InputStream, which is assigned to the InputStream instance input. The size of the file is computed by calling an available() method on the InputStream class. A buffer equal to the file size is defined, and the file content is read via the InputStream object into the buffer. The InputStream object is closed. The file content in the form of bytes stored in the buffer is converted into a string and is assigned to the TextView control for display. After the application is run, we find the content of the file info.txt is displayed through TextView, as shown in Figure 4.26.

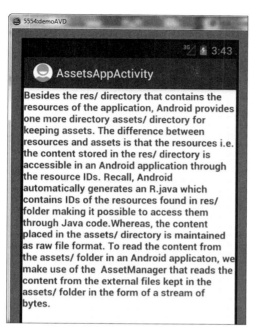

FIGURE 4.26   The content of the file in the `assets` folder displayed via `TextView`

Summary

In this chapter, you learned about different types of resources, such as `Dimension`, `Color`, `Styles`, and `Themes`, and also applied them in Android applications. You learned to create and use string and integer arrays. You learned to use `Drawable` resources and created an Image Switcher application using the `ToggleButton` control. You saw how to play audio and video in an Android application, as well as learned how to load video onto a device/emulator SD card. You learned how to use `ScrollView` to display views that don't fit in a single screen, how to create a `ProgressBar`, and how raw files in the `assets` folder are accessed.

The next chapter focuses on `Selection Widgets`. You learn to use the `ListView`, `Spinner`, `AutoComplete`, and `GridView` controls in Android applications. You learn how to use display options in selection widgets through string arrays and the Array Adapter. You also see how to extend `ListActivity` and use styling for the standard `ListAdapters`. You learn to create an Image Gallery using Gallery Control and the procedure to use the Debugging Tool, Dalvik Debug Monitor Service (DDMS). You also see the procedure involved in debugging applications, placing breakpoints in an application, and using Debug perspective. Finally, you learn to add logging support to Android applications.

CHAPTER 5

Using Selection Widgets and Debugging

As the name suggests, selection widgets refers to the group controls that display a list of choices from which users select items. To constrain users to enter the correct data type or within a specific range and also to show the valid values, lists and drop-down lists are commonly used in applications. Lists and drop-down lists are called `ListView` and `Spinner` controls in Android. Besides `ListView` and `Spinner`, we discuss two more selection widgets in this chapter: `AutoCompleteTextView` and `GridView`.

Let's begin our journey with the first selection widget, the `ListView`.

Using `ListView`

A `ListView` is used to display a list of vertically scrolling items, allowing users to select one or more of them. Several attributes can be used to configure this control. Some of them are listed in Table 5.1.

TABLE 5.1   List of Attributes Used to Configure the `ListView` Control

Attribute	Description
android:entries	Used to refer to an `array` `resource` for displaying options in the `ListView`
android:choiceMode	Used to define the number of items that are selectable from the `ListView`. Valid values are
	`none`—Doesn't allow selection of any option from the `ListView`
	`singleChoice`—Allows selection of a single option from the `ListView`
	`multipleChoice`—Allows selection of more than one option from the `ListView`
multipleChoiceModal	Used to allow selection of more than one item in a custom selection mode
android:drawSelectorOnTop	When set to `true`, the `selector` (an orange bar) is drawn over the selected item. Otherwise, the `selector` is drawn behind the selected item. The default value is `false`.
android:transcriptMode	Used to set the `transcript` mode for the list. The `transcript` mode helps in deciding whether we want the list to automatically scroll to the bottom. The valid values are
	`disabled`—Disables the `transcript` mode (default value). The `ListView` does not scroll automatically.
	`normal`—The `ListView` automatically scrolls to the bottom when a new item is added to the adapter and a notification is generated.
	`alwaysScroll`—The `ListView` always automatically scrolls to the bottom.

A sample `ListView` control may appear as follows:

```
<ListView
    android:id="@android:id/list"
    android:layout_width="match_parent"
    android:layout_height="match_parent"
    android:entries="@array/fruits"
    android:choiceMode="singleChoice"
    android:drawSelectorOnTop="false"
    android:transcriptMode="normal" />
```

This sample defines a `ListView` with the ID `list`, whose items are populated by the string array `fruits`. Only one item is selectable from the `ListView`. No selector appears on the top of the `ListView`, and it also scrolls to the bottom when a new item is added to the data source.

For creating `ListView` controls, we can use either of the following methods:

▶ The regular `Activity` base class

▶ An activity that extends `android.app.ListActivity`

NOTE

The `ListActivity` class already contains a `ListView`; hence while extending this class, we don't need to define the `ListView` control in the layout file.

Let's begin with creating a `ListView` through a regular `Activity` base class.

Creating a `ListView` **with an** `Activity` **Base Class**

In both cases, whether we are creating a `ListView` by extending the `Activity` class or the `ListActivity` class, the `ListView` can be populated by one of the following two methods:

▶ By `ListView` through a string resource

▶ By `ListView` through `Adapter`

Populating `ListView` **Through String Resource**

To understand how a `ListView` is populated through string resources, let's create a new Android project called `ListViewApp`. In this application, we use two controls: `ListView` and `TextView`. `ListView` is populated through string resources to display a list of items for the user to select from. The item or option selected from the `ListView` is displayed via the `TextView` control.

Open the string resource file `/res/values/strings.xml`, and add a `string-array` structure called `fruits` that lists various fruits that we want to display via the `ListView` control. After we add a `string-array`, the `strings.xml` file appears as shown in Listing 5.1.

LISTING 5.1   The `strings.xml` File After Adding the Strings Array

```
<resources>
    <string name="app_name">ListViewApp</string>
    <string name="menu_settings">Settings</string>
    <string name="title_activity_list_view_app">ListViewAppActivity</string>
    <string-array name="fruits">
        <item>Apple</item>
        <item>Mango</item>
        <item>Orange</item>
        <item>Grapes</item>
        <item>Banana</item>
    </string-array>
</resources>
```

The `string resource app_name` is the default `string resource` meant for displaying the application name in the title bar while running the application. The `string-array fruits` is the one that defines the array elements that we use to populate the `ListView` control.

After we define `fruits`, the next step is to define the two controls, `ListView` and `TextView`, in the layout file. Open the layout file `main.xml` and define `ListView` and `TextView`. The code written into `activity_list_view_app.xml` appears as shown in Listing 5.2.

LISTING 5.2   The Layout File `activity_list_view_app.xml` After Defining the `ListView` and `TextView` Controls

```
<LinearLayout xmlns:android="http://schemas.android.com/apk/res/android"
    xmlns:tools="http://schemas.android.com/tools"
    android:orientation="vertical"
    android:layout_width="match_parent"
    android:layout_height="wrap_content">
    <ListView android:id="@+id/fruits_list"
        android:layout_width="match_parent"
        android:layout_height="match_parent"
        android:entries="@array/fruits"
        android:drawSelectorOnTop="false"/>
    <TextView
        android:id="@+id/selectedopt"
        android:layout_width="match_parent"
        android:layout_height="wrap_content" />
</LinearLayout>
```

We can see that the `ListView` and `TextView` controls are assigned the resource IDs `fruits_list` and `selectedopt`, respectively. To populate the `ListView`, the `string-array fruits` is assigned to the `ListView` through the `android:entries` attribute. That is, the `android:entries` attribute in the layout XML file is used for populating `ListView` from the `string resource`. The `android:drawSelectorOnTop` attribute is set to `false`, because we don't want the selector to be drawn over the selected item.

To display the option selected from the `ListView` in the `TextView` control, we need to access the `string-array TextView` and attach an event listener to the `ListView` to sense for the occurrence of an event on it. To do this, we write the code shown in Listing 5.3 into the Java activity file `ListViewAppActivity.java`.

LISTING 5.3   Code Written into the Java Activity File `ListViewAppActivity.java`

```
package com.androidunleashed.listviewapp;

import android.app.Activity;
import android.os.Bundle;
```

```
import android.widget.TextView;
import android.widget.ListView;
import android.widget.AdapterView;
import android.widget.AdapterView.OnItemClickListener;
import android.view.View;

public class ListViewAppActivity extends Activity {
    @Override
    public void onCreate(Bundle savedInstanceState) {
        super.onCreate(savedInstanceState);
        setContentView(R.layout.activity_list_view_app);
        final String[] fruitsArray = getResources().getStringArray(R.array.fruits);
        final TextView selectedOpt=(TextView)findViewById(R.id.selectedopt);
        ListView fruitsList = (ListView)findViewById(R.id.fruits_list);
        fruitsList.setOnItemClickListener(new OnItemClickListener(){
            @Override
            public void onItemClick(AdapterView<?> parent, View v, int position,
long id)
            {
                selectedOpt.setText("You have selected "+fruitsArray[position]);
            }
        });
    }
}
```

The string-array fruits from the resource file strings.xml is accessed and assigned to the string array fruitsArray. Similarly, the TextView selectedopt and the ListView fruits_list are captured from the layout file and assigned to the objects selectedOpt and fruitsList, respectively. To take an action when an item is selected from the ListView, the setOnItemClickListener() method is passed a new AdapterView.OnItemClickListener. This anonymous instance implements the onItemClick() callback method, which is executed when an item is selected from the ListView. In the onItemClick() method, we find the index location (position) of the selected item, use it to access the array element from the string array fruitsArray, and display it through the TextView object selectedOpt.

When the application is run, we see the list of fruits defined in the string-array fruits is displayed in the ListView control as shown in Figure 5.1 (left). When an item is selected from the ListView, it is displayed through the TextView, as shown in Figure 5.1 (right).

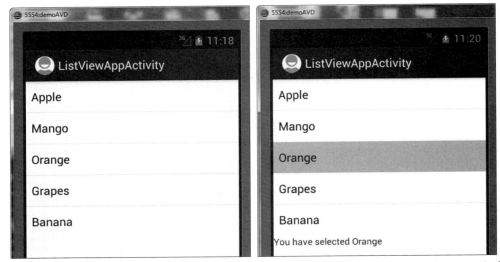

FIGURE 5.1   Options displayed via the string array (string resource) in the ListView control (left) and the selected option from ListView (right) displayed via the TextView control

As mentioned earlier, another way to display items through ListView is to use Adapters, which are the easiest and most flexible way of binding data to a control.

Adapters

Android provides a framework of adapters (also known as data adapters) that are used to provide a data source for displaying content in the form of choices in selection widgets; that is, they help create child elements for the selection widgets. The data source refers to the content, including elements in arrays and data in database tables. The Adapters serve two purposes. First, they provide the data source for a selection widget, and second, they convert individual elements of data into specific Views to be displayed inside the selection widget. The second purpose is important, as it casts the data to suit the selection widget environment, overriding its default behavior, and also enables us to format the data in the available formats. Android provides many basic Adapters such as ListAdapter, ArrayAdapter, and CursorAdapter. We can also create our own Adapter. In this chapter, we use the ArrayAdapter for populating selection widgets, as described in the next section.

Populating ListView Through the ArrayAdapter

The ArrayAdapter is one of the adapters provided by Android that provides data sources (child elements) to selection widgets and also casts the data into specific view(s) to be displayed inside the selection widgets. In this section, we learn to create an ArrayAdapter and use it to populate the ListView control. An ArrayAdapter can be created through string resource, as well as through string arrays defined in Java code. We try the latter method in this section.

Create a new Android project called ListViewDemo1. Again, in this application, we use two controls, ListView and TextView, where ListView displays the items assigned to it through `ArrayAdapter` and the `TextView` displays the item that is selected by the user from the `ListView`. Define the two controls by writing the code shown in Listing 5.4 into the layout file `activity_list_view_demo1.xml`.

LISTING 5.4   The Layout File `activity_list_view_demo1.xml` After Adding the `ListView` and `TextView` Controls

```
<LinearLayout xmlns:android="http://schemas.android.com/apk/res/android"
    xmlns:tools="http://schemas.android.com/tools"
    android:orientation="vertical"
    android:layout_width="match_parent"
    android:layout_height="wrap_content">
    <ListView
        android:id="@+id/fruits_list"
        android:layout_width="match_parent"
        android:layout_height="match_parent"
        android:drawSelectorOnTop="false"/>
    <TextView
        android:id="@+id/selectedopt"
        android:layout_width="match_parent"
        android:layout_height="wrap_content" />
</LinearLayout>
```

Next, we need to write code into the Java activity file `ListViewDemo1Activity.java` to serve the following purposes:

▶ Create an `ArrayAdapter` through a string array and assign it to the `ListView` for displaying items

▶ Display the item selected from the `ListView` in the `TextView`

The code written into the activity file `ListViewDemo1Activity.java` is shown in Listing 5.5.

LISTING 5.5   Code Written into the Java Activity File `ListViewDemo1Activity.java`

```
package com.androidunleashed.listviewdemo1;

import android.app.Activity;
import android.os.Bundle;
import android.widget.AdapterView.OnItemClickListener;
import android.widget.TextView;
import android.widget.ListView;
import android.widget.ArrayAdapter;
import android.widget.AdapterView;
import android.view.View;
```

```
public class ListViewDemo1Activity extends Activity {
    @Override
    public void onCreate(Bundle savedInstanceState) {
        super.onCreate(savedInstanceState);
        setContentView(R.layout.activity_list_view_demo1);
        final String[] fruits={"Apple", "Mango", "Orange", "Grapes", "Banana"};
        final TextView selectedOpt=(TextView)findViewById(R.id.selectedopt);
        ListView fruitsList = (ListView)findViewById(R.id.fruits_list);
        final ArrayAdapter<String> arrayAdpt= new ArrayAdapter<String>(this,
            android.R.layout.simple_list_item_1, fruits);
        fruitsList.setAdapter(arrayAdpt);
        fruitsList.setOnItemClickListener(new OnItemClickListener(){
            @Override
            public void onItemClick(AdapterView<?> parent, View v, int position,
long id){
                selectedOpt.setText("You have selected "+fruits[position]);
            }
        });
    }
}
```

An `ArrayAdapter` is the simplest of the adapters and acts as the data source for the selection widgets `ListView`, `GridView`, and so on. An `ArrayAdapter` makes use of the `TextView` control to represent the child `Views` in a `View`. In the code shown in Listing 5.5, an `ArrayAdapter` is created through the following code:

```
ArrayAdapter<String> arrayadpt=new ArrayAdapter<String> (this,
android.R.layout.simple_list_item_1, fruits);
```

This constructor creates an `ArrayAdapter` called `arrayAdpt` that can display the elements of the specified array, `fruits`, via the `TextView` control.

The `ArrayAdapter` constructor consists of the following:

▶ **this (the current context)**—As the `Activity` is an extension of the `Context` class, we use the current instance as the context.

▶ **android.R.layout.simple_list_item_1**—Points to a `TextView` defined by the Android SDK that will be used for displaying each item in the `ListView`. The elements of the array that is specified next needs to be wrapped or cast in a view before being assigned to any selection widget for display. So, the `android.R.layout.simple_list_item_1` simply turns the strings defined in the string array into a `TextView` for displaying them in a `ListView`.

▶ **array**—The data source—an array of strings for the `ListView`.

We can see that the `ListView` and `TextView` controls from the layout files are accessed and mapped to the objects `fruitsList` and `selectedOpt`, respectively. The `arrayAdpt` `ArrayAdapter` containing the elements of the `fruits` array in `TextView` form is assigned to the `ListView` control for displaying choices to the user. The `OnItemClickListener` interface is implemented via an anonymous class that implements a callback method, `onItem-Click()`. The reference of an anonymous class is passed to the `fruitsList` `ListView` to invoke the callback method `onItemClick()` when any of the items in `ListView` is clicked. In the `onItemClick()` method, the item selected in the `ListView` is displayed via the `TextView` control `selectedOpt`. When we run the application, the list of items is displayed via `ListView`, and the item selected from the `ListView` is displayed via the `TextView` control, as shown in Figure 5.2.

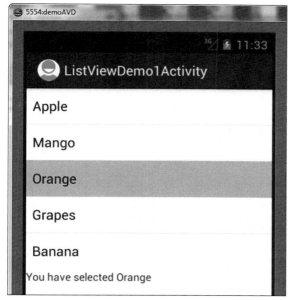

FIGURE 5.2   Options displayed through Java code in the `ListView` control and the selected option from `ListView` displayed through the `TextView` control

Now that we understand how to create a `ListView` through an `Activity` base class, let's create `ListView` by extending the `ListActivity` class.

Creating `ListView` **by Extending** `ListActivity`

The `ListActivity` already contains a `ListView`, and we just need to populate it by calling the `setListAdapter()` method. If we just want to display a `ListView` and no other control in our application, then there is no need of defining any `View` in the layout file `main.xml`, as `ListActivity` automatically constructs a full-screen list for us. Also there is no need of using the `onCreate()` method for defining the content view of the activity for the simple reason that `ListActivity` already contains a `ListView` control. If we want to display some other controls along with `ListView`, we need to define the `ListView` and other desired controls in the layout file `main.xml`.

Let's create a new application to examine the creation of `ListView` by extending the `ListActivity` class. Name the new application `ListViewDemo2`. Because we want to display `ListView` and `TextView` controls in our application, we need to use the layout file `activity_list_view_demo2.xml` and write the code as shown in Listing 5.6.

LISTING 5.6   The Layout File `activity_list_view_demo2.xml` After Adding `ListView` and `TextView` Controls

```
<LinearLayout xmlns:android="http://schemas.android.com/apk/res/android"
    xmlns:tools="http://schemas.android.com/tools"
    android:orientation="vertical"
    android:layout_width="match_parent"
    android:layout_height="wrap_content">
    <ListView
        android:id="@android:id/list"
        android:layout_width="match_parent"
        android:layout_height="match_parent"
        android:drawSelectorOnTop="false"  />
        <TextView
            android:id="@+id/selectedopt"
            android:layout_width="match_parent"
            android:layout_height="wrap_content" />
</LinearLayout>
```

Note that the ID assigned to the `ListView` control defined in `activity_list_view_demo2.xml` must be `@android:id/list`; otherwise, `ListActivity` will not be able to identify it. To populate `ListView` and to display the item selected from it through the `TextView` control, write the code into `ListViewDemo2Activity.java` as shown in Listing 5.7.

LISTING 5.7   Code Written into the Java Activity File `ListViewDemo2Activity.java`

```
package com.androidunleashed.listviewdemo2;

import android.os.Bundle;
import android.app.ListActivity;
import android.widget.TextView;
import android.widget.ArrayAdapter;
import android.widget.ListView;
import android.view.View;

public class ListViewDemo2Activity extends ListActivity {
    TextView selectedOpt;
    String[] fruits={"Apple", "Mango", "Orange", "Grapes", "Banana"};
```

```
@Override
public void onCreate(Bundle savedInstanceState) {
    super.onCreate(savedInstanceState);
    setContentView(R.layout.activity_list_view_demo2);
    selectedOpt=(TextView)findViewById(R.id.selectedopt);
    ArrayAdapter<String> arrayAdpt = new ArrayAdapter<String>(this,
        android.R.layout.simple_list_item_single_choice,fruits);     #1
    getListView().setChoiceMode(ListView.CHOICE_MODE_SINGLE);        #2
    setListAdapter(arrayAdpt);
}

@Override
public void onListItemClick(ListView parent, View v, int position, long id)
{
    super.onListItemClick(parent, v, position, id);
    selectedOpt.setText("You have selected "+fruits[position]);
}
}
```

We can see that an `ArrayAdapter`, `arrayAdpt`, is wrapping an array of strings. The `ListView` is populated by assigning `arrayAdpt` to it via the `setListAdapter()` method. The `onList-ItemClick()` method is overridden to define the action that we want to take place when any item in the `ListView` is clicked. The `onListItemClick()` method is executed when an item from the `ListView` is selected. In the `onListItemClick()` method, the item selected by the user from the `ListView` is displayed through the `TextView` `selected-Opt`. The `simple_list_item_single_choice` term in statement #1 and the `ListView.CHOICE_MODE_SINGLE` in statement #2 allow us to select a single item from the `ListView`. On running the application, we see that items in the `ListView` control appear in the form of a `RadioButton` control, allowing us to select only a single item at a time (see Figure 5.3 (left). The chosen item is displayed through the `TextView` control.

To enable users to select multiple items from the `ListView`, replace `simple_list_item_single_choice` with `simple_list_item_multiple_choice` in statement #1 and change the choice mode in statement #2 from `ListView.CHOICE_MODE_SINGLE` to `ListView.CHOICE_MODE_MULTIPLE`. After we make these two changes, the statements appear as shown here:

```
ArrayAdapter<String> arrayAdpt = new ArrayAdapter<String>(this,
    android.R.layout.simple_list_item_multiple_choice,fruits);
getListView().setChoiceMode(ListView.CHOICE_MODE_MULTIPLE);
```

On running the application, we find that the items in the `ListView` control appear as `CheckBoxes`, allowing us to select more than one item at a time, as shown in Figure 5.3 (right).

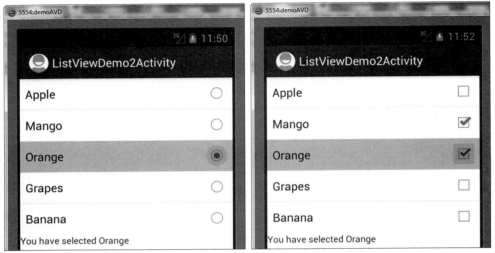

FIGURE 5.3   The `ListView` control with the choice mode set to single (left). and the `ListView` control with the choice mode set to multiple (right)

Using the `Spinner` Control

The `Spinner` is akin to a drop-down list that displays a list of items, allowing the user to select the desired item. After the user touches a Spinner or presses the center button of the `D-pad`, a list of items is displayed, allowing the user to select an item from the list. To populate the `Spinner` control, we use two methods: one via the `string resource` and the other via the `ArrayAdapter` that acts as a data source.

Create a new Android project and name it as `SpinnerApp`. First, we populate the `Spinner` control via the `string resource` and then by `ArrayAdapter`.

Populating a `Spinner` Through Resources

We define two resources, one to display a prompt in the `Spinner` control and the other to display a list of choices. To display a prompt in the `Spinner` control, we define a `string resource`. Open the `strings.xml` file from the `res/values` folder and define a `string resource` in it. The code is shown in Listing 5.8. The new code is shown in bold.

LISTING 5.8   String Resource Defined in the `strings.xml` File

```
<resources>
    <string name="app_name">SpinnerApp</string>
    <string name="menu_settings">Settings</string>
    <string name="title_activity_spinner_app">SpinnerAppActivity</string>
    <string name="choose_msg">Choose a fruit</string>
</resources>
```

We can see that a `string resource` called `choose_msg` is defined to represent the text `Choose a fruit`. Next, we need to define the resource for displaying options in the `Spinner` control. We use a `string-array` to do this. To add a new `xml` file to the `res/values` folder, right-click on the `res/values` folder in the `Package Explorer` window and select the `New, Android XML File` option. Call the file `arrays` (without the extension `.xml`) and then click the `Finish` button. The code written in `arrays.xml` is shown in Listing 5.9.

LISTING 5.9   String Array Defined in the `arrays.xml` File

```xml
<?xml version="1.0" encoding="utf-8"?>
<resources>
    <string-array name="fruits">
        <item>Apple</item>
        <item>Mango</item>
        <item>Orange</item>
        <item>Grapes</item>
        <item>Banana</item>
    </string-array>
</resources>
```

We can see that a `string-array` called `fruits` is defined, consisting of five elements, `Apple`, `Mango`, `Orange`, `Grapes`, and `Banana`. These array elements are used to display options in the `Spinner` control. To display the `Spinner` control in the application, let's define it in the layout file `activity_spinner_app.xml`, as shown in Listing 5.10.

LISTING 5.10   The `activity_spinner_app.xml` File with a Defined `Spinner` Control

```xml
<LinearLayout xmlns:android="http://schemas.android.com/apk/res/android"
    xmlns:tools="http://schemas.android.com/tools"
    android:orientation="vertical"
    android:layout_width="match_parent"
    android:layout_height="match_parent">
    <Spinner
        android:id="@+id/spinner"
        android:layout_width="match_parent"
        android:layout_height="wrap_content"
        android:prompt="@string/choose_msg"
        android:entries="@array/fruits"/>
    <TextView
        android:id="@+id/selectedopt"
        android:layout_width="match_parent"
        android:layout_height="wrap_content" />
</LinearLayout>
```

We can see that a `Spinner` control and a `TextView` control are defined. The `Spinner` control displays a list of choices, and the `TextView` displays the choice selected by the user from the `Spinner` control. The `prompt` attribute is a string that appears at the top of the `Spinner` control to guide the user. The `choose_msg string resource`, representing the string `Choose a fruit` is set to appear as a `Spinner` control prompt. The `entries` attribute is used to specify the data source to populate the `Spinner` control. We set the `entries` attribute to the string array `fruits` that we just defined in `arrays.xml`.

We want the item selected from the `Spinner` control by the user to appear in the `TextView`. To do so, write the code shown in Listing 5.11 into the Java activity file `SpinnerAppActivity.java`.

LISTING 5.11   The Code Written into the Java Activity File `SpinnerAppActivity.java`

```
package com.androidunleashed.spinnerapp;

import android.app.Activity;
import android.os.Bundle;
import android.widget.TextView;
import android.widget.Spinner;
import android.widget.AdapterView;
import android.view.View;
import android.widget.AdapterView.OnItemSelectedListener;

public class SpinnerAppActivity extends Activity {
    @Override
    public void onCreate(Bundle savedInstanceState) {
        super.onCreate(savedInstanceState);
        setContentView(R.layout.activity_spinner_app);
        final TextView selectedOpt=(TextView)findViewById(R.id.selectedopt);
        Spinner spin=(Spinner)findViewById(R.id.spinner);
        final String[] fruitsArray = getResources().getStringArray(R.array.fruits);
        spin.setOnItemSelectedListener(new OnItemSelectedListener() {
            public void onItemSelected(AdapterView<?> parent, View v, int position,
                long id) {
                selectedOpt.setText("You have selected " +fruitsArray[position]);
            }
            public void onNothingSelected(AdapterView<?> parent) {
                selectedOpt.setText("");
            }
        });
    }
}
```

The `Spinner` control is captured from the layout file and is mapped to the `Spinner` object `spin`. Similarly, the `TextView` is captured and mapped to the `TextView` object `selectedOpt`. The `selectedOpt` object is used to display the item selected from the `Spinner` control. An event listener, `setOnItemSelectedListener`, is attached to the `Spinner` control. When an item from the `Spinner` is selected, the `onItemSelected()` callback method that was specified in the anonymous class passed to the Spinner's `setOnItemSelectedListener` is called. The `onItemSelected()` callback method retrieves the item that was selected in the `Spinner` and displays it through the `TextView`. The item selected in the `Spinner` is retrieved from the `fruits` array by specifying its index location—the position of the item selected from the `Spinner` control.

The `onNothingSelected()` method is implemented to make the `selectedOpt TextView` blank; that is, it removes any previous message being displayed through `TextView` control that was selected earlier from the `Spinner` control.

When we run the application, the `Spinner` and `TextView` control appear as shown in Figure 5.4 (left). After we select the drop-down arrow of the `Spinner` control, the items listed in the spinner control are displayed as shown in Figure 5.4 (middle). After we select an item from the `Spinner` control, its name is displayed via the `TextView` control, as shown in Figure 5.4 (right).

FIGURE 5.4   `Spinner` control with a drop-down arrow (left), options displayed through an Arrays Resource in the `Spinner` control (middle), and the option selected in the `Spinner` displayed through `TextView` (right)

Let's now have a look at populating the `Spinner` control by using `ArrayAdapter`.

Populating a `Spinner` **Through** `ArrayAdapter`

Before populating the `Spinner` control with `ArrayAdapter`, we make it empty by removing the `android:entries="@array/fruits"` attribute from the XML definition of the `Spinner` control in the layout file `main.xml`. After we remove the `entries` attribute, the elements of the `fruits` string array no longer are displayed in the `Spinner` control. After we remove the `entries` attribute from the `Spinner` control, the layout file appears as shown in Listing 5.12.

LISTING 5.12   The Layout File `main.xml` After Removing the `entries` Attribute from the `Spinner` Control

```
<LinearLayout xmlns:android="http://schemas.android.com/apk/res/android"
    xmlns:tools="http://schemas.android.com/tools"
```

```
    android:orientation="vertical"
    android:layout_width="match_parent"
    android:layout_height="match_parent" >
    <Spinner
        android:id="@+id/spinner"
        android:layout_width="match_parent"
        android:layout_height="wrap_content"
        android:prompt="@string/choose_msg"/>
    <TextView
        android:id="@+id/selectedopt"
        android:layout_width="match_parent"
        android:layout_height="wrap_content"/>
</LinearLayout>
```

There is no need to make any changes to `strings.xml`, the resource file, and we don't need the `arrays.xml` file either. To create an `ArrayAdapter` and to assign it to the `Spinner` control for populating it, the code shown in Listing 5.13 is written into the Java activity file `SpinnerAppActivity.java`. The code shown in bold is the modified code; the remainder is the same as Listing 5.11.

LISTING 5.13   Code Written into `SpinnerAppActivity.java`

```
package com.androidunleashed.spinnerapp;

import android.app.Activity;
import android.os.Bundle;
import android.widget.TextView;
import android.widget.Spinner;
import android.widget.ArrayAdapter;
import android.widget.AdapterView;
import android.view.View;
import android.widget.AdapterView.OnItemSelectedListener;

public class SpinnerAppActivity extends Activity {

    @Override
    public void onCreate(Bundle savedInstanceState) {
        super.onCreate(savedInstanceState);
        setContentView(R.layout.activity_spinner_app);
        final TextView selectedOpt=(TextView)findViewById(R.id.selectedopt);
        final String[] fruits={"Apple", "Mango", "Orange", "Grapes", "Banana"};
        Spinner spin=(Spinner)findViewById(R.id.spinner);
        ArrayAdapter<String> arrayAdpt=new ArrayAdapter<String>(this,
            android.R.layout.simple_spinner_item, fruits);
        spin.setAdapter(arrayAdpt);
        spin.setOnItemSelectedListener(new OnItemSelectedListener() {
```

```
    public void onItemSelected(AdapterView<?> parent, View v, int position,
        long id) {
        selectedOpt.setText("You have selected " +fruits[position]);
    }
    public void onNothingSelected(AdapterView<?> parent) {
        selectedOpt.setText("");
    }
    });
    }
}
```

An `ArrayAdapter<String>` object called `arrayAdpt` is created from the string array `fruits`, and a standard `simple_spinner_item` view is used to display each bound element in the `Spinner` control. The `arrayAdpt` `ArrayAdapter` is assigned to the `Spinner` control for populating it. After we select an item in the `Spinner` control, the `onItemSelected()` callback method is executed to display the selected item through the `TextView` control. After we run the app⸺⸺tion, the `Spinner` and `TextView` control appears as shown in Figure 5.5 (left). After we ⸺⸺⸺ ⸺drop-down arrow of the `Spinner` control, the items listed in the `Spinner` cont⸺ ⸺⸺⸺shown in Figure 5.5 (middle). After we select an item from the `Sp`⸺⸺⸺ ⸺⸺⸺⸺⸺⸺nlayed via the `TextView` control, as shown in Figure 5.5 ⸺

options displayed in the `Spinner`
⸺layed through the `TextView` (right)

⸺ontrol with auto-complete function-
⸺tered characters appear. The user
⸺n the `EditText` control. To imple-
⸺ayAdapter and set it to display items
⸺ array, and wrap them in a `View`, called
⸺_dropdown_item_1. To understand how
⸺w application called `AutoCompleteApp`.
⸺leteTextView, in the layout file `activity_`
⸺g 5.14.

LISTING 5.14   The Layout File `activity_auto_complete_app.xml` After Defining the `TextView` and `AutoCompleteTextView` Controls

```
<LinearLayout xmlns:android="http://schemas.android.com/apk/res/android"
    xmlns:tools="http://schemas.android.com/tools"
    android:orientation="vertical"
    android:layout_width="match_parent"
    android:layout_height="match_parent" >
    <TextView
        android:text="Enter product name: "
        android:layout_width="match_parent"
        android:layout_height="wrap_content" />
    <AutoCompleteTextView android:id="@+id/product_names"
        android:layout_width="match_parent"
        android:layout_height="wrap_content"/>
</LinearLayout>
```

To display a list of suggestions, we need to create an `ArrayAdapter` and associate it with `AutoCompleteTextView`. To do so, the code shown in Listing 5.15 is written into the `AutoCompleteAppActivity.java` Java activity file.

LISTING 5.15   Code Written into the Java Activity File `AutoCompleteAppActivity.java`

```
package com.androidunleashed.autocompleteapp;

import android.app.Activity;
import android.os.Bundle;
import android.widget.ArrayAdapter;
import android.widget.AutoCompleteTextView;

public class AutoCompleteAppActivity extends Activity {
    @Override
    public void onCreate(Bundle savedInstanceState) {
        String[] products ={"Camera","Handi Cam","Cell phone","Laptop","Car"};
        super.onCreate(savedInstanceState);
        setContentView(R.layout.activity_auto_complete_app);
        ArrayAdapter<String> arrayAdapt = new ArrayAdapter<String>(this,
            android.R.layout.simple_dropdown_item_1line, products);
        AutoCompleteTextView productNames = (AutoCompleteTextView)
            findViewById(R.id.product_names);
        productNames.setThreshold(1);
        productNames.setAdapter(arrayAdapt);
    }
}
```

We can see that an `ArrayAdapter` called `arrayAdapt`, is created and the array elements of the `products` string array are set to display in it. The array elements are wrapped in a `simple_dropdown_item_1line` View to show the suggestions. The `arrayAdapt` `ArrayAdapter` is then associated with the `AutoCompleteTextView`, using the `setAdapter()` method. The `setThreshold()` method is used to indicate the minimum number of characters that a user must enter before the suggestions are displayed. We have set it to value `1` to display suggestions when the user has typed even a single character.

NOTE

`AutoCompleteTextView` is a subclass of the `EditText` class.

On running the application, we get a `TextView` and an `AutoCompleteTextView` control on startup. The `TextView` displays a message, `Enter product name:`, asking the user to type the product name in the `AutoCompleteTextView` control. Figure 5.6 (left) displays the suggestions after typing `c` in the `AutoCompleteTextView`, and Figure 5.6 (middle) displays available options based on the characters `cam` typed in the `AutoCompleteTextView` control. Similarly, Figure 5.6 (right) displays the suggestions after typing `1` in the `AutoCompleteTextView`. As we type more characters in the `AutoCompleteTextView`, suggestions become more specific.

FIGURE 5.6   The `TextView` and the `AutoCompleteTextView` displayed on application startup (left), possible options displayed (middle) based on the characters that are typed, and available result after `1` is entered (right)

Using the `GridView` **Control**

The `GridView` control is a `ViewGroup` used to display text and image data in the form of a rectangular, scrollable grid. To display data in the grid, we first define a `GridView` control in the XML layout, and then bind the data that we want to be displayed to it using the `ArrayAdapter`.

NOTE

As the name suggests, `ViewGroup` is a view that contains other views known as child views. The `ViewGroup` class is a base class for layout managers that are used to contain and arrange several views. `ListView`, `GridView`, and other container controls are good examples of `ViewGroup`s.

Let's create a new Android project called `GridViewApp`. In this application, we display certain strings arranged in a rectangular grid. When a user selects any of the strings, its name is displayed. That is, we require two controls in this application: a `GridView` control for arranging strings and a `TextView` control for displaying the string selected by the user. We write the code shown in Listing 5.16 into the `activity_grid_view_app.xml` layout file to define a `TextView` and `GridView` control.

LISTING 5.16   The Layout File `activity_grid_view_app.xml` After Defining the `TextView` and `GridView` Controls

```
<LinearLayout xmlns:android="http://schemas.android.com/apk/res/android"
    xmlns:tools="http://schemas.android.com/tools"
    android:orientation="vertical"
    android:layout_width="match_parent"
    android:layout_height="match_parent">
    <TextView android:id="@+id/selectedopt"
        android:layout_width="match_parent"
        android:layout_height="wrap_content"
        android:text="Select a fruit " />
    <GridView android:id="@+id/grid"
        android:layout_width="match_parent"
        android:layout_height="match_parent"
        android:verticalSpacing="2dip"
        android:horizontalSpacing="5dip"
        android:numColumns="auto_fit"
        android:columnWidth="130dip"
        android:stretchMode="columnWidth"
        android:gravity="center" />
</LinearLayout>
```

Let's take a look at the different attributes used in `GridView`.

GridView **Attributes**

The number of rows displayed through `GridView` is dependent on the number of elements supplied by the attached adapter. The size and number of columns is controlled through the following attributes:

▶ **android:numColumns**—Defines the number of columns. If we supply a value, auto_ fit, Android computes the number of columns based on available space.

▶ `android:verticalSpacing` and `android:horizontalSpacing`—Define the amount of whitespace between the items in the grid.

▶ `android:columnWidth`—Defines the width of each column.

▶ `android:stretchMode`—The attribute determines whether the column can stretch or expand to take up the available space. The valid values for this attribute are

   ▶ `none`—Does not allow columns to stretch or expand
   ▶ `columnWidth`—Makes the columns take up all available space
   ▶ `spacingWidth`—Makes the whitespace between columns take up all available space

Listing 5.16 defines `TextView` and `GridView` controls with the IDs `selectedopt` and `grid`, respectively. The `GridView` displays items or data in a rectangular grid, and `TextView` displays the item selected by the user from the `GridView`. The horizontal and vertical spacing among items in the `GridView` is set to `5dip` and `2dip`. The width of a column in `GridView` is set to `130dip`. The number of columns in the `GridView` is determined by the number of columns of `130dip` that can be accommodated in the available space. The columns are set to stretch to take up the available space, if any. The `GridView` appears at the center of the `LinearLayout` container. To display content in the `GridView` and to display the item selected from the `GridView` in `TextView`, write the code shown in Listing 5.17 into the Java activity file `GridViewAppActivity.java`.

LISTING 5.17   Code Written into the Java Activity File `GridViewAppActivity.java`

```
package com.androidunleashed.gridviewapp;

import android.app.Activity;
import android.os.Bundle;
import android.widget.TextView;
import android.widget.GridView;
import android.widget.ArrayAdapter;
import android.widget.AdapterView;
import android.view.View;


public class GridViewAppActivity extends Activity implements
    AdapterView.OnItemClickListener {
    TextView selectedOpt;
    String[] fruits={"Apple", "Mango", "Banana", "Grapes", "Orange",  "Pineapple",
        "Strawberry", "Papaya", "Guava", "Pomegranate",  "Watermelon", "Chickoo", "Dates",
        "Plum", "Cherry", "Kiwi"};

    @Override
    public void onCreate(Bundle savedInstanceState) {
        super.onCreate(savedInstanceState);
        setContentView(R.layout.activity_grid_view_app);
```

5

```
        selectedOpt=(TextView) findViewById(R.id.selectedopt);
        GridView g=(GridView) findViewById(R.id.grid);
        ArrayAdapter<String> arrayAdpt=new ArrayAdapter<String> (this,
            android.R.layout.simple_list_item_1, fruits);
        g.setAdapter(arrayAdpt);
        g.setOnItemClickListener(this);
    }
    public void onItemClick(AdapterView<?> parent, View v, int position, long id) {
        selectedOpt.setText("You have selected "+fruits[position]);
    }
    public void onNothingSelected(AdapterView<?> parent) {
        selectedOpt.setText("");
    }
}
```

We access the `TextView` with the `selectedopt` ID from the layout and map it to the `selectedOpt` `TextView` object. We use the `selectedOpt` object to display the item selected by the user in the `GridView`. An array of strings called `fruits` is created. It is the strings in this array that we want to display in the `GridView`. We create an `ArrayAdapter` called `arrayAdpt` that makes the elements in the string array `fruits` appear in the `TextView` form. The `ArrayAdapter` is set to the `GridView` via the `setAdapter()` method to display its content via `GridView`.

By attaching `ItemClickListener` to the `GridView`, we are assured that when any item displayed through `GridView` is clicked, the `onItemClick()` callback method is invoked. Through the `onItemClick()` method, we display the item selected by the user in the `GridView` via the `TextView` `selectedOpt`.

On running the application, we find that all items are displayed in the `GridView`, as shown in Figure 5.7 (left). The item selected in the `GridView` is displayed through the `TextView` control at the top. If we reduce the size of the column width in the `GridView` definition, we can accommodate more columns. For example, modifying the attribute shown in `main.xml` accommodates three columns in the `GridView`:

```
android:columnWidth="100dip"
```

After we set the column width to `100dip`, three columns appear in the `GridView` control, as shown in Figure 5.7 (right).

FIGURE 5.7   Items displayed in two columns in GridView (left), and items displayed in three columns in GridView (right)

We have just seen the procedure for displaying text in a tabular format via the GridView control. Let's move one step further and try displaying images in a GridView control.

Displaying Images in GridView

To display content in the GridView control, we use Adapters, which provide the content to display to the controls. The content can be fetched from the sources such as arrays, databases, or other data sources. In the previous example, we displayed text in the GridView control through an ArrayAdapter. In this section, we learn to create our own custom adapter and subsequently use it to display images in the GridView control.

Let's create a new application called GridImageApp. Assuming the image filenames that we want to display through the GridView control are prod1.png, prod2.png, prod3.png, prod4.png, and prod5.png, copy them into the four res/drawable folders. Our project in the Package Explorer window appears as shown in Figure 5.8.

FIGURE 5.8 The `Package Explorer` window showing the images copied to the `res/drawable` folders

In this application, we want a message to be displayed showing the image number of the picture displayed via the `GridView` control. Our application is therefore going to have two controls: a `TextView` control for displaying the selected image number and a `GridView` control for displaying images in a grid. After we add the `TextView` and `GridView` controls, `activity_grid_image_app.xml` appears as shown in Listing 5.18.

LISTING 5.18 The Layout File `activity_grid_image_app.xml` After Adding the `TextView` and `GridView` Controls

```xml
<LinearLayout xmlns:android="http://schemas.android.com/apk/res/android"
    xmlns:tools="http://schemas.android.com/tools"
    android:layout_width="match_parent"
    android:layout_height="match_parent"
    android:orientation="vertical" >
    <TextView android:id="@+id/selectedopt"
        android:layout_width="match_parent"
        android:layout_height="wrap_content"
        android:text="List of Products " />
    <GridView android:id="@+id/grid"
```

```
            android:layout_width="match_parent"
            android:layout_height="match_parent"
            android:verticalSpacing="2dip"
            android:horizontalSpacing="2dip"
            android:numColumns="auto_fit"
            android:columnWidth="100dip"
            android:stretchMode="columnWidth"
            android:gravity="center" />
</LinearLayout>
```

We can see that the TextView and GridView controls are assigned the IDs selectedopt and grid, respectively. The width of GridView columns is set to 100dip, and the horizontal and vertical spacing between columns is set to 2dip.

To display images in the GridView control and also tell us which image is selected by the user, write the code shown in Listing 5.19 into the activity file GridImageApp-Activity.java.

LISTING 5.19   Code Written into the Java Activity File GridImageAppActivity.java

```
package com.androidunleashed.gridimageapp;

import android.app.Activity;
import android.os.Bundle;
import android.widget.GridView;
import android.view.View;
import android.widget.ImageView;
import android.content.Context;
import android.widget.BaseAdapter;
import android.widget.AdapterView;
import android.widget.TextView;
import android.view.ViewGroup;

public class GridImageAppActivity extends Activity implements
    AdapterView.OnItemClickListener {
    TextView selectedOpt;

    @Override
    public void onCreate(Bundle savedInstanceState) {
        super.onCreate(savedInstanceState);
        setContentView(R.layout.activity_grid_image_app);
        selectedOpt=(TextView) findViewById(R.id.selectedopt);
        GridView g=(GridView) findViewById(R.id.grid);
        g.setAdapter(new ImageAdapter(this));
        g.setOnItemClickListener(this);
    }
```

```java
    public void onItemClick(AdapterView<?> parent, View v, int position, long id) {
        int p=position+1;
        selectedOpt.setText("You have selected the image number "+p);
    }

    public class ImageAdapter extends BaseAdapter {
        private Context contxt;
        Integer[] images = {
            R.drawable.prod1,
            R.drawable.prod2,
            R.drawable.prod3,
            R.drawable.prod4,
            R.drawable.prod5
        };

        public ImageAdapter(Context c) {
            contxt = c;
        }

        public int getCount() {
            return images.length;
        }

        public Object getItem(int position) {
            return position;
        }

        public long getItemId(int position) {
            return position;
        }

        public View getView(int position, View convertView, ViewGroup parent) {
            ImageView imageView = new ImageView(contxt);
            imageView.setImageResource(images[position]);
            imageView.setLayoutParams(new GridView.LayoutParams(100, 120));
            return imageView;
        }
    }
}
```

The TextView and GridView controls defined in activity_grid_image_app.xml with the IDs selectedopt and grid, respectively, are fetched and mapped to the objects selectedOpt and g, respectively. To create our custom adapter, ImageAdapter, we extend the BaseAdapter abstract class that is provided by Android. To display the adapter's content (images) via GridView, ImageAdapter is set to the GridView object, g, via the setAdapter() method.

We instantiate our `ImageAdapter`, passing it the application context. An array called `images` is defined containing the resource IDs of the images that we copied into `res/drawable` folders. The `images` array acts as a data source, providing the images that we want to display. Because `ImageAdapter` is set to the `GridView` control, it can access the adapter methods to display content. The adapter's methods `getCount()`, `getItem()`, and `getItemId()` are used to determine the number of images to be displayed and the unique identifier of the specified image. The `getView()` method is used to retrieve the appropriate `View`, that is, the image at the specified position. In the `getView()` method, the member `Context` is used to create a new `ImageView`. The `ImageView` is assigned an image from the `images` array that we defined earlier. The height and width of the image are set by setting the `GridView.LayoutParams()` method.

An `AdapterView.OnItemClickListener` event handler is attached to the `GridView`, so that when any image displayed through `GridView` is clicked, the callback `onItemClick()` method is invoked. In the `onItemClick()` method, we return the position of the clicked `View`; that is, the image is returned. The position is zero based, so it is incremented by `1` before displaying the image number via the `selectedOpt TextView`.

On running the application, we see that all images are displayed in `GridView`, as shown in Figure 5.9 (left). The image selected in the `GridView` is displayed through the `TextView` control at the top, as shown in Figure 5.9 (right).

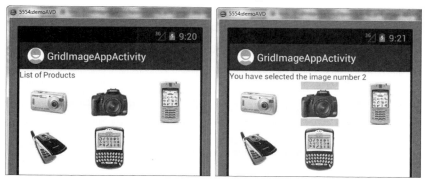

FIGURE 5.9   Images displayed in a `GridView` control (left), and the selected image number displayed via a `TextView` (right)

Creating an Image Gallery Using the `ViewPager` Control

The `ViewPager` control (`android.support.v4.view.ViewPager`) helps in showing data, which may be text, image, and so on, in the form of pages with the horizontal swiping behavior. That is, the pages of data being displayed can be flipped left and right. To identify and to keep track of the pages being displayed through `ViewPager`, a key object is associated with each of them. The `ViewPager` needs a data adapter to define and load the data for each page. The data adapter that is used to define the data for each page to be displayed through the `ViewPager` control is the `PagerAdapter` (`android.support.v4.view.PagerAdapter`) class.

While implementing the `PagerAdapter`, we must override the following methods:

- ▶ `instantiateItem(View container, int position)`—Used for creating and instantiating the page and adding it to the container. Using the `LayoutInflater` service, the method also inflates the appropriate layout and adds it to the specified container.

  Syntax:

  ```
  public ObjectinstantiateItem(View container, int position)
  ```

- ▶ `container`—Represents the container in which the page has to be displayed.

- ▶ `position`—Represents the position of the page to be instantiated.

- ▶ `destroyItem(View container, int position, Object object)`—Used for removing the page of the specified position from the container.

- ▶ `isViewFromObject(View view, Object object)`—Determines whether the specified page is associated with a specific key object.

- ▶ `getCount()`—Defines the size of the paging range, that is, the count of the number of the pages.

The position of the pages is zero based by default; that is, the first page to the left is in position 0, the next page to the right is position 1, and so on. We can also set the initial position of the pager through the `setCurrentItem()` method.

To listen to the change in state of the selected page, we need to define a class that extends `SimpleOnPageChangeListener`. When a page from the `ViewPager` is selected, the callback method `onPageSelected()` is called.

Let's apply all the knowledge gained so far in creating an application that displays a scrollable image gallery, and when an image is selected from the gallery, the selected image number is displayed. Let's name this application `ViewPagerApp`. The first step is to copy the images that we want to display through the gallery into the `res/drawable` folders of the application. Assuming we have the files named `prod1.png`, `prod2.png`, `prod3.png`, `prod4.png`, and `prod5.png` on our local disk drive, copy them into the `res/drawable` folders of our project.

NOTE

To support devices of different resolutions, the images of different resolution and size must be copied to the `res/drawable-xhdpi`, `res/drawable-hdpi`, `res/drawable-mdpi`, and `res/drawable-ldpi` folders.

After copying the images, we define two controls, `TextView` and `ViewPager`, in the layout file `activity_view_pager_app.xml`. The `TextView` control displays a message with the image number selected from the image gallery. The `ViewPager` control displays the images in a horizontally scrolling list. After we define the `TextView` and `ViewPager` control, `activity_view_pager_app.xml` appears as shown in Listing 5.20.

LISTING 5.20   The Layout File `activity_view_pager_app.xml` After Defining the `TextView` and `ViewPager` Controls

```xml
<LinearLayout xmlns:android="http://schemas.android.com/apk/res/android"
    xmlns:tools="http://schemas.android.com/tools"
    android:layout_width="match_parent"
    android:layout_height="match_parent"
    android:orientation="vertical" >
    <TextView android:id="@+id/selectedopt"
        android:layout_width="match_parent"
        android:layout_height="wrap_content"
        android:text="Image Gallery "
        android:gravity="center"
        android:textStyle="bold"   />
    <android.support.v4.view.ViewPager
        android:id="@+id/viewpager"
        android:layout_width="match_parent"
        android:layout_height="100dip"
        android:layout_marginTop="25dip"   />
</LinearLayout>
```

We can see that the `TextView` and `ViewPager` controls are assigned the IDs `selectedopt` and `viewpager`, respectively. To make the image gallery appear at a distance of `25dip` from the top of the LinearLayout container, the `android:layout_marginTop` attribute is set to `25dip`. To constrain the height of the images being displayed to `100dip`, the `android:layout_height` is set to `100dip`.

To display images in the `ViewPager` control and to display the image number selected by the user, write the code shown in Listing 5.21 into the activity file `ViewPagerApp-Activity.java`.

LISTING 5.21   Code Written into the Java Activity File `ViewPagerAppActivity.java`

```java
package com.androidunleashed.viewpagerapp;

import android.os.Bundle;
import android.app.Activity;
import android.support.v4.view.ViewPager;
import android.support.v4.view.PagerAdapter;
import android.widget.TextView;
import android.view.View;
import android.widget.ImageView;
import android.support.v4.view.ViewPager.SimpleOnPageChangeListener;

public class ViewPagerAppActivity extends Activity {
    public TextView selectedOpt;
```

```java
@Override
public void onCreate(Bundle savedInstanceState) {
    super.onCreate(savedInstanceState);
    setContentView(R.layout.activity_view_pager_app);
    selectedOpt=(TextView) findViewById(R.id.selectedopt);
    ViewPager viewPager = (ViewPager) findViewById(R.id.viewpager);
    viewPager.setAdapter(new ImageAdapter());
    viewPager.setOnPageChangeListener(new PageListener());
}

public class ImageAdapter extends PagerAdapter {
    Integer[] images = {
        R.drawable.prod1,
        R.drawable.prod2,
        R.drawable.prod3,
        R.drawable.prod4,
        R.drawable.prod5
    };

    public Object instantiateItem(View container, int position) {
        ImageView view = new ImageView(ViewPagerAppActivity.this);
        view.setImageResource(images[position]);
        ((ViewPager) container).addView(view, 0);
        return view;
    }

    @Override
    public int getCount() {
        return images.length;
    }

    @Override
    public void destroyItem(View arg0, int arg1, Object arg2) {
        ((ViewPager) arg0).removeView((View) arg2);
    }

    @Override
    public boolean isViewFromObject(View arg0, Object arg1) {
        return arg0 == ((View) arg1);
    }
}

private class PageListener extends SimpleOnPageChangeListener{
    public void onPageSelected(int position) {
        selectedOpt.setText("You have selected the page number "+position);
```

```
      }
    }
  }
```

The `TextView` and `ViewPager` controls defined in `activity_view_pager_app.xml` with the IDs `selectedopt` and `viewpager`, respectively, are fetched and mapped to the respective objects `selectedOpt` and `viewPager`. We create our custom adapter, `ImageAdapter`, by extending the `PagerAdapter` class. The `ImageAdapter` is set to the `ViewPager` object, `viewPager`, to display the adapter's content—the images via the `ViewPager` control. An array called `images` is defined, containing the resource IDs of the images that we copied into the `res/drawable` folders. The `images` array acts as a source of images that we want to display. The `instantiateItem()`, `getCount()`, `destroyItem()`, and `isViewFromObject()` methods define the pages, determine the number of images to be displayed via `ViewPager`, and define the respective unique identifier of the selected image.

A `setOnPageChangeListener` is attached to the `ViewPager` so that when any image is selected from it, the `onPageSelected()` callback method is invoked, which in turn displays the position of the clicked image through the `TextView` control. On running the application, we find that all images are displayed through the `ViewPager`, as shown in Figure 5.10 (left). When we select an image from the gallery, its position is displayed on the screen as seen in Figure 5.10 (middle). Figure 5.10 (right) shows the text message when the fourth image is selected in the gallery.

FIGURE 5.10   Image displayed in the gallery control on application startup (left), hidden images displayed on scrolling the gallery (middle), and the selected image number displayed via a `TextView` (right)

We have now created enough applications, but we don't yet know how to fix coding problems. Fortunately, Android supplies debugging tools, so let's take a look at them.

Using the Debugging Tool: Dalvik Debug Monitor Service (DDMS)

The DDMS is a powerful debugging tool that is downloaded as part of the Android SDK. DDMS can be run either by selecting the DDMS icon on the top-right corner of the Eclipse IDE or by selecting the `Window`, `Open Perspective`, `DDMS` option.

When we run DDMS, it automatically connects to the attached Android device or any running emulator. DDMS helps with a variety of tasks, including

▶ Finding bugs in applications running either on an emulator or on the physical device.

▶ Providing several services such as port forwarding, on-device screen capture, incoming call, SMS, and location data spoofing.

▶ Showing the status of active processes, viewing the stack and heap, viewing the status of active threads, and exploring the file system of any active emulator.

▶ Providing the logs generated by LogCat, so we can see log messages about the state of the application and the device. LogCat displays the line number on which the error(s) occurred.

▶ Simulating different types of networks, such as GPRS and EDGE.

Figure 5.11 shows the DDMS tool window.

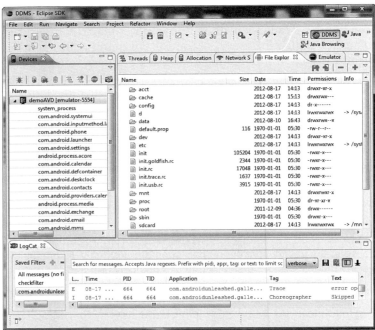

FIGURE 5.11   The DDMS tool window

In the upper-left pane of the DDMS window, we see a Devices tab that displays the list of Android devices connected to your PC, along with the running AVDs (if any). The VMs associated with each device or AVD also is displayed. Selecting a VM displays its information in the right pane. In the Devices tab, you see some icons, described here:

▶ **Debug**—Used to debug the selected process.

▶ **Update Heap**—Enables heap information of the process. After clicking this icon, use the Heap icon on the right pane to get heap information.

▶ **Dump HPROF file**—Shows the HPROF file that can be used for detecting memory leaks.

▶ **Cause GC**—Invokes Garbage Collection.

▶ **Update Threads**—Enables fetching the thread information of the selected process. After clicking this icon, we need to click the `Threads` icon in the right pane to display information about the threads that are created and destroyed in the selected process.

▶ **Start Method Profiling**—Used to find the number of times different methods are called in an application and the time consumed in each of them. Click the `Start Method Profiling` icon, interact with the application, and click the `Stop Method Profiling` icon to obtain information related to the different methods called in the application.

▶ **Stop Process**—Stops the selected process.

▶ **Screen Capture**—Captures our device/emulator screen. If the application is running and its output is being displayed through the device/emulator, clicking the `Screen Capture` icon displays the `Device Screen Capture` dialog box, as shown in Figure 5.12 (left). The text, `Capturing`, tells us that the output of the application or image being displayed in the device/emulator is in the process of being captured. Once the image is captured, it is displayed as shown in Figure 5.12 (right).

FIGURE 5.12   Image shown in the device/emulator is being captured (left), and the captured image of the device/emulator displayed (right)

The meaning of the buttons shown at the top in the `Device Screen Capture` dialog box is shown here:

▶ **Refresh**—Updates the captured image.

▶ **Rotate**—With each click of this button, the captured image rotates 90 degrees in the counterclockwise direction.

▶ `Save`—Saves the captured image as a `.png` file.

▶ `Copy`—Copies the captured image to the clipboard.

▶ `Done`—Closes the `Device Screen Capture` dialog.

Back to DDMS, on the right pane (refer to Figure 5.11), we find the following tabs:

▶ `Threads`—Displays information about the threads within each process, as shown in Figure 5.13 (left). The following information about the threads is displayed:

    ▶ `Thread ID`—Displays the unique ID assigned to each thread

    ▶ `Status`—Displays the current status of the thread—whether it is in running, sleeping, starting, waiting, native, monitor, or zombie state

    ▶ `utime`—Indicates the cumulative time spent executing user code

    ▶ `stime`—Indicates the cumulative time spent executing system code

    ▶ `Name`—Displays the name of the thread

▶ `Heap`—Displays the heap information of the process (provided the `Update Heap` button from the `Devices` tab has been clicked). Select the `Cause GC` button to begin the garbage collection process. The object types and the size of memory allocated to them are displayed. After we select an object type, a bar graph is displayed, showing the number of objects allocated for a particular memory size in bytes (see Figure 5.13—right).

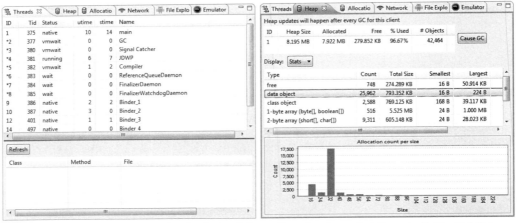

FIGURE 5.13   The `Threads` tab, displaying information about running threads (left), and the `Heap` tab displaying heap information of the current process (right)

▶ `Allocation Tracker`—Tracks the objects allocated to an application. Click the `Start Tracking` button, interact with the application, and then click `Get Allocations` to see the list of objects allocated to the application (see Figure 5.14—left). After we click the `Get Allocations` button again, the newly allocated objects are added to the earlier displayed list of allocated objects. We can also click the `Stop Tracking` button to clear the data and restart.

▶ **Network Statistics**—Helps us in getting information regarding network usage of our application, that is, when our app made network requests, speed of data transfer—and other related information.

▶ **File Explorer**—Displays the file system on the device, as shown in Figure 5.14 (right). We can view and delete files on the device/emulator through this tab. We can even push or pull files from the device using the two icons, `Pull a file from the device` and `Push a file onto the device`, that are shown at the top. To copy a file from the device, select the file in the `File Explorer` and click the `Pull a file from the device` button. The `Get Device File` dialog box opens up, prompting us to specify the path and filename where we want to store the pulled device file. Similarly, to copy a file to the device, click the `Push file onto the device` button in the `File Explorer` tab. The `Put File on Device` dialog box opens up, letting us browse the local disk drive. Select the file we want to copy to the device and click `Open` button to copy it to the device.

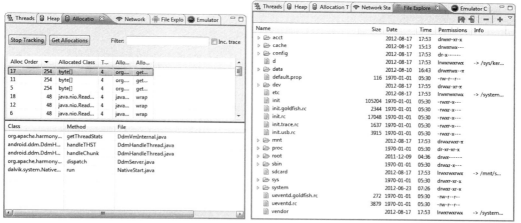

FIGURE 5.14   The `Allocation Tracker` tab, which tracks objects allocated to the application (left) and the `File Explorer` tab, displaying the file system on the device/emulator (right)

Right of the `File Explorer` tab is the `Emulator Control` tab that can be used to simulate incoming phone calls, SMS messages, or GPS coordinates. To simulate an incoming phone call, select the `Voice` option, provide the incoming phone number, and click the `Call` button, as shown in Figure 5.15 (left). In the emulator, an incoming call appears, prompting the user to answer the call in Figure 5.15 (right). The incoming call can be ended either by clicking the `End` button in the emulator or by clicking the `Hang Up` button in the `Emulator Control` tab.

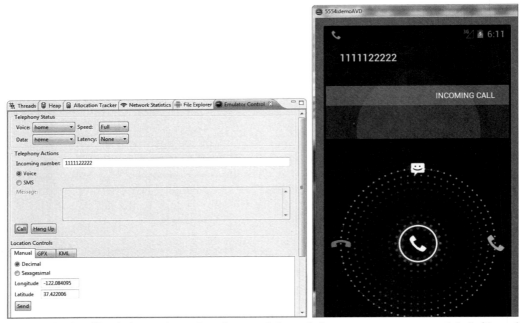

FIGURE 5.15   Simulating an incoming phone call through the `Emulator Control` tab (left), and an incoming phone call appears on the Android emulator (right).

To simulate an SMS message, select the `SMS` option in the `Emulator Control` tab, provide the phone number, write the message, and click the `Send` button, as shown in Figure 5.16 (left). In the emulator, an incoming SMS notification appears at the top (see Figure 5.16—right). We can simulate GPS coordinates (longitude and latitude values) manually, via the `GPX` file or `KML` file through the `Emulator Control` tab. Remember, only GPX 1.1 files are supported.

FIGURE 5.16   Simulating SMS via the `Emulator Control` tab (left), and incoming SMS notification displayed at the top in the Android emulator (right)

The bottom pane of the DDMS is used to show the log of the processes on the selected device or AVD. The pane is meant for performing debugging and tracing tasks. The LogCat tab shows all messages of the device, including exceptions and those placed in the application to see the intermediate results. We can also set up filters to watch filtered log information. The Console tab displays the messages related to the starting of the activity.

Let's move ahead and examine the most critical and essential task in software development—debugging.

Debugging Applications

The two most common ways of debugging an application and finding out what went wrong are placing breakpoints and displaying log messages.

Placing Breakpoints in an Application

Breakpoints are used to temporarily pause the execution of the application, allowing us to examine the content of variables and objects. To place a breakpoint in an application, select the line of code where you want to place a breakpoint and either press Ctrl+Shift+B, select Run, Toggle Breakpoint, or double-click in the marker bar to the left of the line in the Eclipse code editor. You can place as many breakpoints as you want in our application. Let's return to the Android project, HelloWorldApp, that we created in Chapter 1, "Introduction to Android." Add a few statements to its activity file, as shown in Listing 5.22. The statements just perform simple multiplication and display log messages. Only the statements in bold are newly added; the rest of the code is the same as the code in Listing 1.5.

LISTING 5.22   Code Added to the Java Activity File HelloWorldAppActivity.java

```
package com.androidunleashed.helloworldapp;

import android.app.Activity;
import android.os.Bundle;
import android.widget.TextView;
import android.util.Log;

public class HelloWorldAppActivity extends Activity {
    @Override
    public void onCreate(Bundle savedInstanceState) {
        super.onCreate(savedInstanceState);
        setContentView(R.layout.activity_hello_world_app);
        TextView mesg = (TextView)findViewById(R.id.message);
        mesg.setText("Hello World!");
        int a,b,c;
        a=10;
        b=5;
        c=a*b;
```

```
        Log.v("CheckValue1", "a = " + a);
        Log.v("CheckValue2", "b = " + b);
        Log.v("CheckValue3", "c = " + c);
        Log.i("InfoTag", "Program is working correctly up till here");
        Log.e("ErrorTag", "Error--Some error has occurred here");
    }
}
```

Let's place breakpoints at the following three statements in the activity file:

```
c=a*b;
Log.v("CheckValue1", "a = " + a);
Log.v("CheckValue3", "c = " + c);
```

When we place these breakpoints, a blue dot appears on the left, indicating that the breakpoints were successfully inserted (see Figure 5.17).

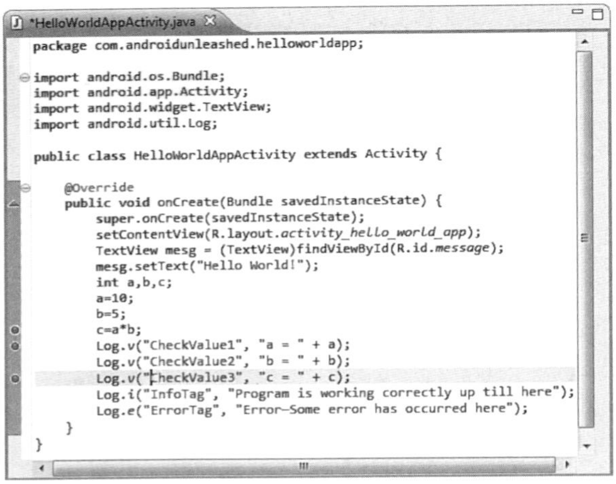

FIGURE 5.17   Activity file displaying the statements where breakpoints are inserted

To stop execution at the breakpoints, don't run the application; instead debug it by either pressing F11, selecting Run, Debug, or right-clicking the project in Package Explorer and selecting Debug As, Android Application. During debugging, the application pauses when the first breakpoint is reached. At the breakpoints, we can highlight variables to see their values and execute certain expressions. When the application reaches a breakpoint for the first time, a window pops up asking whether we want to switch to the Debug perspective, as shown in Figure 5.18. To prevent this window from appearing again, check the Remember my decision check box and click Yes.

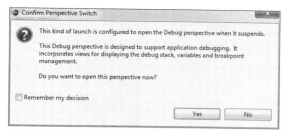

FIGURE 5.18   Dialog prompting to switch to the `Debug perspective`

Using the `Debug Perspective`

When the application switches from the `Java` to the `Debug perspective`, you see the callback stack, console, code view, and variables, as shown in Figure 5.19.

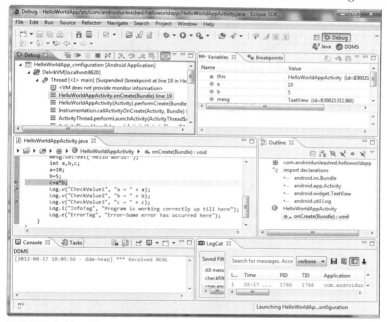

FIGURE 5.19   The `Debug perspective` window showing different panes

The following panes are visible by default in `Debug perspective`:

▶ **Debug**—On the top left, this pane displays the application being debugged, along with its currently running threads.

▶ **Variables**—Displays values of the variables at the specific breakpoints.

▶ **Breakpoints**—Lists all the breakpoints inserted in the code.

▶ **Editor**—At the middle left, this pane displays the application code pointing to the breakpoint where the application is currently suspended.

▶ `Outline`—At the center right, this pane lists the imports, classes, methods, and variables used in the application. When we select an item in the `Outline` pane, the matching source code in the `Editor` pane is highlighted.

▶ `Console`—At the bottom left, the pane displays the status of emulator/device activity, such as the launching of activities.

▶ `LogCat`—At the bottom right, this pane displays the system log messages.

Debug **Pane**

The `Debug` pane displays debug session information in a tree hierarchy. In Figure 5.19, you notice that in the `Debug` pane the call stack starts with a line, `Thread [<1> main]` `(Suspended (breakpoint at line 19))`, telling us that the application is suspended at the breakpoint on line `19`. On selecting the top stack frame icon (horizontal blue bars), in the `Variables` window, you see several gray circles labeled with the variables used in the application and showing their values at the breakpoint. A call stack is a data structure that keeps the sequence or order of different functions or subroutines called in an application. It stores the return address of the subroutines that are called in an application so that when the subroutine is over, the execution resumes from the statement following where the subroutine was called. The following buttons appear starting from the left, at the top of this pane:

▶ `Remove All Terminated Launches`—Clears all terminated processes from the display.

▶ `Resume (F8)`—Resumes execution of the currently suspended debugging session.

▶ `Suspend`—Pauses the selected debugging session.

▶ `Terminate (Ctrl+F2)`—Ends the selected debugging session.

▶ `Disconnect`—Disconnects the debugger from the selected debug target. The disconnected process can be relaunched by right-clicking it in the `Debug` pane and selecting the `Relaunch` option.

▶ `Step Into (F5)`—Executes the current statement or method and proceeds to the next method call/statement.

▶ `Step Over (F6)`—Steps over the next method call/statement. On every `Step-Over`, we can examine the values of the variables and output. The value of the variables can be examined in the `Variables` pane and the output in the `Console` pane. To see the value of any variable, hover over it with the mouse and its content is displayed.

▶ `Step Return (F7)`—Returns from the method that has been stepped into.

▶ `Drop To Frame`—Used to rerun a part of an application. Select a stack frame in the call stack and select this option to rerun the application from there.

▶ `Use Step Filters`—Ensures that all step functions apply step filters. The step filters are used to filter out the classes that we don't want to step into. To specify the classes that we want to filter out while `stepping`, select `Window`, `Preferences`. In the `Preferences` window that opens, navigate to `Java`, `Debug`, `Step Filtering`. We see the list of packages and classes and can select the ones we want to be filtered out (see Figure 5.20).

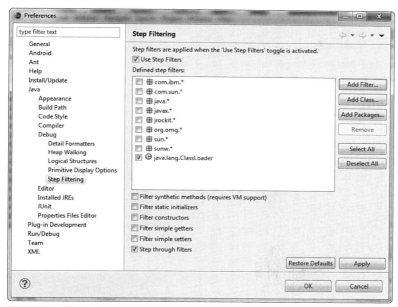

FIGURE 5.20   Dialog box for applying and managing step filters

After selecting the classes/packages to be filtered out, click `OK` to close the `Preferences` window. The selected classes/packages are filtered while stepping through the code, provided the `Use Step Filters` toggle button in the `Debug` view is `On`.

The `Debug` pane also displays a `Debug view` menu to perform tasks, such as changing the layout of debug view (tree, breadcrumb, and so on), controlling view management, and activating or deactivating the child elements shown in the `Debug` pane.

Expressions **Pane**

We can also open an `Expressions` pane that we can use to compute expressions with different variables of the application. The `Expressions` pane is not visible by default. To open it, select `Window`, `Show View`, `Expressions`. The `Expressions` pane appears, as shown in Figure 5.21 (left). We can add our own expressions by clicking the `+ Add new expres-sion` button shown in the last row of the `Expressions` pane. Write the expression in the text entry box. Remember that the variables (if any) used in the expression must exist in the application. After writing an expression, press the `Enter` key to see the result, which is displayed in the `Value` column, as shown in Figure 5.21 (right).

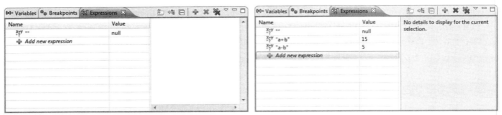

FIGURE 5.21   `Expressions` pane showing the default expression (left), and `Expressions` pane with several expressions and their respective values (right)

`Breakpoints` **Pane**

The `Breakpoints` pane displays all the inserted breakpoints in the application, as shown in Figure 5.22. This pane helps in enabling, disabling, skipping, and removing breakpoints. It also helps in suspending the breakpoint on specific conditions.

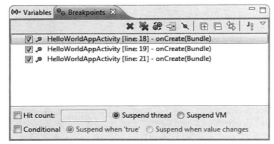

FIGURE 5.22   The `Breakpoints` pane showing applications breakpoints

At the bottom of the `Breakpoints` pane, we find two check boxes: `Hit count` and `Conditional`. The `Hit count` is for specifying the number of times we want the breakpoint to occur before suspending the thread execution. The `Conditional` check box is for specifying a condition when we want to suspend a thread. From the `Editor` pane, right-click the breakpoint (blue dot) in the marker bar and select `Breakpoint Properties` from the context menu that opens. A dialog box appears, as shown in Figure 5.23.

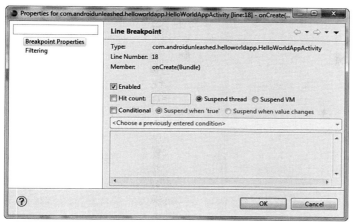

FIGURE 5.23   The `Breakpoint Properties` dialog box

The check boxes are as follows:

▶ **`Enabled`**—This check box is selected by default, indicating the breakpoint is active. When it is unchecked, the breakpoint is disabled and the breakpoint image, which was a solid blue dot, becomes a white hollow dot.

▶ **`Hit Count`**—When a breakpoint is applied to a statement within a loop, the application suspends for the number of times equal to the iteration of the loop. We can select the `Hit count` check box and add a numerical value into the text field, for example, `10`. In this case, the breakpoint is ignored `10` times before being suspended again.

▶ **`Conditional`**—Used to suspend a breakpoint when a specific condition occurs. To write a condition, select the `Conditional` check box and write a Boolean statement in the box below it. For example, the Boolean statement

```
a >=10
```

suspends the breakpoint only if the value of the variable, `a`, is greater than or equal to `10` (see Figure 5.24—left). To suspend the breakpoint every time the specified condition evaluates to `true`, select the `Suspend when 'true'` radio button. The `Suspend when value changes` radio button causes the breakpoint to suspend when the result of the condition changes. Click `OK` to apply the conditional breakpoint. A question mark (`?`) appears on the breakpoint in the `Breakpoints` pane to which the condition is applied, as shown in Figure 5.24 (right).

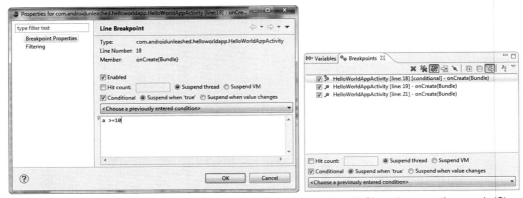

FIGURE 5.24   Applying a condition for suspending a breakpoint (left) and a question mark (?) displayed on the conditional (right)

The following buttons appear at the top of the Breakpoints pane, from left to right:

▶ **Remove Selected Breakpoints**—Removes the selected breakpoint. You can also remove a breakpoint from the Editor pane by double-clicking on the blue dot that represents the breakpoint in the marker bar. You also can right-click on the blue dot and select Toggle Breakpoint from the context menu that opens.

▶ **Remove All Breakpoints**—Removes all breakpoints from the application.

▶ **Show Breakpoints Supported by Selected Target**—Displays the breakpoints that are supported by the currently selected debug target.

▶ **Go to File for Breakpoint**—Highlights the statement in the Editor pane where the breakpoint is suspended.

▶ **Skip All Breakpoints**—Ignores all breakpoints.

▶ **Expand All**—Expands all the collapsed elements in the view.

▶ **Collapse All**—Collapses all the expanded elements in the view.

▶ **Link with Debug View**—Highlights the selected breakpoint when the application moves from one breakpoint to another in the Debug view.

▶ **Add a Java Exception Breakpoint**—Lets you set breakpoints that are suspended when exceptions are thrown. A thread can be suspended when the specified exception occurs, whether it is uncaught, caught, or both. To understand this concept, we need to add some statements, shown in Listing 5.23, to the HelloWorldApp application activity file that throws an exception. Only the statements in bold are newly added code; the remainder is the same as the code in Listing 5.22.

LISTING 5.23   Code Added to the Java Activity File `HelloWorldAppActivity.java`

```java
package com.androidunleashed.helloworldapp;

import android.app.Activity;
import android.os.Bundle;
import android.widget.TextView;
import android.util.Log;

public class HelloWorldAppActivity extends Activity {
    @Override
    public void onCreate(Bundle savedInstanceState) {
        super.onCreate(savedInstanceState);
        setContentView(R.layout.activity_hello_world_app);
        TextView mesg = (TextView)findViewById(R.id.message);
        mesg.setText("Hello World!");
        int a,b,c;
        a=10;
        b=5;
        c=a*b;
        callExcep();
        Log.v("CheckValue1", "a = " + a);
        Log.v("CheckValue2", "b = " + b);
        Log.v("CheckValue3", "c = " + c);
        Log.i("InfoTag", "Program is working correctly up till here");
        Log.e("ErrorTag", "Error--Some error has occurred here");
    }
    public void callExcep() {
        throw new RuntimeException("RuntimeException testing");
    }
}
```

We see that a method, `callExcep()`, that throws a `RuntimeException` is defined. When we don't insert `Java Exception Breakpoint`, if the application is run, it simply crashes when the exception is thrown. To suspend the thread execution when the exception occurs, select the `Add a Java Exception Breakpoint` button from the `Breakpoints` pane. We can then examine the variables and logging messages that might have thrown the exception. After we select the `Java Exception Breakpoint` button, a dialog box showing all of the available exceptions is displayed, as shown in Figure 5.25 (left).

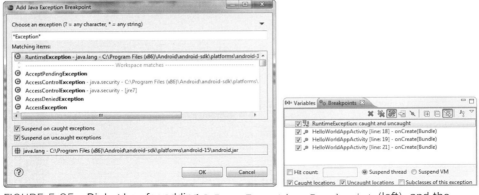

FIGURE 5.25   Dialog box for adding a `Java Exception Breakpoint` (left), and the `Breakpoints` pane showing the `RuntimeException` (right)

Type the name of the exception you want to catch or select it from the list. Two check boxes are displayed at the bottom so you can choose whether you want to suspend the thread execution on `caught` or `uncaught exceptions`. Select `Suspend on caught exceptions` to suspend the thread execution at locations where the exception is thrown and is caught by a `catch` clause. Similarly, select `Suspend on uncaught exception` if you want to suspend thread execution at locations where the exception is thrown but is uncaught. Let's select `RuntimeException` from the list of available exceptions. Keep the two check boxes selected (by default) and select `OK` to add an `Exception Breakpoint` to the application. An exception, `RuntimeException caught and uncaught`, is added and displayed in the `Breakpoints` pane, as shown in Figure 5.25 (right). Now the thread is suspended on the statement that throws the exception, allowing us to examine the variables and the `LogCat` logging pane to see what went wrong.

Variables **Pane**

The `Variables` pane displays values of the variables associated with the stack frame selected in the `Debug` pane, as shown in Figure 5.26 (left). As we step into the application, new variables may be added and the values of the existing variables display their current value, as shown in Figure 5.26 (right). To see the values of the variables up to a particular statement, you can place the cursor on a particular statement in the `Editor` pane and select `Run-To-Line` from the `Run` menu or press `Ctrl+R` to continue execution up to the selected statement.

Name	Value
this	HelloWorldAppActivity (id=830021997648)
a	10
b	5
mesg	TextView (id=830022066864)
savedInstanceState	null

Name	Value
this	HelloWorldAppActivity (id=830021997648)
a	10
b	5
mesg	TextView (id=830022066864)
savedInstanceState	null
c	50

FIGURE 5.26   The `Variables` pane showing the values of the variables at a stack frame (left), and the `Variables` pane displaying variable values after stepping all the breakpoints (right)

Adding Logging Support to Android Applications

LogCat is commonly used for debugging an application. This utility is provided through the Log class of the android.util package and displays the log messages, exceptions, warnings, System.out.println, and intermediate results that occur during runtime. The methods in the android.util.Log class are shown in Table 5.2.

TABLE 5.2   Methods Used in the Log Class

Method	Purpose
Log.e()	Log errors
Log.w()	Log warnings
Log.i()	Log informational messages
Log.d()	Log debug messages
Log.v()	Log verbose messages

These methods display log messages of different severity levels. To add logging support to our application, add the following import statement to the Activity file for the Log class:

```
import android.util.Log;
```

The logging messages need to be tagged as follows:

```
Log.i("debug_tag", "Message to display");
```

Examples:

```
Log.i("InfoTag", "Program is working correctly up till here");
Log.e("ErrorTag", "Error--Some error has occurred here");
```

In these examples, we're logging an Info message and then an Error message, which shows up in Logcat in green and red, respectively. To keep the tags consistent, it is better to create static final String constants, as shown in the following statements:

```
private static final String INFO_TAG = "InfoTag";
Log.i(INFO_TAG, "a = " + a);
Log.i(INFO_TAG, "This is info tag ");
```

We can see that the two logging messages are assigned a consistent tag, INFO_TAG. This consistency in tags helps in filtering out the desired log messages. By default, the LogCat pane shows log messages related to the entire application, as shown in Figure 5.27.

FIGURE 5.27   `LogCat` showing all the log messages of the application

To see only the desired log messages, we can set up a filter by clicking the green plus sign in the `LogCat` pane. We see a dialog box, `Logcat Message Filter Settings`, as shown in Figure 5.28 (left). Here we have to specify the `Filter Name`, the `Log Tag` whose messages we want to see, the `application name` if we want to see log messages related to the entire application, and `Log Level` to filter the log messages on the basis of severity level.

Let's specify the filter name as `checkfilter` and `Log Tag` as `CheckValue1`, as we wish to see the log messages related to this tag only. Specify the `application name` as `com.androidunleashed.helloworldapp` to focus only on the application's logs. After we select `OK`, a filter called `checkfilter` is added and appears as a new tab in `LogCat`. After we select the `checkfilter` tab, only the log messages that satisfy the specified criteria are displayed, as shown in Figure 5.28 (right).

FIGURE 5.28   Dialog box for adding `LogCat` filters (left), and filtered log messages displayed after selecting the filter (right)

Summary

In this chapter, we learned to use different selection widgets—`ListView`, `Spinner`, `AutoComplete TextView`, and `GridView` controls. We learned how to display options in selection widgets via string resources and `ArrayAdapters` and how to extend `ListActivity` and styles with the standard `ListAdapters`. We also saw how to use the debugging tool, Dalvik Debug Monitor Service (DDMS), and learned the techniques of debugging applications, placing breakpoints in an application, and adding logging support to Android applications.

In the next chapter, we learn to use different dialogs in Android applications, including the `AlertDialog` to display important messages to the user, as well as to receive input from the user. We also learn how to display and select dates and times with the `DatePicker` and `TimePicker` dialog boxes, and we learn about fragments, their life cycles, and the procedure of creating fragments through XML and with Java code. Finally, we learn about specialized fragments, `ListFragment`, `DialogFragment`, and `PreferenceFragment`.

5

# CHAPTER 6

Displaying and Fetching Information Using Dialogs and Fragments

A dialog is a smaller window that pops up to interact with the user. It can display important messages and can even prompt for some data. Once the interaction with the dialog is over, the dialog disappears, allowing the user to continue with the application. Fragments, as the name suggests, enable us to fragment or divide our Activities into encapsulated reusable modules, each with its own user interface, making our application suitable to different screen sizes. That is, depending on the available screen size, we can add or remove fragments in our application.

What Are Dialogs?

We usually create a new activity or screen for interacting with users, but when we want only a little information, or want to display an essential message, dialogs are preferred. Dialogs are also used to guide users in providing requested information, confirming certain actions, and displaying warnings or error messages. The following is an outline of different dialog window types provided by the Android SDK:

▶ `Dialog`—The basic class for all dialog types.

▶ `AlertDialog`—A dialog with one, two, or three `Button` controls.

▶ `CharacterPickerDialog`—A dialog that enables you to select an accented character associated with a regular character source.

▶ `DatePickerDialog`—A dialog that enables you to set and select a date with a `DatePicker` control.

▶ `ProgressDialog`—A dialog that displays a `ProgressBar` control showing the progress of a designated operation. We learned to work with the `ProgressBar` control in Chapter 4, "Utilizing Resources and Media."

▶ `TimePickerDialog`—A dialog that enables you to set and select a time with a `TimePicker` control.

A dialog is created by creating an instance of the `Dialog` class. The `Dialog` class creates a dialog in the form of a floating window containing messages and controls for user interaction. In Android, the dialogs are called asynchronously; that is, the dialogs are displayed and the main thread that invokes the dialogs returns and continues executing the rest of the application. The rest of the code continues to execute in the background and also allows users to simultaneously interact with the dialog. That means the dialogs in Android are `modal` in nature. If the dialog is open, users can interact only with the options and controls in the dialog until it is closed. While the user interacts with the dialog, the parent activity resumes its normal execution for efficiency.

Each dialog window is defined within the activity where it will be used. A dialog window can be created once and displayed several times. It can also be updated dynamically.

The following is a list of the Activity class dialog methods:

▶ `showDialog()`—Displays a dialog and creates a dialog if one does not exist. Each dialog has a special `dialog identifier` that is passed to this method as a parameter.

▶ `onCreateDialog()`—The callback method that executes when the dialog is created for the first time. It returns the dialog of the specified type.

▶ `onPrepareDialog()`—The callback method used for updating a dialog.

▶ `dismissDialog()`— Closes the dialog whose dialog identifier is supplied to this method. The dialog can be displayed again through the `showDialog()` method.

▶ `removeDialog()`—The `dismissDialog()` method doesn't destroy a dialog. The dismissed dialog can be redisplayed from the cache. If we do not want to display a dialog, we can remove it from the activity dialog pool by passing its `dialog identifier` to the `removeDialog()` method.

All these methods are deprecated, with the new preferred way being to use the `DialogFragment` with the `FragmentManager` (explained later in the chapter). Older platforms should use the compatibility library to use `DialogFragment` and the `FragmentManager`.

The `onCreateDialog()` method is called only once while creating the dialog for the first time, whereas the `onPrepareDialog()` method is called each time the `showDialog()` method is called, allowing the activity to update the dialog before displaying it to the user. Basically, instead of creating new instances of a dialog each time, `onCreateDialog()` and `onPrepareDialog()` persist and manage dialog box instances. When these methods persist the state information within dialogs, any option selected or data entered in any of its text fields will remain and will be lost while displaying different dialog instances.

By overriding the `onCreateDialog` method, we specify dialogs that will be created when `showDialog()` is called. Several dialog window types are available in the Android SDK, such as `AlertDialog`, `DatePickerDialog`, and `TimePickerDialog`, that we can readily use in an application. All the dialog windows are created by extending the `Dialog` class. Let's begin with `AlertDialog`.

AlertDialog

An `AlertDialog` is a popular method of getting feedback from the user. This pop-up dialog remains there until closed by the user and hence is used for showing critical messages that need immediate attention or to get essential feedback before proceeding further.

The simplest way to construct an `AlertDialog` is to use the static inner class `AlertDialog.Builder` that offers a series of methods to configure an `AlertDialog`. This example creates a new `AlertDialog.Builder` object called `alertDialog`:

```
AlertDialog.Builder alertDialog = new AlertDialog.Builder(this);
```

In this example, `this` refers to the context, that is, the current activity created here. We can add a `title`, icon, and `message` to the `alertDialog` object that we want to display in the dialog. We can define buttons and controls for user interaction to display in the dialog. We can also register event listeners with the dialog buttons for handling events. All these tasks can be easily accomplished through the methods provided by the `AlertDialog.Builder` subclass. Let's have a quick look at the methods provided.

Methods of the `AlertDialog.Builder` Subclass

The methods of the `AlertDialog.Builder` subclass that we can use to configure the `AlertDialog` box are

- ▶ `setTitle()` and `setIcon()`—For specifying the text and icon to appear in the title bar of the dialog box.

- ▶ `setMessage()`—For displaying a text message in the dialog box.

- ▶ `setPositiveButton()`, `setNeutralButton()`, and `setNegativeButton()`—For configuring the following three buttons:
  - ▶ `Positive` button—Represents the `OK` button.
  - ▶ `Negative` button—Represents the `Cancel` button.
  - ▶ `Neutral` button—Represents a button to perform a function other than `OK` or `Cancel`.

Through these three methods, we can set the three buttons to appear in the dialog and also define their location in the dialog box. We can also define the captions and actions of these buttons.

> **NOTE**
>
> The `AlertDialog` can display up to three buttons, and all three buttons cause the `Alert-dialog` to be dismissed.

Let's create an Android application to see how `AlertDialog` is displayed. Name the project `AlertDialogApp`. In this application, we want to display a `Button` control that, when clicked, displays the `AlertDialog`. So, first we need to define a `Button` control in the layout file `activity_alert_dialog_app.xml`, which appears as shown in Listing 6.1.

LISTING 6.1   The Layout File `activity_alert_dialog_app.xml` After Adding the `Button` Control

```
<LinearLayout xmlns:android="http://schemas.android.com/apk/res/android"
    xmlns:tools="http://schemas.android.com/tools"
      android:orientation="vertical"
      android:layout_width="match_parent"
      android:layout_height="match_parent">
    <Button
        android:layout_width="match_parent"
        android:layout_height="wrap_content"
        android:id="@+id/click_btn"
        android:text="Click for Alert Dialog" />
</LinearLayout>
```

To display an `AlertDialog`, we use the `AlertDialog.Builder` subclass to create a `Builder` object. Thereafter, we configure the dialog with a title, message, and buttons with the `Builder` object. We then define actions for the respective buttons, if any. Finally, the dialog is built and shown on the screen through the `Builder` object. To do all this, the code into the `AlertDialogAppActivity.java` Java activity file is as shown in Listing 6.2.

LISTING 6.2   Code Written into the Java Activity File `AlertDialogAppActivity.java`

```
package com.androidunleashed.alertdialogapp;

import android.app.Activity;
import android.os.Bundle;
import android.view.View.OnClickListener;
import android.widget.Button;
import android.view.View;
import android.app.AlertDialog;
import android.content.DialogInterface;

public class AlertDialogAppActivity extends Activity implements OnClickListener    {
    @Override
    public void onCreate(Bundle savedInstanceState) {
        super.onCreate(savedInstanceState);
```

```
        setContentView(R.layout.activity_alert_dialog_app);
        Button b = (Button)this.findViewById(R.id.click_btn);
        b.setOnClickListener(this);
    }


    @Override
    public void onClick(View v) {
        AlertDialog.Builder  alertDialog = new AlertDialog.Builder(this);
        alertDialog.setTitle("Alert window");
        alertDialog.setIcon(R.drawable.ic_launcher);
        alertDialog.setMessage("This is an alert");
        alertDialog.setPositiveButton("OK", new DialogInterface.OnClickListener() {
            public void onClick(DialogInterface dialog, int buttonId) {
                return;
            }
        });
        alertDialog.show();
    }
}
```

Here we see that the `click_btn` `Button` control in the layout file is assigned the caption `Click for Alert Dialog`. The `Button` control is captured from the layout file and is mapped to the `Button` object, `b`. We want the `AlertDialog` to appear when the `click_btn` button is clicked; hence an event listener, `setOnClickListener`, is associated with it. When `click_btn` is clicked, the `onClick()` callback method is executed. In `onClick()` a `Builder` called `alertDialog` is created. To display the alert dialog on the screen, we provide the `Context`—the current activity—to the `builder` object. We then set the `icon` and `title` for the dialog box. The `title` and `text` of the dialog are set to `Alert window` and `This is an alert`, respectively. A `positive` button is configured in the dialog with the caption `OK`. In the button's click handler, we simply do nothing and return. The `AlertDialog` is made visible on the screen through the `show()` method.

After running the application, we see a `Button` control with the caption `Click for Alert Dialog`, as shown in Figure 6.1 (left). When we select the `Button` control, an `AlertDialog` is displayed with the title `Alert window` showing the message `This is an alert`, as shown in Figure 6.1 (right).

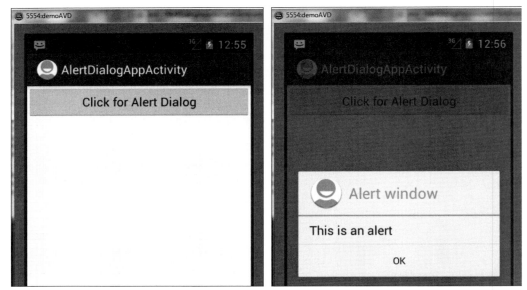

FIGURE 6.1   Button with the caption `Click for Alert Dialog` displayed on application startup (left), and the `AlertDialog` appears on selecting the `Button` control (right)

Besides showing essential or critical messages to the user that require immediate action, the `AlertDialog` can also be used for getting input from the user. Let's see how.

Getting Input via the Dialog Box

We modify our current Android project `AlertDialogApp` to get input from the user. We make the following changes to the application:

▶ Dynamically create an `EditText` control and set it as part of the `AlertDialog` to prompt the user for input.

▶ Add a `TextView` control to the layout file to display the data entered by the user in `AlertDialog`.

To make it more specific, our application asks the user to input a name through `AlertDialog`, and when the user selects the `OK` button after entering a name, a welcome message is displayed through the `TextView` control defined in the layout file. We also add a `Cancel` button to the `AlertDialog`, allowing the user to cancel the operation, which terminates the dialog. We don't have to worry about defining the `EditText` control in the layout file, as it will be created dynamically with Java code in the activity file. The only thing that we need to define in `main.xml` is a `TextView` control that will be used for displaying a Welcome message on the screen. The code shown in Listing 6.3 is added to the layout file for defining the `TextView` control. Only the code in bold is newly added; the rest is the same as we saw in Listing 6.1.

LISTING 6.3   The Layout File `activity_alert_dialog_app.xml` After Adding the `TextView` Control

```
<LinearLayout xmlns:android="http://schemas.android.com/apk/res/android"
    xmlns:tools="http://schemas.android.com/tools"
    android:orientation="vertical"
    android:layout_width="match_parent"
    android:layout_height="match_parent" >
    <Button
        android:layout_width="match_parent"
        android:layout_height="wrap_content"
        android:id="@+id/click_btn"
        android:text="Click for Alert Dialog"/>
    <TextView
        android:layout_width="match_parent"
        android:layout_height="wrap_content"
        android:id="@+id/response"/>
</LinearLayout>
```

We can see that the newly added code defines a `response` `TextView` control in the layout file. Next we add code to the Java Activity file `AlertDialogAppActivity.java` to do the following tasks:

▶ Dynamically create an `EditText` control and set it as the content of the `AlertDialog`.

▶ Access the `TextView` control from the layout file `main.xml` and map it to a `TextView` object.

▶ Fetch the name entered by the user in the `EditText` control and assign it to the `TextView` object for displaying a welcome message.

▶ Register an event listener for the `Cancel` button. Recall that the purpose of the `Cancel` button is to cancel the operation and terminate the `AlertDialog`.

To perform all these tasks, the code shown in Listing 6.4 is added to `AlertDialogAppActivity.java`. Only the code in bold is newly added; the rest is the same as we saw in Listing 6.2.

LISTING 6.4   Code Written into the Java Activity File `AlertDialogAppActivity.java`

```
package com.androidunleashed.alertdialogapp;

import android.app.Activity;
import android.os.Bundle;
import android.view.View.OnClickListener;
import android.widget.Button;
import android.widget.EditText;
import android.widget.TextView;
```

```java
import android.view.View;
import android.app.AlertDialog;
import android.content.DialogInterface;

public class AlertDialogAppActivity extends Activity implements OnClickListener    {
    TextView resp;

    @Override
    public void onCreate(Bundle savedInstanceState) {
        super.onCreate(savedInstanceState);
        setContentView(R.layout.activity_alert_dialog_app);
        resp = (TextView)this.findViewById(R.id.response);
        Button b = (Button)this.findViewById(R.id.click_btn);
        b.setOnClickListener(this);
    }

    @Override
    public void onClick(View v) {
        AlertDialog.Builder   alertDialog = new AlertDialog.Builder(this);
        alertDialog.setTitle("Alert window");
        alertDialog.setIcon(R.drawable.ic_launcher);
        alertDialog.setMessage("Enter your name ");
        final EditText username = new EditText(this);
        alertDialog.setView(username);
        alertDialog.setPositiveButton("OK", new DialogInterface.OnClickListener() {
            public void onClick(DialogInterface dialog, int buttonId) {
                String str = username.getText().toString();
                resp.setText("Welcome "+str+ "!");
                return;
            }
        });
        alertDialog.setNegativeButton("Cancel", new DialogInterface.OnClickListener() {
            public void onClick(DialogInterface dialog, int buttonId) {
                return;
            }
        });
        alertDialog.show();
    }
}
```

We can see here that the TextView control from the layout file is mapped to the TextView object resp. The message set in the AlertDialog is Enter your name. The dynamically created EditText control username is set to appear as content in the AlertDialog, allowing users to enter a name. When a user selects the OK button after entering a name, a

`Welcome` message is displayed, along with the entered name via the `TextView` object `resp`. No action is performed when `Cancel` is clicked; we simply terminate the `AlertDialog` by returning back to the main activity.

After running the application, we see a `Button` control with the caption `Click for Alert Dialog`. When clicked, it displays an `AlertDialog` with the title `Alert window` that shows the message `Enter your name`. There is also an `EditText` control prompting the user to enter a name, as shown in Figure 6.2 (left). After the user enters a name in `EditText` and click the `OK` button, a welcome message is displayed via the `TextView` control, as shown in Figure 6.2 (right).

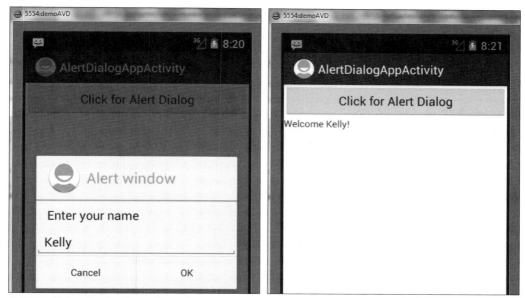

FIGURE 6.2   Getting input from the user via the `AlertDialog` (left), and the data entered by the user displayed through `TextView` (right)

The next dialog we are going to discuss is `DatePickerDialog`, which is used to set the system date.

DatePickerDialog

`DatePickerDialog` is used to see and modify the date. We can supply the day, month, and year values to its constructor to initialize the date initially displayed through this dialog. The constructor includes a callback listener to inform the current `Context` when the date has been set or changed. To initialize the current date to the dialog, we use a `Calendar` instance. To try `DatePickerDialog`, let's create a new Android project and name it `DatePickerApp`. The application contains a `TextView` and a `Button` control. When clicked, the `Button` control displays the `DatePickerDialog`, and the `TextView` control displays the date set by the user.

To define the `Button` and `TextView` control, let's write the code shown in Listing 6.5 into the layout file `activity_date_picker_app.xml`.

LISTING 6.5   The Layout File `activity_date_picker_app.xml` After Adding the `TextView` and `Button` Controls

```
<LinearLayout xmlns:android="http://schemas.android.com/apk/res/android"
    xmlns:tools="http://schemas.android.com/tools"
    android:orientation="vertical"
    android:layout_width="match_parent"
    android:layout_height="match_parent">
    <TextView android:id="@+id/datevw"
        android:layout_width="wrap_content"
        android:layout_height="wrap_content" />
    <Button android:id="@+id/date_button"
        android:layout_width="wrap_content"
        android:layout_height="wrap_content"
        android:text="Set the Date" />
</LinearLayout>
```

We can see that a `TextView` and a `Button` control with the IDs `datevw` and `date_button`, respectively, are defined in the layout file. The caption `Set the Date` is set to display in the `Button` control.

To add action to the application, we need to write some Java code into the activity file `DatePickerAppActivity.java`. The code in the activity file does the following:

▶ Access the system's current date through the `Calendar` instance.

▶ Display the current system date in the `TextView` control.

▶ Display the `DatePickerDialog`, initialized to display the current system date when the `Button` control is clicked.

▶ Access the date set by the user in the `DatePickerDialog` when its `Set` button is clicked and display it through the `TextView` control.

To perform all the preceding tasks, the code shown in Listing 6.6 is written into the Java activity file `DatePickerAppActivity.java`.

LISTING 6.6   Code Written into the Java Activity File `DatePickerAppActivity.java`

```
package com.androidunleashed.datepickerapp;

import android.app.Activity;
import android.os.Bundle;
import android.widget.TextView;
import android.widget.Button;
```

```
import java.util.Calendar;
import android.app.DatePickerDialog;
import android.view.View.OnClickListener;
import android.view.View;
import android.widget.DatePicker;

public class DatePickerAppActivity extends Activity {
    private TextView dispDate;
    private int yr, mon, dy;

    @Override
    public void onCreate(Bundle savedInstanceState) {
        super.onCreate(savedInstanceState);
        setContentView(R.layout.activity_date_picker_app);
        dispDate = (TextView) findViewById(R.id.datevw);
        Button dateButton = (Button) findViewById(R.id.date_button);
        final Calendar c = Calendar.getInstance();
        yr = c.get(Calendar.YEAR);
        mon = c.get(Calendar.MONTH);
        dy = c.get(Calendar.DAY_OF_MONTH);
        dispDate.setText("Current date is: "+(mon+1)+"-"+dy+"-"+yr);
        dateButton.setOnClickListener(new OnClickListener() {
            public void onClick(View v) {
                new DatePickerDialog(DatePickerAppActivity.this, dateListener, yr,
mon, dy).show();
            }
        });
    }

    private DatePickerDialog.OnDateSetListener dateListener = new
        DatePickerDialog.OnDateSetListener() {
        public void onDateSet(DatePicker view, int year, int monthOfYear, int dayOf-
Month){
            yr = year;
            mon = monthOfYear;
            dy = dayOfMonth;
            dispDate.setText("Current date is: "+(mon+1)+"-"+dy+"-"+yr);
        }
    };
}
```

When a user clicks a button, we want the `DatePickerDialog` to be invoked so a date can be selected. A `date_button` `Button` is captured from the layout and mapped to a `Button` object `dateButton`. A `setOnClickListener` event listener is associated with the `Button` so that when it is clicked, the event handler, that is, the callback method, `onClick()`, is invoked. In the `onClick()` method, a new instance of a `DatePickerDialog` is created using the `DatePickerDialog` constructor and is displayed on the screen.

We want to initialize the `DatePickerDialog` to today's date, so we use the `Calendar` class to set the `DatePickerDialog` control to today's date each time the dialog is shown. An instance of `Calendar` is then created, initially set to the current date. The current year, month, and day are fetched from the `Calendar` instance and passed to the `DatePickerDialog` constructor to initialize it to display the current date. The constructor also includes a callback listener to inform the current `Context` when the date is set or changed.

The `DatePickerDialog` provides a callback listener, `OnDateChangedListener` or `OnDateSetListener`, that listens for when the user has finished setting the date. This occurs when the user clicks the `Set` button in the `DatePickerDialog`. The `onDateSet()` method is called when the date is set or changed, and we use it to display the set date through the `TextView`. Note that the month value is zero-based. January is considered month `0` and December month `11`. To display the correct month, the `mon` variable, which carries the month number of the selected month, is incremented by `1` before being displayed through the `TextView`.

After running the application, we see a `Button` control with the caption `Set the Date` (see Figure 6.3—top left). When clicked, it displays a `DatePickerDialog` showing today's date, as shown in Figure 6.3 (top right). We can change the day, month, and year as desired by scrolling them in an up or down direction (see Figure 6.3—bottom left). After we set the date in the `DatePickerDialog`, when the `Done` button is clicked, the currently set date is displayed via the `TextView` control, as shown in Figure 6.3 (bottom right).

FIGURE 6.3   A `TextView` displaying the current date with a `Button` control (top left); the `DatePicker` dialog after clicking the `Button` control (top right); changing the day, month, and year displayed through the `DatePicker` dialog (bottom left); and displaying the date selected from the `DatePicker` dialog in the `TextView` control (bottom right)

Let's now see how system time can be accessed and set via `TimePickerDialog`.

TimePickerDialog

The `TimePickerDialog` allows us to set or select time through the built-in Android `TimePicker` view. We can set the values of hour and minute with values of hour ranging from `0` through `23` and minutes from `0` through `59`. The dialog provides a callback listener, `OnTimeChangedListener` or `OnTimeSetListener`, which tells us when a time is changed or set by the user.

Again, we create a new Android project, called `TimePickerApp`, to see how `TimePickerDialog` works. In this application, we use two controls, `TextView` and a `Button`, where the `TextView` control displays the current system time and the new time set by the user. The `Button` control is used to invoke the `TimePickerDialog`; when the `Button` control is clicked, the `TimePickerDialog` appears. To define `TextView` and `Button`, write the code shown in Listing 6.7 into the layout file `activity_time_picker_app.xml`.

LISTING 6.7   The Layout File `activity_time_picker_app.xml` After Adding the `TextView` and `Button` Controls

```xml
<LinearLayout xmlns:android="http://schemas.android.com/apk/res/android"
    xmlns:tools="http://schemas.android.com/tools"
    android:orientation="vertical"
    android:layout_width="match_parent"
    android:layout_height="match_parent">
    <TextView android:id="@+id/timevw"
        android:layout_width="wrap_content"
        android:layout_height="wrap_content" />
    <Button android:id="@+id/time_button"
        android:layout_width="wrap_content"
        android:layout_height="wrap_content"
        android:text="Set the Time" />
</LinearLayout>
```

We can see here that the `TextView` and `Button` controls are defined with the IDs `timevw` and `time_button`, respectively. The caption on the `Button` control is `Set the Time`.

Next, we need to write code into the Java activity file `TimePickerAppActivity.java` to perform the following tasks:

▶ Invoke the `TimePickerDialog` when the `Button` control is clicked.

▶ Display the current system time in the `TextView` control.

▶ Use the `Calendar` instance to initialize `TimePickerDialog` to display the current system time.

▶ Display the newly set time in the `TextView` control.

To perform these tasks, the code shown in Listing 6.8 is written into the `TimePickerAppActivity.java` file.

LISTING 6.8   Code Written into the Java Activity File `TimePickerAppActivity.java`

```java
package com.androidunleashed.timepickerapp;

import android.app.Activity;
import android.os.Bundle;
import android.widget.TextView;
```

```
import android.widget.Button;
import java.util.Calendar;
import android.app.TimePickerDialog;
import android.view.View.OnClickListener;
import android.view.View;
import android.widget.TimePicker;

public class TimePickerAppActivity extends Activity {
    private TextView dispTime;
    private int h, m;

    @Override
    public void onCreate(Bundle savedInstanceState) {
        super.onCreate(savedInstanceState);
        setContentView(R.layout.activity_time_picker_app);
        dispTime = (TextView) findViewById(R.id.timevw);
        Button timeButton = (Button) findViewById(R.id.time_button);
        final Calendar c = Calendar.getInstance();
        h = c.get(Calendar.HOUR_OF_DAY);
        m = c.get(Calendar.MINUTE);
        dispTime.setText("Current time is: "+h+":"+m);
        timeButton.setOnClickListener(new OnClickListener() {
            public void onClick(View v) {
                new TimePickerDialog(TimePickerAppActivity.this, timeListener,
h,m,true).show();
            }
        });
    }

    private TimePickerDialog.OnTimeSetListener timeListener = new
        TimePickerDialog.OnTimeSetListener() {
        public void onTimeSet(TimePicker view, int hour, int minute) {
            h = hour;
            m = minute;
            dispTime.setText("Current time is: "+h+":"+m);
        }
    };
}
```

In this application, the `timePickerDialog` is displayed when the `Button` is selected. The `Button` with the text `Set the Time` and the ID `time_button` is captured from the layout and mapped to a `Button` object `timeButton`. A `setOnClickListener` event listener is attached to the button so that when it is clicked, the event handler callback method `onClick()` is invoked. In `onClick()`, a new instance of a `TimePickerDialog` is created using the `TimePickerDialog` constructor and is displayed on the screen.

To initialize the `TimePickerDialog` so it displays the current system time, we use the `Calendar` class. An instance of `Calendar` class is created that is initially set to be the current system time. The current hour and minute values are fetched from the `Calendar` instance and passed to the `TimePickerDialog` constructor to initialize it, which sets it to display current system time. We also pass a Boolean value, `true`, to the constructor to indicate that we want to display the 24-hour clock and not the 12-hour clock that displays AM/PM. The constructor also includes a callback listener to inform the current `Context` (i.e., the current activity) when the time is set or changed in the `TimePickerDialog`.

> **NOTE**
>
> If the Boolean value `false` is passed to the `TimePickerDialog` constructor, the hour appears in the 12-hour format with an AM/PM button displayed.

The `TimePickerDialog` provides a callback listener, `OnTimeChangedListener` or `OnTimeSetListener`, that listens for when the user is finished setting the time by selecting the `Done` button. The `onTimeSet()` method is called when the time is set or changed and we use it to display the selected time through the `TextView`.

After running the application, we see a `Button` control with the caption `Set the Time` (see Figure 6.4—top left), which, when clicked, displays a `TimePickerDialog` showing the current time, as shown in Figure 6.4 (top right). The current hour and minute are displayed, and by scrolling them in an up or down direction, we can change them as desired (see Figure 6.4—bottom left). After we set the desired time in the `TimePickerDialog` and select the `Done` button, the currently set time is displayed via the `TextView` control, as shown in Figure 6.4 (bottom right).

FIGURE 6.4   The `TextView` displaying the current time with a `Button` control (top left), the `TimePicker` dialog appears after selecting the `Button` control (top right), changing the hour and minutes displayed via the `TimePicker` dialog (bottom left), and displaying the time selected from the `TimePicker` dialog in the `TextView` control (bottom right)

How about combining the two controls `DatePickerDialog` and `TimePickerDialog` in one application? This is covered in the next section.

Selecting the Date and Time in One Application

To see how the system date and time can be set in an application, let's create a new Android application and name it `DateTimePickerApp`. In this application, we use a `TextView` and two `Button` controls. The `TextView` control displays the current system date and time, and the two `Button` controls, `Set Date` and `Set Time`, are used to invoke the respective dialogs. When the `Set Date` button is selected, the `DatePickerDialog` is invoked, and when the `Set Time` button is selected, the `TimePickerDialog` is invoked.

So, let's write the code shown in Listing 6.9 into the layout file `activity_date_time_picker_app.xml` to define a `TextView` and two `Button` controls.

LISTING 6.9   The Layout File `activity_date_time_picker_app.xml` After Adding the `TextView` and `Button` controls

```xml
<LinearLayout xmlns:android="http://schemas.android.com/apk/res/android"
    xmlns:tools="http://schemas.android.com/tools"
    android:orientation="vertical"
    android:layout_width="match_parent"
    android:layout_height="match_parent" >
    <TextView android:id="@+id/datetimevw"
        android:layout_width="wrap_content"
        android:layout_height="wrap_content" />
    <Button android:id="@+id/date_button"
        android:layout_width="match_parent"
        android:layout_height="wrap_content"
        android:text="Set Date" />
    <Button android:id="@+id/time_button"
        android:layout_width="match_parent"
        android:layout_height="wrap_content"
        android:text="Set Time" />
</LinearLayout>
```

We can see here that the `TextView` and the two `Button` controls are defined with the IDs `datetimevw`, `date_button`, and `time_button`, respectively. The captions for the two `Button` controls are `Set Date` and `Set Time`, respectively.

After defining the controls in the layout file, we write Java code into the `DateTimePickerAppActivity.java` activity file to perform the following tasks:

- ▶ Display the current system date and time in the `TextView` control.
- ▶ Invoke `DatePickerDialog` and `TimePickerDialog` when the `Set Date` and `Set Time` `Button` controls are clicked.
- ▶ Initialize `DatePickerDialog` and `TimePickerDialog` to display the current system date and time via the `Calendar` instance.
- ▶ Display the modified date and time set by the user via the `DatePickerDialog` and `TimePickerDialog` through the `TextView` control.

To perform these tasks, the code shown in Listing 6.10 is written into `DateTimePickerAppActivity.java`.

LISTING 6.10   Code Written into the Java Activity File `DateTimePickerAppActivity.java`

```java
package com.androidunleashed.datetimepickerapp;

import android.app.Activity;
import android.os.Bundle;
import android.widget.TextView;
```

```java
import android.widget.Button;
import java.util.Calendar;
import android.app.TimePickerDialog;
import android.app.DatePickerDialog;
import android.view.View.OnClickListener;
import android.view.View;
import android.widget.TimePicker;
import android.widget.DatePicker;

public class DateTimePickerAppActivity extends Activity {
    private TextView dateTimeView;
    private Calendar c;
    private int h, m,yr,mon,dy;

    @Override
    public void onCreate(Bundle savedInstanceState) {
        super.onCreate(savedInstanceState);
        setContentView(R.layout.activity_date_time_picker_app);
        dateTimeView = (TextView) findViewById(R.id.datetimevw);
        Button timeButton = (Button) findViewById(R.id.time_button);
        Button dateButton = (Button) findViewById(R.id.date_button);
        c = Calendar.getInstance();
        h = c.get(Calendar.HOUR_OF_DAY);
        m = c.get(Calendar.MINUTE);
        yr = c.get(Calendar.YEAR);
        mon = c.get(Calendar.MONTH);
        dy = c.get(Calendar.DAY_OF_MONTH);
        dateTimeView.setText("Current date is "+ (mon+1)+"-"+dy+"-"+yr+" and current
time is: "+h+":"+m);
        dateButton.setOnClickListener(new OnClickListener() {
            public void onClick(View v) {
                new DatePickerDialog(DateTimePickerAppActivity.this, dateListener,
yr, mon, dy).show();
            }
        });
        timeButton.setOnClickListener(new OnClickListener() {
            public void onClick(View v) {
                new TimePickerDialog(DateTimePickerAppActivity.this, timeListener,
h,m,true).show();
            }
        });
    }

    private DatePickerDialog.OnDateSetListener dateListener = new  DatePickerDialog.
OnDateSetListener() {
```

```
        public void onDateSet(DatePicker view, int year, int monthOfYear, int dayOf-
Month)
        {
            yr = year;
            mon = monthOfYear;
            dy = dayOfMonth;
            dateTimeView.setText("Current date is "+ (mon+1)+"-"+dy+"-"+yr+" and
current time is: "+h+":"+m);
        }
    };

    private TimePickerDialog.OnTimeSetListener timeListener = new TimePickerDialog.
OnTimeSetListener() {
        public void onTimeSet(TimePicker view, int hour, int minute) {
            h = hour;
            m = minute;
            dateTimeView.setText("Current date is "+ (mon+1)+"-"+dy+"-"+yr+" and
current time is: "+h+":"+m);
        }
    };
}
```

The respective listeners, OnDateSetListener and OnTimeSetListener, invoke their callback methods, onDateSet() and onTimeSet(), when the Done button in the DatePickerDialog or TimePickerDialog is selected by the user. The two callback methods access the newly set date and time and display them through the TextView control.

After we run the application, the system's current date and time are displayed through the TextView control. Two Button controls with the captions Set Date and Set Time are displayed in Figure 6.5 (left). When the Set Date button is clicked, the DatePickerDialog showing the system's current date is displayed, as shown in Figure 6.5 (middle). If we scroll in an up or down direction, the day, month, and year can be changed as desired. After we set the desired date, the currently set date and time are displayed via the TextView control, as shown in Figure 6.5 (right).

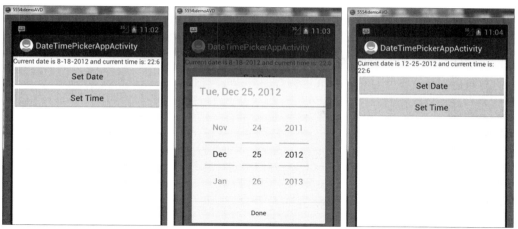

FIGURE 6.5   The `TextView` displaying the current date and time and two `Button` controls (left), the `DatePicker` dialog appears when the `Set Date` button is clicked (middle), and the date selected from the `DatePicker` dialog displayed in the `TextView` (right)

Similarly, when the `Set Time` button is clicked, the `TimePickerDialog` initialized to the system's current time is displayed, as shown in Figure 6.6 (left). If we scroll in an up or down direction, the hour and minute can be changed as desired, as shown in Figure 6.6 (middle). After we set the desired time in the `TimePickerDialog`, the currently set date and time are displayed via the `TextView` control, as shown in Figure 6.6 (right).

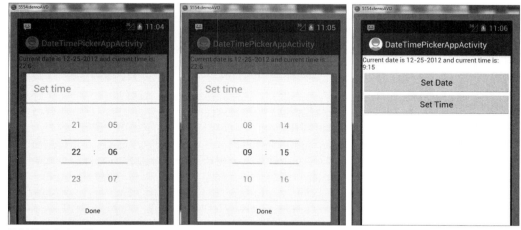

FIGURE 6.6   The `TimePicker` dialog appears when the `Set Time` button is clicked (left), changing the hour and minutes in the `TimePicker` dialog (middle), and the time selected from the `TimePicker` dialog displayed in the `TextView` (right)

We can also format the date and time. Let's modify the `DateTimePickerAppActivity.java` file to appear as shown in Listing 6.11. Only the code in bold is modified; the rest is the same as we saw in Listing 6.10.

LISTING 6.11   Code in the Java Activity File `DateTimePickerAppActivity.java`

```java
package com.androidunleashed.datetimepickerapp;

import android.app.Activity;
import android.os.Bundle;
import android.widget.TextView;
import android.widget.Button;
import java.util.Calendar;
import android.app.TimePickerDialog;
import android.app.DatePickerDialog;
import android.view.View.OnClickListener;
import android.view.View;
import android.widget.TimePicker;
import android.widget.DatePicker;
import java.text.DateFormat;

public class DateTimePickerAppActivity extends Activity {
    private TextView dateTimeView;
    private Calendar c;
    DateFormat DateTimeFormat = DateFormat.getDateTimeInstance();

    @Override
    public void onCreate(Bundle savedInstanceState) {
        super.onCreate(savedInstanceState);
        setContentView(R.layout.activity_date_time_picker_app);
        dateTimeView = (TextView) findViewById(R.id.datetimevw);
        Button timeButton = (Button) findViewById(R.id.time_button);
        Button dateButton = (Button) findViewById(R.id.date_button);
        c = Calendar.getInstance();
        dateTimeView.setText(DateTimeFormat.format(c.getTime()));
        dateButton.setOnClickListener(new OnClickListener() {
            public void onClick(View v) {
                new DatePickerDialog(DateTimePickerAppActivity.this, dateListener,c.
get(Calendar.YEAR), c.get(Calendar.MONTH), c.get(Calendar.DAY_OF_MONTH)).show();
            }
        });
        timeButton.setOnClickListener(new OnClickListener() {
            public void onClick(View v) {
                new TimePickerDialog(DateTimePickerAppActivity.this, timeListener,
c.get(Calendar.HOUR_OF_DAY), c.get(Calendar.MINUTE),true).show();
            }
        });
    }

    private DatePickerDialog.OnDateSetListener dateListener = new  DatePickerDialog.
OnDateSetListener() {
```

```
    public void onDateSet(DatePicker view, int year, int monthOfYear, int dayOf-
Month)
    {
        c.set(Calendar.YEAR,year);
        c.set(Calendar.MONTH,monthOfYear);
        c.set(Calendar.DAY_OF_MONTH,dayOfMonth);
        dateTimeView.setText(DateTimeFormat.format(c.getTime()));
    }
};

private TimePickerDialog.OnTimeSetListener timeListener = new
    TimePickerDialog.OnTimeSetListener() {
    public void onTimeSet(TimePicker view, int hour, int minute) {
        c.set(Calendar.HOUR_OF_DAY, hour);
        c.set(Calendar.MINUTE, minute);
        dateTimeView.setText(DateTimeFormat.format(c.getTime()));
    }
};
}
```

After we run the application, the formatted date and time are displayed, as shown in Figure 6.7.

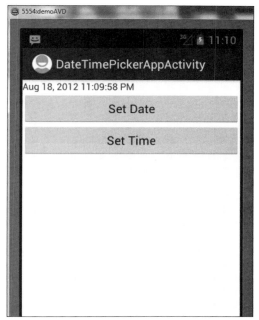

FIGURE 6.7   The formatted date and time

Let's now move ahead to understand the concept called fragments.

Fragments

The size of the screen changes when a device is oriented from portrait to landscape mode. In landscape mode, the screen becomes wider and shows empty space on the right. The height becomes smaller and hides the controls on the bottom of the display. There is a difference in screen sizes between the Android phone and Android tablet, as well. Android tablets have a 7–10 inch display, whereas Android phones are in the range of 3–5 inches.

When developing an application, we need to arrange Views in such a way that the user can view everything in both landscape and portrait mode. If we don't organize the Views with this in mind, problems arise if the user switches modes while running an application. One solution to this problem is one we have already seen—designing an individual layout for each device or screen mode. This solution is time consuming. Another solution is implementing fragments in the application.

The Structure of a Fragment

A fragment is a combination of an activity and a layout and contains a set of views that make up an independent and atomic user interface. For example, one or more fragments can be embedded in the activity to fill up the blank space that appears on the right when switching from portrait to landscape. Similarly, the fragments can be dynamically removed if the screen size is unable to accommodate the Views. That is, the fragments make it possible for us to manage the Views depending on the target device.

Let's assume that we have two fragments, Fragment1 and Fragment2, each having its own set of Views. If the screen size is small, we can create two activities, each having a single fragment, and display one activity at a time. If the device screen is able to accommodate views of both Fragment1 and Fragment2, these can be embedded into a single activity to fill up the screen.

A fragment is like a subactivity with its own life cycle and view hierarchy. We can add or remove fragments while the activity is running. Remember that the fragments exist within the context of an activity, and so cannot be used without one.

> **TIP**
>
> Fragments are self-contained and can be used in multiple activities.

To create a fragment, we need to extend the Fragment class and implement several life cycle callback methods, similar to an activity.

The Life Cycle of a Fragment

The life cycle of a fragments is affected by the activity's life cycle in which it is embedded. That is, when the activity is paused, all the fragments in it are paused. Similarly, if an activity is destroyed, all of its fragments are destroyed, as well. The life cycle of a fragment includes several callback methods, as listed here:

- ▶ `onAttach()`—Called when the fragment is attached to the activity.

- ▶ `onCreate()`—Called when creating the fragment. The method is used to initialize the items of the fragment that we want to retain when the fragment is resumed after it is paused or stopped. For example, a fragment can save the state into a `Bundle` object that the activity can use in the `onCreate()` callback while re-creating the fragment.

- ▶ `onCreateView()`—Called to create the view for the fragment.

- ▶ `onActivityCreated()`—Called when the activity's `onCreate()` method is returned.

- ▶ `onStart()`—Called when the fragment is visible to the user. This method is associated with the activity's `onStart()`.

- ▶ `onResume()`—Called when the fragment is visible and is running. The method is associated with the activity's `onResume()`.

- ▶ `onPause()`—Called when the fragment is visible but does not have focus. The method is attached to the activity's `onPause()`.

- ▶ `onStop()`—Called when fragment is not visible. The method is associated with the activity's `onStop()`.

- ▶ `onDestroyView()`—Called when the fragment is supposed to be saved or destroyed. The view hierarchy is removed from the fragment.

- ▶ `onDestroy()`—Called when the fragment is no longer in use. No view hierarchy is associated with the fragment, but the fragment is still attached to the activity.

- ▶ `onDetach()`—Called when the fragment is detached from the activity and resources allocated to the fragment are released.

A fragment also has a bundle associated with it that serves as its initialization arguments. Like an activity, a fragment can be saved and later automatically restored by the system.

To understand the concept of fragments, let's create an Android project called `FragmentsApp`. In this application, we are going to create two fragments: `Fragment1` and `Fragment2`. `Fragment1` contains a selection widget, `ListView`, that displays a couple of fruits to choose from. `Fragment2` contains a `TextView` control to display the fruit selected from the `ListView` of `Fragment1`. The fragments use individual XML layout files to define their `Views`, so for the two fragments, let's add two XML files called `fragment1.xml` and `fragment2.xml` to the `res/layout` folder.

To define a `ListView` control in the first fragment, the code shown in Listing 6.12 is written into the XML file, `fragment1.xml`.

LISTING 6.12   Code Written into the XML File `fragment1.xml`

```
<?xml version="1.0" encoding="utf-8"?>
<LinearLayout xmlns:android="http://schemas.android.com/apk/res/android"
    android:layout_width="match_parent"
```

```
        android:layout_height="match_parent"
        android:orientation="vertical"
        android:background="#0000FF" >
    <ListView
        android:id="@+id/fruits_list"
        android:layout_width="match_parent"
        android:layout_height="match_parent"
        android:drawSelectorOnTop="false"/>
 </LinearLayout>
```

We can see here that a `ListView` selection widget is defined with the ID `fruits_list`. For distinguishing the two fragments, the background of this fragment is set to blue. To define a `TextView` control for the second fragment, the code shown in Listing 6.13 is written into the XML file `fragment2.xml`.

LISTING 6.13   Code Written into the XML File `fragment2.xml`

```
<?xml version="1.0" encoding="utf-8"?>
<LinearLayout xmlns:android="http://schemas.android.com/apk/res/android"
    android:layout_width="match_parent"
    android:layout_height="match_parent"
    android:orientation="vertical" >
    <TextView
        android:id="@+id/selectedopt"
        android:layout_width="match_parent"
        android:layout_height="wrap_content"
        android:text="Please select a fruit" />
    </LinearLayout>
```

We can see that a `selectedopt` `TextView` control is defined and is set to display `Please select a fruit`. Each fragment has a Java class that loads its UI from the XML file, so for the two fragments, we need to add two Java classes to our application. Add `Fragment1Activity.java` and `Fragment2Activity.java` to the `com.androidunleashed.fragmentsapp` package of the application. The code shown in Listing 6.14 is written into the Java class file of the first fragment, `Fragment1Activity.java`.

LISTING 6.14   Code Written into the Java Class File `Fragment1Activity.java`

```
package com.androidunleashed.fragmentsapp;

import android.app.Fragment;
import android.os.Bundle;
import android.view.ViewGroup;
import android.view.View;
import android.view.LayoutInflater;
import android.widget.ListView;
```

```
import android.widget.ArrayAdapter;
import android.content.Context;
import android.widget.AdapterView;
import android.widget.AdapterView.OnItemClickListener;
import android.widget.TextView;

public class Fragment1Activity extends Fragment {
    @Override
    public View onCreateView(LayoutInflater inflater, ViewGroup container, Bundle
savedInstanceState) {
        Context c = getActivity().getApplicationContext();
        View vw = inflater.inflate(R.layout.fragment1, container, false);
        final String[] fruits={"Apple", "Mango", "Orange", "Grapes", "Banana"};
        ListView fruitsList = (ListView) vw.findViewById(R.id.fruits_list);
        ArrayAdapter<String> arrayAdpt= new ArrayAdapter<String>(c,
android.R.layout.simple_list_item_1, fruits);
        fruitsList.setAdapter(arrayAdpt);
        fruitsList.setOnItemClickListener(new OnItemClickListener(){
            @Override
            public void onItemClick(AdapterView<?> parent, View v, int position,
long id)
            {
                TextView selectedOpt = (TextView) getActivity().findViewById(R.
id.selectedopt);
                selectedOpt.setText("You have selected "+((TextView) v).getText().
toString());
            }
        });
        return vw;
    }
}
```

We can see that the Java class for the fragment extends the `Fragment` base class. To access and draw the UI for the fragment, the `onCreateView()` method is overridden. In the `onCreateView()` method, a `LayoutInflater` object is used to inflate the UI—the `ListView` control we defined in the `fragment1.xml` file. The `ListView` and `TextView` controls are accessed from the layout files and mapped to the objects `fruitsList` and `selectedOpt`, respectively. The `arrayAdpt` Array Adapter containing the elements of the array, `fruits` in `TextView` form, is assigned to the `ListView` control for displaying choices to the user. The `OnItemClickListener` interface is implemented via an anonymous class that implements a callback method, `onItemClick()`. The reference to the anonymous class is passed to the `ListView`, `fruitsList`, to invoke the callback method `onItemClick()` when any item in the `ListView` is clicked. In the `onItemClick()` method, the item selected in the `ListView` is displayed via the `TextView` control `selectedOpt`.

> **NOTE**
>
> Besides the `Fragment` base class, a fragment can also extend a few other subclasses of the `Fragment` class, such as `DialogFragment`, `ListFragment`, and `PreferenceFragment`, as we see later in this chapter.

To load the UI of the second fragment from the XML file `fragment2.xml`, write the code shown in Listing 6.15 into the Java class file of the second fragment `Fragment2-Activity.java`.

LISTING 6.15   Code Written into the Java Class File `Fragment2Activity.java`

```
package com.androidunleashed.fragmentsapp;

import android.app.Fragment;
import android.os.Bundle;
import android.view.ViewGroup;
import android.view.View;
import android.view.LayoutInflater;

public class Fragment2Activity extends Fragment {
    @Override
    public View onCreateView(LayoutInflater inflater, ViewGroup container, Bundle
savedInstanceState) {
        return inflater.inflate(R.layout.fragment2, container, false);
    }
}
```

Like the Java class of the first fragment, this class also extends the `Fragment` base class. The `onCreateView()` method is overridden where a `LayoutInflater` object is used to inflate the `TextView` control we defined in the `fragment2.xml` file.

To accommodate both the fragments in the application, the code shown in Listing 6.16 is written into the layout file `activity_fragments_app.xml`.

LISTING 6.16   The Layout File `activity_fragments_app.xml` After Adding the Two Fragments

```
<LinearLayout xmlns:android="http://schemas.android.com/apk/res/android"
    xmlns:tools="http://schemas.android.com/tools"
    android:layout_width="match_parent"
    android:layout_height="match_parent"
    android:orientation="horizontal" >
    <fragment
        android:name="com.androidunleashed.fragmentsapp.Fragment1Activity"
        android:id="@+id/fragment1"
        android:layout_weight="1"
        android:layout_width="wrap_content"
```

```
            android:layout_height="match_parent" />
    <fragment
            android:name="com.androidunleashed.fragmentsapp.Fragment2Activity"
            android:id="@+id/fragment2"
            android:layout_weight="0"
            android:layout_width="wrap_content"
            android:layout_height="match_parent" />
</LinearLayout>
```

Here we can see that the two fragments are added to the activity through the `<fragment>` elements. The fragments are assigned the IDs `fragment1` and `fragment2`, respectively. The fragments are set to refer to their respective Java class through the `android:name` attribute. The first fragment refers to its Java class file `Fragment1Activity`, which was placed in the `com.androidunleashed.fragmentsapp` package. The orientation of the container `LinearLayout`, was set to `horizontal`, so both the fragments appear beside each other. We don't have to write any code into `FragmentsAppActivity.java`. We can leave the default code unchanged, as shown in Listing 6.17.

LISTING 6.17   Code Written into the Java Activity File `FragmentsAppActivity.java`

```
package com.androidunleashed.fragmentsapp;

import android.app.Activity;
import android.os.Bundle;

public class FragmentsAppActivity extends Activity {
    @Override
    public void onCreate(Bundle savedInstanceState) {
        super.onCreate(savedInstanceState);
        setContentView(R.layout.activity_fragments_app);
    }
}
```

After we run the application, the two UIs defined in `Fragment1` and `Fragment2` appear side by side. The `ListView` of `Fragment1` displays the list of items, and `Fragment2` displays the `TextView` asking the user to `Please select a fruit`, as shown in Figure 6.8 (left). After a fruit has been selected from the `ListView`, its name is displayed through the `TextView`, as shown in Figure 6.8 (right).

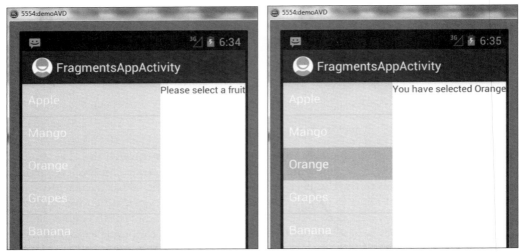

FIGURE 6.8   `ListView` and `TextView` controls displayed via two fragments (left), and the `TextView` of the second fragment, showing the item selected from the `ListView` of the first fragment (right)

In the preceding example, we saw how two fragments were included in an activity. But the main benefit of using fragments lies in the fact that it provides the freedom to add fragments to the activity when a device is switched to landscape mode or when it has empty space on the right. It's also easier to remove fragments when the device switches to portrait mode. So, let's modify our application `FragmentsApp` in such a way that when the device is in portrait mode, only one fragment is made visible, and when the device switches to landscape mode, two fragments are made visible to fill up the empty space on the right.

To be more precise, we want only the `ListView` control to appear when the device is in portrait mode. When an item is selected from the `ListView`, the `TextView` should appear on the next screen in another activity. We also require that when the device is in landscape mode, both controls, the `ListView` and the `TextView`, should appear beside each other, as there will be enough space on the right.

Traditionally, the layout file `activity_fragments_app.xml` contains the UI to display when the device is in portrait mode. Because we want only `Fragment1` to be visible when the device is in portrait mode, let's remove `Fragment2` from the layout file. After we remove the `Fragment2`, the layout file `activity_fragments_app.xml` appears as shown in Listing 6.18.

LISTING 6.18   The Layout File `activity_fragments_app.xml` with a Single Fragment

```
<LinearLayout xmlns:android="http://schemas.android.com/apk/res/android"
    android:layout_width="match_parent"
    android:layout_height="match_parent"
    android:orientation="horizontal" >
```

```
    <fragment
        android:name="com.androidunleashed.fragmentsapp.Fragment1Activity"
        android:id="@+id/fragment1"
        android:layout_weight="1"
        android:layout_width="wrap_content"
        android:layout_height="match_parent" />
</LinearLayout>
```

We can see that `Fragment1` with the ID `fragment1` is added to the layout file, which means only the `ListView` control of `Fragment1` is displayed when the device is in portrait mode.

Because we want the UI of `Fragment1` and `Fragment2` to appear when the device is in landscape mode, create a folder called `layout-land` in the `res` folder and copy the XML file `activity_fragments_app.xml` from the `res/layout` folder to the `res/layout-land` folder.

> **NOTE**
>
> If you recall from Chapter 3, "Laying Out Controls in Containers," when a device switches to the landscape mode, the layout file from the `res/layout-land` folder is used to display `Views` on the screen. When the device switches to portrait mode, the layout file from the `res/layout` folder is used for displaying `Views` on the screen.

To the `activity_fragments_app.xml` file in `res/layout-land` folder, add the two fragments, `Fragment1` and `Fragment2`. After we add these two fragments, the file appears as shown in Listing 6.19.

LISTING 6.19   The Layout File `activity_fragments_app.xml` with Two Fragments

```
<LinearLayout xmlns:android="http://schemas.android.com/apk/res/android"
    android:layout_width="match_parent"
    android:layout_height="match_parent"
    android:orientation="horizontal" >
    <fragment
        android:name="com.androidunleashed.fragmentsapp.Fragment1Activity"
        android:id="@+id/fragment1"
        android:layout_weight="1"
        android:layout_width="wrap_content"
        android:layout_height="match_parent" />
    <fragment
        android:name="com.androidunleashed.fragmentsapp.Fragment2Activity"
        android:id="@+id/fragment2"
        android:layout_weight="0"
        android:layout_width="wrap_content"
        android:layout_height="match_parent" />
</LinearLayout>
```

We can see that `Fragment1` and `Fragment2` were added to the layout file.

Next, we need to modify the Java class of the `Fragment1`, `Fragment1Activity` to appear as shown in Listing 6.20. Only the code in bold is newly added; the rest is the same as we saw in Listing 6.14.

LISTING 6.20 Code Written into the Java Class `Fragment1Activity.java`

```java
package com.androidunleashed.fragmentsapp;

import android.app.Fragment;
import android.os.Bundle;
import android.view.ViewGroup;
import android.view.View;
import android.view.LayoutInflater;
import android.widget.ListView;
import android.widget.ArrayAdapter;
import android.content.Context;
import android.widget.AdapterView;
import android.widget.AdapterView.OnItemClickListener;
import android.widget.TextView;
import android.content.Intent;
import android.content.res.Configuration;

public class Fragment1Activity extends Fragment {

    @Override
    public View onCreateView(LayoutInflater inflater, ViewGroup container, Bundle
savedInstanceState) {
        Context c = getActivity().getApplicationContext();
        View vw = inflater.inflate(R.layout.fragment1, container, false);
        final String[] fruits={"Apple", "Mango", "Orange", "Grapes", "Banana"};
        ListView fruitsList = (ListView) vw.findViewById(R.id.fruits_list);
        ArrayAdapter<String> arrayAdpt= new ArrayAdapter<String>(c,
android.R.layout.simple_list_item_1, fruits);
        fruitsList.setAdapter(arrayAdpt);
        fruitsList.setOnItemClickListener(new OnItemClickListener(){
            @Override
            public void onItemClick(AdapterView<?> parent, View v, int position,
long id)
            {
                if (getResources().getConfiguration().orientation == Configuration.
ORIENTATION_LANDSCAPE){
                    TextView selectedOpt = (TextView) getActivity().findViewById(R.
id.selectedopt);
                    selectedOpt.setText("You have selected "+((TextView)
v).getText().toString());
```

```
                } else {
                    Intent intent = new Intent(getActivity().getApplicationCon-
text(),  ShowItemActivity.class);
                    intent.putExtra("item", ((TextView) v).getText().toString());
                    startActivity(intent);
                }
            }
        });
        return vw;
    }
}
```

Take a look at the `onItemClick()` method in Listing 6.20 that's called when any item in the `ListView` shown through `Fragment1` is selected. In the method, we first check to see whether the device is in landscape mode. We know that the `fragment2` is available when the device is in landscape mode. So, if the device is in landscape mode, the `TextView` UI control defined in `fragment2.xml` is accessed and assigned to the `TextView` object `selectedOpt`. The item selected from the `ListView` is displayed through the `TextView`.

If the `fragment2` is not available, it means that the device is in portrait mode. However, we want to display the `TextView` of the item selected from the `ListView` in another screen. Recall from Chapter 2, "Basic Widgets," that to start an activity, we need to first create a new `Intent` specifying the current application context and the class name of the activity that we want to launch, and pass this `Intent` to the `startActivity()` method. Let's specify the class name of the new activity as `ShowItemActivity`, and specify it while creating a new intent. In the new activity screen, we want to display the item selected from the `ListView`, so we put the selected item in the intent under the key `item`. In the `ShowItemActivity`, we retrieve the selected item using this key.

Let's add a Java class called `ShowItemActivity.java` and write the content as shown in Listing 6.21.

LISTING 6.21   Code Written into the Activity File for the Second Fragment `ShowItemActivity.java`

```
package com.androidunleashed.fragmentsapp;

import android.app.Activity;
import android.content.res.Configuration;
import android.os.Bundle;
import android.widget.TextView;

public class ShowItemActivity extends Activity{
    @Override
    protected void onCreate(Bundle savedInstanceState) {
        super.onCreate(savedInstanceState);
        if (getResources().getConfiguration().orientation == Configuration.
```

```
ORIENTATION_LANDSCAPE) {
            finish();
            return;
        }
        setContentView(R.layout.fragment2);
        Bundle extras = getIntent().getExtras();
        if (extras != null) {
            String selectedItem = extras.getString("item");
            TextView textView = (TextView) findViewById(R.id.selectedopt);
            textView.setText("You have selected "+selectedItem);
        }
    }
}
```

Here we check to see whether the device is in landscape mode. If so, then we `finish` the activity (terminate the screen), as it's not required—the `Views` of both the fragments can be accommodated in a single screen. If the device is in portrait mode, the `getExtras()` method is called to see whether anything is passed to it. If any `Bundle` is passed to the intent, the value stored in it under the `item` key is accessed. The `TextView` from `fragment2.xml` is accessed and mapped to a `TextView` object, `textView`, and the value passed to the intent (the name of the item selected from the ListView) is displayed via the `TextView` control.

Recall that only the components declared in the application's manifest file `AndroidManifest.xml` are visible to Android. Hence, the newly added activity `ShowItemActivity.java` must be declared in `AndroidManifest.xml` to make it visible to Android and hence to start it. The `AndroidManifest.xml` file is shown in Listing 6.22. The statements in bold are added to register the newly created activity `ShowItem-Activity.java`.

LISTING 6.22   Code in the `AndroidManifest.xml` File

```xml
<?xml version="1.0" encoding="utf-8"?>
<manifest xmlns:android="http://schemas.android.com/apk/res/android"
    package="com.androidunleashed.FragmentsApp"
    android:versionCode="1"
    android:versionName="1.0" >
    <uses-sdk android:minSdkVersion="15" />
    <application
        android:icon="@drawable/ic_launcher"
        android:label="@string/app_name" >
        <activity
            android:name=".FragmentsAppActivity"
            android:label="@string/app_name" >
            <intent-filter>
                <action android:name="android.intent.action.MAIN" />
```

```
        <category android:name="android.intent.category.LAUNCHER" />
      </intent-filter>
    </activity>
    <activity android:name=".ShowItemActivity" android:label="@string/app_name" />
  </application>
</manifest>
```

After we run the application, if the device is in portrait mode, only the UI of fragment1 is visible, as shown in Figure 6.9 (left). When an item from the ListView is selected, the selected fruit name is displayed via TextView on the new screen or activity, as shown in Figure 6.9 (right).

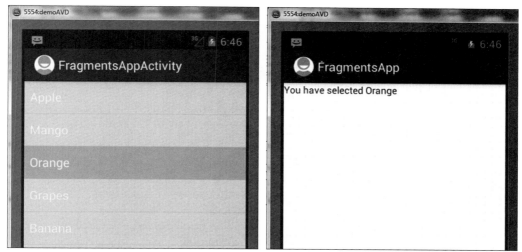

FIGURE 6.9   In portrait mode, only the UI of the first fragment, ListView, is displayed (left), and the item selected from the ListView is displayed via another activity (right).

When the device is switched to landscape mode, the UI of both the fragments, ListView and TextView, is visible side-by-side, as shown in Figure 6.10 (left). The selected item from the ListView is shown via the TextView on the same screen, as shown in Figure 6.10 (right).

FIGURE 6.10   In Landscape mode, the UI of both fragments, `ListView` and `TextView`, is displayed (left); and the item selected from the `ListView` is displayed via the `TextView` of the second fragment (right).

Creating Fragments with Java Code

Until now, we have been defining fragments statically by using `<fragment>` elements in the layout file of the application. Let's now learn how to add fragments to the activity during runtime. For creating, adding, and replacing fragments to an activity dynamically, we use the `FragmentManager`.

FragmentManager

As the name suggests, the `FragmentManager` is used to manage fragments in an activity. It provides the methods to access the fragments that are available in the activity. It also enables us to perform the `FragmentTransaction` required to add, remove, and replace fragments. To access the `FragmentManager`, the method used is `getFragmentManager()`, as shown here:

```
FragmentManager fragmentManager = getFragmentManager();
```

To perform fragment transactions, we use the instance of the `FragmentTransaction` as shown here:

```
FragmentTransaction fragmentTransaction = fragmentManager.beginTransaction();
```

A new `FragmentTransaction` is created using the `beginTransaction()` method of the `FragmentManager`. The following code shows how to add a fragment:

```
FragmentManager fragmentManager = getFragmentManager()
FragmentTransaction fragmentTransaction = fragmentManager.beginTransaction();
Fragment1Activity fragment = new Fragment1Activity();
fragmentTransaction.add(R.id.fragment_container, fragment, "TAG1");
fragmentTransaction.commit();
```

Here the `Fragment1Activity` is the Java class of the fragment, which is also used to load the UI of the fragment from its XML file. We assume that the `fragment_container` is the ID of the container that exists in the layout file where we want to put our fragment. Usually `LinearLayout` or `FrameLayout` is used as the `fragment_container`. The `TAG1` refers to the unique ID to identify and access the fragment. The `commit()` method is used to apply the changes.

> **NOTE**
>
> To add fragments dynamically, a container `View` must exist in the layout in which the `Views` of the fragment are displayed.

Before we add a fragment, it is a wise idea to check whether it already exists by modifying the code as shown here:

```
FragmentManager fragmentManager = getFragmentManager()
FragmentTransaction fragmentTransaction = fragmentManager.beginTransaction();
if(null==fragmentManager.findFragmentByTag(TAG1)){
    Fragment1Activity fragment = new Fragment1Activity();
    fragmentTransaction.add(R.id.fragment_container, fragment, "TAG1");
}
fragmentTransaction.commit();
```

We can see that the `findFragmentByTag()` method of the `FragmentManager` checks to see whether any fragment with the given tag exists. One more method that can be used to identify a fragment is `findFragmentById()`. The `findFragmentById()` method is used to identify the fragment that is added to the Activity layout. Otherwise, `findFragmentByTag()` is preferred. The `Fragment1Activity` is a Java class meant for loading the `Views` defined in the fragment's layout file.

To replace the fragment or content being displayed in the `fragment_container` with the `View` from another fragment, we use the `replace()` method of the `FragmentTransaction` as shown here:

```
fragmentTransact.replace(R.id.fragment_container, fragment2, "TAG2");
```

In this statement, the `Views` of `fragment2` replace the content being displayed in the `fragment_container` of the Activity layout. To remove a fragment, we identify it either through the `findFragmentById()` or `findFragmentByTag()` methods and then use the `remove()` method of `FragmentTransaction`. The following code identifies the fragment via the `findFragmentById()` method and then removes it:

```
FragmentTransaction fragmentTransaction = fragmentManager.beginTransaction();
Fragment fragment = fragmentManager.findFragmentById(R.id.fragment);
fragmentTransaction.remove(fragment);
fragmentTransaction.commit();
```

Here we assume that a fragment with the ID `fragment` exists in the Activity. To identify the fragment through the `findFragmentByTag()` method, the statement can be replaced by the following:

```
Fragment fragment = fragmentManager.findFragmentByTag(TAG1);
```

Communicating Between Fragments

We can also pass information among the fragments. The two methods provided by the `Fragment` class to enable communication between fragments are `setArguments()` and `getArguments()`. The `setArguments()` method stores a `Bundle` in the fragment, whereas the `getArguments()` method retrieves the `Bundle` to fetch the passed information.

The following code passes information from `fragment` 1 to `fragment` 2.We assume that `fragment` is the ID of the fragment container that exists in the layout file where we want to display `fragment` 2.

```
final Fragment2Activity frag2 = new Fragment2Activity();       #1
final Bundle args = new Bundle();                              #2
String selectedItem="Text to send to fragment 2";             #3
if(null==fragmentManager.findFragmentByTag(FRAG2)){           #4
    args.putString("item", selectedItem);                     #5
    frag2.setArguments(args);                                 #6
    fragmentTransaction.replace(R.id.fragment, frag2);        #7
    String tag = null;                                        #8
    fragmentTransaction.addToBackStack(tag);                  #9
    fragmentTransaction.commit();
}
```

Statement #1, `Fragment2Activity`, represents the Java class of the `fragment` 2. A Java class instance called `frag2` is created. Statement #2 creates a `Bundle` object called `args`, and a string, `selectedItem`, is defined in #3 that we want to pass to `fragment` 2. Statement #4 checks to see whether `fragment` 2 doesn't already exist in the layout. The `selectedItem` variable is saved in the `Bundle` object `args` under the key `item` in #5. The `Bundle` object `args` is stored in `fragment` 2 in #6. Through statement #7, `fragment` 2 replaces the `View` in the fragment container of the layout file. The statements #8 and #9 are meant for navigating to the previous fragment as discussed next.

Navigating to Previous Fragments

The Activity stack keeps track of previous Activities. When we press the `back` button, the Activities in the Activity stack pop up, making their `View`s visible. In other words, the Activity stack enables us to navigate back to previous screens by using the `back` button.

The same concept is applicable to fragments as well. To add the `FragmentTransaction` to the `back stack`, we need to call the `addToBackStack()` method of `FragmentTransaction` before calling the `commit()` method.

In the code shown previously, `fragment 2` replaces `fragment 1`, which was being displayed in the fragment container of the layout file. `fragment 1` is added to the back stack, making its `Views` invisible. Pressing the `back` button then reverses the previous `FragmentTransaction` and returns the `View` of the earlier fragment, `fragment 1`.

Retrieving Content Passed Through `Bundle`

We can access the content passed to the fragment via the `Bundle` that was saved through the `setArguments()` method. The `getArguments()` method accesses the `Bundle` that may be passed to the fragment. The following code accesses the `Bundle` object passed to the fragment. It also accesses the content passed under the `item` key and assigns it to the String `selectedItem`:

```
String selectedItem="";
@Override
public void onCreate(Bundle state) {
    super.onCreate(state);
    if (null == state)  state = getArguments();
    if (null != state){
        selectedItem = state.getString("item");
    }
}
```

Saving and Restoring the State of Fragments

Fragments can also save their state to be restored later, just like Activities. The callback methods meant for this purpose are `onSaveInstanceState()` and `onRestoreInstanceState()`.

The `onSaveInstanceState()` Callback

The `onSaveInstanceState()` callback is used for saving the status of the fragment into a `Bundle` object, which is then used while restoring the fragment. The following code saves the status of the fragment. It saves the value of the `selectedItem` variable into the `Bundle` under the `selectedfruit` key.

```
@Override
public void onSaveInstanceState(Bundle savedInstanceState) {
    super.onSaveInstanceState(savedInstanceState);
    savedInstanceState.putString("selectedfruit", selectedItem);
}
```

The `onRestoreInstanceState()` Callback

The `onRestoreInstanceState()` callback is for restoring the fragment to its earlier saved state. It uses the content in the `Bundle` that was used in the `onSaveInstanceState()` for getting the previously saved content of the fragment. The following code restores the fragment status. It retrieves the value under the `selectedfruit` key from the `Bundle` that was saved while calling `onSaveInstanceState()`:

```
@Override
public void onRestoreInstanceState(Bundle savedInstanceState){
    super.onRestoreInstanceState(savedInstanceState);
    selectedItem = savedInstanceState.getString("selectedfruit");
}
```

To understand how fragments are created programmatically, we create an application similar to our `FragmentsApp` application showing a `ListView` and `TextView` in landscape mode and only a `ListView` in portrait mode. When an item from the `ListView` is selected, its name is displayed through a `TextView`. Let's create a new Android project called `FragmentCodeApp`. Add two layout files, `fragment1.xml` and `fragment2.xml`, to the res/layout folder. The `fragment1.xml` file contains the code to display a `ListView` control, and `fragment2.xml` contains code to display a `TextView` control. The code in `fragment1.xml` is the same as that as shown in Listing 6.12. Similarly, the code written into `fragment2.xml` is the same as that shown in Listing 6.13. Write the code shown in Listing 6.23 into the main layout file of the application, `activity_fragment_code_app.xml`.

LISTING 6.23   Code in the Layout File `activity_fragment_code_app.xml`

```
<LinearLayout xmlns:android="http://schemas.android.com/apk/res/android"
    android:layout_width="match_parent"
    android:layout_height="match_parent"
    android:orientation="horizontal" >
    <LinearLayout
        android:id="@+id/fragment1"
        android:layout_weight="1"
        android:layout_width="wrap_content"
        android:layout_height="match_parent" />
    <LinearLayout
        android:id="@+id/fragment2"
        android:layout_weight="0"
        android:layout_width="wrap_content"
        android:layout_height="match_parent" />
</LinearLayout>
```

We can see that two `LinearLayout` elements are added to the layout file instead of the fragments. This is because we are adding fragments dynamically through code. The `Views` of the desired fragments are displayed through these `LinearLayout` containers. The `LinearLayout` elements are assigned the IDs `fragment1` and `fragment2`, respectively, to identify them in the Java code.

To load the `Views` of the two layout files defined in `fragment1.xml` and `fragment2.xml`, add two Java class files called `Fragment1Activity.java` and `Fragment2Activity.java` to the `com.androidunleashed.fragmentcodeapp` package of the application. To load the `Views` defined in `fragment2.xml`, the code that is written into `Fragment2Activity.java` is the same as that shown in Listing 6.15.

To load the `Views` defined in `fragment1.xml`, write the code shown in Listing 6.24 into the Java class file `Fragment1Activity.java`. Only the code shown in bold is new; the rest of the code is the same as Listing 6.20.

LISTING 6.24   Code Written into the Java Class File `Fragment1Activity.java`

```
package com.androidunleashed.fragmentcodeapp;

import android.view.View;
import android.view.LayoutInflater;
import android.app.Fragment;
import android.os.Bundle;
import android.view.ViewGroup;
import android.widget.ListView;
import android.widget.ArrayAdapter;
import android.content.Context;
import android.widget.AdapterView;
import android.widget.AdapterView.OnItemClickListener;
import android.widget.TextView;
import android.content.Intent;
import android.app.FragmentManager;

public class Fragment1Activity extends Fragment{
    protected static final String FRAG2 = "2";
    public View onCreateView(LayoutInflater inflater, ViewGroup container,     Bundle
savedInstanceState) {
        Context c = getActivity().getApplicationContext();
        View vw = inflater.inflate(R.layout.fragment1, container, false);
        final String[] fruits={"Apple", "Mango", "Orange", "Grapes", "Banana"};
        ListView fruitsList = (ListView) vw.findViewById(R.id.fruits_list);
        ArrayAdapter<String> arrayAdpt= new ArrayAdapter<String>(c,
android.R.layout.simple_list_item_1, fruits);
        fruitsList.setAdapter(arrayAdpt);
        final FragmentManager fragmentManager = getFragmentManager();
        fruitsList.setOnItemClickListener(new OnItemClickListener(){
            @Override
            public void onItemClick(AdapterView<?> parent, View v, int position,
long id){
                if(null!=fragmentManager.findFragmentByTag(FRAG2)){
                    TextView selectedOpt = (TextView) getActivity().findViewById(R.
id.selectedopt);
                    selectedOpt.setText("You have selected "+((TextView)
v).getText().toString());
```

```
                    } else {
                        Intent intent = new Intent(getActivity().getApplicationCon-
text(),   ShowItemActivity.class);
                        intent.putExtra("item", ((TextView) v).getText().toString());
                        startActivity(intent);
                    }
                }
            });
            return vw;
        }
    }
}
```

We want only the `View` of the first fragment, `ListView`, displayed in portrait mode, and
when an item from the `ListView` is selected, the name of the selected item is displayed on
the next screen. The new screen is created through a new activity. So, add a Java class file
called `ShowItemActivity.java` to the `com.androidunleashed.fragmentcodeapp` package
of the application. In the `ShowItemActivity.java` file, write the code as shown in Listing
6.21. As said earlier, to inform about the newly added activity file to the application, we
need to write a statement as shown in Listing 6.22 in the `AndroidManifest.xml` file. To
the main activity file of the application `FragmentCodeAppActivity.java`, write the code as
shown in Listing 6.25.

LISTING 6.25   Code Written into the Java Activity File `FragmentCodeAppActivity.java`

```
package com.androidunleashed.fragmentcodeapp;

import android.app.Activity;
import android.os.Bundle;
import android.app.FragmentManager;
import android.app.FragmentTransaction;
import android.content.res.Configuration;

public class FragmentCodeAppActivity extends Activity {
    private static final String FRAG1 = "1";
    private static final String FRAG2 = "2";

    public void onCreate(Bundle savedInstanceState) {
        super.onCreate(savedInstanceState);
        setContentView(R.layout.activity_fragment_code_app);
        FragmentManager fragmentManager = getFragmentManager();
        FragmentTransaction fragmentTransaction =fragmentManager.beginTransaction();
        if (getResources().getConfiguration().orientation == Configuration.ORIENTA-
TION_LANDSCAPE)
        {
            fragmentTransaction.add(R.id.fragment1, new Fragment1Activity(), FRAG1);
            fragmentTransaction.add(R.id.fragment2, new Fragment2Activity(), FRAG2);
```

```
        }
        else
        {
            if(null!=fragmentManager.findFragmentByTag(FRAG2))
                fragmentTransaction.remove(fragmentManager.findFragmentByTag(FRAG2));
            fragmentTransaction.add(R.id.fragment1, new Fragment1Activity(), FRAG1);
        }
        fragmentTransaction.commit();
    }
}
```

After we run the application, the output of the application is the same as that shown earlier in Figures 6.9 and 6.10.

> **TIP**
>
> Besides making a class extend a `Fragment` base class, the fragments are also created by making the class extend certain subclasses of the `Fragment` base class. Such fragments are known as *specialized fragments*.

Creating Special Fragments

After understanding the procedure to create simple fragments, we learn to create specialized fragments such as list fragments, dialog fragments, and preference fragments. To create these, we extend from the following subclasses of the `Fragment` base class:

▶ `ListFragment`

▶ `DialogFragment`

▶ `PreferenceFragment`

Creating a `ListFragment`

A `ListFragment` is a fragment that contains a built-in `ListView` that can be set to display items from a specified data source. The data source can be an array or a cursor. To understand `ListFragments`, let's create an application consisting of a `ListView` and a `TextView`. The `ListView` displays some items to choose from. The item selected from the `ListView` is displayed through a `TextView`. In this application, the `ListView` is displayed via a `ListFragment`, and the `TextView` is displayed via a simple fragment. The item selected from the `ListView` in the `ListFragment` is displayed through the `TextView` in the simple fragment. Let's name the new Android project `ListFragApp`. We first create a fragment to hold the `TextView` control. So, let's add an XML file called `fragment2.xml` to the `res/layout` folder of our project. Listing 6.26 shows how to define a `TextView` control in `fragment2.xml`.

LISTING 6.26   Code in the XML File `fragment2.xml`

```xml
<?xml version="1.0" encoding="utf-8"?>
<LinearLayout xmlns:android="http://schemas.android.com/apk/res/android"
    android:layout_width="match_parent"
    android:layout_height="match_parent"
    android:orientation="vertical" >
    <TextView
        android:id="@+id/selectedopt"
        android:layout_width="match_parent"
        android:layout_height="wrap_content"
        android:text="Please select a fruit" />
</LinearLayout>
```

We can see that a `TextView` control with the ID `selectedopt` is defined in a `LinearLayout` container. The initial text assigned to the `TextView` control is `Please select a fruit`. This `TextView` control is assigned text through Java code to indicate the item selected from the `ListView`.

To load the UI of the fragment from `fragment2.xml`, we need to create a Java class file. So, add a Java class file called `Fragment2Activity.java` under the `com.androidunleashed.listfragapp` package. Write the code as shown in Listing 6.27 into the Java class file, `Fragment2Activity.java`.

LISTING 6.27   Code Written into the Java Class File of the Second Fragment
`Fragment2Activity`

```java
package com.androidunleashed.listfragapp;

import android.app.Fragment;
import android.os.Bundle;
import android.view.ViewGroup;
import android.view.View;
import android.view.LayoutInflater;

public class Fragment2Activity extends Fragment {
    public View onCreateView(LayoutInflater inflater, ViewGroup container, Bundle
savedInstanceState) {
        return inflater.inflate(R.layout.fragment2, container, false);
    }
}
```

We can see that the Java class extends the `Fragment` base class. The `onCreateView()` method is overridden when a `LayoutInflater` object is used to inflate the `TextView` control UI that we defined in the `fragment2.xml` file.

We use `ListFragment` to display the `ListView` control. As I said earlier, the `ListFragment` already contains a `ListView` so we don't need to define a UI for this fragment. We can directly add a Java class file that extends the `ListFragment` class. In this Java class file, we write code to define the items to be displayed through the `ListView` of the `ListFragment` and also to display the item selected from the `ListView` through the `TextView` of the `Fragment2`. So, add a Java class called `Fragment1Activity.java` to the project and write the code shown in Listing 6.28 into it.

LISTING 6.28   Code Written into the Java Class for the First Fragment `Fragment1Activity.java`

```
package com.androidunleashed.listfragapp;

import android.app.ListFragment;
import android.os.Bundle;
import android.widget.ArrayAdapter;
import android.view.View;
import android.widget.ListView;
import android.widget.TextView;

public class Fragment1Activity extends ListFragment {
    final String[] fruits={"Apple", "Mango", "Orange", "Grapes", "Banana"};

    @Override
    public void onCreate(Bundle savedInstanceState) {
        super.onCreate(savedInstanceState);
        ArrayAdapter<String> arrayAdpt = new ArrayAdapter<String>(getActivity(),
android.R.layout.simple_list_item_1, fruits);
        setListAdapter(arrayAdpt);
    }

    @Override
    public void onListItemClick(ListView l, View v, int position, long id) {
        TextView selectedOpt = (TextView) getActivity().findViewById(R.
id.selectedopt);
        selectedOpt.setText("You have selected "+((TextView) v).getText().
toString());
    }
}
```

As expected, the Java class extends the `ListFragment` base class to create a `ListFragment`. To display content through the `ListView` of the `ListFragment`, an array called `fruits` is defined and fruit names are assigned to it. In the `onCreate()` method, an `ArrayAdapter` object called `arrayadpt` is defined to display the elements of the `fruits` array in the `simple_list_item_1` mode. When we use the `setListAdapter()` method, the content in the `ArrayAdapter` object, `arrayadpt`, is assigned to the `ListView` for display. As expected, the `onListItemClick()` method is invoked when any of the fruits displayed through the

ListView control is selected. In this method, we display the name of the selected fruit through the TextView control that we defined in fragment2.xml.

To accommodate both the fragments in the application, code is written into activity_list_frag_app.xml as shown in Listing 6.29.

LISTING 6.29   The activity_list_frag_app.xml Layout File After Adding Two Fragments

```xml
<LinearLayout xmlns:android="http://schemas.android.com/apk/res/android"
    android:layout_width="match_parent"
    android:layout_height="match_parent"
    android:orientation="horizontal" >
    <fragment
        android:name="com.androidunleashed.listfragapp.Fragment1Activity"
        android:id="@+id/fragment1"
        android:layout_weight="1"
        android:layout_width="wrap_content"
        android:layout_height="match_parent" />
    <fragment
        android:name="com.androidunleashed.listfragapp.Fragment2Activity"
        android:id="@+id/fragment2"
        android:layout_weight="0"
        android:layout_width="wrap_content"
        android:layout_height="match_parent" />
</LinearLayout>
```

We can see that the fragment1 and fragment2 fragments are added to the activity through the <fragment> elements. The fragments are set to refer to their respective Java classes through the android:name attribute. We don't have to write any code into the Java activity file of the application ListFragAppActivity.java. We leave the default code in the activity file unchanged, as shown in Listing 6.30.

LISTING 6.30   Default Code in the Java Activity File ListFragAppActivity.java

```java
package com.androidunleashed.listfragapp;

import android.app.Activity;
import android.os.Bundle;
import android.view.Menu;

public class ListFragAppActivity extends Activity {
    @Override
    public void onCreate(Bundle savedInstanceState) {
        super.onCreate(savedInstanceState);
        setContentView(R.layout.activity_list_frag_app);
    }
```

```
    @Override
    public boolean onCreateOptionsMenu(Menu menu) {
        getMenuInflater().inflate(R.menu.activity_list_frag_app, menu);
        return true;
    }
}
```

After running the application, we see the two fragments side-by-side, as shown in Figure 6.11 (left). The `ListView` on the left side appears through the `ListFragment`. The content in the `ListView` is displayed via the Java class file of the `ListFragment`, `Fragment1Activity.java`. The item selected from the `ListView` is displayed through the `TextView` defined in `Fragment2`, as shown in Figure 6.11 (right).

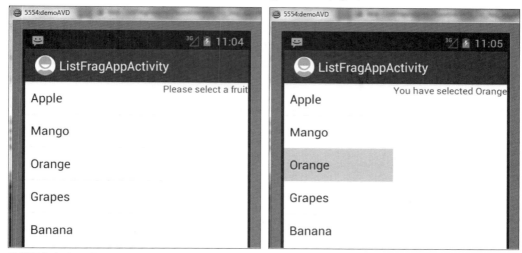

FIGURE 6.11   The `ListView` displayed via `ListFragment` (left), and the Item selected from the `ListView` of `ListFragment`, displayed via the `TextView` of the second fragment (right)

Using a `DialogFragment`

In Android, dialogs are asynchronous. Synchronous dialogs are those in which the activity suspends its execution until a dialog is dismissed. While the user is interacting with the dialog, no further execution takes place. Asynchronous dialogs are those in which activity continues its normal execution, and at the same time users can interact with the dialog. The activity accesses user interaction with the dialog by implementing callback methods. The dialogs in Android are `modal` in nature; while a dialog is open, users cannot access any other part of the application. The benefit of calling dialogs asynchronously is that it not only increases code efficiency, but also provides us with the capability to dismiss the dialog through code.

We can display a `DialogFragment` by extending the `DialogFragment` base class, which in turn is derived from the `Fragment` class. To demonstrate `DialogFragment`, let's create a new Android project called `DialogFragApp`. In this project, we use two fragments. One is used to show a `DialogFragment`, and the other displays a `TextView`. The user's interaction with the `DialogFragment` is conveyed through the `TextView` control in the second fragment. The selected button in the `DialogFragment` is displayed via the `TextView` control in the second fragment.

Before beginning the creation of `DisplayFragment`, let's first define the UI of the simple fragment that consists of a `TextView`. To do so, add an XML file called `fragment2.xml` to the `res/layout` folder. Write the code shown in Listing 6.31 into the `fragment2.xml` file.

LISTING 6.31   Code Written into the XML File `fragment2.xml`

```xml
<?xml version="1.0" encoding="utf-8"?>
<LinearLayout xmlns:android="http://schemas.android.com/apk/res/android"
    android:layout_width="match_parent"
    android:layout_height="match_parent"
    android:orientation="vertical" >
    <TextView
        android:id="@+id/selectedopt"
        android:layout_width="match_parent"
        android:layout_height="wrap_content"
        android:text="Select Open Dialog Button" />
</LinearLayout>
```

We can see that a `TextView` control is defined inside a `LinearLayout` container. The `TextView` is assigned the `selectedopt` ID and is initialized to display the text `Select Open Dialog Button`. This `TextView` is used to display the option selected by the user in the `DialogFragment`.

To load the UI of the fragment from `fragment2.xml`, a Java class file called `Fragment2Activity.java` is added to the project. Write the code shown in Listing 6.32 into the Java file `Fragment2Activity.java`.

LISTING 6.32   Code Written into the Java Class for the Second Fragment `Fragment2Activity.java`

```java
package com.androidunleashed.dialogfragapp;

import android.app.Fragment;
import android.os.Bundle;
import android.view.ViewGroup;
import android.view.View;
import android.view.LayoutInflater;

public class Fragment2Activity extends Fragment {
    @Override
    public View onCreateView(LayoutInflater inflater, ViewGroup container, Bundle
savedInstanceState) {
```

```
        return inflater.inflate(R.layout.fragment2, container, false);
    }
}
```

The Java class extends the `Fragment` base class. The `onCreateView()` method is overridden when a `LayoutInflater` object is used to inflate the `TextView` control UI that we defined in the `fragment2.xml` file.

To accommodate the fragment defined in `fragment2.xml`, we need to write code into the layout file `activity_dialog_frag_app.xml`, as shown in Listing 6.33.

LISTING 6.33   The Layout File `activity_dialog_frag_app.xml` After Adding a `Fragment` and a `Button`

```xml
<LinearLayout xmlns:android="http://schemas.android.com/apk/res/android"
    android:layout_width="match_parent"
    android:layout_height="match_parent"
    android:orientation="horizontal" >
    <fragment
        android:name="com.androidunleashed.dialogfragapp.Fragment2Activity"
        android:id="@+id/fragment2"
        android:layout_weight="0"
        android:layout_width="wrap_content"
        android:layout_height="match_parent" />
    <Button
        android:id="@+id/dialog_button"
        android:layout_width="match_parent"
        android:layout_height="wrap_content"
        android:text="Open Dialog" />
</LinearLayout>
```

A `Button` control is defined because we want the `DialogFragment` to appear only when a button is selected in the application. Both the `Fragment` and `Button` controls are nested inside the `LinearLayout` container. The `Fragment` is assigned the ID `fragment2` and is set to refer to its Java class through the `android:name` attribute. The `Button` control is assigned the ID `dialog_button`, and the caption as `Open Dialog`. `fragment2` is meant to display a `TextView` to show the option selected by the user in the `DialogFragment`.

Now it's time to write code to show a `DialogFragment`. As stated earlier, to show `DialogFragment`, a Java class needs to extend the `DialogFragment` class. Let's add a Java class called `Fragment1Activity.java` under the package `com.androidunleashed.dialogfragapp`. To display a `DialogFragment`, write the code shown in Listing 6.34 into the `Fragment1Activity.java` file.

LISTING 6.34   Code Written into the Java Class File of the First Fragment
Fragment1Activity.java

```java
package com.androidunleashed.dialogfragapp;
import android.app.DialogFragment;
import android.app.Fragment;
import android.os.Bundle;
import android.app.Dialog;
import android.app.AlertDialog;
import android.content.DialogInterface;

public class Fragment1Activity extends DialogFragment{
    static Fragment1Activity newInstance(String title) {
        Fragment1Activity fragment = new Fragment1Activity();
        Bundle args = new Bundle();
        args.putString("title", title);
        fragment.setArguments(args);
        return fragment;
    }

    @Override
    public Dialog onCreateDialog(Bundle savedInstanceState) {
        String title = getArguments().getString("title");
        Dialog diag = new AlertDialog.Builder(getActivity())
        .setIcon(R.drawable.ic_launcher)
        .setTitle(title)
        .setPositiveButton("OK", new DialogInterface.OnClickListener() {
            public void onClick(DialogInterface dialog, int whichButton) {
                ((DialogFragAppActivity) getActivity()).PositiveButton();
            }
        })
        .setNegativeButton("Cancel", new DialogInterface.OnClickListener() {
            public void onClick(DialogInterface dialog, int whichButton) {
                ((DialogFragAppActivity) getActivity()).NegativeButton();
            }
        }).create();
        return diag;
    }
}
```

We can see that to create the DialogFragment, the Java class extends the DialogFragment class. The newInstance() method is used to create a new instance of the fragment. The title of the DialogFragment is passed to this method as an argument, which in turn is stored in the Bundle object and is associated with the fragment that is returned by this method.

To create the view hierarchy of the `DialogFragment`, the `onCreateDialog()` method of
the `DialogFragment` class is overridden, and a `Bundle` object carrying the title of the fragment and other information, if any, is passed to it. In the `onCreateDialog()` method,
an alert dialog builder is used to create a dialog object. In the beginning of this chapter,
we learned that `AlertDialog` is a dialog window that displays a message with optional
buttons. In the `onCreateDialog()` method, an `AlertDialog` with two buttons, `OK` and
`Cancel`, is created, and the title that has to be displayed in the fragment is obtained
from the `title` argument saved in the `Bundle` object. An `onClickListener()` is associated with the two buttons `OK` and `Cancel`, which results in invoking the respective
`onClick()` method when the respective button is clicked. When `OK` is selected, the
`PositiveButton()` method from the activity is called. Similarly, when `Cancel` is selected,
the `NegativeButton()` method from the activity is called. The method returns the created
`AlertDialog`.

In the Java activity file, we need to write code to invoke the `DialogFragment`. The code
must be written to take the necessary action when `OK` or `Cancel` is selected from the
`DialogFragment`. The code written into the Java activity file `DialogFragAppActivity.java`
is shown in Listing 6.35.

LISTING 6.35   Code Written into the Java Activity File `DialogFragAppActivity.java`

```
package com.androidunleashed.dialogfragapp;

import android.app.Activity;
import android.os.Bundle;
import android.widget.Button;
import android.view.View;
import android.widget.TextView;

public class DialogFragAppActivity extends Activity {
    @Override
    public void onCreate(Bundle savedInstanceState) {
        super.onCreate(savedInstanceState);
        setContentView(R.layout.activity_dialog_frag_app);
        Button dialogButton = (Button)findViewById(R.id.dialog_button);
        dialogButton.setOnClickListener(new Button.OnClickListener(){
            @Override
            public void onClick(View arg0) {
                Fragment1Activity dialogFragment = Fragment1Activity.
newInstance("Continue Processing?");
                dialogFragment.show(getFragmentManager(), "Dialog Fragment Example");
            }
        });
    }

    public void PositiveButton() {
```

```
        TextView selectedOpt = (TextView)findViewById(R.id.selectedopt);
        selectedOpt.setText("You have selected OK button");
    }

    public void NegativeButton() {
        TextView selectedOpt = (TextView) findViewById(R.id.selectedopt);
        selectedOpt.setText("You have selected Cancel button");
    }
}
```

We want the `DialogFragment` to appear when the `Button` is selected from the application. So, we see that the `dialogButton` `Button` control is captured from the layout file and is mapped to the `Button` object `dialogButton`. An `OnClickListener` is associated with the `Button` control, and the `onClick()` callback method is called if the `Button` control is selected from the application. In the `onClick()` method, the `DialogFragment` is created by creating a `dialogFragment` instance of the `Fragment1Activity` Java class file, and the title of the `DialogFragment` is passed to it as `Continue processing`.

The `DialogFragment` is made visible by calling its `show()` method. The `show()` method adds the fragment to the given `FragmentManager`. The code also defines the two methods, `PositiveButton()` and `NegativeButton()`, which are invoked when `OK` and `Cancel` from the `DialogFragment` are selected. In both the `PositiveButton()` and `NegativeButton()` methods, the `selectedOpt` `TextView` control that we defined in `fragment2.xml` is accessed and mapped to the `TextView` object `selectedOpt`. When `OK` is selected, a message, `You have selected OK button`, appears in the `TextView` through the `selectedOpt` instance. Similarly, when `Cancel` from the `DialogFragment` is selected, a message, `You have selected Cancel button`, appears in the `TextView` of the second fragment.

After we run the application, a `TextView` and a `Button` control are displayed, as shown in Figure 6.12 (left). The `TextView` is displayed through `fragment2.xml`. The `TextView` displays the initial text `Select the Open Dialog Button`, directing the user to select the `Open Dialog` button. After we click the `Open Dialog` button, a dialog fragment with the title `Continue Processing` opens, showing two buttons, `OK` and `Cancel`, as shown in Figure 6.12 (middle). After we click the `OK` button from the `DialogFragment`, a message, `You have selected OK button`, is shown through the `TextView` control, as shown in Figure 6.12 (right).

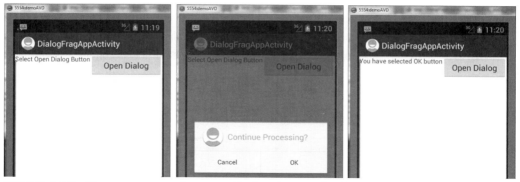

FIGURE 6.12 The `TextView` and `Button` displayed on application startup (left), the `DialogFragment` appears after clicking the button (middle), and the `TextView` showing that the `DialogFragment` `OK` button was clicked (right)

After we click the `Open Dialog` button again, the `DialogFragment` opens up once more. This time, if we select `Cancel` from the `DialogFragment`, the `TextView` displays the message `You have selected Cancel button`, as shown in Figure 6.13.

FIGURE 6.13 The `TextView` showing that the `DialogFragment` `Cancel` button was clicked

Using `PreferenceFragment`

`PreferenceFragment` is a fragment that enables users to configure and personalize an application. The `PreferenceFragment` can contain several `Preference Views` that help in uniformly setting application preferences with minimum effort. Table 6.1 shows the list of `Preference Views` that can be displayed via a `PreferenceFragment`.

TABLE 6.1 `Preference Views` That Can Be Displayed in `PreferenceFragments`

Preference View	Description
PreferenceScreen	The root element of the XML used to define a preference screen
CheckBoxPreference	Displays a simple check box that returns `true` when checkedh otherwise returns `false`

Preference View	Description
ListPreference	Displays a list of radio buttons allowing the user to select one
EditTextPreference	Displays a dialog with an EditText control allowing the user to enter text
RingtonePreference	Displays radio buttons indicating the ringtones available for selection
PreferenceCategory	Used in grouping related preferences in categories
Preference	A custom preference that acts like a Button control

To understand how application preferences are set, let's create a new Android project called PreferenceFragApp. There are two ways of displaying Preference Views in a PreferenceFragment: through an XML file and through code. We prefer the XML approach, so we first add a folder called xml to the res folder. Inside the res/xml folder, we add an XML file called preferences.xml. This file contains the Preference Views we want to display to the user to configure the application. The options selected by the user in Preference Views persist in the application. The code written into the preferences.xml file is shown in Listing 6.36.

LISTING 6.36 Code Written into XML File preferences.xml

```
<?xml version="1.0" encoding="utf-8"?>
<PreferenceScreen xmlns:android="http://schemas.android.com/apk/res/android" >
    <PreferenceCategory android:title="Category 1">
        <CheckBoxPreference
            android:title="Pizza"
            android:defaultValue="false"
            android:key="Pizzakey" />
        <EditTextPreference android:key="Namekey"
            android:title="Enter your name: "
            android:dialogTitle="Enter your information">
        </EditTextPreference>
    </PreferenceCategory>
    <PreferenceCategory android:title="Category 2">
        <RingtonePreference android:showDefault="true"
            android:key="Audio" android:title="Select sound"
            android:ringtoneType="notification">
        </RingtonePreference>
        <ListPreference android:title="Fruits List "
            android:key="fruits_list"
            android:entries="@array/fruits"
            android:entryValues="@array/fruitselected"
            android:dialogTitle="Choose a fruit">
        </ListPreference>
    </PreferenceCategory>
```

```
    <Preference
        android:title="Submit"
        android:key="submitPref" />
</PreferenceScreen>
```

We can see that the `Preference Views` are shown in two categories: `Category 1` and `Category 2`. `Category 1` includes two `Preference Views`: a `CheckBoxPreference` and an `EditTextPreference`. `Category 2` includes the `RingtonePreference` and `ListPreference`. Every `Preference View` needs to have an `android:key` value that is used to identify and access its value. The `android:title` attribute is used to assign initial text to the `Preference View`, and the `android:defaultValue` attribute is used to assign a default value to the `Preference View`.

The `CheckBoxPreference` displays a check box as its UI element, and it stores a value in Boolean form—either `true` or `false`. The value `true` is stored when the check box in `CheckBoxPreference` is selected, and `false` when the check box is not selected. The default value `false` is assigned to the `CheckBoxPreference` using the `android:defaultValue` attribute.

The `EditTextPreference` is assigned the `Namekey` key, and the title `Enter your name:` appears as the text of the `Preference View`. When the `EditTextPreference` is selected, a dialog titled `Enter your information` is displayed, asking the user to enter information. When the user clicks `OK`, the entered information is saved to the preference store.

The `RingtonePreference` opens a dialog box showing the list of ringtones, allowing the user to select a `default ringtone` or `silent` mode. The `key` assigned to the `RingtonePreference` is `Audio`, and the dialog box is assigned the title `Select sound`. The `android:ringtoneType` attribute helps in determining the list of ringtones to be displayed. Valid values for `android:ringtoneType` attribute are `ringtone`, `notification`, `alarm`, and `all`.

The `ListPreference` shows a dialog box listing a set of preferences in the form of radio buttons, allowing the user to select one of them. The dialog box is titled `Choose a fruit` and is assigned the key `fruits_list`. The `android:entries` attribute assigns a string array named `fruits` to the `ListPreference` to show the list of preferences. That is, the elements in the `fruits` array display text for the radio buttons displayed via the `ListPreference`. The `android:entryValues` attribute defines another array, `fruitselected`, to hold the values of the elements defined in the `fruits` array. The `android:entryValues` attribute represents an array that stores the values corresponding to the radio button selected by the user.

The `<Preference>` elements display a `Submit` button in the `PreferenceFragment` that users click after selecting the desired preferences from `Preference Views` to either store the preferences or perform another action. The `Submit` button is assigned the key `submitPref`, which is used to identify it in the Java code.

Next, we need to define two arrays in the `strings.xml` resource file: one to display text for the radio button in the `ListPreference` and the second to store the values of the corresponding elements in the first array. After we define the two arrays, the `strings.xml` file appears as shown in Listing 6.37.

LISTING 6.37   The Strings Resource File `strings.xml` After Defining the Two Arrays

```
<resources>
    <string name="app_name">PreferenceFragApp</string>
    <string name="menu_settings">Settings</string>
    <string name="title_activity_preference_frag_app">PreferenceFragAppActivity</string>
    <string-array name="fruits">
        <item>Apple</item>
        <item>Mango</item>
        <item>Orange</item>
        <item>Grapes</item>
        <item>Banana</item>
    </string-array>
    <string-array name="fruitselected">
        <item>You have selected Apple</item>
        <item>You have selected Mango</item>
        <item>You have selected Orange</item>
        <item>You have selected Grapes</item>
        <item>You have selected Banana</item>
    </string-array>
</resources>
```

The elements in the `fruits` array are used to display text for the radio buttons shown in the `ListPreference`, and the elements in the `fruitsselected` array show the values that are returned if the corresponding elements in the `fruits` array are selected.

To load the `Preference Views` defined in `preferences.xml`, a Java class file called `PrefActivity.java` is added to the project. Write the code shown in Listing 6.38 into the Java class file `PrefActivity.java`.

LISTING 6.38   Code Written into `PreferenceFragment` `PrefActivity.java`

```
package com.androidunleashed.preferencefragapp;

import android.os.Bundle;
import android.app.Activity;
import android.preference.Preference;
import android.preference.Preference.OnPreferenceClickListener;
import android.preference.PreferenceFragment;

public class PrefActivity extends Activity {
    public void onCreate(Bundle savedInstanceState) {
        super.onCreate(savedInstanceState);
```

```
            getFragmentManager().beginTransaction().replace(android.R.id.content, new
        PrefsFragment()).commit();
        }

        public static class PrefsFragment extends PreferenceFragment {
            @Override
            public void onCreate(Bundle savedInstanceState) {
                super.onCreate(savedInstanceState);
                addPreferencesFromResource(R.xml.preferences);
                Preference submitPref = (Preference) findPreference("submitPref");
                submitPref.setOnPreferenceClickListener(new OnPreferenceClickListener()
{
                    public boolean onPreferenceClick(Preference preference) {
                        getActivity().finish();
                        return true;
                    }
                });
            }
        }
    }
```

To create the `PreferenceFragment`, a Java class called `PrefsFragment` is defined that
extends the `PreferenceFragment` class. The `addPreferencesFromResource()` method
is called to load the `Preference Views` in the `PreferenceFragment` from the XML file
`preferences.xml`. The `Submit` button defined in the `preferences.xml` file through
the `<Preference>` element is accessed and mapped to the `Preference` object `sub-
mitPref`. An `OnPreferenceClickListener` event handler is added to the `submitPref`
object. Its callback method, `onPreferenceClick()`, is implemented, which executes
when the `submitPref Button` is clicked. In the `onPreferenceClick()` method, we
finish by closing the `PreferenceFragment` and returning to `PreferenceFragActivity.`
`java` to take necessary action on the selected preferences. Through the Java activity file
`PreferenceFragAppActivity.java`, we display the preferences selected by the user via
`TextView` controls.

To display the options selected from the `Preference Views` shown in the
`PreferenceFragment`, we need to define four `TextView` controls in the layout file
`activity_preference_frag.xml`. After defining the four `TextView` controls `activity_`
`preference_frag_app.xml` appears as shown in Listing 6.39.

LISTING 6.39   The Layout File `activity_preference_frag_app.xml` After Adding the Four
`TextView` Controls

```
<LinearLayout xmlns:android="http://schemas.android.com/apk/res/android"
    android:layout_width="match_parent"
    android:layout_height="match_parent"
    android:orientation="vertical" >
    <TextView
```

```
        android:layout_width="match_parent"
        android:layout_height="wrap_content"
        android:id="@+id/pizza"/>
    <TextView
        android:layout_width="match_parent"
        android:layout_height="wrap_content"
        android:id="@+id/name"/>
    <TextView
        android:layout_width="match_parent"
        android:layout_height="wrap_content"
        android:id="@+id/ringtone"/>
    <TextView
        android:layout_width="match_parent"
        android:layout_height="wrap_content"
        android:id="@+id/fruit"/>
</LinearLayout>
```

We can see that the four `TextView` controls are assigned the IDs `pizza`, `name`, `ringtone`, and `fruit`. The `TextView` controls are vertically arranged inside the `LinearLayout` container. The `pizza` `TextView` is used to indicate whether the user has checked the check box in the `CheckBoxPreference`. The `name` `TextView` is used to display the name entered by the user in the `EditTextPreference`. The `ringtone` `TextView` is used to display the type of ring tone selected by the user in the `RingtonePreference`. The `fruit` `TextView` is used to display the fruit selected by the user in the `ListPreference`.

To display the `PreferenceFragment` and show the preferences selected by the user, we need to write the code shown in Listing 6.40 into the main activity file `PreferenceFragAppActivity.java`.

LISTING 6.40   Code Written into the Main Activity File `PreferenceFragAppActivity.java`

```
package com.androidunleashed.preferencefragapp;

import android.app.Activity;
import android.os.Bundle;
import android.content.Intent;
import android.preference.PreferenceManager;
import android.content.SharedPreferences;
import android.widget.TextView;

public class PreferenceFragAppActivity extends Activity {
    @Override
    public void onCreate(Bundle savedInstanceState) {
        super.onCreate(savedInstanceState);
        setContentView(R.layout.activity_preference_frag_app);
        startActivity(new Intent(this, PrefActivity.class));
```

```
    }

    @Override
    public void onResume() {
        super.onResume();
        SharedPreferences prefs=PreferenceManager.getDefaultSharedPreferences(this);
        TextView pizza=(TextView)findViewById(R.id.pizza);
        TextView name=(TextView)findViewById(R.id.name);
        TextView ringtone=(TextView)findViewById(R.id.ringtone);
        TextView fruit=(TextView)findViewById(R.id.fruit);
        if(Boolean.valueOf(prefs.getBoolean("Pizzakey", false)))
            pizza.setText("You have selected Pizza");
        else
            pizza.setText("");
        ringtone.setText("The ringtone selected is "+prefs.getString("Audio",
"Silent"));
        name.setText("The name entered is "+prefs.getString("Namekey",""));
        String selectedFruit = prefs.getString("fruits_list", "Apple");
        fruit.setText(selectedFruit);
    }
}
```

To display the `PreferenceFragment`, its activity class, `PrefActivity.class`, is started. To show the preferences selected by the user in the `PreferenceFragment`, the TextView controls defined in the layout file `main.xml` are accessed and mapped to the `TextView` objects. The `pizza`, `name`, `ringtone`, and `fruit` TextViews are mapped to the `TextView` objects `pizza`, `name`, `ringtone`, and `fruit`, respectively.

To find the options selected in the `Preference Views`, a `SharedPreferences` object called `prefs` is created. To read the value of `CheckBoxPreference`, we access the shared preferences and call the `getBoolean()` method, passing the key of the `CheckBoxPreference` to it. When the `CheckBoxPreference` `Pizzakey` key is passed to the `getBoolean()` method of the `SharedPreference` instance, it returns `true` or `false`, indicating whether the check box in `CheckBoxPreference` is checked.

Thereafter, `EditTextPreference` is accessed by passing its `Namekey` key to the `getString()` method of the `SharedPreference` instance. Similarly, the `RingtonePreference` and `ListPreference` are accessed by passing their keys, `Audio` and `fruits_list`, to the `getString()` method of the `SharedPreference` instance. The preferences selected by the user in the `Preference Views` are displayed via `TextView` controls.

To make the newly added activity `PrefActivity.java` visible to Android, it is declared in `AndroidManifest.xml` by adding the following statement in it:

```
<activity android:name=".PrefActivity" android:label="@string/app_name" />
```

After running the application, we see the `Preference Views` defined in `Category 1` and `Category 2`. The `CheckBoxPreference` check box is unchecked by default. When the check box is selected, it is checked, as shown in Figure 6.14 (left). When the `EditTextPreference` with the text `Enter your name:` is selected, a dialog box titled `Enter your information` pops up. We can enter a name or cancel the operation by selecting `Cancel`. Let's enter `Troy` as shown in Figure 6.14 (middle), then click `OK` to go back to the `PreferenceFragment`. When `Select sound` is clicked and which represents `RingtonePreference`, a dialog box prompting the user to select a ringtone type is opened, as shown in Figure 6.14 (right).

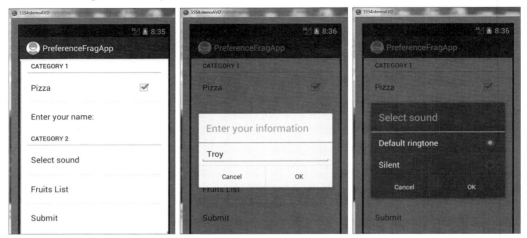

FIGURE 6.14   A `PreferenceFragment` showing different `Preference Views` (left), the `EditTextPreference` prompting for information (middle), and the `RingtonePreference` prompting to select a ringtone type (right)

Let's select a `Default` ringtone followed by clicking the `OK` button to return to the `PreferenceFragment`. After we select the `ListPreference` represented by `Fruits List`, a dialog box titled `Choose a fruit` opens up showing several fruits in the form of radio buttons, as shown in Figure 6.15 (left). Let's select `Orange`. On selecting a fruit, we automatically return to the `PreferenceFragment`. Finally, we click the `Submit` button at the bottom of the `PreferenceFragment` to close the fragment and display the selected preferences. All the selected preferences are shown through the `TextView` controls, as shown in Figure 6.15 (right).

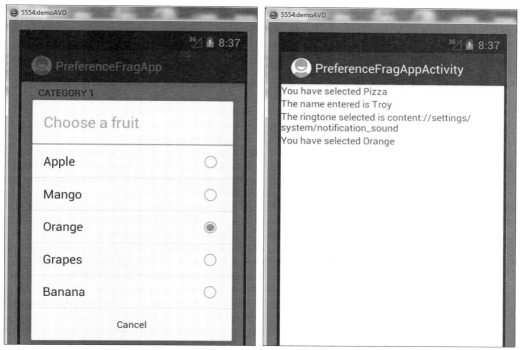

FIGURE 6.15   The `ListPreference` showing selectable fruits in the form of radio buttons (left) and all the selected preferences displayed via `TextView` controls (right)

Summary

In this chapter, we learned about dialogs and their different methods. We learned to use `AlertDialog` for displaying important messages to the user and getting input from the user. We saw how to display and select date and time through the `DatePicker` and `TimePicker` dialogs. We learned about fragments, their role in Android applications, their life cycle, and the procedure for adding them to an activity. We learned about the specialized fragments `ListFragment`, `DialogFragment`, and `PreferenceFragment`.

In the next chapter, we learn about different types of menus and how to create `Options Menus`, `Expanded Menus`, `Submenus`, and `Context Menus` with XML as well as Java code. We learn to handle menu selections, add shortcut keys, and assign icons to menu items. We also learn to use ActionBar, display Action Items, and create a Tabbed ActionBar and a DropDownList ActionBar.

PART III

Building Menus and Storing Data

CHAPTER 7

Creating Interactive Menus and ActionBars

In almost all applications we encounter menus that display options in the form of menu items. Choosing a menu item results in the initiation of the desired task. Menus are therefore the preferred way of indicating the possible actions in an application.

The ActionBar is a widget that replaces the title bar at the top of an Activity displaying navigation and important functionality of an application. It provides a consistent UI of an application. It also displays the key actions that are commonly used in an application and that are constantly visible on the screen. ActionBar is also commonly used to provide a quick link to an application's home.

Menus and Their Types

Android SDK supports three types of menus: Options, Submenu, and Context, as detailed in the following list:

▶ **Options Menu**—Also known as the `Activity` menu, this menu is displayed when a `MENU` button is clicked. In an `Options Menu`, the menu items are displayed in the form of text, check box, or radio buttons. It can display shortcut keys but does not display icons. In older Android API levels (Levels 10 and below), there were two types of `Options Menus`:

  ▶ **Icon Menu**—The `Icon Menu` appears when the user presses the `MENU` button on the device. The `Icon Menu` shows the first six menu items of the menu in the form of large, finger-friendly buttons arranged in a grid at the bottom of the screen. The menu items in the `Icon Menu` can display icons as well as text. The `Icon Menu` does not display check boxes, radio buttons, or the shortcut keys for menu items. It is not mandatory to have icons for `Icon Menu` items; text will also do for the `Icon Menu`.

▶ **Expanded Menu**—If the menu has more than six menu items, the first five items are displayed as an `Icon Menu` and the sixth option appears as a `More` button. Clicking the `More` button displays the `Expanded Menu` that shows the scrollable list of the rest of the menu items that could not be accommodated in the `Icon Menu`. The `Expanded Menu` can display menu items in the form of text, check boxes, or radio buttons. Also, it can display shortcut keys but does not display icons. Pressing the `Back` button from the `Expanded Menu` takes you back to the Activity the menu was launched from.

NOTE

The `Icon Menu` and `Expanded Menu` are not supported in Android API levels 11 and higher.

▶ **Submenu**—Submenu refers to the menu that displays more detailed or specific menu options when a menu item is selected. A submenu is displayed as a floating window showing all of its menu options. The name of the submenu is shown in the header bar, and each menu option is displayed with its full text, check box, radio button (if any), and shortcut key. Icons are not displayed in the submenu options. We cannot add a submenu to any menu option of a submenu as Android does not support nested submenus. Pressing the `Back` button closes the floating window without navigating back to the `Expanded` or `Icon` menus.

▶ **Context Menu**—The `Context Menu` is displayed when we tap-and-hold on the concerned `View` or when a user holds the middle D-pad button or presses the track-ball. `Context Menus` support submenus, check boxes, radio buttons, and shortcuts, but we cannot display icons in a `Context Menu`. In the `Context Menu`'s header bar, we can display a title and icon.

Creating Menus Through XML

Besides through Java code, in Android, menus can be created through `Resources` too. We can define a menu in the form of an XML file, which is then loaded by the Android SDK. As usual, Android generates `resource IDs` for each of the loaded menu items. The XML file for the menu has to be kept in a specific, designated folder that does not exist by default; we need to create it manually.

To understand the procedure of creating menus practically, let's create a new Android application called `MenuApp`. We see that a folder called `menu` already exists in our `res/` directory. The `menu` folder also contains a file `activity_menu_app.xml` by default. We learn to create all three types of menus: `Options Menu`, `Submenu`, and `Context Menu`. Let's begin with the `Options Menu`.

Creating an Options Menu

An Options Menu is the menu displayed when the MENU button on the device is clicked. It shows menu items in the form of text, check boxes, and radio buttons. Also, the shortcut keys can be assigned to the menu items. An Options Menu is defined through an XML file in the res/menu folder of the application. That is, the menu items of the Options Menu are defined in that XML file.

The activity_menu_app.xml file, which is automatically created for us, contains the following data:

```
<menu xmlns:android="http://schemas.android.com/apk/res/android">
    <item android:id="@+id/menu_settings"
        android:title="@string/menu_settings"
        android:orderInCategory="100"
        android:showAsAction="never" />
</menu>
```

We can see that the root node of our menu in the XML file is <menu>. The default menu item with the ID menu_settings shows the text that is defined in the strings.xml file. Let's define certain <item> nodes to display certain menu items. The code written in the activity_menu_app.xml file is as shown in Listing 7.1.

> **NOTE**
>
> Each <item> node represents a menu item in the menu file.

LISTING 7.1   The Menu Items Defined in the File activity_menu_app.xml

```
<menu xmlns:android="http://schemas.android.com/apk/res/android">
    <item android:id="@+id/create_datab"
        android:title="Create Database"
        android:icon="@drawable/ic_launcher" />
    <item android:id="@+id/insert_rows"
        android:title="Insert Rows"
        android:icon="@drawable/ic_launcher" />
    <item android:id="@+id/list_rows"
        android:title="List Rows" />
    <item android:id="@+id/search_row"
        android:title="Search"
        android:icon="@drawable/ic_launcher"/>
    <item android:id="@+id/delete_row"
        android:title="Delete" />
    <item android:id="@+id/update_row"
        android:title="Update"
        android:icon="@drawable/ic_launcher" />
</menu>
```

We can see that we have defined six menu items in the preceding menu, and a unique ID is assigned to each of them. The `android:title` and `android:icon` attribute defines the text and icon for the menu item. The menu items defined in our menu file are `Create Database`, `Insert Rows`, `List Rows`, `Search`, `Delete`, and `Update`. The six menu items are assigned the IDs as `create_datab`, `insert_rows`, `list_rows`, `search_row`, `delete_row`, and `update_row`, respectively. In the application, we want to display a message that asks the user to select the `MENU` button on the device or emulator for displaying the `Icon Menu`. We use the `TextView` control to display messages. To define `TextView`, we write the code as shown in Listing 7.2 in the layout file `activity_menu_app.xml`.

LISTING 7.2   The Layout File `activity_menu_app.xml` on Adding the `TextView` Control

```
<LinearLayout xmlns:android="http://schemas.android.com/apk/res/android"
    android:orientation="vertical"
    android:layout_width="match_parent"
    android:layout_height="match_parent">
    <TextView
        android:layout_width="match_parent"
        android:layout_height="wrap_content"
        android:id="@+id/selectedopt" />
</LinearLayout>
```

We added a `TextView` with the ID `selectedopt` to the default layout `LinearLayout` that we use to display desired text messages to the user. The `TextView` also is used to inform which menu item is selected by the user.

To inflate or merge the menu that we defined in the `mymenu.xml` file in our application and also to inform which menu item is selected by the user, we write the Java code as shown in Listing 7.3 in our Activity file `MenuAppActivity.java`.

LISTING 7.3   Code Written in the Java Activity File `MenuAppActivity.java`

```
package com.androidunleashed.menuapp;

import android.app.Activity;
import android.os.Bundle;
import android.view.Menu;
import android.view.MenuItem;
import android.view.MenuInflater;
import android.widget.TextView;

public class MenuAppActivity extends Activity {
    private TextView selectedOpt;

    @Override
    public void onCreate(Bundle savedInstanceState) {
        super.onCreate(savedInstanceState);
```

```
        setContentView(R.layout.activity_menu_app);
        selectedOpt=(TextView)findViewById(R.id.selectedopt);
        selectedOpt.setText("Please select MENU button to display menu");
    }

    @Override
    public boolean onCreateOptionsMenu(Menu menu) {
        MenuInflater inflater = getMenuInflater();
        inflater.inflate(R.menu.activity_menu_app, menu);
        return true;
    }

    @Override
    public boolean onOptionsItemSelected(MenuItem item) {
        switch (item.getItemId()) {
            case R.id.create_datab:
                selectedOpt.setText("You have selected Create Database option");
                break;
            case R.id.insert_rows:
                selectedOpt.setText("You have selected Insert Rows option");
                break;
            case R.id.list_rows:
                selectedOpt.setText("You have selected List Rows option");
                break;
            case R.id.search_row:
                selectedOpt.setText("You have selected Search Row option");
                break;
            case R.id.delete_row:
                selectedOpt.setText("You have selected Delete Row option");
                break;
            case R.id.update_row:
                selectedOpt.setText("You have selected Update Row option");
                break;
        }
        return true;
    }
}
```

We capture the TextView defined in the layout and assign it to a TextView object named selectedOpt. We use this TextView for displaying an initial message and for informing which menu item is selected by the user. The onCreateOptionsMenu() method of the Activity is called when the user clicks the MENU button of the device. So, we override this method to display our Icon Menu. To display our Icon Menu, we need to inflate or merge our menu that we defined in the activity_menu_app.xml file in the menu provided as a parameter to this method. Initially, there is no menu item defined in the menu parameter.

To inflate the menu that we defined in the `activity_menu_app.xml` file, we get the `MenuInflater` from the Activity class. An object, `inflater`, is created of the `MenuInflater` class and the inflater's `inflate` method is called to inflate, or merge, our own menu defined in the `activity_menu_app.xml` file to the `menu` given as a parameter to this method. The `onCreateOptionsMenu()` method is set to return the Boolean value `true` to allow Android to display the menu. By now, we have learned to display an `Options Menu` consisting of six menu items. But the menu is of no use if no action takes place on selecting its menu items. We have not yet assigned any task to the menu items of our `Options Menu`. Hence, the next step for us is to define the action to take place when the user selects any of the menu items.

Handling Menu Selections

All the menu items selected in the Activity's menu are handled through the `onOptions-ItemSelected()` method. The selected menu item is passed to this method as the `MenuItem` parameter. We override this method in the Activity to write the code that we want to execute when a menu item is selected. In the method, we extract the `Menu Item ID` of the menu item selected for identifying it and then can take the respective action. The `getItemId()` method helps in knowing the ID of the selected menu item.

The following code is part of the previous application and explains how the action is taken when a menu item is selected:

```
public boolean onOptionsItemSelected(MenuItem item) {
    switch (item.getItemId()) {
        case R.id.create_datab:
            selectedOpt.setText("You have selected Create Database option");
            break;
            ..........
            ..........
            ..........
    }
    return true;
}
```

The preceding method is automatically invoked when a menu item is selected from the menu. The selected menu item is passed to this method and assigned to the `MenuItem` object `item`. In preceding code example, `getItemId()` method is called to know the ID of the selected menu item, and through the `switch` statement respective action is taken on the selected menu item. In this code, we are setting a text message through the `TextView` object `selectedOpt` to inform the user which of the menu items is selected.

On running the application, we get a `TextView` showing the message `Please select MENU button to display menu` (see Figure 7.1—left). When we select the `MENU` button of the device or emulator, the `Options Menu` is displayed showing the respective menu items. When we select a menu item, say `Create Database`, the `TextView` responds by showing the message `You have selected Create Database option`, as shown in Figure 7.1 (right).

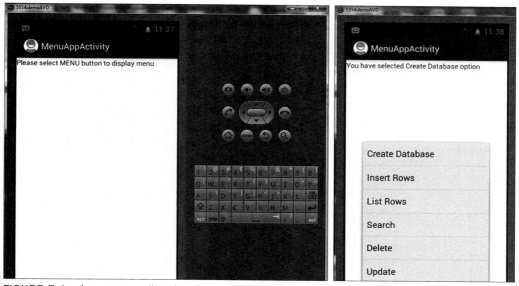

FIGURE 7.1   A `TextView` directing the user to select the MENU button to invoke a menu (left), and the `TextView` displays the option selected from the `Options menu` (right).

Similarly, when we select the `Delete` menu item, the `TextView` responds by showing the message `You have selected Delete Row option`, as shown in Figure 7.2.

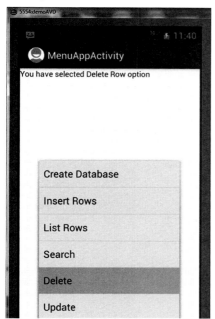

FIGURE 7.2   The message displayed through the `TextView` control changes on selecting another option from the `Icon` menu.

By now, we know how to display simple text as menu items and also how the menu selections are handled. We can also define check boxes, shortcuts, and radio buttons in menu items. Let's learn how.

Defining Check Boxes and Shortcuts

In this section, we learn how to define checkable menu items and shortcuts for them. We add more menu items to the menu in our application `MenuApp`. One of the newly added menu items will be checkable, and the other will be invoked with assigned shortcut keys. The menu file `activity_menu_app.xml` is modified to appear as shown in Listing 7.4. Only the code in bold is newly added; the rest of the code is the same as Listing 7.1.

LISTING 7.4   The Menu File `activity_menu_app.xml` After Defining Checkable Menu Items and Shortcuts

```
<menu xmlns:android="http://schemas.android.com/apk/res/android">
    <item android:id="@+id/create_datab"
        android:title="Create Database"
        android:icon="@drawable/ic_launcher" />
    <item android:id="@+id/insert_rows"
        android:title="Insert Rows"
        android:icon="@drawable/ic_launcher" />
    <item android:id="@+id/list_rows"
        android:title="List Rows" />
    <item android:id="@+id/search_row"
        android:title="Search"
        android:icon="@drawable/ic_launcher"/>
    <item android:id="@+id/delete_row"
        android:title="Delete" />
    <item android:id="@+id/update_row"
        android:title="Update"
        android:icon="@drawable/ic_launcher"   />
    <item android:id="@+id/sort_rows"
        android:title="Sort Table"
        android:checkable="true"
        android:checked="true"/>
    <item android:id="@+id/merge_row"
        android:title="Merge Rows"
        android:alphabeticShortcut="m"
        android:numericShortcut="4"/>
</menu>
```

We can see that the code now has eight menu items. The seventh menu item, `sort_rows`, is set to appear in the form of a check box via the `android:checkable` attribute. When we set the value of the `android:checkable` property to `true`, the menu item appears as a check box. The check box can be initially set to appear in either a checked or unchecked state by the `android:checked` attribute. When we set `android:checked="true"`, the menu item appears as checked by default.

Shortcut keys are assigned to the last menu item, `Merge Rows` (`merge_row`). When we set the `android:alphabeticShortcut="m"` attribute, the shortcut key `m` for the full keyboard is assigned to the menu item. Similarly, the `android:numericShortcut="4"` attribute assigns the shortcut key `4` from the numeric keypad. The shortcut keys are displayed below the menu item text. When the menu is open (or while holding the `MENU` key), if we press the `m` key from the full keyboard or `4` from the numeric keypad, the menu item `Merge Rows` is selected.

On running the application, we get a `TextView` showing the message `Please select MENU button to display menu`. When the `MENU` button of the device or emulator is selected, the `Options Menu` is displayed, showing respective menu items (see Figure 7.3). We can see that the menu item `Sort Table` appears as a checkable menu item. When we select any menu item, the respective text message is displayed on the screen. For example, if `Sort Table` is selected, the `TextView` responds by showing the message `You have selected Sort Table option`. If we press the `m` or `4` key while holding the `MENU` key, the menu item `Merge Rows` is selected (as shortcut keys are assigned to this menu item).

NOTE

Android API Level 10 and below categorize the `Options Menu` as an `Icon Menu` and an `Expanded menu`. If the menu items are less than or equal to six, the menu is called an `Icon Menu`; otherwise it is an `Expanded Menu`. An `Icon Menu` displays menu items in the form of icons and text, whereas the `Expanded Menu` displays menu items in the form of a scrollable list and shows only the menu items that could not fit in the `Icon Menu`. An `Expanded Menu` automatically appears when more than six menu items are defined in the `Options Menu`. When an `Icon Menu` with more than six menu items is displayed, a `More` button appears as a sixth menu item. When we select the `More` button, the rest of the menu items appear in the `Expanded Menu`. In the `Expanded Menu`, when we click the `Back` button we return to the Activity the `Icon Menu` was launched from. `Expanded Menu` items support check boxes, radio buttons, or shortcut keys; `Icon Menu` items do not.

FIGURE 7.3   The Options Menu showing the text and checkable menu items

While creating menu items, we may need a menu item with submenu items. Let's see how submenus are added.

Adding Submenus

A submenu is a collection of menu items invoked when a regular menu item is selected. Usually, a submenu represents more detailed options for the selected menu item. The submenu can be associated with any menu item. A submenu is created by enclosing `<item>` nodes within the `<menu>` node, where `<item>` nodes represent the submenu options and the `<menu>` node acts as the root node of the submenu. To associate a submenu with any menu item, just put the `<menu>` node of the submenu along with its nested `<item>` nodes inside the `<item>` node of the menu item to which we want to assign the submenu.

Let's add a submenu consisting of three menu items—Search on Code, Search on Name, and Search on Price—to the Search menu. To add a submenu to the Search menu item, activity_menu_app.xml is modified to appear as shown in Listing 7.5. The code in bold is newly added; the rest is the same as Listing 7.4.

LISTING 7.5   The Code in the Menu File activity_menu_app.xml After Adding a Submenu

```
<menu xmlns:android="http://schemas.android.com/apk/res/android">
    <item android:id="@+id/create_datab"
        android:title="Create Database"
        android:icon="@drawable/ic_launcher" />
```

```
    <item android:id="@+id/insert_rows"
        android:title="Insert Rows"
        android:icon="@drawable/ic_launcher" />
    <item android:id="@+id/list_rows"
        android:title="List Rows" />
    <item android:id="@+id/search_row"
        android:title="Search"
        android:icon="@drawable/ic_launcher">
        <menu>
            <group android:checkableBehavior="single">
                <item android:id="@+id/search_code"
                    android:title="Search on Code"
                    android:checked="true" />
                <item android:id="@+id/search_name"
                    android:title="Search on Name"
                    android:alphabeticShortcut="n"
                    android:numericShortcut="6" />
                <item android:id="@+id/search_price"
                    android:title="Search on Price" />
            </group>
        </menu>
    </item>
    <item android:id="@+id/delete_row"
        android:title="Delete" />
    <item android:id="@+id/update_row"
        android:title="Update"
        android:icon="@drawable/ic_launcher" />
    <item android:id="@+id/sort_rows"
        android:title="Sort Table"
        android:checkable="true"
        android:checked="true" />
    <item android:id="@+id/merge_row"
        android:title="Merge Rows"
        android:alphabeticShortcut="m"
        android:numericShortcut="4" />
</menu>
```

We can see that a submenu has been created, consisting of three menu items, Search on Code, Search on Name, and Search on Price, with the IDs search_code, search_name, and search_price, respectively. The submenu is assigned to the Search menu item by nesting its <menu> node within the <item> node of the Search menu item. If we want the menu items to appear as radio buttons, we need to nest them within the <group> node, as we have done with the menu items of our submenu.

The `<group>` node is used to collect certain nodes and for collectively applying attributes to all the nested nodes. The `android:checkableBehavior` attribute determines whether to make the menu items nested within the `<group>` node appear as radio buttons, check boxes, or as simple menu items. The attribute can take three values:

▶ **single**—Only one item can be checked at a time, producing radio buttons.

▶ **all**—Any item can be checked, producing check boxes.

▶ **none**—The item appears as simple text, without a check box or radio button.

We have defined an `Expanded Menu` and a `Submenu` for the `Search` menu item of our `Icon Menu` with the menu file `mymenu.xml`. Next, we need to write some Java code to add actions to the menu items defined in the submenu. So, in the `MenuAppActivity.java` Java Activity file, we add statements to the `onOptionsItemSelected()` method. These statements display messages showing which menu item from the `Expanded Menu` or `Submenu` has been selected. The Activity file appears as shown in Listing 7.6. Only the code in bold is newly added; the rest is the same as Listing 7.3.

LISTING 7.6   Code Written into the Java Activity File `MenuAppActivity.java`

```
package com.androidunleashed.menuapp;

import android.app.Activity;
import android.os.Bundle;
import android.view.Menu;
import android.view.MenuItem;
import android.view.MenuInflater;
import android.widget.TextView;

public class MenuAppActivity extends Activity {
    private TextView selectedOpt;

    @Override
    public void onCreate(Bundle savedInstanceState) {
        super.onCreate(savedInstanceState);
        setContentView(R.layout.main);
        selectedOpt=(TextView)findViewById(R.id.selectedopt);
        selectedOpt.setText("Please select MENU button to display menu");
    }

    @Override
    public boolean onCreateOptionsMenu(Menu menu) {
        MenuInflater inflater = getMenuInflater();
        inflater.inflate(R.menu.mymenu, menu);
        return true;
    }
```

```java
    @Override
    public boolean onOptionsItemSelected(MenuItem item) {
        switch (item.getItemId()) {
            case R.id.create_datab:
                selectedOpt.setText("You have selected Create Database option");
                break;
            case R.id.insert_rows:
                selectedOpt.setText("You have selected Insert Rows option");
                break;
            case R.id.list_rows:
                selectedOpt.setText("You have selected List Rows option");
                break;
            case R.id.search_row:
                selectedOpt.setText("You have selected Search Row option");
                break;
            case R.id.delete_row:
                selectedOpt.setText("You have selected Delete Row option");
                break;
            case R.id.update_row:
                selectedOpt.setText("You have selected Update Row option");
                break;
            case R.id.sort_rows:
                selectedOpt.setText("You have selected Sort Table option");
                item.setChecked(!item.isChecked());
                break;
            case R.id.merge_row:
                selectedOpt.setText("You have selected Merge Rows option");
                break;
            case R.id.search_code:
                selectedOpt.setText("You have selected Search on Code option");
                break;
            case R.id.search_name:
                selectedOpt.setText("You have selected Search on Name option");
                break;
            case R.id.search_price:
                selectedOpt.setText("You have selected Search on Price option");
                break;
        }
        return true;
    }
}
```

When the application is run, we see a TextView prompting us to select a MENU button, after which the Icon Menu is displayed. After we select the Search menu item from the Icon Menu, the Search submenu is displayed (see Figure 7.4—left). We can select a menu item from the submenu by either clicking it or using its shortcut key (if any). For example, if we select `Search on Code` as shown in Figure 7.4 (middle), the `TextView` responds showing the message, `You have selected Search on Code` option, as shown in Figure 7.4 (right).

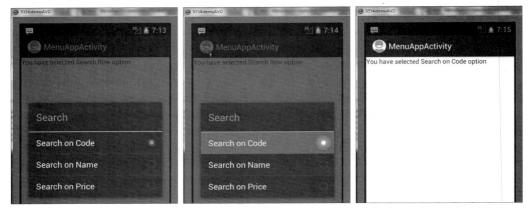

FIGURE 7.4   A submenu appears after selecting a `Search` menu item from the `Icon Menu` (left), selecting a menu item from the submenu (middle), and the text message displayed via `TextView` informs the menu item that was selected (right).

So, we created both an `Icon` and `Expanded Menu` and also defined a submenu. Let's create the last menu type, the `Context Menu`.

Creating a Context Menu

A context menu appears as a floating window and is displayed when the user taps and holds on a widget, holds the middle D-pad button, or presses the trackball. The difference between an options menu and a context menu is that the options menu is invoked when the `MENU` button is pressed. A context menu appears when we press and hold a `View`. An Activity can have multiple views, and each view can have its own context menu. An Activity can have only a single options menu but many context menus. Context menus are removed from memory when closed.

Let's define two context menus that we associate with two different `TextView` controls. For each context menu, we need to add a separate file to the menu folder of our project. Right-click on the `res/menu` folder and add two XML files called `mycontext_menu1.xml` and `mycontext_menu2.xml`. Let's define three menu items—`Cut`, `Copy`, and `Find`—in the first context menu. The code in `mycontext_menu1.xml` is shown in Listing 7.7.

LISTING 7.7   Code Written into the Context Menu `mycontext_menu1.xml` file

```xml
<?xml version="1.0" encoding="utf-8"?>
<menu xmlns:android="http://schemas.android.com/apk/res/android">
    <group android:checkableBehavior="all">
        <item android:id="@+id/cut_item"
            android:title="Cut" />
        <item android:id="@+id/copy_item"
```

```
                    android:title="Copy" />
        </group>
        <item android:id="@+id/find_item"
            android:title="Find">
            <menu>
                <item android:id="@+id/find_next"
                    android:title="Find Next" />
            </menu>
        </item>
    </menu>
```

The file shows that three menu items are added to the context menu. The first two are set to appear as check boxes by nesting them within the <group> node and applying the android:checkableBehavior attribute to them. We just learned that applying the value all to the android:checkableBehavior attribute makes the menu items nested in the <group> node appear as check boxes. A submenu consisting of a single menu item, Find Next (Find), is attached to the third menu item.

Let's define two menu items in the second context menu. The menu file of the second context menu, mycontext_menu2.xml, appears as shown in Listing 7.8.

LISTING 7.8   Code Written into the Context Menu mycontext_menu2.xml file

```
<?xml version="1.0" encoding="utf-8"?>
<menu xmlns:android="http://schemas.android.com/apk/res/android">
    <item android:id="@+id/open_item"
        android:title="Open"
        android:alphabeticShortcut="o"
        android:numericShortcut="5" />
    <item android:id="@+id/close_item"
        android:title="Close"
        android:checkable="true" />
</menu>
```

This context menu consists of two menu items titled Open and Close, respectively. To invoke the Open menu item, the shortcut keys o (full keyboard) and 5 (numeric keypad) can be used. The second menu item, Close, is set to appear as a check box by setting the android:checkable attribute to true. If we want to assign these two context menus to two TextView controls so that the respective context menu appears when we press and hold a TextView control, we have to write some code. Let's modify the layout file activity_menu_app.xml to add these two TextView controls, as shown in Listing 7.9. The newly added code is shown in bold; the rest is the same as in Listing 7.2.

```
<LinearLayout xmlns:android="http://schemas.android.com/apk/res/android"
    android:orientation="vertical"
    android:layout_width="match_parent"
    android:layout_height="match_parent" >
    <TextView
        android:layout_width="match_parent"
        android:layout_height="wrap_content"
        android:id="@+id/selectedopt" />
    <TextView
        android:text="View to invoke first context menu"
        android:layout_width="match_parent"
        android:layout_height="wrap_content"
        android:id="@+id/contxt1_view" />
    <TextView
        android:text="View to invoke second context menu"
        android:layout_width="match_parent"
        android:layout_height="wrap_content"
        android:id="@+id/contxt2_view"/>
</LinearLayout>
```

We can see that two `TextView` controls were initialized to `View to invoke first context menu` and `View to invoke second context menu`. The IDs assigned to these `TextView` controls are `contxt1_view` and `contxt2_view`, respectively.

Next, we need to write some Java code into the Activity file `MenuAppActivity.java`. To create context menus, we need to override the `onCreateContextMenu` method for registering the `Views` that are supposed to use it. The option to register a context menu to `View(s)` enables us to associate context menus for certain selected `Views`. A context menu is registered to a `View` through the `registerForContextMenu()` method (in the Activity file `MenuAppActivity.java`), as shown in the following code:

```
@Override
public void onCreate(Bundle savedInstanceState) {
    super.onCreate(savedInstanceState);
    setContentView(R.layout.main);
    selectedOpt=(TextView)findViewById(R.id.selectedopt);
    selectedOpt.setText("Please select MENU button to display menu");
    TextView contxt1View=(TextView)findViewById(R.id.contxt1_view);
    TextView contxt2View=(TextView)findViewById(R.id.contxt2_view);
    registerForContextMenu(contxt1View);
    registerForContextMenu(contxt2View);
}
```

We can see that the two `TextView` controls with the `contxt1_view` and `contxt2_view` IDs are captured from the layout file `activity_menu_app.xml` and mapped to the `TextView` objects `contxt1View` and `contxt2View`, respectively. The two `TextView` objects are passed to the `registerForContextMenu()` method, as we want to associate them with the two context menu just defined.

Once a `View` is registered, the `onCreateContextMenu()` method is invoked whenever we tap and hold on the registered `View`. The method also receives a `Menu` object as a parameter that we use to add menu items to it. To add menu items to a menu, the `add()` method is used. We need to override the `onCreateContextMenu()` method for displaying the context menu. The method receives the `menu` object as a parameter to which we add the menu items for the context menu. Besides the `menu` object, the method also receives the `View` object that initiated the context menu and a `ContextMenuInfo` object. `ContextMenuInfo` is an interface that belongs to `ContextMenu` and acts as an adapter for passing any other information about menu inflation.

The following code snippet is part of the application that creates the context menu. The `onCreateContextMenu()` method appears as shown here:

```
@Override
public void onCreateContextMenu(ContextMenu menu, View v, ContextMenu.ContextMenu-
Info menuInfo) {
    super.onCreateContextMenu(menu, v, menuInfo);
    if (v.getId()==R.id.contxt1_view) {
        MenuInflater inflater = getMenuInflater();
        inflater.inflate(R.menu.mycontext_menu1, menu);
        menu.setHeaderTitle("Sample Context Menu1");
        menu.setHeaderIcon(R.drawable.ic_launcher);
    }
    if (v.getId()==R.id.contxt2_view) {
        MenuInflater inflater = getMenuInflater();
        inflater.inflate(R.menu.mycontext_menu2, menu);
        menu.setHeaderTitle("Sample Context Menu2");
        menu.setHeaderIcon(R.drawable.ic_launcher);
    }
}
```

We can see that we first identify which `View` has initiated the context menu, and accordingly we inflate or merge the menu that we defined in `mycontext_menu1.xml` or `mycontext_menu2.xml` in the `menu` provided as the parameter to the `onCreateContextMenu()` method. To inflate the menu that we defined in the `mycontext_menu1.xml` and `mycontext_menu2.xml` files, we get the `MenuInflater` from the Activity class. A `MenuInflater` class object, `inflater`, is created and its `inflate` method is invoked to inflate, or merge, our own menu, defined in the respective XML file, with the `menu` parameter of this method.

Recall that the context menu supports check boxes, radio buttons, submenus, and shortcut keys, but not the icons. Two context menus are being created in the preceding code.

One is created if the user taps and holds the `contxt1View` TextView, and the other is created if the user taps and holds the `contxt2View` TextView. The `View.getID()` method is used to identify the `View` that is tapped and held. The first context menu displays two check boxes and a submenu. The second context menu displays two menu items; one is displayed with a shortcut key, and the other is displayed as a check box. The title and icon are set to appear in the context menu's header bar via `setHeaderTitle` and `setHeader-Icon`, respectively.

NOTE

Certain Android widgets provide their own default context menus containing various menu items. Hence, we call `onCreateContextMenu()` on its super class to handle menu items provided by the default context menu.

Handling Context **Menu Selections**

The preferred approach to handling menu items selected in context menus is to override the `onContextItemSelected()` method in the Activity that is automatically invoked whenever a `Context Menu Item` is selected. The menu item that is selected is passed to the method as a parameter, as shown in the following code:

```
@Override
public boolean onContextItemSelected(MenuItem item) {
    switch (item.getItemId()) {
        case R.id.cut_item:
            selectedOpt.setText("You have selected the Cut option");
            item.setChecked(!item.isChecked());
            break;
        ........
        ........
    }
    return true;
}
```

The `Menu Item ID` of the selected menu item is extracted through the `getItemId()` method, and accordingly the message is displayed through the `TextView` to display which context menu item is selected. We toggle the state of the checkable item through the `MenuItem.isChecked()` method. The method returns `true` if the menu item is checked; otherwise it returns `false`. We change the state of the menu item by passing a Boolean value that represents the reverse of the existing state.

The `MenuAppActivity.java` appears as shown in Listing 7.10. Only the code in bold is modified; the rest of the code is the same as we saw in Listing 7.6.

LISTING 7.10   Code Written into the Java Activity File `MenuAppActivity.java`

```java
package com.androidunleashed.MenuApp;

import android.app.Activity;
import android.os.Bundle;
import android.view.Menu;
import android.view.MenuItem;
import android.view.MenuInflater;
import android.widget.TextView;
import android.view.ContextMenu.ContextMenuInfo;
import android.view.View;
import android.view.ContextMenu;

public class MenuAppActivity extends Activity {
    private TextView selectedOpt;

    @Override
    public void onCreate(Bundle savedInstanceState) {
        super.onCreate(savedInstanceState);
        setContentView(R.layout.main);
        selectedOpt=(TextView)findViewById(R.id.selectedopt);
        selectedOpt.setText("Please select MENU button to display menu");
        TextView contxt1View=(TextView)findViewById(R.id.contxt1_view);
        TextView contxt2View=(TextView)findViewById(R.id.contxt2_view);
        registerForContextMenu(contxt1View);
        registerForContextMenu(contxt2View);
    }

    @Override
    public boolean onCreateOptionsMenu(Menu menu) {
        MenuInflater inflater = getMenuInflater();
        inflater.inflate(R.menu.mymenu, menu);
        return true;
    }

    @Override
    public boolean onOptionsItemSelected(MenuItem item) {
        switch (item.getItemId()) {
            case R.id.create_datab:
                selectedOpt.setText("You have selected Create Database option");
                break;
            case R.id.insert_rows:
                selectedOpt.setText("You have selected Insert Rows option");
                break;
            case R.id.list_rows:
```

```
                    selectedOpt.setText("You have selected List Rows option");
                    break;
            case R.id.search_row:
                    selectedOpt.setText("You have selected Search Row option");
                    break;
            case R.id.delete_row:
                    selectedOpt.setText("You have selected Delete Row option");
                    break;
            case R.id.update_row:
                    selectedOpt.setText("You have selected Update Row option");
                    break;
            case R.id.sort_rows:
                    selectedOpt.setText("You have selected Sort Table option");
                    item.setChecked(!item.isChecked());
                    break;
            case R.id.merge_row:
                    selectedOpt.setText("You have selected Merge Rows option");
                    break;
            case R.id.search_code:
                    selectedOpt.setText("You have selected Search on Code option");
                    break;
            case R.id.search_name:
                    selectedOpt.setText("You have selected Search on Name option");
                    break;
            case R.id.search_price:
                    selectedOpt.setText("You have selected Search on Price option");
                    break;
        }
        return true;
    }


    @Override
    public void onCreateContextMenu(ContextMenu menu, View v, ContextMenuInfo menuInfo)
    {
        super.onCreateContextMenu(menu, v, menuInfo);
        if (v.getId()==R.id.contxt1_view)
        {
            MenuInflater inflater = getMenuInflater();
            inflater.inflate(R.menu.mycontext_menu1, menu);
            menu.setHeaderTitle("Sample Context Menu1");
            menu.setHeaderIcon(R.drawable.ic_launcher);
        }
        if (v.getId()==R.id.contxt2_view)
        {
            MenuInflater inflater = getMenuInflater();
            inflater.inflate(R.menu.mycontext_menu2, menu);
```

```java
        menu.setHeaderTitle("Sample Context Menu2");
        menu.setHeaderIcon(R.drawable.ic_launcher);
    }
}


@Override
public boolean onContextItemSelected(MenuItem item) {
    switch (item.getItemId()) {
        case R.id.cut_item:
            selectedOpt.setText("You have selected the Cut option");
            item.setChecked(!item.isChecked());
            break;
        case R.id.copy_item:
            selectedOpt.setText("You have selected the Copy option");
            item.setChecked(!item.isChecked());
            break;
        case R.id.find_item:
            selectedOpt.setText("You have selected the Find Submenu");
            break;
        case R.id.find_next:
            selectedOpt.setText("You have selected the Find Next option");
            break;
        case R.id.open_item:
            selectedOpt.setText("You have selected the Open option");
            break;
        case R.id.close_item:
            selectedOpt.setText("You have selected the Close option");
            item.setChecked(!item.isChecked());
            break;
    }
    return true;
}
}
```

On running the application, we get three `TextView` controls. The first one is to tell the user to click the MENU button to display the menu. The second and third `TextView` controls are meant for invoking context menus. When the `TextView` controls are tapped and held, the respective Context Menu is displayed (see Figure 7.5—left). After we tap and hold the second `TextView`, a context menu titled Sample Context Menu1 is displayed, as shown in Figure 7.5 (middle). After we select the Find menu item from the context menu, a submenu, the Find SubMenu, is displayed, as shown in Figure 7.5 (right).

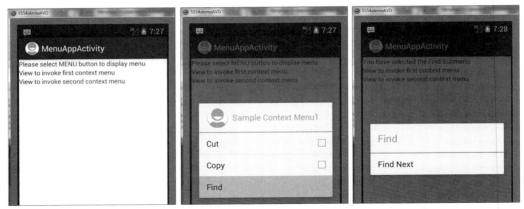

FIGURE 7.5   Three `TextView` controls showing different messages (left), the first `Context Menu` containing two check boxes that appear after pressing and holding the second `TextView` (middle), and a Find submenu appears after selecting a `Find` menu item (right).

After we tap and hold the third `TextView` that shows the text `View to invoke second context menu` (see Figure 7.6—left), a context menu, `Sample Context Menu2`, is displayed, as shown in Figure 7.6 (middle). After we select the `Open` item or press its shortcut key, the first `TextView` responds by displaying the message `You have selected the Open option`, as shown in Figure 7.6 (right).

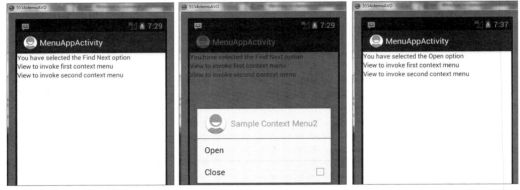

FIGURE 7.6   The first `TextView` shows that the `Find Next` option was selected from the `Find` submenu (left), the second context menu containing a menu item and a check box that appear after pressing and holding the third `TextView` (middle), and the first `TextView` shows that the `Open` menu option was selected from the context menu (right).

Let's create an application that demonstrates the creation of `Submenus` and context menus through coding instead of by using XML files. But before we do that, let's first look at the different methods that we will encounter.

Creating Menus Through Coding

As stated earlier, besides using XML resources, we can create the menus through Java code too. In this next section, we learn to create the three types of menus, Options Menu, Submenu, and Context Menu, with Java coding. We begin by defining Options Menus.

Defining Options Menus

To define an Options or Activity menu, we override the onCreateOptionsMenu method in the Java Activity file MenuAppCodeActivity.java. The method receives a menu object as a parameter, which is used to add menu items to it. To add menu items to the menu object, the add() method is used.

Here is the syntax:

```
add(Group ID, Menu Item ID, Sort order ID, Menu text)
```

The add() method requires following four parameters:

- ▶ Group ID—An integer used for grouping a collection of menu items.

- ▶ Menu Item ID—A unique identifier assigned to each menu item to identify it. Usually a private static variable within the Activity class is assigned to the menu item as a unique identifier. We can also use the Menu.FIRST static constant and simply increment that value for successive menu items.

- ▶ Sort order ID—Defines the order in which the menu items are to be displayed.

- ▶ Menu text—Text to appear in the menu item.

TIP

The group ID, Menu Item ID, and Sort Order ID parameters in the add() method are all optional, and we can use Menu.NONE in place of them if we don't want to specify any of them.

The following code adds a single menu item, Create Database, to the Options Menu:

```
private static final int CREATE_DATAB = Menu.FIRST;
menu.add(0,CREATE_DATAB,0,"Create Database").setIcon(R.drawable.ic_launcher);
```

We can see that the CREATE_DATAB is assigned a static constant, Menu.FIRST, and is used as a Menu Item ID in the add() method. In the add() method, we can see that Group ID is assigned the value 0. All the menu items that we want to be a part of this group are assigned the Group ID of 0. The CREATE_DATAB is assigned to Menu Item ID; the Sort order ID is 0; and the string Create Database is the menu item text. The setIcon() method assigns the ic_launcher.png image to the menu item from the drawable resource (the res/drawable directory).

> **NOTE**
>
> We can avoid the `setIcon()` method if we want only a menu item text without an icon.

Assigning Icons

We can assign icons to the menu items in the `Icon Menu` using the `setIcon()` method.

Here is the syntax:

```
menuItem.setIcon(R.drawable.icon_filename);
```

where `icon_filename` is a drawable resource identifier for the icon to be assigned to the menu item. Icons are only displayed in the `Icon Menu` and not visible in `Extended`, `Submenu`, and `Context` menus.

After we add all the menu and submenu items to the menu, the `onCreateOptionsMenu()` method is set to return the Boolean value `true` to allow Android to display the menu.

Creating Submenus

Submenus appear as single floating windows displaying all of their menu items. A submenu is attached to a regular menu item that, when selected, invokes the submenu, hence displaying all the menu items in it. A submenu is added through the `addSubMenu()` method. It supports the same parameters as the `add()` method used to add menu items in the `Options Menu`: Group ID, Menu Item ID, Sort order ID, and Menu Text. We can also use the `setHeaderIcon` method to specify an icon to display in the submenu's header bar and the `setIcon()` method to display the icon for the menu item to which this submenu is associated.

> **NOTE**
>
> Android does not support nested submenus.

The following code adds a submenu to a regular menu item, `Search`:

```
private static final int SEARCH_ROW = Menu.FIRST + 3;
SubMenu searchSub = menu.addSubMenu(0, SEARCH_ROW, 3, "Search");
searchSub.setHeaderIcon(R.drawable.ic_launcher);
searchSub.setIcon(R.drawable.ic_launcher);
searchSub.add(1, SEARCH_CODE, Menu.NONE, "Search on Code");
```

We can see that a submenu called `searchSub` is created for the regular menu item `Search`. The menu item `Search` to which the submenu `searchSub` is associated is assigned a group ID of 0. SEARCH_ROW, which is assigned the value of the static constant `Menu.FIRST+3`, is assigned as the `Menu Item ID`; 3 is assigned as the `Sort order ID`; and `Search` is assigned as the menu item text. The `ic_launcher.png` file in `Resources` is set to display in the submenu's header bar. The image `ic_launcher.png` is set to display as an icon in the

`Search` menu item, to which the submenu `searchSub` is associated. A menu item, `Search on Code`, is added to the submenu through the `add()` method.

Using Check Boxes/Radio Buttons in Menus

Android supports check boxes and radio buttons in menu items. To set a menu item as a check box, we use the `setCheckable()` method.

Here is the syntax:

```
setCheckable(boolean);
```

The menu item appears as a check box when the Boolean value `true` is passed to the `setCheckable()` method. The following code makes a menu item appear as a check box:

```
menu.add(3, CLOSE_ITEM, Menu.NONE, "Close").setCheckable(true);
```

By default, the check box is unchecked. To make the check box checked by default, we use the `setChecked()` method. By passing the Boolean value `true` to the `setChecked()` method, we can make the check box appear checked by default.

The following code makes a menu item appear as a checked check box by default:

```
menu.add(3, CLOSE_ITEM, Menu.NONE, "Close").setCheckable(true).setChecked(true);
```

Radio buttons are mutually exclusive menu items displayed as a circles; only one menu item can be selected in a group at any time. Selecting a radio button menu item unselects any other previously selected menu items in the same group. To create radio buttons, we need to make them part of the same group; hence we assign the same group identifier to all of them; then we call the `setGroupCheckable()` method.

Here is the syntax:

```
setGroupCheckable(int GroupID, boolean Checkable, boolean Exclusive)
```

where the `GroupID` refers to the group whose menu items we want to appear as radio buttons or check boxes. The second parameter, `Checkable`, should be set to `true` to make the check box or radio button appear as checkable. If we pass a `false` value to the `Checkable` parameter, then the menu items appear neither as check boxes nor radio buttons. The third parameter, `Exclusive`, determines whether we want the menu items to be mutually exclusive. If the `Exclusive` parameter is set to `true`, it means the menu items are mutually exclusive and only one can be selected at a time. So we set the parameter `Exclusive` to `true` if we want the menu items to appear as radio buttons. Passing the value `false` to the `Exclusive` parameter makes all the menu items in the group appear as check boxes.

The following code makes all the menu items of a submenu appear as radio buttons:

```
SubMenu searchSub = menu.addSubMenu(0, SEARCH_ROW, 3, "Search");
searchSub.add(1, SEARCH_CODE, Menu.NONE, "Search on Code").setChecked(true);
```

```
searchSub.add(1, SEARCH_NAME, Menu.NONE, "Search on Name");
searchSub.add(1, SEARCH_PRICE, Menu.NONE, "Search on Price");
searchSub.setGroupCheckable(1, true, true);
```

We can see that a submenu called `searchSub` is created and is associated with a menu item, `Search`. The `searchSub` submenu contains three menu items: `Search on Code`, `Search on Name`, and `Search on Price`. All three menu items are assigned the `Group ID 1`. All the menu items appear as checkable radio buttons, because the `Checkable` and `Exclusive` parameters in the `setGroupCheckable()` method are passed as `true`. The first menu item in the group, `Search on Code`, is set to appear as checked by default by passing the value `true` to the `setChecked()` method.

We can also assign shortcut keys to the menu items. Let's see how.

Assigning Shortcut Keys

The methods used to assign shortcut keys are `setShortcut`, `setAlphabeticShortcut`, and `setNumericShortcut`. Let's begin with `setShortcut` method:

▶ In the `setShortcut()` method, we can assign two shortcut keys through this method. One of the shortcut keys is used with the numeric keypad and the second with the full keyboard. Neither key is case sensitive.

Example:

```
menu.add(0,MERGE_ROW,7,"Merge Rows").setShortcut('4', 'm');
```

This code assigns shortcut keys for both modes to the menu item `Merge Rows`. The number 4 is used as the numeric keypad shortcut, and m acts as the shortcut key while using the full keyboard. This shortcut key also is displayed below the menu item text.

▶ The `setAlphabeticShortcut()` and `setNumericShortcut()` methods can be used to define the shortcut keys for the numeric keypad and full keyboard separately, as shown here:

```
menu.add(0,MERGE_ROW,7,"Merge Rows").setAlphabeticShortcut('m').setNumeric-
Shortcut('4');
```

We have seen all the methods required to define the `Options` menu, assign icons to the menu items, create submenus, make menu items appear as check boxes and radio buttons, and assign shortcut keys to the menu items. Let's apply all these methods to create a menu with Java code.

Trying It Out

We have seen all the methods required for defining Options Menus, Submenus, and Context Menus. Also, we have seen the methods required in assigning Icons, using check boxes/radio buttons in menus and assigning shortcut keys to the menu items. It's now time to try out all the knowledge that we have gained. Let's do it.

Create a new Android project called MenuAppCode. We want to display three Text View controls in the menu in the same way as we saw earlier in Figure 7.4 (left). The first TextView directs the user to click the MENU button to display the menu. The second and third TextView controls are used for displaying Context Menus. When the user taps and holds on either TextView control, a Context Menu appears on the screen. To display the three TextView controls, modify the layout file activity_menu_app_code.xml to appear as shown in Listing 7.11.

LISTING 7.11   The Layout File activity_menu_app_code.xml After Adding Three TextView Controls

```
<LinearLayout xmlns:android="http://schemas.android.com/apk/res/android"
    android:orientation="vertical"
    android:layout_width="match_parent"
    android:layout_height="match_parent">
    <TextView
        android:layout_width="match_parent"
        android:layout_height="wrap_content"
        android:id="@+id/selectedopt" />
    <TextView
        android:text="View to invoke first context menu"
        android:layout_width="match_parent"
        android:layout_height="wrap_content"
        android:id="@+id/contxt1_view" />
    <TextView
        android:text="View to invoke second context menu"
        android:layout_width="match_parent"
        android:layout_height="wrap_content"
        android:id="@+id/contxt2_view"/>
</LinearLayout>
```

In the code, we can see that the three TextView controls are assigned the IDs selectedopt, contxt1_view, and contxt2_view, respectively. To tell the user which Views are meant for displaying Context Menus, the TextView controls are set to display the text View to invoke first context menu and View to invoke second context menu, respectively.

To display the menu items in the Options menu, Submenu, and Context Menu, the Activity file MenuAppCodeActivity.java is modified as shown in Listing 7.12.

LISTING 7.12   Code Written into the Java Activity File `MenuAppCodeActivity.java`

```java
package com.androidunleashed.menuappcode;

import android.app.Activity;
import android.os.Bundle;
import android.view.Menu;
import android.view.MenuItem;
import android.widget.TextView;
import android.view.SubMenu;
import android.view.View;
import android.view.ContextMenu;

public class MenuAppCodeActivity extends Activity {
    private static final int CREATE_DATAB = Menu.FIRST;
    private static final int INSERT_ROWS = Menu.FIRST + 1;
    private static final int LIST_ROWS = Menu.FIRST+2;
    private static final int SEARCH_ROW = Menu.FIRST + 3;
    private static final int DELETE_ROW = Menu.FIRST+4;
    private static final int UPDATE_ROW = Menu.FIRST + 5;
    private static final int SORT_ROWS = Menu.FIRST+6;
    private static final int MERGE_ROW = Menu.FIRST + 7;
    private static final int SEARCH_CODE = Menu.FIRST + 8;
    private static final int SEARCH_NAME = Menu.FIRST + 9;
    private static final int SEARCH_PRICE = Menu.FIRST + 10;
    private static final int CUT_ITEM = Menu.FIRST + 11;
    private static final int COPY_ITEM = Menu.FIRST + 12;
    private static final int OPEN_ITEM = Menu.FIRST + 13;
    private static final int CLOSE_ITEM = Menu.FIRST + 14;
    private static final int FIND_ITEM = Menu.FIRST + 15;
    private static final int FIND_NEXT = Menu.FIRST + 16;
    private TextView selectedOpt;

    @Override
    public void onCreate(Bundle savedInstanceState) {
        super.onCreate(savedInstanceState);
        setContentView(R.layout.activity_menu_app_code);
        selectedOpt=(TextView)findViewById(R.id.selectedopt);
        selectedOpt.setText("Please select MENU button to display menu");
        TextView contxt1View=(TextView)findViewById(R.id.contxt1_view);
        TextView contxt2View=(TextView)findViewById(R.id.contxt2_view);
        registerForContextMenu(contxt1View);
        registerForContextMenu(contxt2View);
    }

    @Override
```

```java
    public boolean onCreateOptionsMenu(Menu menu) {
        menu.add(0,CREATE_DATAB,0,"Create Database").setIcon(R.drawable.ic_
launcher);
        menu.add(0,INSERT_ROWS,1,"Insert Rows").setIcon(R.drawable.ic_launcher);
        menu.add(0,LIST_ROWS,2,"List Rows");
        SubMenu searchSub = menu.addSubMenu(0, SEARCH_ROW, 3, "Search");
        menu.add(0,DELETE_ROW,4,"Delete");
        menu.add(0,UPDATE_ROW,5,"Update");
        menu.add(0,SORT_ROWS,6,"Sort Table").setCheckable(true).setChecked(true);
        menu.add(0,MERGE_ROW,7,"Merge Rows").setAlphabeticShortcut('m').setNumeric-
Shortcut('4');
        searchSub.setHeaderIcon(R.drawable.ic_launcher);
        searchSub.setIcon(R.drawable.ic_launcher);
        searchSub.add(1, SEARCH_CODE, Menu.NONE, "Search on Code").setChecked(true);
        searchSub.add(1, SEARCH_NAME, Menu.NONE, "Search on Name").setShortcut('6',
'n');
        searchSub.add(1, SEARCH_PRICE, Menu.NONE, "Search on Price");
        searchSub.setGroupCheckable(1, true, true);
        return true;
    }


    @Override
    public boolean onOptionsItemSelected(MenuItem item) {
        switch (item.getItemId()) {
            case CREATE_DATAB:
                selectedOpt.setText("You have selected Create Database option");
                break;
            case INSERT_ROWS:
                selectedOpt.setText("You have selected Insert Rows option");
                break;
            case LIST_ROWS:
                selectedOpt.setText("You have selected List Rows option");
                break;
            case SEARCH_ROW:
                selectedOpt.setText("You have selected Search Submenu option");
                break;
            case DELETE_ROW:
                selectedOpt.setText("You have selected Delete Row option");
                break;
            case UPDATE_ROW:
                selectedOpt.setText("You have selected Update Row option");
                break;
            case SORT_ROWS:
                selectedOpt.setText("You have selected Sort Table option");
                item.setChecked(!item.isChecked());
                break;
```

7

```
                case MERGE_ROW:
                    selectedOpt.setText("You have selected Merge Rows option");
                    break;
                case SEARCH_CODE:
                    selectedOpt.setText("You have selected Search on Code option");
                    break;
                case SEARCH_NAME:
                    selectedOpt.setText("You have selected Search on Name option");
                    break;
                case SEARCH_PRICE:
                    selectedOpt.setText("You have selected Search on Price option");
        }
        return true;
    }


    @Override
    public void onCreateContextMenu(ContextMenu menu, View v, ContextMenu.Context-
MenuInfo menuInfo)
    {
        super.onCreateContextMenu(menu, v, menuInfo);
        if (v.getId()==R.id.contxt1_view) {
            menu.setHeaderTitle("Sample Context Menu1");
            menu.setHeaderIcon(R.drawable.ic_launcher);
            menu.add(2, CUT_ITEM, Menu.NONE,"Cut");
            menu.add(2, COPY_ITEM, Menu.NONE, "Copy");
            menu.setGroupCheckable(2, true, false);
            SubMenu subcont = menu.addSubMenu(2, FIND_ITEM, Menu.NONE, "Find");
            subcont.add(3, FIND_NEXT, Menu.NONE, "Find Next");
        }
        if (v.getId()==R.id.contxt2_view) {
            menu.setHeaderTitle("Sample Context Menu2");
            menu.setHeaderIcon(R.drawable.ic_launcher);
            menu.add(3, OPEN_ITEM, Menu.NONE, "Open").setShortcut('5', 'o');
            menu.add(3, CLOSE_ITEM, Menu.NONE, "Close").setCheckable(true);
        }
    }


    @Override
    public boolean onContextItemSelected(MenuItem item) {
        switch (item.getItemId()) {
            case CUT_ITEM:
                selectedOpt.setText("You have selected the Cut option");
                item.setChecked(!item.isChecked());
                break;
            case COPY_ITEM:
                selectedOpt.setText("You have selected the Copy option");
```

```
            item.setChecked(!item.isChecked());
            break;
        case FIND_ITEM:
            selectedOpt.setText("You have selected the Find Submenu");
            break;
        case FIND_NEXT:
            selectedOpt.setText("You have selected the Find Next option");
            break;
        case OPEN_ITEM:
            selectedOpt.setText("You have selected the Open option");
            break;
        case CLOSE_ITEM:
            selectedOpt.setText("You have selected the Close option");
            item.setChecked(!item.isChecked());
            break;
    }
    return true;
}
}
```

In the `onCreate()` method shown in the preceding code, we can see that the `TextView` with the ID `selectedopt` is accessed from the layout file and is mapped to the `TextView` object `selectedOpt`. It is set to display the text `Please select MENU button to display menu`. The two `TextView` controls with the IDs `contxt1_view` and `contxt2_view` are registered for displaying a `Context Menu`.

The `onCreateOptionsMenu()` method defines the menu items for the `Options Menu` as well as for the `Search SubMenu`. The menu items defined for the `Options Menu` are `Create Database`, `Insert Rows`, `List Rows`, `Delete`, `Update`, `Sort Table`, and `Merge Rows`. The menu items defined for the `Search SubMenu` are `Search on Code`, `Search on Name`, and `Search on Price`. Shortcut keys are assigned for the `Merge Rows` menu item and the `Search on Name` menu item of the `Search SubMenu`. The `Sort Table` menu item is set as a checkable menu item. All the menu items of the `Search SubMenu` are set to appear as radio buttons.

The `onOptionsItemSelected()` method informs the menu item that is selected by the user. It displays the text message through the `TextView selectedOpt` to inform which of the menu options is selected by the user.

The `onCreateContextMenu()` method displays the two `Context Menus`. When the user taps and holds on any of the `TextView` controls with the IDs `contxt1_view` and `contxt2_view` the method displays the corresponding `Context Menu` on the screen. The `onContextItemSelected()` method does the job of informing us which menu item of the `Context Menu` is selected by the user.

The output of this application is the same as that shown earlier in Figures 7.2 through 7.5. We have learned that we can display different types of menus via XML files and Java coding too.

Applying a `Context Menu` **to a** `ListView`

We have seen the implementation of `Context Menus` to the two `TextView` controls (refer to Figures 7.4 and 7.5). Instead of having two `TextView` controls, let's try creating a `Context Menu` for a `ListView` control so that when the user taps and holds on any `ListView` item, information about that item is displayed.

To apply `Context Menus` to `ListView` controls, let's create a new Android application called `ContextMenuApp`. To display the `Context Menu` for the item selected from the `ListView`, let's add `Context Menu` files to the `menu` folder. Right-click on the `res/menu` folder in the `Package Explorer` window and select the `New, Android XML File` option. Enter the filename as `mycontext_menu1` (without the extension `.xml`). Keeping the `Root Element:` as `menu` (default), click the `Finish` button to create the context file `mycontext_menu1.xml`. Repeat the procedure to add one more context file called `mycontext_menu2.xml` to our `menu` folder. Write the code as shown in Listing 7.13 in the `mycontext_menu1.xml` file.

LISTING 7.13   Code Written into the Context Menu `mycontext_menu1.xml`

```
<?xml version="1.0" encoding="utf-8"?>
<menu xmlns:android="http://schemas.android.com/apk/res/android">
    <item android:id="@+id/cut_item"
        android:title="Cut" />
    <item android:id="@+id/copy_item"
        android:title="Copy" />
</menu>
```

The code in the second context menu file, `mycontext_menu2.xml`, appears as shown in Listing 7.14.

LISTING 7.14   Code Written into the Second Context Menu `mycontext_menu2.xml`

```
<?xml version="1.0" encoding="utf-8"?>
<menu xmlns:android="http://schemas.android.com/apk/res/android">
    <item android:id="@+id/open_item"
        android:title="Open" />
    <item android:id="@+id/close_item"
        android:title="Close" />
</menu>
```

We want to display a `TextView` and a `ListView` in our application. The `TextView` directs the user to take a desired action and tells the user which item from the `ListView` is selected by the user. The `ListView` control is used to display different items on the screen, which the user can tap and hold to invoke the related `Context Menu`. To display the `TextView` and `ListView` in our application, modify `activity_context_menu_app.xml` to appear as shown in Listing 7.15.

LISTING 7.15   The Layout File `activity_context_menu_app.xml` After Adding the `TextView` and `ListView` Controls

```
<LinearLayout xmlns:android="http://schemas.android.com/apk/res/android"
    android:orientation="vertical"
    android:layout_width="match_parent"
    android:layout_height="match_parent" >
    <TextView
        android:layout_width="match_parent"
        android:layout_height="wrap_content"
        android:id="@+id/selectedopt" />
    <ListView
        android:id="@+id/listvw"
        android:layout_width="match_parent"
        android:layout_height="match_parent"
        android:drawSelectorOnTop="false"/>
</LinearLayout>
```

To add an action, for example, to display the related `Context Menu` and information about the selected item, let's add the code shown in Listing 7.16 to the Activity file `ContextMenuAppActivity.java`.

LISTING 7.16   Code Written into the Java Activity File `ContextMenuAppActivity.java`

```
package com.androidunleashed.contextmenuapp;

import android.app.Activity;
import android.os.Bundle;
import android.view.MenuItem;
import android.view.MenuInflater;
import android.widget.TextView;
import android.view.ContextMenu.ContextMenuInfo;
import android.view.View;
import android.view.ContextMenu;
import android.widget.AdapterView;
import android.widget.ListView;
import android.widget.ArrayAdapter;

public class ContextMenuAppActivity extends Activity {
    private TextView selectedOpt;
    String[] fruits={"Apple", "Mango", "Orange", "Grapes", "Banana"};

    @Override
    public void onCreate(Bundle savedInstanceState) {
        super.onCreate(savedInstanceState);
        setContentView(R.layout.activity_context_menu_app);
        selectedOpt=(TextView)findViewById(R.id.selectedopt);
```

```
        selectedOpt.setText("Tap and hold a menu item to display its context menu");
        ListView myListView = (ListView)findViewById(R.id.listvw);
        final ArrayAdapter<String> arrayAdpt= new ArrayAdapter<String>(this,
android.R.layout.simple_list_item_1, fruits);
        myListView.setAdapter(arrayAdpt);
        registerForContextMenu(myListView);
    }


    @Override
    public void onCreateContextMenu(ContextMenu menu, View v, ContextMenuInfo menu-
Info)
    {
        super.onCreateContextMenu(menu, v, menuInfo);
        if(v.getId()==R.id.listvw) {
            AdapterView.AdapterContextMenuInfo info = (AdapterView.AdapterContext-
MenuInfo)menuInfo;
            if(fruits[info.position]=="Apple"){
                menu.setHeaderTitle(fruits[info.position]);
                MenuInflater inflater = getMenuInflater();
                inflater.inflate(R.menu.mycontext_menu1, menu);
            }
            if(fruits[info.position]=="Mango") {
                menu.setHeaderTitle(fruits[info.position]);
                MenuInflater inflater = getMenuInflater();
                inflater.inflate(R.menu.mycontext_menu2, menu);
            }
        }
    }


    @Override
    public boolean onContextItemSelected(MenuItem item) {
        AdapterView.AdapterContextMenuInfo info=(AdapterView.AdapterContextMenuInfo)
item.getMenuInfo();
        switch (item.getItemId()) {
            case R.id.cut_item:
                selectedOpt.setText("You have selected the Cut option of " +
fruits[info.position]+" menu");
                break;
            case R.id.copy_item:
                selectedOpt.setText("You have selected the Copy option of " +
fruits[info.position]+" menu");
                break;
            case R.id.open_item:
                selectedOpt.setText("You have selected the Open option of " +
fruits[info.position]+" menu");
                break;
```

```
            case R.id.close_item:
                selectedOpt.setText("You have selected the Close option of the " +
fruits[info.position]+" menu");
                break;
        }
        return true;
    }
}
```

When we run the application, a TextView and a ListView are displayed as shown in Figure 7.7 (left). When we tap and hold a list item, the related Context Menu appears. For example, when we tap and hold Apple, the Context Menu titled Apple appears with the menu items Cut and Copy, as shown in Figure 7.7 (middle). When we select a Context Menu Item, a corresponding message is displayed via a TextView. For example, when we select the Cut menu item from the Apple Context Menu, the TextView displays the message You have selected the Cut option of Apple menu, as shown in Figure 7.7 (right).

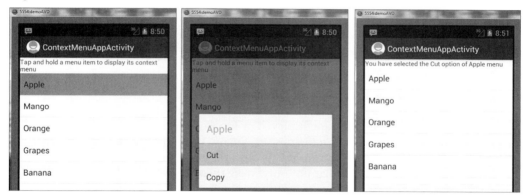

FIGURE 7.7   Items displayed through a ListView and on pressing and holding the Apple item (left), an Apple Context Menu appears and on selecting the Cut menu item (middle), and the TextView tells the user that the Cut menu item is selected from the Apple context menu (right).

Similarly, when we tap and hold Mango from the ListView, the Context Menu titled Mango appears with its menu items, Open and Close, as shown in Figure 7.8 (left). When we select the Close menu item from the context menu, the TextView displays the message You have selected the Close option of the Mango menu, as shown in Figure 7.8 (right).

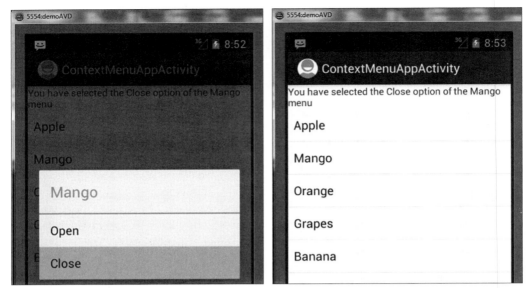

FIGURE 7.8   The `Mango Context Menu` appears on pressing and holding the `Mango` item in the `ListView` (left), and the `TextView` above the `ListView` tells the user that the `Close` menu item is selected from the `Mango Context Menu` (right).

We have learned the procedure of creating menus and their role in initiating different tasks. We have also learned the purpose of different menu types including the `Options Menu`, `SubMenu`, and `Context Menu`. The only drawback you might have observed while working with menus is that they are displayed or invoked on pressing the `Menu` button on the AVD or device. Now, the problem is that many Android devices no longer have a dedicated `Menu` button. The solution to this problem is using the ActionBar. Making the menu items appear in the ActionBar not only make them instantly accessible but also removes the need of pressing the `Menu` button to invoke them. Let's learn more about the ActionBar.

Using the ActionBar

The ActionBar is a widget that replaces the title bar at the top of every Activity displaying navigation and important functionality of an application. By default, the ActionBar includes the application logo on the left side, followed by the Activity title, and menu items (if any) on the right side. The ActionBar provides a consistent UI of an application. It helps in displaying the key actions commonly used in an application that we want to be visible on the screen while running the application. The ActionBar is also commonly used to provide a quick link to an application's home. The application's logo acts as a link to the application's home; that is, wherever we are in the application, if we tap the application logo displayed through the ActionBar, we navigate to the application's home.

NOTE

On Android 3.0 and higher, items from the `Options Menu` are presented by the ActionBar. It also means that beginning with Android 3.0, the `Menu` button is deprecated.

The ActionBar provides the following features:

▶ Customizes the title bar of an Activity.

▶ Follows its own life cycle.

▶ Consistently displays frequently used actions of an application. The menu items from the `Options Menu` are displayed in the ActionBar to be accessed instantly. The menu items displayed in the ActionBar are also called `action items`. The menu items that could not be accommodated in the ActionBar appear in the Overflow Menu. The menu items of the Overflow Menu can be seen by selecting the `Menu` button on the device or the `Overflow Menu` button in the ActionBar.

▶ Appears in three forms: standard, tabbed, and list.

▶ Makes it possible to use the application's icon or logo for navigation.

▶ Through the ActionBar we can even display Action Views, that is, custom views in the Activity's title bar. For example, we can display the search widget in the ActionBar.

The ActionBar includes the components as shown in Figure 7.9.

▶ **Application's Icon/Logo**—Displayed at the upper left on the ActionBar.

▶ **Activity Title**—Displays the title for the ActionBar.

▶ **Tabs**—Displays the tabs of the ActionBar if the navigation mode set is tabs.

▶ **Drop-Down List**—Displays the action items in the form of a drop-down list if the navigation mode set is list navigation. We learn about navigation mode soon.

▶ **ActionItems**—Displays the menu items of the Options menu in the ActionBar.

▶ **ActionViews**—Displays Custom Views in the ActionBar.

▶ **Overflow Menu**—Displays menu items that could not be accommodated in the ActionBar.

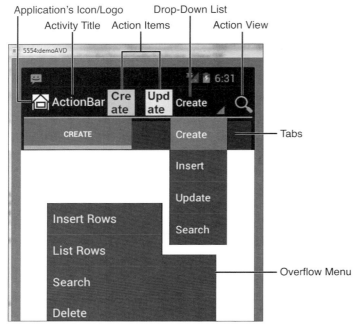

FIGURE 7.9   Different components displayed in an ActionBar

Enabling the ActionBar

The ActionBar is enabled if an application uses the default `Theme.Holo` theme and whose target (or minimum) SDK version is `11` or higher.

Example:

```
<uses-sdk android:targetSdkVersion="15" />
```

To toggle the visibility of an ActionBar at runtime, we can use its show and hide methods as follows:

```
ActionBar actionBar = getActionBar();
actionBar.hide();    // It  hides the actionbar
actionBar.show();    // Makes the actionbar visible
```

In the preceding code, the `getActionBar()` method is called to get an ActionBar object, and its `hide()` and `show()` methods are for hiding and showing the ActionBar, respectively.

To hide the ActionBar in an Activity, we can also apply a theme that doesn't support it. In the `AndroidManifest.xml` file, set the theme for the Activity to `Theme.Holo.NoActionBar` as shown in the following code:

```
<activity android:label="@string/app_name"
android:name=".ActionBarApp"
android:theme="@android:style/Theme.Holo.NoActionBar">
```

The icon or logo displayed in the ActionBar can be modified through the `android:icon` attribute in the configuration file `AndroidManifest.xml`. We can also use the `android:logo` attribute in the same file for the same purpose.

The visibility of the icon or logo in the ActionBar is controlled by passing a Boolean value to the `setDisplayShowHomeEnabled()` method.

The following statement hides the logo or icon in the ActionBar:

```
actionBar.setDisplayShowHomeEnabled(false);
```

The following statement makes the logo or icon visible in the ActionBar:

```
actionBar.setDisplayShowHomeEnabled(true);
```

Similarly, the visibility of the title in the ActionBar can be controlled by passing a Boolean value to the `setDisplayShowTitleEnabled()` method.

The following statement hides the title in the ActionBar:

```
actionBar.setDisplayShowTitleEnabled(false);
```

The following statement shows the title in the ActionBar:

```
actionBar.setDisplayShowTitleEnabled(true);
```

Using an Application's Icon for Navigation

The logo or icon displayed in an ActionBar if clicked navigates you to the home of the application. "Home of the application" here means the application's main Activity, that is, the root of our Activity stack.

By default, the logo or icon displayed in the ActionBar is nonclickable. To make the logo or icon clickable, we must call the ActionBar's `setHomeButtonEnabled()` method, passing the Boolean value `true` to it as shown here:

```
actionBar.setHomeButtonEnabled(true);
```

Clicking the logo or icon is considered a Menu Item click. Like Menu Item clicks are handled by the `onOptionsItemSelected` handler of our Activity; the logo or icon clicks too are handled by the same method. When the logo or icon is clicked, it is considered that a Menu Item with the ID `android.R.id.home` is clicked. In other words, when we click the logo or icon, the `onOptionItemSelected()` method is called passing the Menu Item with the ID `android.R.id.home` to it as a parameter as shown here:

```
@Override
public boolean onOptionsItemSelected(MenuItem item) {
    switch (item.getItemId()) {
        case  (android.R.id.home) :
            Intent intent = new Intent(this, DemoActionBarActivity.class);
            intent.addFlags(Intent.FLAG_ACTIVITY_CLEAR_TOP);
            startActivity(intent);
            break;
        default:
            return super.onOptionsItemSelected(item);
    }
    return true;
}
```

For navigating to the home Activity, we use an intent flag, FLAG_ACTIVITY_CLEAR_TOP, that clears the stack of all activities on top of the home Activity as shown in the preceding code.

Displaying Action Items

To display menu items in the ActionBar as action items, we need to add an android:showAsAction attribute to the menu items while defining them in the menu file. The showAsAction attribute determines how to display the action item. The value of the showAsAction attribute can be any one of the following:

- ▶ **always**—Makes the action item appear on the ActionBar.

- ▶ **ifRoom**—Makes the action item appear in the ActionBar, but only if there is room available on the ActionBar. If there's not enough room, the item appears in the Overflow Menu.

- ▶ **never**—Makes the menu item appear in the Overflow Menu.

To display the Overflow Menu, press the Menu button on the AVD or a soft options menu button that appears as three vertical dots on the physical device.

We need to understand the concept of the ActionBar through a running application. So, let's create a new Android project called DemoActionBar. In this application, we create six Button controls that are used to show/hide the ActionBar, the application's logo, and Activity's title bar. Besides this, the application displays an action item called Create, which when selected navigates us to a new Activity, CreateActivity. From the new Activity, when we select the application's logo, we are navigated back to the main Activity. The application also displays an ActionView in the form of a search widget.

After we create the project, the first thing we do is to define six Button controls in the layout file activity_demo_action_bar.xml. These six Button controls are used to show/hide the ActionBar, the application's logo, and the Activity's title bar, respectively. The code written in the layout file activity_demo_action_bar.xml is as shown in Listing 7.17.

LISTING 7.17   Code Written into the Layout File `activity_demo_action_bar.xml`

```xml
<LinearLayout xmlns:android="http://schemas.android.com/apk/res/android"
    android:layout_width="match_parent"
    android:layout_height="match_parent"
    android:orientation="vertical" >
    <Button
        android:layout_width="match_parent"
        android:layout_height="wrap_content"
        android:id="@+id/show_action"
        android:text="Show ActionBar"/>
    <Button
        android:layout_width="match_parent"
        android:layout_height="wrap_content"
        android:id="@+id/hide_action"
        android:text="Hide ActionBar"/>
    <Button
        android:layout_width="match_parent"
        android:layout_height="wrap_content"
        android:id="@+id/show_title"
        android:text="Show Title"/>
    <Button
        android:layout_width="match_parent"
        android:layout_height="wrap_content"
        android:id="@+id/hide_title"
        android:text="Hide Title"/>
    <Button
        android:layout_width="match_parent"
        android:layout_height="wrap_content"
        android:id="@+id/show_logo"
        android:text="Show Logo"/>
    <Button
        android:layout_width="match_parent"
        android:layout_height="wrap_content"
        android:id="@+id/hide_logo"
        android:text="Hide Logo"/>
</LinearLayout>
```

We can see that the `Button` controls are assigned the IDs `show_action`, `hide_action`, `show_title`, `hide_title`, `show_logo`, and `hide_logo`. Also, the caption assigned to the `Button` controls signifies the task they are supposed to perform. The captions assigned to the Button controls are `Show ActionBar`, `Hide ActionBar`, `Show Title`, `Hide Title`, `Show Logo`, and `Hide Logo`.

Next, we need to define an action item, `Create`, in our application. This action item when selected navigates us to the new Activity in the application. The action item is nothing but the menu item from the `Options Menu` that is displayed in the ActionBar to be accessed instantly. We can define action items in the menu file `activity_demo_action_bar.xml` that is provided by default in the `res/menu` folder of our application. In the menu file, we define two menu items, `Create` and `Search`, where `Create` is displayed in the `ActionBar` as an action item, and `Search` is used to display a search widget in the form of `ActionView`. The `activity_demo_action_bar.xml` file, after defining the two menu items in an `Options Menu`, appears as shown in Listing 7.18.

LISTING 7.18   Code Written into the Menu File `activity_demo_action_bar.xml`

```
<menu xmlns:android="http://schemas.android.com/apk/res/android" >
    <item android:id="@+id/create_datab"
        android:title="Create"
        android:icon="@drawable/create"
        android:orderInCategory="0"
        android:showAsAction="ifRoom|withText" />
    <item android:id="@+id/menu_search"
        android:title="Search"
        android:showAsAction="always"
        android:actionViewClass="android.widget.SearchView"/>
</menu>
```

Because we want to represent the action item `Create` via an icon, an image file, `create.png`, should be copied to the `res/drawable` folders of the application.

On selecting the `Create` action item, we want to navigate to a new Activity. To define `Views` for the new Activity, we need to add an XML file to the `res/layout` folder. So, right-click the `layout` folder in the `Package Explorer` window and select the `New, Android XML File` option. In the dialog box that pops up, specify the filename as `create` and select the `Root Element` as `LinearLayout` as we want the container of this XML file to be `LinearLayout`. Finally, select the `Finish` button to create the XML file called `create.xml`.

When we navigate to the new Activity, we want to display a text message informing that we have navigated to the new Activity. For displaying a text message, we define a `TextView` control in the new Activity's layout file, `create.xml`. The layout file `create.xml`, after defining the `TextView` control, appears as shown in Listing 7.19.

LISTING 7.19   Code Written into the Layout File `create.xml`

```
<?xml version="1.0" encoding="utf-8"?>
<LinearLayout xmlns:android="http://schemas.android.com/apk/res/android"
    android:layout_width="match_parent"
    android:layout_height="match_parent"
    android:orientation="vertical" >
    <TextView
        android:layout_width="match_parent"
        android:layout_height="wrap_content"
```

```
        android:text="This is Create Activity"
        android:textStyle="bold" />"
</LinearLayout>
```

We can see that the preceding layout file defines a `TextView` control with the initial text, `"This is Create Activity"`. The text message is displayed when we navigate to the new Activity.

After defining the layout file `create.xml` for the new Activity, we need a Java class file to load the `Views` defined in the layout file. So, add a Java class file called `CreateActivity.java` to the package `com.androidunleashed.demoactionbar` of our application. In the `CreateActivity.java` file, we need to write code to perform the following tasks:

▶ Load the `Views` defined in the `create.xml` file.

▶ Make the application's logo clickable. Remember, we want the user to be taken to the main Activity of the application on selecting the application's logo.

▶ Navigate to the main Activity file, `DemoActionBarActivity.class`, of the application.

For performing all these tasks, we write the code as shown in Listing 7.20 in the file `CreateActivity.java`.

LISTING 7.20   Code Written into the New Activity File `CreateActivity.java`

```
package com.androidunleashed.demoactionbar;

import android.app.ActionBar;
import android.app.Activity;
import android.content.Intent;
import android.os.Bundle;
import android.view.MenuItem;

public class CreateActivity extends Activity {

    @Override
    protected void onCreate(Bundle savedInstanceState){
        super.onCreate(savedInstanceState);
        setContentView(R.layout.create);
        ActionBar actionBar = getActionBar();
        actionBar.setHomeButtonEnabled(true);
    }

    @Override
    public boolean onOptionsItemSelected(MenuItem item) {
        switch (item.getItemId()) {
            case  (android.R.id.home) :
                Intent intent = new Intent(this, DemoActionBarActivity.class);
```

```
                intent.addFlags(Intent.FLAG_ACTIVITY_CLEAR_TOP);
                startActivity(intent);
                break;
            default:
                return super.onOptionsItemSelected(item);
        }
        return true;
    }
}
```

In the preceding code, we can see that an `ActionBar` object, `actionBar`, is accessed by calling the `getActionBar()` method and then the Boolean value `true` is passed to the `setHomeButtonEnabled()` method to make the application's logo clickable. Clicking the application's logo generates a click event on a menu item with the ID `android.R.id.home`. In the handler method `onOptionsItemSelected()`, we check whether the menu item with the ID `android.R.id.home` is clicked, that is, whether the application's logo is clicked. If the application's logo is found to be clicked, we navigate back to the main Activity of the application, `DemoActionBarActivity.class`, by clearing all the activities (if any) on the top of the stack. For clearing all the top activities, we use an intent flag, `FLAG_ACTIVITY_CLEAR_TOP`.

We know that no Activity is visible to the Android application until it is mentioned in the configuration file `AndroidManifest.xml`. To make the newly added Activity `CreateActivity.java` visible to the Android project, a statement is written in the `AndroidManifest.xml` file. Also, to replace the default application's logo with a new logo, we need to write code as shown in Listing 7.21 in the `AndroidManifest.xml` file. Only the statements in bold are added; the rest is the default code.

LISTING 7.21   Code Written into the Configuration File `AndroidManifest.xml`

```
<manifest xmlns:android="http://schemas.android.com/apk/res/android"
    package="com.androidunleashed.DemoActionBar"
    android:versionCode="1"
    android:versionName="1.0" >
    <uses-sdk
        android:minSdkVersion="11"
        android:targetSdkVersion="15" />
    <application
        android:icon="@drawable/home"
        android:label="@string/app_name"
        android:theme="@style/AppTheme" >
        <activity
            android:name=".DemoActionBarActivity"
            android:label="@string/title_activity_demo_action_bar" >
            <intent-filter>
                <action android:name="android.intent.action.MAIN" />
```

```
              <category android:name="android.intent.category.LAUNCHER" />
          </intent-filter>
      </activity>
      <activity android:name=".CreateActivity" android:label="@string/app_name" />
  </application>
</manifest>
```

To display our application's logo, we need to copy an image, `home.png`, to the `res/draw-able` folders of our application. The statements added to the `AndroidManifest.xml` file replace the default application's logo with the image `home.png` supplied by us. Also the code makes the newly added Activity, `CreateActivity.class`, visible to the rest of the application. To enable the ActionBar, the minimum SDK version, that is, the value of the `android:minSdkVersion` attribute, is set to `11` or higher. Finally, it's time to write code in the main Activity file of the application `DemoActionBarActivity.java`. We need to perform the following tasks through the main Activity file:

▶ Access the six `Button` controls from the layout file `activity_demo_action_bar.xml` and map them to the respective `Button` objects.

▶ Make the three `Button` controls hide the `ActionBar`, Activity's title, and application's logo. Also make the hidden components visible through the rest of the three `Button` controls.

▶ When the user selects the `ActionView`, `Search` widget in the `ActionBar`, a text box should pop up prompting for the text to search for.

▶ Navigate to the new Activity `CreateActivity.class` when the action item `Create` is selected from the ActionBar.

To perform all these tasks, the code as shown in Listing 7.22 is written in the main Activity file `DemoActionBarActivity.java`.

LISTING 7.22   Code Written into the Java Activity File `DemoActionBarActivity.java`

```
package com.androidunleashed.demoactionbar;

import android.app.Activity;
import android.os.Bundle;
import android.view.View;
import android.widget.Button;
import android.app.ActionBar;
import android.view.Menu;
import android.view.MenuInflater;
import android.view.MenuItem;
import android.content.Intent;
```

```java
public class DemoActionBarActivity extends Activity {
    Intent intent;

    public void onCreate(Bundle savedInstanceState) {
        super.onCreate(savedInstanceState);
        setContentView(R.layout.activity_demo_action_bar);
        final ActionBar actionBar = getActionBar();
        Button showAction = (Button) this.findViewById(R.id.show_action);
        Button hideAction = (Button) this.findViewById(R.id.hide_action);
        Button showTitle = (Button) this.findViewById(R.id.show_title);
        Button hideTitle = (Button) this.findViewById(R.id.hide_title);
        Button showLogo = (Button) this.findViewById(R.id.show_logo);
        Button hideLogo = (Button) this.findViewById(R.id.hide_logo);

        showAction.setOnClickListener(new Button.OnClickListener(){
            public void onClick(View v)
            {  actionBar.show();  }  });
        hideAction.setOnClickListener(new Button.OnClickListener(){
            public void onClick(View v)
            {   actionBar.hide();      }  });
        showTitle.setOnClickListener(new Button.OnClickListener(){
            public void onClick(View v)
            { actionBar.setDisplayShowTitleEnabled(true);    }  });
        hideTitle.setOnClickListener(new Button.OnClickListener(){
            public void onClick(View v)
            {  actionBar.setDisplayShowTitleEnabled(false);  }  });
        showLogo.setOnClickListener(new Button.OnClickListener(){
            public void onClick(View v)
            { actionBar.setDisplayShowHomeEnabled(true);  }  });
        hideLogo.setOnClickListener(new Button.OnClickListener(){
            public void onClick(View v)
            {  actionBar.setDisplayShowHomeEnabled(false);  }  });
    }

    @Override
    public boolean onCreateOptionsMenu(Menu menu) {
        MenuInflater inflater = getMenuInflater();
        inflater.inflate(R.menu.mymenu, menu);
        return true;
    }

    @Override
    public boolean onOptionsItemSelected(MenuItem item) {
        switch (item.getItemId()) {
            case R.id.create_datab:
                intent = new Intent(this, CreateActivity.class);
```

```
            startActivity(intent);
            break;
        default:
            return super.onOptionsItemSelected(item);
    }
    return true;
    }
}
```

On running the application, we find six `Button` controls, the action item `Create`, the ActionView `Search` widget, and the application's logo on the screen as shown in Figure 7.10 (left). On selecting the action item `Create`, we navigate to the Activity `CreateActivity`. The text message `"This is Create Activity"` displayed via the `TextView` defined in the layout file `create.xml` confirms that we have navigated to the Activity `CreateActivity` (see Figure 7.10—middle). After we select the `Button Hide ActionBar`, the ActionBar becomes invisible as shown in Figure 7.10 (right).

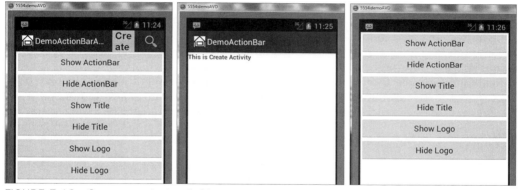

FIGURE 7.10   Screen on startup (left), message displayed in the `Create` activity (middle), and the screen on hiding the ActionBar (right)

When we select the `Button Hide Title`, the title of the Activity, `DemoActionBar`, becomes invisible as shown in Figure 7.11 (left). Similarly, when we select the `Button Hide Logo`, the application's logo, displayed via `home.png` file becomes invisible as shown in Figure 7.11 (middle). When we select the `Search` widget in the `ActionBar`, a text box appears prompting us to enter the text we want to search for as shown in Figure 7.11 (right).

FIGURE 7.11   Activity title is hidden (left), logo is hidden (middle), and a text box opens on selecting the Search widget (right).

Replacing a Menu with the ActionBar

We know by now that menus created in the application MenuApp at the beginning of this chapter are useful in initiation of different tasks in an application but need pressing a Menu button for invoking it. If we make the menu items of the menu created in that application appear in the ActionBar, it not only makes the menu items appear consistently throughout the application but also relieves the user from pressing the Menu button. To understand how a menu can be replaced by ActionBar, let's create a new Android project called ActionBarApp. This application displays the simple menu items, checkable menu items, submenu, and so on—everything that we created in the MenuApp application but this time in the ActionBar.

In the menu that we are going to make, we use icon images for a few menu items. So, let's copy and paste four icon images, namely, create.png, insert.png, search.png, and update.png, into the res/drawable folders. The resolution and size of the icons should be as follows:

▶ **For ldpi**—Resolution should be 120dpi and size 18 × 18px

▶ **For mdpi**—Resolution should be 160dpi and size 24 × 24px

▶ **For hdpi**—Resolution should be 240dpi and size 36 × 36px

▶ **For xhdpi**—Resolution should be 320dpi and size 48 × 48px

---

NOTE

The term *dpi* stands for dots per inch.

After copying the images, define the menu items in the menu file `activity_action_bar_app.xml` as shown in Listing 7.23. On comparing the code in Listing 7.23 with the code in Listing 7.1, which we used for creating menus, you will find that only the statements in bold are newly added; the rest is the same as in Listing 7.1.

LISTING 7.23   Code Written into the Menu File `activity_action_bar_app.xml`

```xml
<menu xmlns:android="http://schemas.android.com/apk/res/android" >
    <item android:id="@+id/create_datab"
        android:title="Create Database"
        android:icon="@drawable/create"
        android:orderInCategory="0"
        android:showAsAction="ifRoom|withText" />
    <item android:id="@+id/insert_rows"
        android:title="Insert Rows"
        android:icon="@drawable/insert"
        android:showAsAction="ifRoom" />
    <item android:id="@+id/list_rows"
        android:title="List Rows"
        android:showAsAction="ifRoom" />
    <item android:id="@+id/search_row"
        android:title="Search"
        android:icon="@drawable/search"
        android:showAsAction="ifRoom|withText" />
    <item android:id="@+id/delete_row"
        android:title="Delete"
        android:showAsAction="never" />
    <item android:id="@+id/update_row"
        android:title="Update"
        android:icon="@drawable/update"
        android:showAsAction="always" />
</menu>
```

In the preceding code, we see that the `showAsAction` attribute is applied to different menu items to determine whether they should appear in the ActionBar or in the `Overflow` menu. To inflate or merge the menu that we defined in the `activity_action_bar_app.xml` file in our application, we write the Java code as shown in Listing 7.24 in our Activity file `ActionBarAppActivity.java`.

LISTING 7.24   Code Written into the Java Activity File `ActionBarAppActivity.java`

```java
package com.androidunleashed.actionbarapp;

import android.app.Activity;
import android.os.Bundle;
import android.view.Menu;
```

```
import android.view.MenuInflater;

public class ActionBarAppActivity extends Activity {

    @Override
    public void onCreate(Bundle savedInstanceState) {
        super.onCreate(savedInstanceState);
        setContentView(R.layout.activity_action_bar_app);
    }

    @Override
    public boolean onCreateOptionsMenu(Menu menu) {
        MenuInflater inflater = getMenuInflater();
        inflater.inflate(R.menu.activity_action_bar_app, menu);
        return true;
    }
}
```

To display the menu or menu items in the ActionBar, we need to inflate or merge our menu defined in the `mymenu.xml` file in the `menu` provided as a parameter to the `onCreate-OptionsMenu()` method. Initially, there is no menu item defined in the `menu` parameter. To inflate the menu that we defined in the `activity_action_bar_app.xml` file, we get the `MenuInflater` from the `Activity` class. An object, `inflater`, is created of the `MenuInflater` class, and its `inflate` method is called to inflate, or merge, our own menu defined in the `activity_action_bar_app.xml` file with the `menu` parameter of this method.

On running the application, we find that the two menu items, `Create` and `Update`, appear in the ActionBar. We can see in the Figure 7.12 (left) that the icons of the menu items appear without pressing the `Menu` button. The rest of the menu items that could not be accommodated in the ActionBar are displayed in the `Overflow Menu` as shown in Figure 7.12 (right). No text of the `action items` appears but only the icons in the ActionBar, as there is not enough space when the device is in portrait mode. We can also compare the output of the ActionBar with the menu by comparing Figure 7.1 with Figure 7.12.

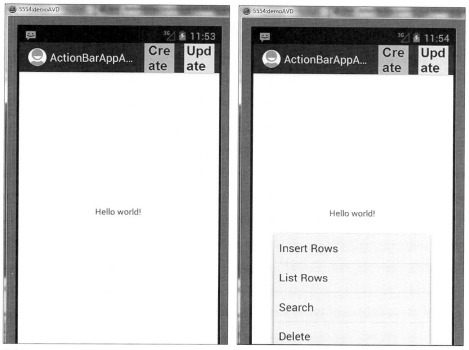

FIGURE 7.12   Screen on startup in portrait mode (left), and hidden actions, that is, Overflow Menu displayed (right)

On switching the device to landscape mode, we find that instead of two, four menu items appear in the ActionBar. Also, because there is enough space, the text of the menu items also appears along with the icons as shown in Figure 7.13 (left). Only two menu items of our menu could not be accommodated in the ActionBar, and hence they appear in the Overflow Menu as shown in Figure 7.13 (right).

FIGURE 7.13   ActionBar in landscape mode (left), and Overflow Menu displayed (right)

To display checkable menu items and submenus, and to apply shortcuts to the menu items in the same way as we did in the MenuApp application, we write the code as shown in Listing 7.25 in the `activity_action_bar_app.xml`. When compared with the code in Listing 7.5, only the code in bold is new; the rest is the same as in Listing 7.5.

LISTING 7.25   Code Written into the Menu File `activity_action_bar_app.xml`

```xml
<menu xmlns:android="http://schemas.android.com/apk/res/android" >
    <item android:id="@+id/create_datab"
        android:title="Create Database"
        android:icon="@drawable/create"
        android:showAsAction="ifRoom|withText" />
    <item android:id="@+id/insert_rows"
        android:title="Insert Rows"
        android:icon="@drawable/insert"
        android:showAsAction="ifRoom" />
    <item android:id="@+id/list_rows"
        android:title="List Rows"
        android:showAsAction="ifRoom" />
    <item android:id="@+id/search_row"
        android:title="Search"
        android:icon="@drawable/search"
        android:showAsAction="ifRoom|withText" >
            <menu>
            <group android:checkableBehavior="single">
                <item android:id="@+id/search_code"
                    android:title="Search on Code"
                    android:checked="true" />
                <item android:id="@+id/search_name"
                    android:title="Search on Name"
                    android:alphabeticShortcut="n"
                    android:numericShortcut="6" />
                <item android:id="@+id/search_price"
                    android:title="Search on Price" />
            </group>
        </menu>
    </item>
    <item android:id="@+id/delete_row"
        android:title="Delete"
        android:showAsAction="never"
        android:alphabeticShortcut="d"
        android:checkable="true" />
    <item android:id="@+id/update_row"
        android:title="Update"
        android:icon="@drawable/update"
        android:showAsAction="always"
        android:alphabeticShortcut="u"
        android:numericShortcut="4" />
</menu>
```

We can see that the preceding code includes the `android:showAsAction` attribute to display the menu items in the ActionBar if the space permits. Also the `<menu>` element defined inside the `Search` menu item defines the submenu consisting of three menu items: `Search on Code`, `Search on Name`, and `Search on Price`. The `Delete` menu item appears as a checkable menu item, as the `android:checkable` attribute is set to the Boolean value `true` for this menu item. The `android:alphabeticShortcut` and the `android:numericShortcut` define shortcut keys of the menu items. The `android:alphabeticShortcut` attribute defines the shortcut key for the full keyboard, whereas the `android:numericShortcut` attribute defines the shortcut key from the numeric keypad.

To show a response when a menu item is selected, we need to define a `TextView` control in the layout file `activity_action_bar_app.xml`. After we define the `TextView` control, the layout file `activity_action_bar_app.xml` appears as shown in Listing 7.26.

LISTING 7.26   Code Written into the Layout File `activity_action_bar_app.xml`

```
<LinearLayout xmlns:android="http://schemas.android.com/apk/res/android"
    android:layout_width="match_parent"
    android:layout_height="match_parent"
    android:orientation="vertical" >
    <TextView
        android:layout_width="match_parent"
        android:layout_height="wrap_content"
        android:id="@+id/selectedopt" />
</LinearLayout>
```

To identify the `TextView` in Java code, it is assigned the ID `selectedopt`. To display the response when a menu item is selected, modify the file `ActionBarAppActivity.java` to appear as shown in Listing 7.27.

LISTING 7.27   Code Written into the Java Activity File `ActionBarAppActivity.java`

```
package com.androidunleashed.actionbarapp;

import android.app.Activity;
import android.os.Bundle;
import android.view.Menu;
import android.view.MenuInflater;
import android.view.MenuItem;
import android.widget.TextView;

public class ActionBarAppActivity extends Activity {
    private TextView selectedOpt;

    @Override
    public void onCreate(Bundle savedInstanceState) {
```

```java
        super.onCreate(savedInstanceState);
        setContentView(R.layout.activity_action_bar_app);
        selectedOpt=(TextView)findViewById(R.id.selectedopt);
    }

    @Override
    public boolean onCreateOptionsMenu(Menu menu) {
        MenuInflater inflater = getMenuInflater();
        inflater.inflate(R.menu.activity_action_bar_app, menu);
        return true;
    }

    @Override
    public boolean onOptionsItemSelected(MenuItem item) {
        switch (item.getItemId()) {
            case R.id.create_datab:
                selectedOpt.setText("You have selected Create Database option");
                break;
            case R.id.insert_rows:
                selectedOpt.setText("You have selected Insert Rows option");
                break;
            case R.id.list_rows:
                selectedOpt.setText("You have selected List Rows option");
                break;
            case R.id.search_row:
                selectedOpt.setText("You have selected Search Row option");
                break;
            case R.id.delete_row:
                selectedOpt.setText("You have selected Delete Row option");
                break;
            case R.id.update_row:
                selectedOpt.setText("You have selected Update Row option");
                break;
            case R.id.search_code:
                selectedOpt.setText("You have selected Search on Code option");
                break;
            case R.id.search_name:
                selectedOpt.setText("You have selected Search on Name option");
                break;
            case R.id.search_price:
                selectedOpt.setText("You have selected Search on Price option");
                break;
        }
        return true;
    }
}
```

Notice that the code shown in Listing 7.27 is the same as we saw in Listing 7.6 of the `MenuApp` application.

On running the application, we find the two menu items `Create` and `Update` appear as action items in the ActionBar (see Figure 7.14—left). When we select the `Create` action item, the `TextView` displays the message, `You have selected Create Database option`. The `Overflow Menu` appears as shown in Figure 7.14 (middle). You can observe that the `Delete` menu item appears as a checkable menu item. Again, when we select any menu item from the `Overflow Menu`, the respective text message appears through the `TextView`. When we select the `Search` menu item from the `Overflow Menu`, a Search submenu appears as shown in Figure 7.14 (right). The `TextView` confirms selection of the `Search` menu item by displaying the message `You have selected Search Row option`.

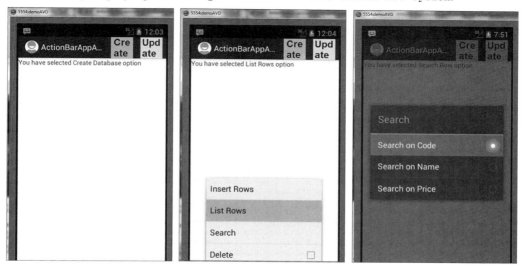

FIGURE 7.14   Message displayed on selecting the `Create` icon (left), message displayed on selecting the `List Rows` option (middle), and a submenu opens on selecting the `Search` menu item (right).

We know that the ActionBar appears in three forms: standard, tabbed, and list. The ActionBars that we have been working with until now are the standard form. Let's now learn about the tabbed ActionBar.

Creating a Tabbed ActionBar

Tabbed and drop-down list ActionBars display menu items in the form of tabs and drop-down lists, respectively. They are popularly used for fragment transitions within an Activity. In tabbed and drop-down ActionBars, only one type of navigation can be enabled at a time. To display navigation tabs in an ActionBar, its `setNavigationMode()` method is called, passing the value `ActionBar.NAVIGATION_MODE_TABS` as a parameter as follows:

```
actionBar.setNavigationMode(ActionBar.NAVIGATION_MODE_TABS);
```

After we determine the navigation mode, we add the tabs to the ActionBar by calling its `addTab()` method:

```
actionBar.addTab(actionBar.newTab().setText("Create").setTabListener(this));
```

The preceding code creates a new tab, sets its text to `Create`, attaches a `TabListener` to it, and finally adds the newly created tab to the ActionBar. Just as the `setText()` method used in the preceding code sets the text of the tab, we can also call the `setIcon()` method to define an image for the tab. Besides this, we can also call the `setContentDescription()` method to supply more detailed information of the tab.

Example:

```
Tab tab1 = actionBar.newTab();
tabOne.setText("Create")
.setIcon(R.drawable.ic_launcher)
.setContentDescription("Creating the Database")
.setTabListener(this));
actionBar.addTab(tab1);
```

The preceding code adds a tab with the text `Create` to the tabbed ActionBar. The icon assigned to the tab is the default icon `ic_launcher`, and a detailed description assigned is "`Creating the Database`" to inform the user about the purpose of the tab. When we click a tab, the event is handled by the `TabListener` that performs the desired task.

We can better understand the concept of the tabbed ActionBar by a running example. So, create a new Android project called `TabbedActionBarApp`. In this application, we create two tabs, `Create` and `Update`. When either tab is selected, a respective log message is displayed. In the Java Activity file of the application, `TabbedActionBarAppActivity.java`, write the code as shown in Listing 7.28.

LISTING 7.28   Code Written into the Java Activity File `TabbedActionBarAppActivity.java`

```
package com.androidunleashed.tabbedactionbarapp;

import android.app.Activity;
import android.os.Bundle;
import android.app.ActionBar;
import android.app.ActionBar.Tab;
import android.app.FragmentTransaction;
import android.util.Log;

public class TabbedActionBarAppActivity extends Activity implements ActionBar.Tab-
Listener {

    @Override
    public void onCreate(Bundle savedInstanceState) {
```

```
        super.onCreate(savedInstanceState);
        final ActionBar actionBar = getActionBar();
        actionBar.setNavigationMode(ActionBar.NAVIGATION_MODE_TABS);
        actionBar.setDisplayShowTitleEnabled(false);
        actionBar.addTab(actionBar.newTab().setText("Create").setTabListener(this));
        actionBar.addTab(actionBar.newTab().setText("Update").setTabListener(this));
    }

    @Override
    public void onTabReselected(Tab tab, FragmentTransaction ft) {
        Log.d("Tab", String.valueOf(tab.getPosition()) + " re-selected");
    }

    @Override
    public void onTabSelected(Tab tab, FragmentTransaction ft) {
        Log.d("Tab", String.valueOf(tab.getPosition()) + " selected");
    }

    @Override
    public void onTabUnselected(Tab tab, FragmentTransaction ft) {
        Log.d("Tab", String.valueOf(tab.getPosition()) + " Unselected");
    }
}
```

In the preceding code, we can see that an ActionBar object, `actionBar`, is created by calling the `getActionBar()` method. To make the ActionBar appear in the form of tabs, its navigation mode is set to `ActionBar.NAVIGATION_MODE_TABS`. The Activity title is made invisible by passing the Boolean value `false` to the `setDisplayShowTitleEnabled()` method. Thereafter, two tabs with the text `Create` and `Update` are respectively created and added to the ActionBar. The event listener `TabListener` is associated with both the tabs. When either tab is selected, the `onTabSelected()` method is invoked, and the selected tab is passed to it as a parameter. The `onTabSelected()` method displays the log message informing the position of the selected tab. The position of the tab is zero numbered; that is, the first tab is considered to have the position 0, the second tab has the position 1, and so on. When a tab is selected, the `onTabUnselected()` method is also called, and the other tab that is not selected is passed to it as the parameter. The `onTabUnselected()` method displays the position of the other tab that is not selected. On running the application, we find the tabbed ActionBar showing two tabs as shown in Figure 7.15 (left). When we select the first tab, `Create`, the log messages `1 Unselected` and `0 selected` are displayed confirming that the first tab, `Create`, is selected and the second tab, `Update`, is unselected. Similarly, when we select the second tab, `Update`, the log messages `0 Unselected` and `1 selected` are displayed as shown in Figure 7.15 (right).

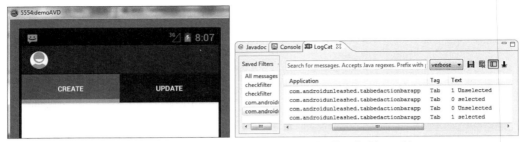

FIGURE 7.15   Screen showing two tabs in the tabbed ActionBar (left), and log messages displayed on selecting the action tabs (right)

After understanding the tabbed ActionBar, let's learn how the drop-down list ActionBar is created.

Creating a Drop-Down List ActionBar

In a drop-down list ActionBar, the menu items are displayed in the form of a drop-down list. It is popularly used for displaying the content within an Activity on the basis of the selection made by the user. To display a drop-down list in an ActionBar, its `setNavigationMode()` method is called, passing the value `ActionBar.NAVIGATION_MODE_LIST` as a parameter to it as shown here:

```
actionBar.setNavigationMode(ActionBar.NAVIGATION_MODE_LIST);
```

The drop-down list as expected appears like a spinner, displaying a list of available options, allowing us to select one of them. For displaying options in the drop-down list, we use the Adapter that implements the `SpinnerAdapter` interface, like an `ArrayAdapter` or `SimpleCursorAdapter`. We use an `ArrayAdapter` in this application. Remember that an `ArrayAdapter` is the simplest of the adapters and acts as the data source for the selection widgets `ListView`, `GridView`, and so on. First, we define a string array containing the strings that we want to be displayed in the drop-down list. Thereafter, we create an `ArrayAdapter` that displays the elements of the array in the form of drop-down items. That is, the elements of the array are wrapped or cast into the spinner drop-down items. Finally, the `ArrayAdapter` is assigned to the ActionBar for displaying the menu items, that is, array elements in the form of drop-down menu items. To assign the `ArrayAdapter` to the ActionBar and to attach the event listener to the drop-down items that are displayed, the `setListNavigationCallbacks()` method is called, passing the `adapter` and `OnNavigationListener` to it as parameters as shown in the following code:

```
String[] items = new String[] { "Create", "Insert", "Update", "Search" };
ArrayAdapter<String> adapter = new ArrayAdapter<String>(this, android.R.layout.sim-
ple_spinner_dropdown_item, items);
ActionBar actionBar = getActionBar();
actionBar.setNavigationMode(ActionBar.NAVIGATION_MODE_LIST);
actionBar.setListNavigationCallbacks(adapter, onNavigationItemSelected);
```

In the preceding code, the string array `items` is defined consisting of the strings that we want to display in the drop-down list ActionBar. An `ArrayAdapter` called `adapter` is created comprising the string array `items` and casting the array elements in the `spinner` drop-down items. An `ActionBar` object `actionBar` is created and its navigation mode is set to `ActionBar.NAVIGATION_MODE_LIST`. The `setListNavigationCallbacks()` method is called on the `actionBar` passing the `ArrayAdapter`, `adapter`, and the listener, `onNavigationSelected`, to it as parameters. That is, we assign the callbacks to handle drop-down selections. When a user selects an item from the drop-down list, the `onNavigationItemSelected` handler is called where we can write the code to perform the desired action.

Let's create a drop-down list ActionBar in an Android project. Create a new Android project called `ListActionBarApp`. In this application, we display a few menu items in the form of a drop-down list, and when any menu item is selected, a respective log message is displayed. In the Java Activity file of the application `ListActionBarAppActivity.java`, write the code as shown in Listing 7.29.

LISTING 7.29   Code Written into the Java Activity File `ListActionBarAppActivity.java`

```
package com.androidunleashed.listactionbarapp;

import android.app.Activity;
import android.os.Bundle;
import android.app.ActionBar.OnNavigationListener;
import android.app.ActionBar;
import android.widget.ArrayAdapter;
import android.util.Log;

public class ListActionBarAppActivity extends Activity  {

    @Override
    public void onCreate(Bundle savedInstanceState) {
        super.onCreate(savedInstanceState);
        String[] items = new String[] { "Create", "Insert", "Update", "Search" };
        ArrayAdapter<String> adapter = new ArrayAdapter<String>(this,
android.R.layout.simple_spinner_dropdown_item, items);
        ActionBar actionBar = getActionBar();
        actionBar.setNavigationMode(ActionBar.NAVIGATION_MODE_LIST);
        actionBar.setListNavigationCallbacks(adapter, onNavigationItemSelected);
    }
    OnNavigationListener onNavigationItemSelected = new OnNavigationListener() {
        @Override
        public boolean onNavigationItemSelected(int itemPosition, long itemId) {
            Log.d("Option ", String.valueOf(itemId) + " is selected");
            return true;
        }
    };
}
```

In the preceding code, we notice that when an item from the drop-down list is selected, the `onNavigationItemSelected()` method is called. The parameters `itemPosition` and `itemId` in the `onNavigationItemSelected()` method contain the information about the `position` and `ID` of the selected item. A log message is displayed in this method displaying the ID of the selected item. The IDs are sequentially assigned to the items in the drop-down list beginning with 0. To enable the ActionBar, don't forget to set the value of the `android:minSdkVersion` attribute to `11` or higher in the `AndroidManifest.xml` file.

On running the application, we get a Spinner as shown in Figure 7.16 (top left). The Spinner shows the first item of the drop-down list, `Create`. The default style shows the first item in a dark color, which is almost invisible in the dark background color. Open the `styles.xml` file from the `res/values` folder and add a custom style called `MyActionBar` to it through the following statement:

```
<style name="MyActionBar" parent="@android:style/Widget.Holo.Light.ActionBar" />
```

After we add this style, the `styles.xml` file appears as shown in Listing 7.30.

LISTING 7.30   Code Written into the `styles.xml` File

```
<resources xmlns:android="http://schemas.android.com/apk/res/android">
<style name="AppTheme" parent="android:Theme.Light" />
<style name="MyActionBar" parent="@android:style/Widget.Holo.Light.ActionBar" />
</resources>
```

To implement the preceding style to our application, open the `AndroidManifest.xml` file and set the value of `android:theme` attribute as shown here:

```
android:theme="@style/MyActionBar"
```

The preceding statement applies the `MyActionBar` style to our application. The output now appears as shown in Figure 7.16 (top right).

When we select the Spinner, the drop-down list opens showing all the available items as shown in Figure 7.16 (bottom left). When we select an item, `Update`, it appears as the Spinner's header as shown in Figure 7.16 (bottom right), informing that it was selected in the previous selection.

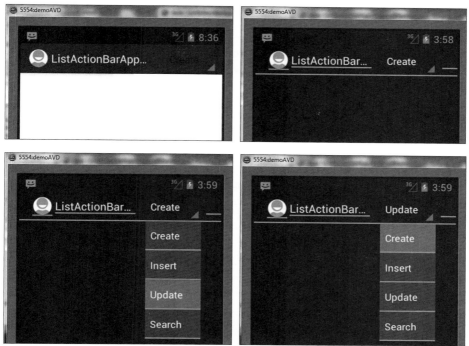

FIGURE 7.16   First Item of the spinner almost invisible (top left), first item of the spinner, `Create`, becomes visible (top right), all actions displayed on selecting the list (bottom left), and selected list item displayed at the header of the list (bottom right)

Figure 7.17 shows the log messages displayed on selecting the two items `Update` and `Create` from the drop-down list. The ID of the selected drop-down item is displayed using the `itemId` parameter in the `onNavigationItemSelected()` method.

FIGURE 7.17   Log messages displayed on selecting the actions from the list ActionBar

Summary

In this chapter, we learned about different types of menus and saw how to create menus through XML, as well as by coding. We learned to create Options Menus, define Icon Menus, and handle menu selections. We saw how to define Expanded Menus, add Submenus, create Context Menus, and handle Context Menu selections. We learned to use check boxes and radio buttons in menus, add shortcut keys, and apply Context Menus to `ListViews`. We learned to create instant access menu items through ActionBars and also saw the procedure of creating tabbed and drop-down ActionBars.

In the next chapter we learn to use databases in Android applications. We use the SQLite `SQLiteOpenHelper`, fetching desired rows from the table and using cursors. We also learn to access databases through ADB and menus, creating data entry forms and displaying table rows through `ListViews`.

CHAPTER 8

Using Databases

U ser-entered data needs to be saved somewhere so that it can be accessed at a later time. Android offers the SQLite relational database library for persisting data. It's an open-source, lightweight, and powerful database available in the form of a C library. It uses SQL (Structured Query Language) for storing and retrieving information and performing database maintenance. SQLite is extremely reliable and is popularly used in devices with restricted computing power. Through SQLite, we can create individual databases for each application and store and manage application-related data.

Using the `SQLiteOpenHelper` Class

Android databases are stored in the `/data/data/<package_name>/databases` folder on devices or emulators.

To create an Android application that stores, accesses, and manipulates user information in a SQLite-relational database, we use the `SQLiteOpenHelper` class. The `SQLiteOpenHelper` class is an abstract class that provides a way to get read or write access to a database. The `SQLiteOpenHelper` class thus makes our task of manipulating the data stored in the database easy.

The `SQLiteOpenHelper` class is an abstract class used to create, open, and upgrade databases. It provides several methods including `getWritableDatabase()`, `getReadableDatabase()`, and `close()` that returns an `SQLiteDatabase` object that lets the calling code do the reading, writing, and closing of the database, respectively.

The `SQLiteDatabase` class also provides methods including `insert()` and `query()`, which are used to insert rows in the database table and execute different SQLite queries on the database table. The `query()` method accepts several parameters such as the database table to query, columns, and criteria, and returns a `Cursor` representing the rows that satisfy the supplied criteria. The `Cursor` class provides several methods to traverse the result set and move to the desired row and column position in the result set.

To understand how the information in an Android application can be stored and accessed from an SQLite database, let's create a new Android application.

Building an SQLite Project

Launch Eclipse IDE and create a new Android project called `DatabaseApp`. In this application, we create a database called `shopping`, and in it we create a table called `products`. The `products` table consists of three columns: `code`, `product_name`, and `price` to store the code, product name, and price, respectively. To the `products` table, we add a couple of rows. Also, we access the rows in the `products` table and display them via the `TextView` control. To take advantage of the `SQLiteOpenHelper` class and its method, we need to extend it. That is, we add a Java class to our application and make it inherit the `SQLiteOpenHelper` class. The `SQLiteOpenHelper` class makes the task of maintaining the SQLite database easier by hiding the complexities of maintaining the database.

To add a Java class to our application, right-click the `com.androidunleashed.database-app` package in the `Package Explorer` window and select `New`, `Class` option. We see a `New Java Class` dialog box used to enter the new Java class information (see Figure 8.1). Enter the Java class name as `DatabaseManager`. The two boxes, `Source folder` and `Package`, appear automatically filled with the `src` folder location and the application package name, respectively. In the `Modifiers` options, `public` is selected by default. Keeping all the default information, click `Finish` to create the new Java file `DatabaseManager.java`.

FIGURE 8.1   Creating a new Java file called `DatabaseManager.java`

The newly added `DatabaseManager.java` file has the initial contents shown here:

```
package com.androidunleashed.databaseapp;
public class DatabaseManager {
}
```

We write code in `DatabaseManager.java` to perform the following tasks:

▶ Inherit from the `SQLiteOpenHelper` class to access and take advantage of the methods defined in it.

▶ Open and return the writable and readable database file instance to perform writing and reading operations on the database, respectively.

▶ Create a database table, `products`, consisting of three columns: `code`, `product_name`, and `price`.

▶ Add rows to the `products` table. The information for the new product is supplied by the activity file `DatabaseAppActivity.java`.

▶ Fetch rows from the `products` table and return them to the activity file `DatabaseAppActivity.java` for displaying on the screen.

The Java file is accessed and executed from the Java activity file of our application `DatabaseAppActivity.java`.

To perform these tasks, the code shown in Listing 8.1 is written into the Java file `DatabaseManager.java`.

LISTING 8.1   Code Written into the Java Class `DatabaseManager.java`

```java
package com.androidunleashed.databaseapp;

import android.database.sqlite.SQLiteDatabase;
import android.content.Context;
import android.content.ContentValues;
import android.database.Cursor;
import android.database.sqlite.SQLiteOpenHelper;
import android.util.Log;

public class DatabaseManager {
    public static final String DB_NAME = "shopping";
    public static final String DB_TABLE = "products";
    public static final int DB_VERSION = 1;
    private static final String CREATE_TABLE = "CREATE TABLE " + DB_TABLE + " (code
        INTEGER PRIMARY KEY, product_name TEXT, price FLOAT);";
    private SQLHelper helper;
    private SQLiteDatabase db;
    private Context context;

    public DatabaseManager(Context c){
        this.context = c;
        helper=new SQLHelper(c);
        this.db = helper.getWritableDatabase();
    }

    public DatabaseManager openReadable() throws android.database.SQLException {
        helper=new SQLHelper(context);
        db = helper.getReadableDatabase();
        return this;
    }

    public void close(){
        helper.close();
    }

    public void addRow(Integer c, String n, Float p){
        ContentValues newProduct = new ContentValues();
```

```java
        newProduct.put("code", c);
        newProduct.put("product_name", n);
        newProduct.put("price", p);
        try{db.insertOrThrow(DB_TABLE, null, newProduct);}
        catch(Exception e)
        {
            Log.e("Error in inserting rows ", e.toString());
            e.printStackTrace();
        }
    }


    public String retrieveRows(){
        String[] columns = new String[]{"code", "product_name", "price"};
        Cursor cursor = db.query(DB_TABLE, columns, null, null, null, null, null);
        String tablerows = "";
        cursor.moveToFirst();
        while (cursor.isAfterLast() == false) {
            tablerows = tablerows + cursor.getInt(0) + ", "+cursor.getString(1)+", "
+ cursor.getFloat(2)+ "\n";
            cursor.moveToNext();
        }
        if (cursor != null && !cursor.isClosed()) {
            cursor.close();
        }
        return tablerows;
    }


    public class SQLHelper extends SQLiteOpenHelper {
        public SQLHelper(Context c){
            super(c, DB_NAME, null, DB_VERSION);
        }

        @Override
        public void onCreate(SQLiteDatabase db) {
            db.execSQL(CREATE_TABLE);
        }

        @Override
        public void onUpgrade(SQLiteDatabase db, int oldVersion, int newVersion) {
            Log.w("Products table","Upgrading database i.e. dropping table and rec-
reating it");
            db.execSQL("DROP TABLE IF EXISTS " + DB_TABLE);
            onCreate(db);
        }
    }
}
```

Before we look at the code in detail, let's examine what the code is doing.

The DatabaseManager is a class where we write all the methods related to database maintenance such as creating databases and tables, upgrading tables, and adding and retrieving rows to and from the database table. To make our task easier, the DatabaseManager class includes a SQLHelper class, which inherits the SQLiteOpenHelper class.

In this code, we see that an SQLHelper class is defined in the DatabaseManager class, which inherits the SQLiteOpenHelper class. The SQLHelper class instance, helper, is created by passing the context to its constructor. The SQLHelper's constructor in turn invokes the constructor of the SQLiteOpenHelper class passing the context database name (shopping) and its version number (1) to it. The helper instance is set to refer to version 1 of the database, shopping. The SQLiteOpenHelper class provides two methods, getWritableDatabase() and getReadableDatabase(), that are used to open and return the writable and readable instance of the referred database. We can see that the getWritableDatabase() method is called on by the helper instance to get an SQLiteDatabase object called db. The SQLiteDatabase object, db, now refers to the shopping database that is opened in write mode, and we can perform write operations on the database.

The SQLiteOpenHelper onCreate and onUpgrade class methods are overridden in the SQLHelper class to create a new database and to upgrade it to a new version. The on-Create() method creates a products table in the shopping database by calling the execSQL()SQLiteDatabase method through its object, db. The products database table consists of three columns: code, product_name, and price, where code is the primary key in the products table. In the onUpgrade method, the existing table, products, is dropped and re-created.

The openReadable() method calls the getReadableDatabase() on the helper object to get the SQLiteDatabase object db that refers to the readable instance of the shopping database. The close() method calls the close() method on the helper class to close it.

The addRow() method accepts the values for the new row of the products table as parameters and inserts them in the products table by calling the SQLiteDatabase insert-OrThrow() method through its object db. The ContentValues is used to insert rows in the products table. Each ContentValues object represents a single table row as a map of column names to values. A ContentValues object, newProduct, is created, and through its put() methods, we supply the code, product_name, and price columns' values. Thereafter, the insertOrThrow() method is called, and the ContentValues object, newProduct, is passed to it to insert a new row in the table, supplying the content specified in the ContentValues object. An exception is thrown in case an error occurs while inserting the row.

The retrieveRows() method fetches all the rows from the products table by executing the query() method of the SQLiteDatabase object and returns in the form of a Cursor object. The query() method helps in running the query with the specified criteria to get the desired number of rows.

Fetching the Desired Rows from Tables

To fetch the desired rows from a database table, we execute queries containing a criterion against the given database. The queries are executed through the `query()` method provided by the `SQLiteDatabase` class. The parameters that are passed to the `query()` method are shown here: `db.query(bool_uniq, db_table, array_columns, where_clause, select_arg, group_by, having_clause, order);`.

Table 8.1 shows the meaning of these parameters.

TABLE 8.1   Parameters Used in the `query()` Method

Parameter	Usage
`bool_uniq`	Optional Boolean value to determine whether the result set should contain only unique values. A `True` value confirms the unique values in the result set.
`db_table`	The database table to be queried.
`array_columns`	A string array containing the list of columns we want in the result set.
`where_clause`	Defines the criteria for the rows to be returned. For specifying values in the clause, ? wildcard(s) are used, which are then replaced by the values stored in the `select_arg` parameter.
`select_arg`	An array of strings that provide values for the ? wildcards used in the `where_clause` parameter.
`group_by`	Defines the condition for grouping the returned result set.
`having_clause`	Defines the conditions to be applied to the groups defined in the `group_by` clause.
`order`	Defines the order of the returned rows.

Examples:

The following two queries return all the `products` table rows for the `code`, `product_name`, and `price` columns. The first query confirms that only unique rows should be fetched:

```
public static final String DB_TABLE = "products";
String[] columns = new String[]{"code", "product_name", "price"};
Cursor cursor = db.query(true, DB_TABLE, columns, null, null, null, null, null);
Cursor cursor = db.query(DB_TABLE, columns, null, null, null, null, null);
```

The following query returns the rows with the product name `Camera` and the result set is sorted on the product code:

```
String whereClause="product_name=Camera";
String order="code";
Cursor cursor = db.query(DB_TABLE, columns, whereClause, null, null, null, order);
```

The returned rows from the query() method are in the form of Cursor objects. A Cursor object does not create a separate result set of the extracted rows, but points at the result set that is part of a database table. When we call the moveToFirst() method on the Cursor object, the cursor is moved to the first row in the result set. Thereafter, all the products table rows that exist in the Cursor object are fetched one by one by calling the moveToNext() method and returned. The Cursor is closed when all the rows pointed at in its result set are traversed.

Using Cursors

Cursors are pointers pointing at the result set of the underlying data and can be set to traverse the rows and retrieve column data of the result set. The Cursor class provides several methods that can be used to set the pointer at the desired row and column position of the result set. Table 8.2 lists the methods provided by a Cursor object to set the pointer at the desired location in the result set.

TABLE 8.2   The Cursor Class Methods Used to Set the Pointer at the Desired Location

Method	Usage
moveToFirst	Moves the cursor to the first row in the result set
moveToNext	Moves the cursor to the next row
moveToPrevious	Moves the cursor to the previous row
getCount	Returns the count of the rows in the result set
getColumn-IndexOrThrow	Returns the index for the column with the specified name. It throws an exception if no column exists with that name
getColumnName	Returns the column name with the specified column index
getColumnNames	Returns a string array that contains all the column names in the current cursor
moveToPosition	Moves the cursor to the specified row
getPosition	Returns the current cursor position

The DatabaseManager class is accessed through an instance created in our Activity file. Let's write the code for it. Modify the DatabaseAppActivity.java file to appear as shown in Listing 8.2.

LISTING 8.2   Code Written into the Java Activity File DatabaseAppActivity.java

```
package com.androidunleashed.databaseapp;

import android.app.Activity;
import android.os.Bundle;
import android.widget.TextView;

public class DatabaseAppActivity extends Activity {
    private DatabaseManager mydManager;
```

```
    private TextView response;
    private TextView productRec;

    @Override
    public void onCreate(Bundle savedInstanceState) {
        super.onCreate(savedInstanceState);
        setContentView(R.layout.activity_database_app);
        response=(TextView)findViewById(R.id.response);
        productRec=(TextView)findViewById(R.id.prodrec);
        mydManager = new DatabaseManager(this);
        mydManager.addRow(101, "Camera", Float.parseFloat("15"));
        mydManager.addRow(102, "Laptop",  Float.parseFloat("1005.99"));
        mydManager.close();
        mydManager = new DatabaseManager(this);
        mydManager.openReadable();
        String tableContent = mydManager.retrieveRows();
        response.setText("The rows in the products table are:");
        productRec.setText(tableContent);
        mydManager.close();
    }
}
```

We can see that `TextView` controls with the `response` and `prodrec` IDs are captured from the layout file `activity_database_app.xml` and mapped to the `TextView` objects, `response` and `productRec`, respectively. To access different methods defined in the `DatabaseManager` Java class that we just created above, its instance is created called `mydManager`. Through the `mydManager` instance, we access the `addRow()` method of `DatabaseManager` to add two rows to the `products` table of our `shopping` database. After we insert the rows in the `products` table, `mydManager` is closed so that it can be re-created to open the database in read mode. The readable database instance is obtained by calling the `openReadable()` method of the `DatabaseManager` class through its instance `mydManager`. The text in the `response` `TextView` control is set to `The rows in the products table are:`. The text is a header for the `products` rows that are displayed through another `TextView` control. All the rows in the `products` table are accessed by calling the `retrieveRows()` method and displayed via the `TextView` object `productRec`.

It's clear that we need to define two `TextView` controls in our applications, one to display the rows in the `products` table and the other as the header or title for the rows being displayed. To define two `TextView` controls in `activity_database_app.xml`, use the code shown in Listing 8.3.

LISTING 8.3   Code Written into the Layout File `activity_database_app.xml`

```
<LinearLayout xmlns:android="http://schemas.android.com/apk/res/android"
    android:orientation="vertical"
    android:layout_width="match_parent"
    android:layout_height="match_parent">
```

```
    <TextView
        android:layout_width="match_parent"
        android:layout_height="wrap_content"
        android:id="@+id/response" />
    <TextView
        android:id="@+id/prodrec"
        android:layout_width="match_parent"
        android:layout_height="wrap_content" />
</LinearLayout>
```

Our application is complete, and we can run it. The rows in the `products` database table are displayed, as shown in Figure 8.2.

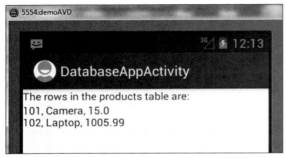

FIGURE 8.2   The rows in the `products` table displayed via the `TextView` control

To confirm whether the two rows we inserted with the previous application were actually inserted into the `products` table of our `shopping` SQLite database, let's learn how to access the database through ADB.

Accessing Databases with the ADB

Recall from Chapter 1, "Introduction to Android," that the ADB (Android Debug Bridge) is a client/server program that is part of the Android SDK and is used to communicate with, control, and manage Android devices and emulators. We can perform several tasks via adb commands, including viewing applications, deleting them, installing new applications, and executing shell commands.

To access the ADB through the Windows operating system, open the command prompt and navigate to the folder where `adb.exe` is located. By default, the file, `adb.exe` is installed in `C:\Program Files (x86)\Android\android-sdk\platform-tools`. We can issue the following commands to interact with a device or emulator.

The `adb devices` command shows the list of currently running emulator(s) and devices:

```
C:\Program Files (x86)\Android\android-sdk\platform-tools>adb devices
List of devices attached
emulator-5554    offline
```

The `adb shell` command activates the shell, where we can issue Unix-like commands:

```
C:\Program Files (x86)\Android\android-sdk\platform-tools>adb shell
#
```

The `ls -l` long listing command shows the list of directories in the emulator/device:

```
# ls -l
ls -l
drwxrwxrwt root      root                    2011-08-06 09:14 sqlite_stmt_journals
drwxrwx--- system    cache                   2011-07-22 23:14 cache
d---rwxrwx system    system                  1970-01-01 05:30 sdcard
lrwxrwxrwx root      root                    2011-08-06 09:14 etc -> /system/etc
drwxr-xr-x root      root                    2009-07-01 05:54 system
drwxr-xr-x root      root                    1970-01-01 05:30 sys
drwxr-x--- root      root                    1970-01-01 05:30 sbin
dr-xr-xr-x root      root                    1970-01-01 05:30 proc
-rwxr-x--- root      root               9075 1970-01-01 05:30 init.rc
-rwxr-x--- root      root               1677 1970-01-01 05:30 init.goldfish.rc
-rwxr-x--- root      root             106568 1970-01-01 05:30 init
-rw-r--r-- root      root                118 1970-01-01 05:30 default.prop
drwxrwx--x system    system                  2009-07-01 05:54 data
drwx------ root      root                    1970-01-01 05:30 root
drwxr-xr-x root      root                    2011-08-06 09:14 dev
```

The `ls /data/data` command shows the list of files and directories in the subdirectory of the data directory. We see the list of all installed applications in the emulator. The installed application's package names are also displayed:

```
# ls /data/data
ls /data/data

com.android.mms
com.android.googlesearch
com.android.launcher
::::::::::::
::::::::::::
com.androidunleashed.databaseapp
```

The following command shows the content of the application package's databases directory:

```
# ls /data/data/com.androidunleashed.databaseapp/databases
ls /data/data/com.androidunleashed.databaseapp/databases
shopping
```

The output, `shopping`, confirms that the `shopping` database has been created in our application package `com.androidunleashed.databaseapp`.

Let's go into the `databases` directory of our application package:

```
# cd /data/data/com.androidunleashed.databaseapp/databases
cd /data/data/com.androidunleashed.databaseapp/databases
```

On executing the `ls` command, we see the list of files and directories in the `databases` subdirectory. As expected, the name of our shopping database is displayed:

```
# ls
ls
shopping
```

Then, we make the `shopping` database active by using the `sqlite3 shopping` command:

```
# sqlite3 shopping
sqlite3 shopping
SQLite version 3.5.9
Enter ".help" for instructions
```

The `SQLite` version information is displayed with the directive to type the `.help` command to see help instructions. We also see an `sqlite>` prompt to issue database-related commands.

The `.tables` command displays the tables that exist in the currently active database:

```
sqlite> .tables
.tables
android_metadata   products
```

The `.schema` command displays the structure (field names, their types, width, and so on) of all the tables that exist in the currently active database:

```
sqlite> .schema
.schema
CREATE TABLE android_metadata (locale TEXT);
CREATE TABLE products (code INTEGER PRIMARY KEY, product_name TEXT, price
FLOAT)
;
```

The SQL `SELECT` command can be used to see the number of rows in the `products` table of our `shopping` database:

```
sqlite> select * from products;
select * from products;
```

```
101|Camera|15.0
102|Laptop|1005.98999023438
```

This output confirms that our `DatabaseApp` application successfully inserted two rows into the `products` table.

We can also issue an SQL `DELETE` command to delete a row. The following command deletes a row from the `products` table that has a product `code` equal to `102`.

```
sqlite> delete from products where code=102;
delete from products where code=102;
```

To confirm that the row was really deleted, we can give a SQL `SELECT` command as shown here:

```
sqlite> select * from products;
select * from products;
101|Camera|15.0
```

This output shows only one row in the `products` table, confirming that one of the two rows was deleted. Similarly we can give an SQL `UPDATE` command to update or modify the information of any row. The following SQL `UPDATE` command updates the product name to `Handy Cam`, whose code is equal to `101`.

```
sqlite> update products set product_name='Handy Cam' where code=101;
update products set product_name='Handy Cam' where code=101;
```

We can confirm whether the row was successfully updated by issuing an SQL `SELECT` command:

```
sqlite> select * from products;
select * from products;
101|Handy Cam|15.0
```

The preceding output confirms that the product name was updated. Similarly, we can give a different SQL command at the `sqlite>` prompt to manipulate our database. When finished, we can leave the `sqlite>` prompt by giving an `.exit` command:

```
sqlite>.exit
```

NOTE

An alternative to viewing all this data is to transfer the database file to the developer machine and then use many of the free SQLite utilities to view the data in a simple GUI-like fashion. Remember, the preceding commands work only on emulators or rooted devices.

Accessing the Database Through Menus

To make our `DatabaseApp` application accessible through menus, we need to define a few menu items in the menu file `activity_database_app` available in the `res/menu` folder.

In the menu file, we define a menu consisting of two menu items called `Insert Rows` and `List Rows`. These are used to initiate the tasks of inserting and accessing rows from the `products` table. The `activity_database_app.xml` file with the two menu items appears as shown in Listing 8.4.

LISTING 8.4   Code Written into the Menu File `activity_database_app.xml`

```
<menu xmlns:android="http://schemas.android.com/apk/res/android">
    <item android:id="@+id/insert_rows"
        android:title="Insert Rows"
        android:icon="@drawable/ic_launcher" />
    <item android:id="@+id/list_rows"
        android:title="List Rows"
        android:icon="@drawable/ic_launcher" />
</menu>
```

We can see that the IDs assigned to the two menu items of the menu are `insert_rows` and `list_rows`, respectively. In addition, the `ic_launcher` image from the `res/drawable` folder is displayed in the menu items. To insert and fetch rows from the database table when a menu item is selected, we need to write some Java code into the `DatabaseAppActivity.java` activity file. Note, there is no need to change the Java file `DatabaseManager.java`.

The Java code we adds performs the following tasks:

▶ Display the menu on the screen. Recall from the previous chapter that the `onCreateOptionsMenu()` method is called when a user clicks the `Menu` button on the device or emulator. So, in the activity file, we need to override this method to inflate the menu defined in the `mymenu.xml` file.

▶ Enclose the commands for inserting and fetching rows from the database table into two separate methods so that they can be invoked when the respective menu item is selected.

▶ Handle menu item selections and direct them to the respective methods for performing desired tasks.

To do all these tasks, the code shown in Listing 8.5 is written into the Java activity file `DatabaseAppActivity.java`. Only the code in bold is added or modified code; the rest of the code is the same as we saw in Listing 8.2.

LISTING 8.5   Code in the `DatabaseAppActivity.java` Activity File

```java
package com.androidunleashed.databaseapp;

import android.app.Activity;
import android.os.Bundle;
import android.widget.TextView;
import android.view.Menu;
import android.view.MenuInflater;
import android.view.MenuItem;

public class DatabaseAppActivity extends Activity {
    private DatabaseManager mydManager;
    private TextView response;
    private TextView productRec;
    @Override
    public void onCreate(Bundle savedInstanceState) {
        super.onCreate(savedInstanceState);
        setContentView(R.layout.activity_database_app);
        response=(TextView)findViewById(R.id.response);
        productRec=(TextView)findViewById(R.id.prodrec);
        response.setText("Press MENU button to display menu");
    }

    @Override
    public boolean onCreateOptionsMenu(Menu menu) {
        MenuInflater inflater = getMenuInflater();
        inflater.inflate(R.menu.activity_database_app, menu);
        return true;
    }

    @Override
    public boolean onOptionsItemSelected(MenuItem item) {
        switch (item.getItemId()) {
            case R.id.insert_rows: insertRec();
                break;
            case R.id.list_rows: showRec();
                break;
        }
        return true;
    }

    public boolean insertRec(){
        mydManager = new DatabaseManager(this);
        mydManager.addRow(101, "Camera", Float.parseFloat("15"));
        mydManager.addRow(102, "Laptop",  Float.parseFloat("1005.99"));
```

```
        response.setText("The rows in the products table are inserted");
        productRec.setText("");
        mydManager.close();
        return true;
    }

    public boolean showRec(){
        mydManager = new DatabaseManager(this);
        mydManager.openReadable();
        String tableContent = mydManager.retrieveRows();
        response.setText("The rows in the products table are:");
        productRec.setText(tableContent);
        mydManager.close();
        return true;
    }
}
```

We can see that the response `TextView` object is set to display the text `Press MENU` button to display menu. The Activity class's `onCreateOptionsMenu()` method is overridden to display the menu defined in the `mymenu.xml` file.

Initially, there is no menu defined in the `menu` parameter of the `onCreateOptionsMenu()` method. To inflate the menu that we defined in `mymenu.xml`, we get the `MenuInflater` from the Activity class and invoke its `inflate` method to inflate, or merge, our own menu defined in `mymenu.xml` to the `menu` parameter of this method. The `onCreateOptionsMenu()` method is set to return the boolean value, `true`, to allow Android to display the menu. Two methods, `insertRec()` and `showRec()`, are defined that contain the code to insert and fetch rows from the database table. In the `insertRec()` method, a `DatabaseManager` class instance is created called `mydManager`, and through this instance, the `addRow()` method is invoked to insert two rows in the `products` table. On successful insertion of the rows, the `TextView` response displays the text: The rows in the products table are inserted.

In the `showRec()` method, the `DatabaseManager` class instance called `mydManager` is created. It obtains the read-only reference of the database and invokes the `DatabaseManager` class's `retrieveRows()` method that fetches all the rows in the `products` table and returns a string. The rows returned as a string by `retrieveRows()` are assigned to the `product-Rec` `TextView` for display. To display the header above the displayed rows, the `response` `TextView` object is set to The rows in the products table are:.

The `onOptionItemSelected()` method handles the menu item selections. It calls the `insertRec()` and `showRec()` methods when the menu items with the ID `insert_rows` and `list_rows` are selected by the user.

After running the application, we get the initial screen shown in Figure 8.3 (left), where the `TextView` control prompts to call the menu. The menu appears with two menu items, `Insert Rows` and `List Rows`. After we select `Insert Rows`, the activity class method `insert-Rec()` is executed, which inserts two rows in the `products` table and displays the message

The rows in the products table are inserted (see Figure 8.3—middle). After we select List Rows, the rows in the `products` database table are accessed and displayed on the screen through the `TextView` control, as shown in Figure 8.3 (right).

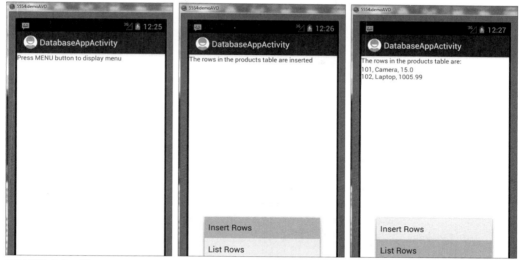

FIGURE 8.3   The `TextView` asking the user to press the MENU button to invoke the application's menu (left), the menu is displayed and the `TextView` shows that the `Insert Rows` menu item was selected (middle), and the rows in the products table displayed after selecting the `List Rows` menu item (right)

Our application looks pretty good, but there seems to be a limitation. It doesn't ask the user to provide information for adding new products to the `products` table. Instead the two rows to be added are hard-coded. To add more user interaction, we need to allow the user to enter new product information to the `products` table. Let's see how it can be done.

Creating a Data Entry Form

To create a form for entering new product information (see Figure 8.5—left), three `TextViews`, three `EditText` controls, and two `Button` controls are arranged in tabular format in the `TableLayout`. The layout file `activity_database_app.xml` is modified to appear as shown in Listing 8.6. Only the code in bold is the newly added code; the rest is the same as we saw in Listing 8.3.

LISTING 8.6   Code Written into the Layout File `activity_database_app.xml`

```
<LinearLayout xmlns:android="http://schemas.android.com/apk/res/android"
    android:orientation="vertical"
    android:layout_width="match_parent"
    android:layout_height="match_parent" >
    <TextView
        android:layout_width="match_parent"
```

```
            android:layout_height="wrap_content"
            android:id="@+id/response" />
    <TextView
            android:id="@+id/prodrec"
            android:layout_width="match_parent"
            android:layout_height="wrap_content" />
    <TableLayout
        android:id="@+id/add_table"
        android:layout_width="match_parent"
        android:layout_height="wrap_content" >
        <TableRow >
            <TextView
                android:text="Product Code:"
                android:padding="3dip" />
            <EditText
                android:id="@+id/prod_code"
                android:layout_width="match_parent"
                android:layout_height="wrap_content"/>
        </TableRow>
        <TableRow >
            <TextView
                android:text="Product Name:"
                android:padding="3dip" />
            <EditText
                android:id="@+id/prod_name"
                android:layout_width="wrap_content"
                android:layout_height="wrap_content"
                android:minWidth="150dip" />
        </TableRow>
        <TableRow >
            <TextView
                android:text="Product Price:"
                android:padding="3dip" />
            <EditText
                android:id="@+id/prod_price"
                android:layout_width="wrap_content"
                android:layout_height="wrap_content"
                android:minWidth="50dip" />
        </TableRow>
        <TableRow >
            <Button
                android:id="@+id/add_button"
                android:text="Add Product"
                android:layout_width="wrap_content"
                android:layout_height="wrap_content"
                android:padding="3dip" />
```

```
            <Button
                android:id="@+id/cancel_button"
                android:text="Cancel"
                android:layout_width="wrap_content"
                android:layout_height="wrap_content"
                android:padding="3dip" />
        </TableRow>
    </TableLayout>
</LinearLayout>
```

We can see that the three TextView controls are set to display the text Product Code:, Product Name:, and Product Price:. The captions in the two Button controls are set to Add Product and Cancel. The IDs assigned to the three EditText controls are prod_code, prod_name, and prod_price. The Button controls are assigned the IDs add_button and cancel_button.

There are no major changes to the Java file DatabaseManager.java. Only three statements are modified, as shown in bold in Listing 8.7.

LISTING 8.7   Code Written into the Java Class DatabaseManager.java

```
package com.androidunleashed.databaseapp;

import android.database.sqlite.SQLiteDatabase;
import android.content.Context;
import android.content.ContentValues;
import android.database.Cursor;
import android.database.sqlite.SQLiteOpenHelper;
import android.util.Log;

public class DatabaseManager {
    public static final String DB_NAME = "shopping";
    public static final String DB_TABLE = "products";
    public static final int DB_VERSION = 1;
    private static final String CREATE_TABLE = "CREATE TABLE " + DB_TABLE + " (code
        INTEGER PRIMARY KEY, product_name TEXT, price FLOAT);";
    private SQLHelper helper;
    private SQLiteDatabase db;
    private Context context;

    public DatabaseManager(Context c){
        this.context = c;
        helper=new SQLHelper(c);
        this.db = helper.getWritableDatabase();
    }
```

8

```
    public DatabaseManager openReadable() throws android.database.SQLException {
        helper=new SQLHelper(context);
        db = helper.getReadableDatabase();
        return this;
    }
    public void close(){
        helper.close();
    }
    public boolean addRow(int c, String n, float p){
        ContentValues newProduct = new ContentValues();
        newProduct.put("code", c);
        newProduct.put("product_name", n);
        newProduct.put("price", p);
        try{db.insertOrThrow(DB_TABLE, null, newProduct);}
        catch(Exception e) {
            Log.e("Error in inserting rows ", e.toString());
            e.printStackTrace();
            return false;
        }
        db.close();
        return true;
    }


    public String retrieveRows(){
        String[] columns = new String[]{"code", "product_name", "price"};
        Cursor cursor = db.query(DB_TABLE, columns, null, null, null, null, null);
        String tablerows = "";
        cursor.moveToFirst();
        while (cursor.isAfterLast() == false) {
            tablerows = tablerows + cursor.getInt(0) + ", "+cursor.getString(1)+",
"+ cursor.getFloat(2)+ "\n";
            cursor.moveToNext();
        }
        if (cursor != null && !cursor.isClosed()) {
            cursor.close();
        }
        return tablerows;
    }


    public class SQLHelper extends SQLiteOpenHelper {
        public SQLHelper(Context c){
            super(c, DB_NAME, null, DB_VERSION);
        }

        @Override
        public void onCreate(SQLiteDatabase db) {
```

```
                db.execSQL(CREATE_TABLE);
         }


         @Override
         public void onUpgrade(SQLiteDatabase db, int oldVersion, int newVersion) {
                Log.w("Products table","Upgrading database i.e. dropping table and rec-
reating it");
                db.execSQL("DROP TABLE IF EXISTS " + DB_TABLE);
                onCreate(db);
         }
     }
}
```

We can see that the addRow() method is set to return a boolean value instead of void, as
it was before. The reason is that we use the returned boolean value to see whether the
row was successfully inserted into the products table. The database is closed after the row
insertion in the products table.

In the activity file, we need to write Java code to perform the following tasks:

▶ Access the TableLayout container and make it visible when the Insert Rows menu
   item is selected. Also make it invisible when the List Rows menu item is selected.

▶ Map the EditText and Button controls defined in the TableLayout to the EditText
   and Button objects, respectively.

▶ Associate ClickListener to the Add Product button defined in the TableLayout to
   listen for the click event occurrence on the Button control.

▶ Through the callback event of the ClickListener, onClick(), access the new
   product information entered by the user and send it to the addRow() method
   defined in DatabaseManager.java as parameters to insert them in the products table.

▶ Hide the soft keyboard when the user is finished entering new product information.

To perform these tasks, add the code shown in Listing 8.8 into the DatabaseAppActivity.
java activity file. Only the code in bold is the newly added code; the rest is the same as
we saw in Listing 8.5.

LISTING 8.8   Code Written into the DatabaseAppActivity.java Java Activity File

```
package com.androidunleashed.databaseapp;

import android.app.Activity;
import android.content.Context;
import android.os.Bundle;
import android.widget.TextView;
import android.view.Menu;
import android.view.MenuInflater;
```

```
import android.view.MenuItem;
import android.view.View;
import android.widget.Button;
import android.widget.EditText;
import android.widget.TableLayout;
import android.view.View.OnClickListener;
import android.view.inputmethod.InputMethodManager;

public class DatabaseAppActivity extends Activity {
    private DatabaseManager mydManager;
    private TextView response;
    private TextView productRec;
    EditText pcode, pname, price;
    Button addButton;
    private TableLayout addLayout;
    private boolean recInserted;

    @Override
    public void onCreate(Bundle savedInstanceState) {
        super.onCreate(savedInstanceState);
        setContentView(R.layout.activity_database_app);
        response=(TextView)findViewById(R.id.response);
        productRec=(TextView)findViewById(R.id.prodrec);
        addLayout=(TableLayout)findViewById(R.id.add_table);
        addLayout.setVisibility(View.GONE);
        response.setText("Press MENU button to display menu");
        Button addButton = (Button) findViewById(R.id.add_button);
        addButton.setOnClickListener(new OnClickListener() {
            public void onClick(View v) {
                mydManager = new DatabaseManager(DatabaseAppActivity.this);
                pcode=(EditText)findViewById(R.id.prod_code);
                pname=(EditText)findViewById(R.id.prod_name);
                price=(EditText)findViewById(R.id.prod_price);
                recInserted=mydManager.addRow(Integer.parseInt(pcode.getText().
toString()), pname.getText().toString(),
                Float.parseFloat (price.getText().toString()));
                addLayout.setVisibility(View.GONE);
                if(recInserted)
                    response.setText("The row in the products table is inserted");
                else
                    response.setText("Sorry, some errors occurred while inserting
the row in the products table");
                InputMethodManager imm = (InputMethodManager)
getSystemService(Context.INPUT_METHOD_SERVICE);
                imm.hideSoftInputFromWindow(price.getWindowToken(), InputMethodMa-
nager.HIDE_NOT_ALWAYS);
```

```
            mydManager.close();
            pcode.setText("");
            pname.setText("");
            price.setText("");
            productRec.setText("");
        }
    });
}


@Override
public boolean onCreateOptionsMenu(Menu menu) {
    MenuInflater inflater = getMenuInflater();
    inflater.inflate(R.menu.activity_database_app, menu);
    return true;
}


@Override
public boolean onOptionsItemSelected(MenuItem item) {
    switch (item.getItemId()) {
        case R.id.insert_rows: addLayout.setVisibility(View.VISIBLE);
            response.setText("Enter information of the new product");
            productRec.setText("");
            break;
        case R.id.list_rows: showRec();
            break;
    }
    return true;
}


public boolean showRec(){
    addLayout.setVisibility(View.GONE);
    mydManager = new DatabaseManager(this);
    mydManager.openReadable();
    String tableContent = mydManager.retrieveRows();
    response.setText("The rows in the products table are:");
    productRec.setText(tableContent);
    mydManager.close();
    return true;
}
}
```

We can see that the `TableLayout` container is captured from the layout file and mapped to the `TableLayout` object `addLayout`. It is initially set to the `GONE` mode and is be displayed only when the `InsertRows` menu item is selected by the user. The `TableLayout` contains controls to enter new product information. The `Button` control defined in the `TableLayout` with the ID `add_button`, is accessed and mapped to the `Button` object `add_button`. A `ClickListener` is associated with the `add_button` object so that the callback method, `onClick()`, is executed when the `Button` with the caption `Add Button` is selected by the user.

In the `onClick()` method, the information entered by the user in the three `EditText` controls, `prod_code`, `prod_name`, and `prod_price`, is accessed, converted into a string data type, and passed as arguments to the `addRow()` method defined in `DatabaseManager.java`. To add a new row in the `products` table, the `addRow()` method accepts three parameters of the string data type. The boolean value returned by `addRow()` is checked to see whether the new row was successfully inserted in the `products` table. If the boolean value returned by `addRow()` is `true`, it means that the new row was successfully inserted and the message `The row in the products table is inserted` is displayed. If not, the message `Sorry, some errors occurred while inserting the row in the products table` is shown instead. Finally, the soft keyboard that appeared while inserting new product information is hidden.

Note, there is no need to make any changes to the menu file `mymenu.xml`.

Our application is complete and is ready to accept new product information from the user. After we run the application, the first screen that we see on startup is shown in Figure 8.4 (left). The screen displays a message via a `TextView` control asking the user to select the `MENU` button. Two menu items, `Insert Rows` and `List Rows`, are displayed. After we select the `List Rows` menu item, the information stored in the `products` table is displayed, as shown in Figure 8.4 (right).

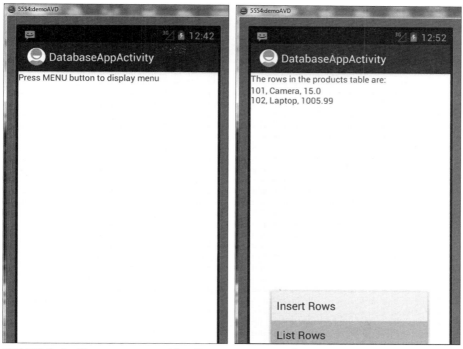

FIGURE 8.4   The `TextView` asking the user to press the `MENU` button to invoke application's menu (left), and the rows in the products table displayed after selecting the `List Rows` menu item (right)

After we select the `Insert Rows` menu item, a form is displayed for entering new product information. A `TextView` at the top displays the text `Enter information of the new product`. The user can enter the new product information, as shown in the Figure 8.5 (left), and then click the `Add Product` button to add a new row into the `products` table. If the row is successfully inserted, the message `The row in the products table is inserted` appears on the screen, as shown in Figure 8.5 (middle). After we select the `List Rows` menu item, the newly added row is displayed on the screen, as shown in Figure 8.5 (right).

FIGURE 8.5   The form filled with the new product information (left), the confirmation message, indicating the row was successfully inserted (middle), and the newly added rows (right)

If, for any reason, the row could not be added to the products table, the error message `Sorry, some errors occurred while inserting the row in the products table` appears on the screen.

We can make our application more attractive and interactive by displaying the `products` table rows via the `ListView` control, shown in Figure 8.6, instead of through the `TextView` control shown in Figure 8.5 (right).

Displaying Table Rows Via `ListView`

To display the information fetched from the database table with the `ListView` control instead of the `TextView` control, the first step is to replace the `response TextView` that we used to display `products` table rows with a `ListView` control. After we replace the `TextView` control with a `ListView` control, `activity_database_app.xml` appears as shown in Listing 8.9. Only the code in bold is modified; the rest of the code is the same as we saw in Listing 8.6.

LISTING 8.9   Code Written into the Layout File `activity_database_app.xml`

```
<LinearLayout xmlns:android="http://schemas.android.com/apk/res/android"
    android:orientation="vertical"
    android:layout_width="match_parent"
    android:layout_height="match_parent">
    <TextView
        android:layout_width="match_parent"
        android:layout_height="wrap_content"
        android:id="@+id/response" />
    <ListView
        android:id="@+id/prodrec"
```

```
    android:layout_width="match_parent"
    android:layout_height="match_parent"
    android:drawSelectorOnTop="false"/>
<TableLayout
    android:id="@+id/add_table"
    android:layout_width="match_parent"
    android:layout_height="wrap_content" >
    <TableRow >
        <TextView
            android:text="Product Code:"
            android:padding="3dip" />
        <EditText
            android:id="@+id/prod_code"
            android:layout_width="match_parent"
            android:layout_height="wrap_content"/>
    </TableRow>
    <TableRow >
        <TextView
            android:text="Product Name:"
            android:padding="3dip" />
        <EditText
            android:id="@+id/prod_name"
            android:layout_width="wrap_content"
            android:layout_height="wrap_content"
            android:minWidth="150dip" />
    </TableRow>
    <TableRow >
        <TextView
            android:text="Product Price:"
            android:padding="3dip" />
        <EditText
            android:id="@+id/prod_price"
            android:layout_width="wrap_content"
            android:layout_height="wrap_content"
            android:minWidth="50dip"/>
    </TableRow>
    <TableRow >
        <Button
            android:id="@+id/add_button"
            android:text="Add Product"
            android:layout_width="wrap_content"
            android:layout_height="wrap_content"
            android:padding="3dip"/>
        <Button
            android:id="@+id/cancel_button"
            android:text="Cancel"
```

```
                android:layout_width="wrap_content"
                android:layout_height="wrap_content"
                android:padding="3dip" />
        </TableRow>
    </TableLayout>
</LinearLayout>
```

In the Java file, `DatabaseManager.java`, we need to modify the `retrieveRows()` method that returns the `products` table rows in string data format. Currently, the `retrieveRows()` method is set to return a data of type `String`, as the information returned by it was displayed via a `TextView` control. Now, because we want to display the data via a `ListView` control, we must modify the method return type to `ArrayList<String>`. A `productRows` of `ArrayList<String>` variable data type is defined, and every row fetched from the `products` table is added to it. The method returns the variable `productRows`, containing the products table rows in the `ArrayList` format. The Java file `DatabaseManager.java` is modified to appear as shown in Listing 8.10. Only the statements shown in bold are modified; the rest of the code is the same as we saw in Listing 8.7.

LISTING 8.10   Code Written into the Java Class `DatabaseManager.java`

```
package com.androidunleashed.databaseapp;

import android.database.sqlite.SQLiteDatabase;
import android.content.Context;
import android.content.ContentValues;
import android.database.Cursor;
import android.database.sqlite.SQLiteOpenHelper;
import android.util.Log;
import java.util.ArrayList;

public class DatabaseManager {
    public static final String DB_NAME = "shopping";
    public static final String DB_TABLE = "products";
    public static final int DB_VERSION = 1;
    private static final String CREATE_TABLE = "CREATE TABLE " + DB_TABLE + " (code
        INTEGER PRIMARY KEY, product_name TEXT, price FLOAT);";
    private SQLHelper helper;
    private SQLiteDatabase db;
    private Context context;

    public DatabaseManager(Context c){
        this.context = c;
        helper=new SQLHelper(c);
        this.db = helper.getWritableDatabase();
    }
```

```java
public DatabaseManager openReadable() throws android.database.SQLException {
    helper=new SQLHelper(context);
    db = helper.getReadableDatabase();
    return this;
}

 public void close(){
      helper.close();
}

public boolean addRow(int c, String n, float p){
    ContentValues newProduct = new ContentValues();
    newProduct.put("code", c);
    newProduct.put("product_name", n);
    newProduct.put("price", p);
    try{db.insertOrThrow(DB_TABLE, null, newProduct);}
    catch(Exception e)
    {
        Log.e("Error in inserting rows ", e.toString());
        e.printStackTrace();
        return false;
    }
    db.close();
    return true;
}
public ArrayList<String> retrieveRows(){
    ArrayList<String> productRows=new ArrayList<String>();
    String[] columns = new String[]{"code", "product_name", "price"};
    Cursor cursor = db.query(DB_TABLE, columns, null, null, null, null, null);
    cursor.moveToFirst();
    while (cursor.isAfterLast() == false) {
        productRows.add(Integer.toString(cursor.getInt(0)) + ", "+cursor.get-
String(1)+",
            "+Float.toString(cursor.getFloat(2)));
        cursor.moveToNext();
    }
    if (cursor != null && !cursor.isClosed()) {
        cursor.close();
    }
    return productRows;
}

public class SQLHelper extends SQLiteOpenHelper {
    public SQLHelper(Context c){
        super(c, DB_NAME, null, DB_VERSION);
    }
```

```
        @Override
        public void onCreate(SQLiteDatabase db) {
                db.execSQL(CREATE_TABLE);
        }

        @Override
        public void onUpgrade(SQLiteDatabase db, int oldVersion, int newVersion) {
                Log.w("Products table","Upgrading database i.e. dropping table and rec-
reating it");
                db.execSQL("DROP TABLE IF EXISTS " + DB_TABLE);
                onCreate(db);
        }
    }
}
```

Again, a small modification is required in `DatabaseAppActivity.java`. In its `showRec()` method, we write the code to access the `ListView` control from the layout file and map it to the `ListView` object, `productRec`. The rows returned by calling the `retrieveRows()` method of `DatabaseManager` in the `ArrayList<String>` format are temporarily stored in the variable `tableContent`. An `ArrayAdapter` called `arrayAdpt` is created through the `tableContent` array. Finally, the `ArrayAdapter`, `arrayAdpt`, is set to the `ListView` control `productRec` to display the `products` table rows in the `ListView` control. The activity file `DatabaseAppActivity.java` is modified to appear as shown in Listing 8.11. Only the code in bold is modified; the rest of the code is exactly the same as we saw in Listing 8.8.

LISTING 8.11   Code Written into the `DatabaseAppActivity.java` Java Activity File

```
package com.androidunleashed.databaseapp;

import android.app.Activity;
import android.content.Context;
import android.os.Bundle;
import android.widget.TextView;
import android.view.Menu;
import android.view.MenuInflater;
import android.view.MenuItem;
import android.view.View;
import android.widget.Button;
import android.widget.EditText;
import android.widget.TableLayout;
import android.view.View.OnClickListener;
import android.view.inputmethod.InputMethodManager;
import android.widget.ListView;
import android.widget.ArrayAdapter;
import java.util.ArrayList;
```

```java
public class DatabaseAppActivity extends Activity {
    private DatabaseManager mydManager;
    private TextView response;
    private ListView productRec;
    EditText pcode, pname, price;
    Button addButton;
    private TableLayout addLayout;
    private Boolean recInserted;
    ArrayList<String> tableContent;

    @Override
    public void onCreate(Bundle savedInstanceState) {
        super.onCreate(savedInstanceState);
        setContentView(R.layout.activity_database_app);
        response=(TextView)findViewById(R.id.response);
        productRec=(ListView)findViewById(R.id.prodrec);
        addLayout=(TableLayout)findViewById(R.id.add_table);
        addLayout.setVisibility(View.GONE);
        response.setText("Press MENU button to display menu");
        Button add_button = (Button) findViewById(R.id.add_button);
        add_button.setOnClickListener(new OnClickListener() {
            public void onClick(View v) {
                mydManager = new DatabaseManager(DatabaseAppActivity.this);
                pcode=(EditText)findViewById(R.id.prod_code);
                pname=(EditText)findViewById(R.id.prod_name);
                price=(EditText)findViewById(R.id.prod_price);
                recInserted=mydManager.addRow(Integer.parseInt (pcode.get-
Text().toString()), pname.getText().toString(),Float.parseFloat(price.getText().
toString())));
                addLayout.setVisibility(View.GONE);
                if(recInserted)
                    response.setText("The row in the products table is inserted");
                 else
                    response.setText("Sorry, some errors occurred while inserting
the row in the products table");
                InputMethodManager imm = (InputMethodManager)
getSystemService(Context.INPUT_METHOD_SERVICE);
                imm.hideSoftInputFromWindow(price.getWindowToken(), InputMethodMa-
nager.HIDE_NOT_ALWAYS);
                mydManager.close();
                pcode.setText("");
                pname.setText("");
                price.setText("");
                productRec.setVisibility(View.GONE);
            }
        });
```

```
    }

    @Override
    public boolean onCreateOptionsMenu(Menu menu) {
        MenuInflater inflater = getMenuInflater();
        inflater.inflate(R.menu.activity_database_app, menu);
        return true;
    }

    @Override
    public boolean onOptionsItemSelected(MenuItem item) {
        switch (item.getItemId()) {
            case R.id.insert_rows:
                addLayout.setVisibility(View.VISIBLE);
                response.setText("Enter information of the new product");
                productRec.setVisibility(View.GONE);
                break;
            case R.id.list_rows: showRec();
                break;
        }
        return true;
    }

    public boolean showRec(){
        addLayout.setVisibility(View.GONE);
        mydManager = new DatabaseManager(this);
        mydManager.openReadable();
        tableContent = mydManager.retrieveRows();
        response.setText("The rows in the products table are:");
        productRec = (ListView)findViewById(R.id.prodrec);
        ArrayAdapter<String> arrayAdpt=new ArrayAdapter<String>(this,
android.R.layout.simple_list_item_1, tableContent);
        productRec.setAdapter(arrayAdpt);
        productRec.setVisibility(View.VISIBLE);
        mydManager.close();
        return true;
    }
}
```

Our application is updated to show the database table rows via a ListView control. After running the application, we get the usual startup screen (as you saw earlier in Figure 8.4—left), asking the user to bring up the menu. The menu shows two menu items, Insert Rows and List Rows, as shown earlier in Figure 8.4 (right). After we select the List Rows menu item, the rows in the products table are fetched and displayed via the ListView control, as shown in Figure 8.6.

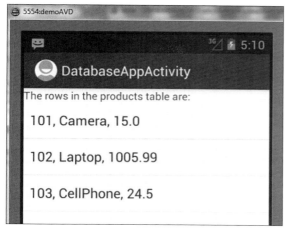

FIGURE 8.6   The products table rows displayed via the `ListView` control

Summary

In this chapter we learned to use databases in Android applications. We saw how to use `SQLiteOpenHelper` and cursors, as well as how to fetch desired rows from the table. We learned to access a database through the ADB and menus. Finally, we learned to create data entry forms and display database table rows via `ListView`.

The next chapter focuses on understanding animation. We learn to use Canvas and Paints, measure screen coordinates, and apply frame-by-frame animation. We also learn about tweening animation and the use of interpolators.

PART IV

Advanced Android Programming: Internet, Entertainment, and Services

Implementing Drawing and Animation

Drawings and animations are two important tools that make an application more attractive and dynamic. Android supports displaying images, text, and different shapes. It supports animation that we can use in developing game applications, educational tutorials, and demonstrations.

Drawing on the Screen

We can draw images, text, and primitive shapes on the screen with Android. We can draw these images in different colors and fill them with the desired styles or gradients. The following are the objects required while drawing in Android applications:

▶ `Canvas` **object**—Used to draw on the screen. A `Canvas` object is obtained by extending the `View` class and implementing the `onDraw()` method to draw the desired content. A `Canvas` is also obtained by instantiating a `Canvas` with a bitmap to draw in to.

▶ `Paint` **object**—Used to provide information such as color, style, and other rendering information to be applied to a graphic, shape, or text.

Using `Canvas` **and** `Paint`

To draw on the screen, we need to use the `Canvas` and `Paint` objects collectively. The `Canvas` object provides the methods available for drawing graphics, text, and shapes. The following steps are required to draw with the `Canvas` and `Paint` objects:

- ▶ Create a custom class that extends the View class.

- ▶ Implement the onDraw() method in the custom class to create a Paint object. Set the graphic color and shade through the Paint object if desired. Draw the desired graphic in the selected color and shade by calling a Canvas class method.

- ▶ Override the onCreate() method in our Activity to draw the content through the custom class, in the same way as a layout.

Let's create a new Android project called CanvasApp. In the Java activity file CanvasAppActivity.java, write the code shown in Listing 9.1.

LISTING 9.1   Code Written into the Java Activity File CanvasAppActivity.java

```java
package com.androidunleashed.canvasapp;

import android.app.Activity;
import android.os.Bundle;
import android.graphics.Paint;
import android.graphics.Canvas;
import android.view.View;
import android.content.Context;
import android.graphics.Color;

public class CanvasAppActivity extends Activity {
    @Override
    public void onCreate(Bundle savedInstanceState) {
        super.onCreate(savedInstanceState);
        MyView myView=new MyView(this);
        setContentView(myView);                              #5
    }

    public class MyView extends View{                        #1
        public MyView(Context context){
            super(context);
        }

        @Override
        protected void onDraw(Canvas canvas) {
            super.onDraw(canvas);
            Paint paint = new Paint();                       #2
            paint.setColor(Color.RED);                       #3
            canvas.drawCircle(200,200,70,paint);             #4
        }
    }
}
```

Statement #1 shows the creation of the MyView custom class that extends the View class. The onDraw() method is overridden and a Paint object called paint is created in statement #2. The color of the graphics to be drawn is set to red in statement #3. The drawCircle() method is called in statement #4, which draws a circle with a radius of 70 pixels and a center location of 200, 200 (at 200 pixels on the X and Y axes). The onCreate() method in the Activity is overridden by the content defined in the custom class MyView. Statement #5 calls the setContentView() method to draw the content (a red circle) defined through the custom class MyView.

After running the application, we see the circle drawn, as shown in Figure 9.1 (left). You can observe that the circle edge appears a bit rough. We learn to make the edges smooth in the following section.

FIGURE 9.1   Filled circle with rough edge (left), and filled circle with smooth edge (right)

Using Colors

Besides red, we can use any color in graphics via the following constants:

- ▶ Color.BLACK
- ▶ Color.BLUE
- ▶ Color.CYAN
- ▶ Color.DKGRAY
- ▶ Color.GRAY

▶ `Color.GREEN`

▶ `Color.LTGRAY`

▶ `Color.MAGENTA`

▶ `Color.RED`

▶ `Color.TRANSPARENT`

▶ `Color.WHITE`

▶ `Color.YELLOW`

Drawing Circles

The `drawCircle()` method used in Listing 9.1 is the `Canvas` class method that draws a circle of a given radius at a specified center using a specified paint. Here is the syntax:

```
drawCircle(float x, float y, float r, Paint p)
```

where `x` and `y` form the center point, `r` represents the circle radius, and `p` is the `Paint` object.

Determining the Height and Width of the `Canvas`

To find the `Canvas`'s height and width, we use the `getHeight()` and `getWidth()` methods. The following code snippet can be added to the `onDraw()` method of the project shown in Listing 9.1 to find the `Canvas`'s width and height:

```
int width=canvas.getWidth();
int height=canvas.getHeight();
Log.d("width", String.valueOf(width));
Log.d("height", String.valueOf(height));
```

Also import the `Log` class by adding the following statement at the top in the `CanvasAppActivity.java` file:

```
import android.util.Log;
```

After we add this code, log messages appear in the `LogCat` pane with the `Canvas`'s width and height, as shown in Figure 9.2.

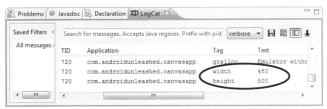

FIGURE 9.2   Log messages showing the width and height of the `Canvas`

To draw a circle at the center of the `Canvas`, replace the code for drawing the circle (statement, #4) in Listing 9.1 with the following code:

```
int width=canvas.getWidth();
int height=canvas.getHeight();
float center_x = (float) width/2;
float center_y = (float) height/2;
canvas.drawCircle(center_x,center_y,70,paint);
```

Applying Paint Antialiasing

The circle we saw in Figure 9.1 (left) has a rough edge. To make it smooth, use the `Paint`'s antialiasing feature. If we enable antialiasing while creating a `Paint` object, the drawings appear smoother. The following code creates a `Paint` object called `paint` with antialiasing enabled:

```
Paint paint = new Paint(Paint.ANTI_ALIAS_FLAG);
```

If this statement replaces statement #2 in Listing 9.1, the circle appears smoother, as shown in Figure 9.1 (right).

Drawing Points

To draw a point, the `Canvas` class's `drawPoint()` method is used. The following is the method signature:

```
void drawPoint(float x, float y, Paint paint)
```

where `x` and `y` represent the X and Y coordinates where the point is to be drawn, and `paint` refers to the `Paint` object.

Setting the Paint Style

`Paint` style refers to the graphic's appearance, specifically whether it appears only as an outline or with a fill. The method used for defining `Paint` style is the `setStyle()` method. The following is the method signature:

```
void setStyle (Paint.Style)
```

where `paint_style` can be any of the following:

▶ `Paint.Style.STROKE`—Graphic and text outlines are stroked in the selected color.

▶ `Paint.Style.FILL`—Graphic and text are filled with the selected color. The stroke-related settings are be ignored when this style is applied. It is the default style.

▶ `Paint.Style.FILL_AND_STROKE`—Graphic and text are filled as well as stroked.

Setting the Stroke Width

When a stroke style is applied, we can control the stroke's width by using the `setStroke-Width()` method. The following is the method signature:

```
void  setStrokeWidth(float width)
```

where we can pass any width parameter value to set the stroke's width. Passing value `0` sets the stroke's width to a single pixel.

Setting the Stroke Cap

We can set the end or cap of the stroke to square or rounded with the `setStrokeCap()` method.

Syntax:

```
setStrokeCap(Print.Cap)
```

where `Print.Cap` can be one of the following:

▶ `Paint.Cap.BUTT`—The stroke ends at the specified coordinate and does not extend beyond it. It is the default.

▶ `Paint.Cap.ROUND`—The stroke extends out as a semicircle, with the center at the end of the specified coordinate.

▶ `Paint.Cap.SQUARE`—The stroke extends out as a square, with the center at the end of the specified coordinate.

The following code displays three square red points at the (20,20), (50,50), and (100,100) coordinate locations:

```
Paint paint = new Paint();
paint.setColor(Color.RED);
paint.setStyle(Paint.Style.STROKE);
paint.setStrokeWidth(10);
canvas.drawPoint(20, 20, paint);
canvas.drawPoint(50, 50, paint);
canvas.drawPoint(100, 100, paint);
```

By default, the dots appear as squares, as shown in Figure 9.3 (left). To make the dot appear wider, the `stroke` width is set to `10` pixels. If the `setStrokeCap()` method is added, passing the `Paint.Cap.ROUND` parameter to it makes the points appear round. This method makes the stroke's cap or end appear round:

```
paint.setStrokeCap(Paint.Cap.ROUND);
```

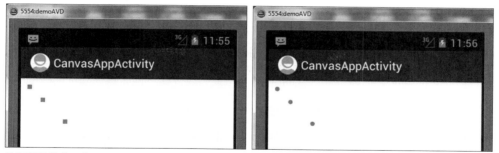

FIGURE 9.3   Square points (left) and round points (right)

Drawing Lines

The `drawLine()` method is used to draw lines between two specified coordinates. The method signature is as follows:

```
void drawLine(float x1, float y1, float x2, float y2, Paint paint)
```

where

`x1, y1`—Represents the X and Y coordinates of the start of the line

`x2, y2`—Represents the X and Y coordinates of the end of the line

`paint`—Represents the `Paint` object used to draw the line

When we draw lines, any style applied to the `Paint` object is ignored.

The following code displays two lines in red with a stroke width set to `10` pixels. The first line is drawn from `20, 100` to `120, 100`, and the second line is drawn from `120,100` to `120,200`:

```
Paint paint = new Paint();
paint.setColor(Color.RED);
paint.setStyle(Paint.Style.STROKE);
paint.setStrokeWidth(10);
canvas.drawLine(20,100,120,100, paint);
canvas.drawLine(120,100,120,200, paint);
```

The lines drawn by this code appear as shown in Figure 9.4 (left).

To draw more than one line with a single method, all the line coordinates need to be stored in an array and passed to the `drawLines()` method. The method signature is as follows:

```
void drawLines(float[] ptsArray, int offset, int count, Paint paint)
```

Table 9.1 provides descriptions of the parameters used in the `drawLines()` method.

9

TABLE 9.1   `drawLines()` Parameters

Parameter	Description
ptsArray	Represents the array containing the coordinates of all the lines to be drawn. The first line is drawn with the values in ptsArray[0], ptsArray[1] as the starting X and Y coordinates and ptsArray[2], ptsArray[3] as the ending X and Y coordinates. Similarly, the second line is drawn with ptsArray[4], ptsArray[5] as the beginning X and Y coordinates and ptsArray[6], ptsArray[7] as the ending X and Y coordinates, and so on.
Offset	Represents the number of elements in the array to skip before drawing. If we enter a value as 1, then the first element of the array, ptsArray[0], is skipped and lines are drawn with the values from ptsArray[1], ptsArray[2]....
count	Represents the number of elements in the array to be used for drawing lines, after skipping the offset number of elements.
paint	Represents the Paint object to draw the lines.

NOTE

Because each line requires four values, the `ptsArray` in the `drawLines()` method must contain at least four values.

The following code displays two lines in red with the stroke width set to 10 pixels. The first line is drawn from 20, 100 to 120, 100, and the second line is drawn from 120,100 to 120,200. All the line coordinates are stored in a ptsArray array, which is then passed to the drawLines() method:

```
float ptsArray[]=new float[8];
ptsArray[0]=20;
ptsArray[1]=100;
ptsArray[2]=120;
ptsArray[3]=100;
ptsArray[4]=120;
ptsArray[5]=100;
ptsArray[6]=120;
ptsArray[7]=200;
Paint paint = new Paint();
paint.setColor(Color.RED);
paint.setStyle(Paint.Style.STROKE);
paint.setStrokeWidth(10);
canvas.drawLines(ptsArray, paint);
```

In the preceding code, we call the `drawLines()` method without passing `offset` and `count` parameters, as we want all the coordinates of the `ptsArray` to be used for drawing lines and don't want to skip any elements. The preceding code displays two lines, as shown in Figure 9.4 (left).

To display only the first line, that is, to use just the first four elements of the `ptsArray` for drawing a line, use the `drawLines()` method with parameters passed to it as shown in the following code:

```
canvas.drawLines(ptsArray,0,4,paint);
```

This statement skips 0 elements of the `ptsArray` and uses its first four elements, `ptsArray[0]`, `ptsArray[1]`, `ptsArray[2]`, and `ptsArray[3]`, for drawing a line. The first line is drawn as shown in Figure 9.4 (middle). Again, to draw both the lines, we use all eight elements of the `ptsArray` without skipping any of its elements, as shown in the following statement:

```
canvas.drawLines(ptsArray,0,8,paint);
```

The output of this statement is same as in Figure 9.4 (left). To draw only the second line, we skip the first four elements of the `ptsArray` and use the next four elements to draw a line, as shown in the following statement:

```
canvas.drawLines(ptsArray,4,4,paint);
```

In this statement, the elements `ptsArray[4]`, `ptsArray[5]`, `ptsArray[6]`, and `ptsArray[7]` are used to draw only the second line, as shown in Figure 9.4 (right).

FIGURE 9.4   Two lines drawn (left), only the first line is drawn (middle), and only the second line is drawn (right)

Defining Drawing Paths

To draw a graphic that consists of lines and curves, we can define a path and draw the graphic collectively with a single method, `drawPath()`. The method signature for using the `drawPath()` method follows:

```
public void drawPath(Path path, Paint paint)
```

where `path` represents the `Path` object and `paint` represents the `Paint` object to draw the graphic.

The following code defines a path composed of two lines and draws it:

```
Paint paint = new Paint();
paint.setColor(Color.RED);
paint.setStyle(Paint.Style.STROKE);
paint.setStrokeWidth(10);
Path path = new Path();
path.moveTo(20, 100);
path.lineTo(120, 100);
path.lineTo(120, 200);
canvas.drawPath(path, paint);
```

Import the `Path` class by adding the following statement at the top in the `CanvasAppActivity.java`:

```
import android.graphics.Path;
```

The two lines drawn in the path appear as shown in Figure 9.5 (left). To give the line round ends, the `setStrokeCap()` method can be added to the preceding code, passing the constant `Paint.Cap.ROUND` to it, as shown in the following statement:

```
paint.setStrokeCap(Paint.Cap.ROUND);
```

If we add this statement, the lines in the path are drawn with the ends rounded, as shown in Figure 9.5 (right).

FIGURE 9.5   Lines with square caps drawn in a path (left), and lines with rounded caps drawn in a path (right)

Drawing Rectangles
To draw rectangles on the screen, the `Canvas` method `drawRect()` is used.

Syntax:

```
void  drawRect(Rect r, Paint paint)
```

where `r` is a `Rect` object that includes four integer coordinates `x1,y1,x2,y2`. These represent rectangle boundaries, where `x1,y1` represent the X and Y coordinates of the top-left corner where the rectangle begins, and `x2,y2` represent the X and Y coordinates of the bottom-right corner, where the rectangle ends. The `paint` represents the `Paint` object used to draw the rectangles. To create a `Rect` object, use the constructor shown here:

```
Rect(int x1, int y1, int x2, int y2)
```

where `x1` and `y1` defines the X and Y coordinates of the top-left corner of the `Rect` object and `x2` and `y2` define the X and Y coordinates of the bottom-right corner of the `rect` object.

The following code draws a rectangle in red from `100,100` coordinates to `300,300` coordinates, where `100,100` represents the X and Y coordinates to begin the rectangle, and `300,300` represents the X and Y coordinates to end the rectangle.

```
Paint paint = new Paint();
paint.setColor(Color.RED);
paint.setStyle(Paint.Style.STROKE);              #1
Rect rect = new Rect();
rect.set(100,100,300,300);
canvas.drawRect(rect, paint);
```

Import the `Rect` class in the activity file `CanvasAppActivity.java` by adding the following statement:

```
import android.graphics.Rect;
```

The preceding code displays the outline of a rectangle (see Figure 9.6—left), because the `Paint`'s style is set to the `STROKE` style. To increase the width of the outline, add the `setStrokeWidth()` method to the preceding code, as shown here:

```
paint.setStrokeWidth(5);
```

This statement make the width `5`, as shown in Figure 9.6 (middle). To fill the rectangle, replace the `STROKE` `Paint`'s style with the `FILL` style. To do so, replace statement `#1` in the previous code with the following statement:

```
paint.setStyle(Paint.Style.FILL);
```

This statement fills the rectangle with the color red, as shown in Figure 9.6 (right).

9

FIGURE 9.6   Square outline drawn with stroke width = 1 (left), square outline drawn with stroke width = 5 (middle), and filled square (right)

Drawing Rounded Rectangles

To draw rounded rectangles, the `Canvas` method used is `drawRoundRect()`.The syntax is as follows:

```
void  drawRoundRect(RectF rect, float rx, float ry, Paint paint)
```

Table 9.2 describes the parameters used in the `drawRoundRect()` method.

TABLE 9.2   `drawRoundRect()` Parameters

Parameter	Description
rect	Represents the `RectF` object. `Rect` defines the rectangle boundaries with integer coordinates; `RectF` defines rectangle boundaries with float coordinates.
rx	Represents the x radius to round the corners.
ry	Represents the y radius to round the corners.
paint	Represents the `Paint` object to draw the rounded rectangle.

NOTE

`RectF` holds four float coordinates that represent rectangle boundaries: `x1,y1` and `x2,y2` where `x1,y1` are the X and Y coordinates of the top-left corner of the rectangle boundaries and `x2,y2` are the bottom-right corner of the rectangle boundaries.

The following code draws a filled, red, rounded rectangle from `100,100` coordinates to `300,300` where `100,100` represents the X and Y coordinates of the top-left corner of the rectangle and `300,300` represents the X and Y coordinates of the bottom-right corner of the rectangle.

```
Paint paint = new Paint();
paint.setColor(Color.RED);
paint.setStyle(Paint.Style.FILL);
```

```
final RectF rectf = new RectF(100, 100, 300, 300);
canvas.drawRoundRect(rectf, 20, 20, paint);
```

Import the `RectF` class by adding the following statement in the activity file
`CanvasAppActivity.java`:

```
import android.graphics.RectF;
```

Here, we can see that the X and Y radius used for rounding the corners is `20, 20`. The
rounded rectangle appears as shown in Figure 9.7 (left). Let's increase the X and Y radius
from `20,20` to `50,50`, as shown in the following statement:

```
canvas.drawRoundRect(rectf, 50, 50, paint);
```

The rounded rectangle now appears as shown in Figure 9.7 (middle). The corners of the
rounded rectangle can be more rounded by increasing the X and Y radius to `100, 100`
with the following statement:

```
canvas.drawRoundRect(rectf, 100, 100, paint);
```

With such a high X and Y radius, the rounded rectangle now appears like a circle, as
shown in Figure 9.7 (right).

FIGURE 9.7   Filled rounded rectangle with the x and y radius = 20,20 (left), filled rounded
rectangle with the x and y radius = 50,50 (middle), and filled rounded rectangle with the x and y
radius = 100, 100 (right)

Drawing Ovals

The method used to draw ovals is `drawOval()`. The method signature is

```
void  drawOval(RectF oval, Paint paint)
```

where `oval` is the `RectF` object that defines the four float coordinates representing the
boundaries within which we want to draw the oval. The `paint` parameter is the `Paint`
object used to draw the oval.

The following code draws a vertical oval with a red fill:

```
Paint paint = new Paint();
paint.setColor(Color.RED);
paint.setStyle(Paint.Style.FILL);
RectF rectf = new RectF(100, 100, 200, 300);
canvas.drawOval(rectf,  paint);
```

Here, the coordinates `100,100` and `200,300` that are used for making the `RectF` object defines the oval boundaries. Because the distance between the X coordinates in the `RectF` object just created is smaller than the distance between the Y coordinates, the oval appears vertical (see Figure 9.8—left). To make the oval appear horizontal, reduce the distance between the Y coordinates and increase the distance between the X coordinates. That is, replace the statement that creates the preceding `RectF` object with the following statement:

```
RectF rectf = new RectF(100, 100, 300, 200);
```

When we use this statement, the horizontal oval appears as shown in Figure 9.8 (right).

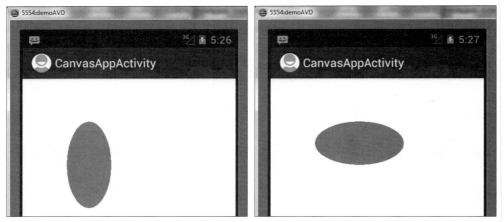

FIGURE 9.8   Filled vertical oval (left) and filled horizontal oval (right)

Drawing Arcs

The `Canvas` method used to draw arcs is `drawArc()`. The method signature is as follows:

```
drawArc(RectF oval, float angle1, float angle2, boolean center, Paint paint)
```

Table 9.3 describes the parameters used in the `drawRoundRect()` method.

TABLE 9.3   `drawRoundRect()` Parameters

Parameter	Description
oval	Represents the `RectF` object comprised of four float coordinates that define the top-left and bottom-right boundaries within which we want to draw the arc.
angle1	Represents the starting angle in degrees from where we want to begin the arc. If this angle is negative or greater than 360, the modulo 360 angle is used.
angle2	Represents the ending angle. The arc is drawn clockwise. If this angle is greater than 360, then instead of the arc, a complete oval is drawn. If this angle is negative, the modulo 360 angle is used.
center	If this Boolean value is set to `true`, it means we want to use the center of the oval to draw and close the arc.
paint	Represents the `Paint` object to draw the arc.

The following code draws an outline of the arc from `90` to `270` degrees in red. The STROKE width is set to 5 pixels and the boundaries within which the arc is drawn are `100,100,300,300`:

```
Paint paint = new Paint();
paint.setColor(Color.RED);
paint.setStyle(Paint.Style.STROKE);                     #1
paint.setStrokeWidth(5);
RectF rectf = new RectF(100, 100, 300, 300);
canvas.drawArc(rectf, 90, 270, true, paint);
```

We can see here that the center of the oval is used for drawing the arc. Hence, the arc appears closed, as shown in Figure 9.9 (top left). If we don't want to use the center of the oval for drawing the arc, we pass a `false` Boolean value to the `drawArc()` method as shown in the following code:

```
canvas.drawArc(rectf, 90, 270, false, paint);
```

An open arc is drawn between the specified angle without using the center of the arc, as shown in Figure 9.9 (top right). To draw the filled arc, remove statement #1 from the previous code. Statement #1 sets the `Paint`'s style to the STROKE style. After we delete this statement, the `Paint` object picks up the default FILL style. The arc appears closed and filled with red (see Figure 9.9—bottom left) if statement #1 is removed and a `true` Boolean value is passed to the center parameter in the `drawArc()` method:

```
canvas.drawArc(rectf, 90, 270, true, paint);
```

Similarly, when we pass a `false` Boolean value for the `center` parameter in the `drawArc()` method, the center of the oval is not used for closing the arc (see Figure 9.9—bottom right).

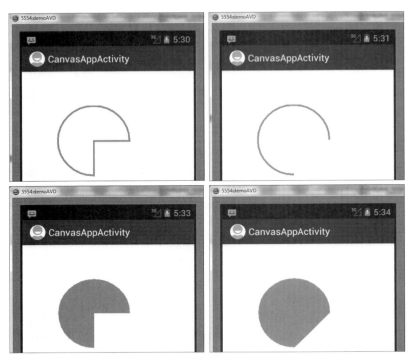

FIGURE 9.9   An arc outline drawn using the center point (top left), an arc outline without using the center point (top right), a filled arc using the center point (bottom left), and a filled arc without using the center point (bottom right)

Using Gradients

We can apply shading to a graphic by creating a color gradient. The three classes that are used for creating color gradients are LinearGradient, RadialGradient, and SweepGradient. Gradients are usually two colors, where the first color defines the start color and the second color defines the end color.

Using LinearGradient

The LinearGradient creates the shader or color gradient in which the color changes linearly along a single straight line. The syntax of its constructor follows:

```
public LinearGradient(float x1, float y1, float x2, float y2, int color1, int
color2, Shader.TileMode tile)
```

Table 9.4 describes the parameters used in the LinearGradient() constructor.

TABLE 9.4 `LinearGradient()` Constructor Parameters

Parameter	Description
`x1, y1`	Represents the X and Y coordinates that define the start of the gradient line.
`x1, y2`	Represents the X and Y coordinates that define the end of the gradient line.
`color1`	Represents the color at the start of the gradient line.
`color2`	Represents the color at the end of the gradient line.
`tile`	Represents the `Shader` tiling mode. The available options are `Shader.TileMode.CLAMP`—Replicates the edge color `Shader.TileMode.MIRROR`—Repeats the gradient horizontally and vertically with alternating mirror images `Shader.TileMode.REPEAT`—Repeats the gradient horizontally and vertically

To apply the color gradient to a graphic, the `setShader()` method is used. The method signature follows:

```
public Shader setShader(Shader shader)
```

where `shader` represents the object of `LinearGradient`, `RadialGradient`, or `SweepGradient`. Pass a null value for this parameter to clear any previously set shader.

The following code applies a `LinearGradient` shade to a circle. The color of the shade begins with red and ends at black. The canvas color is set to blue. The gradient line begins from the `0,0` coordinate and ends at the `25,25` coordinate:

```
Paint paint = new Paint();
canvas.drawColor(Color.BLUE);
paint.setColor(Color.RED);
paint.setStyle(Paint.Style.FILL);
LinearGradient linGrad = new LinearGradient(0, 0, 25, 25, Color.RED, Color.BLACK,
Shader.TileMode.CLAMP);
paint.setShader(linGrad);
canvas.drawCircle(200,200,70,paint);
```

Import the `LinearGradient` and `Shader` classes in the project by adding the following statements in the Java activity file `CanvasAppActivity.java`:

```
import android.graphics.LinearGradient;
import android.graphics.Shader;
```

The circle is drawn with the center at `200, 200` and a radius of `70` pixels. We can see that the shader tiling mode is set to CLAMP, making it so the circle is filled with black, as shown in Figure 9.10 (left). After we set the shader tiling mode to MIRROR, the color gradient is

repeated in the circle with alternating mirror images, as shown in Figure 9.10 (middle).
Similarly, after we set the shader tiling mode to REPEAT, the color gradient repeats in the
circle, as shown in Figure 9.10 (right).

FIGURE 9.10   A linear gradient in CLAMP shade (left), a linear gradient in MIRROR shade
(middle), and a linear gradient in REPEAT shade (right)

Let's modify the LinearGradient in the circle shown previously. Let's make the gradient
line in the LinearGradient begin at the 0,0 coordinate and end at the 50,50 coordinate.
The statement for doing so follows:

```
LinearGradient linGrad = new LinearGradient(0, 0, 50, 50, Color.RED, Color.BLACK,
Shader.TileMode.MIRROR);
```

With shader tiling mode set to the MIRROR style, the circle is filled with the shade shown
in Figure 9.11 (left). After we set the shader tiling mode to REPEAT, the color gradient is
repeated in the circle as shown in Figure 9.11 (right).

FIGURE 9.11   A linear gradient in the MIRROR shade (left), and a linear gradient in the REPEAT
shade (right)

Using RadialGradient

RadialGradient creates a shader or color gradient in which the color changes begin from a point and radiate outward in a circle. For creating a RadialGradient object, the syntax of its constructor is

```
public RadialGradient(float x, float y, float radius, int color1, int color2,
Shader.TileMode tile)
```

Table 9.5 describes the parameters used in the RadialGradient() constructor.

TABLE 9.5   RadialGradient() Constructor Parameters

Parameter	Description
x, y	Represents the X and Y coordinates of the center of the circle.
radius	Represents the radius of the circle for the color gradient.
color1	Represents the color for the center of the circle.
color2	Represents the color for the edge of the circle.
tile	Represents the Shader tiling mode. Available options are Shader.TileMode.CLAMP, Shader.TileMode.MIRROR, and Shader.TileMode.REPEAT.

The following code applies a RadialGradient shade to a circle. The color for the center of the circle is set to red and for the edge of the circle to black. The canvas color is set to blue. The center of the color gradient is 0,0 and the radius is 15 pixels:

```
Paint paint = new Paint();
canvas.drawColor(Color.BLUE);
paint.setColor(Color.RED);
paint.setStyle(Paint.Style.FILL);
RadialGradient radGrad = new RadialGradient(0, 0,15, Color.RED, Color.BLACK, Shader.
TileMode.CLAMP);
paint.setShader(radGrad);
canvas.drawCircle(200,200,70,paint);
```

Import the RadialGradient class in the project by adding the following statement in the Java activity file CanvasAppActivity.java:

```
import android.graphics.RadialGradient;
```

The circle is drawn with the center at 200, 200, with a radius of 70 pixels. If the shader tiling mode is set to CLAMP, the circle is filled with black, as shown in Figure 9.12 (left). When the shader tiling mode is set to MIRROR, the color gradient is repeated with alternating mirror images, as shown in Figure 9.12 (middle). If the shader tiling mode is set to REPEAT, the color gradient repeats, as shown in Figure 9.12 (right).

9

FIGURE 9.12   A radial gradient in the CLAMP shade (left), a radial gradient in the MIRROR shade (middle), and a radial gradient in the REPEAT shade (right)

Using SweepGradient

The SweepGradient creates the shader or color gradient in which the color changes in the form of pie slices, so the color gradient is created around a center point. The syntax of its constructor is as follows:

```
public SweepGradient(float x, float y, int color1, int color2)
```

where

▶ x,y—Represents the center of the color gradient

▶ color1—Represents the color to use at the beginning of the sweep

▶ color2—Represents the color to use at the end of the sweep

The following code applies a SweepGradient shade to a circle. The starting color is set to red, and the ending color is set to black. The canvas color is set to blue. The center of the color gradient is 100, 100:

```
Paint paint = new Paint();
canvas.drawColor(Color.BLUE);
paint.setColor(Color.RED);
paint.setStyle(Paint.Style.FILL);
SweepGradient swpGrad = new SweepGradient(100, 100,Color.RED, Color.BLACK);
paint.setShader(swpGrad);
canvas.drawCircle(200,200,70,paint);
```

Import the SweepGradient class in the project by adding the following statement in the activity file CanvasAppActivity.java:

```
import android.graphics.SweepGradient;
```

The circle is drawn with the center at 200, 200 with a radius of 70 pixels. The color gradient begins with red and transitions to black in the form of pie slices, as shown in Figure 9.13.

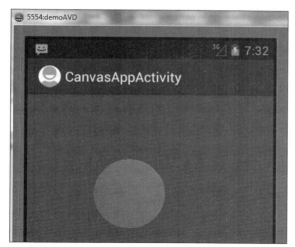

FIGURE 9.13   A circle filled with a `SweepGradient`

Displaying Bitmaps

To draw a bitmap on a screen, use the `drawBitmap()` method. The method signature is

```
void drawBitmap(Bitmap bitmap, float x, float y, Paint paint)
```

where:

- ▶ **bitmap**—Represents the `Bitmap` object we want to draw.
- ▶ **x, y**—Represents the X and Y coordinates from where the bitmap is drawn; that is, the top-left corner of the bitmap appears at the `x,y` location.
- ▶ **paint**—Represents the `Paint` object that draws the bitmap.

The following code draws the bitmap on the canvas with its top corner location at `10,10`. The following code assumes the image called `bintupic.png` is copied to all the four `res/drawable` folders:

```
Bitmap myBitmap = BitmapFactory.decodeResource(getResources(), R.drawable.bintupic);
canvas.drawBitmap(myBitmap, 10, 10, null);
```

Import the `Bitmap` and `BitmapFactory` classes in the project by adding the following statements to the activity file `CanvasAppActivity.java`:

```
import android.graphics.Bitmap;
import android.graphics.BitmapFactory;
```

The bitmap is drawn with its corner placed at `10,10`, as shown in Figure 9.14 (left). If we want to draw the bitmap after applying certain transformations such as clipping, scaling, or translating, the following method signature can be used:

```
void  drawBitmap(Bitmap bitmap, Rect src, Rect dst, Paint paint)
```

where `src` and `dst` represent the source and destination rectangle boundaries. The bitmap is transformed from the source rectangle boundaries to the destination rectangle boundaries.

The following statement makes the bitmap appear in its original size at the top-left corner of the canvas at `0,0`:

```
canvas.drawBitmap(myBitmap, null, new Rect(0, 0,myBitmap.getWidth(), myBitmap.
getHeight()), null);
```

We can see here that we supplied a `null` parameter for the source rectangle and the destination boundaries, as well as the `width` and `height` of the bitmap. The bitmap appears in its original size without applying any scale or other transformations. The bitmap is displayed at `0,0`—the top-left corner of the canvas (see Figure 9.14—middle).

The following code cuts off the part of the bitmap:

```
canvas.drawBitmap(myBitmap, new Rect(20, 20,myBitmap.getWidth()-20, myBitmap.
getHeight()-20),  new Rect(0, 0,myBitmap.getWidth(), myBitmap.getHeight()), null);
```

We can see here that instead of supplying the beginning coordinates of the bitmap as `0,0`, we supplied them as `20,20`, so the top-left corner of the bitmap is clipped. In the destination boundaries, we supplied the actual width and height of the bitmap, so the bitmap is displayed with the original width and height, but with its top-left corner clipped, as shown in Figure 9.14 (right).

FIGURE 9.14   Bitmap drawn at the location `10,10` on the X and Y axis (left), bitmap drawn at the top-left coordinate (middle), and bitmap drawn after being cut off (right)

The following statement scales the bitmap to fill the entire canvas:

```
canvas.drawBitmap(myBitmap, new Rect(0, 0,myBitmap.getWidth(), myBitmap.
getHeight()),  new Rect(0, 0, 480, 800), null);
```

We can see that in the source rectangle boundaries, we supplied the width and height of the bitmap, whereas in the destination boundaries, we supplied the width and height of the entire canvas. The bitmap is scaled as shown in Figure 9.15.

FIGURE 9.15   Bitmap scaled to fill up the entire canvas

To display text in different sizes, styles, and typefaces, we use the `drawText()` method. With this method, we can draw text in any typeface; the `Sans Serif` is the default. The method signature of the `drawText()` method is as follows:

```
void  drawText(String text, float x, float y, Paint paint)
```

where:

- **text**—Represents the text to draw
- **x,y**—Represents the X and Y coordinates where the top-left corner of the text appears
- **paint**—Represents the `Paint` object to draw the text

To specify the size of the text, the `setTextSize()` method is used. The syntax is as follows:

```
public void setTextSize(float size)
```

where `size` represents the text size in which we want to draw the text. This value must be greater than 0.

The following code draws the text in blue. The text size is set to 32 pixels, and the typeface used is the default, Sans Serif.

```
Paint paint = new Paint();
paint.setColor(Color.BLUE);
paint.setTextSize(32);
paint.setTypeface(null);                         #1
canvas.drawText("Hello World!", 20, 50, paint);
```

The top-left corner of the text Hello World! appears at 20,50, as shown in Figure 9.16 (top left). To draw text in the desired typeface, the method used is setTypeface(). The setTypeface() method also clears the previously set typeface, if any. The method signature is

```
public Typeface setTypeface(Typeface typeface)
```

where typeface is a Typeface object that represents the typeface in which we want to draw the text. To clear any previously set typeface, pass the null value to this method. Possible parameters for this method are

▶ **Typeface.MONOSPACE**—Displays text in the default monospace typeface

▶ **Typeface.SANS_SERIF**—Displays text in the default sans serif typeface

▶ **Typeface.SERIF**—Displays text in the default serif typeface

To draw Hello World! in Serif font, we set its typeface by passing the Typeface.SERIF constant to the setTypeface() method. That is, we replace statement #1 in the preceding code with the following statement:

```
paint.setTypeface(Typeface.SERIF);
```

We also need to import the Typeface class in the project by adding the following statement in the activity file CanvasAppActivity.java:

```
import android.graphics.Typeface;
```

Hello World! appears in Serif font, as shown in Figure 9.16 (top right). Replacing statement #1 in the preceding code with the following statement makes the text appear in Serif font and italic style (see Figure 9.16—bottom left):

```
paint.setTypeface(Typeface.create(Typeface.SERIF,Typeface.ITALIC));
```

The create() method of the Typeface class creates a typeface in the specified style. The Typeface.ITALIC style makes the text appear in the italic style. The method signature of the create() method is

```
Typeface create(Typeface typeface, int style)
```

where the value of the `typeface` parameter can be `Typeface.MONOSPACE`, `Typeface.SANS_`
`SERIF`, or `Typeface.SERIF`. Here is the list of style constants for the `style` parameter:

▶ `Typeface.BOLD`

▶ `Typeface.BOLD_ITALIC`

▶ `Typeface.ITALIC`

▶ `Typeface.NORMAL`

If we replace statement #1 in the preceding code with the following statement, `Hello`
`World!` appears in `Serif` font and in `bold` style (see Figure 9.16—bottom right):

```
paint.setTypeface(Typeface.create(Typeface.SERIF,Typeface.BOLD));
```

FIGURE 9.16   Text message in the default font (top left), text message in Serif font (top right),
text message in Serif font and Italic style (bottom left), and text message in Serif font and Bold
style (bottom right)

Now that we've learned to use `Canvas` and `Paint` to draw different shapes, text, bitmaps,
and gradients, let's learn how to add motion or movement to our graphics.

Animations

Broadly, Android supports two types of animations:

▶ **Property animation**—It is a robust framework with which we can animate properties of any object. That is, we can define an animation to change any object property
over a specified length of time. For example, we can change an object's position over
the specified time duration.

▶ **View animation**—The view animation framework enables us to animate view objects. There are two types of animations that we can do with this framework:

 ▶ **Frame-by-frame animation**—A series of images arranged in frames are displayed at regular intervals. Each image differs slightly from the previous image and is displayed for a very short duration to imply motion.

 ▶ **Tweening animation**—This process considers two key images: the beginning and ending states of the images. In-between images that show gradual transformation of the image from the beginning state to the ending state are created automatically. Tweening animation can be applied to any graphic, text, or other view. Android provides tweening animation support for several common image transformations, including alpha, rotate, scale, and translate.

Understanding Frame-by-Frame Animation

Frame-by-frame animations are produced by drawing a series of sequential images, each of which is displayed for a specific duration. To show motion, each image differs slightly from the previous one. All the images involved in a frame-by-frame animation must be copied into the `res/drawable` folder. The image filenames are their IDs while accessing them in Java code. To support devices of different sizes and resolutions, images or drawables of different sizes and resolutions need to be copied to the respective `drawable-ldpi`, `drawable-mdi`, `drawable-hdpi`, and `drawable-xhdpi` folders.

Frame-by-frame animation can be defined with XML and Java code. We begin with defining animation with XML.

Defining Frame-by-Frame Animation with XML

As the name suggests, we need to create an XML file to define the list of images and the duration for which each image is displayed. The first step is to create an Android project called `FrameAnimXMLApp` and copy the images that we want to animate in the `res/drawable` folders. Figure 9.17 shows the four images, `face1.png`, `face2.png`, `face3.png`, and `face4.png`, that we use in this frame-by-frame animation. Observe that each image is slightly different from the previous image to show movement or motion.

FIGURE 9.17   The four images used in frame-by-frame animation

Copy the four image files into the `res/drawable` folders. To control the animation, we define a `ToggleButton` that is used to start and stop the animation. We also need to define an `ImageView` control to display the images to animate. To define the `ImageView` and `ToggleButton` controls, the code shown in Listing 9.2 is written into the `activity_frame_anim_xmlapp.xml` layout file.

LISTING 9.2   Code in `activity_frame_anim_xmlapp.xml` After Defining the `ImageView` and `ToggleButton`

```
<RelativeLayout xmlns:android="http://schemas.android.com/apk/res/android"
    xmlns:tools="http://schemas.android.com/tools"
    android:layout_width="match_parent"
    android:layout_height="match_parent"    >
    <ImageView android:id="@+id/imgview"
        android:layout_width="100dip"
        android:layout_height="120dip"
        android:layout_centerInParent="true" />
    <ToggleButton
        android:id="@+id/startstop_button"
        android:textOn="Stop Animation"
        android:textOff="Start Animation"
        android:layout_width="wrap_content"
        android:layout_height="wrap_content"
        android:layout_centerHorizontal="true" />
</RelativeLayout>
```

Here, `ImageView` determines on which frame the animation is applied. The `ToggleButton` is used to switch the animation `On` or `Off`. The IDs assigned to the `ImageView` and `ToggleButton` controls are `imgview` and `startstop_button`, respectively. The two controls are accessed with Java code through these IDs.

Next, to define the images involved in the animation and to specify the duration of their display, we need to add an XML file to the `res/anim` folder. The `anim` folder does not already exist by default. Right-click the `res` folder in the `Package Explorer` window, select the `New`, `Folder` option, and assign the name `anim` to the newly created folder.

Thereafter, add an XML file by right-clicking on the `res/anim` folder and selecting the `New`, `Android XML File` option. In the dialog box that pops up, the `Drawable Resource Type` is selected by default. Keeping the default `Resource Type`, enter the name of the XML file as `frame_anim` (see Figure 9.18). Select the `Root Element` as the `animation-list` and click `Finish` to create the `frame_anim.xml` file.

9

FIGURE 9.18   Adding an XML file to the `res/anim` folder

Each of the images copied into the `res/drawable` folder acts as a frame. That is, each image is accessed through its resource ID and is displayed sequentially. To show a simple animation that cycles through the series of supplied images, displaying each one for 100 milliseconds, write the code shown in Listing 9.3 into the `frame_anim.xml` file.

LISTING 9.3   Code Written into `frame_anim.xml`

```xml
<?xml version="1.0" encoding="utf-8"?>
<animation-list xmlns:android="http://schemas.android.com/apk/res/android"
android:oneshot="false">
    <item android:drawable="@drawable/face1" android:duration="100" />
    <item android:drawable="@drawable/face2" android:duration="100" />
    <item android:drawable="@drawable/face3" android:duration="100" />
    <item android:drawable="@drawable/face4" android:duration="100" />
</animation-list>
```

Table 9.6 gives a brief description of the attributes used in this file.

TABLE 9.6   Attributes Used in the `frame_anim.xml` File

Attribute	Description
android:drawable	Used to define the drawable resource displayed in the animation.
android:duration	Determines the duration of an animation. The time supplied is in milliseconds. For example, the value `5000` makes the animation complete in 5 seconds: `android:duration="5000"`
android:oneshot	Determines whether we want the animation to run in a continuous loop. The Boolean value `false` makes the animation run in a continuous loop. The Boolean value `true` makes the image animate only once.

We can see that the list of images that we want to animate is collected in the animation list. The `animation-list` tag is converted into an `AnimationDrawable` object representing the collection of images. The `AnimationDrawable` class is available in the graphics package used to display frames in sequential order for a specific duration. Because we want the animation to run in an infinite loop, a `false` Boolean value is assigned to the `android:oneshot` attribute in the previous code.

Next, we need to write Java code to perform the following tasks:

▶ Access the images listed in the `frame_anim.xml` file and draw them via `ImageView`.

▶ Make an object of the `AnimationDrawable` class and access its `start()` and `stop()` methods to start and stop the animation.

To perform these tasks, the code shown in Listing 9.4 is written into the `FrameAnimXMLAppActivity.java` activity file.

LISTING 9.4   Code Written into the `FrameAnimXMLAppActivity.java` Activity File

```
package com.androidunleashed.frameanimxmlapp;

import android.app.Activity;
import android.os.Bundle;
import android.widget.ToggleButton;
import android.widget.ImageView;
import android.view.View;
import android.graphics.drawable.AnimationDrawable;

public class FrameAnimXMLAppActivity extends Activity {
    AnimationDrawable animation;
    @Override
    public void onCreate(Bundle savedInstanceState) {
        super.onCreate(savedInstanceState);
        setContentView(R.layout.activity_frame_anim_xmlapp);
        final ToggleButton startStopButton = (ToggleButton) findViewById(R.
id.startstop_button);
```

```
        final ImageView imgView = (ImageView)findViewById(R.id.imgview);
        startStopButton.setOnClickListener(new View.OnClickListener() {
            @Override
            public void onClick(View v) {
                if (startStopButton.isChecked()) {
                    imgView.setBackgroundResource(R.drawable.frame_anim);
                    animation = (AnimationDrawable) imgView.getBackground();
                    animation.start();
                }
                else
                    animation.stop();
            }
        });
    }
}
```

Here we see that `ToggleButton` and `ImageView` are accessed from the layout file and mapped to the `ToggleButton` and `ImageView` instances called `startStopButton` and `imgView`, respectively. A `ClickListener` is associated with the `ToggleButton`, and when it is clicked, its `onClick()` callback method is invoked. In the `onClick()` method, we refer to the `frame_anim.xml` file that contains the `animation-list` image collection. We set the `Drawable` as a background resource for our `ImageView`.

An object of the `AnimationDrawable` class is called an animation. We access the `start()` and `stop()` methods of the `AnimationDrawable` class to start and stop the animation. On application startup, the `ToggleButton` displays the caption `Start Animation` (see Figure 9.19—left). Recall that when clicked once, the `ToggleButton` switches to the Checked state, and when clicked again, it switches back to the Unchecked state. After clicking the `Start Animation` button, we call the `start()` method of `AnimationDrawable` to begin the frame-by-frame animation (see Figure 9.19—middle). The caption of the `ToggleButton` then changes to `Stop Animation`. After we click the `Stop Animation` button, the `ToggleButton` switches to the Unchecked state, calling the `AnimationDrawable`'s `stop()` method to stop the animation. The `ImageView` shows the image of the frame where it is stopped, and the caption of the `ToggleButton` again changes to `Start Animation` (see Figure 9.19—right).

FIGURE 9.19   Startup screen (left), the animation plays after clicking the Start Animation button (middle), and the animation stops after clicking the Stop Animation button (right).

NOTE

By increasing the number of images, thus reducing the level of difference between two consecutive images, and by choosing an appropriate drawing speed, we can make frame-by-frame animations smooth.

Now that we have frame-by-frame animation with XML, let's learn how to display frame-by-frame via Java code.

Defining Frame-by-Frame Animation with Java Code

While defining frame-by-frame animation with Java, we don't need an XML file to define the animation-list. Instead, we are directly accessing all the images involved in the animation from the Drawable resources and adding them to the AnimationDrawable object. Thereafter, the AnimationDrawable is set as the background resource of an ImageView and the start of the animation.

Let's create an Android project called FrameAnimApp. Again, in this application, we need two controls: ImageView and ToggleButton. ImageView is used for displaying the animation, and ToggleButton is used for starting and stopping it. To define the ImageView and ToggleButton, write the code shown in Listing 9.2 into the activity_frame_anim_app.xml layout file. The IDs assigned to the ImageView and ToggleButton controls are imgview and startstop_button, respectively, and are used to access them with Java code. Don't forget to copy the image files face1.png, face2.png, face3.png, and face4.png into the res/drawable folders, as these are the images used in the animation.

Now we write Java code to do the following tasks:

▶ Create an object of the AnimationDrawable class.

▶ Access the images from the Drawable resources, define their display duration, and add them to the AnimationDrawable object in the form of frames.

▶ Set the `AnimationDrawable` as the background resource of an `ImageView`.

▶ Start and stop the animation when `ToggleButton` is clicked.

To perform the preceding tasks, write the code shown in Listing 9.5 into the `FrameAnimAppActivity.java` Java activity file.

LISTING 9.5   Code Written into the `FrameAnimAppActivity.java` Java Activity File

```
package com.androidunleashed.frameanimapp;

import android.app.Activity;
import android.os.Bundle;
import android.view.View;
import android.graphics.drawable.AnimationDrawable;
import android.widget.ToggleButton;
import android.widget.ImageView;

public class FrameAnimAppActivity extends Activity {
    ImageView imgView;
    AnimationDrawable animation;

    @Override
    public void onCreate(Bundle savedInstanceState) {
        super.onCreate(savedInstanceState);
        setContentView(R.layout.activity_frame_anim_app);
        final ToggleButton startStopButton = (ToggleButton) findViewById(R.
id.startstop_button);
        imgView = (ImageView)findViewById(R.id.imgview);
        createAnimation() ;
        startStopButton.setOnClickListener(new View.OnClickListener() {
            @Override
            public void onClick(View v) {
                if (startStopButton.isChecked())
                    animation.start();
                else
                    animation.stop();
            }
        });
    }

    private void createAnimation(){
        animation = new AnimationDrawable();
        animation.addFrame(getResources().getDrawable(R.drawable.face1), 100);
        animation.addFrame(getResources().getDrawable(R.drawable.face2), 100);
        animation.addFrame(getResources().getDrawable(R.drawable.face3), 100);
```

```
        animation.addFrame(getResources().getDrawable(R.drawable.face4), 100);
        animation.setOneShot(false);
        imgView.setBackground(animation);
    }
}
```

We can see that the `ToggleButton` and `ImageView` controls defined in the layout file are accessed and mapped to the `ToggleButton` and `ImageView` instances `startStopButton` and `imgView`, respectively. An instance of `AnimationDrawable` class is created. The four Bitmap resources, `face1.png`, `face2.png`, `face3.png`, and `face4.png`, are accessed from the Drawable resources and are added as frames to the `AnimationDrawable` object. The time duration for each frame display is defined as `100` milliseconds. Finally, the `AnimationDrawable` is set as the background of the `ImageView` to display the images. The `ClickListener` is associated with the `ToggleButton` depending on the click event that occurs with the `ToggleButton`; the animation is started or stopped by calling the `start()` and `stop` methods of the `AnimationDrawable` class. To make the animation run in a continuous loop, the `setOneShot()` method is called and passed the Boolean value `false`:

```
animation.setOneShot(false);
```

On running the application, we get the same output as shown in Figure 9.19.

Understanding Tweening Animation

Here are four types of tweening animation:

▶ **Alpha animation**—Used to change the opacity or transparency of a `View`.

▶ **Rotate animation**—Used to rotate a `View` by a specific angle around a given axis or pivot point.

▶ **Scale animation**—Used to make a `View` smaller or larger on the X axis, Y axis, or both. We can also specify the pivot point around which we want to scale the `view`.

▶ **Translate animation**—Used to move a `View` along the X or Y axis.

These four animations can be implemented individually and can also be combined, or nested, within each other.

> **NOTE**
>
> When we apply scaling and rotation animations, if the animation extends beyond the screen region, it is clipped.

As with frame-by-frame animation, tweening animation can be defined with either XML or Java code.

Defining Tweening Animations with XML Resources

To define tweening animation with XML, we need to create an XML file for each type of animation and store them in the `/res/anim` folder. For example, for a rotation animation, we need to create a file called `rotate.xml` and place it in the `/res/anim` folder of our application. Similarly, for a scale animation, we need to create a file called `scale.xml` in the `/res/anim/` folder, and so on. The animation sequences defined in the XML files are then loaded through Java code. To understand the procedure clearly, let's create a new Android project called `TweenAnimApp`. The image we want to animate needs to be copied into the `res/drawable` folders. We use the `face4.png` image file (as seen earlier in Figure 9.17—last image) in this application. Copy it into the `res/drawable` folders.

In this application, we want to use an `ImageView` and four `Button` controls. The `ImageView` is used for displaying animation. The four `Button` controls are used to initiate the four tweening animation types, `Alpha`, `Rotate`, `Scale`, and `Translate`. To define an `ImageView` and four `Button` controls, the `activity_tween_anim_app.xml` layout file is modified as shown in Listing 9.6.

LISTING 9.6   Code Written into the `activity_tween_anim_app.xml` Layout File

```
<RelativeLayout xmlns:android="http://schemas.android.com/apk/res/android"
    xmlns:tools="http://schemas.android.com/tools"
    android:layout_width="match_parent"
    android:layout_height="match_parent" >
    <ImageView android:id="@+id/imgview"
        android:layout_width="100dip"
        android:layout_height="150dip"
        android:src="@drawable/face4"
        android:layout_centerInParent="true" />
    <Button
        android:id="@+id/alpha_button"
        android:text="Alpha"
        android:layout_width="wrap_content"
        android:layout_height="wrap_content"  />
    <Button
        android:id="@+id/rotate_button"
        android:text="Rotate"
        android:layout_width="wrap_content"
        android:layout_height="wrap_content"
        android:layout_toRightOf="@id/alpha_button" />
    <Button
        android:id="@+id/scale_button"
        android:text="Scale"
        android:layout_width="wrap_content"
        android:layout_height="wrap_content"
        android:layout_toRightOf="@id/rotate_button" />
    <Button
        android:id="@+id/translate_button"
```

```
        android:text="Translate"
        android:layout_width="wrap_content"
        android:layout_height="wrap_content"
        android:layout_toRightOf="@id/scale_button"   />
</RelativeLayout>
```

We can see that the `ImageView` is assigned the `imgview` ID, which is used for accessing it with Java code. Also, it is set to initially display the `face4.png` image. The width and height assigned to the `ImageView` control are `100dip` and `150dip`, respectively. The four `Button` controls are assigned the text `Alpha`, `Rotate`, `Scale`, and `Translate` to show the kind of animation they play when clicked. The four `Button` controls are assigned the IDs `alpha_button`, `rotate_button`, `scale_button`, and `translate_button`, respectively, to identify and access them with Java code.

As stated earlier, for each type of animation, an XML file needs to be defined and stored in the `/res/anim` folder. So, let's create a folder called `anim` within the `res` folder. Add four XML files called `alpha.xml`, `rotate.xml`, `scale.xml`, and `translate.xml`. We define the code in the XML files of the four animation types separately. Let's begin with Alpha animation.

Defining Alpha Animation

Alpha animation also means *Transparency animation*—it makes the specific `Views` fade in or out. Alpha values ranges from `0.0` (fully transparent or invisible) to `1.0` (fully opaque or visible). The Alpha range is supplied through the attributes explained in Table 9.7.

TABLE 9.7   Attributes Used in Alpha Animation

Attribute	Description
android:fromAlpha	Used to specify the starting transparency value. For example, assigning the value `1.0` to this attribute makes the `View` fade out from the fully opaque visible state. Similarly, assigning the value `0.0` to this attribute makes the `View` fade in from the fully transparent invisible state.
android:toAlpha	Used to specify the ending transparency value. For example, assigning the value `1.0` to this attribute makes the `View` fade in; the value `0.0` makes the `View` fade out.

The XML `alpha.xml` resource file shown in Listing 9.7 changes the opacity of the target `View`; that is, it makes the `View` fade out from fully opaque state (`1.0`) to almost invisible state (`0.0`) in three seconds.

LISTING 9.7   Code Written into the `alpha.xml` File

```xml
<?xml version="1.0" encoding="utf-8"?>
<alpha  xmlns:android="http://schemas.android.com/apk/res/android"
    android:fromAlpha="1.0"
    android:toAlpha="0.1"
    android:duration="3000" />
```

Let's now define XML file for Rotate animation.

Defining Rotate Animation

We can rotate `Views` either clockwise or counterclockwise on a specified axis. The value of the rotation angle is defined in degrees. The attributes shown in Table 9.8 are used in Rotate animation to specify the beginning and ending angle of the `Views`.

TABLE 9.8   Attributes Used in Rotate Animation

Attribute	Description
`android:fromDegrees`	Used to specify the angle to begin rotation from. For example, supplying a 0 value to this attribute begins rotating the `View` from 0 degrees: `android:fromDegrees="0"`

`android:toDegrees`	Used to specify the angle at which we want to end rotation. For example, supplying a value of 360 to this attribute makes the `View` to rotate in the clockwise direction from the angle specified in the `android:fromDegrees` attribute up to 360 degrees:
	 `android:toDegrees="360"`
	 To rotate the `View` in the counterclockwise direction, we need to specify a negative angle. To rotate a `View` 360 degrees in the counterclockwise direction beginning from the angle specified in the `android:from` attribute, we supply a value of −360 to this attribute
	 `:android:toDegrees="-360"`

`android:pivotX`	By default, the axis or pivot point of rotation is at (0,0), that is, the top-left corner of the `View`. We can set a custom pivot point using the `android:pivotX` and `android:pivotY` attributes. The `pivotX` attribute is used to specify the pivot point on the X axis. We can define its value in absolute form or as a percentage. For example, assigning a value of 50% to this attribute sets the pivot point at the midpoint of the X axis: `android:pivotX="50%"`
`android:pivotY`	Used to specify the pivot point on the Y axis. Again, the value assigned to this attribute can be a fixed coordinate or a percentage. For example, assigning a value of 50% to this attribute sets the pivot point at the midpoint of the Y axis: `android:pivotY="50%"`

The `/res/anim/rotate.xml` resource file shown in Listing 9.8 rotates the `View` 360 degrees clockwise with a three-second duration. The axis or the pivot point of the rotating `View` is its center.

LISTING 9.8   Code Written into the `rotate.xml` File

```xml
<?xml version="1.0" encoding="utf-8"?>
<rotate xmlns:android="http://schemas.android.com/apk/res/android"
```

```
    android:fromDegrees="0"
    android:toDegrees="360"
    android:pivotX="50%"
    android:pivotY="50%"
    android:duration="3000" />
```

Next, we need to define the XML file for Scale animations.

Defining Scale Animation

We can increase or reduce the size of `Views` in both the horizontal and vertical direction. Scaling is done in terms of relative scale that ranges from value `0.0` to `1.0`. A `0.0` value means to scale the `View` to 0%, and `1.0` value means to scale the `View` to 100%. For example, if we want to scale a `View` to 50%, we supply a scale value of `0.5`. A `View` can be scaled with the same or different values for the horizontal and vertical direction. Identical values maintain aspect ratio. To scale `Views`, we need to set values for the attributes described in Table 9.9.

TABLE 9.9   Attributes Used in Scale Animation

Attribute	Description
android:fromXScale	Used to specify the starting scale value horizontally
android:fromYScale	Used to specify the starting scale value vertically
android:toXScale	Used to specify the target scale value horizontally
android:toYScale	Used to specify the target scale value vertically
android:android:pivotX, android:android:pivotY	Used to specify the pivot point from which to begin scaling

The following XML snippet applies a scaling animation to a `View`. The `View` is scaled to twice the original size both horizontally and vertically. The scaling is performed taking the center of the `View` as the pivot point and is completed in three seconds:

```
<scale
    android:fromXScale="1.0"
    android:toXScale="2.0"
    android:fromYScale="1.0"
    android:toYScale="2.0"
    android:pivotX="50%"
    android:pivotY="50%"
    android:duration="3000" />
```

Combining and Sequencing Tweening Animations

We can combine tweening animations to occur simultaneously or sequentially by nesting them in a `<set>` tag. The common attribute used while combining animations is `android:startOffset`. The `android:startOffset` attribute inserts a delay in the beginning of an animation. The time to delay animation is supplied in milliseconds. For example, the value `3000` assigned to this attribute makes the animation occur after three seconds:

```
android:startOffset="3000"
```

Let's combine two scaling animations in a resource file. The resource file `/res/anim/scale.xml` shown in Listing 9.9 scales the `View` to double its original size with a three-second duration. The center of the `View` is the pivot point for the scaling operation. After the `View` is scaled, it starts shrinking and scales down to its original size in a three-second duration.

LISTING 9.9   Code Written into the `scale.xml` File

```
<?xml version="1.0" encoding="utf-8"?>
<set xmlns:android="http://schemas.android.com/apk/res/android">
    <scale
        android:fromXScale="1.0"
        android:toXScale="2.0"
        android:fromYScale="1.0"
        android:toYScale="2.0"
        android:pivotX="50%"
        android:pivotY="50%"
        android:duration="3000" />
    <scale
        android:fromXScale="1.0"
        android:toXScale="0.5"
        android:fromYScale="1.0"
        android:toYScale="0.5"
        android:pivotX="50%"
        android:pivotY="50%"
        android:startOffset="3000"
        android:duration="3000" />
</set>
```

Finally, it's time to define Translate animations.

Defining Translate Animation

Translation animation results in moving the `View` from one X and Y coordinate location to another. The `android:fromXDelta` and `android:fromYDelta` attributes are used to specify the starting position to begin the translation. Similarly, the `android:toXDelta` and `android:toYDelta` attributes are used to specify the location at which to stop the translate animation. Table 9.10 shows the attributes used in the translate animation.

TABLE 9.10   Attributes Used in Translate Animation

Attribute	Description
android:fromXDelta	Used to specify the X axis location where the View translation begins.
android:toXDelta	Used to specify the X axis location to end the View translation. A positive value makes the View move right; a negative value moves the View left. For example, the following code makes the View move right by 50 pixels: android:toXDelta="50" Similarly, the following code makes the View move left by 50 pixels: android:toXDelta="-50"
android:fromYDelta	Used to specify the Y axis location where the View translation begins.
android:toYDelta	Used to specify the Y axis location to end the View translation. A positive value makes the View move downward; a negative value moves the View upward. For example, the following code makes the View move down by 50 pixels: android:toYDelta="50" Similarly, the following code makes the View move up by 50 pixels: android:toYDelta="-50"
android:fillAfter	A Boolean value assigned to this attribute that determines whether we want the View to return to its starting location when the animation is over. The Boolean value true stops the View from returning to its starting position: android:fillAfter="true"

The following XML snippet applies a translate animation that moves the View down by 200 pixels on the Y axis with a three-second duration:

```
<translate
    android:toYDelta="200"
    android:fillAfter="true"
    android:duration="3000" />
```

Similarly, the following XML snippet moves the View left by 150 pixels on the X axis with a three-second duration:

```
<translate
    android:toXDelta="-150"
    android:fillAfter="true"
    android:duration="3000" />
```

Let's combine the two translate animations in a single resource file. The resource file /res/anim/translate.xml shown in Listing 9.10 includes a set of two translate animations. First, it takes three seconds to move the View left to -150 pixels on the X axis. After the View is moved to the left after the duration of three seconds, the View moves down 200 pixels on the Y axis with a three-second duration.

LISTING 9.10   Code Written into the `translate.xml` File

```xml
<?xml version="1.0" encoding="utf-8"?>
<set xmlns:android="http://schemas.android.com/apk/res/android"
    android:fillAfter="true">
    <translate android:fromXDelta="0"
        android:toXDelta="-150"
        android:duration="3000"
        android:fillAfter="true"/>
    <translate android:toYDelta="200"
        android:fillAfter="true"
        android:duration="3000"
        android:startOffset="3000"/>
</set>
```

After defining the resource files for all four types of tweening animation, we need to write Java code into the activity file to load animations from the XML files.

Loading Animations

The procedure of applying or associating an animation implemented in a given XML resource file to an `ImageView` or some other `View` is known as loading an animation. To do this, we use the `AnimationUtils` helper class. For example, the following code loads an animation XML resource file called `/res/anim/alpha.xml` and associates it with an `ImageView`:

```java
import android.view.animation.Animation;
import android.view.animation.AnimationUtils;

ImageView imgView = (ImageView)findViewById(R.id.imgview);
Animation animation = AnimationUtils.loadAnimation(TweenAnimAppActivity.this,
R.anim.alpha);
imgView.startAnimation(animation);
```

Next, we need to write Java code into the activity file to listen for a click event on the four `Button` controls, then load the animation XML resource file associated with that `Button` control, and then apply it to the `ImageView` control to display animation on the screen. To accomplish these tasks, the code shown in Listing 9.11 needs to be written into the Java activity file `TweenAnimAppActivity.java`.

LISTING 9.11   Code Written into the `TweenAnimAppActivity.java` Java Activity File

```java
package com.androidunleashed.tweenanimapp;

import android.app.Activity;
import android.os.Bundle;
import android.widget.ImageView;
import android.view.animation.Animation;
```

```java
import android.widget.Button;
import android.view.animation.AnimationUtils;
import android.view.View;

public class TweenAnimAppActivity extends Activity {
    ImageView imgView;
    Animation animation;

    @Override
    public void onCreate(Bundle savedInstanceState) {
        super.onCreate(savedInstanceState);
        setContentView(R.layout.activity_tween_anim_app);
        Button alphaButton = (Button) findViewById(R.id.alpha_button);
        Button rotateButton = (Button) findViewById(R.id.rotate_button);
        Button scaleButton = (Button) findViewById(R.id.scale_button);
        Button translateButton = (Button) findViewById(R.id.translate_button);
        imgView = (ImageView)findViewById(R.id.imgview);
        alphaButton.setOnClickListener(new View.OnClickListener() {
            @Override
            public void onClick(View v) {
                animation = AnimationUtils.loadAnimation(TweenAnimAppActivity.this,
R.anim.alpha);
                imgView.startAnimation(animation);
            }
        });
        rotateButton.setOnClickListener(new View.OnClickListener() {
            @Override
            public void onClick(View v) {
                animation = AnimationUtils.loadAnimation(TweenAnimAppActivity.this,
R.anim.rotate);
                imgView.startAnimation(animation);
            }
        });
        scaleButton.setOnClickListener(new View.OnClickListener() {
            @Override
            public void onClick(View v) {
                animation = AnimationUtils.loadAnimation(TweenAnimAppActivity.this,
R.anim.scale);
                imgView.startAnimation(animation);
            }
        });
        translateButton.setOnClickListener(new View.OnClickListener() {
            @Override
            public void onClick(View v) {
                animation = AnimationUtils.loadAnimation(TweenAnimAppActivity.this,
R.anim.translate);
```

```
            imgView.startAnimation(animation);
        }
    });
  }
}
```

In the preceding code, we can see that the four `Button` controls defined in the layout file with the IDs `alpha_button`, `rotate_button`, `scale_button`, and `translate_button` are accessed and mapped to the `Button` objects `alphaButton`, `rotateButton`, `scaleButton`, and `translateButton`, respectively. `ClickListeners` are associated with all four `Button` controls so that when any `Button` is clicked, its `onClick()` callback method is called. In the `onClick()` method, the XML resource file of the respective animation is loaded from the `/res/anim` folder and applied to the `ImageView` control to start and display the animation on the screen. After running the application, we see four `Button` controls—Alpha, Rotate, Scale, and Translate—and an `ImageView` control displaying `face4.png`, which we copied into the `res/drawable` folders (see Figure 9.20—left). After we click the `Alpha` button, the `alpha.xml` file defined in the `/res/anim` folder is loaded and makes the image fade out from fully opaque to almost transparent in three seconds (see Figure 9.20—middle). After we click the `Rotate` button, the `rotate.xml` file is loaded, which makes the image rotate `360` degrees clockwise. The axis of rotation is the center of the image, and the animation takes three seconds to perform (see Figure 9.20—right).

FIGURE 9.20   The application on startup (left), the image fading out after clicking the `Alpha` button (middle), and the image rotating after clicking the `Rotate` button (right)

After we click the `Scale` button, the `scale.xml` file from the `/res/anim` folder is loaded and scales the image to double its original size both horizontally and vertically. The scaling is performed from the center of the image with a three-second duration (see Figure 9.21—left). After the image is scaled, it will start shrinking to original size with a three-second duration. After we click the `Translate` button, the image moves `150` pixels left on the X axis. The movement is performed with a three-second duration. Then it starts moving down by `200` pixels on the Y axis (see Figure 9.21—right) with a three-second duration.

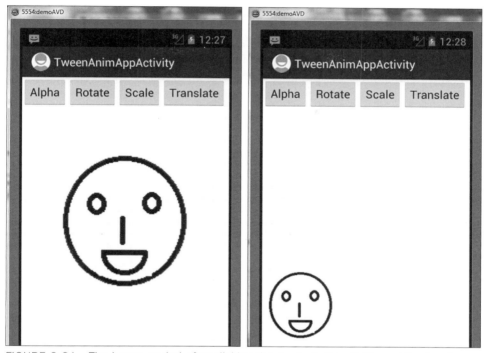

FIGURE 9.21   The image scaled after clicking the Scale button (left), and the image moved after clicking the Translate button (right)

Repeating Animations

We can make all four tweening animations repeat for a specific number of times. The attribute used is android:repeatCount. We can also make the animation restart from the beginning or in reverse by using the android:repeatMode attribute. The two attributes android:repeatCount and android:repeatMode are explained as follows:

▶ **android:repeatCount**—The attribute defines the number of times to repeat the animation. The default value is 0.

For example, the following statement makes the animation repeat 50 times:

```
android:repeatCount="50"
```

If, instead of a positive value, if we supply -1 to this attribute, the animation repeats indefinitely. In Java, the method used to repeat the animation is setRepeatCount(int).

▶ **android:repeatMode**—The attribute determines whether the animation restarts or animates in reverse order when the animation reaches the end. The possible values for this attribute are shown in Table 9.11.

TABLE 9.11   Attributes Used in `android:repeatMode`

Constant	Value	Description
Restart	1	The animation restarts from the beginning.
Reverse	2	The animation starts in reverse.

For example, the following statement makes the animation restart when it reaches the end:

```
android:repeatMode="restart"
```

In Java, the method used to determine the repeat mode is `setRepeatMode(int)`.

NOTE

The `android:repeatMode` attribute works only when the repeat count of the animation is set to greater than 0 or to infinite.

Now that we understand how the four types of tweening animations are performed with XML resource files, let's learn to apply all four tweening animations via Java code.

Defining Tweening Animations with Java Code

Each tweening animation type has a respective class, shown in Table 9.12.

TABLE 9.12   Classes Used in Tweening Animation

Class	Purpose
AlphaAnimation	Defines the opacity or transparency of `Views`
TranslateAnimation	Defines the translate animation and applies motion to the associated `View`
RotateAnimation	Defines the rotate animation and makes the `View` rotate by the specified degree about a specific pivot point or axis, either clockwise or counterclockwise
ScaleAnimation	Defines the scale animation and enlarges or shrinks the specified `View` horizontally, vertically, or both

Using the `AlphaAnimation` Class

The class determines the opacity or transparency of `Views`. The syntax for the constructor of this class follows:

```
public AlphaAnimation(float from_alpha, float to_alpha)
```

The use of the two parameters shown is as follows:

▶ **from_alpha**—Defines the starting `alpha` value to begin animation. Values in the range `0.0` and `1.0` can be supplied to this parameter, where `1.0` means fully opaque and `0.0` means fully transparent.

▶ **To_alpha**—Defines the ending `alpha` value to end the animation. Again, values in the range `0.0` to `1.0` can be supplied.

For example, the following statement makes the `View` animate from the visible to the invisible state:

```
Animation animation = new AlphaAnimation(1.0f, 0.1f);
```

Using the `TranslateAnimation` Class

This class defines the translate animation and applies motion to the associated `View`. The syntax for the constructor of this class is as follows:

```
public TranslateAnimation(float change_from_X, float change_to_X, float change_from_Y, float change_to_Y)
```

Table 9.13 describes the parameters used in the constructor.

TABLE 9.13   Parameters Used in `TranslateAnimation`'s Constructor

Parameter	Description
change_from_X	Represents the change in the X coordinate to apply while beginning an animation. The value o begins the animation from the current X coordinate location.
change_to_X	Represents the change in the X coordinate to end an animation. To move right, the supplied value is positive, and to move left, the supplied value is negative.
change_from_Y	Represents the change in the Y coordinate to apply at the beginning of an animation. A value of o begins the animation from the current Y coordinate location.
change_to_Y	Represents the change in the Y coordinate to end the animation. To move down, the supplied value is positive, and to move up, the supplied value is negative.

For example, the following statement makes the `View` move left from its current location by 150:

```
Animation animation = new TranslateAnimation(0,-150,0,0);
```

Similarly, the following statement makes the `View` animate right by 150 and down by 200; that is, it makes the `View` animate diagonally:

```
Animation animation = new TranslateAnimation(0,150,0,200);
```

Using the `RotateAnimation` **Class**

The class defines the rotate animation and makes the `View` rotate about a specified pivot point or axis in either a clockwise or counterclockwise direction. The syntax for the constructor of this class follows:

```
public RotateAnimation(float from_angle, float to_angle, int pivot_XType, float
pivot_X, int pivot_YType, float pivot_Y)
```

Table 9.14 describes the parameters used in the constructor.

TABLE 9.14   Parameters used in `RotateAnimation`'s Constructor

Parameter	Description
`from_angle`	Defines the angle in degrees at which to begin the `Rotation` animation.
`to_angle`	Defines the angle at which to end the `Rotation` animation. If the angle is positive, the `View` rotates clockwise. A negative angle makes the `View` rotate counterclockwise.
`pivot_XType`	Determines how to interpret the `pivot_X coordinate` value. Valid values for this parameter are
	`Animation.ABSOLUTE`—Interprets the `pivot_X` value as an absolute number of pixels.
	`Animation.RELATIVE_TO_SELF`—Interprets the `pivot_X` value in relation to the current X coordinate of the `View` being animated. The value for the `pivot_X` can be supplied as a percentage. The percentage value is scaled from `0.0` to `1.0`, where `1.0` represents `100%`. If a value `0.5` is assigned to `pivot_X`, it means the midpoint of the `View`'s width.
	`Animation.RELATIVE_TO_PARENT`—Interprets the `pivot_X` value in relation to the X coordinate of the parent of the `View` being animated.
`pivotX`	Defines the X coordinate of the pivot point or axis around which the `View` has to be rotated. If the value assigned to the `pivot_XType` parameter is `Animation.ABSOLUTE`, an absolute value is supplied for this parameter. A value of `0` represents the left edge of the `View`. If the value assigned to the `pivot_XType` parameter is `Animation.RELATIVE_TO_SELF` or `Animation.RELATIVE_TO_PARENT`, a percentage value is assigned to this parameter. The percentage value is supplied in scaled form from `0.0` to `1.0`, where `1.0` represents `100%`.
`pivot_YType`	Determines how to interpret the `pivot_Y` parameter value. Valid values for this parameter are `Animation.ABSOLUTE`, `Animation.RELATIVE_TO_SELF`, and `Animation.RELATIVE_TO_PARENT`.

Parameter	Description
pivotY	Defines the Y coordinate of the pivot or axis around which the `View` has to be rotated. If the value assigned to the `pivot_YType` parameter is `Animation.ABSOLUTE`, an absolute value is supplied to this parameter. Value 0 represents the top edge of the `View`. If the value assigned to the `pivot_YType` parameter is `Animation.RELATIVE_TO_SELF` or `Animation.RELATIVE_TO_PARENT`, a percentage value is assigned to this parameter in scaled form in the range of `0.0` to `1.0`, where `1.0` represents `100%`. If the value `0.5` is assigned to `pivot_y`, it means the Y coordinate of the pivot should be considered the midpoint of the `View`'s height.

For example, the following statement applies a rotate animation to the `View`, rotating it 360 degrees clockwise from the center axis of the `View`:

```
RotateAnimation animation = new RotateAnimation(0,360, Animation.RELATIVE_TO_SELF,0.5f,
Animation.RELATIVE_TO_SELF, 0.5f);
```

Using the `ScaleAnimation` **Class**

The class defines the scale animation and increases or decreases the size of the specified `View` horizontally, vertically, or both. The syntax for the constructor of this class is as follows:

```
public ScaleAnimation(float from_X, float to_X, float from_Y, float to_Y, int
pivot_XType, float pivotX, int pivotYType, float pivotY)
```

Table 9.15 describes the parameters used in the `ScaleAnimation` constructor.

TABLE 9.15   Parameters Used in `ScaleAnimation`'s Constructor

Parameter	Description
from_X	Defines the horizontal initial scaling value to be applied at the beginning of the scale animation. The value supplied is in scaled form. For example, `1.0` represents `100%`, `2.0` represents `200%`, `0.5.` represents `50%`, and so on.
to_X	Defines the horizontal scale value to be applied at the end of a scale animation.
from_Y	Defines the vertical initial scale value to be applied at the beginning of a scale animation.
to_Y	Defines the vertical scale value to be applied at the end of a scale animation.
pivot_XType	Determines how to interpret the `pivot_x` parameter, that is, whether to consider it an absolute value or in percentage form. Valid values are `Animation.ABSOLUTE`, `Animation.RELATIVE_TO_SELF`, and `Animation.RELATIVE_TO_PARENT`. The meanings of these constants are the same as we saw in rotate animation.

Parameter	Description
pivotX	Defines the X coordinate of the pivot point or axis about which the `View` has to be scaled. If the value assigned to the `pivot_XType` parameter is `Animation.ABSOLUTE`, an absolute value is supplied for this parameter. A value of 0 represents the left edge of the `View`. If the value assigned to the `pivot_XType` parameter is `Animation.RELATIVE_TO_SELF` or `Animation.RELATIVE_TO_PARENT`, a percentage value is assigned to this parameter. Again, the percentage value is supplied in scaled form in the range of 0.0 to 1.0, where 1.0 represents 100%.
pivot_YType	Determines how to interpret the `pivot_Y` parameter. Valid values are `Animation.ABSOLUTE`, `Animation.RELATIVE_TO_SELF`, and `Animation.RELATIVE_TO_PARENT`.
pivotY	Defines the Y coordinate of the pivot point or axis about which the `View` has to be scaled. If the value assigned to the `pivot_YType` parameter is `Animation.ABSOLUTE`, an absolute value is supplied for this parameter. A value of 0 represents the top edge of the `View`. If the value assigned to the `pivot_YType` parameter is `Animation.RELATIVE_TO_SELF` or `Animation.RELATIVE_TO_PARENT`, a percentage value is assigned to this parameter in scaled form; that is, in the range of 0.0 to 1.0, where 1.0 represents 100%. If a value of 0.5 is assigned to `pivot_Y`, it means that the middle value of the `View`'s height is the Y coordinate of the pivot.

The values supplied for the `from_X`, `to_X`, `from_Y`, and `to_Y` parameters are always in scaled form. The values supplied for the `pivotX` and `pivotY` parameters can be in absolute or scaled form, depending on the value assigned to `pivotX` and `pivotY`. For example, the following statement scales the `View` to twice its original size horizontally and vertically. The center of the `View` is taken as the axis or pivot point of the scale animation:

```
Animation animation = new ScaleAnimation(1.0f, 2.0f, 1.0f,
2.0f,Animation.RELATIVE_TO_SELF, 0.5f, Animation.RELATIVE_TO_SELF, 0.5f);
```

Collecting and Sequencing Animations

To make animations occur simultaneously or sequentially, we use the `AnimationSet` class. Any number of animation subclasses, such as `AlphaAnimation`, `RotateAnimation`, `ScaleAnimation`, and `TranslateAnimation`, can be added to the `AnimationSet` object. The animation sequences added to the `AnimationSet` object are then applied to the `ImageView` through the `createAnimation()` method. The following statement shows how to apply the animation sequences added in the `AnimationSet` object, `set`, to the `ImageView` object, `imgView`:

```
imgView.startAnimation(set);
```

Let's now create an application that demonstrates the implementation of `alpha`, `rotate`, `scale`, and `translate` animation through Java code. Create a new Android project called `TweenAnimCode`. Copy the `face4.png` file to the `res/drawable` folder. In the

activity_tween_anim_code.xml layout file, write the code shown in Listing 9.6. In the
TweenAnimCodeActivity.java file, write the code shown in Listing 9.12.

LISTING 9.12   Code Written into the TweenAnimCodeActivity.java File

```
package com.androidunleashed.tweenanimcode;

import android.app.Activity;
import android.os.Bundle;
import android.widget.ImageView;
import android.view.animation.Animation;
import android.widget.Button;
import android.view.View;
import android.view.animation.TranslateAnimation;
import android.view.animation.RotateAnimation;
import android.view.animation.AlphaAnimation;
import android.view.animation.ScaleAnimation;
import android.view.animation.AnimationSet;

public class TweenAnimCodeActivity extends Activity {
    ImageView imgView;

    @Override
    public void onCreate(Bundle savedInstanceState) {
        super.onCreate(savedInstanceState);
        setContentView(R.layout.activity_tween_anim_code);
        Button alphaButton = (Button) findViewById(R.id.alpha_button);
        Button rotateButton = (Button) findViewById(R.id.rotate_button);
        Button scaleButton = (Button) findViewById(R.id.scale_button);
        Button translateButton = (Button) findViewById(R.id.translate_button);
        imgView = (ImageView)findViewById(R.id.imgview);
        rotateButton.setOnClickListener(new View.OnClickListener() {
            @Override
            public void onClick(View v) {
                RotateAnimation animation = new RotateAnimation(0,360, Animation.
RELATIVE_TO_SELF,0.5f,Animation.RELATIVE_TO_SELF, 0.5f);
                animation.setDuration(3000);
                imgView.setAnimation(animation);
                animation.start();
            }
        });

        alphaButton.setOnClickListener(new View.OnClickListener() {
            @Override
            public void onClick(View v) {
                Animation animation = new AlphaAnimation(1.0f, 0.1f);
```

```
                animation.setDuration(3000);
                imgView.setAnimation(animation);
                animation.start();
            }
        });


        scaleButton.setOnClickListener(new View.OnClickListener() {
            @Override
            public void onClick(View v) {
                AnimationSet set = new AnimationSet(true);
                Animation animation1 = new ScaleAnimation(1.0f, 2.0f, 1.0f,
2.0f,Animation.RELATIVE_TO_SELF, 0.5f, Animation.RELATIVE_TO_SELF, 0.5f);
                animation1.setDuration(3000);
                set.addAnimation(animation1);
                Animation animation2 = new ScaleAnimation(1.0f, 0.5f, 1.0f, 0.5f,
Animation.RELATIVE_TO_SELF, 0.5f, Animation.RELATIVE_TO_SELF, 0.5f);
                animation2.setDuration(3000);
                animation2.setStartOffset(3000);
                set.addAnimation(animation2);
                imgView.startAnimation(set);
            }
        });
        translateButton.setOnClickListener(new View.OnClickListener() {
            @Override
            public void onClick(View v) {
                AnimationSet set = new AnimationSet(true);
                Animation animation1 = new TranslateAnimation(0,-150,0,0);
                animation1.setDuration(3000);
                animation1.setFillAfter(true);
                set.addAnimation(animation1);
                Animation animation2 = new TranslateAnimation(0,0,0,200);
                animation2.setDuration(3000);
                animation2.setStartOffset(3000);
                animation2.setFillAfter(true);
                set.addAnimation(animation2);
                imgView.startAnimation(set);
            }
        });
    }
}
```

After we run the application, the output is identical to that of the TweenAnimApp application (as you saw earlier in Figures 9.20 and 9.21).

Applying Interpolators

An interpolator defines the rate of change in an animation. It can affect all four types of tweening animations. Interpolators can make the `alpha`, `scale`, `translate`, and `rotate` animations accelerate, bounce, follow a specific pattern, and so on. A number of different interpolators are provided as part of the Android SDK framework. Some of these are described in Table 9.16.

TABLE 9.16 Interpolator Types

Interpolator	Description
AccelerateDecelerateInterpolator	Animation starts slowly, speeds up, and ends slowly.
AccelerateInterpolator	Animation starts out slowly and then accelerates.
AnticipateInterpolator	Animation starts backward and then goes forward.
AnticipateOvershootInterpolator	Animation starts backward, goes forward, over-shoots its destination, and then returns to the destination value.
BounceInterpolator	Animation bounces at the end.
CycleInterpolator	Repeats the animation for a specified number of cycles with smooth transitions.
DecelerateInterpolator	Animation starts quickly and then decelerates.
LinearInterpolator	Animation speed remains constant throughout.
OvershootInterpolator	Animation goes forward, overshoots its destination, and then returns to the destination value.

For example, the following code applies the `translate` animation to the selected graphic. The graphic moves 200 pixels toward the left. Because the `DecelerateInterpolator` interpolator is used, the animation starts quickly and then decelerates:

```
<?xml version="1.0" encoding="utf-8"?>
<set xmlns:android="http://schemas.android.com/apk/res/android"
    android:fillAfter="true"
    android:interpolator="@android:anim/decelerate_interpolator">
    <translate android:fromXDelta="0"
        android:toXDelta="-200"
        android:duration="3000"
        android:fillAfter="true"/>
</set>
```

The following code again applies the `translate` animation to the selected graphic. The graphic is supposed to move 200 pixels toward the left. Because the `AnticipateInterpolator` interpolator is used, the graphic first moves backward (toward the right) and thereafter it goes forward toward the left. The animation stops when the graphic reaches 200 pixels on the left side:

```xml
<?xml version="1.0" encoding="utf-8"?>
<set xmlns:android="http://schemas.android.com/apk/res/android"
    android:fillAfter="true"
    android:interpolator="@android:anim/anticipate_interpolator">
    <translate android:fromXDelta="0"
        android:toXDelta="-200"
        android:duration="3000"
        android:fillAfter="true"/>
</set>
```

The following code makes the graphic move 200 pixels toward the left. Because `BounceInterpolator` is used, the graphic bounces like a ball when it reaches 200 pixels on the left side.

```xml
<?xml version="1.0" encoding="utf-8"?>
<set xmlns:android="http://schemas.android.com/apk/res/android"
    android:fillAfter="true" android:interpolator="@android:anim/bounce_interpolator">
    <translate android:fromXDelta="0"
        android:toXDelta="-200"
        android:duration="3000"
        android:fillAfter="true"/>
</set>
```

Summary

In this chapter we learned to draw circles, points, lines, paths, rectangles, rounded rectangles, ovals, and arcs. We saw how to apply colors, paint antialiasing, paint style, stroke width, and end caps to graphics. We learned to display bitmaps and text, and how to apply color gradients to graphics. We learned how to define frame-by-frame and tweening animations via XML resources and coding. Finally, we saw the role of interpolators in defining the rate of change in animation.

In the next chapter, we learn to display web pages through `WebView` controls, handle page navigation, and add permissions for Internet access. We see how to use the WebViewClient, Google Maps; get Google Keys; and install the Google API. We also learn how to create AVDs for map-based applications, use location-based services, supply latitude and longitude values through DDMS, add zooming, and display map markers.

# CHAPTER 10

Displaying Web Pages and Maps

It is interesting to view web pages and Google Maps through Android applications. The Internet and the web pages found there are a huge source of information today. It also is often beneficial to embed a Google Map in an Android application. Maps provide an easy way to search destinations. They are heavily used in the fields of education, hotel business, travel, and tourism. Besides normal map view, Google Maps also display satellite views of the desired locations.

Displaying Web Pages

`WebView` is a widget commonly used for viewing web applications or pages. It displays web pages as a part of our activity layout.

Let's make a small browser application that prompts the user to enter the URL of a website, and then loads and displays it through the `WebView` control. Launch the Eclipse IDE and create a new Android application. Name the application `WebViewApp`.

In this application, we use `TextView`, `EditText`, `Button`, and `WebView` controls. The `TextView` control displays the text `Address:` to tell the user that the URL of the website must be entered in the adjacent `EditText` control. The `EditText` control displays an empty text box where the user can enter the URL of the site to open. When the user clicks the `Button` control, the website whose URL was entered in the `EditText` control is loaded and displayed via the `WebView` control. To define these four controls, the code shown in Listing 10.1 is written in the `activity_web_view_app.xml` layout file.

LISTING 10.1   Code Written into the `activity_web_view_app.xml` Layout File

```
<LinearLayout xmlns:android="http://schemas.android.com/apk/res/android"
    android:orientation="vertical"
    android:layout_width="match_parent"
    android:layout_height="match_parent">
    <TextView
        android:layout_width="match_parent"
        android:layout_height="wrap_content"
        android:text="Address:"/>
    <EditText
        android:layout_width="match_parent"
        android:layout_height="wrap_content"
        android:id="@+id/web_url"
        android:hint="http://"/>
    <Button
        android:layout_width="wrap_content"
        android:layout_height="wrap_content"
        android:id="@+id/go_btn"
        android:text="Go"
        android:paddingTop="10dip"
        android:paddingBottom="10dip"
        android:paddingLeft="35dip"
        android:paddingRight="35dip"
        android:layout_gravity="center"/>
    <WebView
        android:id="@+id/web_view"
        android:layout_width="match_parent"
        android:layout_height="match_parent" />
</LinearLayout>
```

We can see that the `TextView` control is set to display the text `Address:`. The ID assigned to the `EditText` control is `web_url`, and its `hint` text is set to `http://`. The `hint` text appears in a light color inside the `EditText` control to tell the user about the type of data that should be entered. The ID assigned to the `Button` control is `go_btn`; the button caption set is `Go`; and the spacing of the button text from the left, right, top, and bottom border of the button is set to `35dip`, `35dip`, `10dip`, and `10dip`, respectively. The `Button` control itself is set to appear at the center of the `View`. The last control, `WebView`, is assigned the ID `web_view`.

Modify the Java activity file `WebViewAppActivity.java` to appear as shown in Listing 10.2.

LISTING 10.2   Code Written into the `WebViewAppActivity.java` Java Activity File

```java
package com.androidunleashed.webviewapp;

import android.app.Activity;
import android.os.Bundle;
import android.widget.Button;
import android.widget.EditText;
import android.view.View;
import android.view.View.OnClickListener;
import android.view.View.OnKeyListener;
import android.webkit.WebView;
import android.view.KeyEvent;

public class WebViewAppActivity extends Activity implements OnClickListener {
    EditText url;
    WebView webView;

    @Override
    public void onCreate(Bundle savedInstanceState) {
        super.onCreate(savedInstanceState);
        setContentView(R.layout.activity_web_view_app);
        url = (EditText)this.findViewById(R.id.web_url);
        webView = (WebView) findViewById(R.id.web_view);
        webView.setInitialScale(50);
        webView.getSettings().setJavaScriptEnabled(true);
        url.setOnKeyListener(new OnKeyListener() {
            public boolean onKey(View v, int keyCode, KeyEvent event) {
                if ((event.getAction() == KeyEvent.ACTION_UP) && (keyCode ==
KeyEvent.KEYCODE_ENTER)) {
                    webView.loadUrl(url.getText().toString());
                    return true;
                }
                return false;
            }
        });
        Button b = (Button)this.findViewById(R.id.go_btn);
        b.setOnClickListener(this);
    }

    @Override
    public void onClick(View v) {
        webView.loadUrl(url.getText().toString());
    }

    @Override
```

```
public boolean onKeyUp(int keyCode, KeyEvent event) {
    if ((keyCode == KeyEvent.KEYCODE_BACK) && webView.canGoBack()) {
        webView.goBack();
        return true;
    }
    return super.onKeyUp(keyCode, event);
}
}
```

The `EditText` and `WebView` controls from the layout file are captured and mapped to the `EditText` and `WebView` objects, `url` and `webView`, respectively. The size of the web page that is loaded and viewed through the `WebView` control is resized to `50%`. We want the user-entered website URL loaded into `webView` when either of the following events occurs:

▶ When the user presses the `Enter` key in the `EditText` control

▶ When the user clicks the `Go` button after entering the URL in the `EditText` control

To accomplish this, we need to associate a `KeyListener` with the `EditText` control and a `ClickListener` with the `Button` control so that the `onKey()` callback method is called when any key is pressed in the `EditText` control and the `onClick()` callback method is called when a `Click` event occurs on the `Button` control. In the `onKey()` method, we check for two things:

▶ Whether the event that has occurred is connected to a keypress

▶ Whether the code of the pressed key matches that of the `Enter` key

In short, the `onKey()` method checks for the occurrence of the `Enter` key in the `EditText` control. If the `Enter` key is pressed, the URL of the site entered in the `url` `EditText` control is loaded and displayed in the `WebView` control using the `loadUrl()` method.

The `onKey()` callback method is set to return the Boolean value `true` if we don't want to listen for more keypresses and want to terminate the event handler and exit from the method to do something else. The method is set to return the Boolean value `false` if we do not want to terminate the event handler and want to continue to listen for more keypresses. We can see in the `onKey()` method that when the user presses the `Enter` key, we terminate the `KeyListener` event handler by returning the Boolean value `true` in the callback method. We return the Boolean value `false` from the `onKey()` callback method to have the Key Listener listen for more keys until the `Enter` key is pressed in the `EditText` control.

NOTE

Every keypress consists of several key events. Each key event has an attached key code that helps to identify which key is pressed.

Similarly, in the `onClick()` callback method that is called when a click event occurs on the `Button` control, we simply load the website whose URL was entered in the `url` `EditText` control.

Our web page may not work properly if it contains JavaScript code because the JavaScript is disabled by default in a `WebView`. Let's learn more.

Enabling JavaScript

It may happen that the web page we load through `WebView` contains JavaScript. JavaScript is disabled in a `WebView` by default. To view the web page correctly, we need to enable JavaScript for our `WebView`. The JavaScript is enabled through the WebSettings attached to our `WebView`. We can retrieve the WebSettings with the `getSettings()` method, and then enable JavaScript with `setJavaScriptEnabled()` method.

Handling Page Navigation

When the `WebView` widget is used for loading web pages, it maintains a history of visited web pages. We can use this web page history to navigate backward and forward. To view the previous or next page, the `goBack()` and `goForward()` methods are used.

The function

```
public boolean onKeyUp(int keyCode, KeyEvent event)
```

checks to see whether a key is released. The function calls `goBack()` to navigate to the previous page in the history. The `goBack()` method is called when both conditions are true, that is, if the `Back` key is pressed and the `canGoBack()` function returns `true`. The `canGoBack()` method returns `true` only if there exists a web page history for us to visit. Similarly, we can use `canGoForward()` to check whether there is a forward history.

> **NOTE**
>
> After reaching the end of the history, the `goBack()` or `goForward()` methods do nothing.

Table 10.1 shows an outline of different methods provided by the `WebView` class.

TABLE 10.1   `WebView` Class Methods

Method	Description
reload()	Refreshes or reloads the currently viewed web page.
goBack()	Goes back one step in the browser history.
canGoBack()	Checks to see whether there is any history to go back to.
goForward()	Moves forwards one step in the browser history.
canGoForward()	Checks to see whether there is any history to move forward to.

10

Method	Description
goBackOrForward()	Goes backward or forward in the browser history, depending on whether the number supplied as an argument to the method is positive or negative. A negative number represents the numbers of steps to navigate backward in the history and a positive number represents the number of steps to move forward in the browser history.
canGoBackOrForward()	Checks to see whether the browser can go backward or forward in the browser history for the specified number of steps. The number supplied as the argument to the method depends on whether we want to go backward or forward.
clearCache()	Clears the browser cache.
clearHistory()	Clears the browsing history.

The only step required to complete this application is to add permission to access the Internet from within the application.

Adding Permission for Internet Access

Our application must have access to the Internet to load a web page, so we need to request Internet permission in the `AndroidManifest.xml` file by adding the following statements:

```
<manifest ... >
    <uses-permission android:name="android.permission.INTERNET" />
    ...
</manifest>
```

Our manifest file now appears as shown in Listing 10.3. Only the code in bold is newly added; the rest is the default code automatically created for us by the ADT after creating a new Android project.

LISTING 10.3   The `AndroidManifest.xml` Configuration File

```
<manifest xmlns:android="http://schemas.android.com/apk/res/android"
    package="com.androidunleashed.webviewapp"
    android:versionCode="1"
    android:versionName="1.0">
    <uses-sdk android:minSdkVersion="8"
        android:targetSdkVersion="15"/>
    <uses-permission android:name="android.permission.INTERNET" />
    <application android:icon="@drawable/ic_launcher"
        android:label="@string/app_name"
        android:theme="@style/AppTheme" >
        <activity android:name=".WebViewAppActivity"
```

```
            android:label="@string/title_activity_web_view_app">
            <intent-filter>
                <action android:name="android.intent.action.MAIN" />
                <category android:name="android.intent.category.LAUNCHER" />
            </intent-filter>
        </activity>
    </application>
</manifest>
```

Now our application is complete, and we can run it. The first screen that we see on startup is shown in Figure 10.1 (left). The white space below the Go button represents the WebView control, which is initially blank. We can type the URL of the website we want to view into the EditText control and either press the Enter key or click the Go button to load and view it via the WebView control. After we load my website, http://bmharwani.com, the website is displayed as shown in Figure 10.1 (middle). After we select a link, the WebView control is updated to display information about the linked web page, as shown in Figure 10.1 (right). If we click the Back key, we move back one step in the browsing history, and the web page shown in Figure 10.1 (middle) reappears in the WebView control.

> **NOTE**
>
> After we enter the URL in the EditText control and press Enter, the application doesn't insert a blank line in the EditText box. Instead, it navigates to the entered URL because we have associated a KeyListener with the EditText control.

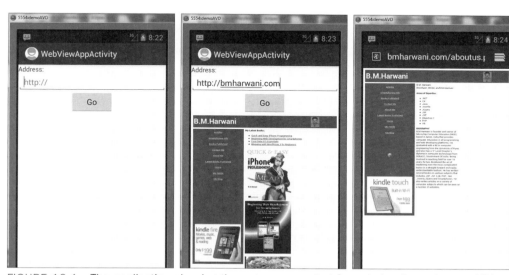

FIGURE 10.1 The application showing the EditText control for entering the web page URL (left), the web page loaded and displayed in the WebView control (middle), and the linked web page opened by the default web browser (right)

10

One thing that you will observe when executing the application is that when any link is selected, the web page loads, but it covers the entire view, making the TextView, EditText, and Button controls invisible. Android invokes the default web browser to open and load the linked web page instead of using the application's WebView control. To override this problem, we use the WebViewClient class.

Using the WebViewClient Class

Android invokes the default web browser to open and load the linked web page. To open links within our WebView, the WebViewClient class and its shouldOverrideUrlLoading() method are used.

So, open the WebViewApp Android application and modify its WebViewAppActivity.java Java activity file to perform the following tasks:

- ▶ Use the WebViewClient class.
- ▶ Use the shouldOverrideUrlLoading() method to load the clicked links in the WebView control.

The code in the file WebViewAppActivity.java is modified to appear as shown in Listing 10.4. Only the code in bold is modified.

LISTING 10.4   Code Written into the WebViewAppActivity.java Java Activity File

```java
package com.androidunleashed.webviewapp;

import android.app.Activity;
import android.os.Bundle;
import android.widget.Button;
import android.widget.EditText;
import android.view.View;
import android.view.View.OnClickListener;
import android.view.View.OnKeyListener;
import android.webkit.WebView;
import android.view.KeyEvent;
import android.webkit.WebViewClient;

public class WebViewAppActivity extends Activity implements OnClickListener {
    EditText url;
    WebView webView;

    @Override
    public void onCreate(Bundle savedInstanceState) {
        super.onCreate(savedInstanceState);
        setContentView(R.layout.activity_web_view_app);
        url = (EditText)this.findViewById(R.id.web_url);
        webView = (WebView) findViewById(R.id.web_view);
```

```
        webView.setInitialScale(50);
        webView.getSettings().setJavaScriptEnabled(true);
        webView.setWebViewClient(new WebViewClient(){
            public boolean shouldOverrideUrlLoading(WebView view, String url) {
                view.loadUrl(url);
                return true;
            }
        });

        url.setOnKeyListener(new OnKeyListener() {
            public boolean onKey(View v, int keyCode, KeyEvent event) {
                if ((event.getAction() == KeyEvent.ACTION_UP) &&  (keyCode ==
KeyEvent.KEYCODE_ENTER)) {
                    webView.loadUrl(url.getText().toString());
                    return true;
                }
                return false;
            }
        });
        Button b = (Button)this.findViewById(R.id.go_btn);
        b.setOnClickListener(this);
    }

    @Override
    public void onClick(View v) {
        webView.loadUrl(url.getText().toString());
    }

    @Override
    public boolean onKeyUp(int keyCode, KeyEvent event) {
        if ((keyCode == KeyEvent.KEYCODE_BACK) && webView.canGoBack()) {
            webView.goBack();
            return true;
        }
        return super.onKeyUp(keyCode, event);
    }
}
```

We use two functions explained here:

▶ setWebViewClient()

The setWebViewClient() function replaces the current handler with the WebViewClient, enabling us to utilize its methods to make all the clicked links open in our WebView control.

▶ `public boolean shouldOverrideUrlLoading (WebView view, String url)`

The `view` and `url` parameters used in the `shouldOverrideUrlLoading()` method refer to the `WebView` that is initiating the callback and the URL of the clicked link, respectively.

By default, the `WebView` asks the `Activity Manager` to choose the proper handler to open a clicked link in a web page. The `Activity Manager` in turn invokes the user's default browser to load the `url` of the linked page. Through this function, we can decide whether we want the host application or the `WebView` to load the linked `url`. If the function returns `true`, it means that we want the host application to handle the `url`. If the function returns `false`, it means we don't want the host application to interrupt and prefer the `WebView` to handle the `url`; that is, we want the `url` to be loaded in our `WebView`.

After making these changes in the activity file, we see a screen prompting for a URL. The web page whose URL was entered in the `EditText` control is then loaded and opened in the `WebView` control, as shown in Figure 10.2 (left). After we select any link, the linked page also opens in the `WebView` control (see Figure 10.2—right). The default browser no longer handles the linked URL.

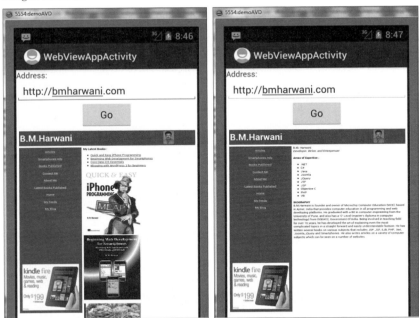

FIGURE 10.2   Loading a web page in the `WebView` control (left), and the linked web page also opens in the `WebView` control (right).

Using Google Maps

We can create map-based applications in Android to display maps in different views. For example, we can have satellite views, traffic views, and street views of different places. We can locate or pinpoint places on the map and zoom in and out. We can also use Location-Based Services (LBS), which use latitude and longitude values to locate the device or emulator.

To access Google Maps in our Android application, we need to have a Google Maps API key first.

Obtaining a Google Maps API Key

You need to apply for a free Google Maps API key before you can integrate Google Maps into your Android application. The steps for obtaining a Google key are as follows:

1. To get a Google key, the application needs to be signed with a certificate and you need to notify Google about the Hash (MD5) fingerprint of the certificate. To test the application on the Android emulator, search for the SDK debug certificate located in the default folder: `C:\Users\<user_name>\.android`. The filename of the debug certificate is `debug.keystore`. For deploying to a real Android device, substitute the `debug.keystore` file with your own keystore file.

2. Copy the `debug.keystore` to any drive.

3. Using the debug keystore certificate, extract its MD5 fingerprint using the `keytool.exe` application provided with the JDK installation. This fingerprint is needed to apply for the free Google Maps key. The `keytool.exe` file can be found in the `C:\Program Files\Java\jdk_version_number\bin` folder.

4. Open the command prompt and go to the `C:\Program Files\Java\jdk_version_number\bin` folder using the `CD` command.

5. Issue the following command to extract the MD5 fingerprint:

```
keytool.exe -list -alias androiddebugkey -keystore "E:\debug.keystore" -store-
pass android -keypass android
```

   You get the MD5 fingerprint, as shown in Figure 10.3.

FIGURE 10.3   Extracting the MD5 fingerprint using the debug certificate

Now you need to sign up for the Google Maps API. Open the browser and go to `http://code.google.com/android/maps-api-signup.html`. Follow the instructions on the page and supply the extracted MD5 fingerprint to complete the signup process and obtain the Google Maps key. After successful completion of the signup process, the Google Maps API key is displayed as shown in Listing 10.5.

LISTING 10.5   Google Maps API Key

```
Your key is:
xxxxxxxxxxxxxxxxxxxxxxxxxxxxxxxxxxxxxx
This key is good for all apps signed with your certificate whose fingerprint is:
XX:XX:XX:XX:XX:XX:XX:XX:XX:XX:XX:XX:XX:XX:XX:XX
Here is an example xml layout to get you started on your way to mapping glory:
<com.google.android.maps.MapView
    android:layout_width="match_parent"
    android:layout_height="match_parent"
    android:apiKey="xxxxxxxxxxxxxxxxxxxxxxxxxxxxxxxxxxxxxx"/>
 <com.google.android.maps.MapView
    android:id="@+id/mapvw"
    android:layout_width="match_parent"
    android:layout_height="match_parent"
    android:enabled="true"
    android:clickable="true"
    android:apiKey="xxxxxxxxxxxxxxxxxxxxxxxxxxxxxxxxxxxxxx"/>
```

Replace xxxxx... with your own map key in the android:apiKey attribute. This output shows the Google Maps API key for the supplied MD5 fingerprint. After we obtain the Google Maps API key, the next step is to install the Google API.

Installing the Google API

For building Google Map-based applications, we need to install the Google API. Recall that in Chapter 1, "Introduction to Android," we installed the Google API. To confirm that it is actually installed, select the Window, Android SDK Manager option. A dialog box opens showing the status of packages and tools on your machine (see Figure 10.4). If the Google API is not yet installed, you can select it in the Android SDK Manager window and then click the Install package button.

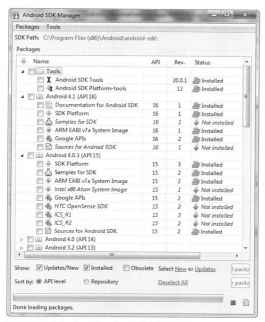

FIGURE 10.4   The Android SDK Manager window showing different packages and tools installed on our machine

To run the Google Maps-based Android application, we need an AVD that targets the Google API platform, so the final step before creating and running the application is to create an AVD that targets it.

AVDs for Map-Based Applications

We need to create a separate AVD to try out Google Maps-based applications. To create a new AVD, select `Window`, `AVD Manager` to open the `AVD Manager` dialog box. The dialog displays a list of existing AVDs. Click the `New` button to define a new AVD. A `Create new Android Virtual Device (AVD)` dialog box opens where we can specify information about the new AVD. Set the `Name` as `GoogleAppAVD` to indicate that it is a virtual device to run Google Map-based applications. Choose `Google APIs (Google Inc.)—API Level 16` for the `Target`, set `SD Card` to `64 MiB`, and leave the `Default (WVGA800)` for `Skin`. Also keep the default in the `Hardware` section. Using the `New` button, we can set the `GPS support` property. Besides the `GPS support`, we can also add several other properties that we want our AVD to emulate, such as `Abstracted LCD density`, `DPad support`, `Accelerometer`, and `Maximum horizontal camera pixels`. Finally, click the `Create AVD` button (see Figure 10.5) to create the virtual device called `GoogleAppAVD`.

10

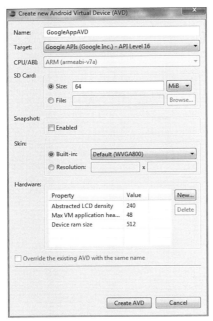

FIGURE 10.5   Creating a new AVD, `GoogleAppAVD` to run the Google Maps-based application

The `GoogleAppAVD` is created and displayed in the list of existing AVDs in the Android SDK and AVD dialog box. Click the `Refresh` button if the newly created AVD doesn't show up in the list. Close the Android SDK and AVD dialog.

Creating a Google Maps-Based Application

Launch the Eclipse IDE and select the `File, New, Android Project` option to create a new Android application. Name the project `GoogleMapApp` and select `Google APIs (Google Inc.) (API 16)` from the `Build SDK` drop-down list. Select `API 16: Android 4.1` from the `Minimum Required SDK` and click `Finish` after supplying all the pertinent information for the new project, as shown in Figure 10.6.

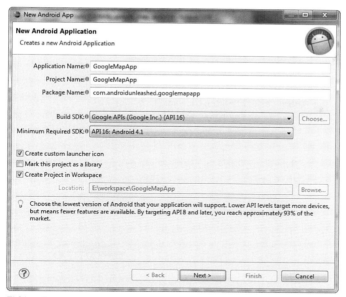

FIGURE 10.6   The dialog box used to specify the information for the new Android project

After we select the Google APIs in the SDK Target list, two files, `maps.jar` and `usb.jar`, are automatically included in our project and thus enable our project to access maps.

To access Google Maps in our application, we have to add the following two statements to the `AndroidManifest.xml` file:

▶ The first statement asks for permission to access the Internet:

```
<uses-permission android:name="android.permission.INTERNET" />
```

▶ The second statement includes the Android map library:

```
<uses-library android:name="com.google.android.maps" />
```

After we add these two code lines, the `AndroidManifest.xml` file appears as shown in Listing 10.6. Only the code in bold is newly added; the rest is the default code.

LISTING 10.6   The `AndroidManifest.xml` Configuration File

```
<manifest xmlns:android="http://schemas.android.com/apk/res/android"
    package="com.androidunleashed.googlemapapp"
    android:versionCode="1"
    android:versionName="1.0">
    <uses-sdk
```

10

```
        android:minSdkVersion="16"
        android:targetSdkVersion="15" />
    <uses-permission android:name="android.permission.INTERNET" />
        <application android:icon="@drawable/ic_launcher" android:label="@string/app_
name"
        android:theme="@style/AppTheme" >
        <uses-library android:name="com.google.android.maps" />
        <activity android:name=".GoogleMapAppActivity" android:label="@string/title_
activity_google_map_app">
            <intent-filter>
                <action android:name="android.intent.action.MAIN" />
                <category android:name="android.intent.category.LAUNCHER" />
            </intent-filter>
        </activity>
    </application>
</manifest>
```

In the `activity_google_map_app.xml` layout file, we add a `MapView` control to display a Google Maps interface element. We need to include the Google Maps API key that we just obtained to use a `MapView` in our application. The Google Maps API key enables our Android application to interact with Google Maps services to obtain map-related information. The `MapView` control is enabled and is also made sensitive to mouse clicks by setting its `android:enabled` and `android:clickable` attributes to `true`. The code shown in Listing 10.7 is written into the `activity_google_map_app.xml` to add the `MapView` control to our application.

LISTING 10.7   Code Written into the `activity_google_map_app.xml` Layout File

```
<LinearLayout xmlns:android="http://schemas.android.com/apk/res/android"
    android:orientation="vertical"
    android:layout_width="match_parent"
    android:layout_height="match_parent">
    <com.google.android.maps.MapView
        android:id="@+id/map_view"
        android:layout_width="match_parent"
        android:layout_height="match_parent"
        android:enabled="true"
        android:clickable="true"
        android:apiKey="xxxxxxxxxxxxxxxxxxxxxxxxxxxxxxxxx" />
</LinearLayout>
```

To use maps, the application Activity needs to extend the `MapActivity` class. We also need to override the `onCreate()` method to lay out the `activity_google_map_app.xml` screen where we have defined our `MapView` control. The code to display Google Maps that we add to `GoogleMapAppActivity.java` is shown in Listing 10.8.

LISTING 10.8   Code Written into the `GoogleMapAppActivity.java` Java Activity File

```
package com.androidunleashed.googlemapapp;

import android.os.Bundle;
import com.google.android.maps.MapActivity;

public class GoogleMapAppActivity extends MapActivity {
    @Override
    public void onCreate(Bundle savedInstanceState) {
        super.onCreate(savedInstanceState);
        setContentView(R.layout.activity_google_map_app);
    }

    protected boolean isRouteDisplayed() {
        return true;
    }
}
```

In the preceding code, we override the `isRouteDisplayed()` method to return the Boolean value `true`, to enable our Activity to display routing information such as traffic directions. After running the application, we see the output shown in Figure 10.7.

FIGURE 10.7   The application showing the startup Google map

We learn to see a specific map later.

10

Using Location-Based Services

Location-Based Services (LBS) help find the device's current location. A location is represented with longitude and latitude values. For using Location-Based Services, we use the following:

▶ **Location Manager**—Provides an interface to the Location-Based Services, enabling applications to obtain periodic updates of the device's geographical location.

▶ **Location Provider**—Used to determine the device's current location. It provides feedback on the geographical location of the device. There may be several Location Providers, and each provider uses a specific technology to determine a device's location. Some use satellites; others use cellular radio, a specific carrier, or the Internet. They differ in battery consumption, monetary cost, and accuracy. The two popular Location Providers are `GPS (Global Positioning System)` and `Android's Network Location Provider`. The former uses satellites, and the latter uses cellular technology to determine device location.

In short, to determine the current device location, Android uses the services of Location Providers through a Location Manager.

To understand the procedure of accessing Location-Based Services, let's create a new Android project called `KnowLocationApp`. In this application, we display the location of the device in terms of longitude and latitude.

Depending on the Location Provider being used, we need to add certain permissions to our application. A GPS provider requires `fine` permission, while the Network provider requires only `coarse`. If we use `fine` permission, then `coarse` permission is implicitly added. The permission tags that need to be added to `AndroidManifest.xml` for `fine` and `coarse` permissions are as follows:

```
<uses-permission android:name="android.permission.ACCESS_FINE_LOCATION"/>
<uses-permission android:name="android.permission.ACCESS_COARSE_LOCATION"/>
```

We are accessing Google Maps in the application; consequently, we also need to add the following two statements in the manifest file:

```
<uses-permission android:name="android.permission.INTERNET" />
<uses-library android:name="com.google.android.maps" />
```

After we add these two statements and the statement for the `fine` permission, `AndroidManifest.xml` appears as shown in Listing 10.9. Only the statements in bold are added; the rest of the code is the default code provided by the ADT after creating the new Android project.

LISTING 10.9   The `AndroidManifest.xml` Configuration File

```
<?xml version="1.0" encoding="utf-8"?>
<manifest xmlns:android="http://schemas.android.com/apk/res/android"
    package="com.androidunleashed.knowlocationapp"
```

```
        android:versionCode="1"
        android:versionName="1.0">
    <uses-sdk android:minSdkVersion="16"
        android:targetSdkVersion="15"/>
    <uses-permission android:name="android.permission.INTERNET" />
    <uses-permission android:name="android.permission.ACCESS_FINE_LOCATION"/>
    <application android:icon="@drawable/ic_launcher"
        android:label="@string/app_name"
        android:theme="@style/AppTheme" >
        <uses-library android:name="com.google.android.maps" />
        <activity android:name=".KnowLocationAppActivity"
            android:label="@string/title_activity_know_location_app">
            <intent-filter>
                <action android:name="android.intent.action.MAIN" />
                <category android:name="android.intent.category.LAUNCHER" />
            </intent-filter>
        </activity>
    </application>
</manifest>
```

In this application, we want to display the location of the device in terms of longitude and latitude, so we have to define two `TextView` controls in the application layout file to display them. After we define two `TextView` controls, `activity_know_location_app.xml` appears as shown in Listing 10.10.

LISTING 10.10   Code Written into the `activity_know_location_app.xml` Layout File

```
<LinearLayout xmlns:android="http://schemas.android.com/apk/res/android"
    android:orientation="vertical"
    android:layout_width="match_parent"
    android:layout_height="match_parent">
    <TextView
        android:text="Latitude: "
        android:layout_height="wrap_content"
        android:layout_width="wrap_content"
        android:id="@+id/latitude_view" />
    <TextView android:text="Longitude: "
        android:layout_height="wrap_content"
        android:layout_width="wrap_content"
        android:id="@+id/longitude_view" />
</LinearLayout>
```

10

Then, modify `KnowLocationAppActivity.java` to appear as shown in Listing 10.11.

LISTING 10.11   The `KnowLocationAppActivity.java` Java Activity File

```java
package com.androidunleashed.knowlocationapp;

import android.app.Activity;
import android.os.Bundle;
import android.widget.TextView;
import android.location.LocationManager;
import android.content.Context;
import android.location.Location;
import android.location.LocationListener;

public class KnowLocationAppActivity extends Activity {
    private TextView latitudeView;
    private TextView longitudeView;
    private LocationManager locationManager;

    @Override
    public void onCreate(Bundle savedInstanceState) {
        super.onCreate(savedInstanceState);
        setContentView(R.layout.activity_know_location_app);
        latitudeView = (TextView) findViewById(R.id.latitude_view);
        longitudeView = (TextView) findViewById(R.id.longitude_view);
        locationManager = (LocationManager) getSystemService(Context.LOCATION_SER-
VICE);    #1
        locationManager.requestLocationUpdates(LocationManager.GPS_PROVIDER, 0, 0,
new LocationListener(){
            public void onProviderDisabled(String provider) { }
            public void onProviderEnabled(String provider) {}
            public void onStatusChanged(String provider, int status, Bundle extras)
{}
            public void onLocationChanged(Location loc) {
                if (loc != null) {
                    int lt = (int) (loc.getLatitude());
                    int lg = (int) (loc.getLongitude());
                    latitudeView.setText("Latitude is: "+String.valueOf(lt));
                    longitudeView.setText("Longitude is: "+String.valueOf(lg));
                }
            }
        });
    }
}
```

The two `TextView` controls defined with the IDs `latitude_view` and `longitude_view` in the layout file are accessed and mapped to the `latitudeView` and `longitudeView` `TextView` objects, respectively.

As mentioned earlier, we need to use the Location Manager to access Location-Based Services. To use the Location Manager, we request an instance of the LOCATION_SERVICE using the getSystemService() method. So, statement #1 provides us with a Location Manager instance called locationManager.

When the location of the device changes, the notifications related to the change in the device's location are received via the Location Manager. To know when the location of the device is changed, we need to register a listener to receive location updates. To register a listener to get updates whenever the location of the device changes, we call the requestLocationUpdates() method. The syntax is

```
requestLocationUpdates(Provider, minTime, minDistance, LocationListener )
```

▶ The Provider parameter refers to the location provider that we are using in the application. The value for this parameter can be LocationManager.GPS_PROVIDER or LocationManager.NETWORK_PROVIDER or any other location provider being used in our application.

▶ The minTime and minDistance parameters are used to specify the minimum time and the minimum distance between location change updates. The minTime and minDistance values are provided in milliseconds and meters. I recommend not to use 0,0 to conserve battery life.

▶ LocationListener is the listener that checks for any change in the device location and other events and executes the respective methods in response.

Example:

```
LocationManager.GPS_PROVIDER, 36000, 1000, new LocationListener(){        }
```

This example invokes the onLocationChanged() method when either of the two events occurs:

▶ After 36000 milliseconds

▶ When the distance traveled by the device is 1000 meters

Four methods may be invoked by the LocationListener, depending on the occurrence of different events. The methods are

▶ **public void onLocationChanged(Location location)**—Called when the location of the device is changed or when the minimum time and distance values are exceeded

▶ **public void onProviderDisabled(String provider)**—Called when the location provider is disabled by the user

▶ **public void onProviderEnabled(String provider)**—Called when the location provider is enabled by the user

10

▶ **public void onStatusChanged(String provider, int status, Bundle extras)**—
Called when the provider status changes from available to unavailable or vice versa

When the location of the device changes, the `onLocationChanged()` method is invoked by the `LocationListener`. Through the `getLatitude()` and `getLongitude()` methods, we access the latitude and longitude values of the current location of the device. The latitude and longitude values are then displayed through the `latitudeView` and `longitudeView` `TextView` controls.

After running the application, we get the output shown in Figure 10.8. We can see that no latitude and longitude values are displayed because we are running our application on an Android emulator instead of an actual device.

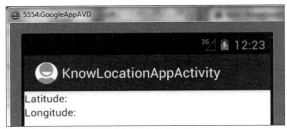

FIGURE 10.8   No output is displayed on an Android emulator

To see whether the application is working correctly, we can set the Android emulator to simulate real hardware and location changes.

Supplying Latitude and Longitude Values Through DDMS

To pass latitude and longitude values to the provider through an emulator, we can use the *Dalvik Debug Monitor Service (DDMS)* interface. In Eclipse, perform the following steps to push the GPS location into the emulator:

1. Ensure the emulator is running. Select the `Window`, `AVD Manager` option. Select the `GoogleAppAVD` virtual device, the one we created in this chapter, and click `Start`. We get a dialog box showing the emulator `Launch Options`. Click `Launch` to run the emulator.

2. Open the DDMS perspective by selecting the `Window`, `Open Perspective`, DDMS option.

3. In the DDMS perspective, open the `File Explorer` by selecting `Window`, `Show View`, `File Explorer`.

4. If you can't see the running emulator anywhere, open the `Devices` view by selecting `Window`, `Show View`, `Device`. You can see all the running emulators and select the one that you want to use for pushing the GPS location.

5. Locate the `Location Controls` section in the `Emulator Control` tab. There are three separate tabs in the `Location Controls` section (see Figure 10.9):

▶ **Manual**—Use this tab to manually send in the coordinates by specifying the latitude and longitude values.

▶ **GPX**—Use the .GPX file to send geographical locations to our application. The *GPX (GPS Exchange Format)* is a lightweight XML data format used for sending GPS data. If we have a .GPX file, we can load it by clicking the Load GPX... button. After loading the .GPX file, we can click the Play button to send a series of coordinates to the Android emulator at regular time intervals. Remember, only GPX 1.1 files are supported.

▶ **KML**—Use *KML (Keyhole Markup Language)* files to send graphical locations to our application. As with .GPX files, we can send a series of coordinates to the Android emulator by clicking the Play button.

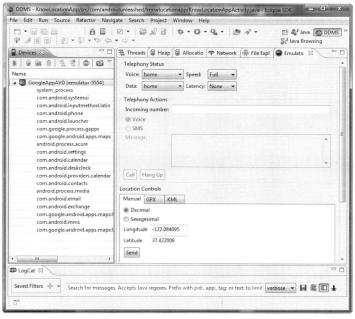

FIGURE 10.9   Sending GPS locations to the application manually

Sending GPS Locations Manually

In the Manual tab, we can enter the Longitude and Latitude values and just click the Send button. After receiving the GPS locations, the LocationListener in our application fires the onLocationChanged() method and displays the new location of the user in the Longitude and Latitude coordinates. If we send the Longitude and Latitude values as -122.084095 and 37.422006, then on running the application, we see the output shown in Figure 10.10.

10

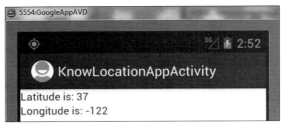

FIGURE 10.10   Latitude and longitude values displayed after manually pushing a GPS location to the emulator

Passing Locations in GPX/KML Format

As mentioned earlier, we can upload a GPX or KML file to the emulator and set the playback speed. The emulator then sends our GPS location to our application at the specified speed.

To load a GPX file, select the GPX tab. A Load GPX button is displayed. Click the Load GPX button to upload the GPX file. The location information contained therein is displayed, as shown in Figure 10.11 (left). After we select a location from the list, it is sent to the emulator. If the Play button is clicked, all the locations are sent to the application at the specified speed, as shown in Figure 10.11 (right).

NOTE

The Speed button is used to send the GPX file location values to the application at the given speed.

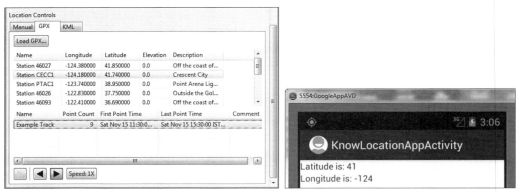

FIGURE 10.11   After we load a GPX file, the location information stored in the GPX file is displayed (left), and the locations displayed when clicking Play button (right).

Displaying Map Locations

To display that location on the map whose latitude and longitude values are supplied, we need to add the MapView control to KnowLocationApp. After we add the MapView control, the `activity_know_location_app.xml` application layout file appears as shown in Listing 10.12. Only the code in bold is newly added; the rest is the same as in Listing 10.10.

LISTING 10.12   Code Written into the `activity_know_location_app.xml` Layout File

```
<LinearLayout xmlns:android="http://schemas.android.com/apk/res/android"
    android:orientation="vertical"
    android:layout_width="match_parent"
    android:layout_height="match_parent">
    <TextView
        android:text="Latitude: "
        android:layout_height="wrap_content"
        android:layout_width="wrap_content"
        android:id="@+id/latitude_view" />
    <TextView android:text="Longitude: "
        android:layout_height="wrap_content"
        android:layout_width="wrap_content"
        android:id="@+id/longitude_view" />
    <com.google.android.maps.MapView
        android:id="@+id/mapvw"
        android:layout_width="match_parent"
        android:layout_height="match_parent"
        android:enabled="true"
        android:clickable="true"
        android:apiKey="xxxxxxxxxxxxxxxxxxxxxxxxxxxxxxxxxxxx" />
</LinearLayout>
```

We can see that the `MapView` control is defined with a `mapvw` ID. It is set to enable mode to listen for the mouse clicks by setting the `android:enabled` and `android:clickable` attributes to `true`. The Google Map API key is supplied to the control, enabling it to access Google Maps.

Next, we need to write Java code into the activity file to perform the following tasks:

▶ Access the `MapView` control from the layout file and map it to the `MapView` object.

▶ Display a default `MapView` zoom control to use the zoom in/out feature.

▶ Select the type of view to display—`satellite`, `street`, or `traffic`.

▶ Convert the GPS location (longitude and latitude values) pushed into the emulator into micro degrees and animate the Google Map to display that location.

▶ Set the zoom level of the Google Map.

To perform these tasks, the code shown in Listing 10.13 is written into the `KnowLocationAppActivity.java` activity file. Only the code in bold is new; the rest is the same as we saw in Listing 10.11.

10

LISTING 10.13   Code Written into the `KnowLocationAppActivity.java` Java Activity File

```java
package com.androidunleashed.knowlocationapp;

import android.os.Bundle;
import android.widget.TextView;
import android.location.LocationManager;
import android.content.Context;
import android.location.Location;
import android.location.LocationListener;
import com.google.android.maps.MapActivity;
import com.google.android.maps.MapController;
import com.google.android.maps.MapView;
import com.google.android.maps.GeoPoint;

public class KnowLocationAppActivity extends MapActivity  {
    private TextView latitudeView;
    private TextView longitudeView;
    private LocationManager locationManager;
    private MapController mapController;
    private MapView mapView;
    private GeoPoint point;

    @Override
    public void onCreate(Bundle savedInstanceState) {
        super.onCreate(savedInstanceState);
        setContentView(R.layout.activity_know_location_app);
        latitudeView = (TextView) findViewById(R.id.latitude_view);
        longitudeView = (TextView) findViewById(R.id.longitude_view);
        locationManager = (LocationManager) getSystemService(Context.LOCATION_SERVICE);
        mapView = (MapView) findViewById(R.id.mapvw);
        mapView.setBuiltInZoomControls(true);
        mapView.setSatellite (true);
        mapController = mapView.getController();
        locationManager.requestLocationUpdates( LocationManager.GPS_PROVIDER, 0, 0,
new LocationListener(){
            public void onProviderDisabled(String provider) { }
            public void onProviderEnabled(String provider) {}
            public void onStatusChanged(String provider, int status, Bundle extras)
{}
            public void onLocationChanged(Location loc) {
                if (loc != null) {
                    int lt = (int) (loc.getLatitude());
                    int lg = (int) (loc.getLongitude());
                    latitudeView.setText("Latitude is: "+String.valueOf(lt));
```

```
                longitudeView.setText("Longitude is: "+ String.valueOf(lg));
                int latit=(int)(loc.getLatitude() * 1E6);
                int longit=(int)(loc.getLongitude()* 1E6);
                point = new GeoPoint(latit, longit);
                mapController.animateTo(point);
                mapController.setCenter(point);
                mapController.setZoom(15);
            }
        }
    });
    }

    @Override
    protected boolean isRouteDisplayed() {
        return true;
    }

    @Override
    protected boolean isLocationDisplayed() {
        return false;
    }
}
```

The `MapView` control is accessed from the layout file and is mapped to the `mapView`
`MapView` object. The `MapView` already has controls that enable us to zoom in and out. By
passing the Boolean value `true` to the `setBuiltInZoomControls()` method, we get the
`MapView`'s default zoom controls. The Google Map displays the `satellite` view by passing
the Boolean value `true` to the `setSatellite()` method.

By default, Google Maps are displayed in a map view that displays streets and important
places. We can set the Google Map to appear in `satellite` and `traffic` view, as well. To
switch among different views, we need to call the respective setter method and pass the
Boolean value `true` to it. The different setter methods are

▶ **setSatellite(boolean)**—Displays the `satellite` view of the Google Map when
passed a `true` boolean value.

▶ **setTraffic (boolean)**—Displays the `traffic` view of the Google Map when passed
a `true` Boolean value. We can zoom in the `traffic` view to see the streets. Different
colors are used to show traffic conditions. Green lines in the map (see Figure 10.13)
represent the smooth traffic, yellow lines represent moderate traffic, and red lines
represent slow traffic. In the print book, you'll find the yellow lines in white, green
lines in gray, and red lines in dark gray.

10

TIP

To turn off a particular map view, pass a `false` Boolean value to it.

After setting the Google Map view, we obtain a controller from the `MapView` instance and assign it to a `mapController MapController` object. The latitude and longitude values passed by us through DDMS are retrieved and assigned to the integers `lt` and `lg`, respectively. Recall that after pushing a GPS location into the emulator through DDMS, the `LocationListener` fires the `onLocationChanged()` method. In this application, we are using a `GeoPoint` object to represent a geographical location. The latitude and longitude of a location in the `GeoPoint` class are represented in micro degrees. Hence, we need to multiply the longitude and latitude entered by us through DDMS by `1,000,000` to convert from degree to micro degree and store these values as `GeoPoint` points.

We used the `animateTo()` method of the `MapController` class to navigate the map to a particular location.

We set the center of the location being displayed through Google Map by passing the point (containing the GPS location in micro degree format) to the `setCenter()` method of the map view's controller.

Finally, we set the zoom level of the map to the value 15 by using the `setZoom()` method.

> **NOTE**
>
> Android defines 22 zoom levels for maps.

The method `isLocationDisplayed()` is set to return the Boolean value `true` to display the current device location.

The method `isRouteDisplayed()` is set to return the Boolean value `true` to display route information such as driving directions.

After we run the application, the Google Map appears, displaying the default location, as shown in Figure 10.12 (left). To see the satellite view of San Francisco, we push its latitude and longitude values `37.775` and `-122.4183333` to the Android emulator through DDMS. The satellite view of San Francisco appears, as shown in Figure 10.12 (middle). The figure also shows the MapView's default zoom controls, and a zoomed satellite view of San Francisco is displayed in Figure 10.12 (right).

> **NOTE**
>
> Android maps support zooming in and out. The "i" key zooms in on the map, and the "o" key zooms out.

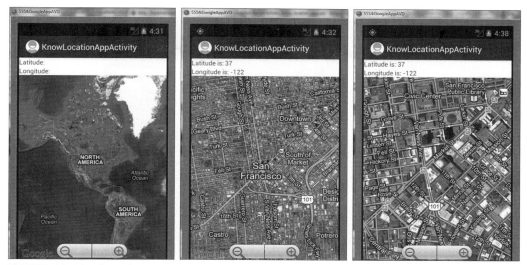

FIGURE 10.12   Satellite view of the default location (left), satellite view of the San Francisco default location at zoom level 15 (middle), and satellite view of San Francisco at zoom level 16 (right)

The following statement superimposes a `traffic` view on top of the San Francisco satellite view when added to the `KnowLocationAppActivity.java` activity file:

```
mapView.setSatellite(true);
```

It can be replaced by the following lines:

```
mapView.setTraffic(true);
mapView.setSatellite(true);
```

After we make these changes, the application shows the San Francisco traffic view zoomed to level 15, as shown in Figure 10.13 (left). After we zoom one more level, the traffic view appears, as shown in Figure 10.13 (right).

10

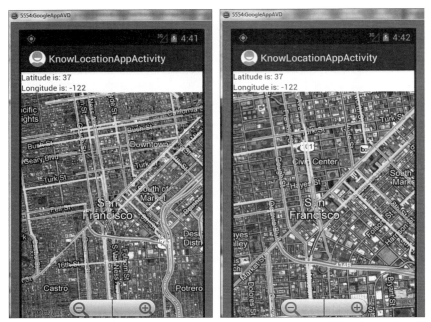

FIGURE 10.13   Traffic view of San Francisco at zoom level 15 (left), and traffic view of San Francisco at zoom level 16 (right)

Printing the GPS Location Address

Android provides a class known as `Geocoder` that helps in getting the street address of supplied GPS coordinates and vice versa. The process of translating between street addresses and longitude/latitude GPS locations is known as geocoding. There are two types of geocoding:

▶ **Forward Geocoding**—Translates street addresses into latitude and longitude values

▶ **Reverse Geocoding**—Translates latitude and longitude values into the street addresses

In both the methods, `Locale` is used to define the location and language. Both geocoding functions return a list of `Address` objects, where each `Address` object contains the details that include the latitude, longitude, phone number, country, street, and house number information.

Reverse Geocoding

For reverse geocoding, we pass the latitude and longitude to a `Geocoder`'s `getFromLocation()` method, and it returns a list of possible matching addresses. If the `Geocoder` could not resolve any addresses for the specified coordinate, it returns `null`:

```
List<Address> result = geocoder.getFromLocation(lat,long, max_no_ofResults);
```

where the `lat` and `long` parameters refer to the `latitude` and `longitude` values whose street address we are looking for, and the `max_no_ofResults` parameter refers to the number of possible addresses we want to have returned. The method returns `null` if no match is found.

Forward Geocoding

Forward geocoding returns latitude and longitude values for the supplied location, where location includes street address, postal codes, train stations, landmarks, and hospitals.

To perform forward geocoding lookup, the `getFromLocationName()` method on a `Geocoder` instance is called, passing the location whose coordinates we are looking for:

```
List<Address> result = geocoder.getFromLocationName(street_address, max_no_ofResults);
```

where `max_no_ofResults` refers to the maximum number of coordinates to return. All possible matches for the supplied address are returned, and each result includes latitude and longitude values, along with additional address information available for the coordinates. If no matches are found, the method returns `null`.

The `Locale` plays an important role in geocoding. It provides the geographical context for interpreting our search requests, as there can be many places with the same location name. To avoid any ambiguity, provide as much detail as possible in the supplied address, as shown in the following example:

```
Geocoder geoGeocoder = new Geocoder(this, Locale.US);
String streetAddress = "2-98 11th St, San Francisco, CA 94103";
List<Address> co_ords = null;
try {
    co_ords = geoGeocoder.getFromLocationName(streetAddress, 10);
} catch (IOException e) {}
```

Let's modify `KnowLocationApp` to print the address of the supplied latitude and longitude values, along with showing that location on the Google Map. To print the address of the supplied coordinates, we have to add one more `TextView` control to our application layout file. After we add the `TextView` control, the `activity_know_location_app.xml` layout file appears as shown in Listing 10.14. Only the code in bold is newly added; the rest of the code is the same as we saw in Listing 10.12.

LISTING 10.14   Code Written into the `activity_know_location_app.xml` Layout File

```
<LinearLayout xmlns:android="http://schemas.android.com/apk/res/android"
    android:orientation="vertical"
    android:layout_width="match_parent"
    android:layout_height="match_parent" >
    <TextView
```

```
            android:text="Latitude: "
            android:layout_height="wrap_content"
            android:layout_width="wrap_content"
            android:id="@+id/latitude_view" />
    <TextView android:text="Longitude: "
            android:layout_height="wrap_content"
            android:layout_width="wrap_content"
            android:id="@+id/longitude_view" />
    <TextView android:text="Address is: "
            android:layout_height="wrap_content"
            android:layout_width="wrap_content"
            android:id="@+id/address_view" />
    <com.google.android.maps.MapView
            android:id="@+id/mapvw"
            android:layout_width="match_parent"
            android:layout_height="match_parent"
            android:enabled="true"
            android:clickable="true"
            android:apiKey="xxxxxxxxxxxxxxxxxxxxxxxxxxxxxxxxxxxxxxxx" />
</LinearLayout>
```

To fetch the address of the supplied longitude and latitude coordinates, we implement reverse geocoding in the KnowLocationAppActivity.java Java activity file (see Listing 10.15). The code added to the file is shown in bold.

LISTING 10.15   Code Written into the KnowLocationoAppActivity.java Java Activity File

```
package com.androidunleashed.knowlocationapp;

import android.os.Bundle;
import android.widget.TextView;
import android.location.LocationManager;
import android.content.Context;
import android.location.Location;
import android.location.LocationListener;
import com.google.android.maps.MapActivity;
import com.google.android.maps.MapController;
import com.google.android.maps.MapView;
import com.google.android.maps.GeoPoint;
import android.location.Geocoder;
import java.util.List;
import android.location.Address;
import java.util.Locale;
import java.io.IOException;

public class KnowLocationAppActivity extends MapActivity  {
```

```java
    private TextView latitudeView;
    private TextView longitudeView;
    private LocationManager locationManager;
    private MapController mapController;
    private MapView mapView;
    private GeoPoint point;

    @Override
    public void onCreate(Bundle savedInstanceState) {
        super.onCreate(savedInstanceState);
        setContentView(R.layout.activity_know_location_app);
        latitudeView = (TextView) findViewById(R.id.latitude_view);
        longitudeView = (TextView) findViewById(R.id.longitude_view);
        locationManager = (LocationManager) getSystemService(Context.LOCATION_SERVICE);
        mapView = (MapView) findViewById(R.id.mapvw);
        mapView.setBuiltInZoomControls(true);
        mapController = mapView.getController();
        locationManager.requestLocationUpdates( LocationManager.GPS_PROVIDER, 0, 0,
new LocationListener(){
            public void onProviderDisabled(String provider) { }
            public void onProviderEnabled(String provider) {}
            public void onStatusChanged(String provider, int status, Bundle extras) {}
            public void onLocationChanged(Location loc) {
                if (loc != null) {
                    int lt = (int) (loc.getLatitude());
                    int lg = (int) (loc.getLongitude());
                    latitudeView.setText("Latitude is: "+String.valueOf(lt));
                    longitudeView.setText("Longitude is: "+ String.valueOf(lg));
                    int latit=(int)(loc.getLatitude() * 1E6);
                    int longit=(int)(loc.getLongitude()* 1E6);
                    point = new GeoPoint(latit, longit);
                    mapController.animateTo(point);
                    mapController.setCenter(point);
                    mapController.setZoom(15);
                    String addr=getAddress(point);
                    TextView addressView = (TextView) findViewById(R.id.address_view);
                    addressView.setText(addr);
                }
            }
        });
    }

    @Override
```

```
    protected boolean isRouteDisplayed() {
        return false;
    }

    @Override
    protected boolean isLocationDisplayed() {
        return false;
    }

    public String getAddress(GeoPoint point) {
        String locationAdd = "";
        Geocoder geoCoder = new Geocoder(getBaseContext(), Locale.getDefault());
        try {
            List<Address> addresses = geoCoder.getFromLocation(point.getLatitudeE6()
/   1E6, point.getLongitudeE6() / 1E6, 1);
            if (addresses.size() > 0) {
                Address address=addresses.get(0);
                for (int index = 0; index < address.getMaxAddressLineIndex(); index++)
                    locationAdd += address.getAddressLine(index);
            }
        }
        catch (IOException e) {
            e.printStackTrace();
        }
        return locationAdd;
    }
}
```

The latitude and longitude supplied by us to the emulator through DDMS is converted into micro degrees and collected into a point GeoPoint. The GeoPoint containing the latitude and longitude values is passed to the getAddress function to perform reverse geocoding. In the getAddress() function, an instance of the Geocoder class called geoCoder is created by supplying a Locale context to it. Thereafter, the geoCoder instance of the getFromLocation() method is called, passing the latitude and longitude values contained in point to it. The latitude and longitude values are converted into degrees while passing to the method. Following the latitude and longitude values, a numerical value 1 is passed to the getFromLocation() method to fetch a single address of the supplied coordinates. The street address returned by the getFromLocation() method is in the form of List<Address>. All the elements in the list are extracted and displayed through the newly added TextView control addressView.

Let's run the application to see how reverse geocoding takes place. After we pass the San Francisco latitude and longitude values 37.775 and -122.4183333 to the Android emulator through DDMS, the location and the address (2-98 11th StSan Francisco, CA) 94103 are displayed on the Google Map, coordinates as shown in Figure 10.14.

FIGURE 10.14   Map view of the supplied coordinates

Displaying Map Markers

We cannot display markers or pin points on the Google Map directly. Instead, we add a transparent layer onto the map and the display markers or text on it. We can add as many layers as we want. The transparent layer we want to create is known as an Overlay.

Creating Overlays

To display markers that pinpoint locations on the map, we need to create transparent overlays on top of a MapView.

To add a new Overlay, a new class is created that extends Overlay. In the class, we may

▶ Override the draw method to show the markers on the map.

▶ Override the onTap method to take the desired action when the user clicks (taps) the marker(s) added through the overlay.

Drag and drop an image called spot.png into the four drawable folders (drawable-xhdpi, drawable-hdpi, drawable-ldpi, and drawable-mdpi) of the res folder. Modify the KnowLocationAppActivity.java activity file to appear as shown in Listing 10.16. Only the code in bold is newly added; the rest is the same as we saw in Listing 10.15.

10

LISTING 10.16   Code Written into the `KnowLocationAppActivity.java` Java Activity File

```
package com.androidunleashed.knowlocationapp;

import android.os.Bundle;
import android.widget.TextView;
import android.location.LocationManager;
import android.content.Context;
import android.location.Location;
import android.location.LocationListener;
import com.google.android.maps.MapActivity;
import com.google.android.maps.MapController;
import com.google.android.maps.MapView;
import com.google.android.maps.GeoPoint;
import android.location.Geocoder;
import java.util.List;
import android.location.Address;
import java.util.Locale;
import java.io.IOException;
import com.google.android.maps.Overlay;
import android.graphics.Canvas;
import android.graphics.Point;
import android.graphics.Bitmap;
import android.graphics.BitmapFactory;

public class KnowLocationAppActivity extends MapActivity  {
    private TextView latitudeView;
    private TextView longitudeView;
    private LocationManager locationManager;
    private MapController mapController;
    private MapView mapView;
    private GeoPoint point;

    @Override
    public void onCreate(Bundle savedInstanceState) {
        super.onCreate(savedInstanceState);
        setContentView(R.layout.activity_know_location_app);
        latitudeView = (TextView) findViewById(R.id.latitude_view);
        longitudeView = (TextView) findViewById(R.id.longitude_view);
        locationManager = (LocationManager) getSystemService(Context.LOCATION_SERVICE);
        mapView = (MapView) findViewById(R.id.mapvw);
        mapView.setBuiltInZoomControls(true);
        mapController = mapView.getController();
        locationManager.requestLocationUpdates(LocationManager.GPS_PROVIDER, 0, 0,
new LocationListener(){
```

```
            public void onProviderDisabled(String provider) { }
            public void onProviderEnabled(String provider) {}
            public void onStatusChanged(String provider, int status, Bundle extras) {}
            public void onLocationChanged(Location loc) {
                if (loc != null) {
                    int lt = (int) (loc.getLatitude());
                    int lg = (int) (loc.getLongitude());
                    latitudeView.setText("Latitude is: "+String.valueOf(lt));
                    longitudeView.setText("Longitude is: "+ String.valueOf(lg));
                    int latit=(int)(loc.getLatitude() * 1E6);
                    int longit=(int)(loc.getLongitude()* 1E6);
                    point = new GeoPoint(latit, longit);
                    mapController.animateTo(point);
                    mapController.setCenter(point);
                    mapController.setZoom(15);
                    String addr=getAddress(point);
                    TextView addressView = (TextView) findViewById(R.id.address_view);
                    addressView.setText(addr);
                    MyOverlay mapOverlay = new MyOverlay();
                    List<Overlay> overlayList=mapView.getOverlays();
                    overlayList.clear();
                    overlayList.add(mapOverlay);
                    mapView.postInvalidate();
                }
            }
        });
        mapView.invalidate();
    }

    @Override
    protected boolean isRouteDisplayed() {
        return false;
    }

    @Override
    protected boolean isLocationDisplayed() {
        return false;
    }

    public String getAddress(GeoPoint point) {
        String locationAdd = "";
        Geocoder geoCoder = new Geocoder(getBaseContext(), Locale.getDefault());
        try {
            List<Address> addresses = geoCoder.getFromLocation(point.getLatitudeE6()
/ 1E6, point.getLongitudeE6() / 1E6, 1);
```

10

```
            if (addresses.size() > 0) {
                Address address=addresses.get(0);
                for (int index = 0; index < address.getMaxAddressLineIndex(); index++)
                    locationAdd += address.getAddressLine(index);
            }
        }
        catch (IOException e) {
            e.printStackTrace();
        }
        return locationAdd;
    }


    class MyOverlay extends Overlay
    {
        @Override
        public boolean draw(Canvas canvas, MapView mapView, boolean shadow, long when)
        {
            super.draw(canvas, mapView, shadow);
            Point screenPoints = new Point();
            mapView.getProjection().toPixels(point, screenPoints);
            Bitmap spotPic = BitmapFactory.decodeResource(getResources(),
R.drawable.spot);
            canvas.drawBitmap(spotPic, screenPoints.x, screenPoints.y-50, null);
            return true;
        }
    }
}
```

Adding Overlays to the Overlay List

Here, MyOverlay is the class that extends Overlay. We create an instance called
mapOverlay of the MyOverlay class to create an overlay. Each MapView contains a list of
overlays currently being displayed, and we can get a reference to that list by calling the
getOverlays() method, as shown here:

```
List<Overlay> overlayList=mapView.getOverlays();
```

This statement gets a reference to the list of overlays, called overlayList. We clear all
the items from the list and add a mapOverlay instance of the MyOverlay class to the list.
Finally, the postInvalidate() method is called on the mapView instance to update the
changes on the map and display the added overlay.

In the `draw()` method, we use a `Canvas` object to draw markers. A `Canvas` object represents a visible display surface, and it includes the methods for drawing lines, text, shapes, and images. To display markers, we need to convert the `GeoPoint` representing the latitude and longitude values where we want to display markers into the screen coordinates by using the `Projection` class. We create an instance of the `Projection` class by calling the `getProjection()` method. We can access the `fromPixel()` and `toPixel()` methods of the projection instance to translate `GeoPoints` coordinates to screen coordinates and vice versa. We call the `toPixels()` method on the `Projection` instance to convert the `GeoPoint` coordinates to the `screenPoints` screen coordinates. Then, we generate a bitmap graphic by using the `BitmapFactory` class. Thus, we use the drawable resource `spot.png` image to generate a bitmap called `spotPic`. The bitmap graphic representing the marker (`spot.png`) is displayed on the canvas using the screen coordinates stored in `screenPoints`.

The output appears as shown in Figure 10.15.

FIGURE 10.15   A marker on the San Francisco map

If we want to display several markers on the map, we use `ItemizedOverlay`, which helps in creating a list of locations to be marked on the map.

Using `ItemizedOverlay`

Android provides a nice class, called `ItemizedOverlay`, to manage drawing `OverlayItems` on a map. It greatly simplifies the process of displaying markers on the map. Let's use the `ItemizedOverlay` class in our application to display several markers.

We do not pass the longitude and latitude information to the Android emulator through DDMS. In addition, we don't want to display the street address of the longitude and latitude values, so let us remove the three `TextView` controls from `KnowLocationApp`. After we remove the three `TextView` controls, our `activity_know_location_app.xml` layout file appears as shown in Listing 10.17.

LISTING 10.17   Code Written into the `activity_know_location_app.xml` Layout File

```
<?xml version="1.0" encoding="utf-8"?>
<LinearLayout xmlns:android="http://schemas.android.com/apk/res/android"
    android:orientation="vertical"
    android:layout_width="match_parent"
    android:layout_height="match_parent">
  <com.google.android.maps.MapView
      android:id="@+id/mapvw"
      android:layout_width="match_parent"
      android:layout_height="match_parent"
      android:enabled="true"
      android:clickable="true"
      android:apiKey="xxxxxxxxxxxxxxxxxxxxxxxxxxxxxxxxxxxxx"/>
</LinearLayout>
```

To apply `ItemizedOverlay`, modify the `KnowLocationAppActivity.java` file to appear as shown in Listing 10.18. Only the code in bold is modified; the rest of the code is the same as we saw in Listing 10.16.

LISTING 10.18   Code Written into the `KnowLocationAppActivity.java` Java Activity File

```
package com.androidunleashed.knowlocationapp;

import android.os.Bundle;
import com.google.android.maps.MapActivity;
import com.google.android.maps.MapController;
import com.google.android.maps.MapView;
import com.google.android.maps.GeoPoint;
import android.app.AlertDialog;
import android.graphics.Canvas;
import com.google.android.maps.OverlayItem;
import android.graphics.drawable.Drawable;
import com.google.android.maps.ItemizedOverlay;
import java.util.ArrayList;
import android.content.DialogInterface;

public class KnowLocationAppActivity extends MapActivity  {
    private MapController mapController;
    private MapView mapView;

    @Override
    public void onCreate(Bundle savedInstanceState) {
```

```
        super.onCreate(savedInstanceState);
        setContentView(R.layout.activity_know_location_app);
        mapView = (MapView) findViewById(R.id.mapvw);
        mapView.setBuiltInZoomControls(true);
        mapController = mapView.getController();
        Drawable marker=getResources().getDrawable(R.drawable.spot);
        marker.setBounds(0, 0, marker.getIntrinsicWidth(),marker.getIntrinsi-
cHeight());
        MyOverlay mapOverlay = new MyOverlay(marker);
        mapView.getOverlays().add(mapOverlay);
        GeoPoint SantaRosa = new GeoPoint((int)(38.4405556*1000000),(int)
(-122.7133333*1000000));
        GeoPoint SanFrancisco = new GeoPoint((int)(37.775*1000000),(int)
(-122.4183333*1000000));
        GeoPoint SanJose = new GeoPoint((int)(37.3394444*1000000),(int)
(-121.8938889*1000000));
        mapOverlay.addPoint(SantaRosa,"Santa Rosa", "Santa Rosa");
        mapOverlay.addPoint(SanFrancisco ,"San Francisco", "San Francisco");
        mapOverlay.addPoint(SanJose ,"San Jose", "San Jose");
        GeoPoint point = mapOverlay.getCenter();
        mapView.getController().setCenter(point);
        mapController.setZoom(8);
    }

    @Override
    protected boolean isRouteDisplayed() {
        return false;
    }

    class MyOverlay extends ItemizedOverlay<OverlayItem> {
        private ArrayList<OverlayItem> overlayItemList = new
ArrayList<OverlayItem>();
        public MyOverlay(Drawable marker) {
            super(boundCenterBottom(marker));
            populate();
        }

        @Override
        protected boolean onTap(int index) {
            AlertDialog.Builder  alertDialog = new   AlertDialog.
Builder(KnowLocationAppActivity.this);
            alertDialog.setTitle("Alert window");
            alertDialog.setMessage("The selected place is "+ overlayItemList.
get(index).getTitle());
            alertDialog.setPositiveButton("OK", new DialogInterface.OnClickLis-
tener() {
```

```
                public void onClick(DialogInterface dialog, int buttonId) {
                    return;
                }
            });
            alertDialog.setIcon(R.drawable.ic_launcher);
            alertDialog.show();
            return true;
        }

        public void addPoint(GeoPoint p, String title, String snippet){
            OverlayItem newItem = new OverlayItem(p, title, snippet);
            overlayItemList.add(newItem);
            populate();
        }

        @Override
        public void draw(Canvas canvas, MapView mapView, boolean shadow) {
            super.draw(canvas, mapView, shadow);
        }

        @Override
        protected OverlayItem createItem(int i) {
            return overlayItemList.get(i);
        }

        @Override
        public int size() {
            return overlayItemList.size();
        }
    }
}
```

The `MyOverlay` class extends `ItemizedOverlay`, which in turn extends Overlay. The `ItemizedOverlay` helps in creating a list of locations that can be used to place markers on a map. The location where we want to place a display marker is supplied to the class constructor, which is then passed to the super class.

The `boundCenterBottom()` method is called on the marker to define the anchor point as the middle of the bottom edge of our marker. That is, the bottom center of the marker is aligned with the geographical coordinates of the Item. Then we call the `populate()` method of `ItemizedOverlay` to cache the `OverlayItem(s)`. The class calls the `size()` method to determine the number of overlay items and executes a loop, calling `createItem(i)` for each item. The `createItem()` method returns the `overlay` item of the given index value. An `overlay` item is composed of the `GeoPoint` coordinate of the place to be marked, along with a title and a snippet.

In the `onCreate()` method, we create an instance of a `Drawable` called `marker` that represents the `spot.png` image file in the drawable resource. We need to define the bounds of our `Drawable` object `marker` before we use it on a map. The `setBounds(Rect)` method is called to decide the location and size of the `Drawable` object. The preferred size of `Drawable` is determined by using the `getIntrinsicHeight()` and `getIntrinsicWidth()` methods. We create an overlay by creating an instance of the `MyOverlay` class called `mapOverlay` and passing the marker to it. We add our overlay to the `mapView`.

We then create three `GeoPoint` instances, `SantaRosa`, `SanFrancisco`, and `SanJose`, through their respective longitude and latitude values. We convert the latitude and longitude values of the locations to micro degrees by multiplying them by 1,000,000 and then converting the result to integers. We call the `addPoint()` method of `MyOverlay` to add the three `GeoPoint` instances as overlay items to the `overlayItemList`.

To make the markers visible on the map, we need to set the center of the displayed map to a point such that all the markers are visible. We choose the first point from the overlay to use as the center point for our map. The `getCenter()` method of the overlay is called to return the first point, and the `setCenter()` method of the `MapView`'s `controller` is called that sets the center of the map. The `setZoom()` method sets the zoom level to 8.

For each item in the overlay, the marker is drawn twice, once for the marker and once to represent its skewed and darkened shadow.

The `onTap()` method defines an `AlertDialog`, sets its title to `Alert` window, and displays a message, `The selected place is`. It then accesses the `overlay` item by using the index value of the tapped marker. The `overlay` item is composed of the `GeoPoint` coordinates, a `title`, and a snippet of the location being marked. The `title` of the marked locations is displayed in the `AlertDialog` dialog.

After running the application, we see three markers displayed on the map on `Santa Rosa`, `San Francisco`, and `San Jose`, as shown in Figure 10.16 (left). After we select a marker, an `Alert` window is displayed showing the location whose marker is selected, as shown in Figure 10.16 (right).

10

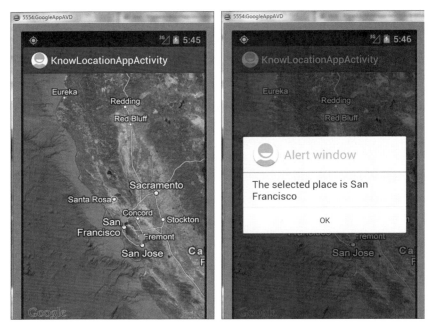

FIGURE 10.16   Showing markers on Santa Rosa, San Francisco, and San Jose (left), and an `Alert` dialog box displayed after selecting a marker (right)

Summary

In this chapter, we learned to display web pages through `WebView` controls, handle page navigation, and add Internet access permission to the Android application. We saw how to use `WebViewClient`, use Google Maps, obtain a Google Key, and install the Google API. We learned to create an AVD for a map-based application, use `Location-Based Services`, supply latitude and longitude values through `DDMS`, add a Zoom facility, and display map markers.

In the next chapter, we learn about `Broadcast Receivers`. We see how to broadcast and receive the broadcasted intent. We also see how the `Notification` system is used, created, configured, and displayed in the status bar. We learn the procedure of sending and receiving SMS programmatically, and, finally, we learn how to send email and use the `TelephonyManager` in making phone calls.

# CHAPTER 11

Communicating with SMS and Emails

Communication with text messages is a popular way to send and receive information via cellular phones. Communicating through text messages not only consumes fewer network resources but also reduces network congestion, making it an inexpensive mode of communication. Moreover, users can respond to such messages at their leisure. We can make our application send and receive text messages via SMS (Short Message Service) automatically at periodic intervals or when a specific event occurs, such as when a button is clicked or when a task is complete.

All, three communication mediums—SMS, email, and voice calls—use the concept of broadcast receivers and notifications. So let's first examine them.

Understanding Broadcast Receivers

A broadcast receiver is a component that responds to different messages that are broadcast by the system or other applications. Messages such as `new mail`, `low battery`, `captured photo`, or `completed download` require attention. Such messages are broadcast as an `Intent` object that is waiting for broadcast receivers to respond. The broadcast receiver responds to such broadcasted `Intents` and takes the necessary actions. The broadcast receivers can, for example, create a status bar notification to alert the user when a broadcast occurs.

> **NOTE**
>
> A broadcast `Intent` can invoke more than one receiver.

We cover two separate aspects of broadcast receivers:

▶ Broadcasting an `Intent`

▶ Receiving the broadcast `Intent`

Broadcasting an `Intent`

To broadcast an `Intent`, we first create an `Intent` object, assign a specific action to it, attach data or a message to the broadcast receiver, and finally broadcast it. We can optionally put an extra message or data on the `Intent`. Table 11.1 lists the methods involved in broadcasting an `Intent`.

TABLE 11.1   Methods Involved in Broadcasting an `Intent`

Method	Description
`putExtra()`	Used to add data or a message to the `Intent` that we want to send to the broadcast receiver.
	Syntax: `putExtra(String name, String value)`
	Where `name` is the key or name of the `value` that we want to pass along with the `Intent`. The `name` is used to identify the `value`.
`setAction()`	Used to set the action to perform on the data or message being sent with the `Intent`.
	Syntax: `setAction(String action)`
	The broadcast receiver uses the `getAction()` method to retrieve the action to be performed on the received data.
`sendBroadcast()`	Available on the `Context` class, this method is used to send the broadcast `Intent` to all the registered `Intent` receivers.
	Syntax: `void sendBroadcast(intent_to_broadcast)`
	Where the `intent_to_broadcast` parameter represents the `Intent` that we want to broadcast.

The following code broadcasts an `Intent`:

```
public static String BROADCAST_STRING = "com.androidunleashed.testingbroadcast";
Intent broadcastIntent = new Intent();
broadcastIntent.putExtra("message", "New Email arrived");
broadcastIntent.setAction(BROADCAST_STRING);
sendBroadcast(broadcastIntent);
```

We can see that an `Intent` object called `broadcastIntent` is created. The data or message to be passed along with the `Intent` is `"New Email arrived"`, and the name or key assigned to this message is `message`. The action string is made unique by using a namespace similar to a Java class. We can see that the `com.androidunleashed.testingbroadcast` is assigned as an action to the `Intent`. Finally, the `broadcastIntent` is sent or broadcasted and received by the broadcast receivers.

Receiving the Broadcast `Intent`

A broadcast receiver is a class that extends the `BroadcastReceiver`. It also needs to be registered as a receiver in an Android application via the `AndroidManifest.xml` file or through code at runtime. The broadcast receiver class needs to implement the `onReceive()` method. The following is sample code of an `onReceive()` method:

```
public void onReceive(Context context, Intent intent) {
    String actionName = intent.getAction();
    if(actionName != null && actionName.equals("com.androidunleashed.testingbroadcast")) {
        String msg = intent.getStringExtra("message");
        Log.d("Received Message: ",msg);
    }
}
```

The `getAction()` and `getStringExtra()` methods used here need some explanation:

▶ **getAction()**—Retrieves the action to be performed from the `Intent` object. It is the action that indicates what task has to be performed on the data passed along with the `Intent`.

   Syntax:

   ```
   getAction()
   ```

▶ **getStringExtra()**—Retrieves the extended data from the `Intent`.

   Syntax:

   ```
   getStringExtra(String name)
   ```

   where `name` represents the `key` or the `name` assigned to the `value` while adding data to the `Intent` through the `putExtra()` method.

In the `onReceive()` method, we access the `Intent` object passed as a parameter. From the `Intent` object, we retrieve the `action` that is supposed to be performed. If the action to be performed is not `null` and matches the one that is sent by the sender activity, the message or data passed along with the `Intent` is extracted from the `Intent` and is logged.

Let's create an Android project called `BroadcastApp`. In this application, a `Button` is displayed with the caption `Send Broadcast`. After we click the `Button`, an `Intent` with a message is broadcast. The broadcasted `Intent` is then received through a broadcast receiver, and the message sent with the `Intent` is extracted and logged. To define a `Button` control, write the code shown in Listing 11.1 into the `activity_broadcast_app.xml` layout file.

LISTING 11.1   Code Written into `activity_broadcast_app.xml`

```xml
<LinearLayout xmlns:android="http://schemas.android.com/apk/res/android"
    android:layout_width="match_parent"
    android:layout_height="match_parent"
    android:orientation="vertical" >
    <Button
        android:id="@+id/broadcast_button"
        android:text="Send Broadcast"
        android:layout_width="wrap_content"
        android:layout_height="wrap_content"
        android:layout_gravity="center"  />
</LinearLayout>
```

We can see that the `Button` control is assigned the `broadcast_button` ID, which is used to identify it in the Java code. The caption assigned to the `Button` control is `Send Broadcast`. Next, we need to write code in the Java activity file to define an `Intent` object, assign action and add data to it, and then broadcast it. To do so, the code shown in Listing 11.2 is written into `BroadcastAppActivity.java`.

LISTING 11.2   Code Written into `BroadcastAppActivity.java`

```java
package com.androidunleashed.broadcastapp;

import android.app.Activity;
import android.os.Bundle;
import android.content.Intent;
import android.widget.Button;
import android.view.View;

public class BroadcastAppActivity extends Activity {
    public static String BROADCAST_STRING = "com.androidunleashed.testingbroadcast";
    @Override
    public void onCreate(Bundle savedInstanceState) {
        super.onCreate(savedInstanceState);
        setContentView(R.layout.activity_broadcast_app);
        Button broadcastButton = (Button) this.findViewById(R.id.broadcast_button);
        broadcastButton.setOnClickListener(new Button.OnClickListener(){
            public void onClick(View v) {
                Intent broadcastIntent = new Intent();
                broadcastIntent.putExtra("message", "New Email arrived");
                broadcastIntent.setAction(BROADCAST_STRING);
                sendBroadcast(broadcastIntent);
            }
        });
    }
}
```

Here we can see that the `Button` control with the `broadcast_button` ID is accessed from the layout file and is mapped to the `Button` object `broadcastButton`. A `ClickListener` is associated with the `Button` control. When the `Button` control is clicked, the callback method `onClick()` is invoked. In the `onClick()` method, an `Intent` object called `broadcastIntent` is defined. A message, `New Email arrived`, is added to the `broadcastIntent` object with the key `message`. With the help of a static string, `BROADCAST_STRING`, a unique action, `com.androidunleashed.testingbroadcast` is assigned to the `Intent` object, `broadcastIntent`. Finally, the `Intent` is broadcasted by calling the `sendBroadcast()` method.

The next step is defining an Activity that acts as a broadcast receiver. So, to the package `com.androidunleashed.broadcastapp` of our application, add a Java file, `ReceiveBroadcastActivity.java`. To respond to the broadcasted `Intent` and to access the data passed along with it, write the code shown in Listing 11.3 in the Java file `ReceiveBroadcastActivity.java`.

LISTING 11.3   Code Written into `ReceiveBroadcastActivity.java`

```
package com.androidunleashed.broadcastapp;
import android.content.BroadcastReceiver;
import android.content.Intent;
import android.content.Context;
import android.util.Log;

    public class ReceiveBroadcastActivity extends BroadcastReceiver {
        @Override
        public void onReceive(Context context, Intent intent) {
            String actionName = intent.getAction();
            if(actionName != null && actionName.equals("com.androidunleashed.test-
ingbroadcast")) {
                String msg = intent.getStringExtra("message");
            Log.d("Received Message: ",msg);
        }
    }
}
```

As mentioned earlier, to receive the broadcasted `Intent`, the Java class needs to extend the `BroadcastReceiver` class. The class also overrides the `onReceive()` method. In the `onReceive()` method, we use the `Intent` parameter, which represents the received `Intent` object. From the `Intent` object, we access the `action` that needs to be performed on the data passed along with the `Intent`. We check to see whether the `action` is not null and match the `action` with the one that was supplied while broadcasting the `Intent`. Thereafter, the data from the `Intent` object is accessed and logged.

The `ReceiveBroadcastActivity.java` file, which is the broadcast receiver, has to be registered in the manifest file. The code for registering the activity is as follows:

```
<receiver android:name=".ReceiveBroadcastActivity">
    <intent-filter>
        <action android:name="com.androidunleashed.testingbroadcast"></action>
    </intent-filter>
</receiver>
```

We can see that the `<receiver>` tag is used in the manifest file to register the broadcast receiver. The tag also designates the `ReceiveBroadcastActivity.class` as the recipient of the `Intent` whose action is `com.androidunleashed.testingbroadcast`. Listing 11.4 shows the code in the `AndroidManifest.xml` file. Only the code in bold is added; the rest is the default code that is auto-generated by the Android SDK.

LISTING 11.4   Code in the `AndroidManifest.xml` File

```
<?xml version="1.0" encoding="utf-8"?>
<manifest xmlns:android="http://schemas.android.com/apk/res/android"
    package="com.androidunleashed.broadcastapp"
    android:versionCode="1"
    android:versionName="1.0" >
    <uses-sdk android:minSdkVersion="8"
        android:targetSdkVersion="15" />
    <application
        android:icon="@drawable/ic_launcher"
        android:label="@string/app_name"
        android:theme="@style/AppTheme" >
        <activity
            android:name=".BroadcastAppActivity"
            android:label="@string/title_activity_broadcast_app" >
            <intent-filter>
                <action android:name="android.intent.action.MAIN" />
                <category android:name="android.intent.category.LAUNCHER" />
            </intent-filter>
        </activity>
        <receiver android:name=".ReceiveBroadcastActivity">
            <intent-filter>
                <action android:name="com.androidunleashed.testingbroadcast"></
action>
            </intent-filter>
        </receiver>
    </application>
</manifest>
```

After running the application, we see a `Button` with the caption `Send Broadcast` displayed on the screen, as shown in Figure 11.1 (left). After we click `Send Broadcast`, an `Intent` with the message `New Email arrived` is broadcast. The `ReceiveBroadcastActivity.class` receives the broadcasted `Intent` and extracts the message, `New Email arrives` from it and logs it. The logged message appears in the `LogCat` window, as shown in Figure 11.1 (right).

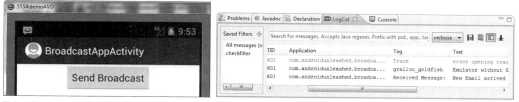

FIGURE 11.1   Application showing the `Send Broadcast` button on startup (left), and logged messages displayed in the `LogCat` window (right)

> **NOTE**
>
> We can have more than one receiver receive the broadcasted `Intent`.

Using the Notification System

The Android notification system provides us with several ways of alerting users. For example, the user can be notified with text, vibration, blinking lights, and sound indicators. Notifications are usually displayed on the status bar at the top of the screen.

> **NOTE**
>
> Not all notifications are supported by all devices.

Notification via the Status Bar

The simplest type of notification is status, which appears in the status bar as an icon along with some optional ticker text. Users can pull down the status bar to see the notification list and clear the notification by clicking the `Clear` button. After tapping the notification, the user navigates to the `Intent` defined by the notification. The status notification never launches an activity automatically, but simply notifies the user and launches the activity only when the notification is selected. Besides an icon and ticker text, the notification can have a title and body text displayed when the full notification is being displayed.

> **NOTE**
>
> The ticker text is briefly displayed in the status bar when the notification fires.

For creating notifications, the following two classes are used:

- **Notification**—The object that defines the information to be displayed, which can be text to be displayed on the status/expanded status bar, an icon displayed with the text, the number of times the notification is triggered, and so on.

- **NotificationManager**—The base object with which notifications are handled. It displays the information encapsulated in the Notification object, which is displayed via the notify() method.

Creating Notifications

The first step is to create a Notification object and configure it by defining notification properties. The following code shows how to do so:

```
Notification notification = new Notification();
notification.icon = R.drawable.ic_launcher;
notification.tickerText = "There is a new notification";
notification.when = System.currentTimeMillis();
notification.flags |= Notification.FLAG_AUTO_CANCEL;
```

Here, we see that a Notification object called notification is created and thereafter its public members are used to configure it:

- **icon**—Assigns the notification icon.

- **tickerText**—Assigns the small notification text.

- **when**—Assigns the time when the notification occurred. We use the system time to specify the time the notification occurred.

- **flag**—Assigns the constant that determines the subsequent action when the notification is selected from the notification window. We usually assign the FLAG_AUTO_ CANCEL constant to this public variable, which specifies that the notification be automatically canceled after it is selected from the notifications.

We can also assign a notification icon, ticker text, and time of occurrence through the Notification object constructor, as shown here:

```
Notification notification  = new Notification(R.drawable.ic_launcher, "There is a
new notification", System.currentTimeMillis());
```

Creating PendingIntent

After receiving the notification, we may choose to take a necessary action. We use the PendingIntent class to switch to the desired Intent when the notification is tapped.

The PendingIntent class enables us to create Intents that can be triggered by our application when an event occurs. The following code creates a PendingIntent called pendIntent:

```
Intent intent = new Intent(getBaseContext(), TargetActivity.class);
PendingIntent pendIntent = PendingIntent.getActivity(getBaseContext(), 0, intent, 0);
```

We can see that we create an `Intent` object by supplying the current application context and the activity name `TargetActivity.class`—the one that we want to launch. Thereafter, a `PendingIntent` object called `pendIntent` is created by supplying the following four parameters to the `getActivity()` method:

▶ The current application context in which the `PendingIntent` starts the activity.

▶ A request code for the sender. Because it is not used, we supply a value of 0 for this parameter.

▶ The `Intent` of the activity to be launched. We supply the `Intent` object for this parameter.

▶ Flags to specify the unspecified parts of the `Intent` to be sent. We supply a value of 0 for this parameter, as there is no unspecified part.

To display text after expanding the notification, and to specify the pending `Intent` that we want to launch, the `setLatestEventInfo()` method of the `Notification` class is used. The method is now deprecated. The syntax of the method is

```
setLatestEventInfo(application_context, title, text, pending_intent);
```

where `application_context` represents the current application context, title represents the title of the notification, and text represents the notification text displayed after expanding the status bar. The `pending_intent` represents the `PendingIntent` object to supply the activity information we want to launch when a notification is tapped.

Example:

```
notification.setLatestEventInfo(getBaseContext(), "New E-mail", "You have one unread
message.", pendInent);
```

The `setLatestEventInfo()` method is deprecated. The task of configuring a notification is done through `Notification.Builder`.

Instead of using the method shown here, we can use the `Notification.Builder`.

Using `Notification.Builder`

`Notification.Builder` is the `Builder` class for `Notification` objects and provides several methods to configure notification, as shown in Table 11.2.

TABLE 11.2   `Notification.Builder` Class Methods

Method	Description
`setSmallIcon()`	Used to supply the small icon resource that is displayed to represent the notification in the status bar. Syntax: `setSmallIcon(int icon)` where the `icon` parameter represents the resource ID of the drawable to be used as the icon of the notification.
`setAutoCancel()`	Used to determine whether we want to make the notification invisible when it is tapped. The Boolean value `true` is supplied to this method to make the notification invisible. Syntax: `setAutoCancel(boolean autoCancel)`
`setTicker()`	Used to supply the ticker text that is displayed in the status bar when the notification arrives. Syntax: `setTicker(CharSequence textMessage)`
`setWhen()`	Used to supply the time of occurrence of the notification. Syntax:`setWhen(long timeOfOccurrence)`
`setContentTi-tle()`	Used to supply the title of the notification when the status bar is expanded. Syntax: `setContentTitle(CharSequence title)`
`setContentText()`	Used to supply the text of the notification. Syntax: `setContentText(CharSequence text)`
`setContentInt-ent()`	Used to supply a `PendingIntent` to be sent when the notification is tapped. Syntax: `setContentIntent(PendingIntent intent)`

The following code shows how to use the `Notification.Builder` methods shown in Table 11.2 to configure the notification:

```
Notification.Builder builder = new Notification.Builder(getBaseContext())
.setSmallIcon(R.drawable.ic_launcher)
.setAutoCancel(true)
.setTicker("There is a new notification")
.setWhen(System.currentTimeMillis())
.setContentTitle("New E-mail")
.setContentText("You have one unread message.")
.setContentIntent(pendIntent);
notification = builder.getNotification();
```

The preceding code configures a notification as shown here:

▶ Sets the `ic_launcher.png` image as the notification icon

▶ Makes the notification invisible when tapped

▶ Assigns the text `There is a new notification` as the ticker text of the notification

▶ Sets the current time as the time of occurrence of the notification

▶ Sets the title of the notification as `New E-mail`

▶ Sets the body text of the notification as `You have one unread message`

▶ Fires the specified pending `Intent`, `pendIntent`, when the notification is tapped

The configuration notification created through the `Notification.Builder` object is assigned to the `Notification` object called `notification`.

Obtaining a `NotificationManager`

The `NotificationManager` class executes and manages all status notifications. To obtain a valid `NotificationManager`, we use the `getSystemService()` method:

```
NotificationManager notificationManager = (NotificationManager)
getSystemService(NOTIFICATION_SERVICE);
```

After obtaining the `NotificationManager` object, we can invoke its `notify()` method to notify the user by displaying the notification.

Syntax:

```
notify(uniqueID, notficationObject)
```

where the `uniqueID` parameter represents the application unique identifier, and the `notificationObject` parameter represents the `Notification` object that we want to display.

Example:

```
notificationManager.notify(0, notification);
```

Let's apply what you've learned so far and create an application that sends notifications to the user. Create a new Android project called `NotificationApp`. In this application, we create a `Button` with the caption `Create Notification`. When clicked, the `Button` creates a notification that displays ticker text in the status bar. When the user expands the status bar, the notification's title and body text are displayed. After we tap the notification, the program jumps to an activity that displays a message indicating that a new activity is launched.

To define a `Button` control, write the code shown in Listing 11.5 into the `activity_notification_app.xml` layout file.

LISTING 11.5   Code Written into `activity_notification_app.xml`

```
<LinearLayout xmlns:android="http://schemas.android.com/apk/res/android"
    android:layout_width="match_parent"
    android:layout_height="match_parent"
    android:orientation="vertical" >
```

```
    <Button
        android:id="@+id/createbutton"
        android:layout_width="wrap_content"
        android:layout_height="wrap_content"
        android:text="Create Notification"
        android:layout_gravity="center" />
</LinearLayout>
```

We can see that the `Button` control is assigned the `createbutton` ID and a caption called `Create Notification`. The ID of the `Button` control identifies it in the Java code.

Because we want to launch an activity when the notification is tapped, let's define the layout file for the new activity. Add an XML file called `target.xml` to the `res/layout` folder. Through the activity that is launched, we need to display a text message through the `TextView` control. To define the `TextView` control in a `LinearLayout` container, write the code shown in Listing 11.6 into the `target.xml` file.

LISTING 11.6   Code Written into `target.xml`

```
<?xml version="1.0" encoding="utf-8"?>
<LinearLayout xmlns:android="http://schemas.android.com/apk/res/android"
    android:layout_width="match_parent"
    android:layout_height="match_parent"
    android:orientation="vertical" >
    <TextView
        android:id="@+id/messageview"
        android:layout_width="wrap_content"
        android:layout_height="wrap_content"
        android:text="This is target activity"
        android:layout_gravity="center" />
</LinearLayout>
```

We can see that the `TextView` control is assigned the `messageview` ID, set to display `This is target activity`, and aligned to appear at the center of the `View`.

For the new Activity, add a Java file to the `com.androidunleashed.notificationapp` package of our project. Assign the name `TargetActivity.java` to the newly added Java file. The new Activity has nothing to do but display the `TextView` defined in its layout file `target.xml`. Write the code shown in Listing 11.7 into the Java file `TargetActivity.java`.

LISTING 11.7   Code Written into `TargetActivity.java`

```
package com.androidunleashed.notificationapp;
import android.app.Activity;
import android.os.Bundle;

public class TargetActivity extends Activity {
```

```
        @Override
        protected void onCreate(Bundle savedInstanceState) {
            super.onCreate(savedInstanceState);
            setContentView(R.layout.target);
        }
}
```

We can see that `target.xml` is set as the `ContentView` of the new Activity `TargetActivity.java`. Next, we need to write the code in the `NotificationAppActivity.java` main activity file to perform the following tasks:

▶ Create a `Notification` object and configure it to display an icon, title, and text.

▶ Create a `PendingIntent` to launch the activity when the notification is tapped.

▶ Create a `NotificationManager` object to display and manage the notification.

To perform these tasks, write the code shown in Listing 11.8 into the `NotificationAppActivity.java` main activity file.

LISTING 11.8   Code Written into `NotificationAppActivity.java`

```
package com.androidunleashed.notificationapp;

import android.app.Activity;
import android.os.Bundle;
import android.view.View;
import android.app.NotificationManager;
import android.app.PendingIntent;
import android.content.Intent;
import android.app.Notification;
import android.widget.Button;
import android.view.View.OnClickListener;

public class NotificationAppActivity extends Activity {
    @Override
    public void onCreate(Bundle savedInstanceState) {
        super.onCreate(savedInstanceState);
        setContentView(R.layout.activity_notification_app);
        Button createButton = (Button) findViewById(R.id.createbutton);
        createButton.setOnClickListener(new OnClickListener() {
            @Override
            public void onClick(View arg0) {
                Intent intent = new Intent(getBaseContext(), TargetActivity.class);
                PendingIntent pendIntent = PendingIntent.
getActivity(getBaseContext(), 0, intent, 0);
                NotificationManager notificationManager = (NotificationManager)
getSystemService(NOTIFICATION_SERVICE);
```

```
                    Notification notification = new Notification();
                    Notification.Builder builder = new Notification.
Builder(getBaseContext())
                .setSmallIcon(R.drawable.ic_launcher)
                .setAutoCancel(true)
                .setTicker("There is a new notification")
                .setWhen(System.currentTimeMillis())
                .setContentTitle("New E-mail")
                .setContentText("You have one unread message")
                .setContentIntent(pendIntent);
                    notification = builder.getNotification();
                    notificationManager.notify(0, notification);
            }
        });
    }
}
```

The Android application never recognizes the newly added activity until it is mentioned
in the `AndroidManifest.xml` configuration file. So, add the statement shown in bold to
`AndroidManifest.xml` (see Listing 11.9).

LISTING 11.9   Code Written into `AndroidManifest.xml`

```xml
<?xml version="1.0" encoding="utf-8"?>
<manifest xmlns:android="http://schemas.android.com/apk/res/android"
    package="com.androidunleashed.notificationapp"
    android:versionCode="1"
    android:versionName="1.0" >
    <uses-sdk android:minSdkVersion="8"
        android:targetSdkVersion="15" />
    <application
        android:icon="@drawable/ic_launcher"
        android:label="@string/app_name"
        android:theme="@style/AppTheme" >
        <activity
            android:name=".NotificationAppActivity"
            android:label="@string/title_activity_notification_app" >
            <intent-filter>
                <action android:name="android.intent.action.MAIN" />
                <category android:name="android.intent.category.LAUNCHER" />
            </intent-filter>
        </activity>
        <activity android:name=".TargetActivity" android:label="@string/app_name" />
    </application>
</manifest>
```

The Android project now can recognize the `TargetActivity.java` activity file. After we run the application, a `Button` control with the caption `Create Notification` is displayed (see Figure 11.2—top left). After we click the `Create Notification` button, a notification is created and its ticker text, `There is a new notification`, is displayed at the top of the screen in the status bar (Figure 11.2—top right). After we pull down the status bar, the title of the notification and its body text are displayed, as shown in Figure 11.2 (bottom left). We can see that the title of the notification is `New E-mail`, and the text reads `You have one unread message`. After we select the notification, a new activity is launched and is confirmed by the message `This is target activity` displayed via its `TextView` control (see Figure 11.2—bottom right).

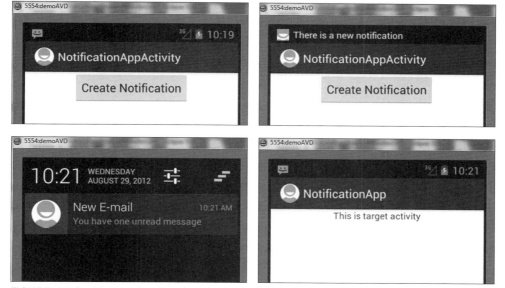

FIGURE 11.2   The application showing the `Create Notification` button on startup (top left), the ticker text of the notification (top right), the notification title and text displayed after expanding the status bar (bottom left), and the new activity launched after selecting the notification (bottom right)

Sending SMS Messages with Java Code

Sending and receiving SMS messages is considered as one of the most economical and popular modes of communication. To implement the SMS Messaging facility in our application, Android provides a built-in class known as `SmsManager`, which we can use to send and receive SMS messages. For testing SMS messaging, we don't need a real device but can easily test it on the Android emulator.

To understand the concept, let's create a new Android project called `SendSMSApp`. The first step is to design the user interface for sending messages via SMS. The user interface consists of three `TextView`, two `EditText`, and two `Button` controls. One of the `TextView` controls is for displaying the title of the screen, `Message Sending Form`. The other two

TextView controls are used on the left of the EditText controls to display text that tells the user what has to be entered in the EditText controls. These two TextView controls are used to display To: and Message:. The two EditText controls are used to enter the phone number of the recipient and the message to be sent.

To define this interface, let's modify the code of the activity_send_smsapp.xml layout file to appear as shown in Listing 11.10.

LISTING 11.10   Code Written into activity_send_smsapp.xml

```xml
<LinearLayout xmlns:android="http://schemas.android.com/apk/res/android"
    android:layout_width="match_parent"
    android:layout_height="match_parent"
    android:orientation="vertical" >
    <TextView
        android:layout_height="wrap_content"
        android:text="Message Sending Form"
        android:textStyle="bold"
        android:textSize="18sp"
        android:layout_width="match_parent"
        android:gravity="center_horizontal"/>
    <TextView
        android:layout_width="wrap_content"
        android:layout_height="wrap_content"
        android:text="To:"  />
    <EditText
        android:id="@+id/recvr_no"
        android:layout_height="wrap_content"
        android:layout_width="match_parent" />
    <TextView
        android:layout_width="wrap_content"
        android:layout_height="wrap_content"
        android:text="Message:" />
    <EditText
        android:id="@+id/txt_msg"
        android:layout_width="match_parent"
        android:layout_height="150dp" />
    <RelativeLayout
        android:layout_width="match_parent"
        android:layout_height="match_parent"
        android:orientation="horizontal">
        <Button
            android:id="@+id/send_button"
            android:text="Send SMS"
            android:layout_width="wrap_content"
            android:layout_height="wrap_content"
            android:layout_marginLeft="40dip"
```

```
            android:paddingLeft="20dip"
            android:paddingRight="20dip" />
        <Button
            android:id="@+id/cancel_button"
            android:text="Cancel"
            android:layout_width="wrap_content"
            android:layout_height="wrap_content"
            android:layout_toRightOf="@id/send_button"
            android:layout_marginLeft="15dip"
            android:paddingLeft="20dip"
            android:paddingRight="20dip" />
    </RelativeLayout>
</LinearLayout>
```

The two `EditText` controls are to be used to enter the phone number of the recipient and the text message; hence the IDs assigned to them are `recvr_no` and `txt_msg`. Because a text message can be long, the `layout_height` attribute of the `txt_msg` `EditText` control is set to `150dp`. The height is large enough to enter long messages. Moreover, the text scrolls vertically within the given height to accommodate longer messages. The two `Button` controls are assigned the text `Send SMS` and `Cancel` to show the kind of task they perform when clicked. The `Send SMS` button is assigned to the `send_button` ID, and the `Cancel` button is assigned to the `cancel_button` ID. The code defined in the `activity_send_smsapp.xml` layout file makes the user interface screen appear as shown in Figure 11.3.

FIGURE 11.3   The screen to enter information about the new SMS

Getting Permission to Send SMS Messages

To send and receive SMS messages in an application, we need to use permissions. All the permissions our application uses are defined in the `AndroidManifest.xml` file, so that when the application is installed on a device, the user is informed of the access permissions that the application uses. We need to add permissions to the `<manifest>` element of our `AndroidManifest.xml` file:

```
<uses-permission android:name="android.permission.SEND_SMS"/>
```

Listing 11.11 shows the code in the `AndroidManifest.xml` file. The statement in bold is the added code; the rest is the default code.

LISTING 11.11   Code Written into `AndroidManifest.xml`

```xml
<?xml version="1.0" encoding="utf-8"?>
<manifest xmlns:android="http://schemas.android.com/apk/res/android"
    package="com.androidunleashed.sendsmsapp"
    android:versionCode="1"
    android:versionName="1.0" >
    <uses-sdk android:minSdkVersion="8"
        android:targetSdkVersion="15" />
    <uses-permission android:name="android.permission.SEND_SMS"/>
    <application
        android:icon="@drawable/ic_launcher"
        android:label="@string/app_name"
        android:theme="@style/AppTheme" >
        <activity
            android:name=".SendSMSAppActivity"
            android:label="@string/title_activity_send_smsapp" >
            <intent-filter>
                <action android:name="android.intent.action.MAIN" />
                <category android:name="android.intent.category.LAUNCHER" />
            </intent-filter>
        </activity>
    </application>
</manifest>
```

Writing Java Code

To add an action to the `send_button` and `cancel_button`, we need to write Java code into the `SendSMSAppActivity.java` activity file. Before we write code, let's define what we want the two buttons to do. We want the button with the `send_button` ID to do the following tasks:

- ▶ Validate the content of the `recvr_no` and `txt_msg` `EditText` controls. Recall that the two `EditText` controls are meant for entering the phone number of the recipient and text message of the SMS. If either of the two `EditText` controls is empty, we want to suspend the process and prompt the user to enter data into both the controls.

- ▶ Send an SMS message to the recipient.

- ▶ Inform the user whether the SMS message was successfully sent and delivered. The difference between SMS Sent and SMS Delivered status is that the former means the SMS message was received by the server or `SMSC` (Short Message Service Center). The latter means that the SMS message was received by the recipient from the server. Remember that if the recipient is out of range or offline the SMS message still can be `Sent`. When the recipient actually receives the message, it is then successfully delivered.

As far as the `cancel_button` is concerned, we want it to cancel the operation and delete the content, if any, in the two `EditText` controls.

To perform these tasks, write the code shown in Listing 11.12 into the `SendSMSAppActivity.java` activity file.

LISTING 11.12   Code Written into `SendSMSAppActivity.java`

```
package com.androidunleashed.sendsmsapp;

import android.app.Activity;
import android.os.Bundle;
import android.telephony.SmsManager;
import android.widget.Button;
import android.view.View;
import android.widget.EditText;
import android.widget.Toast;
import android.app.PendingIntent;
import android.content.BroadcastReceiver;
import android.content.Intent;
import android.content.Context;
import android.content.IntentFilter;

public class SendSMSAppActivity extends Activity {
    EditText phoneNumber, message;
    BroadcastReceiver sentReceiver, deliveredReceiver;
    String SENT = "SMS_SENT";
    String DELIVERED = "SMS_DELIVERED";

    @Override
    public void onCreate(Bundle savedInstanceState) {
```

```
        super.onCreate(savedInstanceState);
        setContentView(R.layout.activity_send_smsapp);
        final PendingIntent sentPendIntent = PendingIntent.getBroadcast(this, 0, new
Intent(SENT), 0);
        final PendingIntent delivered_pendintnet = PendingIntent.getBroadcast(this,
0, new Intent(DELIVERED), 0);
        sentReceiver = new BroadcastReceiver(){
            @Override
            public void onReceive(Context arg0, Intent arg1) {
                switch (getResultCode()) {
                    case Activity.RESULT_OK:
                        Toast.makeText(getBaseContext(), "SMS sent", Toast.LENGTH_
SHORT).show();
                        break;
                    case SmsManager.RESULT_ERROR_GENERIC_FAILURE:
                        Toast.makeText(getBaseContext(), "Generic failure", Toast.
LENGTH_SHORT).show();
                        break;
                    case SmsManager.RESULT_ERROR_NO_SERVICE:
                        Toast.makeText(getBaseContext(), "No service",  Toast.
LENGTH_SHORT).show();
                        break;
                    case SmsManager.RESULT_ERROR_NULL_PDU:
                        Toast.makeText(getBaseContext(), "Null PDU", Toast.LENGTH_
SHORT).show();
                        break;
                    case SmsManager.RESULT_ERROR_RADIO_OFF:
                        Toast.makeText(getBaseContext(), "Radio off",  Toast.LENGTH_
SHORT).show();
                        break;
                }
            }
        };
        deliveredReceiver = new BroadcastReceiver(){
            @Override
            public void onReceive(Context arg0, Intent arg1) {
                switch (getResultCode()) {
                    case Activity.RESULT_OK:
                        Toast.makeText(getBaseContext(), "SMS successfully deliv-
ered",  Toast.LENGTH_SHORT).show();
                        break;
                    case Activity.RESULT_CANCELED:
                        Toast.makeText(getBaseContext(), "Failure—SMS not deliv-
ered",  Toast.LENGTH_SHORT).show();
                        break;
                }
```

```
                }
            };
            registerReceiver(sentReceiver, new IntentFilter(SENT));
            registerReceiver(deliveredReceiver, new IntentFilter(DELIVERED));
            Button sendBtn = (Button) this.findViewById(R.id.send_button);
            sendBtn.setOnClickListener(new Button.OnClickListener(){
                public void onClick(View v) {
                    phoneNumber = (EditText) findViewById(R.id.recvr_no);
                    message = (EditText) findViewById(R.id.txt_msg);
                    if(phoneNumber.getText().toString().trim().length() >0 && message.
getText().toString().trim().length() >0) {
                        SmsManager sms = SmsManager.getDefault();
                        sms.sendTextMessage(phoneNumber.getText().toString(), null,
                        message.getText().toString(), sentPendIntent, delivered_pendint-
net);
                    }
                    else {
                        Toast.makeText(SendSMSAppActivity.this, "Either phone number or
text is  missing", Toast.LENGTH_SHORT).show();
                    }
                }
            });
            Button cancelBtn = (Button) this.findViewById(R.id.cancel_button);
            cancelBtn.setOnClickListener(new Button.OnClickListener(){
                public void onClick(View v) {
                    phoneNumber.setText("");
                    message.setText("");
                }
            });
    }
}
```

To send an SMS message with Java code, we use the `SmsManager` class. We cannot instantiate this class directly and must call the `getDefault()` static method to create its object. The method provided by the `SmsManager` class for sending SMS messages is the `sendText-Message()` method.

The syntax for the `sendTextMessage()` method is

```
sendTextMessage(recipient_phoneno, service_centadd, sms_msg, sent_intent, deliv-
ery_intent)
```

where `recipient_phoneno` is the recipient's phone number, and `service_centadd` is the Service center address. We use the value `null` for the default `SMSC` (`Short Message Service Center`). The `sms_msg` is the text message of the SMS, `sentIntent` is the pending

`Intent` to invoke when the message is sent, and `delivery_Intent` is the pending `Intent` to invoke when the message is delivered.

To monitor the status of the SMS message and confirm if it was sent correctly, we create two `PendingIntent` objects that are then passed as arguments to the `sendTextMessage()` method.

The two `PendingIntent` objects are created with the following statements:

```
String SENT = "SMS_SENT";
String DELIVERED = "SMS_DELIVERED";
final PendingIntent sentPendIntent = PendingIntent.getBroadcast(this, 0, new
Intent(SENT), 0);
final PendingIntent delivered_pendintnet = PendingIntent.getBroadcast(this, 0, new
Intent(DELIVERED), 0);
```

The two `PendingIntent` objects are passed into the last two arguments of the `sendText-Message()` method:

```
SmsManager sms = SmsManager.getDefault();
sms.sendTextMessage(phoneNumber.getText().toString(), null, message.getText().
toString(), sentPendIntent, delivered_pendintnet);
```

We are informed, via the two `PendingIntent` objects, whether the message was success-fully sent, delivered, or failed. The `SmsManager` fires SENT and DELIVERED when the SMS messages are sent and delivered. The two `PendingIntent` objects are used to send broadcasts when an SMS message is sent or delivered. We also create and register two `BroadcastReceivers`, which listen for `Intents` that match SENT and DELIVERED as shown by the following statements:

```
registerReceiver(sentReceiver, new IntentFilter(SENT));
registerReceiver(deliveredReceiver, new IntentFilter(DELIVERED));
```

In the earlier section we saw how to define the `BroadcastReceiver` in the `AndroidManifest.xml` file, but here we are doing it dynamically. Within each `BroadcastReceiver` we override the `onReceive()` method and get the current result code via the `getResultCode()` method. Depending on the value of the result code, we display a successfully sent or failed message.

NOTE

On the Android emulator, only the `sentPendIntent` `PendingIntent` object is fired, but not the `deliveredPendIntent` `PendingIntent` object. On a real device, both `PendingIntent` objects fire.

To run the application and watch its output, we need to have two AVDs (Android Virtual Devices) running. From one AVD, we send the message. We use the other AVD for receiving the message. We already have one AVD created called demoAVD, which we have been using to watch application results. We only need to create one more AVD. Select the Window, AVD Manager option to open the AVD Manager dialog box. Select New to create a new AVD. A dialog box opens, prompting for the name and other configuration settings. Assign the name testSMSAVD with the configuration settings shown in Figure 11.4.

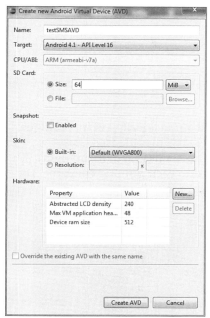

FIGURE 11.4   A dialog box showing configuration settings for the new AVD

Let's designate the SD Card size as 64MB. The Skin and Hardware attributes are set by default. Keeping the default values, click the Create AVD button to create the AVD.

To test the SMS application, both the demoAVD and the testSMSAVD must be running. From the AVD Manager window, select each AVD, followed by the Start button (see Figure 11.5—left). We see a Launch Options dialog box displaying the Skin and Density values of the respective AVD (see Figure 11.5—right). The dialog box also asks whether we want to scale the AVD to real size or wipe user data. Click Launch to launch the AVD. Close the AVD Manager dialog box.

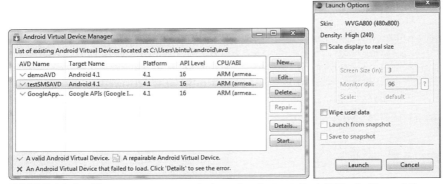

FIGURE 11.5   The `AVD Manager` window showing existing AVDs (left), and the `Launch Options` window showing different options (right)

Both the AVDs run in their respective windows. Android automatically assigns a unique number to each running AVD. For example, the first AVD has the title, `5554:demoAVD`, and the other title displays `5556:testSMSAVD`, as shown in Figure 11.6 (left and right). The numbers `5554` and `5556` are the unique numbers assigned to each running emulator. The numbers keep incrementing with every additional emulator that is run.

FIGURE 11.6   (left) An AVD with the title `5554:demoAVD`, and (right) an AVD with the title `5556:testSMSAVD`

Let's select the `Run` icon from the Eclipse toolbar (or press `Ctrl+F11`) to run our SMS application. We see the `Android Device Chooser` dialog box, asking us to select one of the running AVDs on which we want to run our SMS application. Let's select the `5554`, that is, the `demoAVD` emulator, followed by the `OK` button. Our SMS application executes on the selected AVD, as shown in Figure 11.7 (left). The title bar of the AVD `5554:demoAVD` confirms that our SMS application is running on the selected emulator. We have applied validation checks on the two `EditText` controls that accept the phone number of the recipient and the SMS message. If either of the `EditText` controls is left empty, an error message, `Either phone number or text is missing`, is displayed. When we click the `Send SMS` button after supplying the recipient phone number and a text message, the SMS message is sent to the specified phone number, and a message, `SMS sent`, is displayed, as shown in Figure 11.7 (middle). The SMS message is delivered to the `5556:testSMSAVD` emulator, as shown in Figure 11.7 (right).

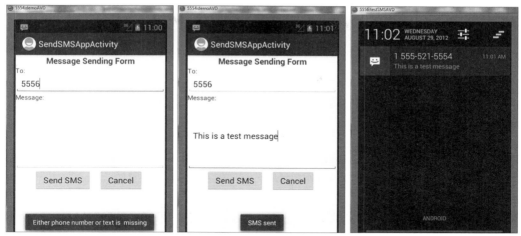

FIGURE 11.7   The error displayed when a field is missing, (left), an SMS message success-fully delivered after delivery of the SMS message (middle), and notification of an SMS message being received (right)

Receiving SMS Messages

To understand the concept of receiving SMS messages, let's create a new Android project called `ReceiveSMSApp`. When a device receives a new SMS message, a new broadcast `Intent` is fired with the `android.provider.Telephony.SMS_RECEIVED` action. To listen for this action, our application must register a `BroadcastReceiver`. That is, we need to create a receiver—a class that extends the `BroadcastReceiver` and then registers it in the manifest file. After we register the receiver, our application is notified whenever an SMS message is received. We see to the process of registering the receiver after creating it.

To create a receiver, add a class file in `ReceiveSMSApp` by right-clicking the `src/com.androidunleashed.receivesmsapp` folder in the `Package Explorer` window and select the `New`, `Class` option. Assign the name `ReceiverSMS` to the class file followed by clicking the `Finish` button. A Java file named `ReceiverSMS.java` is added to our project. To receive the incoming SMS message and display its details, write the code shown in Listing 11.13 into the Java file `ReceiverSMS.java`.

LISTING 11.13   Code Written into `ReceiverSMS.java`

```
package com.androidunleashed.receivesmsapp;

import android.content.BroadcastReceiver;
import android.content.Intent;
import android.content.Context;
import android.os.Bundle;
import android.telephony.SmsMessage;
```

```
import android.widget.Toast;

public class ReceiverSMS extends BroadcastReceiver {

    @Override
    public void onReceive(Context context, Intent intent) {
        Bundle bundle = intent.getExtras();
        SmsMessage[] msg = null;
        String str = "";
        if (bundle != null) {
            Object[] pdus = (Object[]) bundle.get("pdus");
            msg = new SmsMessage[pdus.length];
            for (int i=0; i<msg.length; i++){
                msg[i] = SmsMessage.createFromPdu((byte[])pdus[i]);
                str += "SMS Received from: " + msg[i].getOriginatingAddress();
                str += ":";
                str += msg[i].getMessageBody().toString();
                str += "\n";
            }
            Toast.makeText(context, str, Toast.LENGTH_SHORT).show();
        }
    }
}
```

The broadcast Intent that is fired after receiving a new SMS message includes a bundle containing information about the received message. The information exists in the bundle in the form of an array of SMS PDUs. PDU stands for Protocol Data Unit and is used to encapsulate the SMS message. Hence, the PDU key is used to extract the array of SMS PDUs from the bundle. The array of SMS PDUs is thereafter converted into an array of SmsMessage objects. To convert each PDU byte array into an SMS Message object, the SmsMessage.createFromPdu() method is called, passing in each byte array. This code snippet shows how it is done:

```
Bundle bundle = intent.getExtras();
SmsMessage[] msg = null;
if (bundle != null) {
    Object[] pdus = (Object[]) bundle.get("pdus");
    msg = new SmsMessage[pdus.length];
    for (int i=0; i<msg.length; i++){
        msg[i] = SmsMessage.createFromPdu((byte[])pdus[i]);
    }
}
```

We can see that the information of all received messages is gathered in the SmsMessage array msg. Each array element represents the complete information of a single received SMS that includes the originating address—the phone number, timestamp, and the message body. The following methods are used to fetch the SMS information from the `SmsMessage` array elements:

▶ `getOriginatingAddress()`—Fetches the phone number of the SMS recipient

▶ `getTimestampMillis()`—Fetches the time at which the SMS is received

▶ `getMessageBody()`—Fetches the message body

The code in Listing 11.13 receives the SMS message and uses the `getOriginatingAddress()` and `getMessageBody()` methods to fetch the phone number and message body of the received message. The phone number and message body are then displayed on the screen.

To listen for incoming messages, we need to register our `ReceiverSMS` Broadcast Receiver class using an Intent Filter that listens for the `android.provider.Telephony.SMS_RECEIVED` action String. To do so, the following code is added in the `AndroidManifest.xml` file:

```
<receiver android:name=".ReceiverSMS">
    <intent-filter>
        <action android:name="android.provider.Telephony.SMS_RECEIVED" />
    </intent-filter>
</receiver>
```

Besides registering a receiver, our application has to seek permission to receive incoming SMS messages. To do this, add the `android.permission.RECEIVE_SMS` permission to the manifest file:

```
<uses-permission android:name="android.permission.RECEIVE_SMS" />
```

After we add the preceding code, the code in the `AndroidManifest.xml` file appears as shown in Listing 11.14.

LISTING 11.14   Code Written into `AndroidManifest.xml`

```
<manifest xmlns:android="http://schemas.android.com/apk/res/android"
    package="com.androidunleashed.receivesmsapp"
    android:versionCode="1"
    android:versionName="1.0" >
    <uses-sdk android:minSdkVersion="8"
        android:targetSdkVersion="15" />
    <uses-permission android:name="android.permission.RECEIVE_SMS" />
    <application
        android:icon="@drawable/ic_launcher"
        android:label="@string/app_name"
        android:theme="@style/AppTheme" >
        <activity
```

```
            android:name=".ReceiveSMSAppActivity"
            android:label="@string/title_activity_receive_smsapp" >
            <intent-filter>
                <action android:name="android.intent.action.MAIN" />
                <category android:name="android.intent.category.LAUNCHER" />
            </intent-filter>
        </activity>
        <receiver android:name=".ReceiverSMS">
            <intent-filter>
                <action android:name="android.provider.Telephony.SMS_RECEIVED" />
            </intent-filter>
        </receiver>
    </application>
</manifest>
```

After running the application, we see the output shown in Figure 11.8.

FIGURE 11.8   The output displayed on application startup

To see how an SMS message is received by this application, we need to first send a
message using the SendSMSApp we just created. To run the SendSMSApp, let's run one more
AVD. Select the Window, AVD Manager option. From the AVD Manager dialog box that
pops up, select the testSMSAVD AVD and click the Start button. A dialog box showing
Launch Options opens; click the Launch button to start the AVD with the default options.

The AVD runs, as shown in Figure 11.9 (left). Close the `AVD Manager` window. Select `SendSMSApp` from the `Project Explorer` window and select the `Run` icon from the toolbar at the top. An `Android Device Chooser` dialog box opens, asking in which AVD we want to run the `SentSMSApp`, as shown in Figure 11.9 (right).

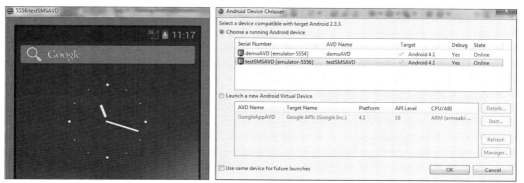

FIGURE 11.9   (left) A running AVD with the title `5556:testSMSAVD`, and (right) the Android Device Chooser to select an AVD

The `SendSMSApp` application is launched in the `5556` AVD, as shown in Figure 11.10 (left). In the `To` box, write the ID of the AVD through which our `ReceiveSMSApp` is running, that is, `5554`. Write some text in the multiline message box and click the `Send SMS` button. The SMS message is sent from the application and received by the `5554` AVD, as is confirmed by the `Toast` message displaying the originating phone number and its message body (see Figure 11.10—middle). The SMS message is received and displayed in the `5554` AVD (see Figure 11.10—right).

FIGURE 11.10   (left) Screen sending an SMS message, (middle) Toast displaying the sender information and received SMS body, and (right) the SMS message received by the receiver

Sending Email

To send an email with Android, we use the following `Intent`:

```
Intent.ACTION_SEND
```

The `Intent.ACTION_SEND` calls an existing email client to send an email. So, for sending email through the Android emulator, we need to first configure the email client. If the email client is not configured, the emulator does not respond to the `Intent`. Through the `ACTION_SEND` Intent, messages of different types, such as text or image, can be sent. The only thing we need to do is to set the type of the `Intent` through the `setType()` method. For example, the following statement declares that the text data type will be sent through the `Intent`:

```
emailIntent.setType("plain/text");
```

The `emailIntent` is the `Intent.ACTION_SEND` object. After we launch this `Intent`, any application on the device that supports plain text messaging may handle this request. To let a user choose the email client to handle the `Intent`, we call `startActivity()` with the `createChooser()` method. As the name suggests, the `createChooser()` method prompts the user to choose the application to handle the `Intent`. This statement shows how to call `startActivity()` with the `createChooser()` method:

```
startActivity(Intent.createChooser(emailIntent, "Sending Email"));
```

This statement displays all the applications that are eligible to handle the `Intent`, allowing the user to choose the application to launch. If there is only one application able to handle the `Intent`, it is launched automatically without prompting the user.

To supply data for the email message fields, we set certain standard extras for the `Intent`. For example, we can set the following:

▶ **EXTRA_EMAIL**—Sets the `To:` address (email address of the receiver)

▶ **EXTRA_CC**—Sets the `Cc:` address (email address of the carbon copy receiver)

▶ **EXTRA_BCC**—Sets the `Bcc:` address (email address of the blind carbon copy receiver)

▶ **EXTRA_SUBJECT**—Sets the `Subject` of the email

▶ **EXTRA_TEXT**—Sets the body of the email

After setting the desired `Intent`'s extras, launch the activity to initiate the sending email task.

Before we go ahead and create an application for sending email, let's configure the email client of the Android emulator in these steps:

▶ Start the emulator and then click on the `Menu` button.

▶ Click on the `System settings` option.

▶ From the `Accounts` section, click on the `Add account` button (see Figure 11.11—left). From the two options, `Corporate` and `Email` (see Figure 11.11—middle), click the `Email` option. We get the `Account setup` form where we need to enter our existing Email ID and password (see Figure 11.11—right) followed by clicking the `Next` button.

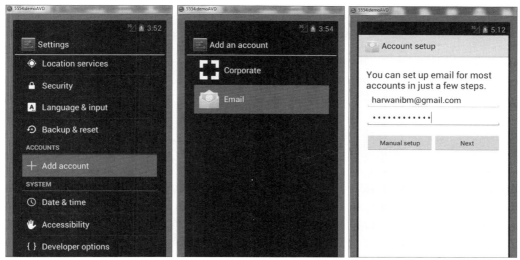

FIGURE 11.11   (left) Settings options in the Android emulator, (middle) two options of adding an account, and (right) account setup form to enter email ID and password

▶ The emulator checks for the incoming and outgoing servers and on finding them displays `Account settings` as shown in Figure 11.12 (left). Select the required check boxes and then click the `Next` button. Our email client is set up, and we are prompted to enter the name to be displayed on the outgoing messages (see Figure 11.12—right). Click the `Next` button to finish configuring the email client.

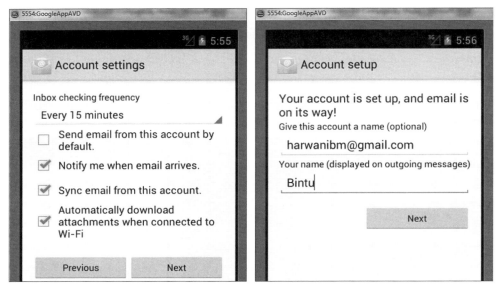

FIGURE 11.12   (left) The `Account settings` form, and (right) the `Account setup` form

Now the email client is successfully configured in the emulator, and we can go ahead and send mail. Let's create an application to send an email. Create a new Android project called `SendEmailApp`. In this application, we provide a user interface to enter the `To`, `Cc`, and `Bcc` addresses of the email receivers; a `Subject`; and the body of the email. After we enter the required information, when the user clicks the `Send` button, the email client on the device is invoked. The email client page is auto-filled with the information entered through the application, and the email is sent after clicking the `Send` button from the email client.

To create the UI for entering email information, we need to use six `TextView` controls, five `EditText` controls, and a `Button` control. To define these controls, write the code shown in Listing 11.15 into the `activity_send_email_app.xml` layout file.

LISTING 11.15   Code Written into `activity_send_email_app.xml`

```
<RelativeLayout
    xmlns:android="http://schemas.android.com/apk/res/android"
    android:layout_width="match_parent"
    android:layout_height="match_parent" >
    <TextView
        android:id="@+id/email_form"
        android:text = "Email Form"
        android:layout_width="wrap_content"
        android:layout_height="wrap_content"
        android:typeface="serif"
        android:textSize="18sp"
        android:textStyle="bold"
```

```
        android:padding="10dip"
        android:layout_centerHorizontal="true"/>
<TextView
        android:id="@+id/to_addressview"
        android:text = "To:"
        android:layout_width="wrap_content"
        android:layout_height="wrap_content"
        android:layout_margin="10dip"
        android:layout_below="@id/email_form" />
<EditText
        android:id="@+id/toaddresses"
        android:layout_height="wrap_content"
        android:layout_width="match_parent"
        android:layout_below="@id/email_form"
        android:layout_toRightOf="@id/to_addressview"
        android:singleLine="true" />
<TextView
        android:id="@+id/cc_addressview"
        android:text = "Cc:"
        android:layout_width="wrap_content"
        android:layout_height="wrap_content"
        android:layout_below="@id/to_addressview"
        android:layout_margin="10dip" />
<EditText
        android:id="@+id/ccaddresses"
        android:layout_height="wrap_content"
        android:layout_width="match_parent"
        android:singleLine="true"
        android:layout_below="@id/toaddresses"
        android:layout_toRightOf="@id/cc_addressview" />
<TextView
        android:id="@+id/bcc_addressview"
        android:text = "Bcc:"
        android:layout_width="wrap_content"
        android:layout_height="wrap_content"
        android:layout_below="@id/cc_addressview"
        android:layout_margin="10dip" />
<EditText
        android:id="@+id/bccaddresses"
        android:layout_height="wrap_content"
        android:layout_width="match_parent"
        android:singleLine="true"
        android:layout_below="@id/ccaddresses"
        android:layout_toRightOf="@id/bcc_addressview" />
<TextView
        android:id="@+id/subjectview"
```

```
        android:text = "Subject:"
        android:layout_width="wrap_content"
        android:layout_height="wrap_content"
        android:layout_below="@id/bcc_addressview"
        android:layout_margin="10dip"
        android:paddingTop="10dip"/>
    <EditText
        android:id="@+id/emailsubject"
        android:layout_height="wrap_content"
        android:layout_width="match_parent"
        android:singleLine="true"
        android:layout_below="@id/bccaddresses"
        android:layout_toRightOf="@id/subjectview"
        android:layout_marginTop="10dip" />
    <TextView
        android:id="@+id/emailtextview"
        android:text = "Message:"
        android:layout_width="wrap_content"
        android:layout_height="wrap_content"
        android:layout_below="@id/subjectview"
        android:layout_margin="10dip" />
    <EditText
        android:id="@+id/emailtext"
        android:layout_height="wrap_content"
        android:layout_width="match_parent"
        android:lines="5"
        android:layout_below="@id/emailsubject"
        android:layout_toRightOf="@id/emailtextview" />
    <Button
        android:id="@+id/send_button"
        android:text="Send"
        android:layout_width="wrap_content"
        android:layout_height="wrap_content"
        android:layout_centerHorizontal="true"
        android:paddingLeft="25dip"
        android:paddingRight="25dip"
        android:layout_marginTop="10dip"
        android:layout_below="@id/emailtext" />
</RelativeLayout>
```

We can see that the six TextView controls are set to display Email Form, To:, Cc:, Bcc:, Subject:, and Message. To identify these in the Java code, the five EditText controls are assigned the IDs toaddresses, ccaddresses, bccaddresses, emailsubject, and emailtext. The Button control is assigned the Send caption and is assigned the ID send_button. To read the addresses, subject, and email body entered by the user, and to use

Intent.ACTION_SEND for sending email, write the code shown in Listing 11.16 into the SendEmailAppActivity.java Java activity file.

LISTING 11.16   Code Written into SendEmailAppActivity.java

```java
package com.androidunleashed.sendemailapp;

import android.app.Activity;
import android.os.Bundle;
import android.view.View;
import android.content.Intent;
import android.view.View.OnClickListener;
import android.widget.Button;
import android.widget.EditText;

public class SendEmailAppActivity extends Activity {
    Button sendbutton;
    EditText toAddress, ccAddress, bccAddress, subject, emailMessage;
    String  toAdds, ccAdds, bccAdds;

    @Override
    public void onCreate(Bundle savedInstanceState) {
        super.onCreate(savedInstanceState);
        setContentView(R.layout.activity_send_email_app);
        sendbutton=(Button) findViewById(R.id.send_button);
        toAddress=(EditText) findViewById(R.id.toaddresses);
        ccAddress=(EditText) findViewById(R.id.ccaddresses);
        bccAddress=(EditText) findViewById(R.id.bccaddresses);
        subject=(EditText) findViewById(R.id.emailsubject);
        emailMessage=(EditText) findViewById(R.id.emailtext);
        sendbutton.setOnClickListener(new OnClickListener(){
            @Override
            public void onClick(View v) {
                final Intent emailIntent = new Intent(Intent.ACTION_SEND);
                if(toAddress.getText().length() >0) {
                    toAdds = '"'+toAddress.getText().toString()+'"';
                    emailIntent.putExtra(Intent.EXTRA_EMAIL, new String[]{ toAdds});
                }
                if(ccAddress.getText().length() >0) {
                    ccAdds = '"'+ccAddress.getText().toString()+'"';
                    emailIntent.putExtra(Intent.EXTRA_CC, new String[]{ ccAdds});
                }
                if(bccAddress.getText().length() >0) {
                    bccAdds = '"'+bccAddress.getText().toString()+'"';
                    emailIntent.putExtra(Intent.EXTRA_BCC, new String[]{ bccAdds});
                }
```

```
                emailIntent.putExtra(Intent.EXTRA_SUBJECT, subject.getText().
toString());
                emailIntent.putExtra(Intent.EXTRA_TEXT, emailMessage.getText());
                emailIntent.setType("plain/text");
                startActivity(Intent.createChooser(emailIntent, "Sending Email"));
            }
        });
    }
}
```

Here, the `toaddresses`, `ccaddresses`, `bccaddresses`, `emailsubject`, and `emailtext` `EditText` controls are accessed and mapped to their respective `EditText` objects. Similarly, the `Button` control with the `send_button` ID is accessed and assigned to the `sendbutton` `Button` object. The `ClickListener` event listener is associated with the `Button` control. After we click the `Button`, the `onClick()` callback method is invoked. In the `onClick()` method, an `Intent` object called `emailIntent` is created, with its action set to `Intent. ACTION_SEND`. Also, to auto-fill the email client's fields, the `Intent` extras, `EXTRA_EMAIL`, `EXTRA_CC`, `EXTRA_BCC`, `EXTRA_SUBJECT`, and `EXTRA_TEXT`, are initialized with the data entered by the user in the `EditText` controls. Finally, the email is sent by launching the email client installed on the device.

After running the application, we see a user interface to enter addresses of the receiver(s), subject, and email body, as shown in Figure 11.13 (top left). When the user clicks the `Send` button, the email client is invoked. The fields of the email client are automatically filled with data entered in the `EditText` controls, as shown in Figure 11.13 (top right). The email is sent to the recipient after it pipes through the email client, as shown in Figure 11.13 (bottom).

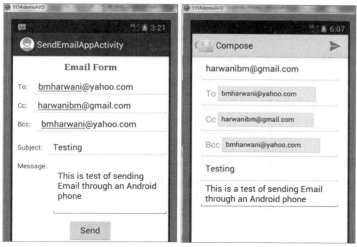

FIGURE 11.13   (top left) Information entered into the Email Form, (top right) information entered into the Email Form appears in the email client fields, and (bottom) email received by the recipient

Working with the Telephony Manager

The Android telephony APIs include the Telephony Manager that accesses the telephony services on the device and enables us to

▶ Provide a user interface for entering or modifying the phone number to dial.

▶ Implement call handling in the application.

▶ Register and monitor telephony state changes.

▶ Get subscriber information.

Making the Outgoing Call

The simplest way to make an outgoing call is to invoke the `Dialer` application by using the `Intent.ACTION_CALL` action. The sample code for doing so follows:

```
Intent callIntent = new Intent(Intent.ACTION_CALL);
callIntent.setData(Uri.parse("tel:1111122222"));
startActivity(callIntent);
```

The preceding code initiates a phone call to `1111122222` using the system in-call Activity. For making the phone call, the application must have the permission to invoke the `Dialer` application. That is, to use this action, the application must request the `CALL_PHONE` uses-permission by adding the following statement to the manifest file:

```
<uses-permission android:name="android.permission.CALL_PHONE"/>
```

Listening for Phone State Changes

To listen for phone state changes, that is, to see when the phone state is changed from idle to ringing, off-hook, and so on, we have to implement a broadcast receiver on `android.intent.action.PHONE_STATE`. That is, we need to implement a `PhoneStateListener` and call the `listen()` method of the `TelephonyManager` to receive notification whenever there is a change in the phone state. When a phone state changes, the `onCallStateChanged()` method of `PhoneStateListener` is called with the new phone state. The phone state is represented by the constants shown here:

▶ **CALL_STATE_IDLE**—The phone is in an idle state.

▶ **CALL_STATE_RINGING**—A phone call has arrived.

▶ **CALL_STATE_OFFHOOK**—The phone is off-hook.

To access the phone state information, the application must have permission for doing so. To ask permission, add following statement to the manifest file:

```
<uses-permission android:name="android.permission.READ_PHONE_STATE" />
```

Let's see how to make a phone call and listen to the phone state. Create a new Android project called `PhoneCallApp`. In this application, there are two controls: `Button` and `TextView`. The `Button` control places the phone call, and the `TextView` displays the phone state. To define the `Button` and `TextView` controls, write the code shown in Listing 11.17 into the `activity_phone_call_app.xml` layout file.

LISTING 11.17   Code Written into `activity_phone_call_app.xml`

```
<LinearLayout xmlns:android="http://schemas.android.com/apk/res/android"
    android:layout_width="match_parent"
    android:layout_height="match_parent"
    android:orientation="vertical" >
    <Button
        android:id="@+id/callbutton"
        android:layout_width="wrap_content"
        android:layout_height="wrap_content"
        android:text="Make Phone Call"
        android:layout_gravity="center" />
    <TextView
```

```
            android:id="@+id/messageview"
            android:layout_width="wrap_content"
            android:layout_height="match_parent"
            android:layout_gravity="center" />
</LinearLayout>
```

We can see that the `Button` control is assigned the caption `Make Phone Call` and assigned the ID `callbutton`. The `TextView` is assigned the ID `messageview`. The IDs are used to access these controls in the Java code.

To make the outgoing call and listen to the phone state changes, write the code shown in Listing 11.18 into `PhoneCallAppActivity.java`.

LISTING 11.18   Code Written into `PhoneCallAppActivity.java`

```
package com.androidunleashed.phonecallapp;

import android.app.Activity;
import android.os.Bundle;
import android.content.Context;
import android.content.Intent;
import android.net.Uri;
import android.telephony.PhoneStateListener;
import android.telephony.TelephonyManager;
import android.view.View;
import android.widget.TextView;
import android.widget.Button;
import android.view.View.OnClickListener;
import android.util.Log;

public class PhoneCallAppActivity extends Activity {
    @Override
    public void onCreate(Bundle savedInstanceState) {
        super.onCreate(savedInstanceState);
        setContentView(R.layout.activity_phone_call_app);
        MyPhoneCallListener phoneListener = new MyPhoneCallListener();
        TelephonyManager telephonyManager = (TelephonyManager)
getSystemService(Context.TELEPHONY_SERVICE);
        telephonyManager.listen(phoneListener,PhoneStateListener.LISTEN_CALL_STATE);
        Button callButton = (Button) findViewById(R.id.callbutton);
        callButton.setOnClickListener(new OnClickListener() {
            @Override
            public void onClick(View arg0) {
                Intent callIntent = new Intent(Intent.ACTION_CALL);
                callIntent.setData(Uri.parse("tel:1111122222"));
                startActivity(callIntent);
```

```
            }
        });
    }


    class MyPhoneCallListener extends PhoneStateListener {
        TextView messageview = (TextView)findViewById(R.id.messageview);
        String msg;

        @Override
        public void onCallStateChanged(int state, String incomingNumber) {
            super.onCallStateChanged(state, incomingNumber);
            switch(state){
                case TelephonyManager.CALL_STATE_IDLE:
                    msg= "Call state is idle";
                    Log.d("idle", msg);
                    break;
                case TelephonyManager.CALL_STATE_RINGING:
                    msg = "Call state is Ringing. Number is "+ incomingNumber;
                    Log.d("ringing", msg);
                    break;
                case TelephonyManager.CALL_STATE_OFFHOOK:
                    msg = "Call state is OFFHOOK";
                    Log.d("offhook", msg);
                    break;
                default:
                    msg = "Call state is" + state + ". Number is " + incomingNumber;
                    Log.d("state", msg);
                    break;
            }
            messageview.setText(msg);
        }
    }
}
```

We can see that to make an outgoing call, an `Intent` object called `callIntent` is created with an `Intent.ACTION_CALL` action. The phone number to call is set to `1111122222`. The `PhoneStateListener` class is implemented to listen for the phone state changes. When the phone state changes, the `onCallStateChanged()` method is called, which displays the phone state through the `TextView` control.

Before running the application, we need to add two permissions to the application. The first permission is for making phone calls, and the second is for accessing the phone state information. After we add the two permissions, `AndroidManifest.xml` appears as shown in Listing 11.19. Only the code in bold is added; the rest is the default code.

LISTING 11.19 Code in `AndroidManifest.xml`

```xml
<manifest xmlns:android="http://schemas.android.com/apk/res/android"
    package="com.androidunleashed.phonecallapp"
    android:versionCode="1"
    android:versionName="1.0" >
    <uses-sdk android:minSdkVersion="8"
        android:targetSdkVersion="15" />
    <uses-permission android:name="android.permission.CALL_PHONE" />
    <uses-permission android:name="android.permission.READ_PHONE_STATE" />
    <application
        android:icon="@drawable/ic_launcher"
        android:label="@string/app_name"
        android:theme="@style/AppTheme" >
        <activity
            android:name=".PhoneCallAppActivity"
            android:label="@string/title_activity_phone_call_app" >
            <intent-filter>
                <action android:name="android.intent.action.MAIN" />
                <category android:name="android.intent.category.LAUNCHER" />
            </intent-filter>
        </activity>
    </application>
</manifest>
```

After running the application, we see the `Button` and `TextView` controls on the screen. Because no phone call has been made, the `TextView` shows the text `Call state is idle` (see Figure 11.14—top left). After we click the `Make Phone Call` button, the phone call is made to the phone number specified in the activity file, as shown in Figure 11.14 (top right). The log messages showing the phone state are displayed in Figure 11.14 (bottom).

FIGURE 11.14   Screen displaying the `Button` and `TextView` showing that the phone state is idle (top left), screen when a phone call is made (top right), and log messages displayed (bottom)

Summary

In this chapter, we learned about broadcast receivers. We saw how to broadcast and receive the broadcasted `Intent`. We saw how the notification system is used, and how the notification is created, configured, and displayed in the status bar. We saw the procedure for sending and receiving SMS messages using Java code. Finally, we saw how to send email and use the Telephony Manager in making phone calls.

In the next chapter, we learn how to define, create, use, and register content providers. We also learn how to define a database, content URI, and MIME types. Also we learn to implement the `getType`, `query`, `insert`, `update`, and `delete` methods required to make a content provider functional.

# CHAPTER 12

Creating and Using Content Providers

Content providers allow users to share data between multiple applications. They also provide access to a structured set of data enabling us to query, modify, add, and delete data.

What Is a Content Provider

A content provider acts as a data store and provides an interface to access its contents. Unlike a database, where information can be accessed only by the package in which it was created, information in a content provider can be shared across packages. The following lists a few characteristics of content providers:

▶ Like in a database, we can query, add, edit, delete, and update data in content providers.

▶ Data can be stored in a database, files, and over a network.

▶ A content provider acts as a wrapper around the data store to make it resemble web services. That is, the data in content providers is exposed as a service.

Android ships with several built-in content providers. Table 12.1 lists a few of them.

TABLE 12.1   Built-In Content Providers

Content Provider	Usage
Contacts	Stores contact details
Media Store	Stores media files such as audio, video, and images
Settings	Stores the device's settings and preferences
Browser	Stores data such as browser bookmarks and browser history
CallLog	Stores data such as missed calls and call details

In this chapter, we learn to use the Contacts content provider. Before doing so, we learn how data is fetched from a content provider.

Understanding the Android Content URI

To fetch data from a content provider, we specify the query string in the form of a URI (universal resource identifier). The syntax of the query URI appears as follows:

```
<standard_prefix>://<authority><data_path>/<id>
```

Table 12.2 lists the meanings of the different tags used in a query URI.

TABLE 12.2   Tags Used in Query URIs

Tag	Meaning
standard prefix	For content providers, the standard prefix is always `content://`.
authority	Specifies the name of the content provider. It appears as a domain name for the content provider. The fully qualified name is not essential for accessing the Android built-in content providers. For third-party content providers, a fully qualified name is recommended. For example, the Android built-in content provider Contacts is accessed as `com.google.android.contacts`. Third-party content providers are referenced via a fully qualified name such as `com.bmharwani.provider`.
data path	Specifies the kind of data requested. For example, to access the `AndroidTutorial` from the `bmharwani` content provider, the URI would appear as `content://com.bmharwani.provider.AndroidTutorial`
id	Specifies the content requested. For example, to access the `AndroidTutorial` with the ID 2 from the `bmharwani` content provider, the URI would look like this: `content://com.bmharwani.provider.AndroidTutorial/2`.

The following examples make the concept of a content provider URI clearer.

The URI to identify a directory or a collection of `AndroidTutorials` in the `bmharwani` database is

```
content://com.bmharwani.provider.AndroidTutorial
```

The URI to identify a specific tutorial is

```
content://com.bmharwani.provider.AndroidTutorial/#
```

where # is the ID of a particular tutorial.

Likewise, the URI to identify collection of people in the contacts database is

```
content://contacts/people/
```

Because `Contacts` is the built-in Android content provider, you do not need a fully qualified URI to identify a specific person. The URI for the person with an ID of 10 in the contacts database is

```
content://contacts/people/10
```

Using Content Providers

In this section, we learn to use the built-in Contacts content provider. Before accessing the contacts information in the Contacts content provider, let's first learn how to insert contact information with the device/emulator. The contacts are named as People in the emulator. To access the contact information, click the People icon on the home page at the bottom of the display (see Figure 12.1—left). A page is displayed telling us that no contact exists in the device emulator. Three buttons are displayed on the screen: `Create a new contact`, `Sign in to an account`, and `Import contacts`, as shown in Figure 12.1 (middle). After we select `Create a new contact`, a dialog appears informing us that new contacts will not be backed up. The dialog also asks whether we want to add an account that backs up contacts online. Two options are displayed: `Keep local` and `Add account`. Select the `Keep local` option. A blank form is displayed asking for information about the new contact, as shown in Figure 12.1 (right). The form asks for personal profile information, such as contact name, phone number, organization, designation, address, home address, and email address.

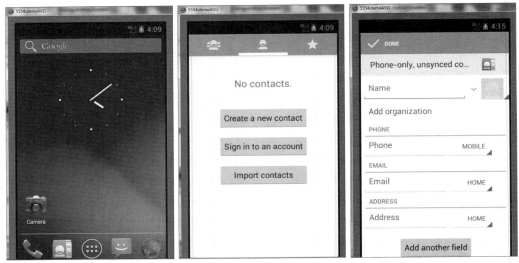

FIGURE 12.1   Icons in the device emulator representing different applications (left), screen showing different options after clicking the People icon (middle), and an empty form to enter information about the new contact (right)

After entering the personal profile information, click DONE at the top to save it (see Figure 12.2—left). After we click DONE, the contact is created, showing the saved information with a left-pointing arrow at the top, as shown in Figure 12.2 (middle). After selecting the arrow, we jump to the screen that shows an alphabetized list of contacts. Because we have a single contact, it appears as shown in Figure 12.2 (right). We can set up the user's contact information by selecting the Set up my profile option. After we select a contact from the list, the profile information is displayed.

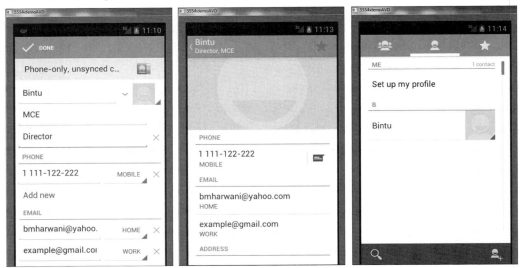

FIGURE 12.2   A form showing information about the new contact (left), a screen showing contact information after creation (middle), and existing contact(s) displayed in alphabetically categorized list (right)

The contact information on our device can be accessed in an Android application. Let's create a new Android project called `ContentProviderApp`. This application accesses the contact information and displays it via `ListView`. To define a `ListView` control, add the code shown in Listing 12.1 into the `activity_content_provider_app.xml` layout file.

LISTING 12.1   Code Written into `activity_content_provider_app.xml`

```xml
<LinearLayout xmlns:android="http://schemas.android.com/apk/res/android"
    android:layout_width="match_parent"
    android:layout_height="match_parent"
    android:orientation="vertical" >
    <ListView
        android:id="@+id/contactslist"
        android:layout_width="match_parent"
        android:layout_height="match_parent"
        android:drawSelectorOnTop="false"
        android:textFilterEnabled="true" />
</LinearLayout>
```

We can see that a `ListView` is defined with the ID `contactslist`. The ID is used to access it in the Java code. To access the contacts information and display it through `ListView`, write the code shown in Listing 12.2 into the Java activity file `ContentProviderAppActivity.java`.

LISTING 12.2   Code Written into `ContentProviderAppActivity.java`

```java
package com.androidunleashed.contentproviderapp;

import android.app.Activity;
import android.os.Bundle;
import android.net.Uri;
import android.database.Cursor;
import android.content.CursorLoader;
import android.provider.ContactsContract;
import android.widget.ListView;
import java.util.ArrayList;
import android.widget.ArrayAdapter;

public class ContentProviderAppActivity extends Activity {
    ArrayList<String> contactRows=new ArrayList<String>();
    final String[] nocontact={"No Contacts on the Device"};

    @Override
```

```
public void onCreate(Bundle savedInstanceState) {
    super.onCreate(savedInstanceState);
    setContentView(R.layout.activity_content_provider_app);
    final ListView contactsList=(ListView) findViewById(R.id.contactslist);
    Uri contactsUri = Uri.parse("content://contacts/people");
    String[] projection = new String[] {ContactsContract.Contacts._ID,
    ContactsContract.Contacts.DISPLAY_NAME };
    Cursor c;
    CursorLoader cursorLoader = new CursorLoader(this, contactsUri, projection,
    null, null , null);
    c = cursorLoader.loadInBackground();
    contactRows.clear();
    c.moveToFirst();
    while(c.isAfterLast()==false){
        String contactID = c.getString(c.getColumnIndex(ContactsContract.
        Contacts._ID));
        String contactDisplayName = c.getString(c.
        getColumnIndex(ContactsContract.Contacts.DISPLAY_NAME));
        contactRows.add(contactID+ " "+contactDisplayName);
        c.moveToNext();
    }
    if (c != null && !c.isClosed()) {
        c.close();
    }
    if(contactRows.isEmpty()) {
        ArrayAdapter<String> arrayAdpt=new ArrayAdapter<String>(this,
        android.R.layout.simple_list_item_1, nocontact);
        contactsList.setAdapter(arrayAdpt);
    }
    else {
        ArrayAdapter<String> arrayAdpt=new ArrayAdapter<String>(this,
        android.R.layout.simple_list_item_1, contactRows);
        contactsList.setAdapter(arrayAdpt);
    }
  }
}
```

We define a contactsUri URI for the Contacts provider. Thereafter, a projection String array is defined to specify the columns that we want to extract from the contacts database. With the help of a CursorLoader, we load rows from the Contacts provider and assign them to the Cursor c. Thereafter, through a while loop, the information in the cursor is extracted. Because we want to display only the ID and contact name, the information in the ContactsContract.Contacts._ID and ContactsContract.Contacts. DISPLAY_NAME columns is accessed and assigned to the contactRows ArrayList. If contactRows is not empty, an ArrayAdapter object called arrayAdpt is defined through it. Finally, a ListView control is filled with the information in the arrayAdpt ArrayAdapter.

To access information in the Contacts Provider in our app, we need to add the following permission into the AndroidManifest.xml file:

```
<uses-permission android:name="android.permission.READ_CONTACTS" />
```

So, add the line in bold to AndroidManifest.xml, as shown in Listing 12.3.

LISTING 12.3   Code in AndroidManifest.xml

```
<manifest xmlns:android="http://schemas.android.com/apk/res/android"
    package="com.androidunleashed.contentproviderapp"
    android:versionCode="1"
    android:versionName="1.0" >
    <uses-sdk android:minSdkVersion="8"
        android:targetSdkVersion="15" />
    <uses-permission android:name="android.permission.READ_CONTACTS"/>
    <application
        android:icon="@drawable/ic_launcher"
        android:label="@string/app_name"
        android:theme="@style/AppTheme" >
        <activity
            android:name=".ContentProviderAppActivity"
            android:label="@string/title_activity_content_provider_app" >
            <intent-filter>
                <action android:name="android.intent.action.MAIN" />
                <category android:name="android.intent.category.LAUNCHER" />
            </intent-filter>
        </activity>
    </application>
</manifest>
```

In the preceding lines, our application can access the information in the Contacts provider. Assuming, there are two contacts on our device/emulator, when we run the application, the contact information is accessed and displayed through the ListView control as shown in Figure 12.3.

FIGURE 12.3   The Contacts information accessed from the device/emulator and displayed via `ListView`

Creating a Custom Content Provider

These are the steps taken to create our own content provider:

▶ Define the content provider—the class that extends the `android.content.ContentProvider` class.

▶ Define the database, URIs, column names, MIME types, and so on.

▶ Implement the `query insert`, `update`, `delete`, and `getType` methods to make the content provider functional.

▶ Register the provider in the manifest file.

Defining a Content Provider

To define our own content provider, we need to create a class that extends the `android.content.ContentProvider` class. Let's create a new Android project called `CreateContentProviderApp`. This application provides the STD (subscriber trunk dialing) code of the specified country. The application allows users to enter the STD codes of different countries, display a scrollable list of existing countries, and delete and update STD code information.

On startup, we want the application to display a form that enables users to enter STD code information of different countries. That is, we want to display `EditText` controls that allow users to enter a country name and its STD code. The form should also display two `Button` controls: one to add STD code information of the supplied country and the other to display the information that already exists in the database table. For displaying such a user interface, write the code shown in Listing 12.4 into the `activity_create_content_provider_app.xml` layout file.

LISTING 12.4   Code Written into `activity_create_content_provider_app.xml`

```xml
<RelativeLayout xmlns:android="http://schemas.android.com/apk/res/android"
    android:layout_width="match_parent"
    android:layout_height="match_parent"  >
    <TextView
        android:id="@+id/stdform"
        android:text = "Enter STD Information of Countries"
        android:layout_width="wrap_content"
        android:layout_height="wrap_content"
        android:textSize="18sp"
        android:textStyle="bold"
        android:padding="10dip"
        android:layout_centerHorizontal="true"/>
    <TextView
        android:id="@+id/country_view"
        android:layout_width="wrap_content"
        android:layout_height="wrap_content"
        android:text="Country Name"
        android:layout_below="@id/stdform" />
    <EditText
        android:id="@+id/country_name"
        android:layout_height="wrap_content"
        android:layout_width="250dp"
        android:layout_below="@id/stdform"
        android:layout_toRightOf="@id/country_view" />
    <TextView
        android:id="@+id/stdcode_view"
        android:layout_width="wrap_content"
        android:layout_height="wrap_content"
        android:text="STD Code"
        android:layout_below="@id/country_name" />
    <EditText
        android:id="@+id/std_code"
        android:layout_height="wrap_content"
        android:layout_width="100dp"
        android:layout_marginLeft="20dip"
        android:layout_toRightOf="@id/stdcode_view"
        android:layout_below="@id/country_name" />
    <Button
        android:text="Add STD Info"
        android:id="@+id/add_stdinfo"
        android:layout_width="wrap_content"
        android:layout_height="wrap_content"
        android:layout_below="@id/std_code"
        android:layout_marginLeft="20dip"  />
```

```
    <Button
        android:text="Show STD Info"
        android:id="@+id/list_stdinfo"
        android:layout_width="wrap_content"
        android:layout_height="wrap_content"
        android:layout_toRightOf="@id/add_stdinfo"
        android:layout_below="@id/std_code"   />
</RelativeLayout>
```

Here we see that the three `TextView` controls are defined and assigned the text `Enter STD Information of Countries`, `"Country Name`, and `STD Code`. The two `EditText` controls are assigned the `ID`s `country_name` and `std_code`. The two `Button` controls are assigned the `ID`s `add_stdinfo` and `list_stdinfo`. The caption assigned to the two `Button` controls is `Add STD Info` and `Show STD Info`. The IDs assigned to the controls are used to access them in Java code.

Next, we add a Java class file to our project that acts as our custom content provider. Let's call the added class `CountriesProvider`. As I said earlier, to become a content provider, the class needs to extend the abstract `ContentProvider` class as shown here:

```
public class CountriesProvider extends ContentProvider
```

Content providers manage their information in databases. So let's go ahead and define a database for our content provider.

Defining a Database

The content provider that we want to create provides information about the countries and their corresponding STD codes. To store country names and their corresponding STD codes, we create a database called `Countries`. In the `Countries` database, we create a single table called `stdinfo`. The `stdinfo` table consists of two columns, `country` and `stdcode`, that store the country names and their respective STD codes. The following constants represent the database, its table, and columns:

```
static final String DB_NAME = "Countries.db";
static final String DB_TABLE = "stdinfo";
static final int DB_VERSION = 1;
static final String CREATE_TABLE ="CREATE TABLE " + DB_TABLE +" (_id INTEGER PRIMARY KEY
AUTOINCREMENT, country TEXT not null, stdcode TEXT not null);";
public static final String ID = "_id";
public static final String COUNTRY = "country";
public static final String STDCODE = "stdcode";
```

We can see that the even the table column names are represented as database constants. Using database constants helps to avoid ambiguity and also makes the database transaction statements readable.

Defining the Content URI

To fetch data from the content provider, a suitable URI is required. The structure of URIs used to retrieve data from a content provider is similar to HTTP URIs. The only difference is that URIs start with `content`. The format of the URI is as follows:

```
content://authority/path-segment1/path-segment2/...
```

For example, the URI that identifies STD information numbered 5 in a `stdinfo` database table is

```
content://com.bmharwani.provider.Countries/stdinfo/5
```

where `com.bmharwani.provider` represents the `Authority` part of the URI and `/stdinfo/5` represents the `path-segment` of the URI. The first part of the `path-segment` refers to a collection of objects. For example, `/stdinfo` indicates a collection or a directory of `stdinfo`, whereas `/5` points to a specific row, that is, the row with the ID `5`.

Similarly, the following content URI represents a request for all rows in the content provider:

```
content://com.bmharwani.provider.Countries/stdinfo
```

This code defines the Authority of the content provider as `com.bmharwani.provider.Countries`. It is through this name that the content provider is registered in the `Android Manifest` file. The authority acts as the base URI for this provider. After the authority, the content URI is defined through a static constant, `CONTENT_URI`:

```
static final String AUTHORITY="com.bmharwani.provider.Countries";
static final Uri CONTENT_URI =Uri.parse("content://"+AUTHORITY+"/stdinfo");
```

The `parse()` method used in the preceding code exposes the content provider's URI address. To make it available to the user, each content provider exposes its authority using a static `CONTENT_URI` property.

Remember, the URI contains a unique identifier for the authority, which is used to locate the provider in the provider registry. The authority and path segments are usually declared as constants in a Java class. The retrieved data is in the form of a set of rows and columns represented by an Android cursor object.

Because the content URI can be either of these two forms (request for a single row or all rows), `UriMatcher` is used to analyze the URIs and identify which form it is.

The following code defines a URI Matcher that analyzes the form of a URI and determines whether the URI is a request for all rows or a single row:

```
private static final int ALLROWS = 1;
private static final int SINGLEROW = 2;
private static final UriMatcher URIMATCHER;
static {
URIMATCHER = new UriMatcher(UriMatcher.NO_MATCH);
URIMATCHER.addURI("com.bmharwani.provider.Countries", "stdinfo", ALLROWS);
URIMATCHER.addURI("com.bmharwani.provider.Countries", "stdinfo/#", SINGLE_ROW);
}
```

Here we see that constants are defined to differentiate between the two URI requests. ALLROWS and SINGLEROW are meant to distinguish the two URI forms. A UriMatcher object called URIMATCHER is defined. Thereafter, the UriMatcher object is populated with the two URIs. The URI ending in stdinfo corresponds to a request for all rows, and the one ending in stdinfo/# represents a request for a single row. If the URI ends with a number, the number is the ID of the specific row. If the URI does not end with a number, it refers to all the rows of the table. The content URIs are used while accessing a content provider using a Content Resolver.

It also means that the content provided by content providers is consumed using a Content Resolver. The Content Resolver isolates the data consumer from the data sources. It also provides a common mechanism to share and consume data. We can access the ContentResolver instance using the getContentResolver() method:

```
ContentResolver contentResolver = getContentResolver();
```

It is the Content Resolver that queries and perform transactions on the content providers. That is, the Content Resolver class includes query and transaction methods corresponding to those defined within a content provider. The methods accept the URI of the content provider with which they need to interact and perform the desired transactions.

Defining MIME Types

After we define the content URI, MIME types are defined for a single row or collection of rows. The provider implementation uses these constants to return the MIME types for the incoming URIs. A content provider returns the MIME type of the data it is returning. The MIME type is either a single row or all the rows for the given URI.

For a single row, the MIME type is

```
vnd.android.cursor.item/vnd.company_name.content_type
```

For a collection of rows, the MIME type is

```
vnd.android.cursor.dir/vnd.company_name.content_type
```

The following are examples of different MIME types:

```
public static final String CONTENT_TYPE ="vnd.android.cursor.dir/vnd.countries.
stdinfo";
public static final String CONTENT_ITEM_TYPE
="vnd.android.cursor.item/vnd.countries.stdinfo";
```

We can see that the first part of the MIME type is either `vnd.android.cursor.item` or `vnd.android.cursor.dir`, depending on whether the type represents a specific row or all rows of a table. The second part of the MIME is a combination of the constant `vnd` followed by our company or application name and the actual content type.

> **NOTE**
>
> If the returned data format is specific to a vendor, the MIME type begins with `vnd`; otherwise, the prefix is not required.

Implementing the `getType`, `query`, `insert`, `update`, **and** `delete` Methods

To make the content provider functional, we need to implement the `getType()`, `query()`, `insert()`, `update()`, and `delete()` methods.

Implementing the `getType()` Method

To identify the data type of the content provider, the `getType()` method is overridden. The syntax for using the method is

```
String getType(uri)
```

where `uri` represents the URI that is passed to the method. In the method, the `UriMatcher` object is used, which returns the `vnd.android.cursor.dir/vnd.countries.stdinfo` MIME type for all rows and `vnd.android.cursor.item/vnd.countries.stdinfo` for a single row. In short, the `getType()` method returns a string based on the passed URI that describes the MIME type, as shown here:

```
@Override
public String getType(Uri uri) {
    switch (URIMATCHER.match(uri)){
        case ALLROWS:
            return "vnd.android.cursor.dir/vnd.countries.stdinfo";
        case SINGLEROW:
            return "vnd.android.cursor.item/vnd.countries.stdinfo";
        default:
            throw new IllegalArgumentException("URI not supported: " + uri);
    }
}
```

Implementing the `query()` **Method**

To enable users to query the content provider for the desired row(s), the `query()` method is overridden. The method definition for the `query()` method is

```
Cursor query(Uri uri, String[] projection, String criteria, String[] criteriaValues, String sortColumn)
```

where

- ▶ **uri**—The URI to the content provider.

- ▶ **projection**—A projection that defines the columns we want in the result set.

- ▶ **criteria**—The criteria that define the rows to be returned. The criteria may include ? wildcards that are then replaced by the values supplied through the `criteriaValues` parameter.

- ▶ **criteriaValues**—An array of string values that replace the ? wildcards in the criteria parameter.

- ▶ **sortColumn**—The column name on which we want to sort the returned rows.

Here is the code for implementing the `query()` method:

```
@Override
public Cursor query(Uri uri, String[] projection, String criteria, String[] crite-
riaValues, String sortColumn) {
    SQLiteQueryBuilder queryBuilder = new SQLiteQueryBuilder();
    queryBuilder.setTables(DB_TABLE);
    if (URIMATCHER.match(uri) == SINGLEROW)
        queryBuilder.appendWhere(ID + " = " + uri.getPathSegments().get(1));
    if (sortColumn==null || sortColumn=="")
        sortColumn = "country";
    Cursor c = queryBuilder.query(CountriesDB,projection,criteria,criteriaValues,nul
    l,null,sortColumn);
    c.setNotificationUri(getContext().getContentResolver(), uri);
    return c;
}
```

An `SQLiteQueryBuilder` object is created to which the database table we want to query is associated. The `SQLiteQueryBuilder` is a helper class in `android.database.sqlite` that is used to create and execute SQL queries on an SQLite database instance. Using the `URIMATCHER` object, it is determined whether the query is for a single row or all rows, and the appropriate `Cursor` object is created and returned. The `Cursor` object carries the row(s) that satisfy the specified criteria and are sorted on the country column.

Implementing the `insert()` **Method**

To insert a new row into the content provider, the `insert()` method is overridden. A `ContentValues` object by name `contentValues` is passed, containing the information for the new row, as shown here:

```
Uri insert(Uri uri, ContentValues contentValues)
```

where `uri` represents the URI of the content provider in which we want to insert a row whose information is stored in `contentValues` parameter.

Here is the code for implementing the `insert()` method:

```
@Override
public Uri insert(Uri uri, ContentValues contentValues) {
    long rowID = CountriesDB.insert(DB_TABLE,null,contentValues);
    if (rowID >0) {
        Uri _uri = ContentUris.withAppendedId(CONTENT_URI, rowID);
        getContext().getContentResolver().notifyChange(_uri, null);
        return _uri;
    }
    throw new SQLException("Error: New row could not be inserted" );
}
```

The information of the new row supplied in the `contentValues` parameter is used to insert a new row into the database table. When the insert operation is successful, the ID of the newly inserted row is returned. When we use the `withAppendedId()` method, the returned `rowID` is appended to the `CONTENT_URI` of the content provider. After we insert the row, the `notifyChange()` method of the `ContentResolver` is called to notify any registered observers about the insert operation.

Implementing the `update()` **Method**

The `update()` method is overridden to update the information in the content provider. Depending on the URI passed to the method, either a single row or all the rows in the content provider are updated. The method signature for the `update()` method follows:

```
int update(Uri uri, ContentValues contentValues, String criteria, String[] criteria-
Values)
```

where

> ▶ **uri**—The URI to the content provider.

> ▶ **contentValues**—Stores the new or modified information of the columns.

> ▶ **criteria**—The criteria that define the rows to be updated. The criteria may include ? wildcards that are then replaced by the values supplied through the `criteriaValues` parameter.

> ▶ **criteriaValues**—An array of string values that replace the ? wildcards in the `crite-ria` parameter.

The method returns the count of the number of rows updated. Here is the code for implementing the `update()` method:

```
@Override
public int update(Uri uri, ContentValues contentValues, String criteria, String[]
criteriaValues) {
    int count = 0;
    switch (URIMATCHER.match(uri)){
        case ALLROWS:
            count = CountriesDB.update(DB_TABLE,contentValues,criteria,criteriaValues);
            break;
        case SINGLEROW:
            count = CountriesDB.update(DB_TABLE, contentValues, ID + " = " +
            uri.getPathSegments().get(1) +(!    TextUtils.isEmpty(criteria) ? " AND
            (" +criteria +
            ')': ""),criteriaValues);
            break;
        default: throw new IllegalArgumentException("URI not found: " + uri);
    }
    getContext().getContentResolver().notifyChange(uri, null);
    return count;
}
```

Using the `URIMATCHER` object, we first determine whether the `URI` parameter passed to the method is meant for updating a single row or multiple rows. If the `URI` passed is for a single row, the `ID` of that row is extracted and the information in the `contentValues` parameter is used to update that row. If the `URI` is for updating multiple rows, all the rows that satisfy the condition mentioned in the `criteria` parameter are updated by the information stored in `contentValues` parameter. After we update the row(s), the `notifyChange()` method of the `ContentResolver` is called to notify registered observers about the update operation. The method returns the count of the updated rows.

Implementing the `delete()` Method

The `delete()` method is overridden to delete information in the content provider. Depending on the URI passed to the method, either a single row or all the rows in the content provider are deleted. The method signature for the `delete()` method follows:

```
int delete(Uri uri, String criteria, String[] criteriaValues)
```

where

- **uri**—The URI to the content provider.

- **criteria**—The criteria that define the rows to be deleted.

- **criteriaValues**—An array of string values that replace the ? wildcards in the criteria parameter.

The method returns the count of the number of rows deleted. Here is the code for implementing the `delete()` method:

```java
@Override
public int delete(Uri rowUri, String criteria, String[] criteriaValues) {
    int count=0;
    switch (URIMATCHER.match(rowUri)){
        case ALLROWS:
            count = CountriesDB.delete(DB_TABLE, criteria, criteriaValues);
            break;
        case SINGLEROW:
            String id = rowUri.getPathSegments().get(1);
            count = CountriesDB.delete(DB_TABLE, ID + " = " + id
            +(!TextUtils.isEmpty(criteria) ? " AND
            (" +criteria + ')': ""),criteriaValues);
            break;
        default: throw new IllegalArgumentException("URI not found: " + rowUri);
    }
    getContext().getContentResolver().notifyChange(rowUri, null);
    return count;
}
```

Using the URIMATCHER object, we determine whether the URI parameter passed to the method is meant for deleting a single row or multiple rows. If the URI passed is for a single row, the ID of that row is extracted and the row is deleted. If the URI is for deleting multiple rows, all the rows that satisfy the condition mentioned in the criteria parameter are deleted. After we delete the row(s), registered observers are notified about the delete operation. The method returns the count of the deleted rows.

To implement all five content provider methods, the code shown in Listing 12.5 is written into the CountriesProvider.java Java file.

LISTING 12.5   Code Written into CountriesProvider.java

```java
package com.androidunleashed.createcontentproviderapp;

import android.content.ContentProvider;
import android.content.UriMatcher;
import android.net.Uri;
import android.database.sqlite.SQLiteOpenHelper;
import android.database.sqlite.SQLiteDatabase;
import android.content.Context;
import android.content.ContentValues;
import android.content.ContentUris;
import android.database.SQLException;
import android.database.Cursor;
import android.text.TextUtils;
```

```
import android.database.sqlite.SQLiteQueryBuilder;
import android.content.ContentResolver;

public class CountriesProvider extends ContentProvider {
    static final String DB_NAME = "Countries.db";
    static final String DB_TABLE = "stdinfo";
    static final int DB_VERSION = 1;
    static final String CREATE_TABLE ="CREATE TABLE " + DB_TABLE +" (_id INTEGER
PRIMARY
KEY AUTOINCREMENT, country TEXT not null, stdcode TEXT not null);";
    static final String ID = "_id";
    static final String COUNTRY = "country";
    static final String STDCODE = "stdcode";
    static final String AUTHORITY="com.bmharwani.provider.Countries";
    static final Uri CONTENT_URI =Uri.parse("content://"+AUTHORITY+"/stdinfo");
    static final int ALLROWS = 1;
    static final int SINGLEROW = 2;
    private static final UriMatcher URIMATCHER;
    static{
        URIMATCHER = new UriMatcher(UriMatcher.NO_MATCH);
        URIMATCHER.addURI(AUTHORITY, "stdinfo", ALLROWS);
        URIMATCHER.addURI(AUTHORITY, "stdinfo/#", SINGLEROW);
    }
    SQLiteDatabase CountriesDB;
    public static final String CONTENT_ITEM_TYPE =  ContentResolver.CURSOR_ITEM_
BASE_TYPE+"/stdinfo";

    @Override
    public boolean onCreate() {
        Context context = getContext();
        SQHelper helper = new SQHelper(context);
        CountriesDB = helper.getWritableDatabase();
        return (CountriesDB == null)? false:true;
    }

    @Override
    public String getType(Uri uri) {
        switch (URIMATCHER.match(uri)){
            case ALLROWS:
                return "vnd.android.cursor.dir/vnd.countries.stdinfo";
            case SINGLEROW:
                return "vnd.android.cursor.item/vnd.countries.stdinfo";
            default:
                throw new IllegalArgumentException("Unsupported URI: " + uri);
        }
    }
}
```

```java
@Override
public Cursor query(Uri uri, String[] projection, String criteria, String[]
criteriaValues, String sortColumn) {
    SQLiteQueryBuilder queryBuilder = new SQLiteQueryBuilder();
    queryBuilder.setTables(DB_TABLE);
    if (URIMATCHER.match(uri) == SINGLEROW)
        queryBuilder.appendWhere(ID + " = " + uri.getPathSegments().get(1));
    if (sortColumn==null || sortColumn=="")
        sortColumn = "country";
    Cursor c = queryBuilder.query(CountriesDB,projection,criteria,criteriaValues
    ,null,null,sortColumn);
    c.setNotificationUri(getContext().getContentResolver(), uri);
    return c;
}


@Override
public Uri insert(Uri uri, ContentValues contentValues) {
    long rowID = CountriesDB.insert(DB_TABLE,null,contentValues);
    if (rowID >0) {
        Uri _uri = ContentUris.withAppendedId(CONTENT_URI, rowID);
        getContext().getContentResolver().notifyChange(_uri, null);
        return _uri;
    }
    throw new SQLException("Error: New row could not be inserted ");
}


@Override
public int update(Uri uri, ContentValues contentValues, String criteria,
String[] criteriaValues) {
    int count = 0;
    switch (URIMATCHER.match(uri)){
        case ALLROWS:
            count = CountriesDB.update(DB_TABLE,contentValues,criteria,criteria
            Values);
            break;
        case SINGLEROW:
            count = CountriesDB.update(DB_TABLE, contentValues, ID + " = " +
            uri.getPathSegments().get(1) +(!    TextUtils.isEmpty(criteria) ? "
            AND (" +criteria +
            ")": ""),criteriaValues);
            break;
        default: throw new IllegalArgumentException("URI not found: " + uri);
    }
    getContext().getContentResolver().notifyChange(uri, null);
    return count;
```

```java
        }

        @Override
        public int delete(Uri rowUri, String criteria, String[] criteriaValues) {
            int count=0;
            switch (URIMATCHER.match(rowUri)){
                case ALLROWS:
                    count = CountriesDB.delete(DB_TABLE, criteria, criteriaValues);
                    break;
                case SINGLEROW:
                    String id = rowUri.getPathSegments().get(1);
                    count = CountriesDB.delete(DB_TABLE, ID + " = " + id +(!TextUtils.
                    isEmpty(criteria) ? " AND (" +criteria + ')': ""),criteriaValues);
                    break;
                default: throw new IllegalArgumentException("URI not found: " + rowUri);
            }
            getContext().getContentResolver().notifyChange(rowUri, null);
            return count;
        }

        private static class SQHelper extends SQLiteOpenHelper {
            SQHelper(Context context) {
                super(context, DB_NAME, null, DB_VERSION);
            }

            @Override
            public void onCreate(SQLiteDatabase db) {
                db.execSQL(CREATE_TABLE);
            }

            @Override
            public void onUpgrade(SQLiteDatabase db, int oldVersion, int newVersion) {
                db.execSQL("DROP TABLE IF EXISTS "+ DB_TABLE);
                onCreate(db);
            }
        }
    }
}
```

We can see that the `onCreate()` method is overridden to initialize the data source to be accessed through the content provider. In the method, we define an `SQHelper` object and open the `Countries.db` database in write mode.

To insert rows into the content provider and access its existing information, we write the code shown in Listing 12.6 into the `CreateContentProviderAppActivity.java` Java activity file.

LISTING 12.6   Code Written into `CreateContentProviderAppActivity.java`

```java
package com.androidunleashed.createcontentproviderapp;

import android.app.Activity;
import android.os.Bundle;
import android.view.View;
import android.content.ContentValues;
import android.widget.Toast;
import android.widget.EditText;
import android.widget.Button;
import android.content.Intent;

public class CreateContentProviderAppActivity extends Activity {
    @Override
    public void onCreate(Bundle savedInstanceState) {
        super.onCreate(savedInstanceState);
        setContentView(R.layout.activity_create_content_provider_app);
        Button addStdButton = (Button)this.findViewById(R.id.add_stdinfo);
        addStdButton.setOnClickListener(new Button.OnClickListener(){
            @Override
            public void onClick(View v) {
                ContentValues contentValues = new ContentValues();
                contentValues.put(CountriesProvider.COUNTRY, ((EditText)
                findViewById(R.id.country_name)).getText().toString());
                contentValues.put(CountriesProvider.STDCODE, ((EditText)
                findViewById(R.id.std_code)).getText().toString());
                getContentResolver().insert(CountriesProvider.CONTENT_URI, content
                Values);
                Toast.makeText(CreateContentProviderAppActivity.this, "Row
                inserted",
Toast.LENGTH_SHORT).show();
            }
        });

        Button listStdButton = (Button)this.findViewById(R.id.list_stdinfo);
        listStdButton.setOnClickListener(new Button.OnClickListener(){
            public void onClick(View v) {
                startActivity(new Intent(CreateContentProviderAppActivity.this,
                ShowSTDActivity.class));
            }
        });
    }
}
```

## 12

We can see that the `add_stdinfo` and `list_stdinfo` Button controls are accessed from the layout file and mapped to the `addStdButton` and `listStdButton` Button objects. The `addStdButton` button performs the insert operation, and `listStdButton` shows the existing information in the content provider.

To insert a row into the content provider, we first collect it in the `ContentValues` object. The `ContentValues` is a dictionary of key/value pairs where we can store the information of a single record. Thereafter, it is the job of the `ContentResolver` to insert that record into the content provider using a URI. `ContentResolver` resolves the URI reference to the right provider and inserts the information held by the `ContentValues` object into the provider.

To add information about the country STD code, we fetch the data entered by the user in the two `EditText` controls. Thereafter, we create a new `ContentValues` object and then populate it with the information entered in the `EditText` controls. Because our content provider is in the same package from where we are accessing it, we use the `CountriesProvider.COUNTRY` and `CountriesProvider.STDCODE` constants to refer to the `country` and `stdcode` columns of the database table. If the content provider is accessed from another package, then instead of using constants, we have to specify the column names. The content URI is referred to via a fully qualified name, as shown here:

```
ContentValues contentValues = new ContentValues();
contentValues.put("country", ((EditText)
findViewById(R.id.country_name)).getText().toString());
contentValues.put("stdcode", ((EditText) findViewById(R.id.std_code)).getText().
toString());
Uri uri = getContentResolver().insert(
Uri.parse("content://com.bmharwani.provider.Countries/stdinfo"), contentValues);
```

When the `listStdButton` is clicked, it starts another `ShowSTDActivity` activity, which we soon add to our project. The `ShowSTDActivity` shows existing information in the content provider by fetching all of its rows and displaying it through the `ListView` control.

To display information in the content provider through a `ListView`, add a layout file called `showstd.xml` to the `res/layout` folder. To define a `ListView` control in the `showstd.xml` file, add the code shown in Listing 12.7.

LISTING 12.7   Code Written into the `showstd.xml` File

```xml
<?xml version="1.0" encoding="utf-8"?>
<LinearLayout xmlns:android="http://schemas.android.com/apk/res/android"
    android:layout_width="match_parent"
    android:layout_height="match_parent"
    android:orientation="vertical" >
    <ListView
        android:id="@android:id/list"
        android:layout_width="match_parent"
        android:layout_height="match_parent"
```

```
            android:drawSelectorOnTop="false" />
</LinearLayout>
```

We can see that a `ListView` control with the ID `list` is defined in the layout file. For the new activity, add a Java class file called `ShowSTDActivity.java` to the `com.androidun-leashed.createcontentproviderapp` package of the project. To fetch all the rows from the content provider and to display them through the `ListView` control, we use loaders.

Using Loaders

As the name suggests, loaders are used to load data asynchronously. They are accessible in an Activity and Fragment through `LoaderManager`. The `LoaderManager` handles the life cycle of loaders, along with the underlying queries and cursors. Loaders can load any kind of data source, but we focus on cursor loading.

Using `CursorLoaders`

The `CursorLoader` class is used for managing cursors. It manages cursor life cycles, performs asynchronous queries against content providers, monitors changes in the included query, and so on. It also confirms whether the `Cursor` is closed when the Activity is terminated.

To show the rows in the content providers through the `ListView` by using `CursorLoaders`, write the code shown in Listing 12.8 into `ShowSTDActivity.java`.

LISTING 12.8   Code Written into `ShowSTDActivity.java`

```java
package com.androidunleashed.createcontentproviderapp;

import android.app.ListActivity;
import android.os.Bundle;
import android.widget.SimpleCursorAdapter;
import android.app.LoaderManager.LoaderCallbacks;
import android.content.CursorLoader;
import android.content.Loader;
import android.database.Cursor;
import android.widget.ListView;
import android.content.Intent;
import android.net.Uri;
import android.view.View;

public class ShowSTDActivity extends ListActivity implements LoaderCallbacks<Cursor>
{
    private SimpleCursorAdapter adapter;

    @Override
    protected void onCreate(Bundle savedInstanceState) {
        super.onCreate(savedInstanceState);
```

```
        setContentView(R.layout.showstd);
        String[] columns = new String[] { CountriesProvider.COUNTRY};
        int[] toIds = new int[] {android.R.id.text1};
        getLoaderManager().initLoader(0, null,this);
        adapter = new SimpleCursorAdapter(this, android.R.layout.simple_list_item_1,
        null, columns, toIds, 0);
        setListAdapter(adapter);
    }

    @Override
    public Loader<Cursor> onCreateLoader(int id, Bundle args) {
        String[] projection = new String[] {CountriesProvider.ID, CountriesProvider.
        COUNTRY, CountriesProvider.STDCODE} ;
        CursorLoader cursorLoader = new CursorLoader(this, CountriesProvider.CON
        TENT_URI, projection, null, null, null);
        return cursorLoader;
    }

    @Override
    public void onLoadFinished(Loader<Cursor> loader, Cursor data) {
        adapter.swapCursor(data);
    }

    @Override
    public void onLoaderReset(Loader<Cursor> loader) {
        adapter.swapCursor(null);
    }

    @Override
    protected void onListItemClick(ListView l, View v, int position, long id) {
        super.onListItemClick(l, v, position, id);
        Intent intent = new Intent(this, MaintainSTDActivity.class);
        Uri uri = Uri.parse(CountriesProvider.CONTENT_URI + "/" + id);
        intent.putExtra(CountriesProvider.CONTENT_ITEM_TYPE, uri);
        startActivity(intent);
    }
}
```

To use a Cursor Loader, we need to create a new `LoaderManager.LoaderCallbacks` implementation:

```
public class ShowSTDActivity extends ListActivity implements LoaderCallbacks<Cursor>
```

We can see that the Loader Manager is accessed by calling the `getLoaderManager()` method. To initialize a new loader, the Loader Manager's `initLoader()` method is called.

The syntax for using the `initLoader()` method follows:

```
getLoaderManager().initLoader(loader_ID, bundle, loader_Callbacks);
```

where

- `loader_ID` represents the loader identifier.
- `bundle` represents the optional arguments bundle. We can pass a null value to this parameter if it isn't required.
- `loader_callbacks` is the reference to the Loader Callback implementation.

Example:

```
Bundle args = null;
getLoaderManager().initLoader(0, args,this);
```

Here, we have user 0 as the loader identifier. If a loader corresponding to the specified identifier does not exist, it is created.

Whenever the `initLoader()` method is called, the existing loader is returned. To re-create a loader, the `restartLoader()` method is called. Here is the syntax for using the method:

```
getLoaderManager().restartLoader(loader_ID, bundle, loader_Callbacks);
```

Through `SimpleCursorAdapter`, the data in the `CountriesProvider.COUNTRY` column of the content provider is accessed and displayed through the `ListView` control.

The Loader Callbacks consist of three handlers:

- **onCreateLoader()**—Called when the loader is initialized. It creates and returns a new `CursorLoader` object. The `CursorLoader` carries the columns specified in the projection `String` array.
- **onLoadFinished()**—When the Loader Manager has completed the asynchronous query, the `onLoadFinished` handler is called, with the data `Cursor` passed in as a parameter. We use this `Cursor` to update our List adapter.
- **onLoaderReset()**—When the Loader Manager resets the Cursor Loader, `onLoaderReset` is called. This handler is used to release any references to data returned by the query. In this method, we remove the existing result `Cursor` from the List adapter.

The `Cursor` is automatically closed by the Loader Manager, so there is no need to explicitly close it.

When any country name item displayed via `ListView` is clicked, the `onListItemClick()` callback method is called. In the `onListItemClick()` method, we start another activity called `MaintainSTDActivity.class`. To the `MaintainSTDActivity.class`, we pass the URI of the row—the selected country. In the `MaintainSTDActivity` we perform two tasks, delete and update content, in the content provider. That is, we display the selected country name and its STD code through `EditText` controls and provide two `Button` controls, `Update` and `Delete`, to the user. The user can modify the information in the content provider by modifying the data displayed in the `EditText` controls followed by clicking `Update`. The user can delete the row from the content provider by clicking `Delete`.

To display the country name and the STD country code selected from the `ListView`, we add a layout file called `maintainstd.xml` to the `res/layout` folder and add the code shown in Listing 12.9.

LISTING 12.9   Code Written into `maintainstd.xml`

```xml
<?xml version="1.0" encoding="utf-8"?>
<RelativeLayout xmlns:android="http://schemas.android.com/apk/res/android"
    android:layout_width="match_parent"
    android:layout_height="match_parent" >
    <TextView
        android:id="@+id/country_view"
        android:layout_width="wrap_content"
        android:layout_height="wrap_content"
        android:text="Country Name" />
    <EditText
        android:id="@+id/country_name"
        android:layout_height="wrap_content"
        android:layout_width="250dp"
        android:layout_toRightOf="@id/country_view" />
    <TextView
        android:id="@+id/stdcode_view"
        android:layout_width="wrap_content"
        android:layout_height="wrap_content"
        android:text="STD Code"
        android:layout_below="@id/country_name" />
    <EditText
        android:id="@+id/std_code"
        android:layout_height="wrap_content"
        android:layout_width="100dp"
        android:layout_marginLeft="20dip"
        android:layout_toRightOf="@id/stdcode_view"
        android:layout_below="@id/country_name" />
    <Button
        android:text="Delete"
        android:id="@+id/delete_stdinfo"
        android:layout_width="wrap_content"
        android:layout_height="wrap_content"
        android:layout_below="@id/std_code"
        android:layout_marginLeft="70dip"  />
    <Button
```

```
            android:text="Update"
            android:id="@+id/update_stdinfo"
            android:layout_width="wrap_content"
            android:layout_height="wrap_content"
            android:layout_toRightOf="@id/delete_stdinfo"
            android:layout_below="@id/std_code"
            android:layout_marginLeft="10dip"/>
</RelativeLayout>
```

We can see that the two EditText controls used for displaying the country names and the STD code are assigned the IDs country_name and std_code. The two Button controls with the Delete and Update captions are assigned the IDs delete_stdinfo and update_stdinfo. The IDs are used to identify and access these controls in the Java code. To create a new activity, add a Java class file called MaintainSTDActivity.java to the com.androidunleashed.createcontentproviderapp package of the project. To delete and update information in the content provider, write the code shown in Listing 12.10 into the MaintainSTDActivity.java file.

LISTING 12.10   Code Written into MaintainSTDActivity.java

```
package com.androidunleashed.createcontentproviderapp;

import android.os.Bundle;
import android.app.Activity;
import android.widget.EditText;
import android.widget.Button;
import android.net.Uri;
import android.content.ContentValues;
import android.database.Cursor;
import android.view.View;
import android.widget.Toast;

public class MaintainSTDActivity extends Activity {
    EditText countryName , stdCode ;
    Uri uri;
    @Override
    protected void onCreate(Bundle savedInstanceState) {
        super.onCreate(savedInstanceState);
        setContentView(R.layout.maintainstd);
        countryName  = (EditText) findViewById(R.id.country_name);
        stdCode  = (EditText) findViewById(R.id.std_code);
        Bundle extras = getIntent().getExtras();
        uri = (extras == null) ? null: (Uri) extras.getParcelable(CountriesProvider.
        CONTENT_ITEM_TYPE);
        if (extras != null) {
            uri = extras.getParcelable(CountriesProvider.CONTENT_ITEM_TYPE);
```

```
            String[] projection = new String[] {CountriesProvider.ID, CountriesPro
            vider.COUNTRY, CountriesProvider.STDCODE} ;
            Cursor cursor = getContentResolver().query(uri, projection, null, null,
            null);
            if (cursor != null) {
                cursor.moveToFirst();
                countryName .setText(cursor.getString(cursor.getColumnIndexOrThrow
                (CountriesProvider.COUNTRY)));
                stdCode .setText(cursor.getString(cursor.getColumnIndexOrThrow
                (CountriesProvider.STDCODE)));
                cursor.close();
            }
        }
        Button deleteStdInfo  = (Button) findViewById(R.id.delete_stdinfo);
        Button updateStdInfo = (Button) findViewById(R.id.update_stdinfo);
        deleteStdInfo .setOnClickListener(new Button.OnClickListener(){
            @Override
            public void onClick(View v) {
                int count = getContentResolver().delete(uri, null, null);
                if(count >0)
                    Toast.makeText(MaintainSTDActivity.this, "Row deleted", Toast.
                    LENGTH_SHORT).show();
            }
        });

        updateStdInfo.setOnClickListener(new Button.OnClickListener(){
            @Override
            public void onClick(View v) {
                ContentValues contentValues = new ContentValues();
                contentValues.put(CountriesProvider.COUNTRY, countryName .getText().
                toString());
                contentValues.put(CountriesProvider.STDCODE, stdCode .getText().
                toString());
                getContentResolver().update(uri, contentValues,null,null);
                Toast.makeText(MaintainSTDActivity.this, "Row updated", Toast.
                LENGTH_SHORT).show();
            }
        });
    }
}
```

We access the EditText controls with the country_name and std_code IDs from the main-tainstd.xml layout file and map them to the countryName and stdCode EditText objects. We access the URI of the selected country name from the ListView that is passed through the Bundle object. Thereafter, we call the query() method to access the row from the content provider with the specified URI. The query() method is called to get the STD code of the selected country so that the country name and its STD code can be assigned and displayed through `EditText` controls.

To delete a row, we call the `delete()` method of the Content Resolver. To the `delete()` method, the content URI of the row to be deleted is passed. To update a row, we call the `update()` method of the Content Resolver. To the `update()` method, we pass the URI of the row to be updated along with the `ContentValues` object that contains the updated or new content of the respective columns.

> **NOTE**
>
> The `criteria` and `criteriaValues` parameters of the `delete()` and `update()` methods are set to null while deleting or updating a single row.

Registering Content Providers

To enable Content Resolvers to discover our content providers, they must be registered in the application manifest file. The provider tag along with its `android:name` and `android:authorities` attributes are used to register the content providers. The `android:name` attribute is the provider's class name, and the `android:authorities` attribute is used to define the base URI of the provider's authority. In our application, the provider's class name is `CountriesProvider`. The format for defining a content provider's authority follows:

```
com.<CompanyName>.provider.<ApplicationName>
```

Assuming the `CompanyName` is `bmharwani` and the `ApplicationName` is `Countries`, the base URI of our provider's authority is `com.bmharwani.provider.Countries`.

Hence, the complete provider tag used to register our content provider is

```
<provider android:name=".CountriesProvider"
android:authorities="com.bmharwani.provider.Countries">
```

Recall that the content provider's authority is used by the Content Resolver to find the database we want to access. Listing 12.11 shows the code in the `AndroidManifest.xml` file. The code in bold is the added code; the rest is the default code. We can see that the `ShowSTDActivity` and `MaintainSTDActivity` activities added to our application are also defined in the manifest file so that our application can identify them.

LISTING 12.11   Code Written into `AndroidManifest.xml`

```
<manifest xmlns:android="http://schemas.android.com/apk/res/android"
    package="com.androidunleashed.createcontentproviderapp"
    android:versionCode="1"
    android:versionName="1.0" >
    <uses-sdk android:minSdkVersion="8"
```

```
        android:targetSdkVersion="15" />
    <application
        android:icon="@drawable/ic_launcher"
        android:label="@string/app_name"
        android:theme="@style/AppTheme" >
        <activity
            android:name=".CreateContentProviderAppActivity"
            android:label="@string/title_activity_create_content_provider_app" >
            <intent-filter>
                <action android:name="android.intent.action.MAIN" />
                <category android:name="android.intent.category.LAUNCHER" />
            </intent-filter>
        </activity>
        <activity android:name=".ShowSTDActivity" android:label="@string/app_name" />
        <activity android:name=".MaintainSTDActivity" android:label="@string/app_
        name" />
        <provider android:name="CountriesProvider"
android:authorities="com.bmharwani.provider.Countries">
        </provider>
    </application>
</manifest>
```

After running the application, we see the screen shown in Figure 12.4 (left). We use this screen to enter country names and their respective STD codes. After entering each record, click Add STD Info to save it in the content provider. A Toast message Row inserted appears after each successful insertion. When we click the Show STD Info button after inserting rows in the content provider, we see all the countries listed in the ListView (see Figure 12.4—middle). After we select a country, its details are displayed, as shown in Figure 12.4 (right).

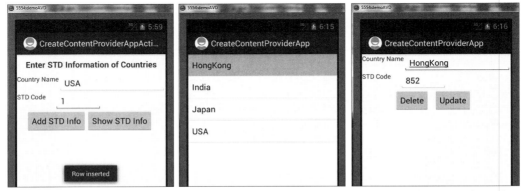

FIGURE 12.4   Entering the country name and STD code information (left), information from the content provider accessed and displayed (middle), and information about the selected country displayed (right)

To modify the country name or STD code, simply modify the content in the `EditText` control and click `Update` (see Figure 12.5—left). After we click the `Update` button, the information in the content provider is updated. Figure 12.5 (middle) shows the updated row. The Toast message `Row updated` appears when a row is successfully updated. After we click the `Delete` button, the selected country and its STD code are deleted from the content provider and a Toast message `Row deleted` appears on the screen, as shown in Figure 12.5 (middle). Figure 12.5 (right) confirms that the selected row was deleted from the content provider, as it is no longer shown in the `ListView` control.

FIGURE 12.5   Updating information in the content provider (left), deleting information from the content provider (middle), and existing information of the content provider accessed and displayed (right)

Summary

In this chapter, we saw how to use the Android Content URI to access built-in content providers. We also created our own content provider. We saw how to define a provider, its database, Content URI, and MIME types. We saw how to implement the `getType`, `query`, `insert`, `update`, and `delete` methods required to make a content provider functional. We learned to use loaders to fetch information from the content providers and saw how to register content providers.

The next chapter focuses on creating and consuming services. We learn to move processes to the background threads using the `Handler` and `AsyncTask` classes and how to download and display images from the Internet. Finally, the chapter explains how to create our own Bind Service and the procedure to consume SOAP Services.

# CHAPTER 13

Creating and Consuming Services

Performing tasks in the background increases application efficiency. One way to handle background processing is to use an Android service. A service is an application component that can perform long-running operations in the background and does not provide a user interface.

Moving Tasks to Background Threads

All Android application components such as activities, services, and broadcast receivers run in the main application thread. That is, all user interface-related tasks are performed by the main application thread. To increase application efficiency, I recommend moving long-running or asynchronous transactions that could affect usability or freeze the UI to background threads. Unimportant processing here means the processing tasks that don't directly interact with the user interface. For example, file operations, database transactions, and other similar tasks for which the time factor is not important can be moved to a background thread.

> **NOTE**
>
> Android supports application of threads to perform asynchronous processing.

There are two ways of moving processing tasks to the background:

▶ Using `Handler` classes

▶ Using `AsyncTask` classes

Using the Handler Class

One of the ways to process tasks in the background is to implement our own threads and use the Handler class to synchronize with them. The handler is associated with the thread from which it is created. That is, we can execute a block of code on the thread from which the handler is instantiated. The two ways with which we can communicate with the handler are through messages and runnable objects. After we create an object from the Handler class, it processes Messages and Runnable objects associated with the current Thread MessageQueue. The tasks to be performed by the current thread are kept in the MessageQueue waiting for their execution.

To process messages, the handleMessage() is overridden. To process Runnable objects, the post() method is used. The thread can post messages via the sendMessage(Message msg) method or via the sendEmptyMessage() method.

To understand the concept of using the Handler class, let's create an application that displays sequence numbers from 1 to 10 using threads. Name the application HandlerApp. Because we just want to display sequence numbers in this application, we only need to use a TextView control. The code shown in Listing 13.1 is written into activity_handler_app. xml to define a TextView control.

LISTING 13.1   Code in the activity_handler_app.xml Layout File

```
<LinearLayout xmlns:android="http://schemas.android.com/apk/res/android"
    android:layout_width="match_parent"
    android:layout_height="match_parent"
    android:orientation="vertical" >
    <TextView
        android:id="@+id/sequenceview"
        android:layout_width="match_parent"
        android:layout_height="wrap_content" />
</LinearLayout>
```

We can see that the TextView control is assigned the sequenceview ID. The ID is used to identify and use it in the Java code. To define a handle and send and receive messages through it, write the code shown in Listing 13.2 into the HandlerAppActivity.java Java activity file.

LISTING 13.2   Code in the HandlerAppActivity.java Java Activity File

```
package com.androidunleashed.handlerapp;

import android.app.Activity;
import android.os.Bundle;
import android.widget.TextView;
import android.os.Handler;
import android.os.Message;
```

```
public class HandlerAppActivity extends Activity {
    TextView seqView;

    @Override
    public void onCreate(Bundle savedInstanceState) {
        super.onCreate(savedInstanceState);
        setContentView(R.layout.activity_handler_app);
        seqView=(TextView)findViewById(R.id.sequenceview);
    }

    Handler handler = new Handler() {
        @Override
        public void handleMessage(Message msg) {
            seqView.setText(msg.obj.toString());
        }
    };

    @Override
    protected void onStart() {
        super.onStart();
        Thread thread=new Thread(new Runnable() {
            @Override
            public void run() {
                for(int i=1;i<=10;i++){
                    try {
                        Thread.sleep(1000);
                        Message msg = new Message();
                        msg.obj=String.valueOf(i);
                        handler.sendMessage(msg);
                    } catch (InterruptedException e) {
                        e.printStackTrace();
                    }
                }
            }
        });
        thread.start();
    }
}
```

Here we see that the TextView control from the layout file is accessed and mapped to the TextView object seqView. In the onStart() method, we use the Thread class together with a Runnable object. The run() method starts the execution of the thread. To display sequence numbers from 1 to 10 through the TextView control in the run() method, we create a Bundle object called b and add the data to it. Because we want to print a sequence of numbers, we add each number from 1 to 10 to the obj variable of the Message instance msg. After we add a sequence value to the `obj` variable, through the `Handler` object, the message is sent.

We also create a `Handler` object called `handler`. In its callback method, `handlemessage()`, the message sent through the `run()` method is received through the `msg` parameter. The `obj` variable (the sequence number in the `msg` parameter) is accessed from the `msg` parameter and displayed through the `TextView` control.

After we run the application, the sequence numbers are displayed beginning from 1 (see Figure 13.1—left). Between every sequence number, there is a time delay of 1 second. The application stops at the number 10, as shown in Figure 13.1 (right).

FIGURE 13.1   The application begins by displaying the sequence number 1 (left) and stops at sequence number 10 (right).

Using the `AsyncTask` Class

The `AsyncTask` class not only creates the `Thread` but manages it and creates an asynchronous task for performing the processing in the background. The `AsyncTask` class provides us with event handlers that synchronize with the `Thread` to show the progress and completion of the task.

To instantiate an `AsyncTask`, we extend the `AsyncTask` class and provide three parameters: `Input Parameters`, `Progress Values`, and `Result Values`. If we don't want to provide any of the parameters, simply replace it with `Void`. The subclass should also override the following event handlers:

▶ **doInBackground**—This method is executed in the background thread. The code that doesn't interact with the user is placed in this handler. `Input Parameters` is passed to this method as input. From within this method, the `publishProgress()` method is called, and the `onProgressUpdate()` method is executed in the main thread. When we use the `publishProgress()` and `onProgressUpdate()` methods, the background thread communicates with the main thread to update the UI elements to indicate progress of the work. Remember, the code in this method runs in a separate background thread.

▶ **onProgressUpdate**—Override this handler to update the UI to indicate progress in the task. This handler receives the set of parameters passed in to `publishProgress()`. This handler is synchronized with the thread when executed, so you can safely modify UI elements.

▶ **onPostExecute**—As the name suggests, this method is called after the `doInBackground()` method is complete. The `Result Values` returned by the `doInBackground()` method are passed in to this event handler. This handler can be used to indicate when the asynchronous task is complete.

The `AsyncTask` class also provides the following two helpful callback methods:

▶ **onPreExecute**—From the name of the method, it is clear that it is called before the `doInBackground()` method is called. This method runs in the main thread, and setup or similar tasks are performed in this method.

▶ **onCancelled**—Manages the cancellation of the thread. The method interrupts the execution of the thread and also prevents execution of the `onPostExecute()` method.

NOTE

Overriding `onPostExecute`, `onPreExecute`, and `onProgressUpdate` is optional.

Let's apply all the knowledge gained so far in creating an application that prints a sequence of numbers from 1 to 10 through a background thread. Name the new application `AsyncApp`. To display a sequence of numbers from 1 to 10, we need a `TextView` control. After we define a `TextView` control, `main.xml` appears as shown in Listing 13.3.

LISTING 13.3   Code in the `main.xml` Layout File

```
<LinearLayout xmlns:android="http://schemas.android.com/apk/res/android"
    android:layout_width="match_parent"
    android:layout_height="match_parent"
    android:orientation="vertical" >
    <TextView
        android:id="@+id/sequenceview"
        android:layout_width="match_parent"
        android:layout_height="wrap_content" />
</LinearLayout>
```

We can see that the `TextView` control is assigned the `sequenceview` ID to identify and use it in the Java code. To extend the `AsyncTask` class and print the sequence numbers from 1 to 10 through it, modify the `AsyncAppActivity.java` file to appear as shown in Listing 13.4.

LISTING 13.4   Code in the `AsyncAppActivity.java` Java Activity File

```
package com.androidunleashed.asyncapp;

import android.app.Activity;
import android.os.Bundle;
```

```java
import android.widget.TextView;
import android.os.AsyncTask;

public class AsyncAppActivity extends Activity {
    TextView seqView;

    @Override
    public void onCreate(Bundle savedInstanceState) {
        super.onCreate(savedInstanceState);
        setContentView(R.layout.activity_async_app);
        seqView=(TextView) findViewById(R.id.sequenceview);
        new PrintSequenceTask().execute(1);
    }

    private class PrintSequenceTask extends AsyncTask<Integer, Integer, Void> {
        @Override
        protected void onPreExecute() {
            seqView.setText("Sequence numbers begins");
        }

        @Override
        protected Void doInBackground(Integer... args) {
            for (int i = args[0]; i <= 10; i++) {
                publishProgress(i);
                try {
                    Thread.sleep(1000);
                } catch (InterruptedException e) {
                    e.printStackTrace();
                }
            }
            return null;
        }

        @Override
        protected void onProgressUpdate(Integer... args) {
            seqView.setText(args[0].toString());
        }

        @Override
        protected void onPostExecute(Void result) {
            seqView.setText("Sequence numbers over");
        }
    }
}
```

We can see in the code that the class `PrintSequenceTask` extends the `AsyncTask` class. Because we want to print the sequence of numbers beginning from 1, it is passed as an `Input Parameter` while instantiating the `PrintSequence` class. Before execution of the `doInBackground()` method, the `onPreExecute()` method is executed that displays the text `Sequence numbers begins` through the `TextView` control. After execution of the `onPreExecute()` method, the `doInBackground()` method is executed, and the value assigned to the `Input Parameter` is passed to this method and assigned to the `args` array.

Inside the `doInBackground()` method, the `for` loop is executed, beginning from the first element in the `args` array (value 1) up to value 10. In the `for` loop, the `publishProgress()` method is executed, and each `for` loop value is passed to this method as a parameter. That is, the sequence numbers from 1 to 10 are assigned as parameters to the `publishProgress()` method. When the `publishProgress()` method is called, the `onProgressUpdate()` method is executed in the main thread with the same parameter value as that assigned to the `publishProgress()` method. This also means that the sequence numbers from 1 to 10 are assigned to the `args` parameter of the `onProgressUpdate()` method.

In the `onProgressUpdate()` method, the sequence numbers assigned to the `args` parameter are displayed through the `TextView` control. Between each sequence number, a time delay of 1 second is introduced. Finally, when the `doInBackground()` method is over and all the sequence numbers have been displayed, the `onPostExecute()` method is executed, which displays `Sequence numbers over` through the `TextView` control.

NOTE

Each `AsyncTask` instance can be executed only once. An exception is thrown if we try to execute it for the second time.

After we run the application, the first message that appears through the `TextView` control is `Sequence numbers begins` (see Figure 13.2—left). The text message is followed by the sequence numbers from 1 to 10. Each sequence number is displayed after the time delay of 1 second (see Figure 13.2—middle). Finally, the message `Sequence numbers over` appears through the `TextView` control (see Figure 13.2—right).

FIGURE 13.2   The text message `Sequence numbers begins` displayed on application startup (left), the sequence numbers from 1 to 10 appear on the screen (middle), and the text message `Sequence numbers over` appears after the sequence numbers (right).

Accessing Data from the Internet

The most common way to access data from the Internet is to use `HttpURLConnection`. `HttpURLConnection` fetches information about the data referenced by the URL. The information includes the length of the content, content type, and date-time information. The steps for accessing data from the Internet using `HttpURLConnection` are as follows:

- ▶ A URL object is created with the URL pointing to the data to be accessed.
- ▶ Use the URL object to open the connection to the server using the `OpenHttpConnection()` method.
- ▶ Configure the request to access data from the remote HTTP server.
- ▶ Define an `InputStream` through the `HttpURLConnection`.
- ▶ Data is read through the `InputStream` and finally it is closed.
- ▶ To access data asynchronously, wrap the code in a subclass of the `AsyncTask` class.
- ▶ Permission for accessing Internet is made by adding the required statement in the `AndroidManifest.xml` file.

To understand how data is downloaded from the Internet, let's create an Android project that downloads an image referenced by the supplied URL. Call the application `HttpApp`. In the application, we display an `EditText` control to enter the URL address of the image to download, a `Button` control to initiate the downloading process, and an `ImageView` control to display the downloaded image. After we define the three controls, `activity_http_app.xml` appears as shown in Listing 13.5.

LISTING 13.5   Code in the `activity_http_app.xml` Layout File

```
<RelativeLayout xmlns:android="http://schemas.android.com/apk/res/android"
    android:layout_width="match_parent"
    android:layout_height="match_parent" >
    <EditText
        android:id="@+id/url_add"
        android:layout_height="wrap_content"
        android:layout_width="250dp"
        android:hint="Enter URL of the image"   />
    <Button
        android:id="@+id/go_button"
        android:text="Go"
        android:layout_width="wrap_content"
        android:layout_height="wrap_content"
        android:layout_toRightOf="@id/url_add" />
    <ImageView
        android:id="@+id/img"
        android:layout_width="wrap_content"
        android:layout_height="wrap_content"
```

```
            android:layout_gravity="center"
            android:layout_below="@id/url_add"   />
</RelativeLayout>
```

To define a URL object, configure the `HttpURLConnection` `InputStream` and read the data through the `InputStream`. To display the read binary data through the `ImageView` control, we need to write the code shown in Listing 13.6 into the `HttpAppActivity.java` Java activity file.

LISTING 13.6   Code in the `HttpAppActivity.java` Java Activity File

```java
package com.androidunleashed.httpapp;

import android.app.Activity;
import android.os.Bundle;
import java.io.IOException;
import java.io.InputStream;
import java.net.URL;
import java.net.URLConnection;
import java.net.HttpURLConnection;
import android.graphics.Bitmap;
import android.graphics.BitmapFactory;
import android.os.AsyncTask;
import android.widget.ImageView;
import android.widget.Button;
import android.widget.EditText;
import android.view.View;

public class HttpAppActivity extends Activity {
    @Override
    public void onCreate(Bundle savedInstanceState) {
        super.onCreate(savedInstanceState);
        setContentView(R.layout.activity_http_app);
        final EditText urlAdd = (EditText) findViewById(R.id.url_add);
        Button goButton = (Button)this.findViewById(R.id.go_button);
        goButton.setOnClickListener(new Button.OnClickListener(){
            public void onClick(View v) {
                new AccessAsync().execute(urlAdd.getText().toString().trim());
            }
        });
    }

    private InputStream openHttpConnection(String urlString) throws IOException {
        InputStream inStream = null;
        int checkConn = -1;
        URL url = new URL(urlString);
```

13

```
        URLConnection conn = url.openConnection();
        try{
            HttpURLConnection httpConn = (HttpURLConnection) conn;
            httpConn.setAllowUserInteraction(false);
            httpConn.setInstanceFollowRedirects(true);
            httpConn.setRequestMethod("GET");
            httpConn.connect();
            checkConn = httpConn.getResponseCode();
            if (checkConn == HttpURLConnection.HTTP_OK) {
                inStream = httpConn.getInputStream();
            }
        }
        catch (Exception ex) {
            throw new IOException("Error connecting");
        }
        return inStream;
    }

    private Bitmap downloadImage(String urladdr) {
        Bitmap bmap = null;
        InputStream inStream = null;
        try {
            inStream = openHttpConnection(urladdr);
            bmap = BitmapFactory.decodeStream(inStream);
            inStream.close();
        } catch (IOException e1) {
            e1.printStackTrace();
        }
        return bmap;
    }

    private class AccessAsync extends AsyncTask<String, Void, Bitmap> {
        protected Bitmap doInBackground(String... urladds) {
            return downloadImage(urladds[0]);
        }
        protected void onPostExecute(Bitmap bmp) {
            ImageView img = (ImageView) findViewById(R.id.img);
            img.setImageBitmap(bmp);
        }
    }
}
```

Here we see that the EditText control with the url_add ID is accessed from the main.xml layout file and is mapped to the EditText object urlAdd. Similarly, the Button control with go_button ID is accessed from the layout file and mapped to the goButton Button object. An `OnClickListener` is associated with the `Button` object. Hence, when the `Button` control is clicked, the `onClick()` callback method is executed. In the `onClick()` method, the `AccessAsync` class is instantiated. The `AccessAsync` class extends the `AsyncTask` class.

The `execute()` method on the `AccessSync` class is called, passing the URL address of the image entered by the user in the `EditText` control to it. The URL address of the image is assigned to the `Input Parameter` of the `AsyncTask` class. As expected, the `doInBackground()` method of the `AsyncTask` class is executed, and the URL address assigned to the `Input Parameter` is assigned to the `urladds` parameter of the `doInBackground()` method. From the `doInBackground()` method, the `downloadImage()` method is called, and the `URL` of the image is passed to it.

In the `downloadImage()` method, the `openHttpConnection()` method is called, passing the URL address of the image to it. In this method, we define an `HttpURLConnection` object called `httpConn`. Through the `HttpURLConnection` object, `httpConn`, an HTTP connection is opened with a remote URL. Various properties of the connection are set. If the HTTP connection is established, we obtain an `InputStream` object. To confirm whether the HTTP connection is established, we compare the response code with the `HTTP_OK` constant. If both are equal, it means the HTTP connection was successfully established.

Through the `inStream InputStream` object that we get from the `HttpURLConnection` object, we download the image data from the server. Remember, it is through an `InputStream` object that we download or read bytes from the `inStream` object.

The data read by the `InputStream` object is decoded into a `bmap Bitmap` object by calling the `decodeStream()` method from the `BitmapFactory` class. This `bmap Bitmap` object is returned by the `downloadImage()` method and hence by the `doInBackground()` method. When the `doInBackground()` method has completed, the `onPostExecute()` method is called, which displays the returned `Bitmap` object by assigning it to the `ImageView` control.

Because we are accessing and downloading the image from the Internet, we need to add an `INTERNET` permission to our application by adding the following line to the `AndroidManifest.xml` file:

```
<uses-permission android:name="android.permission.INTERNET" />
```

After we add this statement, the `AndroidManifest.xml` file appears as shown in Listing 13.7. Only the statement in bold is newly added; the rest is default code.

LISTING 13.7   Code in the `AndroidManifest.xml` File

```
<manifest xmlns:android="http://schemas.android.com/apk/res/android"
    package="com.androidunleashed.httpapp"
    android:versionCode="1"
    android:versionName="1.0" >
    <uses-sdk android:minSdkVersion="8"
        android:targetSdkVersion="15" />
    <uses-permission android:name="android.permission.INTERNET" />
    <application
```

```
        android:icon="@drawable/ic_launcher"
        android:label="@string/app_name"
        android:theme="@style/AppTheme" >
        <activity
            android:name=".HttpAppActivity"
            android:label="@string/title_activity_http_app" >
            <intent-filter>
                <action android:name="android.intent.action.MAIN" />
                <category android:name="android.intent.category.LAUNCHER" />
            </intent-filter>
        </activity>
    </application>
</manifest>
```

After we run the application, the initial screen asks for the URL of the image to download and display (see Figure 13.3—left). The image of the entered URL is displayed on the screen, as shown in Figure 13.3 (right).

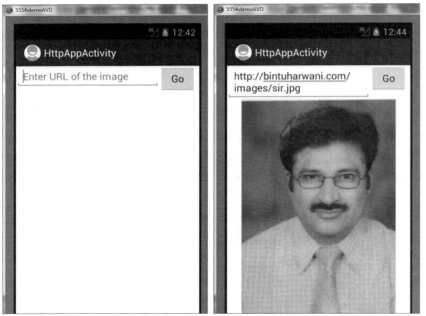

FIGURE 13.3   The screen prompting the URL of the image to download (left), and the image downloaded and displayed from the specified URL (right)

Consuming SOAP Services

Google doesn't provide direct support for calling SOAP Web Services in Android. The following are the two ways to invoke SOAP-based web services via Android:

▶ **Manually sending a request and parsing response**—Use the `HttpClient` and XML parser to manually create a SOAP request and parse the soap response.

▶ **Using a SOAP client library**—Performs the task of parsing and managing SOAP messages. The `kSOAP` library is the one that is popularly used for calling and consuming SOAP Web Services. The library is available at `http://code.google.com/p/ ksoap2-android/`. The filename by which the library is downloaded is `ksoap2- android-assembly-2.6.5-jar-with-dependencies.jar`. For your convenience, the library is provided with the application's source code bundle.

Let's learn about SOAP Services by using an example. Create a new Android project called `ConsumeWebServ`. To link the `kSOAP` library to an Android project, right-click the project in the `Package Explorer` window and select the `Properties` option. From the `Properties` window, select the `Java Build Path` tab. From the `Java Build Path` pane on the right side, click the `Add External JARs...` button (see Figure 13.4—left). Then navigate to the folder where the `kSOAP` library is located and select it. Recall the `kSOAP` library is placed in the application folder, that is, in the `ConsumeWebServ` folder provided with the source code bundle. The `kSOAP` library is attached to our application, and we can use it in consuming a SOAP Service (see Figure 13.4—right).

FIGURE 13.4   The screen to add the `kSOAP` library (left), and the library name displayed after selecting its `jar` file (right)

We are using a web service that converts the temperature value entered in `Celsius` into `Fahrenheit`. The following are the terms that we encounter while using a web service:

▶ **Web Service Namespace**—A logical group of unique identifiers.

▶ **Web Service Method Name**—Method name that users can access to perform an action.

▶ **Web Service URL**—URL of the web service.

▶ **SOAP_ACTION**—Defines the action to be performed. It is the concatenation of the namespace and method name.

The URL of the web service that we are going to use in this application is `http://www.w3schools.com/webservices/tempconvert.asmx`. The method name that performs the conversion is `CelsiusToFahrenheit`, and the namespace of the web service is `http://tempuri.org/`. Because we want to enter temperature in `Celsius` and receive the result in `Fahrenheit`, we need a `TextView`, an `EditText`, and a `Button` control. To define the three controls, the code shown in Listing 13.8 is written into the `activity_consume_web_serv.xml` layout file.

LISTING 13.8   Code in the `activity_consume_web_serv.xml` Layout File

```
<RelativeLayout xmlns:android="http://schemas.android.com/apk/res/android"
    android:layout_width="match_parent"
    android:layout_height="match_parent" >
    <EditText
        android:id="@+id/celsius_value"
        android:layout_height="wrap_content"
        android:layout_width="200dp"
        android:hint="Enter Celsius"  />
    <Button
        android:id="@+id/submit_button"
        android:text="Submit"
        android:layout_width="wrap_content"
        android:layout_height="wrap_content"
        android:layout_toRightOf="@id/celsius_value" />
    <TextView
        android:id="@+id/fahrenheit"
        android:layout_width="match_parent"
        android:layout_height="wrap_content"
        android:layout_below="@id/celsius_value"  />
</RelativeLayout>
```

We can see that the `EditText` control is assigned the ID `celsius_value`, its width is set to `200dp`, and the hint text is set as `Enter Celsius`. The `Button` control is assigned a `Submit` caption and the ID `submit_button`. The `TextView` control is assigned the ID `Fahrenheit`, which is used to identify the control in Java code and assign the result returned by the web service. To access and use the web service for converting the temperature entered in Celsius units into Fahrenheit, write the code shown in Listing 13.9 into the `ConsumeWebServActivity.java` Java activity file.

LISTING 13.9   Code in the `ConsumeWebServActivity.java` Java Activity File

```
package com.androidunleashed.consumewebserv;

import android.app.Activity;
import android.os.Bundle;
import android.view.View;
```

```
import android.widget.Button;
import android.widget.EditText;
import android.widget.TextView;
import org.ksoap2.serialization.SoapObject;
import org.ksoap2.transport.HttpTransportSE;
import org.ksoap2.SoapEnvelope;
import org.ksoap2.serialization.SoapSerializationEnvelope;
import org.ksoap2.serialization.SoapPrimitive;
import org.ksoap2.serialization.PropertyInfo;

public class ConsumeWebServActivity extends Activity {
    private static final String NAMESPACE = "http://tempuri.org/";
    private static final String METHOD_NAME = "CelsiusToFahrenheit";
    private static final String URL = "http://www.w3schools.com/webservices/tempcon
vert.asmx";
    private static final String SOAP_ACTION = "http://tempuri.org/CelsiusToFahren
heit";
    private TextView fahrenheit;

    @Override
    protected void onCreate(Bundle savedInstanceState) {
        super.onCreate(savedInstanceState);
        setContentView(R.layout.activity_consume_web_serv);
        final EditText celsiusVal = (EditText) findViewById(R.id.celsius_value);
        Button submitButton = (Button)this.findViewById(R.id.submit_button);
        submitButton.setOnClickListener(new Button.OnClickListener(){
            public void onClick(View v) {
                fahrenheit = (TextView) findViewById(R.id.fahrenheit);
                SoapObject request = new SoapObject(NAMESPACE, METHOD_NAME);
                PropertyInfo celsiusProp = new PropertyInfo();
                celsiusProp.setName("Celsius");
                celsiusProp.setValue(Integer.parseInt(celsiusVal.getText().
                toString()));
                celsiusProp.setType(double.class);
                request.addProperty(celsiusProp);
                SoapSerializationEnvelope envelope = new SoapSerializationEnvelope(S
                oapEnvelope.VER11);
                envelope.dotNet = true;
                envelope.setOutputSoapObject(request);
                HttpTransportSE androidHttpTransport = new HttpTransportSE(URL);
                androidHttpTransport.debug=true;
                try {
                    androidHttpTransport.call(SOAP_ACTION, envelope);
                    SoapPrimitive resultString = (SoapPrimitive) envelope.getRe
                    sponse();
                    fahrenheit.setText("Value in Farenheit is " + resultString.
                    toString());
```

13

```
            } catch (Exception e) {
                System.out.println(e.toString());
            }
        }
    });
    }
}
```

Here we see that for increasing readability, four string constants are defined—NAMESPACE, METHOD_NAME, URL, and SOAP_ACTION—to represent the namespace, method name, web service's URL, and SOAP action. The celsius_value EditText and submit_button Button controls are accessed from the layout file and mapped to the respective objects. An OnClickListener is associated with the Button control, and the onClick() callback method is called when the Button is clicked. In the onClick() method, we define a SoapObject object called request, as it will be used by kSOAP. Parameters in kSOAP are passed via a PropertyInfo class instance, so a PropertyInfo object called celsiusProp is defined.

The Name attribute of the PropertyInfo object is set to Celsius, its Value attribute is set equal to the value entered by the user in the EditText control, and the Type attribute is set to the double data type. The celsiusProp PropertyInfo object is then added as a property to the SoapObject instance request. Thereafter, we define a SoapSerializationEnvelope called envelope, and as our web service is a .NET-based Service, we set its .dotNet property to true. An HttpTransportSE object called androidHttpTransport is defined, and finally, the web service is invoked. The result returned by the web service is assigned to the resultString SoapPrimitive object, which is then displayed via the TextView control.

Remember, the minSDKVersion should be set to 9, as the higher Android versions don't support web services. After we set the minSDKVersion, the code in AndroidManifest.xml appears as shown in Listing 13.10.

LISTING 13.10   Code in the AndroidManifest.xml File

```
<manifest xmlns:android="http://schemas.android.com/apk/res/android"
    package="com.androidunleashed.consumewebserv"
    android:versionCode="1"
    android:versionName="1.0" >
    <uses-sdk android:minSdkVersion="9" />
    <uses-permission android:name="android.permission.INTERNET" />
    <application
        android:icon="@drawable/ic_launcher"
        android:label="@string/app_name"
        android:theme="@style/AppTheme" >
        <activity
            android:name=".ConsumeWebServActivity"
            android:label="@string/title_activity_consume_web_serv" >
```

```
            <intent-filter>
                <action android:name="android.intent.action.MAIN" />
                <category android:name="android.intent.category.LAUNCHER" />
            </intent-filter>
        </activity>
    </application>
</manifest>
```

After running the application, we get the startup screen shown in Figure 13.5 (left). After we enter any temperature in Celsius units in the EditText control and press the Submit button, the temperature value is converted to Farenheit and displayed via the TextView control, as shown in Figure 13.5 (right).

FIGURE 13.5   The screen prompting for a temperature in Celsius (left), and the temperature that was entered in Celsius is converted into Farenheit (right).

Creating a Service

A service is an application component that performs the desired task without providing a user interface. Hence, services can only be accessed from another application and never invoked by a user. A service does not create its own thread. Instead it runs in the main thread of the application. So, to maintain efficiency of an application, we should create a new thread within the service to perform its processing tasks.

A service can be either started, bound, or both. A started service is one that starts when its startService() method is called. Once started, a service can run in the background indefinitely, even if the component that started it is destroyed. The service automatically stops when its operation is done. The bound service is the one that enables clients to bind to the service by calling the bindService() method. In the case of a bound service, the client must bind to a service to interact with it. A bound service provides an interface, making it possible to interact with the service, send requests to it, get processed results, and so on. A bound service runs as long as it is bound to the application component(s). That is, the service is destroyed when it is unbound from the clients that were bound to it. For using a service, we need to implement the onStartCommand() method to allow components to start it and the onBind() method to allow binding.

To create a service, define a class that extends the Service base class. All services extend the Service class. The methods that we can implement in the class are

▶ **onBind()**—The method returns an IBinder object that enables an activity to use a Service that can directly access members and methods inside it.

▶ **onStartCommand()**—Called when the Service starts. The method is used to check whether any data is passed to the Service for processing. We can also use this method to return a constant that configures the Service. For example, we can make the method return the constant START_STICKY, which makes the Service run until it is explicitly stopped.

▶ **onDestroy()**—Called when the Service is stopped using the stopService() method. With this method, we release resources consumed by the Service.

Let's have a quick look at the methods used for starting, stopping, binding, and unbinding from the service.

To start a Service, use the startService() method. The following example starts the Service represented by HandleService.class file:

```
startService(new Intent(getBaseContext(), HandleService.class));
```

To start a Service from an external application, we need to define its complete package name. The following example starts the HandleService.class Service from an external application:

```
startService(new Intent("com.androidunleashed.handleservice"));
```

To stop a Service, use the stopService() method. The following example stops the HandleService.class Service:

```
stopService(new Intent(getBaseContext(), HandleService.class));
```

A client can bind to the Service with the bindService() method. The following example binds the client to the HandleService.class Service using the servConn ServiceConnection:

```
bindService(new Intent(this, HandleService.class), servConn, Context.BIND_AUTO_CREATE);
```

The client(s) can be unbound from the Service with the unbindService() method. The following example unbinds the Service that is connected through the servConn ServiceConnection:

```
unbindService(servConn);
```

To understand how to use a started Service, we create a new Android project called CreateServiceApp. This application simply consists of a Button control that, when clicked, starts a `Service` displaying a text message. To define a `Button` control, the code shown in Listing 13.11 is written into the `activity_create_service_app.xml` layout file.

LISTING 13.11   Code in the `activity_create_service_app.xml` Layout File

```xml
<LinearLayout xmlns:android="http://schemas.android.com/apk/res/android"
    android:layout_width="match_parent"
    android:layout_height="match_parent"
    android:orientation="vertical" >
    <Button android:id="@+id/start_button"
        android:layout_width="match_parent"
        android:layout_height="wrap_content"
        android:text="Start Service" />
</LinearLayout>
```

To identify the `Button` control in the Java code, the ID assigned to it is `start_button`. The caption assigned to it is `Start Service`, to indicate that it starts the `Service` when clicked. To create the `Service` we want to start using this application, we need to add a Java file to the `com.androidunleashed.createserviceapp` package. Let's call the newly added Java file `HandleService.java`. To enable binding of the `Service` and to define the code that we want to execute when starting a `Service`, we implement the `onBind()` and `onStartCommand()` methods. To do so, the code shown in Listing 13.12 is written into `HandleService.java`.

LISTING 13.12   Code in the `HandleService.java` Java File

```java
package com.androidunleashed.createserviceapp;

import android.app.Service;
import android.content.Intent;
import android.widget.Toast;
import android.os.IBinder;

public class HandleService extends Service {
    @Override
    public IBinder onBind(Intent arg0) {
        return null;
    }

    @Override
    public int onStartCommand(Intent intent, int flags, int startId) {
        Toast.makeText(this, "Welcome to Hello Service", Toast.LENGTH_LONG).show();
        return START_STICKY;
    }
}
```

13

Because we are starting a `Service`, the `onBind()` method returns `null` instead of an `IBinder` object that a client may use to bind to a service. When started, the service displays a `Welcome to Hello Service` message through `Toast`. To enable the Android application to recognize the newly added Java class file, we need to add its entry into the `AndroidManifest.xml` file. After we add the entry, the `AndroidManifest.xml` file appears as shown in Listing 13.13. The code in bold is the added statement; the rest is the default code.

LISTING 13.13   Code in the `AndroidManifest.xml` File

```xml
<manifest xmlns:android="http://schemas.android.com/apk/res/android"
    package="com.androidunleashed.createserviceapp"
    android:versionCode="1"
    android:versionName="1.0" >
    <uses-sdk android:minSdkVersion="8"
        android:targetSdkVersion="15" />
    <application
        android:icon="@drawable/ic_launcher"
        android:label="@string/app_name"
        android:theme="@style/AppTheme" >
        <activity
            android:name=".CreateServiceAppActivity"
            android:label="@string/title_activity_create_service_app" >
            <intent-filter>
                <action android:name="android.intent.action.MAIN" />
                <category android:name="android.intent.category.LAUNCHER" />
            </intent-filter>
        </activity>
        <service android:name=".HandleService" />
    </application>
</manifest>
```

To start the service that we defined through `HandleService.java`, we need to write the code shown in Listing 13.14 into the `CreateServiceAppActivity.java` Java activity file.

LISTING 13.14   Code in the `CreateServiceAppActivity.java` Java Activity File

```java
package com.androidunleashed.createserviceapp;

import android.app.Activity;
import android.os.Bundle;
import android.view.View;
import android.content.Intent;
import android.widget.Button;

public class CreateServiceAppActivity extends Activity {
```

```
@Override
public void onCreate(Bundle savedInstanceState) {
    super.onCreate(savedInstanceState);
    setContentView(R.layout.activity_create_service_app);
    Button startButton = (Button)findViewById(R.id.start_button);
    startButton.setOnClickListener(new Button.OnClickListener(){
        @Override
        public void onClick(View view) {
            Intent service = new Intent(getBaseContext(), HandleService.class);
            startService(service);
        }
    });
}
}
```

We can see that the `Button` control with the `start_button` ID is accessed from the layout file and mapped to the `startButton` `Button` object. An `OnClickListener` is associated with the `Button` control, and its `onClick()` callback method is executed when it is clicked. In the `onClick()` method, an `Intent` object called `service` is defined, referencing our `Service`, that is, the `HandleService.class` Java class. Our `Service` is then started using the `Intent` object.

After running the application, we see the `Button` control in Figure 13.6 (left). After we click the `Start Service` button, the service displays a `Welcome to Hello Service` text message, as shown in Figure 13.6 (right).

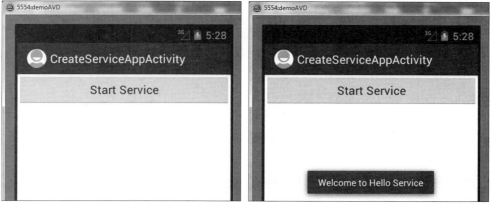

FIGURE 13.6   The screen showing a `Button` control (left), and the service starts on selecting the `Button` control (right).

Interacting with the Service

Let's enhance this application to accept input from the user. We want our service to prompt the user to enter a name. When the user clicks the `Button` control, a welcome message displaying the entered name is shown. Hence, we need to add an `EditText` control to our `activity_create_service_app.xml` layout file. After we add the `EditText` control, the `activity_create_service_app.xml` layout file appears as shown in Listing 13.15.

LISTING 13.15   Code Written in the `activity_create_service_app.xml` Layout File

```
<RelativeLayout xmlns:android="http://schemas.android.com/apk/res/android"
    android:layout_width="match_parent"
    android:layout_height="match_parent" >
    <EditText
        android:id="@+id/username"
        android:layout_height="wrap_content"
        android:layout_width="200dp"
        android:hint="Enter Name"  />
    <Button
        android:id="@+id/submit_button"
        android:text="Submit"
        android:layout_width="wrap_content"
        android:layout_height="wrap_content"
        android:layout_toRightOf="@id/username" />
</RelativeLayout>
```

The `EditText` control displays a hint text, `Enter Name`, inviting the user to enter a name. To identify and access the `EditText` control, the ID assigned to it is `username`. The caption of the `Button` control is set to `Submit`. To access the username entered into the `Service` and display a Welcome message along with the entered username, modify the code in the `HandleService.java` file as shown in Listing 13.16. Only the code in bold is modified; the rest is the same as we saw in Listing 13.12.

LISTING 13.16   Code in the `HandleService.java` Java File

```
package com.androidunleashed.createserviceapp;

import android.app.Service;
import android.content.Intent;
import android.widget.Toast;
import android.os.IBinder;
import android.os.Bundle;

public class HandleService extends Service {
    @Override
    public IBinder onBind(Intent arg0) {
        return null;
    }
```

```
    @Override
    public int onStartCommand(Intent intent, int flags, int startId) {
        Bundle extras = intent.getExtras();
        if(extras !=null) {
            String username=extras.getString("username");
            Toast.makeText(this, "Welcome "+username, Toast.LENGTH_LONG).show();
        }
        return START_STICKY;
    }
}
```

We see that by using the `getExtras()` method, the `Bundle` object that was sent to the service is received. The `username` sent through the `Bundle` is accessed and displayed, along with a Welcome message, through `Toast`.

To access the username entered in the `EditText` control and send it to the service in the form of a `Bundle`, modify the code in the `CreateServiceAppActivity.java` Java activity file to appear as shown in Listing 13.17.

LISTING 13.17   Code in the `CreateServiceAppActivity.java` Java Activity File

```
package com.androidunleashed.createserviceapp;

import android.app.Activity;
import android.os.Bundle;
import android.view.View;
import android.content.Intent;
import android.widget.Button;
import android.widget.EditText;

public class CreateServiceAppActivity extends Activity {
    @Override
    public void onCreate(Bundle savedInstanceState) {
        super.onCreate(savedInstanceState);
        setContentView(R.layout.activity_create_service_app);
        Button submitButton  = (Button)findViewById(R.id.submit_button);
        submitButton .setOnClickListener(new Button.OnClickListener(){
            @Override
            public void onClick(View view) {
                Bundle dataBundle = new Bundle();
                EditText username = (EditText) findViewById(R.id.username);
                dataBundle.putString("username", username.getText().toString());
                Intent service = new Intent(getBaseContext(), HandleService.class);
                service.putExtras(dataBundle);
                startService(service);
            }
```

```
        });
    }
}
```

We see that a `Bundle` object called `dataBundle` is defined. The name entered by the user in the `EditText` control is accessed and stored in the `Bundle` object under the `username` key. The key is used in the service to fetch the username sent through the `Bundle` object. The `Bundle` is associated with our `HandleService.class` `Service`, which is started when the user clicks the `Button` control. After running the application, we see an `EditText` control with `Enter Name` hint text, as shown in Figure 13.7 (left). After we enter the name and click the `Submit` button, the `Service` starts and displays a Welcome message, along with the entered username, as shown in Figure 13.7 (right).

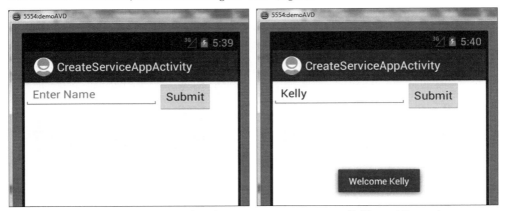

FIGURE 13.7   The screen prompting the user to enter a name (left), and the welcome message displayed after selecting the `Submit` button (right)

Creating a Bound Service

As mentioned earlier, a bound service is one that allows components such as activities to bind to the service, send requests to, receive responses from it, and so on. Recall that the bound service does not run indefinitely, but only for the time it is bound to the application component.

To provide binding for a service, the class must implement the `onBind()` callback method. The method returns an `IBinder` object that the clients can use to interact with the service. A client can bind to the service by calling `bindService()`. Let's modify our existing `CreateServiceApp` Android application that we created in the previous section to create a bound service. Since the bound service is accessed from a client, we need to specify the complete package name of the service. We supply the package name of the service through the `<action>` element in the Android Manifest file. So, modify the `AndroidManifest.xml` file to appear as shown in Listing 13.18. Only the code in bold is new; the rest is the default code of the file.

LISTING 13.18   Code in the `AndroidManifest.xml` File

```xml
<manifest xmlns:android="http://schemas.android.com/apk/res/android"
    package="com.androidunleashed.createserviceapp"
    android:versionCode="1"
    android:versionName="1.0" >
    <uses-sdk android:minSdkVersion="8"
        android:targetSdkVersion="15" />
    <application
        android:icon="@drawable/ic_launcher"
        android:label="@string/app_name"
        android:theme="@style/AppTheme" >
        <activity
            android:name=".CreateServiceAppActivity"
            android:label="@string/title_activity_create_service_app" >
            <intent-filter>
                <action android:name="android.intent.action.MAIN" />
                <category android:name="android.intent.category.LAUNCHER" />
            </intent-filter>
        </activity>
        <service android:name=".HandleService" >
            <intent-filter>
                <action android:name="com.androidunleashed.handleservice" />
            </intent-filter>
        </service>
    </application>
</manifest>
```

Modify the `HandleService.java` to appear as shown in Listing 13.19.

LISTING 13.19   Code in the `HandleService.java` Java File

```java
package com.androidunleashed.createserviceapp;

import android.app.Service;
import android.content.Intent;
import android.widget.Toast;
import android.os.IBinder;
import android.os.Bundle;
import android.os.Handler;
import android.os.Message;
import android.os.Messenger;

public class HandleService extends Service {
    class IncomingHandler extends Handler {
        @Override
```

```
        public void handleMessage(Message msg) {
            Bundle fromActivity=msg.getData();
            if(fromActivity !=null) {
                String    username=fromActivity.getString("username");
                Toast.makeText(HandleService.this, "Welcome "+username, Toast.
                LENGTH_LONG).show();
            }
            super.handleMessage(msg);
        }
    }

    final Messenger messengerToService = new Messenger(new IncomingHandler());
    @Override
    public IBinder onBind(Intent arg0) {
        return messengerToService.getBinder();
    }
}
```

In the service, create a class called IncomingHandler that extends the Handler class.
The Handler is used to handle incoming requests from the clients. Recall that handlers
allow us to send and process Message and Runnable objects associated with a thread's
MessageQueue. They delivers messages and runnables to the message queue and execute
them one by one. A Messenger is created by using the Handler. The Messenger creates
an IBinder that is returned to the clients, enabling them to interact with the service.
The Message Binder is passed to the activity that binds the Message into the service. The
Message sent to the service is in its Handler. So, in the Handler method, we extract
the data passed through the Message. Fetch the username passed to the Handler through
the Message and display it through Toast.

A client can bind to a service by calling the bindService() method. The client needs to
implement the ServiceConnection interface to monitor the connection with the service.

The following are the methods defined in the ServiceConnection interface:

▶ **void onServiceConnected(ComponentName className, IBinder service)**—Called when
  a connection between the client and the service is established. The method returns
  the IBinder that the client can use to interact with the service. A Messenger object is
  also defined in this method.

▶ **void onServiceDisconnected(ComponentName className)**—Called when a connection to the service is lost. The Messenger object is set to null and destroyed in this
  method.

To enable binding to the service and to implement the ServiceConnection interface,
modify the CreateServiceAppActivity.java file to appear as shown in Listing 13.20.

LISTING 13.20   Code in the `CreateServiceAppActivity.java` Java Activity File

```java
package com.androidunleashed.createserviceapp;

import android.app.Activity;
import android.os.Bundle;
import android.view.View;
import android.content.Intent;
import android.widget.Button;
import android.widget.EditText;
import android.os.Messenger;
import android.content.ServiceConnection;
import android.os.IBinder;
import android.content.ComponentName;
import android.os.Message;
import android.os.RemoteException;
import android.content.Context;

public class CreateServiceAppActivity extends Activity {
    private Messenger messengerToService = null;
    boolean mBound;

    private ServiceConnection servConn = new ServiceConnection() {
        public void onServiceConnected(ComponentName className, IBinder service) {
            messengerToService=new Messenger(service);
            mBound=true;
        }
        @Override
        public void onServiceDisconnected (ComponentName className) {
            messengerToService = null;
            mBound=false;
        }
    };

    @Override
    public void onCreate(Bundle savedInstanceState) {
        super.onCreate(savedInstanceState);
        setContentView(R.layout.activity_create_service_app);
        Button submitButton  = (Button)findViewById(R.id.submit_button);
        submitButton .setOnClickListener(new Button.OnClickListener(){
        @Override
        public void onClick(View view) {
            Message msg = Message.obtain();
            Bundle dataBundle = new Bundle();
            EditText username = (EditText) findViewById(R.id.username);
            dataBundle.putString("username", username.getText().toString());
```

```
        msg.setData(dataBundle);
        try {
            messengerToService.send(msg);
        } catch (RemoteException e) {
            e.printStackTrace();
        }
    }
});
}

@Override
protected void onStart() {
    super.onStart();
    Intent intent = new Intent();
    intent.setAction("com.androidunleashed.handleservice");
    bindService(new Intent(this, HandleService.class), servConn, Context.BIND_
    AUTO_CREATE);
}

@Override
protected void onStop() {
    super.onStop();
    if (mBound) {
        unbindService(servConn);
        mBound = false;
    }
}
}
```

Here we see that the Button control with the submit_button ID is accessed from the layout file and is mapped to the submitButton Button object. An OnClickListener is associated with the Button control. The onClick() callback method is invoked when the Button control is clicked. In the onClick() method, a Message object called msg is defined. A Bundle object called dataBundle is also defined. In the Bundle object, the username entered is stored under the username key. The Bundle object carrying the username is added to the Message. A Messenger object called messengerFromService is defined and is associated with the Message so that replies to the message can be sent.

An instance of the ServiceConnection interface called servConn is created. Its two methods, onServiceConnected() and onServiceDisconnected(), are implemented. In the onServiceConnected() method, we get an instance of the IBinder service. A Messenger object called messengerToService is created using the IBinder object, service.

The onStart() method is implemented, and in this method we define an Intent object called intent. Set its action to com.androidunleashed.handleservice and bind the client to the service. After binding, a ServiceConnection is created and passed to the server.

In the `onStop()` method, the client is unbound from the service and the service is stopped.

When the application runs, we get the same output as shown previously in Figure 13.7. That is, the application asks for the username (see Figure 13.7—left). After we enter the username and click the `Submit` button, the username is displayed, along with a welcome message (see Figure 13.7—right).

Can we schedule applications to execute automatically? Yes! Of course. Let's learn how.

Setting Up Alarms

To execute certain events, services, or broadcast intents at a specific time or interval, Android SDK provides a mechanism called `AlarmManager`. The `AlarmManager` provides access to the system alarm services. The alarm services can be either set to occur once or repetitively. Repetitive alarms can be scheduled at a specific time or on the basis of the time since the device booted. The benefit of using alarms is that we can use them to trigger application events or actions even after our application is closed. Alarms remain active even when the device is in sleep mode and can be set to wake the device. When the device reboots, all the alarms are cancelled.

As said earlier, alarms are handled through the `AlarmManager`. To get access to the `AlarmManager`, we call the `getSystemService()` method as shown in the following statement:

```
AlarmManager alarmManager = (AlarmManager) getSystemService(ALARM_SERVICE);
```

To create an alarm that goes off once, we use the `set()` method in the following format:

```
alarmManager.set(alarm_type, trigger_time, pending_intent)
```

where

- `alarm_type` represents the type of alarm that we want to set.
- `trigger_time` represents the time at which we want the alarm to go off. If the `trigger_time` has already passed, the alarm goes off immediately.
- `pending_intent` represents the `PendingIntent` instance to be fired when the alarm goes off.

We can set the following four alarm types:

- **RTC_WAKEUP**—Wakes the device from sleep to fire the `PendingIntent` at the specified time.
- **RTC**—Fires the `PendingIntent` at the specified time but does not wake the device.
- **ELAPSED_REALTIME**—Fires the `PendingIntent` when the specified time since the device booted is passed but does not wake up the device.

▶ **ELAPSED_REALTIME_WAKEUP**—Wakes the device from sleep and fires the `PendingIntent` when the specified time since the device booted is passed.

The following example sets up the alarm that wakes the device from sleep to fire the specified `PendingIntent`:

```
alarmManager.set(AlarmManager.RTC_WAKEUP, calendar.getTimeInMillis(), pendingIntent);
```

When the alarm goes off, the specified `PendingIntent` is broadcast. If another alarm is set using the same `PendingIntent`, it replaces the previously set alarm. To cancel an alarm, the `cancel()` method is called on the `AlarmManager`, passing in the `PendingIntent` that we don't want to trigger, as shown in the following statement:

```
alarmManager.cancel(pendingIntent);
```

Setting Repeating Alarms

We can make the alarms go off repeatedly at the specified interval. To set a repeating alarm, the following two methods on the `AlarmManager` are used:

▶ **setRepeating()**—Repeats the alarm exactly at the specified interval. That is, the alarm is repeated at the specified interval defined in milliseconds.

▶ **setInexactRepeating()**—The method helps in reducing the battery and other resources by synchronizing multiple inexact repeating alarms and triggering them simultaneously. In this method, the time interval is not exactly defined in milliseconds but in terms of the following Alarm Manager constants:

> ▶ INTERVAL_FIFTEEN_MINUTES
> ▶ INTERVAL_HALF_HOUR
> ▶ INTERVAL_HOUR
> ▶ INTERVAL_HALF_DAY
> ▶ INTERVAL_DAY

The benefit of using the method is that instead of each application separately waking the device, the alarms are synchronized, resulting in a reduction of the battery resources.

Setting Up the Time for the Alarm

To set the alarm for a particular date and time, we use the `Calendar` object. A `Calendar` object is defined by calling the `getInstance()` method as shown here:

```
Calendar calendar = Calendar.getInstance();
```

To set the `Calendar`'s current time, we use the `setTimeInMillis()` method. A value representing the time in milliseconds is passed to this method. The following statement sets the `Calendar`'s current time to the current system time:

```
calendar.setTimeInMillis(System.currentTimeMillis());
```

To manipulate `Calendar`'s time, we can add hours, minutes, seconds, days, months, and years to its currently set time. The method used for doing this task is the `add()` method on the `Calendar` instance. The following statement adds a second to the `Calendar`'s current time:

```
calendar.add(Calendar.SECOND, 1);
```

To understand the concept of alarms practically, let's create an Android project that consists of two classes. One class acts as the main `Activity`, and the other `Activity` is launched with the alarm. Call the newly created Android project `AlarmApp`. In this application, the main activity displays a `Button` control that, when clicked, invokes the alarm.

To define the `Button` control, the code as shown in Listing 13.21 is written in the layout file `activity_alarm_app.xml`.

LISTING 13.21   Code in the Layout File `activity_alarm_app.xml`

```
<LinearLayout xmlns:android="http://schemas.android.com/apk/res/android"
    android:layout_width="match_parent"
    android:layout_height="match_parent"
    android:orientation="vertical" >
    <Button
        android:id="@+id/alarm_button"
        android:text="Start Alarm"
        android:layout_width="wrap_content"
        android:layout_height="wrap_content"
        android:layout_gravity="center"  />
</LinearLayout>
```

We can see that the ID assigned to the `Button` control is `alarm_button`, it is set to display the caption `Start Alarm`, and it is set to appear at the horizontally centered position. The `Button` control, when clicked, invokes the alarm, which in turn launches an activity. The target activity displays the text message `Meeting with the Doctor`. To define the layout file for the target activity, add an XML file called `reminder.xml` to the `res/layout` folder. To define the `TextView` control in the `reminder.xml` file, write the code as shown in Listing 13.22.

LISTING 13.22   Code Written in the `reminder.xml` File

```
<?xml version="1.0" encoding="utf-8"?>
<LinearLayout xmlns:android="http://schemas.android.com/apk/res/android"
    android:layout_width="match_parent"
    android:layout_height="match_parent"
```

```
    android:orientation="vertical" >
    <TextView
        android:id="@+id/textView"
        android:layout_width="fill_parent"
        android:layout_height="wrap_content"
        android:text="Meeting with the Doctor" />
</LinearLayout>
```

To identify the `TextView` control in the Java code, an ID `textView` is assigned to it. Also, the control is initialized to display the text message `Meeting with the Doctor`. To define the target activity to be launched by the alarm, add a Java class to the `com.androidunleashed.alarmapp` package. Name the class `ReminderActivity.java`. To display the UI defined in the `reminder.xml` file, write the code as shown in Listing 13.23 in the Java class file `ReminderActivity.java`.

LISTING 13.23   Code in the Java Class File `ReminderActivity.java`

```
package com.androidunleashed.alarmapp;

import android.os.Bundle;
import android.app.Activity;

public class ReminderActivity extends Activity {
    @Override
    public void onCreate(Bundle savedInstanceState) {
        super.onCreate(savedInstanceState);
        setContentView(R.layout.reminder);
    }
}
```

We can see that the preceding code just displays the UI, that is, the `TextView` defined in the layout file `reminder.xml`.

To make the Android application know about this newly added activity, `ReminderActivity.java`, the following statement is added in the `AndroidManifest.xml` file:

```
<activity android:name=".ReminderActivity" android:label="@string/app_name" />
```

After we add this statement, the `AndroidManifest.xml` file appears as shown in Listing 13.24. The statement in bold is the added statement; the rest is the default code.

LISTING 13.24   Code in the `AndroidManifest.xml` File

```
<manifest xmlns:android="http://schemas.android.com/apk/res/android"
    package="com.androidunleashed.alarmapp"
    android:versionCode="1"
```

```
        android:versionName="1.0" >
        <uses-sdk
            android:minSdkVersion="8"
            android:targetSdkVersion="15" />
        <application
            android:icon="@drawable/ic_launcher"
            android:label="@string/app_name"
            android:theme="@style/AppTheme" >
            <activity
                android:name=".AlarmAppActivity"
                android:label="@string/title_activity_alarm_app" >
                <intent-filter>
                    <action android:name="android.intent.action.MAIN" />
                    <category android:name="android.intent.category.LAUNCHER" />
                </intent-filter>
            </activity>
            <activity android:name=".ReminderActivity" android:label="@string/app_name" />
        </application>
</manifest>
```

In this application, we set the alarm at a specific time to call a broadcast receiver. To perform the desired tasks, we follow these steps:

1. Get access to the alarm manager.

2. Set the time of the alarm.

3. Create a receiver to be invoked.

4. Create a pending intent that can be passed to the alarm manager to invoke the receiver at the specified time.

To do all the preceding steps, the code as shown in Listing 13.25 is written in the main Java activity file, `AlarmAppActivity.java`.

LISTING 13.25   Code in the Java Activity File `AlarmAppActivity.java`

```
package com.androidunleashed.alarmapp;

import android.os.Bundle;
import android.app.Activity;
import android.widget.Button;
import android.view.View;
import android.content.Intent;
import android.app.PendingIntent;
import android.app.AlarmManager;
import java.util.Calendar;
```

```
import android.widget.Toast;

public class AlarmAppActivity extends Activity {
    @Override
    public void onCreate(Bundle savedInstanceState) {
        super.onCreate(savedInstanceState);
        setContentView(R.layout.activity_alarm_app);
        Button alarmButton = (Button) this.findViewById(R.id.alarm_button);
        alarmButton.setOnClickListener(new Button.OnClickListener(){
            public void onClick(View v) {
                Intent myIntent = new Intent(AlarmAppActivity.this, ReminderActiv
                ity.class);
                PendingIntent pendingIntent =
                PendingIntent.getActivity(AlarmAppActivity.this, 0,
                myIntent,PendingIntent.FLAG_CANCEL_CURRENT);
                AlarmManager alarmManager = (AlarmManager)getSystemService(ALARM_
                SERVICE);
                Calendar calendar = Calendar.getInstance();
                calendar.setTimeInMillis(System.currentTimeMillis());
                calendar.add(Calendar.SECOND, 1);
                alarmManager.set(AlarmManager.RTC_WAKEUP, calendar.getTimeInMil
                lis(), pendingIntent);
                Toast.makeText(AlarmAppActivity.this, "Alarm will start in a sec
                ond", Toast.LENGTH_LONG).show();
            }
        });
    }
}
```

The activity file just shown does the following tasks:

▶ Accesses the `Button` control defined in the layout file and maps it to the `Button` object.

▶ Associates `setOnClickListener` to the `Button` control to know when it is clicked on.

▶ Creates the intent `myIntent` that refers to the activity that we want to launch, `ReminderActivity.class`.

▶ Creates a `PendingIntent` object that switches to the given intent, `myIntent`, when the alarm is invoked.

▶ The `PendingIntent` object called `pendingIntent` is created with the ID `0`. The `Intent` object, `myIntent`, representing the activity to be launched, and a flag are passed as parameters while creating the `PendingIntent` object. The flag `PendingIntent.FLAG_CANCEL_CURRENT` is passed to inform the `AlarmManager` that any other `PendingIntent` with the same ID, that is, with 0 ID, should be canceled and replaced with this one.

The `AlarmManager` results in waking up the device when the alarm goes off at the set time. The alarm is set to go off after a second from the current time.

When an alarm goes off, the `Intent` that had been registered for it is broadcast by the system, hence starting the target application. On running the application, we find a `Button` control with the caption `Start Alarm` on the screen (see Figure 13.8—left). When we click the `Start Alarm` button, the alarm is invoked. A toast message, `Alarm will start in a second`, appears to confirm the same. The alarm launches `ReminderActivity.java`, which displays the message `Meeting with the Doctor` (see Figure 13.8—right).

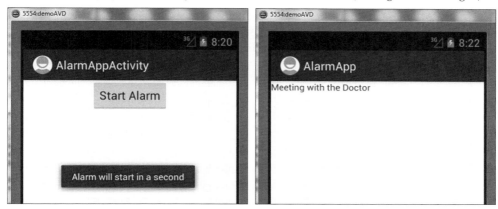

FIGURE 13.8   The toast message displayed on selecting the `Button` control (left), and the activity invoked by the alarm showing a text message (right)

To make the alarm go off repetitively in a time interval, the `AlarmManager`'s `set()` method is used with `setRepeating()` method. For example, the following statement makes the alarm to go off after every five seconds:

```
alarmManager.setRepeating(AlarmManager.RTC_WAKEUP, calendar.getTimeInMillis(),
5*1000, pendingIntent);
```

We can also schedule the alarm event for our application to trigger at the specific time. The following code, when used in the Java activity file `AlarmAppActivity.java`, makes the alarm to go off at 7:50 AM:

```
Calendar calendar = Calendar.getInstance();
calendar.set(Calendar.HOUR_OF_DAY, 7);
calendar.set(Calendar.MINUTE, 50);
calendar.set(Calendar.SECOND, 0);
alarmManager.set(AlarmManager.RTC_WAKEUP, calendar.getTimeInMillis(), pendingIntent);
```

Next, we learn to exploit the sensors of the devices and use them in Android applications.

Using Sensors

Although they may vary from device to device, hardware sensors exist in almost all modern mobile phone devices. Android supports different types of sensors, including accelerometer sensors, magnetic field sensors, orientation sensors, proximity sensors, and so on. Table 13.1 lists some different types of sensors.

TABLE 13.1   Brief Descriptions of Different Types of Sensors

Sensor	Description
Sensor.TYPE_AMBIENT_TEMPERATURE	Returns the ambient room temperature in degrees Celsius.
Sensor.TYPE_ACCELEROMETER	A three-axis accelerometer that returns the current acceleration along three axes in m/s^2 (meters per second, per second).
Sensor.TYPE_GRAVITY	A three-axis gravity sensor that returns the current direction and magnitude of gravity along three axes in m/s^2.
Sensor.TYPE_LINEAR_ACCELERATION	A three-axis linear acceleration that returns the acceleration, not including gravity, along three axes in m/s^2.
Sensor.TYPE_GYROSCOPE	A three-axis gyroscope that returns the rate of device rotation along three axes in radians/ second.
Sensor.TYPE_ROTATION_VECTOR	Returns the orientation of the device as a combination of an angle around an axis.
Sensor.TYPE_MAGNETIC_FIELD	A magnetometer that finds the current magnetic field in microteslas (µT) along three axes.
Sensor.TYPE_PRESSURE	An atmospheric pressure sensor that returns the current atmospheric pressure in millibars (mbars).
Sensor.TYPE_RELATIVE_HUMIDITY	Returns the current relative humidity as a percentage.
Sensor.TYPE_PROXIMITY	Indicates the distance between the device and the target object in centimeters. Usually used to detect whether the device is being held up against the user's ear to manage screen brightness or voice setting.
Sensor.TYPE_LIGHT	Returns ambient illumination and is usually used to control the screen brightness dynamically.

The class that accesses the sensors of devices is SensorManager. SensorManager is a system service running in Android. We get an instance of this service by calling the Context.getSystemService() method with SENSOR_SERVICE as the argument as shown in the following statement:

```
SensorManager    sensorManager=(SensorManager)getSystemService(SENSOR_SERVICE);
```

Because a device may or may not have the specific sensor, it is a wise idea to first check its presence. We can check the presence of the sensors using either the `SensorManager.getDefaultSensor()` or `ServiceManager.getSensorList()` method. While using the `getSensorList()` method on the `SensorManager`, we pass `Sensor.TYPE_ALL` as the parameter:

```
List<Sensor> sensorsList = sensorManager.getSensorList(Sensor.TYPE_ALL);
```

To find a list of all the available sensors of a particular type, the `getSensorList()` method is called passing the type of sensor we are looking for as a parameter to it. The following statement returns the list of available accelerometers:

```
List<Sensor> accelerometersList = sensorManager.getSensorList(Sensor.TYPE_ACCELEROM-
ETER);
```

After knowing the presence of the required sensor in the device, we use the `SensorManager.registerListener()` method to listen to the events that might occur in the sensor. This method accepts one `SensorEventListener` callback interface that is used by `SensorManager` to inform about the occurrence of the sensor events. The occurrence of events is informed via the `onSensorChanged()` and `onAccuracyChanged()` methods:

▶ **abstract void onAccuracyChanged(Sensor sensor, int accuracy)**—The method is called when there is a change in the sensor accuracy or in the degree of error. The first parameter, `sensor` in this method, is the registered sensor, and the second parameter is the accuracy value. The accuracy value can be one of the following:

  ▶ **SensorManager.SENSOR_STATUS_ACCURACY_HIGH**—Represents high accuracy
  ▶ **SensorManager.SENSOR_STATUS_ACCURACY_MEDIUM**—Represents medium accuracy
  ▶ **SensorManager.SENSOR_STATUS_ACCURACY_LOW**—Represents low accuracy
  ▶ **SensorManager.SENSOR_STATUS_UNRELIABLE**—Indicates accuracy is unreliable

▶ **abstract void onSensorChanged(SensorEvent event)**—The method is called when there is a change in the sensor values. The parameter `SensorEvent` in the method represents the sensor values. Basically, `SensorEvent.values` is an array of float values that contain the sensor values. The length and content of this array depend on the type of sensor used.

Don't forget to unregister the event listener and disable the sensor when not used, or else it keeps consuming CPU and battery resources. The event listener is unregistered through the `unregisterListener()` method as shown in the following statement:

```
sensorManager.unregisterListener(event_listener);
```

It is recommended to register the listener to get event notifications in the `onResume()` method and unregister it in the `onPause()` method. It is so because the sensor's data comes in random intervals and can consume a lot of CPU and battery power. So, it is better to get the event notifications only while the application is in the running state.

NOTE

You cannot test the accelerometer on the Android emulator.

We know by now that the sensor returns data when the listener is registered to it. The rate of data returned is determined by the argument passed while registering the listener. The argument determining the rate of data can be any of the following:

- **SENSOR_DELAY_NORMAL**—Data is sent at the normal rate.

- **SENSOR_DELAY_UI**—Data is sent at the rate desired in UI interaction.

- **SENSOR_DELAY_GAME**—Data is sent at the rate desired in games.

- **SENSOR_DELAY_FASTEST**—Data is sent at the fastest rate.

The following example registers a listener to the accelerometer sensor, and the rate of data returned by the sensor is normal:

```
sensorManager.registerListener(this, sensorManager.getDefaultSensor(Sensor.TYPE_
ACCELEROMETER), SensorManager.SENSOR_DELAY_NORMAL);
```

Let's understand the concept of sensors through a running example. Create a new Android project called `AccelerometerApp`. The application shows the acceleration of the device in the X, Y, and Z axes. When not moving, the application shows the values for each axis if the device is oriented in any direction.

To display the values of the three axes, we need to define three `TextView` controls in the layout file `activity_accelerometer_app.xml`. After we define three `TextView` controls, the layout file `activity_accelerometer_app.xml` appears as shown in Listing 13.26.

LISTING 13.26   Code in the Layout File `activity_accelerometer_app.xml`

```
<LinearLayout xmlns:android="http://schemas.android.com/apk/res/android"
    android:layout_width="fill_parent"
    android:layout_height="fill_parent"
    android:orientation="vertical" >
    <TextView
        android:id="@+id/xaxisview"
        android:layout_width="wrap_content"
        android:layout_height="wrap_content"
        android:text="X Axis" />
    <TextView
        android:id="@+id/yaxisview"
        android:layout_width="wrap_content"
        android:layout_height="wrap_content"
        android:text="Y Axis"  />
    <TextView
        android:id="@+id/zaxisview"
```

```
        android:layout_width="wrap_content"
        android:layout_height="wrap_content"
        android:text="Z Axis"  />
  </LinearLayout>
```

To identify and access in the Java code, the three `TextView` controls are assigned the IDs `xaxisview`, `yaxisview`, and `zaxisview`. Also, the three `TextView` controls are set to display the texts `X Axis`, `Y Axis`, and `Z Axis`, respectively.

After defining the layout file, we need to do the following tasks:

▶ Access the Accelerometer sensor in the device.

▶ Register the event listener to it.

▶ Access the data returned by the Accelerometer sensor.

▶ Access the three `TextView` controls defined in the layout file and map them to the `TextView` objects.

▶ Access the data returned by the Accelerometer sensor and display them via the three `TextView` controls.

To perform all these tasks, the code as shown in Listing 13.27 is written in the Java activity file `AccelerometerAppActivity.java`.

LISTING 13.27   Code in the Java Activity File `AccelerometerAppActivity.java`

```java
package com.androidunleashed.accelerometerapp;

import android.app.Activity;
import android.hardware.Sensor;
import android.hardware.SensorEvent;
import android.hardware.SensorEventListener;
import android.hardware.SensorManager;
import android.os.Bundle;
import android.widget.TextView;

public class AccelerometerAppActivity extends Activity implements SensorEventListener {
    TextView xAxisView,yAxisView, zAxisView;
    SensorManager sensorManager;

    @Override
    public void onCreate(Bundle savedInstanceState) {
        super.onCreate(savedInstanceState);
        setContentView(R.layout.activity_accelerometer_app);
        xAxisView=(TextView)findViewById(R.id.xaxisview);
        yAxisView=(TextView)findViewById(R.id.yaxisview);
```

```
        zAxisView=(TextView)findViewById(R.id.zaxisview);
        sensorManager=(SensorManager)getSystemService(SENSOR_SERVICE);
        sensorManager.registerListener(this,
            sensorManager.getDefaultSensor(Sensor.TYPE_ACCELEROMETER),
            SensorManager.SENSOR_DELAY_NORMAL);
    }

    public void onAccuracyChanged(Sensor sensor, int accuracy) {
    }

    public void onSensorChanged(SensorEvent event) {
        if(event.sensor.getType()==Sensor.TYPE_ACCELEROMETER) {
            float x=event.values[0];
            float y=event.values[1];
            float z=event.values[2];
            xAxisView.setText("X: "+x);
            yAxisView.setText("Y: "+y);
            zAxisView.setText("Z: "+z);
        }
    }
}
```

Let's run the application. Assuming the device is in stationary mode, the values of the X, Y, and Z axes are displayed as shown in Figure 13.9 (left). When we orient the device to landscape mode, the values of the X, Y, and Z axes appear as shown in Figure 13.9 (right).

FIGURE 13.9   The data of X, Y, and Z axes returned by the Accelerometer sensor (left), and the data of the X, Y, and Z axes returned by the Accelerometer sensor when the device switched to landscape mode (right).

Summary

In this chapter, we learned how to move processes to background threads using `Handler` classes as well as `AsyncTask` classes. We learned how to download and display images from the Internet. We learned how to create and bind to our own service and the procedure for consuming SOAP Services. Finally, we learned to set alarms and use sensors in Android applications.

In the next chapter, we learn how to publish Android applications. We learn about versioning and digitally signing our applications, deploying APK files, and publishing to the Google Play Store.

# CHAPTER 14

Publishing Android Applications

After developing an Android application, we need to thoroughly test it. The next step is to publish it to make it available to users. We can publish an Android app through Google Play, the Amazon Appstore, or any another Android app store.

Following are the steps to publish an Android application:

1. Set the versioning information of the application.

2. Generate a certificate, digitally sign the Android application, and generate the APK (Android Package) file. Android applications are distributed as Android package files (.APK).

3. Distribute to Google Play or other marketplace to host and sell our application.

Setting Versioning Information of an Application

Every Android application must include a version number to inform users about the enhanced or improved versions of the application if any. Also, we must define the version name, label, and icon of the application. The attributes used in the `AndroidManifest.xml` file to define the version number, name, label, and icon of the application are as follows:

▶ **android:versionCode**—Written within the `<manifest>` element, this attribute represents the version number of our application. Usually, we begin with version 1, and with every revised version of the application, we increment the value by 1. The `android:versionCode` attribute is used by Google Play to determine whether a newer version of your application is available.

▶ **android:versionName**—Written within the `<manifest>` element, this attribute contains versioning information that is visible to users. The versioning information is provided in any format that the developer chooses. The common format is `<major>.<minor>.<point>`. For example, the `versionName="1.0.0"` indicates the versioning information of the application that is published for the first time. If the application is upgraded drastically, the `<major>` value is incremented by 1 making the `versionName` as `"2.0.0"`. If small enhancements are made, either the `<minor>` or `<point>` value is incremented by 1, setting the `versionName` as `"1.1.0"` or "1.0.1".

▶ **android:icon**—Written within the `<application>` element, this attribute represents the icon of the application.

▶ **android:label**—Written within the `<application>` element, this attribute represents the name of our application.

After we set the preceding attributes, our `AndroidManifest.xml` file may appear as shown in Listing 14.1.

LISTING 14.1   Code in the `AndroidManifest.xml` File

```xml
<manifest xmlns:android="http://schemas.android.com/apk/res/android"
    package="com.androidunleashed.createserviceapp"
    android:versionCode="1"
    android:versionName="1.0" >
    <uses-sdk android:minSdkVersion="8"
        android:targetSdkVersion="16" />
    <application
        android:icon="@drawable/ic_launcher"
        android:label="@string/app_name"
        android:theme="@style/AppTheme" >
        <activity
            android:name=".CreateServiceAppActivity"
            android:label="@string/title_activity_create_service_app" >
            <intent-filter>
                <action android:name="android.intent.action.MAIN" />
                <category android:name="android.intent.category.LAUNCHER" />
            </intent-filter>
        </activity>
        <service android:name=".HandleService" >
            <intent-filter>
                <action android:name="com.androidunleashed.handleservice" />
            </intent-filter>
        </service>
    </application>
</manifest>
```

Also, to inform the user about the minimum version of the Android OS required to run the application, the `android:minSdkVersion` attribute is used. The following statement indicates that the application requires the minimum SDK version `"8"` to run the application:

```
<uses-sdk android:minSdkVersion="8" />
```

This statement informs that Android 2.2 is required for running the application. That is, the application cannot be installed on devices running lower versions of the OS. Also, Google Play automatically filters out the application in the search results.

We can also set the `android:targetSdkVersion` that informs the API level the application targets. For example, the following example informs that the application targets Android 4.1:

```
android:targetSdkVersion="16"
```

We need three things to essentially inform users about our application:

▶ The features that our application requires to run—for example, whether it requires Bluetooth, multitouch screen, and so on, to operate

▶ The necessary hardware configuration that our application requires for running

▶ The permissions that our application requires to operate

To inform users about these three things, we use the three tags `<uses-feature>`, `<uses-configuration>`, and `<uses-permissions>` in our `AndroidManifest.xml` file. Table 14.1 gives a brief description of the three tags.

TABLE 14.1   Brief Description of the `<uses-feature>`, `<uses-configuration>`, and `<uses-permissions>` Tags

Tag	Description
`<uses-feature>`	This tag informs that our application requires the specified feature, and if not provided, the application still can operate without it. To indicate the feature essentially required to run the application, the `android:required` attribute is used. The value of the `"android:required"` attribute can be set to either `true` or `false` where the value "true" means the feature is necessarily required to operate the application, and the value "false" means the application will still operate if the feature is missing in the device.
	For example, if our application requires multitouch but will still operate if the feature is not available in the device, the following statement is used:`<uses-feature android:name="android.hardware.touchscreen.multitouch" android:required="false"/>`

Tag	Description
`<uses-configu-ration>`	This specifies the hardware requirements that the device is desired to have to run the application. We can use this tag to inform the keyboard type, touchscreen, navigation controls, and so on required by the application. For example, if an application requires a five-way navigation control and a touchscreen that can be operated with a finger, the following statement is used:`<uses-configuration android:reqFiveWayNav="true" android:reqTouchScreen="finger" />`
	Similarly, if the application requires a standard QWERTY keyboard, the following statement is used:`<uses-configuration android:reqKeyboardType="qwerty" />`
	Google Play uses the configuration and feature requirements and does not display our application on a device that doesn't support the specified essential feature or configuration.
`<uses-permis-sions>`	Used to specify the permissions that our application requires to operate. If our application needs to access the Internet, then a request for `INTERNET` permission is made through the following statement:`<uses-permission android:name="android.permission.INTERNET" />`
	If ours is a location-based application, it needs to have either fine permission or coarse permissions. That is, either of the following two statements has to be added to the `AndroidManifest.xml` file:
	`<uses-permission android:name="android.permission.ACCESS_FINE_ LOCATION"/>`
	`<uses-permission android:name="android.permission.ACCESS_ COARSE_LOCATION"/>`
	Cell tower and wifi use `ACCESS_COARSE_LOCATION`, and GPS requires `ACCESS_FINE_LOCATION`. If both are used by the application, then only `ACCESS_FINE_LOCATION` is needed, because the `ACCESS_FINE_LOCATION` implies permission for `ACCESS_COARSE_LOCATION`.

The Play Store uses the `uses-feature` and `uses-configuration` tags to filter out devices; that is, on incompatible devices, the applications do not appear as available to download.

The permission feature is key, and users at the time of installation are shown these permissions. So, it is essential for developers to ensure that only required permissions are used in the application.

Generating a Certificate, Digitally Signing the Android Applications, and Generating the APK

All Android applications must be digitally signed with a certificate before they are deployed onto a device or emulator. We can generate our own self-signed certificate and use it to sign our Android applications. Whenever we deploy our application to an emulator, Eclipse automatically signs it for us. Eclipse uses the default digital certificate in `debug.keystore` to sign our application. Eclipse provides a wizard that guides us to generate a certificate and also sign our application with the generated certificate.

> **NOTE**
>
> Using the JDK tools `keytool.exe` and `jarsigner.exe`, we not only can manually generate our own certificate but also sign our application with the generated certificate.

Signing Applications Using the Export Android Application Wizard

The Export Android Application Wizard simplifies the process of creating and signing our application package. To launch the wizard, follow these steps:

1. Select the Android project in the `Package Explorer` window and select the `File`, `Export` option or right-click the project in the `Package Explorer` window and select the `Export` option.

2. In the `Export` dialog, expand the `Android` item and select `Export Android Application`. Click `Next`.

3. Our Android project name, `CreateServiceApp`, is displayed in the `Project` box. Click `Next`.

4. The next dialog prompts us to either select an existing keystore or create a new one. Select the `Create new keystore` option to create a new certificate, that is, keystore, for our application. In the `Location` box, specify the name and path of the keystore. Assign the name as `CreateService` to our new keystore. In the `Password` and `Confirm` boxes, enter the password to protect the keystore. After entering the password (see Figure 14.1), click `Next`.

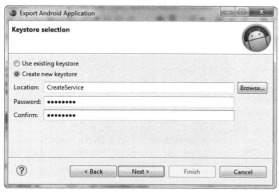

FIGURE 14.1   The `Export Android Application` dialog for entering keystore information

> **NOTE**
>
> To upgrade an installed application, it must be signed with the same key, so we must always sign an application using the same release key.

5. Provide an `alias` for the private key and enter a password to protect the private key (see Figure 14.2). Applications published on Google Play require a certificate with a validity period ending after October 22, 2033. Hence, enter a number that is greater than 2033 minus the current year in the `Validity` box. Also fill the `First and Last Name` box with your name and click `Next`.

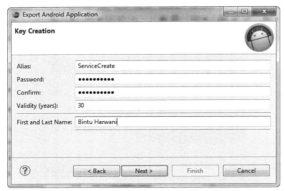

FIGURE 14.2   Dialog prompting information for key creation

6. Enter a path to store the destination APK file (see Figure 14.3). Click `Finish`.

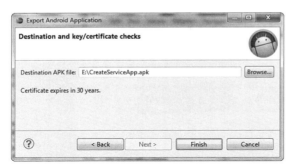

FIGURE 14.3   Entering the path for the generated APK file

The APK file now is generated. That is, our signed package is ready for distribution.

Distributing Applications with Google Play

Google Play, created by Google, is the most common and popular distribution channel. We can also distribute applications through other markets, social networks, and websites. The Google Play Store provides a platform to sell and distribute applications with few restrictions. There is no need for any approval or review of the application before it is listed in Google Play. Google Play provides all the tools and mechanisms required for application distribution, updating the application, selling, and promoting it.

Getting Started with Google Play

For uploading applications to the Google Play, we need to first create a developer account. To do so, we need to have a Google account, for example, an email account in gmail.com. Then, we create a developer account by signing up at the `https://play.google.com/apps/publish/signup`. We get the Android Developer Console at the given URL. The Developer Console is used for managing our applications in Google Play (see Figure 14.4).

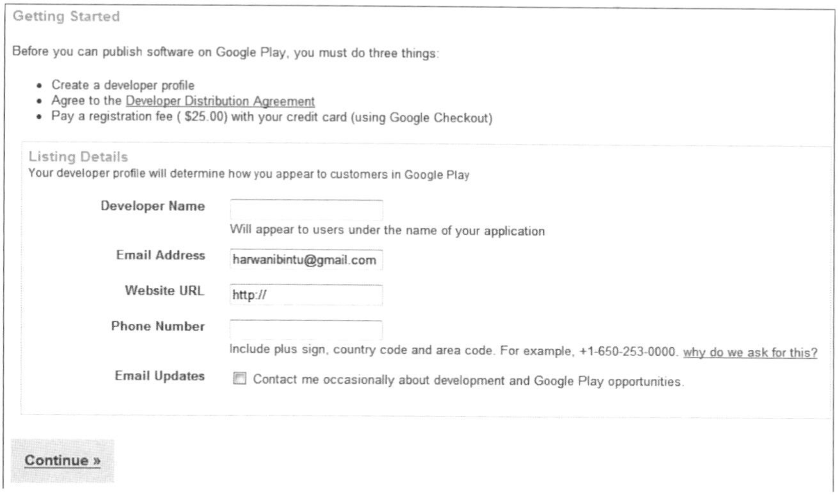

Getting Started

Before you can publish software on Google Play, you must do three things:

- Create a developer profile
- Agree to the Developer Distribution Agreement
- Pay a registration fee ($25.00) with your credit card (using Google Checkout)

Listing Details
Your developer profile will determine how you appear to customers in Google Play

Developer Name	
	Will appear to users under the name of your application
Email Address	harwanibintu@gmail.com
Website URL	http://
Phone Number	
	Include plus sign, country code and area code. For example, +1-650-253-0000. why do we ask for this?
Email Updates	☐ Contact me occasionally about development and Google Play opportunities.

Continue »

FIGURE 14.4   Form for creating developer account on Google Play

In the Developer Console, we need to enter the `Developer Name`, `Email Address`, and `Website URL` of the developer and a `Phone Number`. The Developer can select the `Email Updates` check box to get feedback about development and Google Play opportunities. On selecting the `Continue` link, we get a screen that displays the `Android DDA (Developer Distribution Agreement)` showing the terms and conditions of using Google Play. After reading all the terms, select the `I agree` check box and select the `I agree, Continue` link to move ahead.

The next screen prompts us to pay a one-time registration fee of $25 to complete the registration. After creating a developer account, we see the screen shown in Figure 14.5, which enables us to upload our application(s) so that users can find and download them.

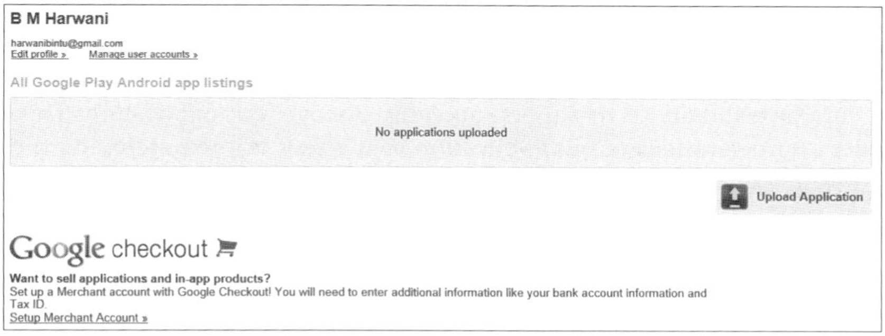

B M Harwani

harwanibintu@gmail.com
Edit profile »   Manage user accounts »

All Google Play Android app listings

No applications uploaded

⬆ Upload Application

Google checkout 🛒

Want to sell applications and in-app products?
Set up a Merchant account with Google Checkout! You will need to enter additional information like your bank account information and Tax ID.
Setup Merchant Account »

FIGURE 14.5   Screen after creating a developer account on Google Play

We can distribute products for free or for a price. The payments are processed through `Google Checkout`. For uploading applications that have a price, click the `Setup Merchant Account` link located at the bottom of the screen. While creating a Merchant Account, we are prompted to supply our `Private contact information` comprising of `Location`, `Address`, `City`, `State`, `Zip`, and `Phone number`. The private contact information is used by Google Play and is not displayed to the users. Also, we have to enter our `Public contact information` including business name, customer support email, website that displays our business information or about the information of the application being sold, and business address. We also are asked to enter `Financial Information`, such as our current monthly sales volume, Federal tax ID, credit card number, Social Security number, and so on. We are shown the Terms of Service, which we need to agree on to create the `Merchant Account`. Remember, the paid applications incur a transaction fee.

Publishing paid applications is currently not available to residents of all countries due to ongoing negotiations or making available the Google Checkout facility in those countries.

For free applications, click the `Upload Application` link from the Android Developer Console. We are prompted to supply information about the application, as shown in Figure 14.6 (left). That is, we have to upload our application's APK file.

FIGURE 14.6   Dialog for uploading the APK file (left), and the dialog displaying information about the application whose APK file is uploaded (right)

After we upload the APK file, the information about the application, including its version name, version code, package name, and so on, is displayed (see Figure 14.6—right). Click the `Save` button to continue. We get a form that asks for complete details of the application being uploaded (see Figure 14.7). We need to supply at least two of its screenshots, a high-resolution application icon, promotional graphic if any, promotional video if any, URL that dictates Privacy Policy, and so on. The form also prompts us to select a language of the application, its title, description, any recent updates, promo text, application type, and category under which we want to display our application in Google Play. The title and description should be elaborate so that users can easily discover our application. This information provides a sufficient idea of our application to the user before purchasing the application.

FIGURE 14.7   Filling in the information of the application being uploaded

We can also select the countries in which we want our application to be available. Also, we need to supply contact information where users can ask for help. Finally, click the Publish button to publish the application on Google Play. Our application will be live and available for download almost immediately. Users can purchase our application, submit comments, and rate the application. We can also upgrade our application and can even unpublish our application through the Developer Console.

We need to provide complete support for the application, or else users can request refunds, which might affect our application ratings. The rating is based on user feedback, install rates, refund rates, and so on. Based on the uploaded APK file, the users are warned about any specific permission required to run the application.

Localizing Android Applications

So that our application is popular all over the world, it needs to support different languages. We can use an application's string resources to localize our applications by providing alternative translated resources. Also, Google Play provides support for adding local language titles and descriptions for our applications. To maximize sales, it is better to have the title and description of our application translated into several languages.

To localize our application, we simply create another folder under /res. For example, create a /res/values-ja folder to store the Japanese version of strings.xml. Similarly, we can create a res/values-fr folder to hold the French version of strings.xml, and so on. The strings in the `strings.xml` file in the respective folders contain strings converted into the Japanese and French languages. While running the application, if the device's language is set to Japanese, Android automatically picks up the `strings.xml` file placed in `/res/values-ja` folder.

Monetizing Our Applications

Google Play provides three options to distribute our applications:

▶ **Applications at a price**—Users need to pay a certain amount before they download and install our application.

▶ **Free applications with In-App Billing (IAB)**—Allow users to freely download and install the application, but charge for upgrades and other add-ons.

▶ **Applications with embedded advertisements**—Allow users to freely download and install applications and generate revenue by displaying advertisements.

We need to create a Google Checkout Merchant Account if we are selling applications at a price or with IAB; also, a transaction fee is charged by Google Play.

Summary

In this chapter we learned the step-by-step approach to publishing Android applications. We learned to set versioning information of the application, generate a certificate, and digitally sign the Android application. The chapter also discussed distributing applications, getting started with Google Play, localizaing applications, and monetizing our applications.

In this book, I have tried my best to keep things easy to understand. You now have all the necessary information for building and maintaining your own applications in Android.

Have fun creating your own applications, and thanks for reading!

Index

B

FreeType library, 11

fromAlpha attribute, 455

fromDegrees attribute, 456

fromPixel() method, 511

fromXDelta attribute, 458

fromXScale attribute, 457

fromYDelta attribute, 458

fromYScale attribute, 457

Froya code name, platform and API levels, 55

full_horizontal value, gravity attribute, 43

full_vertical value, gravity attribute, 43, 108

G

/gen folder, 57

geocoding

    forward geocoding, 502-506

    reverse geocoding, 502-503

Gesture Mode combined with voice, 10

getAction() method, 519

getActionBar() method, 360, 366, 379

getActivity() method, 525

getAddress() method, 506

getArguments() method, 296-297

getAssets() method, 206

getBoolean() method, 317

getCenter() method, 515

getColor() method, 158

getColumnIndexOrThrow() method, 392

getColumnName() method, 392

getColumnNames() method, 392

getContentResolver() method, 570

getCount() method, 235, 239, 392

getDefault() method, 537

getDefaultSensor() method, 627

getDimension() method, 155

getDrawable()method, 178, 194

getExtras() method, 292, 613

getFromLocation() method, 503-506

getFromLocationName() method, 503

getHeight() method, 424-425

getIntrinsicWidth() method, 515

getItem() method, 235

getItemId() method, 235

getLoaderManager() method, 583

getMessageBody() method, 543

getOriginatingAddress() method, 543

getOverlays() method, 510

getPosition() method, 392

getReadable() method, 390

getReadableDatabase() method, 385, 390

getResources() method, 155, 158, 178

getResultCode() method, 538

getSensorList() method, 627

getString() method, 317

getStringExtra() method, 519

getSystemService() method, 493, 527, 619, 626

getTimestampMillis() method, 543

getType() method, 571

getWidth() method, 424-425

getWritableDatabase() method, 385, 390

GIF files, 125, 170

Gingerbread code name, platform and API levels, 55

goBack() method, 477-478

goBackOrForward() method, 478

goForward() method, 477-478

Google Maps API

    AVD-based applications, 485-486

    displaying

        map markers, 507-515

        satellite view, 499

I

J

K

L

M

P

package attribute, <manifest> tags, 62

Package Explorer

  Android Manifest Editor, 64

  Android XML File, 78

  project tree, 56

padding attribute, 101, 103, 114

paddingBottom attribute, 114

paddingLeft attribute, 114

paddingRight attribute, 114

paddingTop attribute, 114

PagerAdapter, 235-236, 239

Paint and Canvas objects, 421-423

  colors, 423-424

  displaying text, 443-444

  drawing

    arcs, 434-435

    bitmaps, 441-443

    canvas height and width, 424-425

    circles, 424

    defining drawing paths, 429-430

    lines, 427

    ovals, 433-434

    points, 425

    rectangles, 430-431

    rectangles, rounded, 432-433

  gradients, 436

    LinearGradient, 436-438

    RadialGradient, 439

    SweepGradient, 440

  paint antialiasing, 425

  paint styles, 425

  strokes

    cap, 426

    width, 426

password attribute, 83

paths, drawing, 429-430

pause() method, 191, 204

PendingIntent class, 524-525, 529, 554

  alarms, 619-620, 624-625

  getActivity() method, 525

phone value, 84

PhoneStateListener class, 554-556

  onCallStateChanged() method, 554, 556

pivotX and pivotY attributes, 456-457

Places card, 10

Play Store. See Google Play Store

PNG files, 125, 170-171

points, 425

populate() method, 514

portrait mode, 140-142, 144, 282

  description, 138

  fragments, 282, 288

PositiveButton() method, 309-310

post() method, 592

postInvalidate() method, 510

predictive keyboard, 10

Preference View, 312-313

PreferenceCategory View, 312

PreferenceFragment, 311-318. See also DialogFragment; FragmentManager; fragments; ListFragment

  methods

    addPreferencesFromResource(), 315

    onPreferenceClick(), 315

  Views, 312-313. See also specific views

Preferences, SDK installation, 24

PreferenceScreen View, 312

PRESSURE sensor type, 626

ProgressBar controls

  definition, 199

S

How can we make this index more useful? Email us at indexes@samspublishing.com

How can we make this index more useful? Email us at indexes@samspublishing.com

    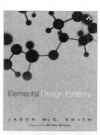

FREE
Online Edition

Safari
Books Online

Your purchase of **Android Programming Unleashed** includes access to a free online edition for 45 days through the Safari Books Online subscription service. Nearly every Sams book is available online through Safari Books Online, along with thousands of books and videos from publishers such as Addison-Wesley Professional, Cisco Press, Exam Cram, IBM Press, O'Reilly Media, Prentice Hall, Que, and VMware Press.

Safari Books Online is a digital library providing searchable, on-demand access to thousands of technology, digital media, and professional development books and videos from leading publishers. With one monthly or yearly subscription price, you get unlimited access to learning tools and information on topics including mobile app and software development, tips and tricks on using your favorite gadgets, networking, project management, graphic design, and much more.

Activate your FREE Online Edition at
informit.com/safarifree

STEP 1:   Enter the coupon code: TXCMOGA.

STEP 2:   New Safari users, complete the brief registration form.
Safari subscribers, just log in.

If you have difficulty registering on Safari or accessing the online edition,
please e-mail customer-service@safaribooksonline.com